The Georgetown Logic Group: Justyna Japola, Robert Leider, Chauncey Maher, David Pierce, Diana
Puglisi, Dan Quattrone and Matthew Rellihan
LSAT Editors: Robert Leider and Matthew Rellihan
Editors: Claire Bonin, Brian Thurbon and Juan Garcia-Arriola
Layout Editor: Dan Quattrone
Editorial/Production Supervision & Book Design: Anne Walsh

Printed by Kunos Press

Printed in the United States of America
10   9   8   7   6   5   4   3   2   1

ISBN 978-0-9785445-4-6

TABLE OF CONTENTS

THE OUTSKIRTS OF LOGIC

REFERENCE SHEETS

FOREWARD

Dear Students,

The Georgetown Logic Group is pleased to present you with an updated version of Wayne Davis's *An Introduction to Logic*. As past students of Professor Davis, and present teachers of his book, we recognized that the manuscript should be put back into print for at least four reasons.

First, Professor Davis introduces a new, practical and easily understood approach to modern logic that is well suited to the introductory student. Second, *An Introduction to Logic* opens with an emphasis on informal and scientific reasoning. This is a natural starting place for a beginning logic course, easing students into the use of formal resources for assessing validity. Third, Professor Davis's book offers an extended treatment of Aristotle and Venn, providing a helpful historical cast, which in turn allows students to appreciate the achievement of predicate logic. Far from being a foray into a defunct logic, the work on Aristotle and Venn affords students a richer understanding of the procedures developed in the later chapters. Third, sprinkled throughout the text are treatments of certain subtleties and nuances that you do not find in other books, such as the discussion on the difficulties posed by conditionals. These bits provide more sustenance for the curious student and afford the teacher unique material upon which to expand in lecture. And fourth, as graduate students we are sympathetic to the outrageously high cost of text books and therefore jumped at the chance to help put together a lower cost book that we believe just happens to be best available.

Putting the book back into print required, among other things, updating a massive range of exercises. The text you have before you is the result of our volunteer work. This shows just how committed we were to seeing the book back on the shelf! And, of course, it indicates that we are proud to present it to you.

Last, but not least, despite our abiding commitment to the project of updating *Introduction*, we are grateful to have had the organizing guidance of Anne Walsh without whom we would have been so many blind scavengers.

Enjoy the new and improved *An Introduction to Logic*!

The Georgetown Logic Group

PREFACE TO THE SECOND EDITION

It is an honor to present a second edition of *An Introduction to Logic*, because the project was initiated by outstanding graduate students (the "Georgetown Logic Group") who chose to use the book in their own teaching. A number of examples, references, and exercises were making the book increasingly dated.

Soon after the first edition appeared more than twenty years ago, I was pleasantly surprised to learn from my undergraduate students that they found it very helpful as preparation for the standard entrance exam for law school. The Georgetown Logic Group agreed, and took the text one step further, using questions and exercises from previously released LSAT exams provided by the Law School Admission Council (LSAC) as "Prep Tests" and applying methods from the book to arrive at solutions. The graduate students who initiated this project had a second motive: to make a more reasonably priced introductory text available to college students. I am proud to help toward this end.

Gratifyingly few typos were found in the first edition, but these have been corrected. Substantive changes are few. The treatment of formal validity acknowledges that there are argument forms all of whose instances are inductively valid. Formally valid arguments are now defined as those all of whose instances are deductively valid. The definition of question-begging arguments was broadened to cover those whose premises "assume" the conclusion as well as those whose premises include the conclusion. Finally, I explain why "p unless q" is not taken to entail "$q \Rightarrow -p$."

The distinctive features outlined in the preface to the first edition remain distinctive. The most popular textbooks currently on the market continue the theoretically and pedagogically unsound practices that motivated me to write an alternative logic book in the first place. For example, Patrick J. Hurley (*A Concise Introduction to Logic, Ninth Edition*, Wadsworth 2006, p. 294) notes that the material interpretation of English conditionals diverges from its ordinary meaning, but justifies using it anyway on the grounds that if a teacher tells a student *"If you get an A on the final, you will get an A in the course,"* we would not say that she lied if it turns out that he did not get an A on the final. But we would most certainly say the teacher has lied (and acted irresponsibly) if she knows that the student failed every previous exam so badly that no matter what he gets on the final she will not give him an A in the course.

Even in this case, however, her conditional statement would be true if it were a material conditional, and she would have had good reason to believe that it would be true because its antecedent would likely turn out to be false. Later, Hurley notes unhelpfully that "when the truth-functional interpretation of a conditional statement conflicts with the ordinary language interpretation, using the horseshoe operator to translate it may not be appropriate" (p. 299). How then should the student do the exercises provided, or apply what is learned to real life?

In the chapter on quantification theory, Hurley instructs students to symbolize "All S are P" in terms of the material conditional, as "$(x)(Sx \supset Px)$"—the Boolean interpretation. This makes "All flying elephants are flightless" true, along with "Everyone who is the student in the previous example and gets an A on the final will get an A in the course," and entails that "All cats are animals" and "No cats are animals" are logically compatible. In the chapter on categorical propositions, Hurley notes that logicians following Aristotle take a different approach. But it is unclear from the discussion whether it suffices for "All S are P" to have "existential import" that there are in fact some S, or whether it is required that "All S are P" implies that there are some S. The latter is more accurate. But if that requirement defines the Aristotelian interpretation, then "All S are P, $\therefore$ Some S are P" is not rendered invalid by the mere fact that there are no S, as the text asserts in one place (p. 212ff). On the contrary, it can easily be proven valid as Hurley does in another place (p. 222). If the former requirement defines the Aristotelian interpretation, then "All S are P, $\therefore$ Some S are P" does not come out valid either as the text asserts (p. 213). For the mere fact that there are some S is not enough to make it impossible for the premise to be true and the conclusion false.

The latest edition of Copi (I. M. Copi & Carl Cohen, *Introduction to Logic*, 12th edition, Pearson/Prentice Hall, 2005, pp. 202-4) notes that use of the Boolean interpretation of Aristotelian categoricals creates serious problems, such as the conclusion that "All S are P" and "No S are P" are logically compatible. They also note that these problems can be avoided by introducing the concept of a presupposition, as I do. Nevertheless, Copi and Cohen say that the cost of doing this is too heavy to bear because sometimes we do not presuppose the existence of an S, as when physicists claim that bodies not acted upon by any external forces move in a straight line. But such claims can be understood as made within the implicit idealizing condition "if there are any such bodies." The same goes for "All trespassers will be prosecuted," which has an implicit "if there are any." The Boolean interpretation is no help here at all. For if it provided the correct analysis of Aristotelian categoricals, then the physicist could just as truly claim that bodies not acted upon by any external force do *not* move in a straight line, since the emptiness of the subject class would make that claim true as well.

Copi and Cohen also note that most conditional statements assert more than a material conditional, but still teach the student to translate them as material conditionals (p. 327ff). They justify this practice by claiming that "the validity of all valid arguments of the general type with which we will be concerned is preserved." But the invalidity of many patently invalid arguments is *not* preserved, such as "$-p$, $\therefore$ If p then q." Moreover, some of the valid arguments they cite have known counterexamples, such as hypothetical syllogism and contraposition. Copi and Cohen continue to claim that some conditionals in English do express the material conditional by citing "If Hitler was a military genius, then I am a monkey's uncle." But such a claim is obviously not intended as the serious assertion of a truth, but rather as a humorous denial by implication of its antecedent. Their conclusion that there are four different senses of "if p then q" from the premise that there are four different relationships between "p" and "q" that would make "if p then q" true is known to be fallacious. Aside from the fact that there are many more than four such relationships, one could just as well argue that there are four different senses of "All S are P."

The first edition was written on one of the first personal computers, the TRS-80, but was produced non-electronically. As a result, no electronic copy existed in a format readable by current word processors. The editorial team scanned the text and scrubbed the results for errors in transcription. I am pleased to have digital files that can easily be revised. So I invite readers who spot defects to send them directly to me.

I am deeply grateful to Jeff Engelhardt, Justyna Japola, Robert Leider, Chauncey Maher, David Pierce, Diana Puglisi, Daniel Quattrone, and Matthew Rellihan for all the fine work they volunteered to make this second edition better than the first. Thanks go to George Bowles who pointed out the possibility of argument forms all of whose instances are inductively valid. I am also thankful to the editorial team who spent long hours digitizing and editing the text: Claire Bonin, Juan Garcia-Arriola, Sophia Pryce Rodney, Megan Smith and Brian Thurbon. I am especially grateful to Anne Walsh, Administrator for the Georgetown University Philosophy Department and Director of Kunos Press, for overseeing the whole project and organizing the work so that it got done properly (down to the minutest details) and in a timely fashion. Without her vision, energy, and direction, it would not have been possible. Finally, I again give thanks to Georgetown University and especially my wife for providing happy homes in which large-scale projects are possible.

August 14, 2007

PREFACE TO THE FIRST EDITION

This introduction to logic is designed to serve two purposes. The first and primary objective is to develop the student's ability to reason logically and think critically. The second is to introduce the student to the terminology, methods, and results of modern logic. There are no prerequisites other than motivation and a good high school education. The text is aimed at the general reader, who is presumed to have little mathematical inclination and no intention of taking further courses in logic. The material is therefore presented as intuitively as possible, and the level of formality and technical difficulty begins low and increases gradually throughout the text. The student will, however, be well prepared to take more advanced courses in logic, and will hopefully be stimulated to do so. For those who have already taken courses in symbolic or mathematical logic, the text will introduce a broader range of topics, from informal inductive logic to formal and deductive logic, while also focusing attention on the application of logic to arguments presented in natural languages. While there are numerous introductions to logic with the same goals, this one is unique in several significant respects. which will be detailed below.

Plan and Use Of the Book

The book is divided into chapters, sections, and subsections, with the section being the unit of assignment. Each section is followed by a glossary and a set of exercises. The glossary defines the main technical terms, and should be committed to memory. As in other technical disciplines, definitions are taken very seriously in logic. One little word can make a big difference. The exercises develop the student's skill at analyzing the logical structure of statements and arguments, at distinguishing sound arguments from fallacies, and at applying various formal techniques for proving arguments valid or invalid. Since the primary objective is to develop a skill, practice is essential. The exercises are therefore plentiful, and are graduated in difficulty. There are so many exercises, in fact, that students should not feel they have to do all of them. Since immediate feedback is highly beneficial, the solutions to nearly all the odd-numbered exercises are presented at the end of the book. This will enable many students to master the material without the assistance of an instructor. At the same time, enough unsolved exercises have been provided for instructors to use for homework or exams. As with any skill, "distributed" practice is more effective than "massed" practice. It is better, for example, to do logic problems an hour every day than to do them once a week in a seven-hour stint. The student is advised not to write the answers near the exercises, since this spoils their practice value. The text of each section should be read at least twice, once before and again after doing the exercises. A general review of the entire text after working through all the chapters will greatly deepen the student's understanding of many points.

There is more material than can comfortably be covered in one semester, The extra material is available for students who wish to go further, and for teachers who wish to tailor their courses to their own interests. Instructors desiring to concentrate on formal deductive logic can use Chapters 1, 2, and 5-9, for example, while those preferring a more informal focus can use Chapters 1-8. Chapters 1-4 provide a good background for courses in epistemology, philosophy of mind, and scientific methodology. I have organized the text so that the level of formality progressively increases. But other arrangements are possible. The two chapters on inductive logic can be presented after those on deductive logic, and the chapters on propositional logic can be presented before those on syllogistic logic.

A very casual approach to use-mention has been adopted. Symbolic expressions usually double as their own names, to avoid thousands of quotation marks. Quotes are occasionally used. though, for smoothness or extra clarity. Quotes or emphasis are always used to form the names of English words and sentences.

Because I have assigned a higher priority to the goal of developing logical reasoning than to that of preparing for further work in logic, I have departed from standard texts in several major ways. These include the treatment of conditionals, general categorical propositions, singular propositions, and validity. Other minor differences concern the treatment of variants of the inference rules, fallacies, inductive logic, and coverage.

Approach Of This Text

Conditionals. Introductory logic texts customarily teach students to treat conditionals in English as material conditionals. The student is therefore taught that an absurd statement like "If President Nixon was a Democrat, then he was not a Democrat" is *true*. and that "If the sun has less than five planets, then it has more than thirty" *follows validly* from the fact that the sun does not have less than five planets. In a course designed to develop a student's ability to reason logically, this practice is counterproductive, to put it mildly. The "paradoxes of the material conditional" have been known for a long time. Recent work has shown that natural language conditionals differ from material conditionals in many further ways. Robert Stalnaker and David Lewis, for example, have produced counterexamples to contraposition and hypothetical syllogism.[1] Some authors justify the translation of conditionals as material conditionals with the claim that the validity of valid arguments is preserved. Unfortunately, the invalidity of invalid arguments is not. This text focuses on "strong" indicative conditionals, those expressing implication. They are treated as compounds that are partially but not completely truth functional. The strong conditional is determinately false in case its antecedent is true and its consequent false, but may be either true or false in the other three cases. This yields a truth table with seven rows, which is sufficient, among other things, to prove the validity of modus ponens, modus tollens, and the dilemmas, and to prove the invalidity of conversion, affirming the consequent, and denying the

---

[1] R. Stalnaker, "A Theory of Conditionals," American Philosophical Quarterly Monographs, 2, 1968, 98-112; D. Lewis, *Counterfactuals* (Harvard University Press, 1973).

antecedent. Modus ponens and modus tollens are taken as rules of inference in the system of deduction developed for propositional logic. Contraposition and hypothetical syllogism are presented as valid only under certain commonly satisfied conditions, which are briefly and intuitively explained. While the text focuses on strong indicative conditionals, the logical properties studied are common to all natural language conditionals. For the sake of students who will be going on in logic, and for teachers who may still wish to adopt the standard approach, the material conditional is defined, and its logical properties explored, in the last section of Chapter 7.

General Categorical Propositions. Logic texts usually give general categorical propositions the Boolean interpretation. "All S are *P*," for example. is treated as equivalent to "Nothing is *S* and not *P*." The student is thus taught that "All flying elephants are hippos" is true, that "All students passed" and "No students passed" are *compatible,* and that "All musicians are humans and no humans are reptiles. so some musicians are not reptiles" is *invalid.* Students are taught in chapters on syllogistic logic that "Every thing is imperfect, therefore some thing is imperfect" is invalid, while in chapters on quantification theory they are taught that "Everything is imperfect, therefore something is imperfect" is valid. Again, when the goal is to teach logical reasoning, these practices are counterproductive.

This text distinguishes Aristotelian categoricals like "All *S* are *P*" from Venn categoricals like "Nothing is *S* and not *P*." Aristotelian categoricals are studied in Chapter 5. The method of refutation by counterinstance is used to prove invalidity, and the method of deduction is introduced to prove validity.

The standard rules of "immediate inference" and a few basic syllogisms provide a powerful but easy-to-use system of natural deduction. Venn categoricals are studied in Chapter 6. where the Venn diagram test is used to prove both validity and invalidity. Corresponding Aristotelian and Venn categoricals are then distinguished in terms of their presuppositions. The former presuppose that there is something to which their subject terms apply, while the latter do not. Consequently, corresponding Aristotelian and Venn categoricals are equivalent except when their subject terms apply to nothing, in which case the Aristotelian categoricals are neither true nor false, while universal Venn categoricals are true and particular Venn categoricals are false. An argument involving Aristotelian categoricals is then tested for validity using Venn diagrams; both the presuppositions and the Venn transforms of the premises are diagramed, and then both the presupposition and Venn transform of the conclusion are checked to see if they have also been diagramed. Basically the same procedure is used in Chapter 9 on quantification theory. The symbols of quantification theory provide an exact translation of Venn categoricals, but not of Aristotelian categoricals. Confronted with an argument containing Aristotelian categoricals, the student symbolizes the Venn transforms and presuppositions of the premises, and tries to deduce the Venn transform and presupposition of the conclusion. In other words, to prove the validity of an argument involving Aristotelian categoricals. the student is taught to prove the validity of an argument involving Venn categoricals that is equivalent with respect to validity.

Singular Propositions. After discussing the logic of general categorical propositions, logic texts generally teach students to treat singular propositions as general. Thus "Socrates is a man" is equated with something like "All people who are Socrates are men," and "Socrates is not a man' is equated with something like "No people who are Socrates are men." This erroneously makes the two singular propositions contrary rather than contradictory (or neither contrary nor contradictory if the Boolean interpretation of general propositions is adopted). This practice furthermore conflicts with the chapters on quantification theory in the very same texts, where singular and general propositions are treated differently. In this text propositions are introduced at the end of Chapter **5,** where the relationships among singular propositions and between general propositions are discussed. The methods of refutation and deduction are then applied to arguments involving singular propositions. In Chapter 6, the Venn diagram test is applied to singular propositions. "Socrates is a man" is diagramed by putting an s (instead of the *x* used to diagram particular propositions) in the man circle, and "Socrates is not a man" is diagramed by putting an s outside the man circle. In Chapter 9, finally, the transition to quantification theory is made simply by telling the student that "*s* is *P*" will now be reduced to *Ps*, and "*s* is not *P*" to *–Ps*.

The student is similarly not taught that "Most *S* are *P*" can be "rendered" as "Some *S* are *P*." nor that "Almost all *S* are *P*" should be "translated" as "Some *S* are *P* and some *S* are not *P*," or anything of the kind. This procedure is misleading at best. While students should be encouraged to generalize what they have learned, they should not be trained to misapply it. In general, the customary section ("the Procrustean Bed") in which the student is shown how to "reduce" other forms of argument to standard-form categorical syllogisms has been deleted. Even when legitimate, this procedure is pointless given the methods of deduction and refutation, and given the chapters on propositional logic and quantification theory. A section on suppressed premises has been included, however, since they are common phenomena, and since failure to acknowledge them constitutes misunderstanding an argument.

Validity and Soundness. Introductions to logic often begin by defining a valid argument as one in which the conclusion follows with necessity from the premises, and end up defining a valid argument as one in which it is impossible for the premises to be true and the conclusion false. These definitions are not exactly equivalent. For example, "The sky is blue, therefore two is the square foot of four" is valid on the second definition but not the first. Since such an argument constitutes poor reasoning, and could not possibly count as a proof of its conclusion, the first definition is preferable given the priorities of this text. Even the first definition is not perfectly suitable, however, since many inductive arguments constitute excellent reasoning even though their conclusions do not follow with necessity. Consequently, this text defines a valid argument as one in which the conclusion follows with necessity or probability, and distinguishes between "deductively valid" and "inductively valid" arguments. I have adopted this terminology to emphasize that whether or not the premises support the conclusion is more important than whether the premises support the conclusion with necessity or probability.

Many texts claim that deductive validity depends exclusively on form. But this is incorrect on either definition given above. For example, while "This is red, therefore it is colored" is deductively valid, most arguments with the same form are invalid. This text explicitly distinguishes deductive validity from formal validity. Finally, a sound argument is customarily defined as a valid argument with true premises. This leads to the result that question begging arguments with true premises are sound, as are valid arguments with wholly unwarranted premises that happen to be true, even though such arguments constitute poor reasoning. Soundness is therefore defined more stringently in this text: it refers to a good argument, one that counts as proving or verifying its conclusion. Since students are generally puzzled about the logician's distinction between soundness and validity, I spend more time than usual on it (see Chapter 2).

Variants of the Rules of Inference. In many texts, the rules of inference are defined by listing a set of argument forms. For example, simplification is commonly defined as the argument form "*p & q* ∴ *p*." Thus defined. the student is allowed to infer "Aristotle was a philosopher" but not "Aristotle was a mathematician" from "Aristotle was a philosopher and mathematician" by simplification. The student has to commute first, and then simplify, to get "Aristotle was a mathematician." This strikes most students as needlessly arbitrary, and they feel unjustly penalized when they lose points for "simplifying from the right." One solution is to include "*p & q* ∴ *q*" as one of the forms defining simplification. But if such additions are made for all similar cases, the result is an unmanageable list of forms. Another solution is to give verbal statements of the rules. Simplification would then be "From a conjunction, you can infer either conjunct." But verbally stated rules of inference are not as graphic, and therefore not as easy to use. This text combines the two approaches. The rules are given a general verbal definition and presented with a representative argument form. The student is allowed to use that representative form or any of its variants.

Fallacies. The customary chapter on informal fallacies has been omitted. Instead, there is a short section on fallacies in Chapter 2, where the purpose is to clarify by contrast the concept of a sound argument. Begging the question, equivocation, *ad hominem* arguments, and arguments from ignorance are briefly discussed there because they illustrate important general points about sound arguments. Other informal fallacies are described throughout the book in connection with related forms of valid inductive argument. Thus *post hoc* arguments are discussed with Mill's methods, and hasty generalization with enumerative induction. This procedure makes the student "compare and contrast," and thereby increases his or her understanding of both the valid and the invalid arguments. Appeals to pity, force, and the like are classified as "biasing influences," not fallacies, because they are seldom if ever presented as arguments. Appeals to authority are discussed not as fallacies but as arguments that are inductively valid under specified conditions, since much of any individual's knowledge is based on arguments from authority. Some commonly discussed fallacies, like composition and division, are omitted altogether because they hardly ever occur in practice. On the other hand, an entire section of Chapter 3 is devoted to what I call the "fallacy of exclusion," which results when undermining evidence is excluded. This fallacy is possibly the most common of all in practice, and is very important theoretically. yet most texts ignore it. I have omitted Latin names unless they have become part of English (like 'ad hominem' or are firmly entrenched in modern logic (like "modus ponens" Names like "*argumentum ad verecundiam,*" rare even in educated discourse, serve only to annoy the student.

Inductive Logic. The primary focus of this text is on the formulation and evaluation of patterns of argument. To maintain this focus throughout required a departure from typical treatments of inductive logic, which concentrate on methods of inquiry like Mill's methods and the hypothetico-deductive method. This text focuses on the argument forms that underlie the methods of inquiry. More important, I have tried to formulate with greater explicitness than usual the conditions under which specific types of inductive argument are valid. And I have devoted a lengthy section to the criteria determining the "best" explanation of a given phenomenon.

Coverage. The traditional three rules of syllogistic logic have been omitted, since they do not exemplify any generally applicable technique in logic. The method of indirect proof and a simple method of conditional proof are introduced, since they are important and can be learned very easily once the method of direct proof has been mastered. (These sections can, however, be omitted.) Quantification theory is presented as a *generalization* of syllogistic logic. And I have gone more deeply into monadic quantification theory than is usual, if only to keep students from thinking that quantifiers must always come at the beginning of a line. The rules of quantifier negation are given more than the usual emphasis, since they forge an important link with the chapters on syllogistic logic, and formulate simple but extremely useful conceptual relationships. I believe that the student's understanding of quantification theory can be greatly deepened with little additional effort. The chapter on quantification theory concludes with a brief section on relational statements, to show students the limits of what they have learned, and to invite them to take more advanced logic courses. The quantification rules are not generalized to cover relational statements, since the added complexity requires weeks to master. A subsection on modality appears in Chapter 2 because a large percentage of arguments found in ordinary discourse contains modal terms, while the main part of introductory logic avoids them. The purpose of the section is to enable the student in a rough and ready way to apply what is subsequently learned to discourse that does contain modal notions. The first section in Chapter 10 goes more deeply into modal logic without rising above the general level of conceptual difficulty represented by the rest of the text. I believe a treatment of elementary modal logic is very desirable in an introductory logic text, given that students generally have difficulty with even the simplest modal arguments, and given the close connections between modal logic and syllogistic logic. and between modal logic and probability theory. The section should be especially useful for philosophy students. Finally, Chapter 10 includes a section on digital logic circuits, which shows how propositional logic can be applied outside its usual domain. It should also be intrinsically interesting in this age of computers.

Acknowledgments

It gives me great pleasure to thank the many people who have contributed to this text. My major debt is to Irving M. Copi, whose fine *Introduction to Logic* served as a model (and also provided some exercises). I am indebted principally to P. F. Strawson, Robert C. Stalnaker, and David Lewis for the intellectual developments leading to the major innovations in this text. Especial gratitude is due to Robert B. Barrett of Washington University and Donald Kalish of UCLA. The former provided encouragement at two key stages of the project and wrote detailed chapter-by-chapter comments, nearly all of which led to improvements. The latter's incisive criticism of the chapter on quantification theory suggested how to increase the degree of rigor without exceeding the level of formality aimed at. David Benfield of Montclair State College also played a key role, first reviewing the project for Prentice-Hall and later trying it out on his classes and conveying a steady stream of constructive feedback. Thanks are also due to Jeremy Horne of Louisiana State University, Evelyn M. Barker of the University of Maryland, Baltimore County, and the other (anonymous) reviewers for Prentice-Hall. Readers seldom appreciate how much a textbook owes to the services of reviewers. I would also like to thank Doris S. Michaels, whose enthusiasm and wise advice as editor for Prentice-Hall turned a modest endeavor into a major production, and Emily Baker, who took over as philosophy editor with equal devotion. Hilda Tauber, production editor, carefully and sympathetically transformed a difficult manuscript into a beautiful book. Working with her was a delight.

Closer to home, my friend and colleague Tom L. Beauchamp gave me helpful advice on a variety of matters. I am grateful to Georgetown University for a summer grant in 1983 that enabled me to complete the second draft, and for providing me with the hundreds of fine logic students who inspired the project in the first place. I am deeply indebted to those students who used the book in manuscript form, and had to suffer its inevitable typos, errors, and infelicities. Among the students who were kind enough to bring errors to my attention, Chris Bard, Bob Nucci, Reggie Noble, Rita Dillon, Anthony Lepore, and Sharon Fekrat were especially helpful. Thanks are due also to Jameson Kurasha. my TA ("trusty assistant") for many years. Above all, I am indebted to Kathryn M. Olesko, who *qua* historian of science provided assistance with the chapters on inductive logic, and *qua* friend and wife provided the background of happiness necessary for such a large project.

CHAPTER ONE

Arguments

1.1 Logic, Reasoning, and Arguments

Logic. Reasoning is a vital human activity. For unlike some animals able to function instinctively, we need knowledge in order to survive. At the very least, knowledge facilitates the pursuit of happiness. Some knowledge can be gained directly. In this way we know, for example, that an object in front of us looks orange and tastes sweet. But we cannot know that it is edible and nutritious, or that it contains vitamin C, which prevents scurvy, without a process of reasoning. Similarly, we do not need reasons to believe that every triangle has three angles. But we cannot know that the angles of a triangle add up to 180° without evidence or proof. The vast bulk of human knowledge is based on reasoning. Indeed, our knowledge can be likened to a building, in which what is directly evident provides the foundation on which all other beliefs are based.

Not just any old reasoning gives us knowledge. Knowledge—as opposed to misguided opinion—requires *correct* reasoning, reasoning that is logical and rational. Everyone can reason correctly to some extent. It is a skill we acquire while growing up. But the ability can be improved by study and reflection. People differ just as markedly in their native logical ability as in their athletic ability. Natural talent can be augmented by training in both areas.

Logic is the discipline that studies correct reasoning. Logic seeks in particular to develop methods for distinguishing correct from incorrect reasoning. Psychologists also study reasoning, but their viewpoint is quite different. Psychologists seek to describe how people actually do reason. Psychologists are concerned with the conditions under which reasoning occurs, the effects it or its absence has on a person's behavior and life, its possible neurological correlates, and so on. Logicians, on the other hand, seek to prescribe how people *should* reason. Logic also differs from psychology in its methods. In any empirical science, observations are made with the senses and experiments performed. Logic, in contrast, is a "pencil-and-paper" discipline in which intellectual reflection and insight replace the senses as a source of data. In this respect, logic is more like mathematics. Indeed, great advances in logical theory have been made in the last century by mathematicians and mathematically trained philosophers. *All* reasoning, though, falls within the purview of logic, including that used in the sciences and mathematics, as well as history, philosophy, ethics, theology, law, business, and even logic itself.

Like scientists as well as mathematicians, logicians tend to be theorists. They pursue their subject in the abstract, which makes it seem remote from practical affairs. But their results can be applied and used to develop the art of reasoning. That is our primary goal here. You will get some idea of the nature and methods of modern logical theory. You will develop some techniques far beyond the point of practical utility "just for the fun of it." But the main purpose of the book is to impart information and develop skills which, if applied conscientiously, will enable you to reason more successfully.

Arguments and Reasoning. What is *reasoning*? It is an inference, or chain of inferences. An *inference* is a mental state or process in which one or more beliefs support or lead to another belief. Thus I may observe that Bob has a temperature, and infer that he is sick. From the fact that Bob is sick, I may infer further that he should rest. I have described two inferences which constitute a two-step reasoning process. Inferences can be expressed in language in another way, as arguments. An ***argument*** is a sequence of statements, some of which are offered as providing a sufficient reason to believe the others. The supporting statements are called ***premises***; the statements they support are called ***conclusions***. An argument, therefore, is a linguistic unit in which premises are stated from which conclusions are drawn.[1] The first inference represented above can be expressed as follows:

> Bob has a temperature, so he is sick.

"Bob has a temperature" is the premise, which corresponds to the starting point of the inference. "He is sick" is the conclusion, corresponding to the end point. An argument may appear as a simple compound sentence, as above, or as a sequence of sentences:

> Bob has a temperature. Therefore he is sick.

In either case, we have a linguistic unit consisting of the same elements logically related in the same way. The grammatical differences are unimportant. Arguments are easy to observe, describe, produce, and manipulate. It will therefore be convenient to study correct reasoning by studying sound arguments.

Note that "premise" and "conclusion" are *relative terms*. A statement may be a conclusion in one argument and a premise in another.

> Bob is sick, therefore he should rest.

The premise here was the conclusion in our previous argument. Note also that while an argument must contain at least one premise, it may contain any number.

> If Alan goes to the party, he will flirt with Monique.
> If Alan flirts with Monique, he will make his wife jealous.
> If Alan makes his wife jealous, she will get mad at him.
> If Alan's wife gets mad at him, he will be miserable.
> Therefore, if Alan goes to the party, he will be miserable.

There is obviously no limit, save exhaustion, on how many premises an argument like this can have.

In every argument, two or more statements are made. But an argument is not just a sequence of statements, nor simply a narrative.

---

[1] Note that "argument" has another almost completely unrelated sense in which it means *quarrel*. A quarrel is an unpleasant personal interaction, not a unit of speech or writing. Quarreling spouses typically do not draw conclusions from premises. On the other hand, philosophers may argue for positions that no one would disagree with.

It was sunny today. It was also very humid.

There is no indication here that either statement is a conclusion drawn from the other statement. Arguments have more structure. It is vitally important to distinguish *conclusions* from *unsupported claims*. Reasons must be offered for accepting a statement before we can classify it as the conclusion of an argument. Unsupported claims may be true, but we will have to look elsewhere for reasons to believe them.

Argument Indicators. How can we recognize arguments? And how can we distinguish the conclusion from the premises? By looking for words like *so* and *therefore.* These two inform us that the statement they are attached to is a conclusion drawn from the immediately preceding statements. Since "so" and "therefore" typically *precede* the conclusion, I call them **conclusion leaders.** Others are frequently used, such as *thus, hence, then,* and *consequently.* In logic and mathematics, the symbol $\therefore$ is used as a conclusion leader, and read "therefore." Arguments do not have to be stated with the premise preceding the conclusion. Our sample argument can be reformulated to read:

Bob is sick, since he has a temperature.
Bob is sick. For he has a temperature.

The tell-tale words here are *since* and *for*, which are **premise leaders.** They inform us that the statement following is the premise. Other common premise leaders are *because* and *as.*

In arguments with more than one premise, the conclusion can occur anywhere.

Bob is sick, and therefore should rest, for rest will help him to get better.

Here the conclusion "Bob should rest" occurs between the premises. Also, while conclusion leaders typically precede the conclusion, they sometimes occur in the middle of it, or at the end:

Bob has a temperature; he is therefore sick.
Bob has a temperature; he is sick therefore.

Premise leaders, on the other hand, always occur at the beginning of the premise. In arguments with more than one premise, sometimes only the first will be marked with a premise leader:

If Alan goes to the party he will be miserable. For he will flirt with Monique if he goes. And his wife will fly into a jealous rage if he flirts with anyone.

"His wife will fly into a jealous rage…" is a premise in this argument, even though it is not marked with a premise leader.

Premise and conclusion leaders may both be described as ***argument indicators***. The list of argument indicators is quite long. Table 1-1 presents the most common ones.

TABLE 1-1: ARGUMENT INDICATORS

Conclusion Leaders	Premise Leaders
therefore	for
hence	since
consequently	because
thus	as
then	inasmuch as
as a result	as indicated by the fact that
it follows that	which follows from the fact that
I conclude that	my reason for saying this is that
which shows that	which is shown by the fact that
which proves that	which is proven by the fact that
we may infer that	the evidence for this is the fact that
which implies that	which is implied by the fact that
which means that	in view of the fact that

Unfortunately, not all arguments are marked with argument indicators. They are often omitted for stylistic reasons, to avoid labored or turgid writing, or to avoid unnecessary words. Consider the following passage from one of John F. Kennedy's messages to Congress:

A strong and sound Federal tax system is essential to America's future. Without such a system, we cannot maintain our defenses and give leadership to the free world. Without such a system, we cannot render the public services necessary for enriching the lives of our people and furthering the growth of our economy.[2]

There is an argument here, whose conclusion is "A strong and sound Federal tax system is essential to America's future." The premises are the two statements following the conclusion. How can we tell in the absence of premise leaders? The truth is that we cannot tell for sure. However, the claim that a strong Federal tax system is essential is not self-evident. Indeed, it has been actively debated throughout American history. Rationality therefore demands that Kennedy defend his position in the controversy. Some supporting premises are therefore to be expected. The statements that such a tax system is needed for defense, leadership, and public services are at least relevant, and do tend to support the conclusion. So it makes good sense of the passage to interpret the statements about defense, and so on, as the needed premises. The accuracy of this interpretation is confirmed by the fact that if we insert a premise indicator like "for" before "Without such a system…," the sense of the passage does not seem to change. Inserting a conclusion indicator like "therefore" in the same place, in contrast, would make the passage seem obviously fallacious.

Interpretation. In short, in the absence of explicit indicators, you must *interpret*, making the best sense of things you can. Interpretation is an art, and an uncertain business at best. Two principles should guide your interpretations: *fidelity* and *charity*. Fidelity requires that an interpretation be as faithful to the author's express intention as possible. So whenever the author indicates what his intentions are, respect them. Charity demands that if two interpretations are compatible with the evidence as to the author's intentions, but one interpretation makes the author's argument more reasonable than the other, then you should assume that he intended the more reasonable interpretation. The principle of charity guided our interpretation of the above passage from Kennedy's message on taxes. These principles are only rough guidelines. Even when they are used, there will be many cases in which it is just not clear which analysis of a passage is correct, especially when that passage is quoted out of context (as in our exercises). This will often be due to the passage's vagueness or ambiguity rather than to your lack of logical acumen.

The identification of premises and conclusions is not an automatic process even when there are argument indicators. Consider the following passage from Robert J. Ringer's *Restoring the American Dream* (Fawcett Crest, 1979, p. 24):

> I also feel duty bound, at the outset, to remind the reader that no system of philosophy is perfect, because man himself is imperfect.

It is clear that there is an argument here, and that the premise is "Man himself is imperfect." But what is the conclusion? It appears to be "I (Robert J. Ringer) also feel duty bound, at the outset, to remind the reader that no system of philosophy is perfect." But appearances are deceiving. The real conclusion is "No system of philosophy is perfect." Ringer's book is on political philosophy, after all, not himself. Even if the book were an autobiography, we could simply take it on Ringer's authority that he feels duty bound to do this or that. What he needs to argue for is the claim that no system of philosophy is perfect. Arguments often contain such *personal intrusions,* as we may call them. "I believe" is an especially common one. All personal intrusions should be deleted when arguments are analyzed.

Diagrams. In the exercises, you will be asked to identify the premises and conclusions in argumentative passages. An efficient way to do this, which will be especially useful in later sections, is to number all the statements in the passage:

> [1] A strong and sound Federal tax system is essential to America's future. [2] Without such a system, we cannot maintain our defenses and give leadership to the free world. [3] Without such a system, we cannot render the public services necessary for enriching the lives of our people and furthering the growth of our economy.

Having numbered the statements, we can then simply say that [2] and [3] are the premises, and [1] the conclusion. This saves us rewriting each of the premises and the conclusions, and gives us a convenient method of referring to particular statements. Later, it will be especially helpful to *diagram* arguments.[3] In this case, which is so simple that a diagram is not very useful, we would bracket together the premises and draw an arrow pointing to the conclusion, like this: {[2] [3]} → [1]; or:

We have considered the speaker who advances his own argument, which is the primary case. But speakers often report or describe arguments that others advance. This is very common in law and philosophy, for example, where the speaker typically goes on to criticize or clarify the reported argument. Consider the following passage from *Furman* v. *Georgia*, which is part of Supreme Court Justice Brennan's opinion.

> Indeed, as my Brother Marshall establishes, [1] the available evidence uniformly indicates, although it does not conclusively prove, that the threat of death has no greater deterrent effect than the threat of

---

[3] I have adapted the method of diagramming presented by I. M. Copi, *Introduction to Logic*, 6th ed. Macmillan, 1982), pp. 18-39. Copi credits Monroe C. Beardsley, *Practical Logic* (Prentice-Hall. Inc., 1950).

imprisonment. The States argue, however, that...[2] death must be a more effective deterrent than any less severe punishment. Because [3] people fear death the most, the argument runs, [4] the threat of death must be the greatest deterrent.

There is a clear argument here, in which [3] is the premise and [4] the conclusion. It is equally clear that Justice Brennan himself does not subscribe to the argument, since he mentions approvingly that the available evidence contradicts its conclusion. Justice Brennan, however, is trying to consider all sides of the issue. After reporting this argument, he goes on to criticize and then dismiss it. Our goal—and an important aspect of critical thinking—is to identify and assess arguments wherever they occur. It is relatively unimportant for us whether an argument is accepted by the speaker, or is merely being reported.

How does statement [2] fit into the argument justice Brennan is reporting? It should be clear that [4] is merely a *repetition* of [2]. People often repeat or restate their premises and conclusions, for various reasons; restatements are typically signaled by phrases like *in other words*, *that is*, or *i.e.* When this happens, we can simply use the same number for the two formulations. Thus we could have written [2] where [4] is, in which case the States' argument is [3] → [2]. Alternatively, if we number two equivalent formulations differently as above, we can connect them with the equal sign = when diagramming the argument; then the above argument would be [3] → {[4] = [2]}. Why doesn't statement [1] appear in our diagrams? Because it is neither a premise nor a conclusion in the argument being analyzed. Statement [1] simply represents **background information**, material relevant to the argument but not one of its premises or conclusions.

Glossary

Logic: the discipline that studies correct reasoning or sound argumentation, and seeks to develop methods to distinguish it from incorrect reasoning or fallacious argumentation.

Argument: a linguistic unit in which one or more statements, called premises, are offered as providing a sufficient reason to believe other statements, called conclusions.

Premise: one of the statements in an argument from which a conclusion is drawn.

Conclusion: one of the statements in an argument that the premises are intended to support.

Repetition: a premise or conclusion repeated, possibly in different words, in the course of an argument.

Background information: material relevant to an argument but not one of its premises or conclusions.

Argument indicators: words like "therefore" and "for" that signal an argument and point out the premises or conclusion.

Premise leaders: argument indicators like "for" and "since" that precede the premises.

Conclusion leaders: argument indicators like "therefore" and "so" that precede the conclusion.

Fidelity: the principle requiring that an interpretation be faithful to the author's express intentions.

Charity: the principle requiring that the most reasonable interpretation be selected that is compatible with the author's express intentions.

Exercises

A. Analyze the following simple arguments. That is, identify the premises and conclusions; classify the argument indicators as premise or conclusion leaders; and then diagram the argument if you wish. Indicate if the author is giving someone else's argument.

1. All the evidence goes to show that what we regard as our mental life is bound up with brain structure and organized bodily energy. Therefore it is rational to suppose that mental life ceases when bodily life ceases. –Bertrand Russell, *Why I Am Not a Christian* (Simon and Schuster, 1957), p. 51.

2. If God exists, then the grounding reality itself is not ultimately groundless. Why? Because God is then the primal ground of all reality. –Hans Kung, *Does God Exist?* (Vintage Books/Random House, 1981), p. 566; emphasis deleted.

3. Whatever space may be in itself—and, of course, some moderns think it finite—we certainly perceive it as three-dimensional, and to three-dimensional space we can conceive no boundaries. By the very forms of our perceptions, therefore, we must feel as if we lived somewhere in infinite space. –C. S. Lewis. *The Grand Miracle* (Ballantine Books, 1970), p.16.

4. Yet if our agriculture-based life depends on the soil, it is equally true that soil depends on life, its very origins and the maintenance of its true nature being intimately related to living plants and animals. For soil is in part a creation of life, born of a marvelous interaction of life and nonlife long eons ago…. Life not only formed the soil, but other living things of incredible abundance and diversity now exist within it; if this were not so the soil would be a dead and sterile thing. –Rachel Carson, *Silent Spring* (Fawcett Publications Inc., 1964), p. 56.

5. In the beginning of his first book Ptolemy shortly recapitulates the fundamental assumptions of astronomy. The heavens is a sphere, turning round a fixed axis, as may be proved by the circular motion of the circumpolar stars and by the fact that other stars always rise and set at the same points of the horizon. –J. L. E. Dreyer, A *History of Astronomy from Thales to Kepler,* 2nd ed. (Dover, 1953), p. 192.

6. Our overriding obligation in the months ahead is to fulfill the world's hopes by fulfilling our own faith. That task must begin at home. For if we cannot fulfill our own ideals here, we cannot expect others to accept them. –John F. Kennedy, *To Turn the Tide*, pp. xv-xvi.

7. As for Federal supervision of elections in the South, I wholeheartedly support the Administration's referee proposal. I believe it is far superior to the well-intentioned but less effective recommendation of the Civil Rights Commission, because the referee proposal will deal not only with registrations, but also with voting itself. After all, what good does it do to be able to register if you cannot vote? –Richard M. Nixon, *The Challenges We Face* (Popular Library, 1960), p. 166.

8. The initial premise underlying the philosophy of libertarianism (and of this book) is that each man owns his own life and therefore has the right to do anything he wishes with that life, so long as he does not forcibly interfere with the life of any other man. –Robert J. Ringer, *Restoring the American Dream,* p. 30.

9. All governments restrain and rule people; therefore, all governments are totalitarian and authoritarian to one extent or another. (*Totalitarianism* refers to a centralized form of government in which those in control grant neither recognition nor tolerance to parties differing in opinion. *Authoritarianism*

is a system of governing that calls for unquestioning submission to authority.) –Robert J. Ringer, *Restoring the American Dream,* pp. 45-46.

10. We still have to learn how to live peacefully, not only with our fellow men but also with nature and, above all, with those Higher Powers which have made nature and have made us; for, assuredly, we have not come about by accident and certainly have not made ourselves. –E. F. Schumacher, *Small Is Beautiful: Economics as if People Mattered* (Perennial Library/Harper & Row. 1975), p. 21.

11. I suggest that the foundations of peace cannot be laid by universal prosperity, in the modern sense, because such prosperity, if attainable at all, is attainable only by cultivating such drives of human nature as greed and envy, which destroy intelligence, happiness, serenity, and thereby the peacefulness of man. –E. F. Schumacher, *Small Is Beautiful,* p. 32.

12. In these years Germany and Japan, their arms expenditures restricted by the victorious powers after World War II and their enthusiasm for warlike activity usefully diminished by defeat, were using their savings to build new and efficient industrial plants. This, in turn, was producing civilian goods at low cost. The United States, by contrast, had come through World War II with its prewar industrial plants intact and...by comparison, obsolescent. And a large share of its savings was going into weapons systems and later into its eccentric misadventure in Vietnam. So, apart from the pull of demand and the press of wage claims, the United States was suffering also in these years from the higher costs of relatively inefficient production. –John Kenneth Galbraith, *Money: Whence It Came, Where It Went* (Bantam Books, 1978). p. 357.

13. There is little more worth citing from this report, except that the authors recognize that "the criteria conventionally used for measuring aggregate economic damage significantly *understate*...the destructiveness of nuclear attacks, since they do not account for either the indirect or the long-term consequences of widespread destruction for both the society and the economy." –Solly Zuckerman, *Nuclear Illusion and Reality* (Vintage Books/Random House, 1983), p. 39.

14. The threshold between conventional war and nuclear war is more easily crossed than the threshold between war and peace; and so the surest way to avoid nuclear conflict is to avoid all conflict. –Leon Wieseltier, *Nuclear War, Nuclear Peace* (Holt, Rinehart & Winston, 1983), p. 26.

15. It is important to understand that assured destruction is the very essence of the whole deterrence concept. We must possess an actual assured-destruction capability, and that capability also must be credible. The point is that a potential aggressor must believe that our assured-destruction capability is in fact actual, and that our will to use it in retaliation to an attack is in fact unwavering. The conclusion, then, is clear: if the United States is to deter a nuclear attack in itself or its allies, it must possess an actual and a credible assured-destruction capability. –from "Mutual Deterrence," a speech by Robert McNamara, Sep. 18, 1967.

16. As slaves, compulsory labor overshadowed every other aspect of women's existence. It would seem, therefore, that the starting point for any exploration of black women's lives under slavery would be an appraisal of their role as workers. –Angela Y. Davis, *Women, Race and Class* (Vintage Books/Random House, 1983), p. 5.

17. Since all behavior springs from desire, it is clear that ethical notions can have no importance except as they influence desire. –Bertrand Russell, *Why I Am Not a Christian,* p. 61.

18. The apparently depressing thing is not merely that the universe is not to be pushed heedlessly around, but that the very state of mind in which we attempt to do so is an illusion. For if man is one with nature in a seamless unity, his beneficent ideals must after all be rationalizations of the great

primordial forces of lust and terror, of blind striving for survival, which we believe to be the basic impulses of nature. –Alan W. Watts, *Nature, Man, and Woman* (Vintage Books/Random House, 1970), p. 5

19. *Over the long run—and it may be very long—stocks should outperform bonds.* The reason is that stock and bond prices are set in the open market—and the market rewards risk. –Andrew Tobias. *The Only Investment Guide You'll Ever Need* (Harcourt Brace Jovanovich, 1978), p 65.

20. When the punishment of death is inflicted in a trivial number of the cases in which it is legally available, the conclusion is virtually inescapable that it is being inflicted arbitrarily. –Supreme Court Justice Brennen, *Furman v. Georgia,* 1972.

B. Analyze the following passages, which contain simple arguments even though there are no argument indicators.

1. To live a good life in the fullest sense a man must have a good education, friends, love, children (if he desires them), a sufficient income to keep him from want and grave anxiety, good health, and work which is not uninteresting. All these things, in varying degrees, depend upon the community and are helped or hindered by political events. The good life must be lived in a good society and is not fully possible otherwise. –Bertrand Russell, *Why I Am Not a Christian*, pp. 74-75.

2. God's *existence is not empirically ascertainable…*; God would not be God if man could perceive and observe him with his own senses at certain places and times. –Hans Kung, *Does God Exist?,* p. 549.

3. The thin layer of soil that forms a patchy covering over the continents controls our own existence and that of every other animal of the land. Without soil, land plants as we know them could not grow, and without plants no animals could survive. –Rachel Carson, *Silent Spring,* p. 56.

4. Medical research has achieved new wonders, but these wonders are too often beyond the reach of too many people, owing to a lack of income (particularly among the aged), a lack of hospital beds, a lack of nursing homes and a lack of doctors and dentists. Measures to provide health care for the aged under Social Security, and to increase the supply of both facilities and personnel, must be undertaken this year. –John F. Kennedy, *To Turn the Tide*, p. 48.

5. There are drawbacks to efforts to achieve racial progress by way of law. Even the most necessary laws are considered by some to be a challenge and an intrusion. Legislation in this area tends to provoke the extremists on both sides. It can have the effect of silencing moderate and constructive elements that have been trying for years by education and persuasion and the force of example—to bring justice and harmony into our racial picture. –Richard M. Nixon, *The Challenges We Face*, pp. 163-64.

6. Clearly, if one insisted that needs and desires were relevant, then moral standards would be out the window. It would mean that one man's desire to steal would be on an equal moral footing with another man's desire to work. One man's desire to be free would not have greater moral validity than another man's desire to violate his freedom. –Robert J. Ringer, *Restoring the American Dream,* p. 127.

7. The supporters of tariffs treat it as self-evident that the creation of jobs is a desirable end, in and of itself, regardless of what the persons employed do. That is clearly wrong. If all we want are jobs, we can create any number—for example, have people dig holes and then fill them up again, or perform

other useless tasks. Work is sometimes its own reward. Mostly, however, it is the price we pay to get the things we want. Our real objective is not just jobs but productive jobs—jobs that will mean more goods and services to consume. –Milton and Rose Friedman, *Free to Choose* (Avon Books, 1981), p. 33.

8. The management of money [by central banks] is no longer a policy but an occupation. Though it rewards those so occupied, its record of achievement in this century has been patently disastrous. It worsened both the boom and the depression after World War I. It facilitated the great bull market of the 1920's. It failed as an instrument for expanding the economy during the Great Depression. When it was relegated to a minor role during World War II and the good years thereafter, economic performance was, by common consent, much better. Its revival as a major instrument of economic management in the late '60s and early '70s served to combine massive inflation with serious recession. And it operated with discriminatory and punishing effect against, not surprisingly, those industries that depend on borrowed money, of which housing is the leading case. –John Kenneth Galbraith, *Money*, p. 369.

9. I do not believe that books on worthless science, promoted into bestsellers by cynical publishers, do much damage to society except in areas like medicine, health, and anthropology. There are people who have died needlessly as a result of reading persuasive books recommending dangerous diets and fake medical cures. The idiocies of Hitler were strengthened in the minds of the German people by crackpot theories of anthropology. In recent years many children have become seriously disturbed by reading books and seeing movies about haunted houses and demon possession. Psychotic mothers have killed their children in attempts to exorcise devils. –Martin Gardner, *Science: Good, Bad, and Bogus* (Avon Discus, 1981), p. xiv.

10. There is a sense in which deterrence is certainly immoral… We prevent them from using their weapons by threatening to [murder] millions of people, and by making them believe that we mean it; and they do the same. If the deed cannot be called moral, the threat cannot be called moral. –Leon Wieseltier, *Nuclear War, Nuclear Peace*, p. 73.

11. But the most common and durable source of factions has been the various and unequal distribution of property. Those who hold and those who are without property have ever formed distinct interests in society. Those who are creditors, and those who are debtors, fall under a like discrimination. A landed interest, a manufacturing interest, a mercantile interest, a moneyed interest, with many lesser interests, grow up of necessity in civilized nations, and divide them into different classes, actuated by different sentiments and views. –James Madison, "Federalist #10."

12. From the protection of different and unequal faculties of acquiring property, the possession of different degrees and kinds of property immediately results; and from the influence of these on the sentiments and views of the respective proprietors, ensues a division of the society into different interests and parties. The latent causes of faction are…sown in the nature of man; and we see them everywhere brought into different degrees of activity, according to the different circumstances of civil society. –James Madison, "Federalist #10."

13. One of the most closely guarded secrets of advanced capitalist societies involves the possibility— real possibility—of radically transforming the nature of house-work…. Teams of trained and well-paid workers, moving from dwelling to dwelling, engineering technologically advanced cleaning machinery could swiftly and efficiently accomplish what the present-day housewife does so arduously and primitively. –Angela Y. Davis, *Women, Race and Class*, p. 223.

14. In the constitution of the judiciary department in particular, it might be inexpedient to insist rigorously [that members of one branch should not be dependent on members of the other branches]: first,… peculiar qualifications being essential in the members, the primary consideration ought to be to select that mode of choice which best secures these qualifications; secondly…the permanent tenure by which the appointments are held in that department, must soon destroy all sense of dependence on the authority conferring them. –James Madison, "Federalist #51."

15. The record of black, Hispanic and female candidates this year has indeed been impressive. The very able mayors of San Francisco and Houston, who happen to be women, won reelection with whopping margins. Incumbent black mayors kept their jobs by comfortable margins, and several promising new figures from Philadelphia and Charlotte, NC, joined their ranks. Hispanic big-city mayors are fewer in number, but carry weight by their evident quality. –"The Rainbow Issue," *The Wall Street Journal* (November 17, 1983), p. 30.

16. Nothing need be said to illustrate the importance of the prohibition of titles of nobility. This may truly be denominated the corner-stone of republican government;…so long as they are excluded, there can never be serious danger that the government will be any other than that of the people. –Alexander Hamilton, "Federalist #84."

17. The President will have only the occasional command of such part of the militia of the nation as by legislative provision may be called into the actual service of the Union. The king of Great Britain and the governor of New York have at all times the entire command of all the militia within their several jurisdictions. In this article,…the power of the President would be inferior to that of…the monarch. –Alexander Hamilton, "Federalist #69"

18. "Grenada Proves We'll Fight" was the headline of one self-congratulatory piece. The fact that we have shown ourselves mighty enough to defeat Grenada will no doubt make the Russians think twice. Or will it?

It certainly should make Americans think twice.

The sneak attack on Grenada was undertaken without declaration of war or specific congressional authorization. It was undertaken in violation of the charters of the United Nations and of the Organization of American States, as well as of nonintervention pledges constantly made (if too often forgotten) by the United States to the Western Hemisphere ever since the Montevideo conference of 1933, when we first subscribed to the declaration that "no state has the right to intervene in the internal or external affairs of another."

The sneak attack was undertaken without any effort to determine what the real situation in Grenada was or where the new regime was headed. It was undertaken against the counsel of even such faithful friends of Mr Reagan as Margaret Thatcher. The U.N. resolution deploring the attack encountered no opposition save our own in the Security Council. The attack produced dismay and indignation throughout Latin America…. –Arthur Schlesinger Jr., "Grenada, Without Warning," *The Wall Street Journal* (November 9, 1983), p.30.

19. The Executive not only dispenses the honors, but holds the sword of the community. The legislature not only commands the purse, but prescribes the rules by which the duties and rights of every citizen are to be regulated. The judiciary, on the contrary, has no influence over either the sword or the purse; no direction either of the strength or of the wealth of the society; and can take no active resolution whatever. It may truly be said to have neither FORCE nor WILL, but merely judgment;

and must ultimately depend upon the aid of the executive arm even for the efficacy of its judgments. –Alexander Hamilaton, "Federalist #78."

20. The calculated killing of a human being by the State involves, by its very nature, a denial of the executed person's humanity. The contrast with the plight of a person punished by imprisonment is evident. An individual in prison does not lose "the right to have rights." A prisoner retains, for example, the constitutional rights to the free exercise of religion, to be free of cruel and unusual punishments, and to treatment as a "person" for purposes of due process of law and the equal protection of the laws. A prisoner remains a member of the human family. Moreover, he retains the right of access to the courts. His punishment is not irrevocable. –Supreme Court Justice Brennen, *Furman* v. *Georgia*, 1972.

LSAT Prep Questions

1. Ambiguity inspires interpretation. The saying "We are the measure of all things," for instance, has been interpreted by some people to imply that humans are centrally important in the universe, while others have interpreted it to mean simply that, since all knowledge is human knowledge, humans must rely on themselves to find the truth.

   The claim that ambiguity inspires interpretation figures in the argument in which one of the following ways?

   (a) It is used to support the argument's conclusion.

   (b) It is an illustration of the claim that we are the measure of all things.

   (c) It is compatible with either accepting or rejecting the argument's conclusion.

   (d) It is a view that other statements in the argument are intended to support.

   (e) It sets out a difficulty the argument is intended to solve.

   Preptest 29, Section 4, Question 15

1.2 Nonarguments

In the exercises of the previous section, you practiced analyzing arguments. That is, you were given that the passage contained an argument, and your task was to separate the premises from the conclusions, and both from background material. A further problem is to *recognize* arguments, and distinguish them from nonarguments. This is especially difficult when a passage contains no argument indicators. For such a passage could be simply a series of unsupported assertions rather than an argument. Interpretation is required. But the problem of recognizing arguments is difficult even when there seem to be premise and conclusion leaders. For most leaders have other functions or senses. We will examine some of the principal alternative meanings, without attempting an exhaustive survey.

Conditionals. Let us begin with "then," which functions as a conclusion leader in the following:

> Bob has a temperature. Then he is sick.

But "then" also occurs in *conditional statements,* which are closely related to arguments, and are therefore often confused with them. Compare the above argument with:

> If Bob has a temperature, then he is sick.

Here the antecedent of the conditional—namely, "Bob has a temperature"—looks very much like a premise. And the consequent "he is sick" looks like a conclusion. But note that if we used this conditional we would not thereby *state* that Bob has a temperature. Nor would we state that Bob is sick. All we would state is that *if* Bob has a temperature, he is sick. Since only one statement is made, and no conclusion is drawn, a conditional statement is not itself an argument. "Then" only functions as a conclusion leader when it is not preceded by "if" or equivalent devices. Conditionals often occur without "then," but are still not arguments. Conditionals may nevertheless occur as premises or conclusions in arguments, as in "The power is on, so the light will come on now if you flip the switch." "If" clauses also appear as independent sentences, in which case "if" is replaced by "suppose."

> Suppose Bob has a temperature. Then he is sick.

Again, this is not an argument since the author asserted neither that Bob has a temperature, nor that he is sick. Note that "then" cannot be replaced by "therefore" without radically changing the meaning. We will treat such passages as conditionals. How should we analyze the following?

> Suppose Bob has a temperature. Then he is sick, and therefore should rest.

This is clearly an argument, as indicated by "therefore." The premise, however, is conditional: Bob is sick if he has a temperature. The conclusion is too: Bob should rest if he has a temperature. We should give the same analysis to "If Bob has a temperature, then he is sick and therefore should rest." Repetitive if-clauses are often deleted.

Temporal Sequences, Examples, and Comparisons. Besides its logical sense, "since" has a purely *temporal* meaning, as in:

> Since Marilyn Monroe died, men have walked on the moon.

This *could* be interpreted as an argument—a very poor one!—but it is more plausibly interpreted as saying simply that in the period of time following the actress's death, men have walked on the moon. "Then" also has a temporal sense, as in "It rained, then it snowed." "Thus" is a conclusion leader in sentences like "Bob is sick, and thus should rest." But it has a very different function in:

> Many scientists turn to music for rest and relaxation. Thus Einstein played the violin.

"Thus" cannot be reasonably construed as a conclusion leader here: the fact that *many* scientists turn to music provides little support for the claim that *Einstein* did, and no support at all for the claim that Einstein specifically played the violin. "Thus" looks more like a premise leader here, but even that interpretation is implausible: the fact that Einstein played the violin provides little support for the claim that many scientists do, and provides no support for the claim that they turn to music specifically for rest and relaxation. In contexts like this, "thus" simply means *for example* or *in this manner.* "So" has a very different meaning after "just as," when it is used to make *comparisons:*

> Just as normal men would die without water, so Jack would die without wine.

A compound like this points out a similarity between Jack's need for wine and the normal need for water, but no claim is made that Jack's need for wine can be inferred from the normal man's need for water.

Explanations. "Because" and the other terms used to indicate arguments are just as commonly used to offer *explanations.* Compare the following sentences.

> The missing plane crashed, because the wreckage was found.
> The missing plane crashed because an instrument malfunctioned.

On its most natural interpretation, the first sentence is an argument. The speaker is trying to show that the missing plane crashed, and the wreckage is offered as *proof* or *evidence,* as a *reason to believe* that it did. The second sentence, in contrast, is most naturally interpreted as an explanation. The speaker is trying to explain the plane crash, and the instrument malfunction is offered as the *cause,* as the *reason why* the crash occurred. Note that the explanation would be rejected as false if it were discovered that the plane crashed, but as a result of something other than the instrument malfunction, such as pilot error. In contrast, the fact that the plane must have crashed for reasons other than finding the wreckage does not have the slightest tendency to show that the argument is faulty.

There are a number of clues to help determine whether an argument or an explanation is being offered. First, the conclusion of an argument is generally something regarded by the arguer as in need of support, while the premises are regarded as already well known. In an explanation, on the other hand, the fact being explained is generally regarded as already well established, while the explanatory factors cited are often highly speculative. Second, when "because" or its cousins are used as explanation indicators, they can be replaced without change of sense with "as a result of" or "due to." Thus "The plane crashed as a result of an instrument malfunction" captures the gist of the second passage. But "The plane crashed as a result of the wreckage being found" differs radically in meaning from the first. Furthermore, when modified by adverbs like "definitely," "probably," and "possibly," or by conjunctions like "either-or" or "not-but," "because" can only be interpreted as an explanation indicator. Thus we are forced to interpret "The plane crashed probably because the wreckage was found" as a ludicrous statement asserting that the finding of the wreckage caused the plane to crash. Despite these aids, it may still be difficult or impossible to determine whether a given passage was intended as an explanation or argument, especially when that passage is quoted out of context. Consider:

> Mary visited her father, because she said she would.

This can easily be interpreted as saying that Mary's visit was a result of her having said she would visit. It can also be naturally interpreted as providing evidence for the claim that she visited her father. Out of context, we just cannot say whether or not this is an argument or an explanation. Recall the warning given in §1.1: many passages will have no uniquely correct interpretation due to their inherent ambiguity or vagueness.

While explanations differ from arguments, explanatory statements may appear as premises or conclusions of arguments. Indeed, in Chapter 4 we will be studying one important pattern of argument that has a causal statement as a conclusion, and another pattern with an explanatory statement as a premise.

Recommendations and Rhetorical Questions. Arguments, by definition, are sequences of statements. Questions or commands, therefore, can never be parts of arguments. Consider, however, the following paraphrase of a passage from Andrew Tobias's *The Only Investment Guide You'll Ever Need* (p. 22):

> Life insurance premiums vary by 50 percent and more for equivalent coverage. So shop around.

"Shop around" appears to express a conclusion. But it is an imperative sentence, and therefore would not seem capable of expressing a conclusion. However, Tobias is not simply giving a *command,* the way a parent or a drill sergeant would. He is making a *recommendation.* That is, he is *advising* you as to what you *should* do. Recommendations need to be defended, and indeed, Tobias has provided a good reason for believing that you should shop around when buying life insurance. So the above passage is best interpreted as an argument:

> Life insurance premiums vary by 50 percent and more for equivalent coverage. So you *should* shop around.

Consider next a passage from Milton and Rose Friedman's *Free to Choose (*p. 41), where they are discussing the view that tariffs and other restrictions on free trade are needed to protect "infant industries" until they are able to compete with foreign industries:

> It is worthwhile for consumers to subsidize the industry initially—which is what they in effect do by levying a tariff—only if they will subsequently get back at least that subsidy in some other way. But in that case, is a subsidy needed? Will it then not pay the original entrants into the industry to suffer initial losses in the expectation of being able to recoup them later?

This may not seem to contain an argument because of the interrogative sentences. But the questions asked are *rhetorical*. It is clear that the Friedmans thought there was only one possible answer to them. But the expected answer to the first question ("No") is hardly obvious, so they supported it with the next question, to which the answer ("Yes, it will") is evident at least upon reflection. So this passage too is best interpreted as an argument:

> If the consumers will eventually get back their subsidy, a subsidy is not needed. For it will then pay the original entrants into the industry to suffer the initial losses in the expectation of being able to recoup them later.

The Friedmans' use of rhetorical questions rather than statements was merely a stylistic device. We need to see through such devices to spot the underlying arguments.

Exercises

Only some of the following passages are arguments. Identify those that are, and analyze them. If the passages are not arguments, try to describe what they are (conditional, explanation, narrative, or whatever).

1. On August 6, a bomb was dropped on the city of Hiroshima; 79,000 persons were killed, and many more exposed to radiation which might cause future disease and even death. Three days later, a similar attack on Nagasaki followed. On August 10, the Japanese ministers sued for peace.

    Yet their action was not unconditional... They demanded that they be allowed to keep their Emperor. Secretary of State Byrnes…replied on the next day. He did not demand the removal of the Emperor but stipulated that "the authority of the Emperor and the Japanese Government to rule the state should be subject to the Supreme Commander of the Allied powers." There followed a final reply from Tokyo that brought the war to an end. –Dexter Perkins and Glyndon G. Van Deusen, *The United States of America: A History*, vol. II (Macmillan, 1962), p. 664.

2. Some historians have raised the question as to whether the war might not have been terminated sooner if the Tokyo government had been assured at an earlier date that the Emperor would be left on the throne…. Would a clear and early statement have shaken the position of the militarists? The answer is certainly doubtful. The decision to surrender nearly provoked a revolt, even after the dropping of the bomb. Some members of the Japanese government argued that the United States did not possess many bombs (on this at least they were right) and that defense was still possible and the only honorable cause. –Perkins and Van Deusen, *The United States of America*, vol. II, pp. 664-65.

3. The Victorian age, for all its humbug, was a period of rapid progress, because men were dominated by hope rather than fear. –Bertrand Russell, *Why I Am Not a Christian*, p 79.

4. With very few exceptions, the religion which a man accepts is that of the community in which he lives, which makes it obvious that the influence of environment is what has led him to accept the religion in question. –Bertrand Russell, *Why I Am Not a Christian*, p. v.

5. What God is in Himself, how He is to be conceived by philosophers, retreats continually from our knowledge. The elaborate world pictures which accompany religion and which look each so solid while they last, turn out to be only shadows. It is religion itself—prayer and sacrament and repentance and adoration—which is here, in the long run, our sole avenue to the real. Like mathematics, religion can grow from within, or decay. The Jew knows more than the Pagan, the Christian more than the Jew, the modern vaguely religious man less than any of the three. But, like mathematics, it remains simply itself, capable of being applied to any new theory of the material universe and outmoded by none. –C.S. Lewis, *The Grand Miracle*, p. 22.

6. Since many of its compounds are tasteless, [arsenic] has been a favorite agent of homicide from long before the time of the Borgias to the present. –Rachel Carson, *Silent Spring*, p. 26.

7. Because these small amounts of pesticides are cumulatively stored and only slowly excreted, the threat of chronic poisoning and degenerative changes of the liver and other organs is very real. –Rachel Carson, *Silent Spring, p. 30*.

8. A 1975 study showed that it cost the city's Sanitation Department $297 per year to provide garbage-collection service twice a week to single-family homes in the Queens section of New York, but that a private firm was providing *three-times-a-week* service, just a few miles away, in a similar neighborhood in Nassau County, at a cost of only $72 a year. –Robert J. Ringer, *Restoring the American Dream, p. 153*.

9. The Great Depression occurred because by 1929 government intervention in the economy had become pronounced and had begun to disrupt the workings of the free market. –Robert J. Ringer, *Restoring the American Dream*, p. 86 (paraphrase).

10. Just as no society operates entirely on the command principle, so none operates entirely through voluntary cooperation. –Milton and Rose Friedman, *Free to Choose*, p. 3.

11. The key insight of Adam Smith's *Wealth of Nations* is misleadingly simple: if an exchange between two parties is voluntary, it will not take place unless both believe they will benefit from it. –Milton and Rose Friedman, *Free to Choose*, p. 5.

12. In recent times conservatives have reacted adversely to inflation, though not with great enthusiasm to the measures for preventing it. Liberals have thought unemployment the greater affliction. In fact no economy can be successful which has either. Inflation causes discomfort and frustration for many. Unemployment causes acute suffering for a lesser number. There is no certain way of knowing which causes the most in the aggregate of pain. –John Kenneth Galbraith *Money*, p *364*.

13. However much damage cities suffered, the total area that conventional bombs could destroy was the sum of a varying number of pockmarks of damage. Thus sixteen square miles of Tokyo were burnt out in March 1945 by tens and tens of thousands of small incendiary bombs that rained down over more than one hundred square miles. –Solly Zuckerman, *Nuclear Illusion and Reality*, p. 15.

14. If, under the influence of films like "The Day After" and the propaganda of the peace movement, a substantial constituency in the United States and in the principal allied nations demands, in effect, unilateral renunciation of nuclear deterrence and defense, credible deterrence will become

impossible. –William V. O'Brien, "An Anti-Deterrent Film," *The New York Times* (November 20, 1983), p. E21.

15. The President of the United States would be liable to be impeached, tried, and, upon conviction of treason, bribery, or other high crimes or misdemeanors, removed from office; and would afterwards be liable to prosecution and punishment in the ordinary course of law. The person of the king of Great Britain is sacred and inviolable; there is no constitutional tribunal to which he is amenable; no punishment to which he can be subjected without involving the crisis of a national revolution. [Fed #69]

16. While the rapists have seldom been brought to justice, the rape charge has been indiscriminately aimed at black men, the guilty and innocent alike. Thus, of the 455 men executed between 1930 and 1967 on the basis of rape convictions, 405 of them were black. –Angela Y. Davis, *Women, Race and Class*, p. 175.

17. The alternatives have become clear. Both affirmation and denial of God are possible. Are we not therefore faced with a stalemate, with indecision? –Hans Kling, *Does God Exist?*, p. 569.

18. *Don't waste money subscribing to investment letters or expensive services.* The more expensive investor newsletters and computer services only make sense for investors with lots of money—if then. Besides their (admittedly tax-deductible) cost there is the problem that they are liable to tempt you into buying and scare you into selling much too often, thereby incurring much higher brokerage fees and capital gains taxes than you otherwise might. There is the added problem that half the experts, at any given time, are likely to be wrong. –Andrew Tobias, *Investment Guide*, p. 86.

19. On a crucial point, the fundamental and common assumption of any debate over our foreign policy, there can be no disagreement. American foreign policy must be defensible in moral terms, as well as in expediential ones. Our nation is founded on moral propositions regarding the "rights of man," not simply the rights of Americans. –Irving Kristol, "Toward a Moral Foreign Policy," *The Wall Street Journal* (November 15, 1983), p. 34.

20. The U.S. budget deficit is now running at a record level. In Britain, public expenditure makes up a higher proportion of gross national product than it did when Mrs. Thatcher came to office. So two right-wing governments on different sides of the Atlantic have failed conspicuously in recent years to achieve their public spending goals. –Geoffrey Smith, "The Folly of Pretending to Cut Spending," *The Wall Street Journal* (November 16, 1983), p. 31.

1.3 Complex Arguments

In §1.1 we confined our attention to *simple arguments*, in which just one conclusion is drawn from one set of premises. Any number of simple arguments, however, can be combined to form a *complex argument*. For example, two of the arguments in §1.1 could be combined into one complex argument as follows:

Bob has a temperature, so is sick and hence should rest.

"So" indicates that a conclusion is being drawn from the premise that Bob has a temperature. "Hence" indicates that from that conclusion a further conclusion is being drawn. So "Bob is sick" is in this one passage both a conclusion (relative to "Bob has a temperature") and a premise (relative to "Bob should rest").

Argument Diagrams. Complex arguments require *analysis*. We need to break them down into simple arguments in order to properly understand and evaluate them. Even simple arguments require analysis, of course, to the extent of discerning their premises and conclusions. The analysis of written arguments can be aided in the following way. First, go through the passage and underline or circle every premise and conclusion leader.

> Bob has a temperature, <u>so</u> is sick and <u>hence</u> should rest.

Don't miss any, otherwise you will miss an entire argument. Second, number all the statements that make up the argument.

> [1] Bob has a temperature, <u>so</u> [2] is sick and <u>hence</u> [3] should rest.

At this stage, it does not matter whether the statement is a premise or a conclusion. Bear in mind, of course, that in this example [3] stands for the entire sentence "Bob should rest," while [2] stands for "Bob is sick." Subjects are often deleted for economy. The third step is to construct an **argument diagram**. This is done by connecting the numbers with an arrow pointing from the premises to the conclusion.

$$[1] \longrightarrow [2] \longrightarrow [3]$$

A diagram like this represents the structure of the argument very clearly. It shows that we have one complex argument consisting of a chain of two simple arguments. The analysis of complex arguments is especially difficult when some or all of the argument indicators have been omitted. A passage with a single indicator is not necessarily a simple argument. You may find it helpful to insert argument indicators first, before diagramming. There may however be several equally reasonable diagrams.

In a complex argument, two conclusions may be drawn independently from one premise:

> [1] John has recently filed for divorce. It follows that [2] he no longer sees any hope of salvaging his marriage. It also follows that [3] he is in for a long legal battle.

How did we know not to draw an arrow connecting the two conclusions in this case, as we did in Bob's case? The word *also* in the conclusion leader "it also follows that" indicates that two independent conclusions are being drawn—that is, one conclusion is not being drawn from the other. If "also" were replaced by *further*, in contrast, we would know that one conclusion was being drawn from the other. Indeed, the argument concerning Bob can be reexpressed as follows:

> [1] Bob has a temperature. It follows that [2] he is sick. It follows further that [3] he should rest.

Just as two conclusions may be drawn independently from one premise, so one conclusion may be drawn independently from two premises:

> [1] 51 is divisible by 3, so [2] it is not a prime number. This conclusion also follows from the fact that [3] 51 is divisible by 17.

Again, the word "also" in the premise leader indicates that two independent arguments for the conclusion are being offered, rather than one simple argument with two premises.

One simple argument may, of course, have two or more premises. In that case, we bracket the premises together before drawing the arrow to the conclusion, as follows:

> [1] If Alan goes to the party, he will be miserable. For [2] if he goes to the party, Alan will flirt with Monique. And [3] if he flirts with Monique, his wife will get very mad at him and he will be miserable.

How do we know that this conclusion is being drawn from both premises *taken together* and not from each premise *taken separately?* First, there is no explicit indication that two separate arguments are intended, as there is in the prime number argument. Second, the argument is valid as it stands, but it would be grossly invalid if two separate arguments were intended. While the premises taken together support the conclusion, neither premise alone does. Hence it is best to interpret the passage as one simple argument with two premises. Arguments in which one conclusion is drawn from several premises are generally simple rather than complex. So the following rule of thumb will be a useful practical guide: *When there is more than one premise for a given conclusion, bracket them together unless it is very clear that they represent separate arguments for the conclusion.*

The more complex the argument, the more useful diagrams are in understanding it. Consider:

> [1] If Mary fails the final exam, she will fail the course, for [2] her score on the midterm was 30 and [3] she received a D and an F on her papers. [4] If Mary fails the course, her grade point average will dip below 1.5. [5] If her average dips below 1.5, she will be suspended, since [6] the dean is very strict. [7] Mary's parents have threatened to cut off all financial aid if she ever fails a course. So [8] if Mary fails the final exam, she is in big trouble. [9] Now you know why Mary is studying so hard.

The diagram would look like this:

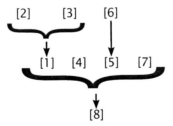

Statement [9] is neither a premise nor a conclusion, so it is not represented in the diagram. Note that treating [2] and [3] as separate premises is arbitrary. We could just as well have treated "her score on the midterm was 30 and she received a D and an F on her papers" as one compound premise. It would be definitely incorrect, however, to break [1] up into two statements. For [1] is a conditional, and its antecedent ("Mary fails the final") and consequent ("she will fail the course") were not stated.

Suppressed Premises. We have one final complication to deal with. Speech takes time, a precious commodity. Writing takes up space, which sometimes is in even shorter supply. An audience's attention span and grasp are also limited. Language accordingly tends to be compressed and abbreviated. Anything that can safely remain unexpressed tends to be unexpressed. We have seen many cases above where a premise or conclusion was stated elliptically, as in "Bob has a temperature so is sick, and hence should rest." But we have a more radical type of ellipsis to contend with. There is generally little point in proclaiming a piece of common knowledge: belaboring the obvious is dull and distracting. Consequently, a speaker will commonly omit an entire premise he thinks is so obviously true and relevant that it will occur to his audience and be accepted without hesitation. A proposition intended as a premise but omitted because it is obvious is called a **suppressed premise.** Consider the following argument:

> [1] Socialism is a system built on belief in human goodness; so [2] it never works. [3] Capitalism is a system built on belief in human selfishness; [4] given checks and balances, it is nearly always a smashing, scandalous success.[4]

It is perfectly acceptable to diagram this passage without reading too much between the lines:

However, the author is obviously taking two very important things for granted:

> [5] Human beings are generally selfish.
> [6] Selfishness is evil.

These are suppressed premises. So a more penetrating analysis of the argument would be:

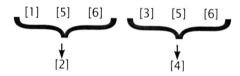

In this case, stylistic considerations undoubtedly led to the suppression of premises [5] and [6]. The passage would not have sounded very "cute" with their weight. Unfortunately, what seems obvious to a writer in one context may not be obvious to a reader in another context. So the recognition of suppressed premises is often difficult.

In complex arguments, intermediate conclusions are often suppressed. Consider:

> [1] In several studies with laboratory rats, cyclamates were found to produce cancer. [2] The FDA, therefore, should ban the use of cyclamates in soft drinks.

We could diagram this as follows: [1] → [2]. But there is clearly an implied intermediate step here, namely:

> [3] There is a significant chance that cyclamates cause cancer in human beings.

So given a more complete analysis, the argument could be diagramed: [1] → [3] → [2]. Such an intermediate conclusion is obviously intended, however, so [3] can safely be suppressed. The argument is less cumbersome, and therefore clearer, without it. In order to *evaluate* this argument, however, the intermediate conclusion must be made explicit, and the amount of support for it assessed.

---

[4] Michael Novak. "A Closet Capitalist Confesses," quoted in I. M. Copi, *Introduction to Logic*, 5th ed. (Macmillan, 1978), p. 17. Reprinted from *The Wall Street Journal* (April 20, 1976), p. 22.

> ### Glossary
>
> **Simple argument:** an argument in which one conclusion is drawn from one set of premises.
>
> **Complex argument:** a combination of one or more simple arguments.
>
> **Argument diagram:** a diagram representing the structure of an argument, constructed by numbering the premises and conclusions, and then drawing arrows from the numbers representing premises to the numbers representing conclusions.
>
> **Suppressed premise or conclusion:** a proposition intended as a premise or conclusion but omitted because it is obvious.

Exercises

A. Diagram the following passages, which may contain more than one simple argument.

1. *Over the long run—and it may be very long—stocks should outperform bonds.* The reason is that stock and bond prices are set in the open market-and the market, over the long run, rewards risk. From 1926 to 1975, the total compounded annual rate of return you would have had from buying risk-free United States Treasury bills was 2.3 percent; the return from slightly riskier corporate bonds would have been 3.89 percent, and the return from stocks would have been 9 percent. –Andrew Tobias, *Investment Guide*, pp. 65-66.

2. If, then, that is to be meaningful which is understandable at all, God is verifiable. But this hermeneutic verification criterion is too broad inasmuch as it is possible with its aid to judge the meaning or absurdity of the word "God," of the proposition "God exists," but not to decide the actual existence or nonexistence of God. Even that which is completely understood, like a "golden mountain," does not necessarily exist. –Hans Kung, *Does God Exist?,* p. 549.

3. If someone says that there is no God, this cannot be positively refuted…. For this negative statement rests in the last resort on a *decision,* a decision that is connected with the fundamental decision for reality as a whole…. And if someone says that there is a God, this, too, cannot be positively refuted…. The affirmation of God also rests, in the last resort, on a *decision*, which, again, is connected with the fundamental decision for reality as a whole. –Hans Kung, *Does God Exist?*, p. 569.

4. One of the most gratifying, and informative, election outcomes we've seen was the overwhelming defeat in Los Angeles County last week of Proposition M, an initiative that would have installed an especially repressive rent-control system.

   The voting pattern made a mockery of the insistent claims by rent-control promoters that they are representing the poor and downtrodden. The poor and downtrodden vigorously rejected Proposition M. Hispanics voted 2 to 1 against it and blacks stomped it 3 to 1.

   Who voted for it? Mainly the swinging singles of glitzy enclaves like Marina del Rey and Malibu. –"Hot-Tub Populism," *The Wall Street Journal* (November 17, 1983), p. 30.

5. Tolstoy condemned all war; others have held the life of a soldier doing battle for the right to be very noble. Here there was probably involved a real difference as to ends. Those who praised the soldier usually consider the punishment of sinners a good thing in itself; Tolstoy did not think so. On such

a matter no argument is possible; I can only state my view and hope that as many as possible will agree. –Bertrand Russell, *Why I Am Not a Christian*, p. 56.

6. Conscience is a most fallacious guide, since it consists of vague reminiscences of precepts heard in early youth, so that it is never wiser than its possessor's nurse or mother. –Bertrand Russell, *Why I Am Not a Christian*, p. 74.

7. Every increase of courage in the ruling caste was used to increase the burdens on the oppressed, and therefore to increase the grounds for fear in the oppressors, and therefore to leave the causes of cruelty undiminished. –Bertrand Russell, *Why I Am Not a Christian*, p. 80.

8. Auroras are emitted by molecules in the earth's upper atmosphere excited by electrically charged particles in the "wind" of thin gas expanding outward from the sun. The particles plunge into the atmosphere because they are trapped in the earth's magnetic field, which is generated by slow flows in the earth's metallic core. Therefore the aurora is a manifestation of the dynamic activity of the core. –Preston Cloud, "The Biosphere," *Scientific American*, 249, no. 3 (1983). p. 4. Copyright © 1983 by Scientific American, Inc. All rights reserved.

9. Differences in the mass of the rock on the sea floor result in variations in gravity: seamounts have a high gravity field and trenches have a low field. Hence water tends to "pile up" over seamounts and to do the opposite over trenches. Therefore the ocean bottom can be inferred from the height of the sea trenches. –Jean Francheteau, "The Oceanic Crust," *Scientific American*, 249, no. 3 (1983), p. 117. Copyright © 1983 by Scientific American, Inc. All rights reserved.

10. Storage [of DDT] in human beings has been well investigated, and we know that the average person is storing potentially harmful amounts. According to various studies, individuals with no known exposure (except the inevitable dietary one) store an average of 5.3 parts per million to 7.4 parts per million; agricultural workers 17.1 parts per million; and workers in insecticide plants as high as 648 parts per million! So the range of proven storage is quite wide and, what is even more to the point, the minimum figures are above the level at which damage to the liver and other organs or tissues may begin. –Rachel Carson, *Silent Spring*, p. 31.

11. Government actions affect your daily life beginning with the moment you wake up in the morning. The clock radio that awakens you is subject to many manufacturing and sales regulations. The music set off by the alarm mechanism comes from a station that is able to broadcast only because it has been granted a special government license; it must comply with the government's idea of "good programming" or run the risk of having its license revoked. –Robert J. Ringer, *Restoring the American Dream*, p. 28.

12. One must remain steadfast to the moral belief that no matter how "worthy" the cause for which a man's rights are violated, the end *never* justifies the means. That is to say, no matter how moral or humane one may believe a cause to be, if its attainment requires a violation of the rights of even one man, then the end has been achieved through immoral action. Therefore, while the needs and desires of certain individuals (whether they be the "poor" or any other vaguely defined group) may constitute a legitimate concern to many people, they nonetheless fall outside the scope of man's natural rights. –Robert J. Ringer, *Restoring the American Dream*, p. 31.

13. In 1960, 37 percent of the voting-age population did not vote. In the 1976 presidential election, the figure had grown to 45 percent. That means that almost 70 million eligible voters did not participate in the last presidential election. It also means that Jimmy Carter was, *at best,* the choice of about

one-fourth of the eligible voters (a little more than half of the 54 percent who voted). –Robert J. Ringer, *Restoring the American Dream,* p. 58.

14. Instead of listening to Gandhi, are we not more inclined to listen to one of the most influential economists of our century, the great Lord Keynes? In 1930, during the world-wide economic depression, he felt moved to speculate on the "economic possibilities for our grandchildren" and concluded that the day might not be all that far off when everybody would be rich. We shall then, he said, "once more value ends above means and prefer the good to the useful."

    "But beware!" he continued. "The time for all this is not yet. For at least another hundred years we must pretend to ourselves and to everyone that fair is foul and foul is fair; for foul is useful and fair is not. Avarice and usury and precaution must be our gods for a little longer still. For only they can lead us out of the tunnel of economic necessity into daylight." –E. F. Schumacher, *Small Is Beautiful*, p. 24.

15. Nothing, or anyhow not much, lasts forever. But what is well established is likely to last for a time. So the forces that have shaped past policy (or which past policy has resisted), if they have been correctly identified in this history, will, one may assume, continue to operate for at least a while in the future. They are, in the fullest sense, historical imperatives. This means that they are not matters for ideological preference as commonly imagined. –John Kenneth Galbraith, *Money,* p. 368.

16. There is another prospect—one for which we can profoundly pray. It is that policy in the future will be based not on forecasts but on the current reality. The reason for this we have sufficiently seen; not only is economic forecasting highly imperfect, something that is conceded even by the forecasters except when offering a new forecast, but official forecasting has an ineluctable tendency to error. On all but the rarest occasions it is biased by what policy-makers hope to have happen or need to have happen. –John Kenneth Galbraith, *Money*, p. 376.

17. I cannot sit idly by in Atlanta and not be concerned about what happens in Birmingham. Injustice anywhere is a threat to justice everywhere. We are caught in an inescapable network of mutuality, tied in a single garment of destiny. Whatever affects one directly, affects all indirectly. Never again can we afford to live with the narrow, provincial "outside agitator" idea. Anyone who lives inside the United States can never be considered an outsider anywhere within its bounds. –Martin Luther King, *Letter From a Birmingham Jail.*

18. On the positive side, there is another reason why the United Kingdom should retain its nuclear arsenal, and which, to the best of my knowledge has never been deployed. Paradoxically, its continued possession could help in the process of world disarmament, not because the United Kingdom might be allowed to argue the case in the conference chamber, but because the scale of what it has, and what the French have, is an indication to the two superpowers of the forces that are adequate to maintain a deterrent threat. –Solly Zuckerman, *Nuclear Illusion and Reality*, p. 142.

19. If and when a historian sets the record straight on the experiences of enslaved black women, she (or he) will have performed an inestimable service. It is not for the sake of historical accuracy alone that such a study should be conducted, for lessons can be gleaned from the slave era which will shed light upon black women's and all women's current battle for emancipation. –Angela Y. Davis, *Women, Race and Class,* p. 4.

20. For most girls and women, as for most boys and men, it was hard labor in the fields from sunup to sundown. Where work was concerned, strength and productivity under the threat of the whip

outweighed considerations of sex. In this sense, the oppression of women was identical to the oppression of men.

But women suffered in different ways as well, for they were victims of sexual abuse and other barbarous mistreatment that could only be inflicted on women. –Angela Y. Davis, *Women, Race and Class*, p. 6.

B. Diagram the following passages. These are more difficult, and the structures of many are unclear.

1. What we call our "thoughts" seem to depend upon the organization of tracks in the brain in the same sort of way in which journeys depend upon roads and railways. The energy used in thinking seems to have a chemical origin; for instance, a deficiency of iodine will turn a clever man into an idiot. Mental phenomena seem to be bound up with material structure. If this be so, we cannot suppose that a solitary electron or proton can "think"; we might as well expect a solitary individual to play a football match. We also cannot suppose that an individual's thinking survives bodily death, since that destroys the organization of the brain and dissipates the energy which utilized the brain tracks. –Bertrand Russell, *Why I Am Not a Christian*, p. 50.

2. Whatever experiences we may have, we shall not regard them as miraculous if we already hold a philosophy which excludes the supernatural. Any event which is claimed as a miracle is, in the last resort, an experience received from the senses; and the senses are not infallible. We can always say we have been the victims of an illusion; if we disbelieve in the supernatural this is what we always shall say. Hence whether miracles have really ceased or not, they would certainly appear to cease in Western Europe as materialism became the popular creed. –C. S. Lewis, *The Grand Miracle*, p. 1.

3. The belief in such a supernatural reality itself can neither be proved nor disproved by experience. The arguments for its existence are metaphysical, and to me conclusive. They turn on the fact that even to think and act in the natural world we have to assume something beyond it and even assume that we partly belong to that something. In order to think we must claim for our own reasoning a validity which is not credible if our own thought is merely a function of our brain, and our brains a by-product of irrational physical processes. In order to act, above the level of mere impulse, we must claim a similar validity for our judgments of good and evil. –C. S. Lewis, *The Grand Miracle*, p. 3.

4. Aggression may be thought of as force or fraud or as the threat of force or fraud. Hence, from a Natural-Law standpoint, only *one* thing is against the law: aggression against others. When aggression occurs, man's rights are violated. It naturally follows that violence for any reason other than self-defense is a violation of Natural Law. –Robert J. Ringer, *Restoring the American Dream*, p. 30.

5. But that command method can be the exclusive or even principal method of organization only in a very small group. Not even the most autocratic head of a family can control every act of other family members entirely by order. No sizable army can really be run entirely by command. The general cannot conceivably have the information necessary to direct every movement of the lowliest private. At every step in the chain of command, the soldier, whether officer or private, must have discretion to take into account information about specific circumstances that his commanding officer could not have. –Milton and Rose Friedman, *Free to Choose*, p. 1.

6. There could be simply enormous and altogether unheard-of discoveries of new reserves of oil, natural gas, or even coal. And why should nuclear energy be confined to supplying one-quarter or one-third of total requirements? The problem can thus be shifted to another plane, but it refuses to go

away. For the consumption of fuel on the indicated scale—assuming no insurmountable difficulties of fuel supply—would produce environmental hazards of an unprecedented kind.

Take nuclear energy.... It is hard to imagine a greater geological threat, not to mention the political danger that someone might use a tiny bit of this terrible substance for purposes not altogether peaceful.

On the other hand, if fantastic new discoveries of fossil fuels should make it unnecessary to force the pace of nuclear energy, there would be a problem of thermal pollution on quite a different scale from anything encountered hitherto. –E. F. Schumacher, *Small Is Beautiful,* p. *29.*

7. While the materialist is mainly interested in goods, the Buddhist is mainly interested in liberation. But Buddhism is "The Middle Way" and therefore in no way antagonistic to physical well-being. It is not wealth that stands in the way of liberation but the attachment to wealth; not the enjoyment of pleasurable things but the craving for them. The keynote of Buddhist economics, therefore, is simplicity and nonviolence. –E. F. Schumacher, *Small Is Beautiful,* p. 57.

8. It is, of course, just conceivable that were war ever to break out, and were either of the engaged sides to resort to nuclear weapons, one shot would be enough to end hostilities, without the side that was struck ever retaliating. However conceivable such an outcome, it is in the highest degree unlikely. The more probable reaction would be retaliation in kind. Only utter desperation and fear could lead one side in a conflict to a "rational" decision to use a nuclear weapon, and if one warhead, why not more than one? The side that had not initiated the exchange would in all reason reckon that it had to respond in order to deny its enemy any advantage. –Solly Zuckerman, *Nuclear Illusion and Reality,* p. 35.

9. There are again two methods of removing the causes of faction: the one, by destroying the liberty which is essential to its existence; the other, by giving to every citizen the same opinions, the same passions, and the same interests.

It could never be more truly said than of the first remedy, that it was worse than the disease. Liberty is to faction what air is to fire, an ailment without which it instantly expires. But it could not be less folly to abolish liberty, which is essential to political life, because it nourishes faction, than it would be to wish the annihilation of air, which is essential to animal life, because it imparts to fire its destructive agency. –James Madison, "Federalist #10."

10. What is the moral dimension of American foreign policy? Well, it can be summed up in one proposition: The only governments whose moral legitimacy we recognize are those that are (a) based on popular consent, and (b) are respectful of the rights of the citizenry to life, liberty and property.... It follows from this basic proposition—which both liberals and conservatives ought to find acceptable—that most existing governments in the world are, in our eyes, if to varying degrees, morally illegitimate. One of the reasons that the United Nations is such a noxious organization is that it affirms precisely the opposite point of view, and our participation in that organization is therefore a source of serious mental confusion for Americans.

It also follows that—as Rep. Jack Kemp recently emphasized—we have not only the moral right but also the moral duty to encourage the peoples of those nations to strive for a degree of self-government that we find morally congruent with our political ideas. –Irving Kristol, "Toward a Moral Foreign Policy," *The Wall Street Journal* (November 15, 1983), p. 34.

LSAT Prep Questions

1. The folktale that claims that a rattlesnake's age can be determined from the number of sections in its rattle is false, but only because the rattles are brittle and sometimes partially or completely break off. So if they were not so brittle, one could reliability determine a rattlesnake's age simply from the number of sections in its rattle, because one new section is formed each time a rattlesnake molts.

    Which one of the following is an assumption the argument requires in order for its conclusion to be properly drawn?

    (a) Rattlesnakes molt exactly once a year.

    (b) The rattles of rattlesnakes of different species are identical in appearance.

    (c) Rattlesnakes molt more frequently when young than when old.

    (d) The brittleness of a rattlesnake's rattle is not correlated with the length of the rattlesnake's life.

    (e) Rattlesnakes molt as often when food is scarce as they do when food is plentiful.

    Preptest 30, Section 2, Question 22

2. Historian: Leibniz, the seventeenth-century philosopher, published his version of calculus before Newton did. But then Newton revealed his private notebooks, which showed he had been using these ideas for at least a decade before Leibniz's publication. Newton also claimed that he had disclosed these ideas to Leibniz in a letter shortly before Leibniz's publication. Yet close examination of the letter shows that Newton's few cryptic remarks did not reveal anything important about calculus. Thus, Leibniz and Newton each independently discovered calculus.

    Which one of the following is an assumption required by the historian's argument?

    (a) Leibniz did not tell anyone about calculus prior to publishing his version of it.

    (b) No third person independently discovered calculus prior to Newton and Leibniz.

    (c) Newton believed that Leibniz was able to learn something important about calculus from his letter to him.

    (d) Neither Newton nor Leibniz knew that the other had developed a version of calculus prior to Leibniz's publication.

    (e) Neither Newton nor Leibniz learned crucial details about calculus from some third source.

    Preptest 31, Section 2, Question 14

3. Joseph: My encyclopedia says that the mathematician Pierre de Fermat died in 1665 without leaving behind any written proof for a theorem that he claimed nonetheless to have proved. Probably this alleged theorem simply cannot be proved, since—as the article points out—no one else has been able to prove it. Therefore it is likely that Fermat was either lying or else mistaken when he made his claim.

    Laura: Your encyclopedia is out of date. Recently someone has in fact proved Fermat's theorem. And since the theorem is provable, your claim—that Fermat was lying or mistaken—clearly is wrong.

    Joseph's statement that "this alleged theorem simply cannot be proved" plays which one of the following roles in the argument?

    (a) an assumption for which no support is offered

    (b) a subsidiary conclusion on which his argument's main conclusion is based

    (c) a potential objection that his argument anticipates and attempts to answer before it is raised

    (d) the principal claim that his argument is structured to refute

    (e) background information that neither supports nor undermines his argument's conclusion

    Preptest 30, Section 4, Question 13

4. On the basis of the available evidence, Antarctica has generally been thought to have been covered by ice for at least the past 14 million years. Recently, however, three-million-year-old fossils of a kind previously found only in ocean-floor sediments were discovered under the ice sheet covering central Antarctica. About three million years ago, therefore, the Antarctic ice sheet must temporarily have melted. After all, either severe climatic warming or volcanic activity in Antarctica's mountains could have melted the ice sheet, thus raising sea levels and submerging the continent.

    Which one of the following is the main conclusion of the argument?

    (a) Antarctica is no longer generally thought to have been covered by ice for the past 14 million years.

    (b) It is not the case that ancient fossils of the kind recently found in Antarctica are found only in ocean-floor sentiments.

    (c) The ice sheet covering Antarctica has not been continuously present throughout the past 14 million years.

    (d) What caused Antarctica to be submerged under the sea was the melting of the ice sheet that had previously covered the continent.

    (e) The ice sheet covering Antarctica was melted either as a result of volcanic activity in Antarctica's mountains or as a result of severe climatic warming.

    Preptest 35, Section 1, Question 16

5. Columnist: Almost anyone can be an expert, for there are no official guidelines determining what an expert must know. Anybody who manages to convince some people of his or her qualifications in an area—whatever those may be—is an expert.

The columnist's conclusion follows logically if which one of the following is assumed?

(a) Almost anyone can convince some people of his or her qualifications in some area.

(b) Some experts convince everyone of their qualifications in almost every area.

(c) Convincing certain people that one is qualified in an area requires that one actually be qualified in that area.

(d) Every expert has convinced some people of his or her qualifications in some area.

(e) Some people manage to convince almost everyone of their qualifications in one or more areas.

Preptest 35, Section 1, Question 20

6. Marian Anderson, the famous contralto, did not take success for granted. We know this because Anderson had to struggle early in life, and anyone who has to struggle early in life is able to keep a good perspective on the world.

The conclusion of the argument follows logically if which one of the following is assumed?

(a) Anyone who succeeds takes success for granted.

(b) Anyone who is able and to keep a good perspective on the world does not take success for granted.

(c) Anyone who is able to keep a good perspective on the world has to struggle early in life.

(d) Anyone who does not take success for granted has to struggle early in life.

(e) Anyone who does not take success for granted is able to keep a good perspective on the world.

Preptest 35, Section 4, Question 14

CHAPTER TWO

Soundness and Validity

2.1 Soundness

In Chapter 1 we studied the interpretation of arguments. We learned how to determine whether a passage is an argument, and what reasoning if any it expresses. The goal in logic, however, is to evaluate arguments. There are two standards by which an argument may be judged as good or bad. For an argument may serve two different purposes, both served by producing reasons for believing its conclusion. One purpose is to persuade or convince someone that the conclusion is true. A second is to prove or verify the conclusion. In other words, an argument may be used to produce belief, or it may be used to justify belief. Justification is necessary to produce knowledge as opposed to mere opinion. We shall use the term **sound** to describe arguments that verify their conclusion, and that consequently are good for the purposes of justification. In all arguments, the premises are offered as providing a sufficient reason to believe the conclusion. Sound arguments are those in which the premises do provide a sufficient reason to believe the conclusion, so that you may infer the conclusion from the premises. Only sound arguments express correct reasoning. Arguments that are not sound are termed **fallacious**. Logic is concerned with an argument's soundness and not its persuasiveness. Persuasiveness is a psychological matter studied in rhetoric. It is a basic and lamentable fact of human nature that convincing arguments are often fallacious, and sound arguments often unconvincing. It would be harder to be a propagandist and easier to be an educator if this weren't so. Fortunately, the defect can be corrected to some extent by studying logic.

A *complex* argument is sound if, and only if, all of the *simple* arguments making it up are sound. As the saying goes, "A chain is only as strong as its weakest link." Hence all of our attention will be devoted to the soundness of simple arguments. "Argument," henceforth, shall mean "simple argument."

There are three requirements for a sound argument. First, *the premises must be true and justified.* Falsehoods, mere speculations, or improbabilities do not verify anything. Consider:

There are exactly five planets, so there are less than eight planets.
IBM stock will go up 25 percent this year, so it is a good investment.

These arguments are fallacious even though their conclusions follow. The premise of the first argument is false: we know there are more than five planets. That of the second argument might be true, but we do not yet know whether it is or not. If an argument has more than one premise, *all* of them must be true and justified. One bad premise spoils an argument. An argument with a false or unjustified premise may be termed a **nonstarter.**

The second requirement of a sound argument is that *the conclusion must follow from the premises, at least with probability.* The probability qualification will be explained below. To say that the conclusion follows from the premises is to say that the premises *imply* the conclusion. In other words, *if* the premises are true, *then* the conclusion is true too. Speaking metaphorically, the argument is a conductor of truth. The conclusions of the arguments in the previous paragraph follow. *If* it is true that IBM will go up 25 percent this year, then it is a good investment. It is not in fact true that there are just five planets; but if it *were* true, it would also be true that there are less than eight planets. The conclusions of the arguments below do not follow.

There are eight planets, therefore Paris is the capital of France.
All dogs are animals, therefore all animals are dogs.

Such arguments, whose conclusions do not follow from the premises at all, are said to be **non sequiturs.** "Non sequitur" is an often used Latin phrase meaning "it does not follow." It is very important to grasp the fact that the first two requirements of soundness are *independent.* As our examples have shown, there are arguments with true premises in which the conclusion does not follow, and there are arguments in which the conclusion follows even though the premises are false.

The third and final requirement of soundness is that *the conclusion must not be assumed by any of the premises.* In other words, *you cannot assume what you are trying to prove.* Consider:

Whales are mammals, therefore whales are mammals.

This argument is fallacious even though the premise is known to be true and the conclusion follows (trivially—if anything is true, then it is true). The argument cannot be used to establish that whales are mammals, because its premise is that very conclusion. When our third requirement is violated, the argument is said to be **question-begging.**[1] A complex argument may be question-begging even though none of the simple arguments making it up are. Such reasoning is *circular.* Consider:

What the Bible says is true because it is the word of God; the
Bible is the word of God because it says so in the Bible and
what the Bible says is true.

This argument cannot be used to justify the conclusion that what the Bible says is true, for that conclusion is used as a premise from which that very conclusion is drawn indirectly. Note, though, that neither simple argument here is question-begging.

Unfortunately, question-begging arguments are seldom as obvious as the ones above. If they were, they would be easy to spot. More often, the question-begging premise is a *reformulation* of the conclusion: something that *says the same thing* as the conclusion, but in different words. Consider:

Unicorns do not exist, for there is no such thing as a unicorn.

---

[1] The Latin term for begging the question is *petitio principii*; it is used mainly in logic books.

The conclusion follows here, but we need to ask ourselves: just what does it mean to say that "there is no such thing as" a unicorn? Simply that unicorns do not exist. So this argument is question-begging too. Or consider:

> All whales are mammals, for no whales are nonmammals.

The premise and conclusion here are not exactly the same (see ch. 5), but they are so obviously equivalent that the conclusion is still assumed by the premise. So the question has been begged. Finally, consider:

> God created the universe in six days.
> Therefore, God created the universe.

While the premise of this argument is not identical to the conclusion, it does *assume* the conclusion. *A premise assumes the conclusion if the premise cannot be known without already knowing that the conclusion is true.* So the premise cannot be used in an argument designed to justify believing that the conclusion is true.

If an argument is sound, then we can justifiably infer that the conclusion is true. However, having a conclusion that is true and justified does not suffice to make an argument sound. Consider:

> All mortal beings are gods.
> The author is a god.
> ∴ The author is mortal.

There is overwhelming evidence supporting the conclusion, so we are fully justified in believing it to be true. However, the premises of this argument are not what justify belief in the conclusion. For not only are the premises false, but the conclusion does not follow. Consequently, this argument is fallacious even though the conclusion is certainly true. The fact that an argument is unsound, therefore, does not even tend to prove that its conclusion is false.

Glossary

Sound argument: an argument in which the premises provide a sufficient reason to believe the conclusion. The premises must be true and justified, the conclusion must follow from the premises at least with probability, and the conclusion must not be one of the premises.

Fallacious argument: one that is not sound.

Non sequitur: an argument whose conclusion does not follow, even with probability; an invalid argument.

Nonstarter: an argument with a false or unjustified premise.

Question-begging argument: an argument whose conclusion is assumed by one of the premises from which the conclusion is drawn.

Exercises

Determine whether the following arguments are sound or fallacious. If an argument is fallacious, classify it as a nonstarter, non sequitur, or question begger (it may be more than one). An almanac or an atlas might be useful

1. All humans are animals, for all humans are mammals and all mammals are animals.

2. All musicians are violinists, for all violinists are stringed-instrument players and all stringed-instrument players are musicians.

3. California is more populous than New York, and New York is more populous than Rhode Island. Therefore, California is more populous than Rhode Island.

4. Pennsylvania is more populous than Rhode Island. The population of New York is much greater than the population of Rhode Island. So New York is more populous than Pennsylvania.

5. Kansas is west of Colorado and Colorado is west of Nevada, so Kansas is west of Nevada.

6. North Dakota is considerably west of Illinois. Arizona is considerably south of North Dakota. Therefore Arizona is southwest of Illinois.

7. California and Oregon are neighboring states. California and Nevada are neighboring states. Hence Oregon and Nevada must be neighboring states.

8. Texas is the largest state, so it must be larger than New York.

9. California is the best state, for it is better than all the other states.

10. The Missouri River is the longest river in the United States. The Mississippi River is longer than any river in Europe. Therefore, the longest river in the United States is longer than any river in Europe.

11. The Missouri River is longer than the Mississippi. The Nile is longer than the Mississippi. Therefore the Nile is longer than the Missouri.

12. The Amazon River is longer than the Nile, the Mississippi, and the Missouri. Therefore the Amazon is the longest river in the world.

13. London is both the capital of, and the largest city in, Great Britain. Tokyo is both the capital of, and the largest city in, Japan. Hence the capital city of a country is its largest city.

14. New York City has a population of about 20 million. Therefore New York City has a greater population than some states, for Rhode Island only has a population of about 1 million.

15. The sun has risen every day for at least the last billion years. Therefore it will probably rise tomorrow.

16. Cigarette smoking causes cancer, emphysema, and heart disease. Therefore if you smoke cigarettes, you are endangering your health.

17. Cigarette smoking is harmful to health. Pipe smoking is different in many ways from cigarette smoking. Therefore pipe smoking is probably not harmful to health.

18. Women in the army should not be allowed to serve in combat, for fighting ought to be done by men.

19. Women should not be allowed to fly combat planes in the Air Force since women are not as strong as men.

20. Men should not do housework, for housework is women's work.

21. Anacin contains the pain reliever doctors recommend most. Therefore Anacin is a more effective pain remedy than Bayer aspirin.

22. Even a one-day-old fetus is a human being. For a nine-month-old fetus is clearly an unborn human being, and there is no precise point in the development of the fetus at which we can say "Now it is a human being, but before this it wasn't."

23. If Richmond is in Virginia, then Richmond is in the South. Richmond is in Virginia. Therefore Richmond is in the South.

24. If Fort Worth is in Texas, then Fort Worth is in the South. Fort Worth is in the South. Therefore Fort Worth is in Texas.

25. Bismarck is in either North Dakota or South Dakota. Bismarck is not in North Dakota. Therefore Bismarck is in South Dakota.

26. California is on the Pacific coast. If a state is on the Pacific coast, then it is west of the Mississippi. A state is west of the Mississippi only if it is west of the Appalachian Mountains. A state that is west of the Appalachian Mountains must not be on the Atlantic coast. Therefore, California is not on the Atlantic coast.

27. California is west of the Rockies. The Rockies are west of the Appalachians. A state is west of the Appalachians only if it is not on the Atlantic coast. A state is not on the Atlantic coast only if it is on the Pacific coast. Therefore California is on the Pacific coast.

28. California is on the Pacific coast. Hence it is west of the Appalachians. If a state is west of the Appalachians, then it is not on the Atlantic coast. So California is not on the Atlantic coast. California is a coastal state, but it is not on the Gulf coast. A coastal state must be either on the Gulf coast, the Atlantic coast, or the Pacific coast. Therefore California is on the Pacific coast.

29. Members of the House of Representatives are members of Congress. Senators are members of Congress too. The president, however, is not a member of Congress. Therefore he is neither a representative nor a senator.

30. All Senators are members of Congress. Only politicians are congressmen. Some politicians are from Massachusetts. Therefore some Senators are from Massachusetts.

31. We [the United States] cannot claim the world's largest land surface, for Brazil, Australia, China, and Russia are larger. –Tim LaHaye, *The Battle for the Mind* (Fleming H. Revell Co., 1979), p. 37.

LSAT Prep Questions

1. The current pattern of human consumption of resources, in which we rely on nonrenewable resources, for example, metal ore, must eventually change. Since there is only so much metal ore available ultimately we must either do without or turn to renewable resources to take its place.

Which one of the following is an assumption required by the argument?

(a) There are renewable resource replacements for all of the nonrenewable resources currently being consumed.

(b) We cannot indefinitely replace exhausted nonrenewable resources with other nonrenewable resources.

(c) A renewable resource cannot be exhausted by human consumption.

(d) Consumption of nonrenewable resources will not continue to increase in the near future.

(e) Ultimately we cannot do without nonrenewable resources.

Preptest 35, Section 1, Question 18

2.2 Argument Strength and Modality

Argument Strength. Some sound arguments are stronger than others. The *strength of an argument* is the degree to which the premises support the conclusion. The premises of all sound arguments provide a *sufficient* reason to believe the conclusion. But some provide *more conclusive* reasons than others. The premises must justify *belief* in the conclusion. But some warrant *greater certainty*. Imagine an urn filled with thousands of balls, ten of which are selected at random, one after another. Then compare the following arguments:

> (1) The first ball is red, for all balls in the urn are red.
> (2) The first ball is red, for at least 90 percent of the balls are red.

Let us assume that their premises are known to be true. Then both arguments are sound. Both premises provide more than enough reason to believe that the first ball is red. Nevertheless, the strength of the reasons differ. The fact that all balls in the urn are red provides an absolutely conclusive reason to believe that the first one is red, and warrants complete certainty in the conclusion. For it is impossible for the first ball not to be red given that all are. The fact that 90 percent of the balls are red is not conclusive, and leaves room for some doubt about the conclusion. For it is possible, though highly unlikely, that the first ball is some other color unless it is given that 100 percent are red. Note that as the known percentage of red balls increases from 90 percent, the strength of the argument increases. As the percentage decreases, the strength decreases. Indeed, if the percentage is reduced sufficiently, the resulting argument will be too weak to be sound. As an example, consider:

> (3) The first ball is red for at least 10 percent of the balls are red.

While the premise provides some reason to believe the conclusion, it does not provide anything near a sufficient reason. Argument (3) is therefore inconclusive.

Statement Strength. The *strength of a statement* has to do not with how well supported it is, but with how much it implies or asserts. One statement is said to be stronger than another if the former implies the latter, but the latter does not imply the former. Thus the statement that 100 percent of the balls in the urn are red is stronger than the statement that at least 90 percent of the balls are red, which in turn is stronger than the statement that at least 10 percent of the balls are red. In general, the strength of a statement of the form "*r* percent of all the balls are red" increases as the percentage *r* increases. While argument strength (how well the premises support the conclusion) and statement strength (how much a statement implies) are different quantities, they are related: *The strength of an argument depends on the strength of its premises and conclusion.* Thus we saw that the strength of the arguments discussed in the previous paragraph is determined by the strength of the premise. The greater the percentage cited in the premise, the greater the support provided for the conclusion. This illustrates a general rule: *The strength of an argument is directly related to the strength of its premises.* That is, if the premises of an argument are strengthened, while everything else (such as the conclusion) is kept the same, the strength of the argument will typically increase. As we go from argument (3) to argument (1), the strength of the argument increases. On the other hand, if the premises are weakened, the argument is generally weakened (everything else remaining constant). As we go from argument (1) to argument (3), the strength of the argument decreases. An obvious exception to this rule occurs when the strength of the argument is already maximal. Thus "At least one ball in the urn is red, for all are" is no stronger than "At least one ball in the urn is red, for over 90 percent are," even though the premise of the former is stronger than the premise of the latter. For the latter argument already has maximal strength. The strength of an argument also fails to increase when its premises are strengthened in irrelevant respects. Thus "The first ball is red, for at least 90 percent of the balls in the urn are *bright* red" is no stronger than (2), even though its premise is stronger.

The strength of an argument also depends on its conclusion. Compare:

> (4) The first ball is red, for 90 percent the balls are red.
> (5) The first five balls are red, for 90 percent of the balls are red.
> (6) The first ten balls are red, for 90 percent of the balls are red.

The conclusions of these arguments increase in strength from (4) to (6). As a result, the arguments *decrease* in strength from top to bottom. The premise that 90 percent of the balls are red does not support the conclusion that the first ten balls are red as well as it supports the conclusion that the first ball is red. Whereas the strength of an argument is *directly* related to the strength of its premises, *the strength of an argument is inversely related to the strength* of *its conclusion*. That is, strengthening the conclusion typically weakens the argument, and weakening the conclusion typically strengthens it (other things equal). The greater the claim made by the conclusion, the greater the evidence needed to justify any particular degree of certainty. The weaker the claim, the less evidence is needed. Arguments of maximal strength again constitute an exception to the rule: weakening their conclusions cannot strengthen them any further.

Several things need to he noted. First, our rules relating the strength of an argument to the strength of its premises and conclusion can be used only to judge *comparative* strength. There is as of yet no way to *measure* argument strength or statement strength. Second, there are exceptions to both rules, as we have seen. Other exceptions will be noted in later chapters. The rules should therefore be treated as rules of thumb and not universal laws of logic. And third, the principle that the strength of an argument is directly related to the strength of its premises and inversely related to the strength of its conclusion does not even enable us to judge comparative strength when the premises and conclusion of an argument are strengthened at the same time. Thus it is hard to say whether "The first two balls are red, for 95 percent of all the balls are red" is stronger or weaker than "The first ball is red, for 90 percent of the balls are red." The greater strength of the premise of the former argument may or may not compensate for the greater strength of its conclusion.

Finally, the strength of an argument depends on more than just the *strength* of its premises and conclusion. An argument's strength also depends on *how well supported* its premises are. Consider: "You will have bad luck today, for you walked under a ladder and whenever a man walks under a ladder he has bad luck." This *would* be a strong argument if the premises were known to be true. But since the second premise is certainly false, the argument is perfectly flimsy. *The strength of an argument is directly related to the probability of its premises*. Other things equal (such as the strength of the premises), the more probable the premises are, the stronger the argument. Consider argument (1). The more certain it is that all balls in the urn are red, the more certain we can be that the first ball is red. Compare (1) and (2). The rule relating argument strength to premise strength tells us that (1) is stronger than (2) *if other things are equal*. One of the other things that needs to be held constant, however, is the probability of the premises. If it is completely certain that at least 90 percent of the balls in the urn are red, while it is probable but not certain that all of the balls in the urn are red, then we cannot say whether (1) or (2) is stronger. The greater certainty of the premise in (2) may or may not compensate for its weaker strength.

Modality. An important determinant of the strength of arguments is the ***modality*** of their premises and conclusions. Consider the following argument from Chapter 1:

> Bob has a temperature.
> ∴. He is sick.

The conclusion of this argument is that Bob is sick, which is to say that he is *actually* sick. The conclusion, we shall say, has the modality of *actuality*. There are other modalities, as can be seen by examining the following argument form:

> Bob has a temperature.
> ∴. He is _____ sick.

The blank here can be filled with "actually," or it can be deleted, which amounts to the same thing. But the blank can also be filled by any of the following adverbs: *necessarily, possibly, certainly,* and *probably*. Consider, for example:

> Bob has a temperature.
> ∴. He is *necessarily* sick.

The conclusion of this argument has the modality of *necessity*. Similarly, if the conclusion of an argument says that something is possible, certain, or probable, it has the modality of *possibility, certainty,* or *probability*. The conclusion of our example is a present-tense statement. Statements about what was or will be the case can have the same modalities.

The modalities can be ranked in order of strength. First of all, if something is necessarily the case, then it is actually the case. Since triangles necessarily have three sides, they actually have three sides. However, something may be actual without being necessary. Washington is the actual capital of the United States. But it is not necessary that Washington be the capital of the United States: there could be a different capital city. So necessity is stronger than actuality. In a similar way actuality is stronger than possibility. If something is actually the case, then it must be possible. However, something may be possible without being actual. New York could be the capital of the United States, but it isn't. Since necessity is stronger than actuality, and actuality is stronger than possibility, it follows that necessity is stronger than possibility.

We get a similar ordering for necessity, certainty, probability, and possibility. Probability varies in degrees. Something is certain if it has the highest degree of probability. Something is probable if its probability is greater than 50 percent, so that it is more likely than not to happen. It follows that if something is certain, then it is probable; but something may be probable without being certain. It is certain and therefore probable that I will not live forever; but while it is probable that I will not live to be 80 it is not certain. Consequently, certainty is stronger than probability. Necessity is stronger than certainty: if something is necessary then it is certain, but something may be certain without being necessary. Since triangles necessarily have three sides, it is certain that they do. But even though it is certain that Washington is the capital of the United States, it is not necessary. Necessity therefore is stronger than certainty. Probability, finally, is stronger than possibility. If something is not possible, its probability is 0 percent. The ordering of the modalities is summarized by Figure 2-1, in which the arrows express implication.

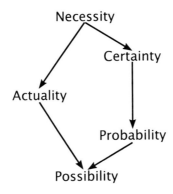

Figure 2-1

Why are there no arrows in Figure 2-1 connecting actuality with certainty or probability? Because actuality cannot be compared in strength with certainty or probability. What will actually be the case may or may not be certain, and it may or may not be probable. Just think about the weather tomorrow. Rain may be likely, even though in fact it will not rain. Snow may be unlikely, even though in fact it will snow. It is natural to feel that actuality is equal in strength to certainty, and that probability is weaker. For people generally do not assert that something is the case unless they believe it is certain, and generally do not assert that something is probable unless they believe it is not certain. People tend to be cautious and to avoid understatement. Thus if I say that it *is* going to rain, you will infer that I am sure it is going to rain; whereas if I say that it is *probably* going to rain, you will infer that I am not sure it is. As we shall frequently see, the act of making a particular statement often has implications that the statement itself does not have.

The modality of a proposition is often expressed not by adverbs, but by modal auxiliaries. *Must* or *have to* express necessity; *is bound to* expresses certainty; *should* expresses probability; and *may* or *can* express possibility. In "The index of leading economic indicators rose for the twelfth consecutive month, so the economy should continue to expand for at least the next six months," the conclusion could be reexpressed as "The economy will probably continue to expand." Similarly, in "51 is divisible by 17 and 3, so it must not be a prime number," the conclusion could be reexpressed as "51 is necessarily not a prime number." The modal auxiliaries also have a prescriptive, or normative, sense, however, in which they do not indicate the descriptive or factual modality we are discussing. In "The president should raise taxes because the budget deficit is much too high," the conclusion is a value judgment, not a prediction, so it has a normative modality. The conclusion cannot be reexpressed as "The president will probably raise taxes." It would be a better world if it were always likely that people did what they ought to do. We will concentrate on the descriptive modalities.

When a proposition is negative, *can't* and *impossible* express the modality of necessity, while *shouldn't, improbable,* and *unlikely* express probability. The impossible is what necessarily will not happen, while the improbable is what probably will not happen. Thus in "The sky is clear, so it is unlikely to rain," the modality of the conclusion is probability. The conclusion can be reexpressed as "It probably will not rain." In "John can't get here before 10:00, for he left at 9:00," the modality of the conclusion is necessity. The conclusion says "John necessarily will not get here before 10:00." We shall refer to adverbs like "necessarily" and "probably," and modal auxiliaries like "should" and "must" as **modality indicators,** because they indicate the modality of the conclusion. The absence of an explicit modality indicator indicates the modality of actuality, as in "Bob has a temperature, so he is sick."

Statements of what is necessary, possible, and impossible are called *modal statements*. The study of arguments involving them is an advanced branch of logic called *modal logic*. The subject is difficult and somewhat controversial. We will briefly introduce modal logic in Chapter 10, but until then we will concentrate on arguments involving nonmodal statements. Statements of what is certain, probable, or improbable, which may be called *qualitative probability statements,* are closely related in many ways to modal statements, but have not received as much attention from logicians. *Quantitative probability statements* are studied in the branch of mathematics called *probability theory,* which we will also look at briefly in Chapter 10. The study of probability statements is just as difficult and controversial as the study of modal statements. We will also generally ignore arguments involving probability statements. In other words, actuality will be our standard modality. It should be borne in mind at all times, however, that other modalities exist, and that changing the modality of a conclusion will generally strengthen or weaken an argument in accordance with the rules discussed above.

Glossary

Argument strength: the degree to which the premises support the conclusion; the strength of an argument tends to be directly related to the strength and probability of the premises, and inversely related to the strength of the conclusion.

Statement strength: how much a statement asserts or implies; one statement is stronger than another if the former implies the latter but the latter does not imply the former.

Modality: the property of a statement according to which it asserts that something is necessary, actual, certain, probable, possible, and so on.

Modality indicators: a term or phrase that expresses the modality of a proposition.

Exercises

A. Using only the rules relating the strength of an argument to the strength of its premises and conclusion, determine, if possible, whether the lettered arguments are stronger or weaker than the numbered arguments. Assume that the premises of the arguments are equally probable.

1. The sun has risen every day for the last thousand years, so it will rise again tomorrow.

    (a) The sun has risen every day for the last billion years, so it will rise again tomorrow.

    (b) The sun has risen every day for the last thousand years, so it will rise every day for the next thousand years.

    (c) The sun has risen every day for the last billion years, so it will rise every day for the next thousand years.

    (d) The sun has risen every day for the last thousand years, so it must rise again tomorrow.

    (e) The sun has risen every day for the last thousand years, so it might rise again tomorrow.

    (f) The sun has risen every day for the last thousand years, so it will probably rise again tomorrow.

    (g) The sun might have risen every day for the last thousand years, so it will rise again tomorrow.

2. Since 90 percent of all college students with athletic scholarships graduate, 90 percent of all students with athletic scholarships at the University of Michigan graduate.

(a) Since 90 percent of all college students with athletic scholarships graduate, over 80 percent of all students with athletic scholarships at Michigan graduate.

(b) Since over 80 percent of all college students with athletic scholarships graduate, 90 percent of all students with athletic scholarships at Michigan graduate.

(c) Since 90 percent of all college students with athletic scholarships graduate, about 90 percent of all students with athletic scholarships at Michigan graduate.

(d) Since over 80 percent of all college students with athletic scholarships graduate, over 80 percent of all students with athletic scholarships at Michigan graduate.

(e) Since 90 percent of all college students with athletic scholarships graduate, 90 percent of all students with athletic scholarships at Michigan and Ohio graduate.

(f) Since 90 percent of all college students with athletic scholarships graduate, the percentage of all students with athletic scholarships at Michigan that graduate might be 90 percent.

(g) Since 90 percent of all college students with athletic scholarships graduate, the percentage of all students with athletic scholarships at Michigan that graduate must be 90 percent.

B. Determine the modality of the conclusion in each of the following arguments. Identify the modality indicator if there is one.

1. It is evident as a matter of logic that, since [the great religions of the world] disagree, not more than one of them can be true. –Bertrand Russell, *Why I Am Not a Christian* (Simon and Schuster, 1957), p. v.

2. With very few exceptions, the religion which a man accepts is that of the community in which he lives, which makes it obvious that the influence of environment is what has led him to accept the religion in question. –Bertrand Russell, *Why I Am Not a Christian*, p. v.

3. If everything must have a cause, then God must have a cause. If there can be anything without a cause, it may just as well be the world as God, so that there cannot be any validity in [the First Cause] argument. –Bertrand Russell, *Why I Am Not a Christian*. pp. 6-7.

4. I conclude that other human beings have feelings like me, because, first, they have bodies like me, which I know in my own case, to be the antecedent condition of feelings; and because, secondly, they exhibit the acts, and other outward signs, which in my own case I know by experience to be caused by feelings. –John Stuart Mill, *An Examination of Sir William Hamilton's Philosophy*, 4th ed. (Longmans, 1872), p. 243.

5. All the evidence goes to show that what we regard as our mental life is bound up with brain structure and organized bodily energy. Therefore it is rational to suppose that mental life ceases when bodily life ceases. –Bertrand Russell, *Why I Am Not a Christian*, p. 51.

6. Whatever space may be in itself…we certainly perceive it as three-dimensional, and to three-dimensional space we can conceive no boundaries. By the very forms of our perceptions, therefore, we must feel as if we lived somewhere in infinite space. –C. S. Lewis, *The Grand Miracle* (Ballantine Books, 1970), p. 16.

7. A nationally reputable consumer organization found that Volvos lasted an average of more than sixteen years. Therefore a Volvo bought today could make it through the next decade.

8. If the "poor" suddenly used as much fuel as the "rich," world fuel consumption would treble right away…. But this cannot happen, as everything takes time. –E. F. Schumacher, *Small Is Beautiful: Economics as if People Mattered* (Perennial Library/ Harper & Row, 1975), p. 32.

9. Since a war in the Middle East, whether brief or protracted, would almost certainly be bloody, and since the likelihood is that a war elsewhere would also be bloody, it is surely right that if one wants to avoid a war in the Middle East one should also want to avoid a war elsewhere.

10. When the true history of the anti-slavery cause shall be written, women will occupy a large space in its pages; for the cause of the slave has been peculiarly women's cause. –Frederick Douglass, *The Life and Times of Frederick Douglass* (Macmillan/Collier Books, 1962 [1892] p. 469.

11. The occupation of Iraq is now the most unpopular it has been in United States opinion polls. In Great Britain, polls have long suggested a similar lack of support. So, two western governments on different sides of the Atlantic have failed to keep the support of their people.

12. That Christianity grew up in cities, at a time when, as today, the big city was the center of economic and cultural attraction, is a circumstance which must have had a deep influence upon the whole character of the religion. For Christianity as a whole has a decidedly urban style, and this is true not only of Roman Catholicism but also of Protestantism, which first arose in the burgher cities of Western Europe. –Alan W. Watts, *Nature, Man, and Woman* (Vintage Books/Random House), p. 25.

13. *Over the long run—and it may be very long—stocks should outperform bonds.* The reason is that stock and bond prices are set in the open market—and the open market rewards risk. –Andrew Tobias, *The Only Investment Guide You'll Ever Need* (Harcourt Brace Jovanovich, 1978). p. 65.

14. The truth is that the welfare state, which politicians would have you believe was designed to aid the "poor," is, in reality, devastating to the "poor." Among other things, it kills incentive, which decreases productivity, which in turn increases unemployment. In addition, it is a major contributor to inflation…, which is one of the worst enemies of the poorest people in our society. –Robert J. Ringer, *Restoring the American Dream* (Fawcett Crest, 1979), p. 130.

15. No voluntary exchange that is at all complicated or extends over any considerable period of time can be free from ambiguity. There is not enough fine print in the world to specify in advance every contingency that might arise and to describe precisely the obligations of the various parties to the exchange in each case. –Milton and Rose Friedman, *Free to Choose* (Avon Books, 1981), p. 21.

16. In a free trade world, as in a free economy in any one country, transactions take place among private entities—individuals, business enterprises, charitable organizations. The terms at which any transaction takes place are agreed on by all the parties to that transaction. The transaction will not take place unless all parties believe they will benefit from it. As a result, the interests of the various parties are harmonized. –Milton and Rose Friedman, *Free to Choose*, p. 43.

17. We should develop the practice of examining both the benefits and the costs of proposed government interventions and require a very clear balance of benefits over costs before adopting them. This course of action is recommended not only by the difficulty of assessing the hidden costs of government intervention but also by another consideration. Experience shows that once government undertakes an activity, it is seldom terminated. The activity may not live up to expectation but that is more likely to lead to its expansion, to its being granted a larger budget, than to its curtailment or abolition. –Milton and Rose Friedman, *Free to Choose*, p. 24.

18. We still have to learn how to live peacefully, not only with our fellow men but also with nature and, above all, with those Higher Powers which have made nature and have made us; for, assuredly, we have not come about by accident and certainly have not made ourselves. –E. F. Schumacher, *Small Is Beautiful,* p. 21.

19. The military buildup that is being proposed is three times as large as the one that took place during the years of the Vietnam War, and it is argued that this is bound to have a highly damaging effect on the whole U.S. economy, partly because of the competition that must occur between the defense and civil sectors for scarce materials and trained manpower, and partly because so large an increase in defense spending without any rise in taxation cannot but lead to rapid inflation. –Solly Zuckerman, *Nuclear Illusion and Reality,* p. 126.

20. The rapid rate of expansion of the United States economy during the first three quarters of 1983 seems sure to slow in 1984. Much of the rise this year resulted from the big swing from inventory cutting to inventory building. –Leonard Silk, "Sustaining the Recovery—and Spurring It Abroad," *The New York Times* (November 20, 1983), 12, p. 13.

21. Some historians have raised the question as to whether the war might not have been terminated sooner if the Tokyo government had been assured at an earlier date that the Emperor would be left on the throne.... Would a clear and early statement have shaken the position of the militarists? The answer is certainly doubtful. The decision to surrender nearly provoked a revolt, even after the dropping of the bomb. Some members of the Japanese government argued that the United States did not possess many bombs (on this at least they were right) and that defense was still possible and the only honorable course. –Dexter Perkins and Glyndon G. Van Deusen, *The United States of America: A History,* vol. II (Macmillan, 1962), pp. 664-65.

22. There can be no doubt that [Cro-Magnon men] were members of the white, or Caucasoid, racial stock, because the features of their skulls and facial skeletons all have that stamp. The one actual painting of a man so far known, a small bas-relief at Angles-sur-Anglin, gives us a white man (actually a lightish purple, but the effect is "white") with black hair and black beard. –William Howells, *Mankind in the Making,* rev. ed. (Doubleday & Co, 1967), pp. 208-9.

23. Getting a high rate of interest doesn't help if you don't save money in the first place. Many people won't save unless "forced" to. For this reason, a payroll-savings plan or whole life insurance contract, or some other form of poor-return saving...may be better than planning to buy bonds or stocks and never getting around to doing it. –Andrew Tobias, *Investment Guide,* p. 49.

LSAT Prep Questions

1. Social critic: The whole debate over the legal right of rock singers to utter violent lyrics misses the point. Legally, there is very little that may not be said. But not everything that may legally be said, ought to be said. Granted, violence predates the rise in popularity of such music. Yet words also have the power to change the way we see and the way we act.

   Which one of the following is most strongly supported by the passage?

   (a) If rock music that contains violent lyrics is morally wrong, then it should be illegal.

   (b) The law should be changed so that the government is mandated to censor rock music that contains violent lyrics.

(c) Violent rock song lyrics do not incite violence, they merely reflect the violence in society.

(d) If rock musicians voluntarily censor their violent lyrics, this may help to reduce violence in society.

(e) Stopping the production of rock music that contains violent lyrics would eliminate much of the violence within society.

Preptest 31, Section 2, Question 7

2.3 Deductive vs. Inductive Soundness

In a sound argument, the conclusion must follow from the premises *at least with probability.* It is time to explain the qualification, "The conclusion *follows* from the premises" means that the conclusion is true if the premises are true. "The conclusion *necessarily* follows" or "follows *with necessity*" means that the conclusion is *necessarily* true if the premises are true. Similarly, the conclusion is said to *probably* follow, or follow *with probability,* provided that the conclusion is *probably* true if the premises are true. "Follows with certainty," "with considerable probability," "with some probability," and so on, can be explained similarly. *"Logically* follows" is often used to mean "necessarily follows." Let us recall the first three arguments presented at the beginning of 2.2.

> (1) The first ball is red, for all balls in the urn are red.
> (2) The first ball is red, for at least 90 percent of the balls are red.
> (3) The first ball is red, for at least 10 percent of the balls are red.

The conclusion that the first ball is red follows with probability from the premise that over 90 percent of the balls are red. For it is highly probable (it is unlikely to be false) that if at least 90 percent are red then the first one is red. The same conclusion follows with necessity from the premise that all balls in the urn are red. For it is necessary (it could not possibly be false) that if all balls are red then the first one is red. So the conclusion that the first ball is red follows with both necessity and probability from the premise that all balls in the urn are red, but only with probability from the premise that *at least* 90 percent are red. Both arguments are sound, because in both the conclusion follows at least with probability. In contrast, argument (3) is not sound, since the conclusion does not follow even with probability: given simply that at least 10 percent of the balls are red, it is not probable that the first ball is red. The conclusion of argument (3) follows "with possibility," but that is not sufficient for soundness.

It is customary and useful to use the terms "deductive" and "inductive" to classify arguments on the basis of whether the conclusion follows with necessity or probability. We will define a ***deductively sound argument*** to be a sound argument in which the conclusion follows with necessity from the premises. An ***inductively sound argument*** is a sound argument in which the conclusion follows with probability but not necessity. Then argument (1) is deductively sound, (2) is inductively sound, and (3) is neither inductively nor deductively sound. Note that as we have defined the terms, an inductively sound argument is *any* sound argument that is not deductively sound.[2] Consequently, every sound argument must be either inductively or deductively sound, and cannot be both. Our two kinds of soundness divide logic into two branches. *Deductive logic* studies one kind, *inductive logic* the other. Chapters 5 to 9 are devoted to deductive logic. Chapters 3 and 4 concern inductive logic.

---

[2] "Inductive" is also commonly used in a narrower sense to denote a certain type of non-deductively sound argument—namely, enumerative induction and its relatives (see 3.3).

It is natural to think that deductively sound arguments are stronger than inductively sound arguments. *Other things equal*, this is true. But other things may not be equal. The strength of an argument is determined by two factors: *the probability with which the conclusion follows from the premises*, and *the probability of the premises*. While the first factor is always maximal in deductively sound arguments, the second may be greater in inductively sound arguments. Compare:

> (4) The sun has risen in the past.
>   ∴ It will rise tomorrow.

> (5) The sun has risen in the past.
>   If it has risen in the past, it will rise tomorrow.
>   ∴ It will rise tomorrow.

We cannot really say which argument is stronger here. For while the conclusion that the sun will rise tomorrow does not follow with complete certainty from the premise that the sun has risen in the past, the additional premise that the sun will rise tomorrow if it has risen in the past is not known with complete certainty. As this example illustrates, an inductively sound argument can always be converted to a deductively sound argument of equal strength by adding an extra premise.

We distinguish between inductively and deductively sound arguments on the basis of whether the conclusion follows with probability or necessity. The question naturally arises at this point as to how to classify arguments in which the modality of the conclusion is something other than actuality, like the following:

> (6) The first ball is *necessarily* red, for all of the balls are.
> (7) The first ball is *probably* red, for at least 90 percent are.
> (8) The first ball is *possibly* red, for at least 10 percent are.

Unfortunately, any attempt to answer the question raises issues too complex for an introductory text. One problem is that the italicized terms are all ambiguous—that is, there are several senses in which something may be necessary, possible, and so on. Furthermore, the terms may be expressing either the strength of the conclusion or the strength of the argument. Another problem is that we may have to deal with "iterated modalities," which are hard to understand. We have to ask, for example, whether it is necessarily necessary, or only probably necessary that the first ball is red if all the balls in the urn are red. These difficulties will not impede our work, for we will be focusing on arguments whose conclusions have the modality of actuality, as in (1), (2), and (3).

Glossary

Deductively sound argument: a sound argument whose conclusion follows with necessity from the premises.

Inductively sound argument: a sound argument whose conclusion follows with probability, but not necessity, from the premises.

Exercises

Assume that the following arguments are sound. Determine whether they are deductively or inductively sound.

1. All human beings are mammals. The president is a human being. Therefore the president is a mammal.

2. Mammals normally have two kidneys. The president is a mammal. Hence the president has two kidneys.

3. Most if not all human beings get colds. The president is a human being. Therefore the president gets colds.

4. It is customary to applaud after a good performance. Yo-Yo Ma is one of the world's greatest cellists. Therefore, there will be applause after his next concert.

5. *The Wall Street Journal* reported today that retail sales rose 1.9 percent in November to $102.46 billion. 102.46 divided by 1.019 is 100.55. So retail sales in October were $100.55 billion.

6. Retail sales rose 1.9 percent in November to $102.46 billion. 102.46 divided by 1.019 is 100.55. So retail sales in October were $100.55 billion.

7. Cigarette smoking always causes cancer, emphysema, and heart disease. Therefore you will ruin your health if you smoke cigarettes.

8. Cigarette smoking has been observed to cause lung cancer in laboratory rats, and a high correlation between cigarette smoking and lung cancer has been found in humans. In many studies, the incidence of cancer was especially high among people who smoked two or more packs a day, and increased the longer they had smoked. So if you smoke three packs of cigarettes a day, and are not killed by something else first, you will eventually get lung cancer.

9. The diameter of Earth at the equator is 7,927 miles. The diameter of Venus at the equator is 7,700 miles. Therefore Earth is larger than Venus.

10. The average high temperature for Minneapolis in January is 22°F. The average high temperature for Miami in January is 73°F. Therefore it will be warmer in Miami next January 16 than in Minneapolis.

11. The tallest building in Baltimore is the U.S. Fidelity & Guaranty building. Baltimore is the largest city in Maryland. Hence the U.S. Fidelity & Guaranty building is the tallest building in Maryland.

12. The tallest building in Baltimore is 529 feet tall. The tallest building in New York City is 1,350 feet tall. Therefore the tallest building in New York City is over twice as tall as the tallest building in Baltimore.

13. Nielsen Media Research estimated that as of January 1, 2007, 98 percent of all homes in the United States had at least one television. Therefore, nearly all homes in Chicago have at least one television.

14. As of January 1, 2007, 60 percent of all U.S. homes had a desktop computer, while only 12 percent had only a laptop computer. 32 percent had only one computer. Therefore there are more desktop computers in the United States than laptop computers.

15. The Dow Jones Industrial Average recently closed above 12,000, an all-time high. The Nikkei index of Japan, however, has not done as well. So, two different modern economies on different sides of the Pacific have had differing degrees of success.

16. Since [the great religions of the world] disagree, not more than one of them can be true. –Bertrand Russell, *Why I Am Not a Christian,* p. v.

17. All the evidence goes to show that what we regard as our mental life is bound up with brain structure and organized bodily energy. Therefore it is rational to suppose that mental life ceases when bodily life ceases. –Bertrand Russell, *Why I Am Not a Christian,* p. 49.

18. When the true history of the anti-slavery cause shall be written, women will occupy a large space in its pages; for the cause of the slave has been peculiarly women's cause. –Frederick Douglass, *The Life and Times of Frederick Douglass,* p. 469.

19. The total contribution of alternative energy sources to humankind's total energy requirements is miniscule. In 2000, in Great Britain it constituted 2 percent; in the E.U., it constituted 3 percent; and in the United States it constituted 4 percent. And these are the highest contributions.

20. Nothing, or anyhow not much, lasts forever. But what is well established is likely to last for a time. So the forces that have shaped past policy (or which past policy has resisted), if they have been correctly identified in this history, will, one may assume, continue to operate for at least a while in the future. –John Kenneth Galbraith, *Money,* p. 368.

2.4 Validity, Deductive and Inductive

There are three requirements for an argument to be sound: it must have true and justified premises, the conclusion must follow from the premises at least with probability, and the conclusion must not be assumed by the premises. The second requirement, that the conclusion follow from the premises at least with probability, will be called **validity**. In ordinary English, the term "valid" is simply a synonym of "sound." In logic, however, we give "valid" a broader sense. It will be our most important technical term, since the primary goal in logic is to develop criteria and methods for distinguishing between valid and invalid arguments. We shall say that an argument is **deductively valid** when the conclusion follows from the premises with necessity, and **inductively valid** when the conclusion follows from the premises with probability but not necessity. An argument is valid, then, if it is either inductively or deductively valid—that is, if the conclusion follows from the premises *at least* with probability.[3] An argument is **invalid** if it is not valid—that is, if it is neither inductively nor deductively valid. An invalid argument, in other words, is a non sequitur.

It is very important to remember that thus defined, *validity is necessary but not sufficient for soundness.* That is, sound arguments must be either deductively or inductively valid. But valid arguments may not be sound. First, *valid arguments may have false premises.* Consider:

> All Americans are Republicans.
> All Republicans are conservatives.
> So, all Americans are conservatives.

Here both premises are in fact false. They could be true, though. Every American who is not currently a Republican could change, for example. Furthermore, if the premises *were* true, the conclusion would necessarily be true too. So the argument is deductively valid. It is nevertheless unsound, because it has false premises. Second, *question-begging arguments are always valid.* Consider once again:

> Whales are mammals.
> So, whales are mammals.

---

[3] Many logicians use "valid" more narrowly where I have used "deductively valid," and use "probable" in place of "inductively valid." Many also use "sound" in a technical sense, to mean a valid argument with true premises.

This argument is valid because it is necessary that if whales are mammals then whales are mammals. Nevertheless, the argument is unsound because it is question-begging. The two arguments displayed in this paragraph illustrate the two ways in which a valid argument can be fallacious.

Validity is an essential property of sound arguments, which is why we will spend so much time studying validity. Nevertheless, soundness requires more than validity, so the two properties should be clearly differentiated. Note that a deductively sound argument is a sound argument that is deductively valid. "Inductively sound" and "inductively valid" are similarly related. Figure 2-2 may help clarify all the relationships.

FIGURE 2-2

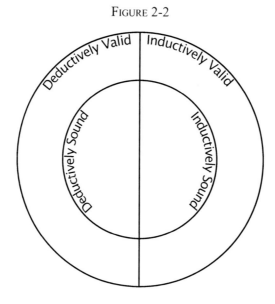

The area within the outer circle represents the set of all valid arguments. The inner circle represents the smaller subset of sound arguments. Both sets are divided by the line separating induction from deduction.

Traditional vs. Modern Definition. It is customary in logic to use "valid" as a technical term with a broader application than "sound." While this is true, no single definition of "valid" has become standard. According to the definition we have adopted, which was used almost exclusively from the time of Aristotle to the nineteenth century, a valid argument is one in which *the conclusion follows from the premises with necessity or probability.* According to another definition, which is widely used in modern logic texts, a valid argument is one in which *it is impossible or improbable for the premises to be true and the conclusion false.* The two definitions are nearly equivalent. For *if* the conclusion of an argument follows from the premises with necessity or probability, then *in all cases* it is impossible or improbable for the premises to be true and the conclusion false. Furthermore, *if* it is impossible or improbable for the premises to be true and the conclusion false, then *with few exceptions* the conclusion follows from the premises with necessity or probability. Thus the following argument is valid on both definitions:

All gods are immortal.
The president is a god.
∴ The president is immortal.

If the premises here were true, the conclusion would have to be true; so this argument is valid on the traditional definition. Furthermore, it would be impossible for the premises to be true and the conclusion false, so the argument is valid on the modern definition as well.

The exceptional cases in which the two definitions of validity diverge are those in which the conclusion is *independently* necessary or probable, or in which the premises are independently impossible or improbable. The conclusion of an argument is independently necessary or probable if it is necessary or probable for reasons other than the truth of the premises. The premises are independently impossible or improbable if they are impossible or improbable for reasons other than the falsity of the conclusion. Consider:

> Some men are tall.
> ∴ All pink cars are pink.

Whether or not some men are tall, it is impossible for the conclusion of this argument to be false. For pink cars are necessarily pink. Hence it is impossible for the premise of this argument to be true and the conclusion false, and the argument is deductively valid according to the modern definition. It is not valid according to the traditional definition we are adopting, however, for the conclusion that all pink cars are pink does not follow from, and is not implied by, the totally irrelevant premise that some men are tall. Note that the premise of the argument is true, and that the argument is not question-begging. The argument fails to be sound, therefore, only because the conclusion does not follow. Consider also:

> The moon is made of green cheese.
> ∴ The sun will rise tomorrow.

The premise here is certainly false, and the conclusion is in all probability true. Hence it is improbable that the premise is true and the conclusion false. So this argument is inductively valid according to the modern definition. It is not valid according to our definition, however, for the conclusion does not follow at all from the premise. Since our primary goal is to develop methods for distinguishing those arguments in which the conclusion follows from those in which it does not, we have adopted the traditional definition. This is not to say that the modern definition is incorrect. It is simply less convenient for our purposes.

Validity and Truth. The arguments displayed in the previous paragraph illustrate another important point: the invalidity of an argument does not imply or require the falsity of its conclusion. The argument about the president displayed two paragraphs back shows similarly that the falsity of a conclusion does not imply the invalidity of the argument. The validity of an argument is independent of the actual truth or falsity of its conclusion or premises, and requires only that *if* the premises are true, *then* (necessarily or probably) the conclusion is true too.

Glossary

Valid argument: an argument whose conclusion follows from the premises at least with probability. Validity is necessary but not sufficient for soundness.

Deductively valid argument: an argument whose conclusion follows from the premises with necessity.

Inductively valid argument: an argument whose conclusion follows from the premises with probability but not necessity.

Invalid argument: an argument that is not valid; a non sequitur.

Exercises

Are the following arguments deductively valid, inductively valid, or invalid? Are they sound or fallacious?

1. All humans are animals, for all humans are mammals and all mammals are animals.

2. All humans are reptiles, for all humans are rodents and all rodents are reptiles.

3. All musicians are violinists, for all violinists are stringed-instrument players and all stringed-instrument players are musicians.

4. California is more populous than New York, and New York is more populous than Rhode Island. Therefore California is more populous than Rhode Island.

5. Pennsylvania is more populous than Rhode Island. New York is more populous than Rhode Island. Therefore Pennsylvania is more populous than New York.

6. Pennsylvania is more populous than Rhode Island. New York is more populous than Rhode Island. Therefore New York is more populous than Pennsylvania.

7. Texas is the largest state, so it must be larger than the state of New York.

8. Alaska is the largest state, so it must be larger than the state of Texas.

9. California is the best state, for it is better than all the other states.

10. No human has ever lived to be 200 years old. Therefore the president will not live to be 200 years old.

11. No human has ever lived to be 100 years old. Therefore the president will not live to be 100 years old.

12. No one lives forever, therefore the president will die soon.

13. Cigarette smoking is harmful to health. Cigarette smoking is similar in many ways to pipe smoking. Therefore pipe smoking is harmful to health.

14. Cigarette smoking is harmful to health. Pipe smoking is different in many ways from cigarette smoking. Therefore, pipe smoking is not harmful to health.

15. Men should not do housework, for housework is women's work.

16. New York City has a population of about 20 million. Therefore New York City has a greater population than some states, for the state of Rhode Island's population is only about 1 million.

17. Kansas is west of Colorado and Colorado is west of Nevada, so Kansas is west of Nevada.

18. California and Oregon are neighboring states. California and Nevada are neighboring states. Hence Oregon and Nevada must be neighboring states.

19. Some beautiful women are beautiful. Therefore all beautiful women are beautiful.

20. The president either is or is not a Republican. Therefore the president both is and isn't a man.

21. Snow is white. Therefore the president will not live to be 145 years old.

22. The Amazon River is longer than the Nile and the Mississippi-Missouri. Therefore, the Amazon River is the longest river in the world.

23. The Mississippi River is longer than the Missouri, which is longer than the Nile. Therefore the Mississippi is longer than the Nile.

24. The Nile is longer than the Missouri, which is longer than the Mississippi. Therefore the Nile is longer than the Mississippi.

25. If Richmond is in Virginia, then Richmond is in the South. Richmond is in Virginia. Therefore Richmond is in the South.

26. If Detroit is in Virginia, then Detroit is on the west coast. Detroit is in Virginia. Therefore Detroit is on the west coast.

27. If Detroit is in Illinois, then Detroit is in the Midwest. Detroit is in the Midwest. Therefore, Detroit is in Illinois.

28. You tossed a silver dollar one million times. Therefore it came up heads about five hundred thousand times.

29. You tossed a silver dollar one million times. Therefore it came up heads at least once.

30. You tossed a silver dollar one million times. Therefore it came up heads most of the time.

2.5 Formal Validity

An argument is deductively valid provided the conclusion follows with necessity from the premises. Consider:

> Every congressman is a Republican.
> Every senator is a congressman.
> So, every senator is a Republican.

This argument does not have true premises. Both premises could conceivably be true, though. And if we imagined them true, we would have to imagine that the conclusion is true too. So this argument is deductively valid. This argument has a further interesting property. Many other arguments have the same form, such as:

> Every mammal is an animal.   Every pilot is an athlete.
> Every cat is a mammal.   Every woman is a pilot.
> So, every cat is an animal.   So, every woman is an athlete.

The logical form of all these arguments can be represented by using blanks.

> Every_____ is a _ _ _ _ _ _ _ _.
> Every .... is a _____.
> So, every .... is a _ _ _ _ _ _ _

We generate different arguments possessing this form by filling in the blanks consistently with appropriate terms. Consistency here requires that different occurrences of the same type of blank be filled with the same term. Thus we get the first argument above by writing "congressman" on each "_____," "Republican" on each "_ _ _ _ _ _ _ _" and "senator" on each "..........." This procedure will become quite familiar later. For now, simply note that *no matter what terms we choose*, we will never get an invalid argument as long as we fill in the blanks consistently. We will get many arguments with false conclusions, such as those about the pilots and the Republicans; but they will also have at least one false premise. And if all the premises *were* true, the conclusion would be true as well.

An argument is said to be ***formally valid*** provided all arguments with the same logical form are deductively valid. All three arguments in the preceding paragraph are formally valid. The branch of logic that develops procedures for identifying formally valid arguments is called *formal logic*. Most of this book is devoted to formal logic, because it is the most tractable, and consequently the most highly developed, part of logic.

All formally valid arguments are deductively valid. If the conclusion follows with necessity from the premises merely by virtue of the logical structure of the argument, then the conclusion follows from the premises with necessity. Not all deductively valid arguments are formally valid, however. Consider:

> Every apple is red.
> So, every apple is colored.

If an object is red, then necessarily it is colored; so this argument is deductively valid. However, the form of this argument is:

> Every............is_____.
> So, every............is _ _ _ _ _ _ _ _.

Innumerable arguments with this form have a true premise and a false conclusion, and therefore must be invalid, such as:

> Every bachelor is unmarried.
> So, every bachelor is handsome.

Our original apple argument is valid not because of its *form,* but rather because of its specific *content,* In particular, the argument is valid because of the necessary connection between the properties expressed by the terms "red" and "colored," a connection that is lacking between the properties expressed by "unmarried" and "handsome."

Since all formally valid arguments are deductively valid, while not all deductively valid arguments are formally valid, the class of formally valid arguments can be represented by taking a slice out of the deductive half of the pie drawn earlier, as in Figure 2-3.

FIGURE 2-3

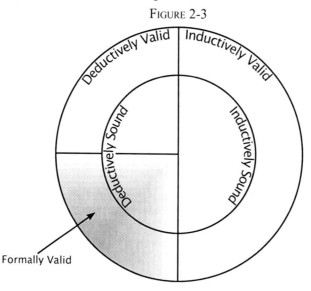

By definition, inductively valid arguments cannot be formally valid. The term "formally valid" is restricted to arguments that are deductively valid because of their form. Some inductively valid arguments have a similar property, however: all arguments with the same form are inductively valid. An example is:

> The probability that it will rain is 99%.
> So, it will rain.

This argument is not deductively valid, since the truth of the premise allows a 1% chance that the conclusion is false. However, the conclusion of this argument does follow with probability from the premise. If the premise is true, then it is at least probable that it will rain. The form of this argument can be represented as follows:

> The probability that _____ is 99%.
> So, _____.

Our original example about rain can be obtained by filling in the blank with "It will rain." No matter how we fill in this blank, the resulting argument will be inductively valid. So the argument about rain is inductively valid because of its form. Arguments with this property have received little attention from logicians. The most important forms that inductively valid arguments take have some substitution instances that are not inductively valid, as we shall see in Chapters 3 and 4.

The use of blanks to represent form, while familiar and graphic, is cumbersome and inconvenient when extensive. Letters of the alphabet are considerably more efficient. The form of the argument "Every congressman is a Republican, every senator is a congressman, so every senator is a Republican," could be represented using letters of the alphabet as follows:

> Every Y is a Z.
> Every X is a Y.
> So, every X is a Z.

Letters are not as graphic as blanks because you cannot generate arguments with the given form by simply filling in the blanks. We now have to *replace* letters with appropriate words. When letters function this way as placeholders, they are called *variables*. The extensive use of variables and other symbols in modern formal logic has earned it the name *symbolic logic*. The symbols, though, are simply a notational convenience.

Glossary

Formally valid argument: an argument whose logical form is such that all arguments with the same form are deductively valid. Formal validity is sufficient but not necessary for validity.

Exercises

Are the following statements true or false?

1. All sound arguments are valid.

2. All valid arguments are sound.

3. All valid arguments are formally valid.

4. All formally valid arguments are valid.

5. All formally valid arguments are sound.

6. All sound arguments are formally valid.

7. All deductively sound arguments are valid.

8. All deductively sound arguments are deductively valid.

9. Some deductively sound arguments are inductively valid.

10. Some deductively valid arguments are not deductively sound.

11. All deductively sound arguments are sound.

12. All valid arguments are either inductively or deductively valid.

13. All valid arguments are either inductively or deductively sound.

14. All inductively sound arguments are inductively valid.

15. All formally valid arguments are deductively valid.

16. All formally valid arguments are sound.

17. All deductively valid arguments are formally valid.

18. All sound arguments have true premises.

19. All valid arguments have true premises.

20. All formally valid arguments have true premises.

21. If an inductively valid argument has true premises (i.e. if all of its premises are true), then its conclusion must be true.

22. If a deductively valid argument has true premises, then its conclusion must be true.

23. If an inductively sound argument has true premises, then its conclusion may be false.

24. If a deductively valid argument has a true conclusion, then its premises (all of them) are true.

25. If a deductively valid argument has a false conclusion, then some of its premises must be false.

26. If an argument is deductively sound and has a true conclusion, then its s premises (all of them) must be true.

27. If an inductively valid argument has a false conclusion, then some of its premises must be false.

28. If an argument is sound, then the premises must follow from the conclusion (at least with probability).

29. If an argument is sound, then the conclusion must follow from the premises (at least with probability).

30. If an argument is valid, then the conclusion must follow from the premises (at least with probability).

31. If an argument is formally valid, then the conclusion must follow from the premises.

32. If an argument is deductively sound, then the premises may be true and the conclusion false.

33. If an argument is inductively valid, then the premises may be true and the conclusion false.

34. If an argument is inductively valid, then the premises are probably true if the conclusion is true.

35. If an argument has true premises and a false conclusion, then it is not valid.

36. If an argument has true premises and a false conclusion, then it is not deductively valid.

37. If an argument has true premises and a false conclusion, then it is not inductively valid.

38. If an argument has true premises and a false conclusion, then it is not formally valid.

39. If an argument has true premises and a false conclusion, then it is necessarily not inductively sound.

40. If an argument has true premises and a false conclusion, then it is probably not inductively sound.

41. Some valid arguments have false premises.

42. Some sound arguments have false premises.

43. Some formally valid arguments have false premises.

44. Some formally valid arguments are fallacious.

45. Some deductively valid arguments are fallacious.

46. Some inductively valid arguments are fallacious.

47. Some inductively sound arguments are fallacious.

48. Some deductively sound arguments are fallacious.

49. Some fallacious arguments have true conclusions.

50. Some fallacious arguments are valid.

51. Some fallacious arguments are formally valid.

52. Some fallacious arguments have true premises and true conclusions.

53. Some sound arguments are invalid.

54. No arguments are true.

55. Some arguments are false.

2.6 Fallacies and Biasing Influences

The term *fallacy* is used in logic to denote fallacious arguments.[4] Many fallacies are common and persuasive. Others are theoretically instructive. All, of course, are to be avoided. We have already met the fallacy of ***begging the question***, which occurs when the conclusion is assumed by the premises— that is, when our third requirement for soundness is violated. Any argument in which the other two requirements are violated—that is, in which either the premises are false or the conclusion does not follow—is also fallacious.

The Fallacy of Equivocation. A word, phrase, or sentence that has more than one meaning is said to be *ambiguous,* or *equivocal.* For example, "Monique is a pretty tall girl" is equivocal, meaning either that Monique is tall and good-looking, or that Monique is fairly tall. If an argument has an equivocal

---

[4] In English, "fallacy" is also applied to false statements.

premise or conclusion, the argument may be sound on one interpretation, fallacious on another. The conclusion that Monique is not ugly follows from the premise that she is a pretty tall girl only if "pretty" means "good-looking." An ambiguous argument may also be fallacious on all interpretations. A theoretically interesting case is called the ***fallacy of equivocation***, which occurs when the premises of an ambiguous argument are true only on one interpretation, while the conclusion follows only on another. Consider:

> A plane is a carpenter's tool.
> A Boeing 747 is a plane.
> So, a Boeing 747 is a carpenter's tool.

This argument appears to be formally valid. And its premises can be interpreted in a way that will make them both true. But the conclusion is false, so something is wrong. The conclusion follows only if the word "plane" is given the same sense in both premises. However, both premises are true only if "plane" is interpreted differently in each. So one way or another, this argument is fallacious: either the conclusion does not follow, or a premise is false. Note that the fallacy of equivocation is not simply the use of equivocal language. The Boeing 747 is a magnificent plane. In saying this, I commit no fallacy, even though "plane" is ambiguous. Ambiguity is one of the most pervasive features of language. There is nothing wrong with it per se.

The fallacy of equivocation forces us to make explicit an important restriction on the use of blanks or similar devices to represent argument forms. Consider:

> A_____ is a _____.
> A .... is a_____.
> So, a .... is a _____.

Our argument about planes has the valid form displayed above *only* when "plane" has the same sense in both premises. Repetitions of the same blank are intended to be filled with the same term in the same sense. If "plane" has a different sense in the two premises, then the argument has the invalid form

> A_____ is a _____.
> A .... is a ....
> So, a .... is a _____.

Another argument with this form is "A cow is a mammal, a rose is a plant, so a rose is a mammal," which is just as bad as the plane argument when "plane" is interpreted differently in the two premises. The logical form of an argument is determined by its meaning, not by the superficial way it is expressed using letters or sounds.

Arguments from Ignorance. Lack of proof is not proof. Despite its seeming obviousness, this point is often overlooked, resulting in a non sequitur known as the ***argument from ignorance.*** This fallacy is committed whenever the conclusion that something is false is drawn from the premise that it has not been shown to be true, or whenever the conclusion that something is true is drawn from the premise that it has not been shown to be false. Such arguments were very common during the McCarthy era, when people were accused of being communists merely because they could not prove they weren't. The same mistake is made if someone argues that a new product is unsafe, dangerous, or ineffective merely because it has not yet been tested adequately. If the argument from ignorance weren't fallacious we would get some very paradoxical results. Scientists currently do not have enough evidence to establish either that life exists on Mars or that it does not. The argument from ignorance would then lead to the conclusion *both* that there is life on Mars (because the contrary has not been proven) *and* that there isn't (for the same reason).

We all believe that unicorns are merely fictitious creatures. If asked why, we would probably say simply that none have ever been found. Is this an argument from ignorance? No. We have suppressed a crucial premise—namely, that people have looked in all the places unicorns are likely to live. Failure to find something after a thorough search constitutes proof that it is not there. One of the cornerstones of American law also appears to be an argument from ignorance—namely, the principle that a person is innocent until proven guilty. Taken at face value, such a statement would represent an argument from ignorance. But in the context of the law, this statement means that conviction requires proof of guilt, whereas failure to prove guilt suffices for acquittal. In opposing legal systems ("guilty until proven innocent"), acquittal must be based on proof of innocence, while failure to prove innocence is sufficient for conviction. Neither system sanctions the argument from ignorance.

Ad Hominem Arguments. The soundness of an argument does not in general depend upon who propounds it. Suppose I argue that the federal budget should always be balanced because deficits cause inflation. The soundness of my argument depends entirely on whether deficits do cause inflation and on whether it indeed follows that federal budgets should be balanced. Facts about myself, such as whether I am Republican or Democrat, male or female, healthy or sick, are irrelevant. The argument would be just as sound or fallacious if you put it forward, or the president, or Bill Gates. The fact that the proponent is an expert may give us reason to believe that his argument is sound (see 3.1). But even here, the argument's soundness does not depend on the fact that he propounded it, and would not be diminished if others less authoritative repeated it. Similarly, someone's bias, ignorance, or dishonesty may prevent our accepting an argument merely on his say-so. But the argument may nevertheless be sound. The only exception to our rule is when the argument is about the very person offering it. The soundness of my argument that *I* would not enjoy Willie Nelson's music because *I* dislike country music depends on the truth of my premise, and that depends directly enough on my taste in music.

The rule that the soundness of an argument does not depend on the arguer is frequently breached. The result is a non sequitur called the ***ad hominem argument***,[5] in which the premises describe someone's personal characteristics, from which the conclusion is drawn that his opinions or reasoning about matters unrelated to himself are fallacious. A classic example occurred in the 1980 presidential campaign. Senator Kennedy was running against President Carter for the Democratic nomination. Kennedy argued in a speech at Georgetown University that Carter should be held responsible for the crisis in Afghanistan because Carter had advance signals of the Soviet invasion, and had encouraged the invasion by his indecisive action concerning Soviet troops in Cuba. How did Carter reply? By dismissing Kennedy's argument on the grounds that it was "politically motivated." Of course Kennedy gave the speech for political reasons. Carter undoubtedly issued his reply for the same reasons. But Kennedy's motives were completely irrelevant to the soundness of his argument. That Kennedy had presidential aspirations provided no reason to doubt that Carter had advance notice of the invasion, nor that Carter should as a result be held responsible. Kennedy's motivation could only establish one thing: that his argument should not be accepted merely because *he* propounded it.

Biasing Influences. One of the most difficult requirements of clear thinking and correct reasoning is to resist ***biasing***, or ***prejudicial, influences.*** It would be nice if our beliefs were affected only by evidence and argument, but they aren't. Many factors have a subtle but important influence on our judgment even though they are logically irrelevant to the issue under consideration. These sources of bias are not generally used as premises in arguments. But if they were, the arguments would be blatantly fallacious. For example, good salespeople generally pay as much attention to their appearance as they

---

[5] The Latin phrase *ad hominem* means "to the man."

do to their sales pitch. Their pitch may consist of cogent arguments as to why their product is useful or better than competing products, and why therefore we should buy it. A Toyota saleswoman, for example, may point out that the Prius gets 54 miles per gallon, has an excellent repair record, and costs less than other cars of comparable quality. These claims may not be true, and may not give the whole story about the Toyota Prius. But at least they are relevant considerations when evaluating a car. But consider the saleswoman's appearance. She will make sure that her hair is done up, that she is dressed neatly and appropriately, and that she speaks well. Consider especially the appropriate dress. A saleswoman will not dress like a nurse, a waitress, or a prostitute. She could, but then she wouldn't sell many cars. Consumers are influenced even though the appearance of the salesperson is completely irrelevant to whether one should buy a particular car. Now the saleswoman who carefully manages her appearance cannot be accused of any fallacy. She is not *arguing* at all. She does not even imply that you should buy the car she is selling because she looks a certain way. So obvious a fallacy would insult your intelligence, and would make you less likely to buy the car. The saleswoman nevertheless expects her appearance to affect your judgment. Fortunately, we do not *have* to succumb to such irrational influences. We can disregard irrelevant considerations, and clear thinking requires that we do so. Although the list of irrelevancies to be ignored is endless, here are a few of the more common ones.

Characteristics of the speaker and the setting. The speaker's appearance is only one characteristic that may influence our acceptance of the speaker's claims and arguments in an irrational way. Others include the speaker's occupation, social status, party affiliation, associates, wealth, fame, or notoriety. Personal attacks citing one or another of the speaker's shortcomings are sometimes used as premises to support rejection of the speaker's opinions or arguments; if so, we have an *ad hominem* fallacy. But *ad hominem* attacks more often function as prejudicial influences. In either case, they are to be disregarded as irrelevant. Relevance, of course, is relative. Nothing is irrational *per se* about attacks on a person's character. We do not, for example, want a crook for president. Hence those who urged that Nixon should not be reelected in 1972 because evidence was starting to come in that he was involved in the Watergate break-in were not being swayed by an irrelevant consideration. The setting in which statements are made is another source of strong but irrelevant influences. Stockbrokers generally sell securities in quiet, well-appointed offices; their recommendations would not go over as well from a concession stand at a carnival.

Appeals to pity or other emotions. A standard trick of defense attorneys is to make the jury feel sorry for the defendant, perhaps by describing what a hard life he has led since childhood, or how the defendant's family will suffer if he is sent to prison. By inducing pity, these factors may influence the jury's judgment of guilt, even though they are logically irrelevant to whether or not the defendant committed the crime in question. (These same factors may well be relevant, though, when a guilty verdict has been given and the judge is deciding on the proper sentence.) In general, when trying to decide whether a given proposition is true, our emotions should not affect our judgment.

Popular appeals. A standard trick of the demagogue is to tell the audience plenty of what it wants to hear in the process of getting across his own message. A presidential candidate addressing a veterans' group will mention the valor of our boys, the might of our great nation, and his own fond memories of being a soldier; he might even wear a veteran's cap. The same candidate addressing a group of union leaders will be sure to mention the honest toil of the working man, the solidarity of the union, and his own fond memories of being a construction worker; a hard hat here. By flattering the audience and making them think he shares their attitudes, the demagogue may make them more receptive to what he has to say.

Poisoning the well. A speaker is often unprepared to argue for certain propositions. He may feel that a proposition is so obvious that it needs no argument, or he may simply have no argument for it. Bare assertion, however, may lack rhetorical force. So the speaker may embellish a little, saying perhaps "It is obvious to everyone that the government cannot keep running a deficit of $400 billion a year."

Such a device may be harmless, especially when the proposition *is* obvious. But the attempt to forestall disagreement by prejudicing the issue can be abused. For example, in a debate on how to put the Social Security system on a sound financial basis, a congresswoman might say "It would be indecent to even suggest that Social Security payments should be cut." Note that all the congresswoman has really said is that Social Security payments should not be cut; she has not given so much as a suggestion as to why. Nevertheless, she has made it very difficult to disagree. Anyone doing so faces the charge of being "indecent," which might be embarrassing. Forestalling disagreement by positively characterizing those who would agree with the speaker's position or negatively characterizing those who would disagree is called "poisoning the well." It takes courage not to be publicly subdued by such tactics, and it takes vigilance not to be privately duped.

Emotive language. Prejudicial language is not always so blatant. The biasing may be done by connotation. Words with the same denotation may have very different connotations. That is, two words that apply to the same set of objects, in virtue of the same properties, may nevertheless have very different emotions and ideas associated with them. "House" and "home" are familiar examples. Some words commonly express either approval or disapproval, and are therefore said to have an emotive connotation or meaning. For example, "bureaucrat," "government official," and "public servant" all have about the same denotation. But "bureaucrat" has a strong negative connotation, while "government official" is neutral, and "public servant" is positive. The connotations of the words used to express a statement are logically irrelevant to its truth, but may prejudice us nonetheless. It is easier to concur if someone says we do not need any more bureaucrats than if he says we do not need any more public servants.

Personal wishes. Perhaps the hardest biasing influences to avoid are our own wishes. We have some tendency to believe what we want to believe. Many people, for example, have a desperate desire to believe in God. They would feel utterly lost and alone in a universe not guided by a Divine Providence. Such individuals may therefore be more inclined to accept arguments supporting the existence of God and may resist unfavorable arguments, regardless of their merits. Confirmed atheists may have the opposite inclination. Despite extensive testing and FDA approval, new drugs sometimes have to be taken off the market. When evidence starts accumulating that the drug has dangerous side-effects, company officials commonly insist publicly that their drug is safe. Their statements may, of course, be self-serving lies. But they may simply be striking expressions of wishful thinking. When making up our minds about issues of personal interest, we should clearly identify our desires and take special care not to let them bias our reasoning.

We will identify many more fallacies and biasing influences in the course of this book. There is no hope of compiling a complete catalogue, however. The ways we can go wrong in our reasoning are unlimited.

Glossary

Fallacy: a fallacious argument.

Begging the question: the fallacy of using a question-begging argument.

Fallacy of equivocation: the fallacy committed when the premises of an ambiguous argument are true only on one interpretation while the conclusion follows and is non-question-begging only on another.

Argument from ignorance: the fallacy of concluding that something is false from the premise that it has not been shown to be true, or of concluding that something is true from the premise that it has not been shown to be false.

> **Ad hominem argument:** a fallacious argument in which the premises describe someone's biases, moral failings, or other personal characteristics, and from which the conclusion is drawn that his opinions or arguments about matters unrelated to himself are false or fallacious.
>
> **Biasing (or prejudicial) influences:** factors other than evidence and argument that influence our judgment but are logically irrelevant to the issue under consideration.

Exercises

Identify which, if any, fallacies discussed in this section are committed in the following arguments. Point out any biasing influences.

1. By *Expediency Factor*, I am referring to the instinct to seek quick, short-term, convenient solutions to problems. This almost always entails irrational action, because any behavior that does not take into consideration the long-term effects on one's own well-being is irrational. –Robert J. Ringer, *Restoring the American Dream*, p. 39.

2. We are concerned with the fundamental question of the *source* of the explanation of utterly uncertain reality. What makes it possible? What, then, is the *condition of the possibility of this uncertain reality?* ... These ultimate questions   which are also primary—call inescapably for an answer. For—in particular—from the quite concrete experience of life's insecurity, the uncertainty of knowledge and man's manifold fear and disorientation, which we were able to follow from the time of Descartes and Pascal throughout the whole of modern times, there arises the irrecusable question: *What is the source* of this radically *uncertain reality,* suspended between being and not-being, meaning and meaninglessness, supporting without support, evolving without aim? –Hans Küng, *Does God Exist?* (Vintage Books/Random House, 1981), pp. 565-66.

3. Montana is west of Missouri, and Louisiana is south of Montana, hence Louisiana is southwest of Missouri.

4. Utah is west of Colorado, and Arizona is south of Utah, so Arizona is southwest of Colorado.

5. The *Wall Street Journal's* arguments that restoring the "death tax" would be bad for the country can be dismissed at once. The *Journal* is a wealthy person's newspaper, and can be expected to tell its readers what they want to hear.

6. You may disbelieve in the Mons Angels [which allegedly protected British troops in their retreat from Mons, Belgium, on August 26, 1914] because you cannot find a sufficient number of sensible people who say they saw them. But if you found a sufficient number, it would, in my view, be unreasonable to explain this by collective hallucination. For we know enough of psychology to know that spontaneous unanimity in hallucination is very improbable, and we do not know enough of the supernatural to know that a manifestation of angels is equally improbable. The supernatural theory is the less improbable of the two. –C. S. Lewis, *The Grand Miracle*, pp. 3-4.

7. God's *existence is not empirically ascertainable,* it is not there to be discovered in space and time; [for] God would not be God if man could perceive and observe him with his own senses at certain places and certain times. –Hans Küng, *Does God Exist?*, p. 549.

8. The Utilitarian doctrine is, that happiness is desirable, and the only thing desirable, as an end; all other things being only desirable as a means to that end. What ought to be required of this

doctrine—what conditions is it requisite that the doctrine should fulfill—to make good its claim to be believed?

The only proof capable of being given that an object is visible is that people actually see it. The only proof that a sound is audible, is that people hear it; and so of the other sources of our experience. In like manner, I apprehend, the sole evidence it is possible to produce that anything is desirable, is that people do actually desire it…. No reason can be given why…happiness is desirable, except that each person, so far as he believes it to be attainable, desires his own happiness. This, however, being a fact, we have not only all the proof which the case admits of, but all which it is possible to require, that happiness is a good. –John Stuart Mill, *Utilitarianism* (Bobbs-Merrill, 1971), p. 73.

9. If the distinction of degrees is infinite, so that there is among them no degree, than which no higher can be found, our course of reasoning reaches this conclusion: that the multitude of natures themselves is not limited by any bounds. But only an absurdly foolish man can fail to regard such a conclusion as absurdly foolish. There is, then, necessarily some nature which is so superior to some nature or natures, that there is none in comparison with which it is ranked as inferior. –St, Anselm, *Monologium*, trans. S. N. Deane, 2nd ed. (Open Court Publishing Co., 1962), p. 43.

10. Furthermore, if one observes the nature of things he perceives, whether he will or no, that not all are embraced in a single degree of dignity; but that certain among them are distinguished by inequality of degree. For, he who doubts that the horse is superior in its nature to wood, and man more excellent than the horse, assuredly does not deserve the name of man. –St. Anselm, *Monologium,* p. 43.

On February 20, 1950, Senator Joe McCarthy [Republican, Wisconsin] made a speech before the Senate in which he announced his intention to "give detailed records of certain individuals in the State Department who have very definite communistic connections." He claimed to have 81 such cases, but he refused to give their names. "I shall not attempt," he said, "to present a detailed case on each one, a case which would convince a jury. All I am doing is to develop sufficient evidence so that anyone who reads the *[Congressional] Record* will have a good idea of the number of communists in the State Department." Exercises 11-14 deal with two of his cases, together with other passages from the speech.

11. The man involved in case no. 1 is employed in the office of an assistant secretary of state. The intelligence unit shadowed him and found him contacting members of an espionage group. A memorandum of December 13, 1946, indicates that he succeeded in having a well-known general intervene with an assistant secretary in behalf of one man who is an active communist with a long record of Communist party connections. There is another individual who is very closely tied up with a Soviet espionage agency. There is nothing in the file to indicate that the general referred to knew those two individuals were communists. –Senator Joe McCarthy, *Major Speeches and Debates of Senator Joe McCarthy delivered in the United States Senate, 1950-1951* (reprinted from the *Congressional Record),* p. 17.

12. Case no. 40 is that of another individual in research, in the State Department since 1947. I do not have too much information on this, except the general statement by the agency that there is nothing in the files to disprove his communistic connections. He is still with the government. –Senator Joe McCarthy, *Major Speeches and Debates,* p. 51.

13. About ten days ago, at Wheeling, W. Va., in making a Lincoln Day speech, I made the statement that there are presently in the State Department a very sizable group of active communists… The secretary of state [Dean Acheson] promptly denied my statement and said there was not a single

communist in the State Department. I thereafter sent a telegram to the president [Harry S. Truman], which I should like to read at this time:

> … I believe the following is the minimum which can be expected of you in this case.
>
> (1) That you demand that Acheson give you and the proper congressional committee the names and a complete report on all of those who were placed in the department by Alger Hiss [charged with espionage and convicted of perjury], and all of those still working in the State Department who were listed by your board as bad security risks because of their communistic connections.
>
> (2) That you promptly revoke the order in which you provided under no circumstances could a congressional committee obtain any information or help in exposing communists.
>
> Failure on your part will label the Democratic party of being the bedfellow of international communism. Certainly this label is not deserved by the hundreds of thousands of loyal American Democrats throughout the nation, and by the sizable number of able loyal Democrats in both the Senate and the House.

–Senator Joe McCarthy, *Major Speeches and Debates,* p. 5.

14. I do not feel that the Democratic Party has control of the executive branch of the government any more. If it had, with the very able members on the other side of the aisle, we would not find the picture which I intend to disclose. I think a group of twisted-thinking intellectuals have taken over the Democratic Party. –Senator Joe McCarthy, *Major Speeches and Debates*, p. 6.

15. Until the 1980s, there had been no female members of the United States Supreme Court, and even now there is but one. Consequently, the various opinions handed down by the Supreme Court on issues of sex and gender are bound to be insensitive to the needs and concerns of female citizens.

16. Computers can do many things better than humans, and can do some things we can't, but they still have to be programmed by men. As we all know so well, women are not men. Therefore, women cannot be computer programmers.

17. No sizable army can really be run entirely by command. The general cannot conceivably have the information necessary to direct every movement of the lowliest private. –Milton and Rose Friedman, *Free to Choose*, p. 1.

18. The following advertising copy was accompanied by a large picture of a smiling black family and a smaller picture of Clairol products. The ad originally appeared in the magazine *Essence,* which is oriented to the black reader.

> *Clairol knows what it is like to have a family you can be proud of:*
> We've got a family, too. A big one.
> We've got hair coloring for bringing out even more of your natural beauty.
> We've got detanglers and conditioners for making your hair more manageable.
> We've got electric hair setters, styling brushes, skin cleaners, and makeup mirrors.
> Not to mention cosmetics, shampoos and hair relaxers.
> And we've taken the time to develop and nurture each one of them to work best for you.
> To us, they're more than just a line of hair products—they're a family we've put together with care and pride.
> Kind of like yours.

©Clairol Incorporated 1976. Reprinted with permission of the copyright owner.

19. The following advertising copy, run by the New York archdiocese, was accompanied by a picture of Father O'Leary talking to an inmate through the bars of a jail cell.

> Father John O'Leary.
> If he's not in church, he's probably in jail.
> He was put in for good behavior… .
> His "flock" is an ever-changing group of 1,400 men who are waiting for trial or sentencing. They're packed in, two men to a cell barely big enough for one, and from where they sit God can seem to be very far away.
> But what can one priest do?
> A prisoner put it pretty well: "He brings you your freedom." It's that simple and that complicated. It's exactly what Christ brought to a world of prisoners 2,000 years ago… .
> The New York Priest.
> God Knows What He Does For a Living.

20. John Kerry did not have a distinguished record in Vietnam. There simply are no documents that support the suggestion that he did. Moreover, the only fellow servicemen that have stood in support of the suggestion that he did are fellow Democrats, people in the very same political party as Kerry. Surely, if he did indeed have a distinguished record, we would know about it.

21. Today, actual photographs of every form of immoral, perverted, and even masochistic acts are readily available in livid color. No wonder we encounter so many bizarre sex crimes against mankind. Who is to blame? The humanist controllers of the American Civil Liberties Union and their humanist partners in moral crime—the judges who were appointed by the humanist politicians. Any morally minded citizen recognizes what the humanist refuses to admit: The free use of pornography increases immorality and sex crimes. –Tim LaHaye, *The Battle for the Mind*, p. 143.

22. Dr. Morris has said, "There is no evidence that vertically upward evolution is possible, that it over occurs in the present or that it ever occurred in the past. If one believes in evolution, he must do so by faith, not by observation." –Tim LaHaye, *The Battle for the Mind*, p. 51.

23. During the past ten or fifteen years, parents and pro-moral citizens have become increasingly alarmed over the atheistic amorality of our schools, until today a coalition of antihumanist pro-moralists is becoming quite vocal and active. Gradually they are coming to realize that a humanist is a humanist is a humanist! That is, he believes as a humanist, thinks as a humanist, acts as a humanist, and makes decisions as a humanist. Whether he is a politician, government official, or educator, he does not think like a pro-moral American, but like a humanist. Consequently, he is not fit to govern us or to train our young. –Tim LaHaye, *The Battle for the Mind*, pp. 45-46.

24. Professor, I know my average in the course was less than a D, but I think I deserve to pass. I had a heavy course-load this semester, and I almost passed the final. I was recovering from a serious accident. Besides, I really have to pass this course. If I don't, I won't graduate. My parents have already come for graduation and will be very disappointed if I don't graduate. I have already been accepted into law school, but my admission is contingent on my graduating. I don't think I will be able to get into a good law school if I don't graduate on time. – One of my students.

25. The average American family has 2.3 children. It is impossible to have three-tenths of a child. So, the average American family is an impossibility.

LSAT Prep Questions

1. City council member: Despite the city's desperate need to exploit any available source of revenue, the mayor has repeatedly blocked council members' attempts to pass legislation imposing real estate development fees. It is clear that in doing so the mayor is sacrificing the city's interests to personal interests. The mayor cites figures to show that, in the current market, fees of the size proposed would significantly reduce the number of building starts and thus, on balance, result in a revenue loss to the city. But the important point is that the mayor's family is heavily involved in real estate development and thus has a strong financial interest in the matter.

    The reasoning in the city council member's argument is flawed because

    (a) the issue of the mayor's personal interest in the proposed legislation is irrelevant to any assessment of the mayor's action with respect to that legislation

    (b) the mayor's course of action being personally advantageous is not inconsistent with the mayor's action being advantageous for the city

    (c) the council member's own absence of personal interest in the proposed legislation has not been established

    (d) that a person or a municipality has a need for something does not, in itself, establish that that person or that municipality has a right to that thing

    (e) the possibility remains open that the mayor's need to avoid loss of family revenue is as desperate as the city's need to increase municipal revenue

    Preptest 32, Section 1, Question 14

2. Attorney: I ask you to find Mr. Smith guilty of assaulting Mr. Jackson. Regrettably, there were no eyewitnesses to the crime, but Mr. Smith has a violent character: Ms. Lopez testified earlier that Mr. Smith, shouting loudly, had threatened her. Smith never refuted this testimony.

    The attorney's argument is fallacious because it reasons that

    (a) aggressive behavior is not a sure indicator of a violent character

    (b) Smith's testimony is unreliable since he is loud and aggressive

    (c) since Smith never disproved the claim that he threatened Lopez, he did in fact threaten her

    (d) Lopez's testimony is reliable since she is neither loud nor aggressive

    (e) having a violent character is not necessarily associated with the commission of violent crimes

    Preptest 35, Section 4, Question 7

3. Cotrell is, at best, able to write magazine articles of average quality. The most compelling pieces of evidence for this are those few of the numerous articles submitted by Cotrell that are superior, since Cotrell, who is incapable of writing an article that is better than average, must obviously have plagiarized superior ones.

The argument is most vulnerable to criticism on which one of the following grounds?

(a) It simply ignores the existence of potential counterevidence.

(b) It generalizes from atypical occurrences.

(c) It presupposes what it seeks to establish.

(d) It relies on judgment of experts in a matter to which their expertise is irrelevant.

(e) It infers limits on ability from a few isolated lapses in performance.

Preptest 36, Section 1, Question 10

CHAPTER THREE

Inductive Logic: Authority and Analogy

3.1 The Argument From Authority

Simple Form. In this era of specialization, the vast bulk of any individual's knowledge is based on the testimony of knowledgeable authorities. All of us know, for example, that Jupiter is the largest planet. But few of us have done the measurements needed to establish this conclusion. We learned that Jupiter is the largest planet from science teachers, textbooks, encyclopedias, and similar sources. The author of a textbook may have learned the fact himself by consulting an astronomer specializing in the planets, or reading his publications.

The Argument From Authority: Simple Form
a affirmed p.
$\therefore p$ is true.
CONDITIONS OF VALIDITY: a affirmed what he believes, his belief is based on careful observation or sound reasoning, and no equally reliable source denies p.

The letter a here stands for the name of any individual cited as an authoritative source of information. We shall refer to a as the **source**. The letter p stands for any proposition. We shall call it the **information**. We argue from authority when we conclude that it is true that Jupiter is the largest planet from the premise that the author of an astronomy textbook affirmed that Jupiter is the largest planet. The source here is the author of the textbook, and the information is that Jupiter is the largest planet. The same pattern of reasoning is used extensively in legal proceedings, where experts and eyewitnesses routinely testify. The information gained by police investigators from witnesses and informants comprises the bulk of their evidence in most cases. Reporters cultivate informed sources, who provide important leads and information. And while most scientists conduct experiments or make observations of their own, they rely on published reports to learn about the experiments and observations of other scientists. Students rely on teachers and textbooks for most of what they learn in school, and preschool children rely on their parents for information about the world outside the home. In short, we make the inference represented by the argument from authority whenever people say something and we *believe them*.

Truthfulness and Knowledgeability. The argument from authority is not deductively valid. There is always the possibility that a proposition is false no matter who affirms it. We are all fallible. Saying that something is true does not *make* it true. Someone's affirmation may nevertheless be a *sign* of truth—that is, it may be unlikely that *p* is false, given that a particular source affirmed *p*. So an argument from authority may be inductively sound. The validity of an argument from authority depends on the *credibility* or *reliability* of the source of the information. That reliability depends on two conditions. First, *the source must have affirmed what he believes.* Second, *the source's belief must be based on careful observation or sound reasoning.* In brief, the source must be *truthful* and *knowledgeable.* If either requirement is unsatisfied, the argument from authority is fallacious.[1]

The truthfulness condition requires that the source was in the proper frame of mind when he gave his testimony. He must have been *sober, lucid, unhurried,* and *in control of himself.* The word of a drunken scientist, an insane medical examiner, or a witness under hypnosis is unreliable. The source may not be able to get the truth out due to circumstances beyond his control. More important, and more difficult to ascertain, the source must be speaking *honestly, freely,* and *seriously.* He must be trying to tell the truth. Obviously, if Stephen Hawking is just joking around on Jay Leno's 'Tonight Show," we cannot take his remarks as the truth. But we must also reject testimony if we suspect it was made under duress. This means that we cannot appeal to the authority of North Korean scientists under pressure to toe the party line, or of government employees in politically sensitive positions. It also means that confessions exacted by the police by torture or threats are not reliable indications of guilt. Appeals to authority are also fallacious if we have reason to believe that the cited authority is not being honest. Thus we should not rely too strongly on an individual's assertions if he stands to gain significantly by our doing so. We cannot trust the endorsements of noted personalities in paid television commercials, or the protestations of innocence of suspects in a criminal investigation. On the other hand, voluntary admissions and confessions are especially reliable. Since the individual stands to lose if we accept his word, the possibility of lying is minimized. Note that paying for information differs significantly from paying for endorsements. When a detective pays an informant, the detective does not specify what proposition the informant is supposed to affirm. In contrast, a personality is paid to endorse a particular product, and usually to read a specified script. Consequently, informants can provide reliable information, but endorsements have little evidential value. In court, witnesses are placed under oath to promote honest testimony. The severe penalty for perjury provides a strong motive to tell the truth.

Truthfulness is saying what one *believes* to be true, not necessarily saying what *is* true. The statements of an ignorant liar may inadvertently correspond to the facts. The validity of an appeal to authority therefore requires that the source be knowledgeable as well as truthful. *A knowledgeable source must be an unbiased, current, and relevant authority.* An *authority* is one who is especially knowledgeable, and can therefore provide information. A *relevant* authority is knowledgeable about the specific subject in question. If the cited authority was not able to make the requisite observations or does not know all the pertinent evidence, then we cannot be sure his opinions are correct. It would be

---

[1] The argument from authority is inductively sound under certain conditions. We are therefore considering it as a pattern of sound inductive reasoning. Since the argument from authority is fallacious when these conditions are not met, we could equally well classify it as a fallacy. Indeed, many logic texts do just that. The important thing is to remember the conditions that determine whether an argument from authority is sound or fallacious.

fallacious, therefore, to appeal to the authority of a specialist in nuclear physics on matters of economic policy. The physicist may be supremely rational, but he will be ignorant of the complexities of economic theory and unfamiliar with the mountains of economic data. The physicist may be an authority on his specialty, but that does not make him an authority on every-thing. The appeal to an irrelevant authority is one of the most common fallacies. Note that while there are relatively few authorities on things like nuclear physics, since expert status in such areas generally requires specialized formal study, we are all authorities on some matters: our whereabouts, the things we have done, what we have seen or heard, and our state of mind.

A *current* authority knows the latest developments in the field. Nineteenth-century physics texts or encyclopedias should not be consulted for information about the structure of the atom, since so much has been learned about the atom since then. Out-of-date medical texts, or physicians out of touch with their profession, cannot be relied on except for the unchanging basics, since the beliefs they express are no longer based on all the available evidence. An *unbiased* authority is unprejudiced, one whose mind was not made up before considering the evidence and whose judgment is not influenced by factors other than evidence and argument. Bias often leads to errors of observation, suppression of evidence, and faulty inferences. It would be fallacious therefore to appeal to the authority of a fundamentalist minister on the theory of evolution. For not only would he probably lack training in biology, geology and physical anthropology, but his own background and strong faith in the literal truth of the Bible would constitute a powerful bias against the theory. The same minister might nevertheless be legitimately cited about what the Bible says. Note that a firm opinion is not proof of bias. Bias requires that the opinion have an irrational basis, that it not be held solely on the evidence.

An argument from authority is fallacious if the cited authority is lying, ignorant of the relevant subject, or biased. We can therefore refute an argument from authority by attacking the source. Indeed, the purpose of cross-examination in trials is often to establish such defects. This may seem like an *ad hominem* argument, a fallacy discussed in Chapter 2. It is not. An *ad hominem* argument would conclude that the cited authority's statements are false from the fact that he is a liar or whatever. But in refuting an argument from authority, we only conclude that his say-so is *unreliable*. If an authority is biased, we cannot conclude that his views are false, but we should not conclude that they are true either. We would also commit the *ad hominem,* fallacy if we attempted to refute an argument from authority by discrediting the person making the appeal rather than the authority he cites. Suppose a juror concludes that the accused was at the scene of the crime because a witness said she saw him there. Showing that the juror was biased would not refute the juror's argument, but showing that the witness was biased would.

Appeals to *popular opinion* and *rumor* may be regarded as fallacious appeals to authority. Such appeals are made by the faithful who justify their belief in God with the claim that "everyone" believes in God, by atheists who justify their lack of belief by claiming that "no one" believes in God anymore, and by gossips who conclude that someone is committing adultery because they've "heard" she is having an affair. Arguments from authority are sound only if the sources are known to be qualified. We can hardly regard an indefinite "everyone" or "someone" as an honest and unbiased authority on any subject. There are relatively few subjects on which all, or even most, people are legitimate authorities. And the word of a source whose credentials cannot be checked should not be trusted.

Our *personal feelings toward the source of information* constitute a strong biasing influence. We tend to trust the word of those we like and to discount the word of those we dislike. Parents often believe their children's protestations of innocence, for example, even when presented with powerful counterevidence by the police, teachers, and other authorities. In wartime, citizens on both sides find their own government's reports more credible than those of the enemy. Within any given country, "establishment types" believe what the government says, while "antiestablishment types" assume the government is lying or misinformed. When evaluating arguments from authority, we must carefully identify and disregard our personal feelings toward the source. For they are logically irrelevant except insofar as they are based on the source's honesty and knowledge.

Types of Testimony. Authoritative testimony may be *firsthand* or *secondhand*. Someone's affirmation that *p* is secondhand testimony when based on someone else's affirmation that *p*. Firsthand testimony does not rely on another's testimony in this way. If Mary tells us that Bob got drunk because she saw him, then her statement is firsthand testimony. If Mary tells us that Bob got drunk because Bob told her he got drunk, then Mary's testimony is secondhand. With secondhand testimony, we appeal to the authority of someone who in turn appealed to the authority of someone else. A secondhand appeal is sound only if the firsthand appeal on which it is based is sound—which means, among other things, that we have two potential liars to worry about. Secondhand testimony, therefore, is less reliable. It is classified as *hearsay evidence* in the law and is generally inadmissible in court for several reasons: the primary source was not under oath; there is no opportunity to observe or cross-examine the primary source; there is that extra possibility of error in the passage of information from one individual to another; and it is difficult to prove perjury. Out of court, where the stakes are not as high, and there is no need to prove things beyond a reasonable doubt, secondhand testimony may be quite acceptable. There is also thirdhand testimony, fourthhand, and so on. Consider what happens when a friend tells you what he heard on the news, which was read by an anchorwoman, who got the story from a reporter, who got it from an informed source. The more "hands" involved, the weaker the argument from authority.

Firsthand authoritative testimony may be further classified as *eyewitness* or *expert*. Eyewitness testimony is a description of something the source personally experienced: what he saw, heard, felt, and so on. Expert testimony goes into matters beyond the personal experience of the source, and therefore depends on specialized training or education. The reliability of eyewitness testimony depends on several special factors relating to the observer and the conditions of observation: the acuity of the witness's eyesight or hearing; the amount of light or background noise; the amount of time the witness had; the extent of the witness's familiarity with the people, things, or events observed: how observant the witness generally is; how much attention was paid; how good the witness's memory is; how free the witness is from possibly distorting bias; and so on.

The reliability of expert testimony also depends on several special factors. The greater the expertise and eminence of the authority, the better his track record, and the more developed his field, the more likely it is that what he says is true. These are complex variables, difficult to define or measure. The *expertise* of an authority refers to how much he knows about his subject, and *eminence* to how well known and respected he is by other experts in the field. Of course, someone relying on an argument from authority will not be an independent judge of the authority's expertise, and will therefore have to rely on eminence as a sign of expertise, or on credentials such as degrees, positions held, and the like. An authority's *track record* refers to how much of his past testimony has turned out to be correct. A stockbroker's predictions of where the market is headed should not be given much weight if his past predictions have usually been wide of the mark. The *development of a field* has to do with how much is known about it, how well that knowledge is organized, how much agreement there is on methods to acquire new knowledge, and so on. Physics and mathematics are highly developed, in contrast to psychology and sociology. A respected mathematician's claims about a well-understood subject like calculus should be reliable; a respected psychologist's claims about a poorly understood subject like the unconscious may be worthy of serious consideration, but cannot be accepted as the absolute truth.

Consensus of Authority. Experts and even eyewitnesses often disagree. We know then that one is wrong. But without further information, we cannot say which. We may still be able to use an argument from authority, though, if one source is more reputable than others holding contrary views, or is in a better position to know, or if the source's view represents the consensus among the most reputable and best-placed authorities. We have, then, a third condition of validity for the argument from authority: there must be no equally (or more) reliable authority who denies p. If one witness was standing two feet from the robber while another witness was across the street, we should (other things equal) rely on the first witness's description of the robber if there is a conflict. Conflict among experts is illustrated by the case of Linus Pauling, the Nobel laureate chemist who advocated that vitamin C is effective against the common cold. Despite Pauling's prestige, we should not appeal to his authority on this matter. Pauling's training was in chemistry, not medicine, so he is not clearly a relevant authority. This is not decisive, though, because he claimed to have become an expert on the subject, and independent evidence exists to that effect. What is decisive is that almost all physicians and medical researchers agree that Pauling's claims are totally without merit. In a case like this, we should rely on the consensus view. The dissenting view might be right, of course, but without further information it is more likely that the dissenting view is wrong than it is that numerous independent minds have reached the wrong conclusion.

In general, the greater the consensus, the stronger the argument from authority. The argument is strongest when there is unanimity. No conclusion can be reached when the authorities are equally divided. Such a situation occurred in the widely publicized trial of John Hinckley, Jr., who attempted to assassinate President Reagan. Hinckley's defense attorneys claimed that he was insane at the time of the crime. Under the laws of the District of Columbia, the prosecuting attorneys had to prove beyond a reasonable doubt that Hinckley was sane. To do so, they produced several eminent psychiatrists who testified that Hinckley was sane. The defense attorneys produced other eminent psychiatrists who testified that Hinckley was insane. The jury consequently could not conclude that Hinckley was sane, and he was acquitted. If the law had required the defense attorneys to prove insanity, they would have failed. For the jury could not conclude that Hinckley was insane either. Given the divided expert opinion, no conclusion could be drawn about Hinckley's sanity.

Consider a more complex example. For years now, few presidents have wished to take the steps necessary to bring government spending in line with revenue. Spending cuts are politically unpopular, as are tax increases. Treasury secretaries, budget directors, and other administration officials nevertheless have often appeared before the press and various congressional committees to give official projections of the federal deficit. Given the enormous pressure on these men and women to issue rosy projections, we cannot be sure they are telling the truth (the whole truth, and nothing but the truth). Even if the official's integrity is unimpeachable, the same pressures create a powerful bias, which means we cannot be sure that all the evidence was weighed rationally in arriving at the projection. Finally, budget projections of the other party and of private economists routinely differ enormously. A consensus among economists is rare on such matters. The net result is that we cannot safely appeal to the authority of politicians and their appointees for budgetary or other economic projections.

Variations on the Simple Form. There are a number of variations on the simple form of the argument from authority. First, the premise that *a* affirmed *p* may be *implied*. For there are many specific ways of affirming, such as predicting, warning, and accusing. A citizen who concludes that General Motors withheld safety data from government accusations to that effect is arguing from authority. Second, the premise may say that *a believes p* and not that *a affirms p*. Expressed this way, we do not have to infer that *a* believes *p* from that fact that he affirmed *p*; consequently, the truthfulness condition drops out as a requirement of validity for such a variant. But the requirement that *a* believes *p* still remains as a condition of soundness, because sound arguments must have true premises. Third, the conclusion of an argument from authority is often implied, and a further conclusion is drawn. Consider an example used earlier:

> The *Wall Street Journal* reported today that retail sales rose 1.9 percent in November to $102.46 billion. So retail sales in October must have been $100.55 billion.

Clearly, anyone using this argument has relied on the authority of *The Wall Street Journal*. The intermediate conclusion, that retail sales in fact rose 1.9 percent in November to $102.46 billion, has simply been suppressed. This intermediate conclusion follows from the premise by the argument from authority, and leads to the conclusion stated by simple mathematics. The argument would be pedantic, and less clear, if the intermediate conclusion were made explicit, so there is good reason for its suppression. Nevertheless, the validity of the argument as a whole depends on the validity of the implied argument from authority, which in turn depends on the reliability of *The Wall Street Journal* in such matters. We must be vigilant for suppressed arguments from authority, and not let them slip by unevaluated.

We have focused on arguments from authority in which the conclusion is drawn that p is true, which means that p is *actually* true. The conclusion of an argument from authority may, however, have any of the other modalities, such as "p *must* be true," "p is *probably* true," or "p *might be* true." The weaker the conclusion, the stronger the argument; the stronger the conclusion, the weaker the argument.

Arguments from authority may also be more complex than the simple form schematized above. Suppose, for example, we used the following argument:

> *The New York Times* reported that the president said in a news conference that his secretary of the interior has resigned. ∴ The interior secretary has resigned.

We in essence used the simple argument from authority twice. First, we inferred, on the authority of *The New York Times,* that the president said his interior secretary resigned. We then inferred further, on the authority of the president, that his interior secretary has in fact resigned. The president in this case is the *primary source,* while *The New York Times* is the *secondary source*. There is no theoretical limit on how complex such an argument from authority can be: the conclusion that p is true might be drawn from the fact that a affirmed that b affirmed that c affirmed p (c would then be the primary source); or from the fact that a affirmed that b affirmed that c affirmed that d affirmed p (d would be the primary source); and so on. We shall represent the general pattern as follows:

The Argument From Authority: Complex Form

a affirmed that b affirmed that c affirmed...p.

∴ p is true.

CONDITION OF VALIDITY: **All of the implied simple arguments from authority are valid.**

Note that the premise of our resignation argument may well be firsthand testimony: the reporter who wrote the article may have attended the news conference. The premise could also be secondhand testimony: the staff member who wrote the article may not have been the reporter at the news conference. So the difference between simple and complex arguments from authority does not coincide with the difference between first- and secondhand testimony: primary sources may provide secondhand testimony. However, as with secondhand testimony, the more authorities on which we rely in an argument from authority, the weaker the argument. For if any one of the simple arguments making up the complex argument from authority is invalid, the complex argument is invalid.

As we have defined the argument from authority, the source must be a person. However, we often consult inanimate sources of information like computers, calculators, and telephone directories. The pattern of inference is similar: from the fact that the inanimate source "said" that p, we infer that p is true. But the conditions of validity are somewhat different: the source must have said what it was supposed to say, and the person or persons who determined what it was supposed to say must have been knowledgeable. The first condition, analogous to the truthfulness condition, requires that there be no serious misprints, flaws in the programming, malfunctions, or other foul-ups.

Finally, we should note that statements about what someone said or believes are not always, or even typically, used as premises in arguments from authority. Consider:

> The key insight of Adam *Smith's Wealth of Nations* is misleadingly simple: if an exchange between two parties is voluntary, it will not take place unless both believe they will benefit from it. –Milton and Rose Friedman, *Free to Choose* (Avon Books, 1981), p. 5.

The Friedmans are telling you what Adam Smith said. They clearly approve, since they refer to Adam Smith's point as an "insight" not a "mistake." But there is no evidence that the Friedmans are arguing. They are not saying "Adam Smith said it, so it must be true." It would surely be beneath the dignity of a Nobel laureate economist in the twentieth century to invoke the authority of an eighteenth-century economist on a simple point of theory: So arguments from authority must be distinguished from mere reports about what someone says or believes. Arguments from authority must also be distinguished from arguments designed to establish what someone says or believes, such as:

> Bob takes vitamin E daily, so he must believe that it does some good.

In this argument, the statement of the form "*a* affirms or believes *p*" is the conclusion, not the premise. This cannot, therefore, be an argument *from* authority. One might go on to argue that since Bob thinks vitamin E supplements are beneficial, they must be beneficial: that would be an argument from authority. But the given argument is quite different.

Glossary

Argument from authority: the argument in which the conclusion that a proposition is true is drawn from the premise that a reliable source of information affirmed it; to be valid, the source must be truthful and knowledgeable, and must represent the consensus.

Source: an individual, group, book, and so on, whose affirmation or opinion provides the premise of an argument from authority.

Information: the proposition inferred to be true in an argument from authority.

Exercises

The following passages contain reports of statements or opinions. Determine whether or not each passage contains an argument from authority. If it does, identify the source used and the information obatined, and identify any factors suggesting that the argument is fallacious.

1. The following table appeared in *The Economics of Petroleum* by Joseph Pogue (John Wiley and Sons, 1921) p. 7.

ASSETS OF THE AMERICAN PETROLEUM INDUSTRY IN 1921, COMPILED FROM ANNUAL REPORTS		
Rank	**Number of Companies**	**Assets**
Above $100,000,000	12	$3,722,873,637
$50,000,000 - $100,000,000	16	$1,147,417,412
$10,000,000 - $50,000,000,000	36	$944,689,248
$1,000,000 - $10,000,000	28	$164,717,016
Total	92	$6,029,697,313

2. According to the *Economics of Petroleum Production*, in 1921, the United States exported 641 million gallons of gasoline. Of that amount, 327 million gallons were exported to France and the United Kingdom. This means that over half the oil exports of the United States went to Western European countries.

3. The annals of the emperors exhibit a strong and various picture of human nature, which we should vainly seek among the mixed and doubtful characters of modern history. –Edward Gibbon, *History of the Decline and Fall of the Roman Empire Vol. 1.* (Source: Project Gutenberg).

4. "How did life get here?" The answer to this question appears in the first verse of divine revelation: Genesis 1:1. The details of that creation, found in Genesis 2:1-7, make it clear that the formation of our physical universe was not the result of a lengthy process, but an instantaneous act of creation. –Tim LaHaye, *The Battle for the Mind* (Fleming H. Revell, 1979) p. 50.

5. In The Eugenic Marriage, Grant Hague M.D. writes "It is estimated that there are more than ten million victims of venereal disease in the United States today. In New York City alone there are two million men and women--not including boys and girls from six to twelve years of age--actively suffering from gonorrhea and syphilis. Eight out of every ten young men, between seventeen and thirty years of age, are suffering directly or indirectly from the effects of these diseases, and a very large percentage of these cases will be conveyed to wife and children and will wreck their lives. No one but a physician can have the faintest conception of the far-reaching consequences of infection of this character. The great White Plague is merely an incident compared to it. These diseases are largely responsible for our blind children, for the feeble-minded, for the degenerate and criminal, the incompetent and the insane. No other disease can approximate syphilis in its hideous influence upon parenthood and the future. The women of the race, and particularly the mothers, should fully appreciate the real significance of the situation as it applies to them individually. That they do not appreciate it is well known to every physician and surgeon. (The Review of Reviews Company, 1916), pp. 11-12. (Source: Project Gutenberg).

6. "The [price] trends... will not maintain themselves through the price depression of 1921, but revealing the habit of oil prices on a rising market they may be expected to reassert themselves when oil prices next begin to advance under pressure from the crude petroleum situation." –Joseph Pogue, *The Economics of Petroleum* (John Wiley and Sons, 1921), p. 105.

7. Greece and Rome paved the way for their ultimate annihilation when their beautiful women ceased to bear children and their men sought the companionship of courtesans. –Grant Hague, *The Eugenic Marriage* (The Review of Reviews Company, 1916).

8. *The National Enquirer* reported that a doctor and two psychics teamed up to perform an astonishing exorcism on a man possessed by an evil spirit that was trying to kill him. Hence, demons and exorcisms must be real phenomena after all.

9. Contrary to popular belief, global warming might not be occurring at all. According to a 1998 memo from ExxonMobil, it is not known whether or not global climate change was occurring or whether or not humans had any influence on climate at all.

10. An advertisement by Ike Berger Enterprises, appearing in *The National Enquirer* (December 20, 1983, p. 37). claims that fat can be turned into muscle using a device called the "Speed Shaper" for just seven minutes a day. The ad is accompanied by the testimonial of an unnamed man over fifty, who claimed the Speed Shaper worked for him. There is also a statement from Ike Berger, winner of an Olympic gold medal in weightlifting, who says that the Speed Shaper works because it combines the principles of isometrics and isotonics. Borger also says that the Speed Shaper enables him to keep in shape in just a fraction of the time he used to spend working out.

11. Far more important [as a cause of the Spanish-American War] was the destruction of the American battleship *Maine* in the harbor of Havana. The vessel had been sent there on what was described as a visit of courtesy, but really because it was believed that protection might be necessary for American lives and property. On the evening of February 15, 1898, a terrific explosion shook the ship, which sank with a loss of over 250 officers and men. There was not then, and there is not now, the slightest evidence that the Spaniards were responsible for this destruction....

But the yellow press proceeded to exploit the episode, and there has perhaps been no more remarkable burst of unregulated emotionalism than what followed. The cry "Remember the Maine" swept over the country, and without a scintilla of proof, Theodore Roosevelt declared, "The Maine was sunk by an act of dirty treachery on the part of the Spaniards." –Dexter Perkins and Glyndon G. Van Deusen, *The United States of America: A History, vol. II* (Macmillan, 1962), p. 250.

12. According to Perkins and Van Deusen, Theodore Roosevelt declared that "The *Maine* was sunk by an act of dirty treachery on the part of the Spaniards," even though there was no evidence that the Spanish were responsible for the destruction of the *Maine*. Roosevelt's statement, therefore, was unjustified and reprehensible.

13. In the far-reaching debate (over annexation of the Philippines) which followed, the Democrats found it especially easy to oppose the administration. However, there were important opponents of annexation on the Republican side of the aisle as well, the most important being George Frisbie Hoar, the senior senator from Massachusetts.

The anti-imperialist point of view had support outside the Senate as well as in it. Such a well-known industrialist as Andrew Carnegie opposed annexation, and such respected independent newspapers as the *Springfield Republican* and the *New York Evening Post* took the same view. In the fall of 1898, the Anti-Imperialist League was organized. Though never very effective, it included many distinguished citizens from all over the country. –Perkins and Van Deusen, *The United States of America,* vol. II, pp. 257-58.

14. An old woman interviewed during the 1930s described her childhood initiation to field work on an Alabama cotton plantation:

> We had old ragged huts made out of poles and some of the cracks chinked up with mud and moss and some them wasn't. We didn't have no good beds, just scaffolds nailed up the wall out of poles and the old ragged bedding throwed on them. That sure was hard sleeping, but even that felt good to our weary bones after them long hard days' work in the field. I 'tended to the children when I was a little gal and tried to clean house just like Old Miss tells me to. Then as soon as I was ten years old, Old Master, he say, "Git this here nigger to that cotton patch."[2]

Jenny Proctor's experience was typical. For most girls and women as for most boys and men, it was hard labor in the fields from sunup to sundown. –Angela Y. Davis, *Women. Race and Class* (Vintage Books/Random House, 1983), p. 6.

15. Slaveowners naturally sought to ensure that their "breeders" would bear children as often as biologically possible, but they never went so far as to exempt pregnant women and mothers with infant children from work in the fields. While many mothers were forced to leave their infants lying on the ground near the

[2] Benjamin A. Botkin, ed., *Lay My Burden Down: A Folk History of Slavery* (University of Chicago Press, 1945); quoted in Mel Watkins and Jay David, eds., *To Be a Black Woman: Portraits in Fact and Fiction* (William Morrow and Co., 1970), p. 16.

area where they worked, some refused to leave them unattended and tried to work at the normal pace with their babies on their backs. An ex-slave described such a case on the plantation where he lived:

> One young woman did not, like the others, leave her child at the end of the row, but had contrived a sort of rude knapsack, made of a piece of coarse linen cloth, in which she fastened her child, which was very young, upon her back; and in this way carried it all day, and performed her task at the hoe with the other people.[3]

–Angela Y. Davis, *Women, Race and Class*, pp. 8-9.

16. *Don't waste money subscribing to investment letters or expensive services....* Half the experts, at any given time, are likely to be wrong....

On May 27, 1977, Dr. Martin Zweig issued a special bulletin to his $95-a-year subscribers. "A *Bear Market is* now underway," his bulletin began. "Sell EVERYTHING."

Three weeks later, *Smart Money* issued a special bulletin to *its* $50-a-year subscribers. (The market, meanwhile, had moved *up* 2 or 3 percent.)..." This could well be an *outstanding buying opportunity,*" the bulletin began. "The ingredients are there for a significant upward move (100 points). New all-time highs are not out of the question. As usual, we'd like to factor in as many pertinent investment considerations as possible. They're all screaming *buy!*"

The market dropped 100 points. –Andrew Tobias, *The Only Investment Guide You'll Ever Need* (Harcourt Brace Jovanovich, 1978), p. 87.

17. *The Wall Street Journal* reported today that Keith F. Pinsoneault, research director at Underwood Neuhaus, expects technical factors to move the market higher in January. Therefore now would be a good time to invest in the stock market.

18. About 1883, Van Benden made the important discovery that the nuclei of the ovum and the spermatozoon which unite in fertilization each contain one-half the number of chromosomes characteristic of the body-cells. [This] may now be regarded as a general fact. –J. Arthur Thomson, *Heredity 2nd Ed.* (John Murray, London 1912).

19. Many nonsmokers are annoyed by cigarette smoke. This is a reality that's been with us for a long time. Lately, however, many nonsmokers have come to believe that cigarette smoke in the air can actually cause disease. *But, in fact there is little evidence—and certainly nothing which proves scientifically— that cigarette smoke causes disease in nonsmokers.*

We know this statement may seem biased. But it is supported by findings and views of independent scientists—including some of the tobacco industry's biggest critics. Lawrence Garfinkel of the American Cancer Society, for example. Mr. Garfinkel, who is the society's chief statistician, published a study in 1981 covering over 175,000 people, and reported that "passive smoking" had "very little, if any" effect on lung cancer rates among nonsmokers. –R. J. Reynolds Tobacco Co., "Second-Hand Smoke: The Myth and the Reality," a paid commentary appearing in *The Wall Street Journal* (October 14, 1984), p. 3.

20. We are concerned here with the nature of the function which relates performance to the amount of reinforcement. In general, these studies have yielded results in agreement on the point that performance

---

[3] Charles Ball, *Slavery in the United States: A Narrative of the Life and Adventures of Charles Ball, a Black Man* (J. W. Shugert, 1836), pp. 150-51

increases as a negatively accelerated function with increases in the amount of reinforcement. Among the investigations leading to this conclusion are those of…and Hutt (1954)….[4]

The results of the experiment appear in Table 12, where mean response rate appears for each of the 9 subgroups in the experiment on the fifth day of training.

TABLE 12 MEAN RATES OF BAR-PRESSING UNDER DIFFERENT COMBINATIONS OF AMOUNT AND QUALITY OF REINFORCEMENT (HUTT, 1954)				
Quantity	Citric	Basic	Saccharin	Mean
Small	3.0	3.9	5.0	3.9
Medium	4.2	6.9	8.0	6.4
Large	8.2	11.1	13.9	11.0
Mean	5.1	7.3	8.9	

The mean rates entered in the table show that both variables had an effect, that of quantity being somewhat greater than that of quality. –Gregory A. Kimble, *Hilgard and Marquis' Conditioning and Learning* (Appleton-Century-Crofts, 1961), pp. 138-39.

21. In point of fact, astronomers have found that the theory of Newton does not suffice to calculate the observed motion of Mercury with an exactness corresponding to that of the delicacy of observation attainable at the present time. After taking account of all the disturbing influences exerted on Mercury by the remaining planets, it was found (Leverrier: 1859 and Newcomb: 1895) that an unexplained perihelial movement of the orbit of Mercury remained. –Albert Einstein, *Relativity: The Special and General Theory* (Methuen & Co., 1924).

22. What is the fossil evidence for the appearance of eukaryotes between 2 and 1.4 billion years ago…? G. R. Licari and I have observed cell diameters up to 60 micrometers among microfossils of eastern California that may be 1.3 billion years old. Such dimensions imply a change then or earlier from an entirely prokaryotic microflora to a partly eukaryotic one. –Preston Cloud, "The Biosphere," *Scientific American*, 249, no. 3 (1983), p. 187. Copyright © 1983 by Scientific American, Inc. All rights reserved.

23. Stature is the character which Dr. Galton used to get and exact measurement of the amount of regression… When large numbers are taken in, it is now abundantly proved that if parents exceed the average stature of their race by a certain amount their offspring will, in general, exceed the racial average by only one-half as much as their parents did. This is due, as Galton said, to the "drag" of the more remote ancestry, which when considered as a whole must represent very nearly mediocrity, statistically speaking. –Roswell Johnson and Paul Propane, *Applied Eugenics* (Macmillan, 1918).

24. An advertisement for Teacher's Scotch appeared in *The New York Times Magazine* (October 23, 1983, p, 34), The ad consisted largely of a picture of Timothy P. King, Director of Advertising, J. P. Stevens & Co., Inc., and the following testimonial. "Teacher's has a full-bodied flavor that's smooth and mellow. It's my Scotch. I've had rich Scotch, and I've had poor Scotch. Believe me rich is better." The ad concluded with a picture of a bottle of Teacher's Scotch, and copy that said, "The taste of Teacher's. Rich is better™."

25. Since Timothy P. King says that rich Scotch is better, it must be better.

---

[4] "Rate of Bar Pressing as a Function of Quality and Quantity of Food Reward," *Journal of Comparative and Physiological Psychology*, 47 (1954), pp. 235-39.

26. Had the rebellion succeeded a continent would have been split into fragments, and the only great Republic—the light and hope of the peoples of the world—would have gone down in anarchy and confusion. Under Providence we are indebted for national existence itself to General Grant and the legion of brace men living and dead. –*President Grant, His Official Record as Statesman* (The Republican Congressional Committee, 1872.), p. 2.

27. We shall not go back too far at first. A.D. 1290 is as good a place to begin as any. We have on our right, ladies and gentlemen, an old manuscript discovered at Ampleforth Abbey in January 1953, which gives a very clear account of a flying saucer passing over the startled community of Byland Abbey in Yorkshire....

A. X. Chumley, who, supplied this information, gives the following translation:

> Took the sheep from Wilfred and roasted them on the feast of S. S. Simon and Jude. But where Henry the Abbot was about to say grace, John, one of the brethren, came in and said there was a great portent outside. Then they all ran out, and Lo! *a large round silver thing like a disk flew slowly* over them and excited the greatest terror. Whereat Henry the Abbot immediately cried that Wilfred was an adulterer, wherefore it was impious to...

It is a pity the rest of the manuscript is missing. I long to hear what Brother Wilfred had been up to, and what the abbot thought would be impious.

What probably happened is that a flying saucer did, in fact, pass over Byland Abbey at the close of the thirteenth century and that the astute Abbot Henry took the opportunity to admonish Wilfred for his carryings-on, and the community for their lack of piety. –Desmond Leslie and George Adamski, *Flying Saucers Have Landed* (The British Book Centre, 1953), pp. 22-23.

28. Accepting the creation of man by the direct act of God has always been a matter of faith in the revelation of God.... Today, however, it is easier to believe than it once was, for many men of science have sifted through the evidence and offered scientific documentation for creationism. In fact, one of my colleagues, Dr. Henry M. Morris, is known as "Mr. Creation." This scientist, an educator for 38 years (13 years as the head of the third-largest engineering school in America), who holds a Ph.D. in hydrology from the University of Minnesota, is a prolific writer. He has written a classic engineering textbook currently in use. In 1970, he founded the Institute for Creation Research, which presently employs ten well-known creation scientists. Dr. Morris also served several years as president of over 600 members of the Creation Research Society. Membership of this society is limited to men who hold graduate degrees in science and have signed a statement of their belief in creation.... Dr. Morris has said, "There is no evidence that vertically upward evolution is possible, that it ever occurs in the present or that it ever occurred in the past. If one believes in evolution, he must do so by faith, not by observation." The facts of science do not prove creation to be true (only the Word of the Creator can do that), but they do advance creationism as a much more effective scientific "model" of the origins than evolutionism. –Tim LaHaye, *The Battle for the Mind*, p. 50.

LSAT Prep Questions

1. Harrold Foods is attempting to dominate the soft-drink market by promoting "Hero," its most popular carbonated drink product, with a costly new advertising campaign. But all survey results show that, in the opinion of 72 percent of all consumers, "Hero" already dominates the market. Since any product with more than 50 percent of the sales in a market is, by definition, dominant in

that market, Harrold Foods dominates the market now and need only maintain its current market share in order to continue to do so.

The argument commits which one of the following errors in reasoning?

(a) failing to exclude the possibility that what appears to be the result of a given market condition may in fact be the cause of that condition

(b) mistaking a condition required if a certain result is to obtain for a condition that by itself is sufficient to guarantee that result

(c) treating the failure to establish that a certain claim is false as equivalent to a demonstration that that claim is true

(d) taking evidence that a claim is believed to be true to constitute evidence that the claim is in fact true

(e) describing survey results that were obtained in the past as if they are bound to obtain in the future as well

Preptest 32, Section 4, Question 13

2. Advertisement: At most jewelry stores, the person assessing the diamond is the person selling it, so you can see why an assessor might say that a diamond is of higher quality than it really is. But because all diamonds sold at Gem World are certified in writing, you're assured of a fair price when purchasing a diamond from Gem World.

The reasoning in the advertisement would be most strengthened if which one of the following were true?

(a) Many jewelry stores other than Gem World also provide written certifications of their diamonds.

(b) The certifications of diamonds at Gem World are written by people with years experience in appraising gems.

(c) The diamonds sold at Gem World are generally of higher quality than those sold at other jewelry stores.

(d) The diamond market is so volatile that prices of the most expensive diamonds can change by hundreds of dollars from one day to the next.

(e) The written certifications of diamonds at Gem World are provided by an independent company of gem specialists.

Preptest 37, Section 2, Question 6

3. In determining the authenticity of a painting, connoisseurs claim to be guided by the emotional impact the work has on them. For example, if a painting purportedly by Rembrandt is expressive and emotionally moving in a certain way, then this is supposedly evidence that the work was created by Rembrandt himself, and not by one of his students. But the degree to which an artwork has an emotional impact differs wildly from person to person. So a connoisseur's assessment cannot be given credence.

The reasoning in the argument is most vulnerable to criticism on the grounds that the argument

(a) ignores the fact that anybody, not just a connoisseur, can give an assessment of the emotional impact of the painting

(b) is based on the consideration of the nature of just one painter's works, even though the conclusion is about paintings in general

(c) neglects the possibility that there may be widespread agreement among connoisseurs about emotional impact even when the public's assessment varies wildly

(d) presumes, without justification, that a painting's emotional impact is irrelevant to the determination of that painting's authenticity

(e) presumes, without offering evidence, that Rembrandt was better at conveying emotions in painting than were other painters

Preptest 37, Section 4, Question 16

3.2 The Argument From Analogy

Simple Form. Imagine opening a bottle of a wine you have never tasted before. You pour yourself a glass and find that it tastes very good. As you pour yourself a second glass, you will undoubtedly expect it to taste very good too. Your reasoning has a very simple pattern, called the *argument from analogy,* or *analogical argument.*

The Argument From Analogy: Simple Form
d is like *i*.
d has *A*.
∴ *i* has *A*.
CONDITIONS OF VALIDITY: *d* is sufficiently like *i* in relevant respects, and is sufficiently large and varied.

The symbols *d* and *i* represent any two numerically different objects (or non-intersecting groups of objects). The symbol *A* represents any attribute they might possess. The first premise of a simple argument from analogy states that *d* and *i* are similar, or analogous, which means that they have some common properties. The second premise attributes another property to *d*, and the conclusion is drawn that *i* shares that property too. Henceforth, the two premises will be referred to as the ***similarity premise*** and the ***attribution premise,*** for obvious reasons. *d* will be called the ***data object*** (or group), because it is *given* in the attribution premise that *d* has *A*. *i* will be called the ***inference object*** (or group), because it is *inferred* in the conclusion that *i* has *A*. *A* will be called the ***projected attribute,*** because it is being projected from the data group to the inference group. In our example, *d* is the first glass of wine, *i* the second, and *A* the attribute of tasting very good:

> The first glass of wine is like the second.
> The first glass has the attribute of tasting very good.
> ∴ The second has the attribute of tasting very good.

The first premise here is the similarity premise, the second the attribution premise.

The strength of a simple argument from analogy may vary greatly, depending on several factors. The first is *the degree* of *similarity between the data and inference objects.* In our example, *d* and *i* are highly similar: both glasses of wine came from the same bottle. The conclusion of the argument would follow with less probability if the glasses of wine came from different bottles from the same winery, and with still less probability if the glasses came from bottles from different wineries. We are concerned here with the *overall* similarity between d and i, not just their similarity in any given respect. The dissimilarities between them must be weighed against their similarities. The greater the similarities between d and i, and the fewer the dissimilarities, the greater the overall resemblance and the stronger the argument. An argument from analogy has its maximum strength when the data and inference objects are *exactly* similar. The argument would be even stronger if d and i were one and the same object, for then the argument would be deductively valid: d and i would have to have *all* properties in common. Such an argument would not be called an argument from analogy, however. Consequently, arguments from analogy are at best inductively valid: two glasses of wine *could* taste different, even though they came from the same bottle. This is unlikely but not impossible.

At the other extreme, the analogy between two objects may be so superficial that any analogical argument from one to the other would be fallacious. To find flimsy analogies, we need only examine the metaphors and similes that enliven good writing. Suppose someone says of an attractive girl that "her smile is like a ray of sunshine." If this is an appropriate simile, there must be some resemblance between the young lady's smile and a ray of sunshine. But the analogy would obviously be too weak to support an argument. We could not argue, for example, that her smile probably consists of a mixture of different wavelengths because rays of sunshine do. There is, unfortunately, no known way to measure degree of similarity. Consequently, we cannot specify just how similar d and i must be for an argument from analogy to be valid.

The second factor influencing the strength of an argument from analogy is *the relevance of the similarities between the data and inference objects*. The fact that two glasses of wine came from the same bottle is relevant when determining whether the second glass will taste as good as the first. The fact that they contain the same quantity of wine is irrelevant. Consider another example. There are many similarities between men and women. These similarities would be relevant when studying the effectiveness of a new sleeping pill. We could test the pills on men and infer that their effect on women would be similar. The similarities between men and women would not be relevant, though, when testing the effectiveness of a new birth control pill. In this case, the differences in reproductive systems would outweigh the similarities in nervous, digestive, and circulatory systems. In general, if d and i are similar only in respects known to be irrelevant to A, the argument from analogy is completely invalid. Furthermore, increased similarity in irrelevant respects will not strengthen the argument. Relevance is even less well understood than degree of similarity. We can say this much, however: for the respects of similarity between d and i to be relevant for the purposes of an argument from analogy it suffices if they are *causally related* to A. Thus, the quantity of wine in the glass is irrelevant, because it has no effect on taste. In contrast, the different grapes, soils, climates, and production methods characteristic of different wineries have a marked influence on taste, so the winery is relevant. We will study methods for establishing causal relationships in Chapter 4.

Arguments from analogy must be distinguished from mere statements of analogy and from other types of argument involving analogy. The following passage, for example, merely states that two things are similar.

> The Isuzu Rodeo is just like the Honda Passport, except for minor matters of trim.

No conclusion is drawn from this similarity, so no argument—and therefore no argument from analogy— is present here at all. If the passage had continued with something like "The Rodeo gets good mileage, so the Passport should too," then we would have had an argument from analogy. Now a statement of similarity, like any other statement, may need to be defended. So a statement of similarity may also occur as the conclusion in an argument rather than a premise, as in:

> Fascist and communist states are very similar. For in both, civil liberties are severely restricted, opposition and criticism are not tolerated, and the control of property is vested in the state. The one difference between the two, that private ownership of property exists under fascism but not communism, is negligible, since ownership without control is tantamount to lack of ownership.

This is an argument *to* analogy rather than an argument *from* analogy. Of course, once an analogy has been established, it can be used in an analogical argument. So from the premise that fascist and communist governments are similar and the further premise that fascist states are prone to bloody coups and purges, it can be inferred by analogy that communist states tend to suffer from the same internal strife.

The presentation of a simple argument from analogy may deviate in several minor ways from the standard form. First, the order of the premises may be reversed. It makes no difference whether the similarity premise comes first or the attribution premise. The validity of an argument is never influenced by the order of presentation. Second, d and i may be switched in the similarity premise. It does not matter whether we have "d is like i" or "i is like d," since the two statements are equivalent. Third, the similarity premise may be suppressed. For example, when d and i are described as "the first glass of wine" and "the second," there is little point in adding that they are similar. Fourth, the similarity premise may be implied, often by enumerating the common properties shared by d and i. Thus "The first glass of wine and the second both came from the same bottle" or "The first glass of wine is similar to the second in the respect of coming from the same bottle" might occur in place of "The first glass is like the second." Note that if projected attribute A is one of the respects of similarity mentioned in the similarity premise, the argument will be deductively valid; but it will also be unsound because it begs the question. Finally, the attribution premise might appear in a number of equivalent forms. In place of "The first glass has the attribute of tasting very good," we could say simply "The first glass tastes very good."

The simple argument from analogy can also be generalized in many ways. We shall describe as an ***analogical argument*** any argument in which, from the premise that two or more objects are similar in some respects, the conclusion is drawn that they are similar in further respects. Analogical arguments come in a myriad of forms. We will single out only a few for special attention. Analogical arguments are among the most useful patterns of inductive reasoning. They enable us to extend our knowledge from things we have observed to other things of the same kind. We use them to predict the future, based on our knowledge of the past.

Straight vs. Cautious or Rash Forms. Let us now consider some variations on the simple argument from analogy. The simple form is ***straight,*** meaning that the attribute in the conclusion is exactly the same as the one in the attribution premise. Analogical arguments may, however, be ***cautious,*** in which case the attribute in the conclusion is broader or less specific than the one in the attribution premise. Consider:

> The first glass of wine is like the second.
> The first glass tasted very good.
> ∴ The second glass will at least taste good.

From the premises here we could conclude by a straight analogical argument that the second glass will taste just as good as the first. But we increase the strength of the argument by allowing for some deviation in the taste of the wine. Suppose, to take another example, we begin measuring how many miles per gallon a car travels, finding that the first tank yielded 25 mpg. We might infer that the mileage on the second tank will also be 25 mpg. But it is much more likely that the mileage on the second tank will be between 24 and 26 mpg, and more likely still that the mileage will be between 20 and 30 mpg. In general, from the premise that some objects have A, we can infer by analogy that similar objects have A', as long as A implies A'. In a straight argument from analogy, A implies A' because A and A' are the same attribute (getting 25 mpg implies getting 25 mpg). In a cautious analogical argument, A implies A' because A represents a special case of A' (getting 25 mpg is more specific than getting between 24 and 26 mpg).

Which of the two attributes in a cautious argument from analogy should be called the *projected attribute?* The attribute in the conclusion, since it is the one projected from the data group to the inference group. The attribute in the premise, we will say, is the **given attribute**. So in the argument displayed above, the projected attribute is "tasting at least good," whereas the given attribute is "tasting very good." In a straight argument from analogy, then, the projected attribute is the same as the given one, whereas in a cautious argument, the projected attributed is less specific. An argument from analogy in which the projected attribute is *more* specific than the given attribute is fallacious; we shall refer to it as **rash.** Given that a car got between 20 and 30 mpg on one tank of gas, we could hardly infer that it will get exactly 25 mpg on the next. The conclusion would be too strong, since we were not given that the data object has the projected attribute.

When A is more specific than A' the statement that something has A is *stronger* than the statement that it has A', and the latter statement is *weaker* than the former. An additional factor influencing the strength of an analogical argument, then, is *the strength of the conclusion and the attribution premise*. The strength of an analogical argument is *inversely* related to the strength of the conclusion, and *directly* related to the strength of the attribution premise. That is, strengthening the attribution premise strengthens the argument; but strengthening the conclusion weakens the argument. Conversely, weakening the premise weakens the argument, while weakening the conclusion strengthens the argument. If premise and conclusion are strengthened or weakened equally, the strength of the argument may not change: it is the *relative* strength of the premise and conclusion that is important.

Another way to weaken the conclusion of an argument from analogy is to weaken the modality, by changing "i has A" to "i *might* have A." The conclusion can be strengthened by changing it to "i *must* have A." Again, the weaker the conclusion, the stronger the argument.

Forms Involving More Than Two Objects. Thus far we have only considered analogical arguments involving two objects, d representing one, i the other. Analogical arguments in general may involve any number of objects. Consider:

> The 1st and 2nd glasses of wine are like the 3rd, 4th, and 5th.
> The 1st and 2nd glasses taste good.
> ∴ The 3rd, 4th, and 5th taste good.

This is a simple argument from analogy in which the first and second glasses of wine are d while the third, fourth, and fifth are i. When d and i represent more than one object, we shall call them the **data group** and the **inference group**. Borrowing a term from statistics, we will refer to the set of all objects represented by d and i as the **population**. Relative to a given argument from analogy, the population is the set of all objects mentioned in its similarity premise. The population in the argument given immediately above consists of the first five glasses of wine. In our initial example, the population consisted of just the first two glasses. When the data group is a subset of the population, as it is in an argument from analogy, it is called a **sample**. In an argument from analogy, the properties of the rest of the population are inferred from the properties of the sample. Figure 3-1 summarizes the relationships among the groups involved in an analogical argument. Note that "populations" as defined here are not restricted to populations in the common sense of a group of people inhabiting a specified area. Any group of things thought to be similar can be a population in our sense: two glasses of wine, a batch of tennis racquets, a group of friends, a class of students, a box full of objects, and so on.

FIGURE 3-1: ARGUMENT FROM ANALOGY

FIGURE 3-1: ARGUMENT FROM ANALOGY

Data Group
(Sample)   Inference
                Group

Population

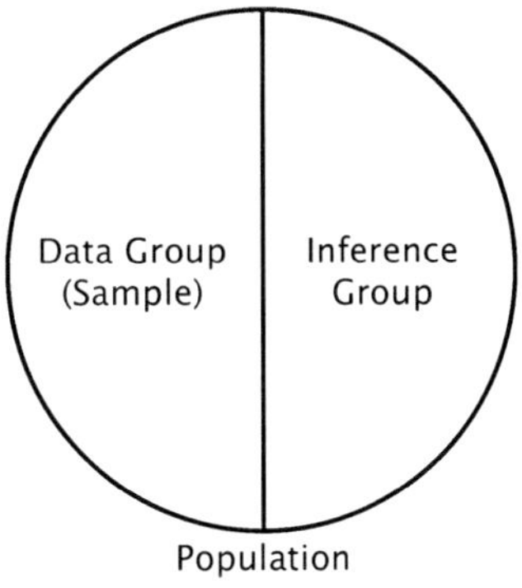

When more than two objects are involved in an analogical argument, two new factors influence its strength. The first is *the number of objects in the data group and the inference group.* The strength of an analogical argument is *directly* related to the size of the data group, and *inversely* related to the size of the inference group. The larger the data group the stronger the analogical argument. Thus the greater the number of friends you have, the more likely it is that you will like *Star Wars,* given that they all liked it. The larger the inference group, the weaker the analogical argument. The more friends you have, the less likely it is that they all will like *Casablanca,* given only that you liked it.

In general, the greater the number of objects in the data group and the smaller the number in the inference group, the stronger the argument from analogy. If both the data group and the inference group increase or decrease proportionately, however, the strength may not change. The weakest case is that with only one object in the data group and a large number in the inference group. Given only that you liked a movie, it is not very likely that everyone else in the world did. The strongest case is that with only one object outside a large data group. If everyone else liked a movie, it is overwhelmingly probable that you will like it too. The argument would be stronger still if the data group contained 100 percent of the population, in which case the inference group would be a subset of the data group. Then the conclusion would follow with necessity, and the argument would be deductively valid. If it were given that everyone you know liked *Star Wars,* including yourself, then it would obviously follow with necessity that you liked it. But an argument in which the data group is the entire population is called a *syllogism,* not an argument from analogy. Syllogisms will be discussed in §3.3 of this chapter, and in Chapter 5. Since the data group is never the entire population in an argument from analogy, it can only be inductively valid.

The larger the inference group, the stronger the conclusion is (other things equal): the conclusion that the third, fourth, and fifth glass of wine will taste good is stronger, for example, than the conclusion that the third glass will taste good. Similarly, the larger the data group, the stronger the attribution premise is: the premise that all ten of your friends liked *Star Wars* is stronger than the premise that all five of your friends liked *Star Wars.* So the principle that the strength of an analogical argument is directly related to the size of the data group and inversely related to the size of the inference group is a special case of the principle that such an argument's strength is directly related to the strength of the attribution premise and inversely related to the strength of the conclusion.

The second new factor influencing the strength of an analogical argument involving many objects is *the variety in the data group.* We want the objects in the data group to be as similar as possible to those in the inference group, which as the first variable discussed in connection with analogical arguments. *The more homogeneous the population, the stronger the argument.* But we also want the objects in the data group *to* differ among themselves as much as possible, which is our new variable. *The more heterogeneous the data group, the stronger the analogical argument.* The conclusion that you will get cancer as a result of cigarette smoke might be drawn from a study in which cigarette smoke caused cancer in 100 monkeys. The same conclusion could be drawn with greater probability if the same result was found in a more diverse group of 100 animals consisting of dogs and rats as well as monkeys. This would eliminate the possibility that the observed result of smoking was due to some peculiarity of the simian system, and increase the chances that it was due to the general nature of the mammalian system that you share. Since few objects are exactly similar, increasing the size of the data group generally increases the variety as well. A sample of one has no variety at all.

Pure vs. Statistical Forms. Given that all your friends liked Star Wars, we can infer by analogy that you will like it too. Unanimity of acclaim is not necessary, however. Indeed, the conclusion that you will like the movie can be drawn with some probability, as long as at least a majority of your friends liked it. Although the evidence for your liking it would be mixed, the positive evidence would outweigh the negative.

> Your friends are like you.
> Most of your friends liked *Star Wars*.
> ∴ You will like *Star Wars*.

When the conclusion that the inference group has *A* is drawn from the premise that all objects in the data group have *A*, we shall describe that argument from analogy as ***pure***. An analogical argument in which a conclusion is drawn from a percentage less than 100 (and more than 0) will be described as ***statistical***. The strength of an analogical argument clearly depends on *the proportion of the data group that has the projected attribute.* Holding constant the number of friends surveyed, whether five or twenty-five, the conclusion that you will enjoy *Star Wars* has the greatest support if all of them liked it. As the percentage liking the movie drops from 100, the probability decreases that you will enjoy the movie too. When the percentage drops to 50 or less, the argument becomes fallacious. Note that the greater the percentage of the data group to which *A* is attributed, the stronger the attribution premise; then recall the general rule that the stronger the attribution premise the stronger the argument.

When the projected attribute is *quantitative,* another type of statistical argument from analogy is possible. Suppose that in her first three games, the center on the women's basketball team has scored 19, 21, and 20 points, respectively. How many points will she score in the next game? We might answer that she will probably get between 19 and 21 points, since she got between 19 and 21 points on each of her previous games. This would be a pure argument from analogy in which *A* is "getting between 19 and 21 points." But we might also argue as follows:

> The next game will be like previous games.
> On average, the center scored 20 points in the previous games.
> ∴ She will score about 2 points in the next game.

This would be a statistical argument from analogy, in which the projected attribute is "scoring about 20 points." Her 20 points in the third game is clear evidence she will score 20 on the next game. But her 21 in the second game suggests she will score more, while her 19 in the first game suggests she will score less. Taking averages is one way of reconciling mixed evidence.

The strength of any analogical argument depends on the size of the data and inference groups, the variety of the data group, and the homogeneity of the population. Thus the above argument about the center becomes stronger the greater the number of previous games, the greater the number of teams played, and the greater the similarity between previous games and the next game. In a statistical analogical argument based on proportions the specific proportion is an additional factor influencing strength, as we saw above. In a statistical analogical argument based on averages, proportions are meaningless. There is still an additional factor however—namely, *the dispersion in the data group.* If the center had scored 0, 5, and 55 points in the previous games, her average would still be 20 points per game; but the conclusion that she will score about 20 points her next game would be much less likely. The conclusion would be most secure if she had scored 20 points in each game, which would then give us a pure analogical argument. Statisticians have several measures of dispersion such as the "variance" and the "standard deviation." (They also define several types of averages.) We shall not pursue the matter further, however.

When averages are used, an analogical argument must be cautious. Hence the "around" in the conclusion above. We could not justifiably conclude that the center will score *exactly* 20 points in her next game. Some margin for error must be allowed. The conclusion could be made more precise by specifying a confidence *interval*. Thus we might conclude that the center will score between 19 and 21 points, or between 15 and 25 points. The broader the confidence interval, the weaker the conclusion and so the stronger the argument.

Forms Without an Attribution Premise. All arguments from analogy have a similarity premise, although it may be suppressed. An attribution premise, however, is not essential. Consider:

> The Isuzu Rodeo and the Honda Passport differ in matters of trim, but are basically
> the same model car: they have the same shape, size, engine, drive train, and so on.
> ∴ If the Passport gets 35 mpg, the Rodeo should get 35 mpg

Here we have a conditional conclusion and no attribution premise; it isn't even suppressed. "The Passport gets 35 mpg," which looks like one, is not asserted as a premise. Instead, it is the antecedent of the conclusion. From the same premise, the more general conclusion might be drawn that the Passport and the Rodeo should get the same gas mileage.

Despite the absence of an attribution premise, these are both analogical arguments: from the fact that the Rodeo and the Passport are similar in some respects, the conclusion is drawn that they are similar in other respects. In an argument from analogy without an attribution premise, the terms "data group," "inference group," "given attribute," and "projected attribute" are undefined. All we have is a population of objects known to be similar in some respects, and inferred to be similar in others. Consequently, in arguments from analogy without attribution premises, the only factor determining strength is the degree and relevance of the similarity between the objects in the population, and the strength of the conclusion.

Summary. We have examined a family of arguments whose major premise states that a number of objects are similar in some respects, and whose conclusion states or implies that they are similar in certain other respects. A sample drawn from a larger population of similar elements is described, and the inference is made that the properties of the sample hold throughout the rest of the population. The strength of any such argument depends on how similar the members of the population are, how relevant the respects of similarity are, how strong the conclusion is relative to the attribution premise, how varied the data group is, and how large it is in relation to the inference group. In statistical arguments from analogy, there are additional factors such as the proportion of the data group having the property in question, or the dispersion in the data group. Analogical arguments come in many forms, but all are variations on the basic theme represented by the simple argument from analogy.

Glossary

Argument from analogy, or analogical argument: any argument in which, from the premise that two objects, or nonintersecting groups of objects, are similar in some respects, the conclusion is drawn that they are similar in further respects.

Argument from analogy, simple form: the argument in which, from the premise that two objects or groups of objects are similar, and that one has a given attribute, the conclusion is drawn that the other has that attribute; to be valid, the data group must be sufficiently like the inference group in relevant respects, and must be sufficiently large and varied.

Similarity premise: the premise in an analogical argument which says that two or more objects are similar.

Attribution premise: the premise in an analogical argument which says that one or more of the objects have a specified attribute.

Data object or group: the object or objects whose attributes are given in the premises of an analogical argument, enumerative induction, or statistical syllogism.

Inference object or group: the object or objects whose attributes are inferred in the conclusion of an analogical argument, enumerative induction, or syllogism.

Projected attribute: the attribute projected from the data group to the inference group.

Given attribute: the attribute of the data group that is given in the premise.

Population: the set of all objects in either the inference group or the data group.

Sample: the data group when it is a subset of the population.

Straight: an argument from analogy, enumerative induction, or syllogism in which the projected attribute is the same as the given attribute.

Cautious: an argument from analogy, enumerative induction, or syllogism in which the projected attribute is less specific, and therefore weaker, than the given attribute.

Rash: an argument from analogy, enumerative induction, or syllogism in which the projected attribute is more specific, and therefore stronger, than the given attribute.

Pure: an analogical argument, enumerative induction, or syllogism in which the inference group is inferred to have a given attribute from the premise that all of the data group does.

Statistical: an analogical argument, enumerative induction, or syllogism in which the inference group is inferred to have a given attribute, even though not all of the data group does.

Exercises

A. All of the following passages contain statements of analogy, but only some contain analogical arguments. If the passage contains an analogical argument, do the following: (a) Identify the data group and the inference group (or the population if these are undefined). (b) Identify any specific similarities that are mentioned in the similarity premise. (c) Identify the projected attribute (or the conclusion if this is undefined). (d) Classify the argument as straight, cautious, or rash, and as pure or statistical. (e) Finally, if the argument is weak, explain why (data group too small, similarities too weak or irrelevant, and so forth).

1. Dick "The Ends Always Justify the Means" Smith and Willie "Nicest Guy in the World" Jones are the only two candidates for the prestigious position of Small County Drain Commissioner. Dick is losing badly in the polls and decides the only way to save his campaign is to dramatically increase his mudslinging efforts. He takes out an advertisement in the local newspaper. The headline, in a bold, accusatory font, reads "How can you trust Willie when he is so Evil?" The article continues, "Hitler and Stalin had mustaches and so does Willie!" No further similarities are noted. However, photographic

evidence is provided and there is some discussion of the atrocities committed by Hitler and Stalin. It is claimed numerous times that Willie is a dastardly, evil fellow. The rest of the article is standard election-time boilerplate.

2. The civil wars of modern Europe have been distinguished, not only by the fierce animosity, but likewise by the obstinate perseverance, of the contending factions. They have generally been justified by some principle, or, at least, colored by some pretext, of religion, freedom, or loyalty. –Edward Gibbon, *History of the Decline and Fall of the Roman Empire Vol. 1*. (Source: Project Gutenberg).

3. Colour and constitutional peculiarities go together, of which many remarkable cases could be given among animals and plants…; hairless dogs have imperfect teeth; long-haired and coarse-haired animals are apt to have, as is asserted, long or many horns; pigeons with feathered feet have skin between their outer toes; pigeons with short beaks have small feet, and those with long beaks large feet. Hence if man goes on selecting, and thus augmenting, any peculiarity, he will almost certainly modify unintentionally other parts of the structures, owing to the mysterious laws of correlation. –Charles Darwin, *On the Origin of Species 6th Ed.*

4. An exact register was kept at Alexandria of all the citizens entitled to receive the distribution of corn. It was found, that the ancient number of those comprised between the ages of forty and seventy, had been equal to the whole sum of claimants, from fourteen to fourscore years of age, who remained alive after the reign of Gallienus. Applying this authentic fact to the most correct tables of mortality, it evidently proves, that above half the people of Alexandria had perished; and could we venture to extend the analogy to the other provinces, we might suspect, that war, pestilence, and famine, had consumed, in a few years, the moiety of the human species. –Edward Gibbon, *History of the Decline and Fall of the Roman Empire Vol. 1*. (Source: Project Gutenberg).

5. I conclude that other human beings have feelings like me, because, first, they have bodies like me, which I know in my own case, to be the antecedent condition of feelings; and because, secondly, they exhibit the acts, and other outward signs, which in my own case I know by experience to be caused by feelings. –John Stuart Mill, *An Examination of Sir William Hamilton's Philosophy,* 4th ed. (Longmans, 1872) p. 243.

6. The lying-in section of Vienna General Hospital was a breeding place of puerperal fever during the eighteen-forties. In the month in which Semmelweis assumed his duties, no less than 36 of 208 mothers died in his wards….

Semmelweis…drove himself to find the explanation. Again and again he and his students went to the morgue and dissected the bodies of the women who had died. The clinical picture was always the same: suppuration and inflammation in almost all parts of the body, not only in the uterus but also in the liver, the spleen, the lymph glands, the peritoneum, the kidneys, the meninges.

In the course of an autopsy a clumsy student had nicked Kolletschka's arm with his scalpel. It was only a tiny cut, and Kolletschka paid no attention to it. But the following night he was attacked by chills and fever, A few days later, after delirious ravings, he died.

Semmelweis asked for the report on the autopsy which had been performed on Kolletschka's body, As he read this report, he felt altogether stunned. The symptoms listed were: suppuration and inflammation of the lymph glands, the veins, the pleura, the peritoneum, the pericardium, the meninges! He felt as if he were reading, not the autopsy on his deceased friend, but one among hundreds of reports which he himself had written on mothers who had died of puerperal fever while under his care. The symptoms were very much the same….

If the autopsies revealed the same symptoms, he asked himself, then were not the causes for the death of Kolletschka and for the deaths of his puerperal fever victims exactly the same? Kolletschka had died because the knife had introduced poisonous traces of cadaverous substances into a wound. Had he, Semmelweis. and his students, with their own hands introduced similar material into the genital canals of his patients when they proceeded from their work in the dissecting room to examination of the maternity cases? That question pursued Semmelweis day and night thereafter. –Jürgen Thorwald, *The Century of the Surgeon* (Bantam Books, 1963). pp. 188-92.

7. [*Homo erectus* was an excellent walker.] His legs were long and straight, and except for individual or racial variations their bones are scarcely distinguishable from those of modern man. In the rest of his skeleton, from the picture that fossil recoveries give us, he was fundamentally like modern man, although slightly shorter. –F. Clark Howell and the Editors of *Life*, Life Nature Library/*Early Man* (Time Life Books, 1980). pp. 81-82. © 1965 Time-Life Books Inc.

8. As a general rule, all apes and men share the same basic pattern of brain configuration. Certain parts are known to be associated with certain functions. Toward the rear are areas that have to do with vision and the storage of information. In the center and sides are areas concerned with speech, memory, bodily sensations, and also movements of the body. The forebrain is where man does his thinking—and presumably where an ape does whatever thinking it is capable of. –F. Clark Howell and the Editors of *Life, Early Man*, p. 82.

9. The term "barrier" has been generally applied to that vast reef which fronts the N.E. shore of Australia, and by most voyagers likewise to that on the western coast of New Caledonia. At one time I thought it convenient thus to restrict the term, but as these reefs are similar in structure, and in position relatively to the land, to those, which, like a wall with a deep moat within, encircle many smaller islands, I have classed them together. –Charles Darwin, *Coral Reefs* (Source: Project Gutenberg).

10. In all these reasonings we cannot but have the most profound admiration for the genius of Ptolemy, even though he had made an error so enormous in the fundamental point of the stability of the earth. Another error of a somewhat similar kind seemed to Ptolemy to be demonstrated. He had shown that the earth was an isolated object in space, and being such was, of course, capable of movement. It could either be turned round, or it could be moved from one place to another. We know that Ptolemy deliberately adopted the view that the earth did not turn round; he had then to investigate the other question, as to whether the earth was animated by any movement of translation. He came to the conclusion that to attribute any motion to the earth would be incompatible with the truths at which he had already arrived. –Sir Robert S. Ball *Great Astronomers* (Source: Project Gutenberg).

11. Kepler had intended to write a systematic treatise on astronomy, like the *Syntaxis* of Ptolemy, doing for the other planets what he had already done for Mars…. He wrote instead a more elementary text-book, *Epitome Astronomiae Copernicanae*…In this work the two first laws of Kepler, which in the first instance had only been proved for Mars, were assumed to extend to the other planets. –J. L. E. Dreyer, *A History of Astronomy from Thales to Kepler,* 2nd ed. (Dover, 1953), p. 403.

12. "We must find a way to *tame* the virus now," said Pasteur to his men, who agreed, but were perfectly certain that there was no way to tame that virus.

"Try this experiment today!" Pasteur would tell them.

"But that is technically impossible!" they protested.

"No matter—plan it any way you wish, provided you do it well," Pasteur replied. (He was, those days, like old Ludwig van Beethoven writing unplayable horn parts for his symphonies—and then miraculously discovering hornblowers to play those parts.) For, one way or another, the ingenious Roux and Chamberland devised tricks to do those crazy experiments. –Paul De Kruif, *Microbe Hunters* (Pocket Books, 1964), p. 166.[5]

13. One month later, Pasteur and his men, at the end of three years of work, knew that victory over hydrophobia [rabies] was in their hands. For, while the two vaccinated dogs romped and sniffed about their cages with never a sign of anything ailing them, the two that had not received the fourteen protective doses of dried rabbit's brain—these two had howled their last howls and died of rabies.

Now immediately—the lifesaver in this man was always downing the mere searcher—Pasteur's head buzzed with plans to wipe hydrophobia from the earth.

"How easy! After a person has been bitten by a mad dog, it is always weeks before the disease develops in him. The virus has to crawl all the way from the bite to the brain. While that is going on we can shoot in our fourteen doses and protect him!" –Paul De Kruif, *Microbe Hunters,* pp. 168-69.

14. By now Grassi had read of those experiments of Ronald Ross with birds. "Pretty crude stuff!" thought this expert Grassi, but when he came to look for those strange doings of the circles and warts and spindle-shaped threads in the stomachs and saliva glands of his she-anopheles, he found that Ronald Ross was exactly right! The microbe of human malaria in the body of his zanzarone [anopheles mosquito] did exactly the same things the microbe of bird malaria had done in the bodies of those mosquitoes Ronald Ross hadn't known the names of. –Paul De Kruif, *Microbe Hunters* p. 286.

15. The word "affinity" in common language means, sometimes resemblance, and sometimes relationship and ties of family. It is from the latter sense that the metaphor is borrowed when we speak of "chemical affinity." By the employment of this term we do not indicate resemblance, but disposition to unite. Using the word in a common unscientific manner, we might say that chlorine, bromine, and iodine, have a great natural affinity with each other, for there are considerable resemblances and analogies among them; but these bodies have very little chemical affinity for each other. –William Whewell, *History of Scientific Ideas Vol. II 3rd Ed.* (Parker, 1858), p. 15.

16. Science tries to find in each bit of earth the record of the causes which made it precisely what it is; those forces have left their trace, she knows, as much as the tact and hand of the artist left their mark on a classical gem. –Walter Bagehot. *Physics and Politics.* (Source: Project Gutenberg).

17. Serving and pitching a baseball, although not identical motions, share many similarities you should be aware of. The strongest correlation is in the wrist snap. When you snap the wrist in serving or throwing the baseball, you let your fingers and hands do the work rather than your arm. –Dennis Ralston et al., "Improve with Other Sports," *World Tennis* (December 1983), p. 34.

18. In the famous 1964 report of the Surgeon General's Advisory Committee on smoking and health, the committee concluded that cigarette smoking is causally related to lung cancer. This conclusion was based on three main kinds of scientific evidence, including the results of animal experiments. "In numerous studies, animals have been exposed to tobacco smoke and tars, and to the various chemical compounds

---

[5] The numerous ellipsis marks used in *Microbe Hunters* for effect have been deleted. Other deletions are indicated by ellipsis marks as usual.

they contain. Seven of these compounds (polycyclic aromatic compounds) have been established as cancer-producing (carcinogenic). Other substances in tobacco and smoke, though not carcinogenic themselves, promote cancer production or lower the threshold to a known carcinogen. Several toxic or irritant gases contained in tobacco smoke produce experimentally the kinds of non-cancerous damage seen in the tissues and cells of heavy smokers. This includes suppression of ciliary action that normally cleanses the trachea and bronchi, damage to the lung air sacs, and to mucous glands and goblet cells which produce mucous." –U.S. Department of Health, Education, and Welfare, *Smoking and Health* (D. Van Nostrand Co., Inc., 1964), p. 26.

19. The sun has risen every day for at least the last billion years. Therefore it will probably rise tomorrow.

20. Cigarette smoking is harmful to health. Pipe smoking is different in many ways from cigarette smoking. Therefore pipe smoking is probably not harmful to health.

21. Soave tastes a lot like Chablis. You like Chablis? Then you'll love Soave.

22. As with any product, financial or otherwise, if you buy in quantity, you get discount prices. To buy and sell 50 shares of AT&T costs the little guy roughly four percent in commissions, which takes some of the bloom off AT&T's dividend. To buy and sell 5,000 shares costs Big Money less than a half a percent. Similarly, the typical $15 service charge on a purchase of $10,000 90-day Treasury bills cuts the effective annual interest rate by .6 percent. There is no service charge on "round lots"—multiples of $100,000. –Andrew Tobias, *Investment Guide*, p. 32.

23. For most girls and women, as for most boys and men, it was hard labor in the fields from sunup to sundown. Where work was concerned, strength and productivity under the threat of the whip outweighed considerations of sex. In this sense, the oppression of women was identical to the oppression of men. –Angela Y. Davis, *Women, Race and Class*, p. 6.

24. That is the heart of the teleological argument—the claim that adaptation can be explained only in terms of a designer. It rests, more or less explicitly, on an analogy with human artifacts. Thus, Paley compared the eye to a watch and argued as follows: If one were to find a watch on a desert island, one would be justified in supposing that it was produced by an intelligent being. By the same token (the adjustment of means to ends) one is entitled, upon examination of the human eye, to conclude that it was produced by an intelligent being. –William P. Alston, "Teleological Argument for the Existence of God." *The Encyclopedia of Philosophy*, vol. 8 (Collier-Macmillan, 1967), p. 85.

25. The plum pudding model of the atom was proposed by J. J. Thomson, the discoverer of the electron in 1897. The plum pudding model was proposed in 1906 before the discovery of the atomic nucleus. In this model, the atom is composed of electrons…, surrounded by a soup of positive charge to balance the electron's negative charge, like plums surrounded by pudding. –"Plum Pudding Model," *Wikipedia*.

26. In Europe we meet with the plainest evidence of the Glacial period, from the western shores of Britain to the Ural range, and southward to the Pyrenees. We may infer from the frozen mammals and nature of the mountain vegetation, that Siberia was similarly affected. –Charles Darwin, *On The Origin of Species* 6th ed. (Source: Project Gutenberg).

27. If you cut up a large diamond into little bits, it will entirely lose the value it had as a whole; and an army divided up into small bodies of soldiers loses its strength. So a great intellect sinks to the level of an ordinary one, as soon as it is interrupted and disturbed, its attention distracted and drawn off from the matter in hand: for its superiority depends upon its power of concentration—of bringing all its strength to bear upon one theme, in the same way as a concave mirror collects into one point all the rays of light

that strike it. –Arthur Schopenhauer, "On Noise," in *Studies in Pessimism* (Swan Sonnenschein & Co., 1893), pp. 127-28.

28. One of the nation's most influential medical eccentrics, whose work is still accepted by many thousands of intelligent but ill-informed people, was Dr. William Horatio Bates, an eye, ear, nose, and throat specialist of New York City. He was the first important figure in the modern cult of revolt against spectacles and the reliance on eye exercises for the treatment of visual defects…. At the heart of Dr. Bates' views is his theory of accommodation. "Accommodation" is a term for the focusing process which takes place within each eye when you shift attention to objects at varying distances. One of the best established facts in eye anatomy is the fact that this adjustment involves an alteration in the shape of the lens. A tiny muscle called the ciliary muscle causes the lens to become more convex as the eye is focused on closer objects. This change of the lens has been photographed in detail, and measured with a high degree of accuracy. Dr. Bates, however, denied all this categorically. The lens, he stated, is "not a factor in accommodation."…To support this odd theory, Dr. Bates records (with many photographs) some experiments he performed on the eye of a fish. After the lens of the fish eye had been removed, the eye was still able to accommodate. –Martin Gardner, *Fads and Fallacies in the Name of Science* (Dover, 1957) pp. 230-32.

29. Time [can be taken to be] a quantity of one dimension; it has great analogy with a line [which is one dimensional], but none at all with a surface or solid. Time may be considered as consisting of a series of instants, which are before and after one another; and they have no other relation than this, of before and after. Just the same would be the case with a series of points taken along a line; each would be after those on one side of it, and before those on another. Indeed the analogy between time, and space of one dimension, is so close, that the same terms are applied to both ideas….Times and lines are alike called long and short; we speak of the beginning and end of a line; of a point of time, and of the limits of a portion of duration. –William Whewell, *The Philosophy of the Inductive Sciences, Vol. 1, 2ⁿᵈ Ed.* (Parker, 1840), p. 129.

30. In short, if Mabel complained of the Scottish arms in ancient times, Mr. Osbaldistone inveighed no less against the arts of these modern Sinons; and between them, though without any fixed purpose of doing so, they impressed my youthful mind with a sincere aversion to the northern inhabitants of Britain, as a people bloodthirsty in time of war, treacherous during truce, interested, selfish, avaricious, and tricky in the business of peaceful life, and having few good qualities, unless there should be accounted such, a ferocity which resembled courage in martial affairs, and a sort of wily craft which supplied the place of wisdom in the ordinary commerce of mankind. In justification, or apology, for those who entertained such prejudices, I must remark, that the Scotch of that period were guilty of similar injustice to the English, whom they branded universally as a race of purse-proud arrogant epicures. Such seeds of national dislike remained between the two countries, the natural consequences of their existence as separate and rival states. –Sir Walter Scott, *Rob Roy Vol.1.*

31. See 1.3, exercise A16.

32. See 1.3, exercise B1.

B. In the following exercises, you will be given an argument from analogy. Then various modifications of the argument will be suggested, or additional information supplied. In each case, determine whether the alteration strengthens or weakens the original argument (or has no effect on strength) and explain why.

1. Your basketball team has played four games so far this year, against four different teams, and won all of them; therefore it will probably win its next game, which is against a fifth team.

    (a) The team has played two games so far this year.

    (b) The team has played ten games so far this year.

    (c) The team has played four games and won three of them.

    (d) The previous games were at home, but the next game is away.

    (e) The previous games were at home, and the next game is at home.

    (f) Your team's star center played in the previous games, but will not play in this game.

    (g) Your team's star center played in only two of the previous games.

    (h) The four previous games were against the same team, but the next game is against a different team.

    (i) The four previous games were against four different teams, but the next game is against one of those same teams.

    (j) The four previous games were against one team, and the next game is against the same team.

    (k) The previous games were played in December, while the next game will be played in January.

    (l) The previous games were played in December and so will the next games.

    (m) Therefore the team will certainly win the next game.

    (n) Therefore the team might win the next game.

    (o) The team won all its previous games by a margin of twenty points.

    (p) Therefore the team will probably win the next game by a substantial margin.

    (q) Therefore the team will probably win its next four games.

    (r) The team wore white uniforms in the previous games, and will wear white uniforms in the next game.

    (s) The team wore white uniforms in the previous games, and will wear blue uniforms the next game.

2. John has flown from Washington to Boston three times before, and each time the flight took about 75 minutes. So John's next flight from Washington to Boston should take about 75 minutes.

    (a) John has flown from Washington to Boston thirty times before.

    (b) John has flown from Washington to Boston once.

    (c) Therefore John's next flight will take exactly 75 minutes.

    (d) Therefore John's next flight will take between 60 and 90 minutes.

    (e) The previous flights took an average of 75 minutes.

    (f) The first two flights took 75 minutes, but the third took 90.

(g) John's previous flights were on United, and his next flight will be on United too.

(h) John's first flight was on United, the second on Delta, and the third on Northwest.

(i) John's previous flights were in poor weather, but the weather will be good for his next flight.

(j) The same pilot that flew the previous flights will fly the next one.

(k) The same flight attendants who flew the previous flights will fly the next one.

(l) John had Scotch on the first trip, bourbon on the second, and beer on the third.

(m) The first flight was in a Boeing 727, the second in a Boeing 757, and the third in a McDonnell-Douglas DC-10.

(n) The previous flights were in a 727, and the next flight will be in a 727.

(o) On the previous flights, there was a strong headwind, but on the next flight there will be a weak headwind.

(p) Therefore John's next flight is bound to take about 75 minutes.

(q) Therefore John's next flight might take about 75 minutes.

(r) Therefore John's next three flights will take about 75 minutes.

(s) Therefore whenever John flies from Washington to Boston in the future, the flight will take about 75 minutes.

(t) Therefore John's next flight from Washington to Detroit should take about 75 minutes.

(u) John has flown hundreds of times, between all major U.S. cities. Every time the flight has taken about 75 minutes.

LSAT Prep Questions

1. Sheila: It has been argued that using computer technology to add color to a movie originally filmed in black and white damages the integrity of the original film. But no one argues that we should not base a movie on a novel or a short story because doing so would erode the value of the book or story. The film adaptation of the written work is a new work that stands on its own. Judgments of it do not reflect on the original. Similarly, the colorized film is a new work distinct from the original and should be judged on its own merit. It does not damage the integrity of the original black-and-white film.

Sheila's argument uses which one of the following techniques of argumentation?

(a) It appeals to an analogy between similar cases.

(b) It offers a counterexample to a general principle.

(c) It appeals to popular opinion on the matter at issue.

(d) It distinguishes facts from value judgments.

(e) It draws an inference from a general principle and a set of facts.

Preptest 33, Section 1, Question 2

2. In our solar system only one of the nine planets—Earth—qualifies as fit to sustain life. Nonetheless, using this ratio, and considering the astonishingly large number of planetary systems in the universe, we must conclude that the number of planets fit to sustain some form of life is extremely large.

    The argument is questionable because it presumes which one of the following without providing justification?

    (a) If a planet is Earthlike, then life will arise on it.

    (b) Our solar system is similar to many other planetary systems in the universe.

    (c) The conditions necessary for life to begin are well understood.

    (d) Life similar to Earth's could evolve under conditions very different from those on Earth.

    (e) Most other planetary systems in the universe have nine planets.

    Preptest 31, Section 3, Question 25

3. Opponent of offshore oil drilling: The projected benefits of drilling new oil wells in certain areas in the outer continental shelf are not worth the risk of environmental disaster. The oil already being extracted from these areas currently provides only four percent of our country's daily oil requirement, and the new wells would only add one-half of one percent.

    Proponent of offshore oil drilling: Don't be ridiculous! You might just as well argue that new farms should not be allowed, since no new farm could supply the total food needs of our country for more than a few minutes.

    The drilling proponent's reply to the drilling opponent proceeds by

    (a) offering evidence in support of drilling that is more decisive than is the evidence offered by the drilling opponent

    (b) claiming that the statistics cited as evidence by the drilling opponent are factually inaccurate

    (c) pointing out that the drilling opponent's argument is a misapplication of a frequently legitimate way of arguing

    (d) citing as parallel to the argument made by the drilling opponent an argument in which the conclusion is strikingly unsupported

    (e) proposing a conclusion that is more strongly supported by the drilling opponent's evidence than is the conclusion offered by the drilling opponent

    Preptest 30, Section 2, Question 7

4. Which one of the following, if true, most weakens the drilling proponent's reply?

    (a) New farms do not involve a risk analogous to that run by new offshore oil drilling.

    (b) Many of the largest oil deposits are located under land that is unsuitable for farming.

    (c) Unlike oil, common agricultural products fulfill nutritional needs rather than fuel requirements.

    (d) Legislation governing new oil drilling has been much more thoroughly articulated than has that governing new farms.

(e) The country under discussion imports a higher proportion of the farm products it needs than it.

Preptest 30, Section 2, Question 8

5. Kostman's original painting of Rosati was not a very accurate portrait. Therefore, your reproduction of Kostman's painting of Rosati will not be a very accurate reproduction of the painting.

   Which one of the following is most similar in its flawed reasoning to the flawed reasoning in the argument above?

   (a) George's speech was filled with half-truths and misquotes. So the tape recording made of it cannot be of good sound quality.

   (b) An artist who paints a picture of an ugly scene must necessarily paint an ugly picture, unless the picture is a distorted representation of the scene.

   (c) If a child's eyes resemble her mother's, then if the mother's eyes are brown the child's eyes also must be brown.

   (d) Jo imitated Layne. But Jo is different from Layne, so Jo could not have imitated Layne very well.

   (e) Harold's second novel is similar to his first. Therefore, his second novel must be enthralling, because his first novel won a prestigious literary prize.

Preptest 36, Section 1, Question 21

6. Professor Beckstein: American Sign Language is the native language of many North Americans. Therefore, it is not a foreign language, and for that reason alone, no student should be permitted to satisfy the university's foreign language requirement by learning it.

   Professor Sedley: According to your argument, students should not be allowed to satisfy the university's foreign language requirement by learning French or Spanish either, since they too are the native languages of many North Americans. Yet many students currently satisfy the requirement by studying French or Spanish, and it would be ridiculous to begin prohibiting them from doing so.

   Professor Sedley uses which one of the following strategies of argumentation in responding to Professor Beckstein's argument?

   (a) attempting to demonstrate that the reasoning used to reach a certain conclusion leads to another conclusion that is undesirable

   (b) trying to show that a certain conclusion contradicts some of the evidence used to support it

   (c) questioning an opponent's authority to address the issue under discussion

   (d) offering an alternative explanation of the facts used to arrive at a specific conclusion

   (e) agreeing with the conclusion of a particular argument while rejecting the evidence used to support the conclusion

Preptest 31, Section 3, Question 20

3.3 Enumerative Induction and the Statistical Syllogism

Pure Enumerative Induction. An important part of the scientific method is to generalize the results found in the relatively small number of examined cases. For instance, Galileo studied objects falling freely at the surface of the earth, taking careful measurements. Those he examined fell with an acceleration of 32 feet per second squared. He inferred that *all* objects do, including those he had not yet studied. This pattern of inference is called *induction by simple enumeration,* or simply *enumerative induction.*

Enumerative Induction: Pure Form

All observed *P* have *A*

∴ All *P* have *A.*

CONDITIONS OF VALIDITY: The group of observed *P*s is sufficiently large and varied, and is sufficiently similar to the group of unobserved *P*s in relevant respects.

The letter *P* denotes classes or populations of objects, such as ravens or objects falling freely at the surface of the earth. The letter *A* stands for attributes, such as being black or falling with an acceleration of 32 feet per second squared. "Observed" must be interpreted more narrowly than "known." An observed *P* must be a *P* that has been measured or tested or in some way examined to see whether or not it has *A*. Galileo undoubtedly knew of many falling objects he had not measured: just think of all the raindrops he must have seen in his lifetime! Galileo could not have included in his *premise,* however, the fact that they fell with an acceleration of 32 feet per second squared.

Enumerative inductions are often expressed in negative terms. Thus from the observation that *no* dogs he tested *died* from his rabies vaccine, Pasteur inferred that no dogs would die from it. This is clearly equivalent to inferring that *all* dogs would *survive* the vaccine from the fact that all dogs he tested did. Similarly, Galileo could just as well have inferred that no falling objects fail to accelerate 32 feet per second squared from the fact that none of the objects he observed failed to fall at that rate. Any enumerative induction expressed negatively can be reformulated in positive terms, and vice versa. We shall focus on positive formulations.

Why is enumerative induction called what it is? Because the premise "All observed *P* have *A,*" which summarizes the results of observing a finite number of *P*s, can be replaced by an enumeration of the results for each of the observed *P*s:

> The first observed *P* has *A*.
> The second observed *P* has *A*.
> ...
> The *n*th and last observed *P* has *A*.
> ∴ All *P* have *A*.

This formulation is equivalent to the one given above, though less economical.

How is enumerative induction related to the analogical argument? In enumerative induction, the data group is the set of all observed *P*: we are given in the premise that all observed *P* have *A*. The inference group is the set of all *P*: we infer in the conclusion that all *P* have *A*. *A* is both the given attribute and the projected attribute. In enumerative induction, then, the data group is a *subset* of the inference group (everything in the data group is in the inference group). The inference group is the entire population, in other words, from which a sample comprising the data group has been drawn. This situation is represented by Figure 3-2.

FIGURE 3-2: ENUMERATIVE INDUCTION

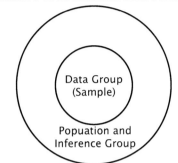

In an argument from analogy, on the other hand, the data group and the inference group are *nonintersecting* (nothing in one is in the other). Part of the population is in the data group, while the rest is in the inference group. Figure 3-2 should be compared to Figure 3-1 (see p. 81).

Despite this formal difference, enumerative induction differs only superficially from the argument from analogy. We are given that all *observed P* have *A*. It follows that *all P* have *A* if, and only if, it follows that all *unobserved P* have *A*. Consequently, the factors influencing the strength of an enumerative induction are the same as those influencing analogical arguments: the degree of similarity between the data group (the observed *P*s) and the rest of the population (the unobserved *P*s); the relevance of the similarities among the objects in the population to the projected attribute *A*; and the number and variety of objects in the data group. A sample that is sufficiently large and varied, and sufficiently similar to the rest of the population, is a ***representative sample***. A nonrepresentative sample is ***biased***. The condition of validity for enumerative induction, then, is that a representative sample of Ps has been observed.[6]

Hasty Generalization. Concluding that all *P* have *A* when the conditions of validity for enumerative induction have not been met is a fallacy called ***hasty generalization***. Suppose the A. C. Neilson Company surveyed three Americans and found that each watched at least six hours of television a day. The ratings company would commit the fallacy of hasty generalization if it concluded that all Americans watch at least six hours of television per day. The sample is not sufficiently large. Or suppose the conclusion were drawn that all Americans know of Michael Bloomberg (mayor of New York City in 2007) from the premise that all Americans surveyed knew of him. The argument would be fallacious, no matter how many millions were surveyed, if they were all New Yorkers. In this case, the sample would not be sufficiently diverse. Although statistics—a branch of applied mathematics—provides some guidelines, no one yet can specify generally and precisely just how large or varied a sample must be before an enumerative induction is valid rather than hasty. One problem is that the sample size necessary depends on how similar one *P* is to another, and on how relevant *P* is to *A*. For example, people differ markedly in their personality traits. Consequently, an enormously large and varied sample is needed to conclude that all people have a particular personality trait. People differ far less in their biological nature, so smaller samples suffice for medical generalizations. Electrons, at the other extreme, differ very little from one another; hence observation of relatively few can support a generalization. One case may even

---

[6] The validity of an enumerative induction, or any other relative of the argument from analogy, depends also on the specific meaning of the term replacing A. Let "grue" mean "observed and green or unobserved and blue." Since all observed emeralds have been green, they have all been grue. But the argument "All observed emeralds are grue, therefore all emeralds are grue" is invalid, for the conclusion implies that unobserved emeralds are blue, not green. This ingenious example was devised by Nelson Goodman in *Fact, Fiction, and Forecast* (Bobbs-Merrill, 1965), who used it in a considerably more complex argument.

suffice if the population is homogeneous enough. For example, we can safely infer that all Pioneer SX-7 receivers have digital tuning given that one does.

The term "hasty generalization" in our sense denotes an enumerative induction based on a small or biased sample. In another sense, it denotes the conclusion of such a fallacious inference. Thus the statement that all Americans watch at least six hours of television a day would be classified as a hasty generalization if it were inferred from a survey of just three Americans. *Stereotypes* are common hasty generalizations. Since movie stars like Cary Grant and Elizabeth Taylor get married and divorced several times, some infer that all (or most) movie stars do. As a result, marital instability has become part of the stereotype of a movie star. In fact, movie stars are a widely varied group of individuals. Many do have several marriages, but many do not. Racial and ethnic stereotypes are especially invidious.

Inductive Generalizations. Enumerative induction is often called *inductive generalization* because it has a generalization as a conclusion, and because the argument is inductive valid under certain conditions. The term "inductive generalization" is more often applied to the conclusion of such an argument, such as Galileo's law of free fall. An inductive generalization, in this sense, is a generalization inferred by the rule of enumerative induction. Inductive generalizations are also called empirical generalizations, since "empirical" means "based on observation." An inductive generalization can receive further support in several ways. The sample can be increased, of course, providing more support of the same kind. Support of a different nature is received if the generalization *explains* phenomena other than the observations on which it was based, or if it can be *explained by* other inductive generalizations or hypotheses. For example, Galileo's law of free fall was based on observations of objects dropped from buildings, and balls rolled down inclined planes. His law is strengthened every time a freshman physics class repeats his experiments. The increase is minimal, however. Something like a "law of diminishing returns" applies. The support for Galileo's law was dramatically increased, though, by two findings. First, his law explained the law of ballistics, which states that projectiles such as cannon balls follow a parabolic trajectory. This sort of inductive support will be discussed at length in the next chapter. Second, Galileo's law was explained by Newton's law of universal gravitation, according to which all objects attract each other with a force inversely proportional to the square of the distance between them. This showed that Galileo's law was just a special case of a broader generalization, which means that all the observations for the broader generalization become support for the special case. In short, if an inductive generalization has explanatory connections with other inductive generalizations, it is supported by them and hence by the observations supporting them.

Generalizations lacking such explanatory connections are described pejoratively as *mere* empirical generalizations, and are treated with caution or skepticism by scientists. Astronomy provides a famous example known inaccurately as Bode's law, which states that the mean distances of the planets from the sun form a certain regular progression. An astronomer named Johann Titius formulated the mathematical equation describing the progression in 1772, and it was championed by Johann Bode. The formula implied, for example that Saturn is about twice as far from the sun as Jupiter, and that the next most distant planet should be about twice as far as Saturn. When Uranus was discovered in the 1780s, it had the proper distance, confirming Bode's law. A gap in the series between Mars and Jupiter was filled when the minor planets, or asteroids, were discovered in 1801 and later; they were nearly twice the distance of Mars and half that of Jupiter. Despite its inductive support, Bode's law never gained universal acceptance. For it could not be explained by any more fundamental laws, and had no additional explanatory power of its own. The caution was rewarded, for Neptune and Pluto were subsequently found to be much closer than Bode's law predicted.[7] It should not be inferred that enumerative induction is an invalid method

---

[7] See M. Grosser, *The Discovery of Neptune* (Harvard University Press, 1962), esp. pp 27-38 and 140; William G. Hoyt, *Planets X and Pluto* (University of Arizona Press, 1980), esp. pp. 24-29, 37-47, and 61.

of inference. Examples like Bode's law do, however, emphasize that enumerative inductions are only inductively valid which means that inductive generalizations are always subject to possible refutation. It should not even be inferred that mere empirical generalizations are always suspect. It is well known, for example, that aspirin is an effective pain reliever, even though it is not known why.

Statistical Enumerative Induction. Earlier, we discussed statistical analogical arguments, in which the conclusion that an object outside the sample has *A* is drawn from the premise that *most* objects in the sample have *A*. From the fact that most people surveyed liked *Star Wars,* we can infer by analogy that you will probably like it too. In this example, only one object in the population lies outside the sample. If many objects lie outside the sample, we cannot safely conclude that all of them have *A* from the fact that most objects in the sample have *A*. Suppose you surveyed 1,000 college students and found that most, but not all, of them liked *Star Wars*. You could not infer that *all* other college students would like it. The best you could conclude is that *most* would. No matter what proportion of the sample has *A*, whether it be more or less than 50 percent, we can (under certain conditions) infer by analogy that *the same* percentage holds for the rest of the population. Thus if 7 out of 10 (or 3 out of 10) of the students you surveyed liked *Star Wars,* you could infer that 7 out of 10 (or 3 out of 10) students you did not survey would like it. Your inference is an enumerative induction, but ***statistical***, not pure, because the percentage observed and inferred is less than 100 (and more than 0). The statistical form of enumerative induction can be represented as follows. Let *r* be any percentage except 100 or 0.

Enumerative Induction: Statistical Form
r % of all observed *P* have *A*.
∴ *r* % of all *P* have *A* (± *e* %).
CONDITIONS OF VALIDITY: The group of observed *P*s is sufficiently large and varied, and is sufficiently similar to the group of unobserved *P*s in relevant respects.

The pure form of enumerative induction represents the limit approached by the statistical form as the percentage *r* approaches 100 (or 0 if the argument is expressed negatively).

The statistical form of enumerative induction is used frequently by actuaries. Insurance premiums are determined by mortality tables, which tell what percentage of all people born on the same date will be alive a specified number of years later. The Commissioners' 1941 Standard Mortality Table was established by observing 1,023,102 American men from birth to death. Because 66 percent were still alive at age 60, the conclusion was drawn that 66 percent of all newborn American males live to be at least 60 years old. An insurance company therefore expects to pay the death benefit to 34 percent of all newborn American males with 60-year term life insurance. Statistical enumerative inductions are also common in quality-control procedures. The cost of developing a completely reliable manufacturing process is generally prohibitive, so a certain percentage of defects is accepted. The output is sampled periodically, and if one percent of the products tested are defective, it may be inferred that about one percent of all items produced are defective. If this rate is too high, steps are taken to bring it down. Statistical enumerative induction is even used in pure science. It is used in physics to determine the half-life of a radioactive element, which is the number of years it takes for half of a given number of atoms to decompose. Many samples of carbon-14 were observed, for example, each containing billions of atoms. The observed atoms decayed at a rate of about one-half per 5,700 years, which led to the conclusion that the half-life of carbon-14 is 5,700 years.

We discussed hasty generalization in connection with the pure form of enumerative induction. But the fallacy occurs whenever a conclusion is drawn about an entire population on the basis of a nonrepresentative sample. So hasty generalization can occur with statistical enumerative induction as well. Given that 90 percent of all students observed are over 6 feet tall, we cannot legitimately infer that 90 percent of all students are over 6 feet tall, if we observed only 10 students all on the men's basketball team. The conclusion that 66 percent of newborn American males live to be 60 years old would be a hasty generalization if the sample of 1,023,102 men on which it was based contained only men whose families had a history of longevity.

From the premise that *r* percent of all observed *P* have *A*, we cannot always conclude that *exactly* *r* percent of all *P* have *A*. Thus, suppose you surveyed 4 of your 21 friends, and found that 3 liked *Star Wars*. You could hardly infer that exactly 75 percent of all your friends liked *Star Wars*. It would be safer to infer that between 65 percent and 85 percent did, and safer still to infer that between 55 percent and 95 percent did. In general, we often must specify a **confidence interval** around *r* percent, which is why "± *e* %" appears in parentheses in the general form of statistical enumerative induction. Plus or minus *e* percent is referred to as the *margin of safety*, or *margin of error*; and *e* is the amount of error that is allowed on either side of the estimated percentage *r*. The limits of the confidence interval are *r* + *e* percent and *r* - *e* percent, since we are inferring that between *r* + *e* percent and *r* - *e* percent of all *P* have *A*, The broader the confidence interval the weaker the conclusion, and so the stronger the argument. Confidence intervals need not be specified in precise numerical terms. Instead of inferring that between 65 percent and 85 percent of your friends liked *Star Wars*, you might infer that *about* 75 percent of them did. Such a conclusion is vague, but for most practical purposes greater precision is pointless. "Most all" and "almost all" are also used to vaguely specify a confidence interval.

Representative Samples. Let us look more closely at the similarity condition. The sample must be sufficiently like the population in relevant respects. With a pure enumerative induction, it is only necessary that the members of the two groups resemble each other. But with a statistical enumerative induction, the two groups must resemble each other *as groups*. The "make-up" of the data group and the rest of the population must be the same. Suppose we survey 25 senators to determine how much support exists for a new tax cut, and find that 92 percent of our sample favors one. Before we conclude that 92 percent of all senators favor a tax cut, we must compare the make-up of our sample to that of the population. Support for such a measure is known to depend on party affiliation. So a representative sample would have to resemble the population in the percentage of Republicans and Democrats. If 65 percent of all senators are Democrats, while 20 senators in our sample (80 percent) are Republicans (or Democrats), the sample is biased. A statistical enumerative induction based on such a biased sample commits the fallacy of hasty generalization.

A representative sample for statistical purposes must be sufficiently large and varied. Size and variety alone, however, do not guarantee representativeness. A sample containing 65 percent Democrats and 35 percent Republicans is just as varied as one containing 35 percent Democrats and 65 percent Republicans (other things equal). But at most one of the samples will be representative for political polling. In a statistical induction, the *distribution* of variety in the sample is as important to representativeness as the *amount* of variety. In a pure induction, only the amount of variety matters.

Perhaps the major difficulty in statistical research is selecting representative samples. Two methods are commonly used. One is called **random sampling**. A sample is random if every member of the population has an equal and independent chance of being selected. Random selection does not guarantee a representative sample, but does make it likely, at least if the sample is large. Random sampling is especially useful when little or nothing is known in advance about the population. Suppose we wish to determine what percentage of Salvadorans favored increased U.S. involvement in their country. If we know nothing about the Salvadoran people, we should select our sample randomly.

A second method used to select representative samples is called **stratified sampling**. A stratified sample is obtained by dividing the population into groups, or "strata," based on characteristics like party affiliation, determining the percentage of the population in each group, and then randomly selecting the same proportion of the sample from each group. Thus, if we want to know how the student body feels about some issue, and we know that the student body is evenly divided among freshmen, sophomores, juniors, and seniors, then we can select stratified sample by randomly selecting 5 freshmen, 5 sophomores, 5 juniors and 5 seniors. Random sampling has the advantage of not requiring advance knowledge of the population. Stratified sampling has the advantage of ensuring that the sample is representative in selected respects.

We have been discussing one type of statistical inference, in which the proportion of the population having a given property is inferred from the proportion of the sample possessing it. Samples can also be used to estimate other parameters of the population, such as averages. We could estimate the average height of Americans, for example, by selecting a random sample of Americans, and calculating the average height in the sample. If the average height of the sample was 5 feet 8 inches, we could infer that the average height of the American population was about 5 feet 8 inches. The strength of our argument would depend notably on the size and representativeness of the sample. An estimate based on a sample of five would not be very reliable, nor would one based on a sample of five hundred basketball players.

We have made *qualitative* assessments of statistical and other inferences. We noted, for example, that the broader the confidence interval, the stronger the argument and the more reliable the estimate. One goal of statistics is to *quantify* the risk of error in making an inference. Statisticians devise procedures for determining just how likely it is that the estimated parameter falls within a specified confidence interval. Random samples are important in statistics not because they are likely to be representative, but because they make it possible to calculate such probabilities.

The Statistical Syllogism. Enumerative induction enables us to establish empirical generalizations. Once verified, we can apply them to new cases. A bombardier can infer from Galileo's law that a bomb will accelerate at a rate of 32 feet per second squared. An insurance company can infer that a new applicant named John, age 25, will probably live to be at least 50, since 86 percent of all 25-year-old American men live to be 50. This pattern of inference, *from* a generalization *to* a specific instance, is called a **syllogism**. Whereas in an argument from analogy or enumerative induction, the inference group contains objects that are not in the data group, in a syllogism the inference group is a subset of the data group. Figure 3-3, which represents the relationships among the groups involved in a syllogism, should be contrasted with Figures 3-1 and 3-2 (pp. 81 and 95).

FIGURE 3-3: SYLLOGISTIC ARGUMENT

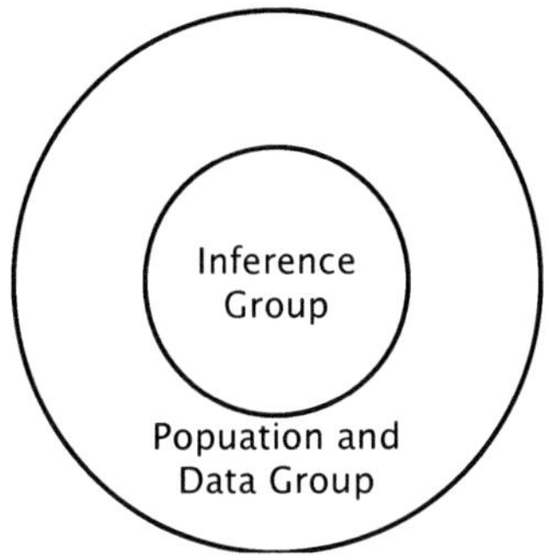

In an enumerative induction, the properties of a population are inferred from the observed properties of a subset of that population. In a syllogistic argument, the properties of a subset of the population are inferred from the known properties of the entire population. In other words, while a syllogistic argument proceeds from the general to the specific, an enumerative induction proceeds from the specific to the general. To continue in these terms, one might say that an analogical argument proceeds from the specific to the specific.

Syllogisms can be pure or statistical. The bombardier's syllogism is **pure**, since the generalization on which the conclusion is based makes a statement about *all* objects falling freely at the surface of the earth. The insurance company's syllogism is **statistical**, since the generalization involved makes a statement about less than 100 percent (and more than 0 percent) of all 25-year-old American males. As we shall see in Chapter 5, there are many types of pure syllogism, some deductively valid (like the example about the bomb), others invalid. Statistical syllogisms have many varieties too. But the pattern illustrated by the insurance example is so common it is called *the* statistical syllogism. Let r again be any percentage other than 100 (or 0).

The Statistical Syllogism

r% of all P have A.

i is P.

∴ i has A.

CONDITIONS OF VALIDITY: r greater than 50 percent, and i is a sufficiently small group of objects.

The symbol i stands for the inference group, while the set of all P—the entire population—is the data group. A is both the given and the projected attribute. The statistical syllogism is inductively valid under certain conditions. The strength of the argument depends principally on the percentage r. The greater the percentage, the stronger the argument. The argument that John (our 25-year-old American male) will live to be 50 years old would be stronger if it were given that 95 percent of all 25-year-old American males live to be 50, and stronger still if 99 percent do. When r is 100, the syllogism is pure, and deductively valid. As r recedes from 100, the strength of the statistical syllogism declines, the chances become greater that i is an "exception to the rule." When r is 50 or less, the argument is invalid. Since no more than 50 percent of all 25-year-old American males live to be 70 years old, we cannot infer that John will reach the age of 70, for we have just as much reason to believe that he will not. Since only 34 percent of all 25-year-old American males reach 75, we should infer that John will probably not live to be 75.

The other factor influencing a statistical syllogism's strength is the number of objects represented by i. The strongest case is that in which i represents just one object, as in our example about John. But we can also infer by the statistical syllogism that John and George will *both* reach age 50 from the premise that 86 percent of all 25-year-old American males do. The larger the inference group i, the stronger the conclusion, and so the weaker the argument, Whereas the strength of a statistical syllogism is directly related to the percentage r, it is inversely related to the size of i. There are limits to how large i may be in any given case. The conclusion that John and George and a million other 25-year-old American males will all live to be 50 cannot validly be drawn from the premise that 86 percent of 25-year-old Americans do. It is not possible, however, to specify precisely and generally the maximum size of i. For it depends on the specific percentage r. Further discussion of the statistical syllogism must await 10.2, which introduces the probability calculus.

Glossary

Enumerative induction: the argument in which, from the premise that all (or a certain percentage) of the observed members of a class have a property, the conclusion is drawn that it or the same percentage) of the members do; to be valid, the sample must be sufficiently large and varied, and sufficiently similar to the rest of the population in relevant respects.

Hasty generalization: an enumerative induction that is fallacious because the sample is insufficiently large, varied, or similar to the rest of the population; or, the conclusion of such an argument.

Inductive generalization: enumerative induction; or, a general statement inferred by enumerative induction.

Confidence interval: a precise interval in which an inference group or population parameter is inferred to fall on the basis of statistics describing the data group.

Representative sample: a sample that is sufficiently large and varied, and sufficiently similar to the rest of the population.

Biased sample: a sample that is not representative.

Random sample: a sample selected in such a way that every member of the population had an equal and independent chance of being included.

Stratified sample: a sample obtained by dividing the population into groups possessing certain characteristics, determining the percentage of the population in each group, and then randomly selecting the appropriate proportion of the sample from each group.

Statistical syllogism: the argument in which, from the general premise that a percentage of a population has a property, the conclusion is drawn that specific members do; to be valid, the percentage must exceed 50 percent, and the inference group must be sufficiently small.

Exercises

A. Classify the following arguments as arguments from analogy, enumerative inductions, or syllogisms, and classify them further as pure or statistical. If the argument is weak or invalid, explain why.

1. The famed biologist Ricky D is trying to determine what effect, if any, certain bird songs have on the behavior of other birds of the same species. Specifically, he is interested in how patterns of sound sung by one bird can alter the behavior of another bird for evolutionary reasons (reproduction, predation, etc.). He notes that since the experiments of Galvani, researchers have used electrical probes to send patterns of electricity to certain areas of bird brains. Furthermore, it is not uncommon for the electrical signal to result in some change in the bird's behavior (depending on where the probes are located). Ricky is a bright guy, and realizes that ears convert mechanical vibrations (e.g. bird songs) into electrical signals that can be interpreted by the brain. He concludes that it is quite plausible that the song of one bird can alter the behavior of another bird, perhaps even for evolutionary reasons.

2. How the market behaves in the first five trading days of the new year frequently points the way for the full year. So the behavior of the market in the first five trading days of this year should point the way for the year as a whole.

3. If we turn our eyes upon the fabric of our fellow animals, we find they are supported with bones, covered with skins, moved by muscles; that they possess the same senses, acknowledge the same appetites, and are nourished by the same aliment with ourselves; and we should hence conclude from the strongest

analogy, that their internal faculties [e.g. mental processes, consciousness, etc.] were also in some measure similar to our own. –Erasmus Darwin, *Zoonomia Vol. 1.*

4. An older man named Biff has just stolen Marty's time machine and traveled back to the year 1955 in an attempt to reclaim his lost youth. He notices a bag on the seat from a bookstore and decides to stop off at a café and do some light reading. It is late in the evening and there is a television tuned to the sports channel in the corner. Biff opens the book and realizes that it is an almanac of outcomes for sporting events for the entire 20th century. He looks up at the recap and sees that for every sporting event of the day, be it horseracing, baseball, racecar-driving, etc., the book has accurately predicted the outcome. Old Biff realizes that he knows the outcome of every sporting event for the next 45 years. He jumps up and runs off to find young Biff and a bookie.

5. What the conditions within the Earth and Moon were in the distant past is uncertain, but these bodies probably passed through viscous stages which endured through enormously long periods of time. No one seriously doubts that Jupiter, Saturn, Uranus and Neptune are now largely gaseous, and that they will evolve, through various degrees of viscosity, into the solid and comparatively elastic state. It is natural to assume that the Earth has already passed through an analogous experience. –William Campbell, "The Evolution of the Stars and the Formation of the Earth," *Popular Science Monthly* Vol. 86 (Oct-Dec 1915).

6. Santa Claus is really a woman—and she's better known as Mom, says a consumer report. Sociologist Theodore Caplow of the University of Virginia surveyed 110 families.... Summing up his findings, Caplow concluded: "Women do most of the shopping, most of the decorating and most of the wrapping. They give more gifts than men do." –*The Star* (December 27, 1983), p. 11.

7. There is another and curious class of cases in which close external resemblance does not depend on adaptation to similar habits of life, but has been gained for the sake of protection. I allude to the wonderful manner in which certain butterflies imitate, as first described by Mr. Bates, other and quite distinct species. This excellent observer has shown that in some districts of South America, where, for instance, an Ithomia abounds in gaudy swarms, another butterfly, namely, a Leptalis, is often found mingled in the same flock; and the latter so closely resembles the Ithomia in every shade and stripe of colour, and even in the shape of its wings, that Mr. Bates, with his eyes sharpened by collecting during eleven years, was, though always on his guard, continually deceived. When the mockers and the mocked are caught and compared, they are found to be very different in essential structure, and to belong not only to distinct genera, but often to distinct families. Had this mimicry occurred in only one or two instances, it might have been passed over as a strange coincidence. But, if we proceed from a district where one Leptalis imitates an Ithomia, another mocking and mocked species, belonging to the same two genera, equally close in their resemblance, may be found. Altogether no less than ten genera are enumerated, which include species that imitate other butterflies. The mockers and mocked always inhabit the same region; we never find an imitator living remote from the form which it imitates. –Charles Darwin, *On the Origin of Species 6th Ed.*

8. The Biorhythm Research Association claims that good luck is immensely greater on a person's "multi-high jackpot days." This must be true, for the association prepared a biorhythm analysis for hundreds of people around the country, who then reported what happened on their jackpot days. Eight of the reports were published in an advertisement for the association which appeared in *The Star* (December 27, 1983, p. 33), and each reported winnings of hundreds and even thousands of dollars at various games of chance.

9. "Not a single one of all my dogs has ever died from a vaccine," Pasteur pondered.... "It must work the same way on humans—it must" –Paul De Kruif, *Microbe Hunters*, p. 169.

10. They put mad dogs in cages with healthy ones, and the mad dogs bit the normal ones. Roux injected virulent stuff from rabid rabbits into the brains of other healthy dogs. Then they treated these beasts, certain to die if they were left alone—they shot the fourteen stronger and stronger doses of vaccine into them. It was an unheard-of triumph! For every one of these creatures lived—threw off perfectly, mysteriously, the attacks of their unseen assassins, and Pasteur—who had a bitter experience with his anthrax inoculations—asked that all of his experiments be checked by a commission of the best medical men of France, and at the end of these severe experiments the commission announced: "Once a dog is made immune with the gradually more virulent spinal cords of rabbits dead of rabies, nothing on earth can give him the disease." –Paul De Kruif, *Microbe Hunters*, p. 169.

11. The learned doctors gaped. Then Patrick Manson read out a telegram from Ronald Ross. It was the final proof: the bite of a malarial mosquito had given a healthy bird malaria! The congress—and this is the custom of congresses—permitted itself a dignified furor, and passed a resolution congratulating this unknown Major Ronald Ross on his "Great and Epoch-Making Discovery." The congress—and it is the habit of congresses—believed that what is true for birds goes for men too. –Paul De Kruif, *Microbe Hunters*, p. 279.

12. Walts was 26 years old… when he learned in October 1981 that he had testicular cancer. He had three operations: one to eliminate the malignancy, another to remove his lymph nodes when it was determined the disease had advanced to a second stage, and a third to remove scar tissue. For six months, he underwent periodic injections of two powerful drugs that drained his strength, leaving him weak and nauseated….

The last treatment was a year ago June 4, on his twenty-seventh birthday…. Little more than a month later, remarkably, he started his comeback, playing for the Friars of Team Tennis….

Three in every 100,800 men age 16 to 45 get testicular cancer, and 93 percent recover…. Having passed the six-month critical period after chemotherapy when reoccurrence of cancer is most likely, Walts seems safe. –Barry Lorge, "Butch Walts vs. Cancer: A Happy Epilogue," *World Tennis* (December 1983), pp. 18-19.

13. Subsequently to my experiments, M. Martens tried similar ones, but in a much better manner, for he placed the seeds in a box in the actual sea, so that they were alternately wet and exposed to the air like really floating plants. He tried ninety-eight seeds, mostly different from mine, but he chose many large fruits, and likewise seeds, from plants which live near the sea; and this would have favoured both the average length of their flotation and their resistance to the injurious action of the salt-water. On the other hand, he did not previously dry the plants or branches with the fruit; and this, as we have seen, would have caused some of them to have floated much longer. The result was that 18/98 of his seeds of different kinds floated for forty-two days, and were then capable of germination…. Therefore, it would perhaps be safer to assume that the seeds of about 10/100 plants of a flora, after having been dried, could be floated across a space of sea 900 miles in width, and would then germinate. –Charles Darwin, *On the Origin of Species 6th Ed.*

14. If we look even to the two main divisions—namely, to the animal and vegetable kingdoms—certain low forms are so far intermediate in character that naturalists have disputed to which kingdom they should be referred…. It does not seem incredible that, from some such low and intermediate form, both animals and plants may have been developed; and, if we admit this, we must likewise admit that all the organic beings which have ever lived on this earth may be descended from some one primordial form. –Charles Darwin, *On the Origin of Species 6th Ed.*

15. Bill has been late for nearly all his previous appointments. Therefore, he will probably be late for his next appointment.

16. Bill is late for nearly all his appointments. Therefore, he will probably be late for his next appointment.

17. Bill is always late for his appointments. Therefore, he will be late for his next appointment.

18. Bob is seldom late for his appointments. Therefore, he will be late for his next appointment.

B. In this exercise, you will be given an enumerative induction. Then various modifications of the argument will be suggested, or additional information supplied. In each case, determine whether the alteration strengthens or weakens the original argument (or has no effect on strength) and explain why.

1. One hundred students, seniors and juniors, from four different Catholic universities around the country were surveyed, and 80 percent professed belief in God. Therefore, about 80 percent of all college students in the United States believe in God.

    (a) One thousand students were surveyed.

    (b) Ten students were surveyed.

    (c) One hundred seniors and juniors were surveyed from the Catholic University in Washington, D.C.

    (d) One hundred seniors and juniors were surveyed from ten different Catholic universities around the country.

    (e) One hundred seniors and juniors were surveyed from four different colleges, one a Catholic school, one with a Protestant affiliation, and two with no religious affiliation at all.

    (f) The one hundred students were all theology majors.

    (g) The one hundred students were all seniors.

    (h) There were equal numbers of freshmen, sophomores, juniors, and seniors.

    (i) The one hundred students were all Sagittarians.

    (j) The one hundred students all had grade point averages of 3.5 or better.

    (k) Half of the students liked football the other half did not.

    (l) Therefore, about 80 percent of all students at Catholic universities believe in God.

    (m) Therefore, more than 50 percent of all students at U.S. universities believe in God

    (n) Therefore, about 80 percent of all college students around the world believe in God.

    (o) Therefore, exactly 80 percent of all U.S. college students believe in God.

LSAT Prep Questions

1. Journalist: One reason many people believe in extrasensory perception (ESP) is that they have heard of controlled experiments in which ESP is purportedly demonstrated. However, ESP is a myth and the public is deluded by these experiments, for a prominent researcher has admitted to falsifying data on psychic phenomena in order to obtain additional grants.

    The reasoning in the journalist's argument is flawed because this argument

    (a) uses an irrelevant personal attack on the integrity of someone

    (b) infers that something must be a myth from the fact that the general public believes it

    (c) presupposes that, in general, only evidence from experiments can support beliefs

    (d) implies that all scientists who depend on grants to support their research are unreliable

    (e) overgeneralizes from the example of one deceptive researcher

    Preptest 31, Section 3, Question 1

2. One thousand people in Denmark were questioned about their views on banning cigarette advertising. The sample comprised adults who are representative of the general population, and who, ten years previously, had been questioned on the same issue. Interestingly, their opinions changed little. Results show that 31 percent are in favor of such a ban, 24 percent are against it, 38 percent are in favor, but only for certain media, and 7 percent have no opinion.

    The survey results in the passage best support which one of the following conclusions?

    (a) People's opinions never change very much.

    (b) A minority of Denmark's population feels that banning cigarette advertising would set a bad precedent.

    (c) Most of Denmark's population is not seriously concerned about cigarette advertising.

    (d) Most of Denmark's population favor some sort of ban on cigarette advertising.

    (e) Most of Denmark's population does not smoke cigarettes.

    Preptest 31, Section 3, Question 6

3. Several recent studies establish that most people would want to be informed if they had any serious medical condition. In each study, over 80 percent of the people surveyed indicated that they would want to be told.

    Each of the following, if true, weakens the argument EXCEPT:

    (a) In another recent study, most of the people surveyed indicated that they would not want to be told if they had a serious medical condition.

    (b) People often do not indicate their true feelings when responding to surveys.

    (c) Some of the researchers conducting the studies had no background in medicine.

    (d) Some questions asked in the studies suggested that reasonable people would want to be told if they had a serious medical condition.

(e) The people surveyed in the studies were all young students in introductory psychology courses.

Preptest 31, Section 3, Question 12

4. Columnist: George Orwell's book *1984* has exercised much influence on a great number of this newspaper's readers. One thousand readers were surveyed and asked to name the one book that had the most influence on their lives. The book chosen most often was the Bible; *1984* was second.

The answer to which one of the following questions would most help in evaluating the columnist's argument?

(a) How many books had each person surveyed read?

(b) How many people chose books other than *1984*?

(c) How many people read the columnist's newspaper?

(d) How many books by George Orwell other than *1984* were chosen?

(e) How many of those surveyed had actually read the books they chose?

Preptest 36, Section 1, Question 24

3.4 The Fallacy Of Exclusion

We have been studying some important forms of inductive inference. Others will be analyzed in the next chapter. Most, if not all, sound inductive arguments have one of these forms, or variants of them. By studying these forms you can improve your ability to analyze, criticize, and construct inductive arguments. However, it was said in §2.5 that inductive arguments are generally not *formally* valid. Some analogical arguments are valid, for example, while others are invalid. An inductive argument's validity depends on factors other than form. We have discussed some factors applying to specific patterns of inductive argument. For example, an enumerative induction is valid only if a sufficient number of *P*s has been observed. The fallacy of hasty generalization results otherwise. We shall now discuss a general factor applicable to all inductive arguments.

Undermining Counterevidence. Imagine that Ivan Lendl is about to play John McEnroe in the finals of the U.S. Open tennis tournament. In the last few years, Lendl has won over 90 percent of his matches. However, he has lost to McEnroe more than he has won, and Lendl has seldom won a major tournament like the U.S. Open. Now consider the following argument from analogy:

> Lendl will win his upcoming match, since he has won over 90
> percent of his matches in the last few years.

The premise is true. Moreover, many inductively sound arguments have the same form. Nevertheless, the premise does not in this case constitute a sufficient reason to believe the conclusion. For we have *additional* information that undermines the argument—namely, that Lendl's upcoming match is the finals of a major tournament, and that his opponent is McEnroe. Given this information, it is not at all improbable that Lendl will lose his upcoming match, even though he has won over 90 percent of his matches in the last few years. Hence the argument is invalid. Note that when the additional information is added as a premise to the original argument, the premises remain true, but the argument no longer seems valid.

> Lendl will win his upcoming match, for (1) he has won over 90 percent of his matches in the last few years, and (2) his match is the finals of a major tournament, which he has seldom won.

The first premise represents positive evidence, since it supports the conclusion. The second premise represents negative evidence, since it supports the contrary conclusion. The negative evidence here overrides the positive, due to its greater specific relevance. Other things equal, Lendl's upcoming match is more similar to finals matches in previous major tournaments than to other previous matches. So his performance in major finals matches should be given greater weight.

Negative evidence is called **counterevidence**, since it supports the contrary conclusion. Counterevidence **undermines** an argument if it supports the falsity of the conclusion to such an extent that the conclusion is not probable even if the premises are true. Note that undermining counterevidence, as defined, affects the conclusion of an argument, not its premises. Clearly, an argument that excludes any undermining counterevidence is invalid: the conclusion does not follow from the premises even with probability. So we have a condition of validity that applies to all arguments:

The General Condition of Validity
There is no undermining counterevidence.

We shall say that an argument whose premises exclude counterevidence, thereby violating the general condition of validity, commits the *fallacy of exclusion*. An exclusionary argument is fallacious because the premises constitute a biased selection from the available evidence; that is, the premises present only evidence that is favorable to the conclusion, even though equal or greater evidence exists that is unfavorable to the conclusion.

To prevent exclusion, many logicians lay down what is called "the principle of total evidence," stating that a sound inductive argument must take into account all relevant evidence. There is no harm, however, in excluding positive evidence. While this may be disadvantageous from a rhetorical point of view, it is not logically fallacious. An argument is sound as long as there is sufficient evidence for the conclusion. The argument does not have to present the strongest possible evidence. Not only is it unnecessary to present the evidence, it is usually both impracticable and undesirable to do so. We generally do not know all of it; and even if we did there would be too much to present effectively: our audience would miss the forest for the trees. Furthermore, while it is misleading to exclude *any* counterevidence since excluding it will make the conclusion appear more probable than it is, doing so is not fallacious unless the counterevidence is strong enough to be undermining. Note that to be undermining, the counterevidence does not have to make the conclusion improbable: it merely has to prevent the conclusion from being probable.

The fallacy of exclusion is probably the most common of all fallacies. For one thing, the available evidence relevant to a given conclusion is often too extensive to keep in mind all at once. Second, even individuals who would never consciously select only favorable evidence have an unconscious tendency to suppress unfavorable evidence. Charles Darwin was so aware of this human frailty he used to make special written notes of any observation casting doubt on his theory of evolution. Third, the exclusion of counterevidence is a favorite device of those whose motive is persuasion rather than proof. Consider the commercial suggesting that Anacin is better than competing products because it contains "the pain reliever doctors recommend most." The undermining information excluded is that countless other products contain the same pain reliever (aspirin), and that the pain reliever doctors recommend next most often (acetaminophen—the active ingredient in Tylenol) is equally effective. As is generally the case, the validity of an argument does not depend on personal facts about the arguer. So an exclusionary argument is equally fallacious whether the undermining evidence was deliberately excluded, unconsciously suppressed, overlooked, or merely forgotten. The arguer, on the other hand, should be judged more guilty of a breach of rationality if his was a sin of commission rather than of omission.

A flagrant form of exclusion is to ignore statistical evidence in favor of one vivid example. Here's a typical case: Michele was buying a new car and was primarily interested in trouble-free transportation. She consulted such sources as *Consumers' Reports,* whose studies show that Toyotas have the best frequency-of-repair record. Properly impressed, she bought one. Alas, it turned out to be a lemon. Soured by her experience, she has vowed never to buy a Toyota again. She is now being irrational. Her decision whether or not to buy another Toyota should be based on the likelihood that it will be reliable. The fact that her current Toyota is a lemon is certainly relevant, and does support the conclusion that the next Toyota she bought would be a lemon too. But this evidence is thoroughly undermined by the statistical data gathered by *Consumers' Reports*, which *is* based on thousands of other cases. While natural to ignore cold and impersonal statistics in favor of experiences close to home, it is irrational.

The fallacy of exclusion has been illustrated with analogical arguments, but it can arise with any pattern of inductive argument. Consider the argument from authority: A juror in the Hinckley trial who reasoned that Hinckley was sane because a psychiatrist said he was, would have committed the fallacy since other equally reputable psychiatrists had testified that Hinckley was insane. The conflicting testimony, not included in the argument, constitutes undermining counterevidence. The juror's argument would violate both the general condition of validity and the third condition of validity specific to arguments from authority. Indeed, in light of the general condition, that third condition is redundant. It is so important, however, and so often violated, that it warrants special emphasis. The general condition is not redundant, though, for it may be violated by an argument from authority even when none of the specific conditions are violated. For example, if Kathy infers that Clay will arrive at 8:00 from the fact that he said he would, she would have committed the fallacy of exclusion if it were well known that Clay is nearly always late.

Consider next enumerative induction: Every time we have stretched a spring, it has returned to its original shape. We would commit the fallacy of exclusion if we inferred that the spring would always return to its original shape when stretched. For we have additional information that is relevant—namely, that all springs eventually fatigue and lose their elasticity.

Dogmatism and Pseudoscience. If an argument is inductively sound. it is improbable but not impossible that new information will undermine it. An inductively valid argument may therefore cease to be valid when further information becomes available. An argument that is deductively valid at one time, however, is valid at all times. For an argument is deductively valid only if it is impossible for the premises to be true and the conclusion false. A deductively valid argument with true premises will never violate the general condition of validity.

Since scientific laws and theories are based on inductive reasoning, scientists can never be *dogmatic.* They can never refuse to consider new evidence claiming that it could not possibly prove them wrong. Dogmatism has often obstructed progress in science. The most dramatic illustrations come from the Scientific Revolution, wrought by Copernicus, Galileo, and others in the Renaissance. During the Middle Ages, the Bible and the works of Aristotle were considered ultimate authorities on matters of fact. Since those revered sources said that the earth did not move, scholars rejected Copernicus's theory that the earth moved around the sun. Galileo nevertheless discovered, using a telescope for the first time, that Jupiter had four moons revolving around it in just the way Copernicus thought the planets revolved around the sun. This observation supported the Copernican theory, but many scholars ignored the evidence. One reportedly refused even to look through Galileo's telescope! The Church eventually suspended publication of Galileo's major work on astronomy, seized existing copies, and ordered Galileo to cease advocating his views. Episodes like these gave the argument from authority a very bad name. In his day, Aristotle was the leading authority in many fields, including biology and physics. At that time, laymen could validly cite Aristotle. But once evidence was gathered that was unknown to Aristotle, appeals to his authority became fallacious; they committed the fallacy of exclusion.

We should immediately suspect the fallacy of exclusion whenever an argument from authority inclines us to believe something incredible, such as the fantastic claims of pseudoscientists, psychics, and the like. For example, an amazing number of people believe in psychokinesis, the ability to move or alter material objects merely by an act of thought. Why? Because they've read or heard about people like Uri Geller. Geller claims in his autobiography *My Story* that he teleported himself from Manhattan to Ossining, New York (about 30 miles).[8] Incredible! Should we believe him? Of course not. But why not? Why is an argument from authority valid in other cases but not here? Geller certainly seems to be in a position to know whether he teleported himself from one place to another, so that requirement of validity seems satisfied. But is he telling the truth? He may *seem* sincere, lucid, and so on. And we would beg the question if we argued that he must be lying because he did not teleport himself anywhere. So the truthfulness as well as the knowledgeability requirements seem unassailable. The question therefore remains, why shouldn't we believe Geller's claims of teleportation? The answer is simple: because we have an incredible amount of evidence undermining the conclusion that he teleported himself anywhere. First, billions and billions of other human beings have been incapable of teleportation, including, I am sure, you and your acquaintances. Indeed, there have been no *proven* cases of teleportation in all of human history. Second, teleportation would violate the known laws of physics. According to those laws, the motion of a material object requires an expenditure of physical energy. Telekinesis, by definition, involves motion without an expenditure of physical energy. So an argument from authority based on Geller's claim would commit the fallacy of exclusion in a big way. The same evidence provides legitimate grounds for thinking that Geller was either lying or suffering from psychotic delusions, which means that an argument from authority in this case would also fail to satisfy the truthfulness or knowledgeability requirements.[9] Now as we have seen, scientists cannot be dogmatic. Despite colossal amounts of evidence, current physical theories could be wrong and teleportation might be possible. But Geller's mere claim hardly suffices to override the carefully obtained and documented experimental evidence those physical theories are based on.

A useful rule of thumb is that *incredible claims require extraordinary evidence.* While the testimony of a single witness generally suffices to establish that a man moved a knife with his hand, it does not suffice to establish that a man moved a knife with his thoughts, or that he moved a mountain with his hand. You may feel vaguely guilty about dismissing out of hand claims by people like Geller, thinking that to be rational you should be unbiased and keep an open mind. But rationality also demands that you weigh *all* evidence available to you, and form your opinions accordingly. A belief that is unshakeable because it is based on solid evidence is not a bias, although individuals who are biased may try to convince you that it is.

The Exclusionary Rule. There has been considerable controversy over the exclusionary rule in American law, which makes illegally obtained evidence inadmissible in court. As a result of this rule, many defendants have been acquitted who, in light of all the available evidence, were known to be guilty. It may seem as if the exclusionary rule sanctions fallacious reasoning, but it does not. For acquittal in American law is based not on proof of innocence but on failure to prove guilt. It would be fallacious to

---

[8] See Martin Gardner, *Science: Good, Bad, and Bogus* (Avon Discus 1981) pp. 160-61.
[9] There is independent evidence that Geller is a charlatan. See Martin Gardner, *Science: Good, Bad, and Bogus.*

conclude that the defendant was innocent when incriminating evidence was excluded for any reason. The exclusionary rule is a compromise designed to reconcile two conflicting rights: the defendant's right to due process, which requires that evidence be gathered legally; and the state's right to punish the guilty, which can be fully exercised only if all available evidence can be used to prove guilt.

Glossary

Counterevidence: evidence supporting a conclusion contrary to that of a given argument.

Undermining counterevidence: counterevidence which supports the falsity of a conclusion to such an extent that the conclusion is not probable even if the premises are true.

General condition of validity: a condition of validity applying to all arguments requiring that there be no undermining counterevidence.

Fallacy of exclusion: the fallacy committed when the premises of an argument exclude undermining counterevidence.

Exercises

For each of the following arguments, determine whether it involves an argument from authority, argument from analogy, enumerative induction, syllogism, or none of the above, Then determine whether the passage commits the fallacy of exclusion, and if so state the undermining counterevidence it excludes.

1. The president of the United States is a human being like you and me. We do not have the power to appoint Justices to the Supreme Court. Therefore, the President does not have the power to appoint Justices to the Supreme Court.

2. The great apes have physiological structures which are homologous to those in humans. The physiological structures of humans degrade through age and disease. Therefore, the physiological structures of great apes are subject to similar degradation.

3. Mary had a baby. She claimed that she was still a virgin. Therefore, some virgins have had babies.

4. Flying saucers are real, for George Adamski has reported that during a meteor shower on October 9, 1946, he saw with his naked eyes a gigantic space craft hovering high above a mountain ridge to the south of Mount Palomar. (See Leslie and Adamski, *Flying Saucers Have Landed*. p. 172.)

5. It is true that man resulted from divine creation rather than evolution, for Dr. Henry M. Morris and other scientists of the Creation Research Society have signed a statement of their belief in creation. (See Tim LaHaye, *The Battle for the Mind*, pp. 50-51.)

6. The mind continues to live after the body dies. This conclusion is based on Dr. Kubler-Ross's study of patients whose brain and other vital organs have stopped for a while, and were clinically dead, only later to be revived. Many of them report having vivid "out of body" experiences while they were dead. Some are even able to describe what went on in the hospital while they were dead.

7. Venus is larger than Mars, for it says in Hammond's *Whole Earth Atlas* (1976) that the diameter of Venus is 7,700 miles, while the diameter of Mars is 4,200 miles.

8. The members of the United States Congress are people like you and me. We can be arrested on our way to work for charges less than felonies, treasons, or breach of peace. Therefore, the members of U.S. Congress can be arrested for such offenses.

9. The sun has risen every day for the last forty years. So it will probably continue to rise every day for a long time.

10. Psychokinesis is real. That is, some people do have the ability to move external objects merely by willing them to move. This was the conclusion of Dr. Joseph Banks Rhine, who was for many years director of the Parapsychology Laboratory at Duke University and editor of the *Journal of Parapsychology,* and who conducted many experiments in which subjects were asked to try to influence the roll of dice.

11. This penny has been tossed a hundred times, and has come up heads every time. Hence, it will probably continue to come up heads.

12. This penny has been tossed a hundred times, and has come up heads every time. Hence, it is bound to come up tails pretty soon.

13. The cards in this deck have been turned up one-by-one, and the ace of spades hasn't shown up in forty-five tries. So it will probably never show up.

14. The cards in this deck have been turned up one-by-one, and the ace of spades hasn't shown up in forty-five tries. So it is bound to show up on the next few turns.

15. Mary has spent many summers lying on the beach getting a gorgeous tan without wearing a sunscreen, and her face has not shown any of the effects doctors warn of; so her skin must be immune to damage from the sun's ultraviolet rays.

16. "I have driven safely for years without using a seatbelt," John says, "so there is no reason for me to start using one now."

17. I have been alive every day since I was born, over 10,000 days ago. Therefore I will probably live forever.

18. I have been alive every day since I was born, over 10,000 days ago. Therefore, I will probably be alive tomorrow.

19. Most human beings have died before they are 100, and none have ever lived to be more than 200, so I will undoubtedly not live forever.

20. All humans are mortal and I am a human, therefore I am mortal.

21. The Biorhythm Research Association claims that when two or more biorhythm cycles hit high on the same day, you experience a "biorhythm multi-high jackpot day," and that on such days your luck will be especially good in lotteries, drawings, raffles, bingo, horse races, cards, slot machines, and other games of chance. How is a biorhythm analysis prepared? By feeding your birth date into an IBM 370-145 computer. There must be something to biorhythm analysis, for in a full page advertisement in *The Star* (December 27, 1983, p. 33) the Biorhythm Research Association printed the stories of nine people from around the country who hit the jackpot on their multi-high jackpot days, including the winner of Ohio's first million-dollar lottery. The ad said that the association had reports from hundreds of people who had their biorhythm analysis prepared but that because of limited space, it listed only a few of their remarkable stories.

22. The idea of a sun millions of miles in diameter and 91,000,000 miles away is silly. The sun is only 32 miles across and not more than 3,000 miles from the earth. It stands to reason it must be so. God made the sun to light the earth, and therefore must have placed it close to the task it was designed to do. What would you think of a man who built a house in Zion [Illinois] and put the lamp to light it in Kenosha, Wisconsin? –Wilbur Glen Voliva, quoted in Martin Gardner, *Fads and Fallacies,* p. 17.

23. A special May 10, 1930, issue of the [Christian Apostolic Church's] periodical, *Leaves of Healing*, is devoted entirely to astronomy. This 64-page number of the magazine is the most complete statement in print of Voliva's scriptural and scientific reasons for thinking the earth flat and motionless. "Can anyone who has considered this matter seriously," one article asks, "honestly say that he believes the earth is traveling at such an impossible speed? If the earth is going so fast, which way is it going? It would be easier to travel with it than against it. The wind always should blow in the opposite direction to the way the earth is traveling. But where is the man who believes that it does?" –Martin Gardner, *Fads and Fallacies,* p. 17.

24. Another argument offered by Voliva in *Leaves of Healing* for thinking that the earth must be flat is that on a clear day one can see across Lake Winnebago, Wisconsin, which is about ten miles across: "With a good pair of binoculars one can see small objects on the opposite shore, proving beyond any doubt that the surface of the lake is a plane, or a horizontal line." –Quoted in Martin Gardner, *Fads and Fallacies*, p. 18.

25. That is the heart of the teleological argument—the claim that adaptation can be explained only in terms of a designer. It rests, more or less explicitly, on an analogy with human artifacts. Thus, Paley compared the eye to a watch and argued as follows: If one were to find a watch on a desert island, one would be justified in supposing that it was produced by an intelligent being. By the same token (the adjustment of means to ends) one is entitled, upon examination of the human eye, to conclude that it was produced by an intelligent being. –William P. Alston, "Teleological Argument for the Existence of God," *The Encyclopedia of Philosophy*, vol. 8, p. 85.

26. *The National Enquirer* (December 20, 1983, p. 3) has reported that a man who had been in a coma for six weeks was saved by exorcism from a demon trying to kill him. According to *The Enquirer,* a doctor and two psychics drove the demon out of the man and into a rat, which began shrieking until it was burned to death, at which point the man stood up and began to talk. This report was based on the statements of unnamed "amazed witnesses," and a Dr. Paul Borgogno.

27. See 3.1, exercise 10.

28. See 3.1, exercise 23

 LSAT Prep Questions

1. Archaeologist: The fact that the ancient Egyptians and the Maya both built pyramids is often taken as evidence of a historical link between Old- and New-World civilizations that is earlier than any yet documented. But while these buildings are similar to each other, there are important differences in both design and function. The Egyptian pyramids were exclusively tombs for rulers, whereas the Mayan pyramids were used as temples. This shows conclusively that there was no such link between Old- and New-World civilizations.

    Which one of the following most accurately describes a flaw in the archaeologist's argument?

    (a) The argument equivocates with respect to the term "evidence."

(b) The argument appeals to emotion rather than to reason.

(c) The argument assumes the conclusion it is trying to prove.

(d) The argument incorrectly relies on words whose meanings are vague or imprecise.

(e) The argument presumes that no other evidence is relevant to the issue at hand.

Preptest 30, Section 4, Question 8

2. Because addictive drugs are physically harmful, their use by athletes is never justified. Purists, however, claim that taking massive doses of even such nonaddictive drugs as aspirin and vitamins before competing should also be prohibited because they are unnatural. This is ridiculous; almost everything in sports is unnatural, from high-tech running shoes to padded boxing gloves to highly-specialized bodybuilding machines. Yet, none of these is prohibited on the basis of its being unnatural. Furthermore, we should be attending to far more serious problems that plague modern sports and result in unnecessary deaths and injuries. Therefore, the use of nonaddictive drugs by athletes should not be prohibited.

Which one of the following statements, if true, would be the strongest challenge to the author's conclusion?

(a) Massive doses of aspirin and vitamins enhance athletic performance.

(b) Addictive drugs are just as unnatural as nonaddictive drugs like aspirin and vitamins.

(c) Unnecessary deaths and injuries occur in other walks of life besides modern sports.

(d) There would be more unnecessary deaths and injuries if it were not for running shoes, boxing gloves, and bodybuilding machines.

(e) Taking massive doses of aspirin or vitamins can be physically harmful.

Preptest 31, Section 2, Question 16

3. Combustion of gasoline in automobile engines produces benzene, a known carcinogen. Environmentalists propose replacing gasoline with methanol, which does not produce significant quantities of benzene when burned. However, combustion of methanol produces formaldehyde, also a known carcinogen. Therefore the environmentalists' proposal has little merit.

Which one of the following, if true, most supports the environmentalists' proposal?

(a) The engines of some automobiles now on the road burn diesel fuel rather than gasoline.

(b) Several large research efforts are under way to formulate cleaner-burning types of gasoline.

(c) In some regions, the local economy is largely dependent on industries devoted to the production and distribution of automobile fuel.

(d) Formaldehyde is a less potent carcinogen than benzene.

(e) Since methanol is water soluble, methanol spills are more damaging to the environment than gasoline spills.

Preptest 29, Section 4, Question 1

CHAPTER FOUR

Inductive Logic:
Causes and Hypotheses

4.1 Causal Induction and Elimination

From a theoretical point of view, the most important product of scientific investigation may be the discovery of laws of nature—that is, general statements describing the nature of things. In the previous chapter, we examined one method used to verify laws of nature—namely, enumerative induction. From a practical standpoint, however, the most important product of scientific inquiry is undoubtedly the discovery of causes. All of mankind is indebted, for example, to the medical researchers who found the causes of malaria, typhus, and puerperal fever, the cures for strep throat and syphilis, and the way to prevent smallpox, polio, whooping cough, and tetanus. Investigation into causes is not limited to scientists, of course. Fire investigators, detectives, safety engineers, and insurance companies routinely investigate the causes of crimes and accidents. And in our private lives, we are always trying to figure out why something does not work, or how something could work better.

Post Hoc Reasoning. Our question now is: What methods can be used to discover or verify causal connections? Let us begin by examining a spurious method, the fallacy of inferring that *c caused e* simply from the fact that *c preceded or accompanied e*, which we shall call ***post hoc reasoning***.[1] This fallacy is committed by every presidential candidate who claims the economy deteriorated because of the incumbent's policies, citing as his only evidence the economy's deterioration after those policies were enacted. The day after a binge, a man could argue with equal cogency that since he got sick after eating the olives in his ten martinis, the olives must be what made him sick. *Post hoc* reasoning is typical of superstitious thought. A stunning example comes from the Middle Ages. In about 1350, a perfectly preserved Greek statue was found near Siena, Italy. It was universally acclaimed for its perfection. A short time later, though, Siena's war with Florence began to go badly. Finally, the Sienese citizens met in

---

[1] The traditional Latin name for this fallacy is *post hoc ergo propter hoc* ("after this therefore because of this").

council. "One citizen arose and spoke in this vein of the statue: 'Signori, citizens, consider that since we found this statue we have always been overtaken by misfortune…. I am one of those who would advise taking it down, destroying it entirely and smashing it, and sending [it] to be buried in the land of the Florentines."[2] And so they did. As this example illustrates, the causal conclusion of a *post hoc* argument is usually implied, while a further practical conclusion is explicitly drawn.

The premise of a *post hoc* argument is certainly relevant to the truth of its conclusion. For causes can never follow their effects in time. The Great Depression of the 1930s might have been a result of policies Hoover enacted in 1929, but could not possibly have resulted from Bush's policies in 2001. Yet the premise of a *post hoc* argument does not provide anything near a sufficient reason to believe the conclusion. For countless other events besides *c* preceded or accompanied *e*, and would therefore have an equal claim to be selected as the cause of *e*. In our example, the economic deterioration (*e*) was preceded not only by certain presidential actions (*c*) but also by congressional actions, by political, economic, and military upheavals overseas, by changes in the weather, by numerous marriages and divorces, and so on. We therefore cannot select Hoover's policies as the cause *solely* because they preceded the decline.

Mill's Methods of Agreement and Difference. Given only the information that *c* preceded or accompanied *e,* we may legitimately infer that *c* is a *possible* cause of *e*. But before we conclude that *c* is the actual cause, we need further information to eliminate other antecedent conditions. Previous investigations, or even common knowledge, may show that certain antecedents are causally irrelevant to the effect under study, and are therefore not possible causes. But generally such background information will not narrow the list of possible causes to *c* alone. New information is required. It may be gathered in two ways, both involving research into cases besides the one in which *c* preceded or accompanied *e*. Let *c′* be another antecedent condition. We can eliminate *c′* by finding cases in which *e* occurred without *c′* or *c′* without *e*. We can identity *c* as the actual cause of *e* if *c* is found in either way to be the only possible cause correlated with *e*.

Suppose John painted his car a new color, installed clean fuel injectors, and installed radial tires. Suppose further that he wonders why his gasoline mileage improved on the next tank of gas. John can immediately rule out the new color, because it is well known that the color of a car has no effect on its performance. He may suspect that the radials were responsible for the improvement, but he cannot yet rule out the possibility that the fuel injectors were responsible. The clean injectors would be a *confounding factor.* Two simple tests might reveal the cause. First, John could put the dirty fuel injectors back in, leaving the new tires on. Second, he could put the old tires back on, leaving the clean injectors in. If John finds in the first test case that the improved mileage is maintained, or that in the second test case it is not, he can rule out the clean injectors. If in either way John can rule out all other possible causes, he may conclude that the new tires caused his improved mileage.

The two procedures for investigating causes just outlined are called *Mill's methods*, after the great logician, philosopher, and economist John Stuart Mill (1806-1873), who gave them their classic formulation. The first method, called the *method of agreement,* is to compare all cases in which the effect under investigation occurred, looking for common antecedents. An antecedent absent in any case can be eliminated as the cause. If all but one antecedent can be eliminated in this way, it may be identified as the cause. The second method, called the *method of difference,* is to contrast cases in which the effect occurred with cases in which it did not occur, looking for differences in the antecedent conditions. An antecedent present in any case in which the effect did not occur can be eliminated as the cause. If all but

---

[2] From a letter written to Lorenzo Ghiberti by Fra Jacopino del Torchio; in Elizabeth G. Holt, ed., A *Documentary History of Art,* Vol. 1 (Doubleday, 1957), pp. 165-66. I am indebted for this example to W. Ward Fearnside, *About Thinking* (Prentice-Hall, 1980), p. 39.

one antecedent can be eliminated in this way, it may be identified as the cause. Mill observed that both methods could be employed jointly.

Causal Induction. A method of inquiry must be distinguished from a method of argument. A *method of argument* is a pattern that functions as a rule of inference. It tells us what data is needed to draw a given conclusion, but does not tell us how to gather that data. A *method of inquiry,* on the other hand, includes a plan or strategy for gathering the data needed to draw a given conclusion. Mill's methods tell us how to gather the data needed to establish the cause of a given effect. In logic, we are interested in the rules of inference on which rational methods of inquiry are based. Mill himself formulated separate rules for his two methods. But in both cases, the cause is identified as the only antecedent condition that was correlated with the effect in the cases examined. Both methods are therefore sanctioned by the following rule of inference, which we shall call *causal induction:*

Causal Induction
c occurred when and only when e occurred (in b)
$\therefore$ c caused e (in b)
CONDITIONS OF VALIDITY: c is a possible cause of e, e is not a possible cause of c, and there are no confounding factors.

As usual, the conclusion can have different modalities, such as "e *probably* caused e," or "c *must have* caused e." The stronger the conclusion, the weaker the argument. The premise may be expressed in a number of equivalent ways, such as: c occurred where and only where e occurred; e occurred in all and only the cases in which e occurred; c never occurred without e and e never occurred without c; and so on. Note that if c was correlated with e, then e was correlated with e. That is, "e occurred when and only when e occurred" is equivalent to "e occurred when and only when e occurred"; so the premise can be expressed in either way. Since "e resulted from c" is synonymous with "c caused e," the conclusion may take the former form as well as the latter. Indeed, the word "cause" has many synonyms or near-synonyms, such as "produce" and "bring about." Furthermore, the concept of causation is contained in many other concepts. Thus killing entails causing death, and opening a window entails causing it to be open. So causal induction may be employed when showing that one of these concepts applies. Finally, the conclusion of a causal induction may be suppressed, and further conclusions drawn, often of a practical nature.

The premise of a causal induction is often implied rather than explicitly stated. Suppose c was identified as the cause of e by the method of agreement. Rather than summarizing what was found, and stating that c occurred when and only when e did in the observed cases, the premise may enumerate the possible causes, stating which occurred in each of the cases. Let c, x, y, and z represent the suspected causes of e. Then the argument that c caused e may be formulated as follows:

> c, x, y, and e occurred without z in the first case; c, x, z, and e occurred without y in the second case; c, y, z and e occurred without x a in the last
> $\therefore$ c caused e.

The premise here implies that c occurred in all and only the cases in which e occurred, so this argument is an implicit causal induction. The details of the premise in such an implicit causal induction may vary greatly, depending on how many cases of e were observed, how many possible causes e has, many possible causes occurred in each of the cases, and so on. Suppose next that c was identified as the cause of e by the method of difference. The premise may enumerate cases in which e did not occur as well as cases in which e did occur. Given the same possible causes, the argument might be presented thus:

$c, x, y, z,$ and e occurred in the first case; x and y occurred without c or e in the second case; z occurred without $c, x, y,$ or e in the last.

∴ c caused e.

The premise implies that c occurred when and only when e did, so this is again an implied causal induction.

When trying to identify whether the methods of agreement or difference were used, it may help to make a table listing what occurs or fails to occur in each case investigated. The information in the premise of the first argument of the previous paragraph is presented in Table 4-1. Table 4-1 shows that in the first case, the event e whose cause we are seeking occurred; among the possible causes, $c, x,$ and y occurred, but z failed to occur. In case 2, the effect e again occurred; among the possible causes, $c, x,$ and z occurred but y failed to occur. In case 3, the effect e occurred; $c, y,$ and z occurred but x did not. The table makes it obvious that the method of agreement was used, because the effect occurred in all the cases investigated, and was the only possible cause that occurred in all the cases.

Case	Possible Causes	Effect
1	c x y –	e
2	c x – z	e
3	c – y z	e

TABLE 4-1: THE METHOD OF AGREEMENT

Table 4-2, which summarizes the premise of the second argument discussed two paragraphs back, looks different. Table 4-2 shows clearly that cases in which e failed to occur were investigated as well as those in which it did occur. Furthermore, c was the only possible cause occurring when e occurred that failed to occur when e failed to occur.

Case	Possible Causes	Effect
1	c x y z	e
2	– x y –	–
3	– – – z	–

TABLE 4-2: THE METHOD OF DIFFERENCE

Look finally at Table 4-3.

Case	Possible Causes	Effect
1	c – x y z	e
2	c w – – –	e
3	– w x – –	–
4	– – – – y z	–

TABLE 4-3: THE METHOD OF AGREEMENT AND DIFFERENCE

Both of Mill's methods can be used with Table 4-3 to identify c as the cause of e. The only possible cause common to the two cases in which e occurred was c; so the method of agreement can be used. And *c* was the only possible cause that occurred in neither of the two cases in which *e* failed to occur; so the method of difference can be used.

Background Conditions. The variable *b* in the formula for causal induction stands for ***background conditions*** or ***circumstances***. The parenthetical restrictions are necessary because an event may have different causes and effects in different circumstances. Indeed, this is the rule, not the exception. An incision may cause death in a hemophiliac, but save the life of a normal person. Exercising a damaged tendon may strengthen it once healing has reached a certain point, but weaken it before. Flipping a switch may turn the lights on when the power is on, but not otherwise.

Once the background conditions are specified, the facts determine objectively what causes what. We have considerable freedom, however, in how we specify the background conditions. For instance, we ordinarily consider it part of the background conditions that a car has enough gasoline and that all systems are in good order; in such circumstances, turning the ignition key is what causes the car to start. But sometimes it is useful to specify as the background conditions that the ignition key is turned to the start position and that all systems are in good order. In these circumstances, having enough gasoline is what causes the car to start. Again we see that a phenomenon may have different causes in different circumstances. Despite their importance, background conditions are seldom explicitly or precisely identified in applications of causal induction. This often happens because the intended circumstances are obvious and do not need to be mentioned But sometimes it happens because the background conditions are complex and incompletely known.

One circumstance is commonly omitted because it is nearly universal. Investigators rarely examine *every* case in which the effect *e* occurred. Cancer researchers, for example, could never hope to examine all cases of even one type of cancer. Causal induction is consequently used to establish that *c* caused *e* *in the observed cases*, and then enumerative induction is used to infer that *c* caused *e* *in all cases*. The strength of this enumerative induction depends, as discussed in Chapter 3, on the number and variety of cases in which *e* was observed to occur. Causal conclusions can also be extended by arguments from analogy. For example, researchers seek the causes of cancer in human beings, but there are severe ethical constraints on the experiments with human subjects. Laboratory animals are used, therefore, in place of humans. By forcing some rats to inhale cigarette smoke, and having others inhale fresh air, experimenters may establish that cigarette smoke causes lung cancer *in laboratory rats*. The inference is then drawn, by analogy, that cigarette smoke causes lung cancer *in humans*. The strength of this inference depends on the degree and relevance of the similarities between the respiratory systems of rats and humans.

Possible Causes. How does causal induction differ from *post hoc* reasoning? Under the latter, the conclusion that *c* causes *e* may be inferred simply from the fact that *c preceded e* (or accompanied it). Mere temporal precedence, however, does not establish a correlation. Suppose a rain dance is performed, and rain falls an hour later. Then the rain dance precedes the rain. But we cannot infer that it rains when and only when a rain dance is performed. A fortiori, we cannot infer that the rain dance *caused* the rain. Even when *c* both precedes and correlates with *e,* however, we can validly infer causation only under certain very strict conditions. Whenever these conditions are violated, the result is *post hoc* reasoning. *Post hoc* reasoning, then, may be defined as the fallacy of inferring that *c* caused *e* from the premise that *c* preceded or accompanied *e* when a correlation has not been established between *c* and *e* or when the conditions of validity on causal induction have not been satisfied.

Let us now examine those conditions of validity in detail. When John painted his car and did other things to it, his gas mileage immediately improved. There was, then, a correlation between the color of John's car and its gas mileage. When the car was the old color, it got lower gas mileage; when the new color, it got higher gas mileage. So the car got higher gas mileage when and only when it was the new color. But we cannot conclude that the new color of John's car caused the higher gas mileage. For we have abundant previous information showing that a car's color is not causally related to its performance. Hence the new color of John's car could not have caused the improved gas mileage. The first condition for the validity of causal induction, then, is that *c must be a possible cause of e*. A **possible cause** is a condition that, in light of previously available information, might have caused the effect. To illustrate further the force of this condition, imagine that whenever Jane has eaten chocolate, she has broken out in a peculiar rash a few hours later, and that she has only broken out in that rash after she has eaten chocolate. Then breaking out in the rash and eating the chocolate are correlated. What caused what in this case? While eating the chocolate might have caused Jane to develop the rash, developing the rash could not have caused Jane to eat the chocolate. For causes cannot follow their effects. The possible causes of a phenomenon must precede or accompany it.

Now if *c* preceded *e*, *e* will automatically not be a possible cause of *c*. However, if *c* accompanied *e*—that is, if *c* and *e* occurred at the same time—it could happen that *c* is a possible cause of *e and* *e* a possible cause of *c*. If this does happen, then we can draw no definite causal conclusion from a correlation between *c* and *e*. Given the symmetry of the situation, we have no reason to infer "*c* caused *e*" rather than "*e* caused *c*," and we cannot infer both. Suppose, for example, an astronomer observes two distant objects of an unknown sort, and finds that the first moves when and only when the second moves. It could be that the movement of the first object is causing the movement of the second; but it could also be that the movement of the second is causing that of the first. So without further information, we cannot say which is the case. The second condition of validity for causal induction, then, is: *e must not be a possible cause of c*. You might think no cases of simultaneous causation exist. But think of a boat sailing across the ocean. The pressure of the water against the hull is causing the boat to float rather than sink. Yet the floating and the pressure are simultaneous.

While relatively few cases of genuine simultaneous causation exist, there are many cases in which the exact timing of two events is unknown. If it is known only that two events occurred at *approximately* the same time, then each may be a possible cause of the other, preventing any conclusion as to which is cause and which effect. Imagine a psychiatrist, for example, who finds that clinically depressed patients have a certain chemical in their brain not found in normal subjects. He does not yet know, though, whether the presence of the chemical preceded the onset of depression, or whether the depression preceded the chemical. Then he cannot yet draw a definite conclusion about the direction of causation. That is, he cannot conclude that the chemical causes the depression, nor that the depression causes the chemical. His data provides no reason to infer one conclusion or the other.

Confounding Factors. The third condition for the validity of causal induction is that *there must be no confounding factors*. A **confounding factor** is *another possible cause besides c that occurred when and only when e did, but was not previously known to have caused e*. If *c'* were such a factor, we would have no justification for concluding that *c* rather than *c'* caused *e*. This is why Mill's methods require us to consider additional cases until only one suspected cause remains that is correlated with the effect. Return to John, who is trying to figure out why his gas mileage improved. Suppose he examined three cases: new tires and clean fuel injectors; new tires and dirty fuel injectors; old tires and clean fuel injectors. Suppose the improved mileage is confined to the first two cases, leading him to conclude that the new tires caused the increase. John's causal induction would be fallacious if he drove mostly on the highway with the new tires on, but mostly in the city with the old tires on. His driving on the highway would be the confounding factor. It is a possible cause of the improved mileage John failed to eliminate. Indeed, a veritable mockery can be made of causal induction by overlooking confounding variables. Consider the case of the ignorant tippler who wondered why he got drunk. He recalled that the first night he drank Scotch and water and became drunk; the second night he drank rye and water and became drunk; and the third night he drank bourbon and water and became drunk. So his problem, he concluded, was drinking too much water!

Special attention must be paid to the definition of confounding factors. Suppose we are investigating the cause of thunder, and find that an electrical discharge in the atmosphere is correlated with it. There is, however, another antecedent correlated with the thunder—namely, a flash of light. Can we infer that the discharge caused the thunder, or is the flash of light confounding? There is abundant independent information proving that light does not cause sound, which means that the flash of light is not a possible cause of the thunder. So the flash is not a confounding factor. Since possible causes are defined in terms of previously available information, the list of possible causes of any phenomenon must be supported by prior research on related phenomena, as reported in professional journals or as embodied in common knowledge. Generally, the more that is known in advance, the shorter the list of possible causes, and the easier the investigation.

Causal research therefore has a cumulative nature essential to its success in practice, for it is nearly always impossible for reasons of time, money, patience, and the like, to gather enough new information to eliminate all but one condition preceding or accompanying the effect we are studying. Progress in science would be much slower if the results of previous research were not utilized. Every scientist is accordingly trained to make a thorough search of the relevant literature before undertaking further study. A literature search doesn't always shorten the list of possible causes, however, for sometimes the search turns up previously unknown antecedent conditions. In this case, the additional knowledge enables us to avoid confounding factors.

A second aspect of the definition of confounding factors needs explanation and emphasis. Confounding factors are not just other possible causes correlated with the effect. Other correlated possible causes are confounding only if they were not previously known to have caused the effect. That is, if it were known that c' caused e before it was observed that c' occurred when and only when e did (and known therefore without using causal induction), then c' is not a confounding factor. Suppose we walk into an unfamiliar room and wish to determine how to illuminate it. We find that flipping one switch to the *off* position is correlated with a lamp's glowing brightly. There is, however, another antecedent condition perfectly correlated with the lamp's glowing—namely, the flow of electrons through its filament. Can we conclude that flipping the switch to the *off* position causes the lamp to glow, or is the flow of electrons through the filament a confounding factor? The flow is certainly a possible cause, and we know that it occurs when and only when the lamp glows. Nevertheless, it is not confounding, since we knew in advance of our investigation that the flow of electrons through the filament is what causes an incandescent lamp to glow. We knew this from experiments on *other* lamps that flipping the switch to the off position causes this lamp to glow. Given previous information, the lamp's being on must be caused by the flow of electrons through its filament. Here again, a thorough knowledge of the relevant data facilitates causal research: by expanding the list of known causes, we reduce the list of confounding factors.

Undermining Evidence. The general condition of validity discussed in §3.4 also applies to causal induction: *there must be no undermining evidence.* If there is, the argument commits the fallacy of exclusion. Suppose Mike wants to determine the cause of dieseling in gasoline engines, a condition in which the engine continues to run after the ignition has been turned off. He investigates twenty cases and finds that the only common factor is the use of inexpensive gasoline. Employing the method of agreement, Mike might conclude that the dieseling is caused by the inexpensive gasoline in the cases be examined. He would be committing the fallacy of exclusion, however, if there are other known cases in which dieseling occurs even when expensive brands of gas are used. This additional information would not make it impossible that the inexpensive gas caused the dieseling in the cases Mike examined, so the first condition of validity is not violated; but the additional information does make it unlikely that the inexpensive gas is the cause, so the general condition has been violated. The ignorant tippler mentioned above also committed the fallacy of exclusion: his argument ignored all those times when he drank straight water and did not get drunk.

Causal Elimination. The premise of causal induction requires that c occur *when and only when* e occurs. Such a correlation is said to be *perfect* and *positive* (or *direct*). Two events are perfectly correlated if there are no exceptions to the rule relating them, imperfectly correlated if there are. Two events are positively (or directly) correlated if one tends to occur when the other does, negatively (or inversely) correlated if one tends to occur when the other does not. Let us imagine two variations on Jane's case. Suppose first that Jane's rash has developed most of the time after eating the chocolate, but not always, and that she has occasionally developed the rash when she has not eaten chocolate. Then eating chocolate is still correlated with developing the rash, perhaps even highly correlated. But we can no longer conclude that the chocolate is what causes the rash. For while eating the chocolate is positively correlated with the rash, the correlation is imperfect. Suppose next that Jane develops the rash when and only when she does not eat chocolate. Then eating chocolate has a perfect but negative correlation with developing the rash. Clearly we cannot infer that chocolate causes the rash. Indeed, we should infer instead that eating chocolate prevents the rash.

Given a valid argument, we can infer that the conclusion is true if the premises are true. We cannot generally infer that the conclusion is false, however, from the fact that the premises are false. Causal induction is an exception to this rule. As the cases in the previous paragraph illustrate, when the premise of a causal induction is false, we may infer that the conclusion is false. That is, if c ever occurred without e, or e without c, we can conclude that c did *not* cause e. We shall refer to this rule of inference as *causal elimination,* since it enables us to eliminate suspected causes of e.

Causal Elimination
c occurred without e
e occurred without c (in b).
∴ c did not cause e (in b).

Causal induction and causal elimination are partners in all causal research. While the former leads to positive causal conclusions, the latter leads to negative ones. A negative result may be frustrating for those intent on finding a cause, but even negative results may be important contributions to knowledge. It is important to know, for example, that drinking Coca-Cola does not cause cancer. Note that causal elimination plays an important role in Mill's methods.

While causal elimination has no specific conditions of validity, the general condition does apply. Consider the case of malaria.[3] Battista Grassi did a thorough study of Italy in 1898. He suspected that mosquitoes carried malaria, but found many places with mosquitoes but no malaria. He could not, however, conclude that mosquitoes do not carry malaria. For there are between twenty and forty kinds of mosquitoes in Italy. And Grassi found one kind, *Anopheles claviger*, that was present in all places, and only those places, where there was malaria. This latter information led by causal induction to the conclusion that *Anopheles* mosquitoes carry malaria, and therefore thoroughly undermined the conclusion that mosquitoes do not carry it. Consider next the sore throat. Many cases of sore throat are observed without streptococcus bacteria. We cannot conclude, though, that streptococcus bacteria do not cause sore throats. For again, there are different kinds of sore throat, with different causes. Cold

[3] From Paul De Kruif, *Microbe Hunters* (Pocket Books, 1964), pp. 280-88.

viruses, for example, also cause sore throats. Just yelling and screaming can cause a sore throat. This additional information undermines the argument that streptococcus bacteria do not cause sore throats.

Necessary and Sufficient Conditions. To further our understanding of causal induction and elimination, we need to introduce the notions of **necessary** and **sufficient conditions**. Running is a *sufficient* condition of exercising, for you will exercise *if* you run. Indeed, you cannot run without exercising. Running is not a *necessary* condition, however, for there are other ways of exercising, such as swimming. Being alive is a necessary condition of exercising, for you will exercise *only if* you are alive. You cannot exercise without being alive. Being alive is not sufficient, however, for other things are necessary, such as motivation and a properly functioning nervous system. Whether a condition is necessary or sufficient generally depends on the circumstances. In my current circumstances, which include an abundance of oxygen, striking this match is a sufficient condition of its lighting. In different circumstances, without oxygen, striking the match would not be sufficient. In my current circumstances, in which no oxygen tanks are handy, the presence of oxygen in the atmosphere is a necessary condition of my staying alive. In different circumstances, such as exist on most airplanes, atmospheric oxygen would not be necessary.

Causal induction identifies as the cause that antecedent condition which is *both* necessary *and* sufficient for the effect (in the circumstances). The premise states in part that *e* never occurs without *c*, which is strong evidence that *c* is a necessary condition of *e*. The premise also states that *c* never occurs without *e* in the cases examined, which is evidence that *c* is a sufficient condition of *e*. That evidence for sufficiency is weak, however, unless some cases are observed in which *e* does not occur, as when the method of difference is used. Even when the method of agreement is used, however, it is usually common knowledge that many cases exist with neither *c* nor *e*, so this information may safely be suppressed. Causal elimination, on the other hand, infers that *c* does not cause *e* from the fact that *c* occurs without *e*, which implies that *c* is not a sufficient condition of *e*, or from the fact that *e* occurs without *c*, which implies that *c* is not a necessary condition of *e*.

Experimental vs. Correlational Studies. Someone investigating the cause of *e* needs to examine some cases in which *e* occurs and some in which *e* does not occur. The selection of these cases is fundamentally important, for they must be representative if the investigator wishes to generalize his results to unobserved cases. The cases in any event must contain no confounding factors. One basic choice is whether the investigator will examine naturally occurring cases over which he has no control, or artificially created cases of his own devising. If naturally occurring cases are selected, the investigation is called a **correlational study**. If the investigator creates his own cases, it is an **experimental study**. Experimental studies are generally superior, for they allow greater certainty that there are no confounding variables.

Consider the case of Edward Jenner, who discovered how to produce immunity to smallpox. Over a period of years, Jenner observed many people who had come into contact with cowpox, a disease similar to smallpox that affects cows. All were immune to smallpox. Jenner tentatively concluded that cowpox produced immunity to smallpox. Up until this point, Jenner's study was correlational. As a result, his evidence was inconclusive. For his subjects were selected because they had been exposed to cowpox, and consequently had many other things in common: they lived on farms and milked cows, for example. One of these other common conditions might have been the real cause of the immunity to smallpox. To eliminate this doubt, Jenner conducted an experiment. He picked a healthy young boy and injected him with cowpox. Jenner subsequently found that he too was immune to smallpox. Since the subject was randomly selected, the chances that he had anything else relevant in common with the original group were minimal. So Jenner could confidently conclude that cowpox produced immunity to smallpox.

Experiments designed to implement the method of difference always involve two groups of cases: one called the **test group** (also called the *experimental* or *treatment* group), the other called the **control group**. The suspected cause c is introduced into the test group, and withheld from the control group. The experimenter then observes both groups to see if the effect e occurs. If the effect occurs every time in the test group, and never in the control group, the conclusion that c caused e may be drawn in accordance with causal induction. Consider the famous public experiment conducted by Louis Pasteur to silence, once and for all, the skepticism of his critics.[4] Before the agricultural society of Melun, Pasteur gathered forty-eight sheep, two goats, and several cattle, all healthy. Half the animals were injected with his anthrax vaccine. This was Pasteur's test group. The other animals, comprising the control group, were not vaccinated. After several weeks, all animals in both groups were injected with a normally fatal dose of anthrax bacilli. Within two days all animals in the control group died. None of the vaccinated animals died. Everyone then realized that Pasteur's vaccine really did produce immunity to anthrax. Experiments implementing the method of agreement, like Jenner's, have a test group but no control group. Jenner's test group was the boy into whom he injected cowpox. Correlational studies have neither test nor control groups, for the investigator is not responsible for the occurrence or nonoccurrence of the suspected cause.

The great virtue of experiments is the amount of control the investigator has over the composition of the test and control groups. This enables her to minimize the possibility of confounding factors by making sure that the presence or absence of the suspected cause c is the only known relevant difference between the groups. The experimenter is said to *control* for other possible causes by making sure they are present in both groups. Thus, Pasteur's groups contained animals of the same species. Failure to control for relevant variables is the most common flaw in experimental design.

Correlational studies have their virtues too, it should be noted. Researchers looking for the causes of cancer, for example, can seldom perform experiments on humans, because of ethical constraints. There aren't many volunteers for the test group. Experiments are performed on dogs and mice, but the results cannot be generalized with certainty to humans. Furthermore, such experiments all have one limitation: the results are obtained in laboratory settings and may not hold in natural settings. Causal conclusions are most secure, therefore, when based on a combination of experimental and correlational studies.

Mill's Method of Concomitant Variation. To infer that c caused e using causal induction, we need to establish that e is the only possible cause present or absent when e is. It is sometimes difficult or impossible, however, to separate c from some other antecedent $c\square$, or to eliminate c entirely. In such cases, neither the method of agreement nor the method of difference can be used. It may still be possible to determine the cause, however, if e varies in magnitude. We can examine cases in which the effect varies, looking for an antecedent condition that varies with it. Any antecedent not varying with the effect can be eliminated. If all but one antecedent can be eliminated in this way, we may be able to identify it as the cause. Mill called this the **method of concomitant variation**. Experimental studies using this method have several test groups, on which different magnitudes of the suspected cause are imposed, and no control group, unless the method of difference is used jointly.

Consider the problem posed by the Torricelli tube. In 1643, a student of Galileo named Evangelista Torricelli took a glass tube about 36 inches long that was sealed at one end, and filled it with mercury, placing his finger over the open end. He then immersed the open end in a bowl of mercury, and released his finger. Torricelli found that the mercury dropped in the tube until it stood at a height of about 30 inches. The question then arose, "What supported the column of mercury?" Because Galileo had already shown that air had weight, Torricelli proposed that the air pressing down on the mercury in the bowl

---

[4] From Paul de Kruif, *Microbe Hunters*, pp. 150-55.

supported the column of mercury. This hypothesis was difficult to test, since at the time there was no way to completely remove the air from around the bowl of mercury, and no place to go without air. A few years later, however, Blaise Pascal reasoned that air pressure would be less on a mountain top than at sea level. The air at sea level would be more compressed since it is supporting a greater load of air above it So Pascal took a Torricelli tube up a mountain, and found that the column of mercury fell with increasing height. At about the same time, Robert Boyle enclosed a Torricelli Tube in a sealed glass vessel and, using the recently invented air pump, pumped air into and out of the vessel. As air was pumped out of the vessel, thereby reducing the air pressure the column of mercury dropped below 30 inches. The more air pumped out, the lower the mercury. On the other hand, if extra air was pumped into the vessel, increasing the air pressure, the mercury rose above 30 inches.[5] Boyle and Pascal inferred that the air pressure caused the column of mercury from the fact that the height of the mercury increased or decreased as the pressure of the air did.

Case	Possible Causes	Effect
1	$c^{+++} \ x^{+} \ y^{++} \ z^{++}$	e^{+++}
2	$c^{++} \ ^{x++} \ y^{+} \ z^{++}$	e^{++}
3	$c^{+} \ x^{+} \ y^{++} \ z^{++}$	e^{+}

TABLE 4-4: THE METHOD OF CONCOMITANT VARIATION

Table 4-4 tabulates the results of a typical experiment employing the method of concomitant variation. Increasing numbers of + 's represent increasing magnitudes of an event. Since Table 4-4 shows that c alone varies with e, c is identified as the cause of e by the method of concomitant variation.

The method of concomitant variation does not always enable us to identify the cause of a given effect, however, even if we find only one antecedent condition varying with it. For before we can conclude that c causes e, we need to establish that e is present or absent when c is. The data must therefore allow us to extrapolate that e would be completely absent provided c were. If c could be completely absent when e is present in any magnitude, then c would not be a necessary condition of e. And if e could be completely absent even though c was present in some magnitude, then c would not be a sufficient condition of e. In either case, c would not be the cause of e in the circumstances.

At this point, let us distinguish *quantitative* from *qualitative* correlations. Two factors are qualitatively correlated, provided one tends to *occur* when and only when the other one does; this is the sort of correlation we have focused on until now. Two factors are quantitatively correlated, provided one tends to *increase* when and only when the other one does. To establish causation, we must establish a perfect qualitative correlation: c must occur when and only when e does. The method of concomitant variation, however, looks for a quantitative correlation. A causal conclusion can be drawn using that method only if the quantitative correlation provides evidence of a perfect qualitative correlation. Consider the experiments of Pascal and Boyle. Neither examined any case with zero air pressure. But the relationship found with the air pressures they did examine enabled them to infer that the column of mercury would be eliminated, provided the air pressure were completely eliminated. So their data implied that the air pressure had a perfect correlation with the column of mercury, which enabled them to conclude that air pressure is what caused the column of mercury.

In contrast, suppose we are studying the effects of Miracle Gro on plant growth. We select four groups of plants, fed at the rate of 1, 10, 20, and 50 drops per week. The plants grow at the rate of 1.01, 1.10, 1.20, and 1.50 inches per week. Then the rate of growth varies with the amount of Miracle

---

[5] From A. R. E. McKenzie, *The Major Achievements of Science*, vol. I (Cambridge University Press, 1960), ch. 5.

Gro. But we cannot conclude that the Miracle Gro causes the growth. For the evidence suggests that the plants would grow at a rate of 1 inch per week without Miracle Gro. The fertilizer is therefore not a necessary condition of growth in the circumstances. The method of concomitant variation does yield some causal conclusions in this case. We can conclude that the Miracle Gro caused the rate of growth to exceed 1 inch per week, which means that the fertilizer caused *some* of the growth. For the evidence does suggest that the growth rate would not exceed 1 inch per week in the absence of the fertilizer. We can also conclude that the amount of Miracle Gro *determines* the rate of growth. But while this sort of determination is similar to causation, the two are not the same relationship. Note that we can infer that c causes e only if c and e are found to be *directly* related. If we find that as the amount of acid in the soil increases, the rate of plant growth decreases, we can conclude that acidity determines the rate of plant growth, but we can hardly conclude that acidity causes plant growth.[6]

Special care must be taken when interpreting the results of statistical studies employing the method of concomitant variation. Consider, for example, one of the studies showing that cigarette smoking may be harmful to your health. The American Cancer Society followed 440,000 men for twelve years. The men were divided into groups based on the number of cigarettes they smoked per day. The number of men who died from lung cancer was recorded. The data was then adjusted to factor out the influence of age. The nonsmokers were divided into five-year age-groups, and the percentage of deaths per age-group calculated. Those percentages were then used to determine the number of deaths that could have been expected in the other groups if they contained nonsmokers. The actual number of deaths in the smoking groups was then divided by the expected number to produce a statistic called the *mortality ratio*. If a smoking group had the same composition by age as the nonsmoking group, a mortality ratio of 2.0 would signify that twice as many deaths occurred in the smoking group. If the smoking group was older on average than the non-smoking group, there would be more than twice as many deaths, but only half could be attributed to the smoking. The results are tabulated in Table 4-5.[7]

Cigarettes per man per day	Mortality Ratios for lung cancer deaths
0	1.00
1-9	4.62
10-19	8.62
20-39	14.62
Over 40	18.77

TABLE 4-5: CIGARETTE SMOKING AND MORTALITY RATIOS

What conclusions can be drawn from this data? While the mortality ratio increased with the number of cigarettes smoked, we cannot conclude that smoking caused the deaths from lung cancer. For some men who smoked did not die from lung cancer, and some men who did not smoke died from lung cancer anyway. We can conclude, however, that the number of cigarettes smoked per day determined the mortality ratio, that smoking caused the mortality ratio to increase, and that smoking therefore caused enough of the deaths to account for that increase. The mortality ratios enable us to estimate what

[6] Mill, and others following him, state the method of concomitant variation more generally: if c and e vary in *any* way, then c and e are causally related in *some* way. I have formulated all our methods of causal investigation so that the specific conclusion that c caused e can be established.

[7] From U.S. Department of Health, Education, and Welfare, *Smoking and Health: A Report of the Surgeon General* (U.S. DHEW, Public Health Service, Office on Smoking and Health, 1979; Publication No. [PHS] 79-50066) ch. 2, pp. 12-13, and ch. 5, pp. 12-13.

proportion of the deaths were attributable to the smoking, but not to identify the specific individuals or circumstances involved.[8]

Glossary

Post hoc reasoning: the fallacy of concluding that c caused e from the premise that c preceded or accompanied e, when a correlation between c and e has not been established or when the conditions of validity on causal induction have not been satisfied.

Mill's methods: the methods of causal inquiry formulated by John Stuart Mill including the methods of agreement, difference, and concomitant variation.

Method of agreement: looking for causes by examining occurrences of a phenomenon for common antecedents; an antecedent absent in any case is eliminated; if all but one antecedent is eliminated, it is identified as the cause.

Method of difference: looking for causes by examining occurrences and nonoccurrences of a phenomenon for different antecedents; an antecedent present when the phenomenon did not occur is eliminated; if all antecedents but one are eliminated, that one is identified as the cause.

Causal induction: the argument in which, from the premise that c occurs when and only when e does in certain circumstances, the conclusion is drawn that c causes e in those circumstances; to be valid, c must be a possible cause of e, e must not be a possible cause of c, and there must be no confounding factors.

Possible cause: a condition which, in light of previously obtained information, might have caused a given phenomenon.

Confounding factor: When c is inferred to cause e by causal induction, a confounding factor is another possible cause perfectly correlated with e that was not previously known to have caused e.

Background conditions or circumstances: specific conditions in which events may or may not be correlated or causally related.

Causal elimination: the argument in which, from the premise that c occurred without e, or e without c, the conclusion is drawn that c did not cause e.

Necessary conditions: conditions such that a given phenomenon occurs only if they do.

Sufficient conditions: conditions such that a given phenomenon occurs if they do.

Correlational study: the use of Mill's methods with naturally occurring cases.

Experimental study: the use of Mill's methods with artificially created cases.

Test group: the group in experimental studies in which the suspected cause is introduced.

---

[8] In addition to the method of agreement, the method of difference, the joint method of agreement and difference, and the method of concomitant variation, Mill formulated a fifth method, which he called the *method of residues*. "Subduct from any phenomenon such part as is known by previous inductions to be the effect of certain antecedents, and the residue of the phenomenon is the effect of the remaining antecedents." First, there will seldom if ever be only one event whose cause is unknown or one antecedent whose effect is unknown; so this method will seldom lead to specific causal conclusions. Second, the residue of the phenomenon might be due to the *joint* action of some or all of the antecedents whose individual effects are known; so this method is problematic. In any event, the method of residues is not sanctioned by either causal induction or causal elimination. The examples Mill and others have used to illustrate the method of residues are best viewed as instances of other valid rules of inference, such as hypothetical induction, discussed in §4.2.

Control group: the group in experimental studies in which the suspected cause is withheld.

Method of concomitant variation: looking for causes by examining occurrences of a phenomenon for antecedent conditions that vary with it; any antecedent not varying with the phenomenon is eliminated; if all antecedents but one are eliminated, that one is identified as the cause.

Exercises

The following passages contain arguments involving causal statements. Identify the suspected cause and the effect, and classify the arguments as *post hoc* reasoning, causal induction, causal elimination, or "other." If the argument is an application of causal induction, determine which of Mill's methods are used; determine whether the study is correlational or experimental; identify, if possible, the control and test groups; and point out any violations of the conditions of validity.

1. Can living things arise spontaneously, or does every living thing have to have parents?… In Spallanzani's time the popular side was the party that asserted that life could arise spontaneously…. Spallanzani's eyes nearly popped out with wonder, with excitement, as he read of a little experiment that blew up this nonsense, once and for always.

   "A great man, this fellow Redi, who wrote this book," thought Spallanzani…. "See how easy he settles it! He takes two jars and puts some meat in each one. He leaves one jar open and then puts a light veil over the other one. He watches—and sees flies go down into the meat in the open pot—and in a little while there are maggots there, and then new flies, He looks at the jar that has the veil over it—and there are no maggots or flies in that one at all. How easy! It is just a matter of the veil keeping the mother flies from getting at the meat…." –Paul De Kruif, *Microbe Hunters, pp.* 26-28.

2. At this time another priest, named Needham … was becoming notorious in England and Ireland, claiming that little microscopic animals were generated marvelously in mutton gravy. Needham sent his experiments to the Royal Society, and the learned Fellows deigned to be impressed.

   He told them how he had taken a quantity of mutton gravy hot from the fire, and put the gravy in a bottle, and plugged the bottle up tight with a cork, so that no little animals or their eggs could possibly get into the gravy from the air. Next he even went so far as to heat the bottle and its mutton gravy in hot ashes. "Surely," said the good Needham, "this will kill any little animals or their eggs that might remain in the flask." He put this gravy flask away for a few days, then pulled the cork and—marvel of marvels—when he examined the stuff inside with his lens, he found it swarming with animalcules.

   "A momentous discovery, this," cried Needham to the Royal Society, "these little animals can only have come from the juice of the gravy. Here is a real experiment showing that life *can* come spontaneously from dead stuff!" –Paul De Kruif, *Microbe Hunters*, pp. 28-29.

3. Spallanzani suspected that the little animals arose in Needham's experiment because the bottles were not heated long enough and were not sealed tightly enough. So Spallanzani took numerous flasks, filled them with pure water and different "stews" made from seeds and the like. He then formed a glass seal on some of the flasks by melting their necks, figuring that the glass was impenetrable. The other flasks he corked, as Needham had done. He boiled some of the flasks in both groups for an hour, and others

for only a few minutes. Several days later, Spallanzani examined his flasks, and found that the corked flasks were teaming with animalcules, large and small. The glass-sealed flasks boiled for only a few minutes contained a few small animalcules. The glass-sealed flasks boiled for an hour contained nothing. Spallanzani concluded that little animals get into Needham's flasks from the air, and that animalcules can survive boiling water unless they are boiled long enough. (Based on Paul De Kruif, *Microbe Hunters*, pp. 29-32.)

4. In *Makers of Electricity* (Fordham UP, 1909), Potamian and Walsh translate an excerpt from Luigi Galvani's journal. The excerpt reads: "I had dissected a frog and had prepared it…and had placed it upon a table on which there was an electric machine, while I set about doing certain other things. The frog was entirely separated from the conductor of the machine, and indeed was at no small distance away from it. While one of those who were assisting me touched lightly and by chance the point of his scalpel to the internal crural nerves of the frog, suddenly all the muscles of its limbs were seen to be so contracted that they seemed to have fallen into tonic convulsions. Another of my assistants, who was making ready to take up certain experiments in electricity with me, seemed to notice that this happened only at the moment when a spark came from the conductor of the machine…. I was at once tempted to repeat the experiment, so as to make clear whatever might be obscure in it. For this purpose I took up the scalpel and moved its point close to one or the other of the crural nerves of the frog, while at the same time one of my assistants elicited sparks from the electric machine. The phenomenon happened exactly as before. Strong contractions took place in every muscle of the limb, and at the very moment when the sparks appeared, the animal was seized as it were with tetanus." Potamian and Walsh go on to note that Galvani ran through a number of controls with no electric shock present and other variations in charge strength and elapsed time before Galvani concluded "that the contact with the scalpel was only effective in producing twitchings when there was a simultaneous electric spark."

5. It is interesting to note that one of the frequent symptoms of extreme combat anxiety cases is an interference with speech that may run from complete muteness to hesitation and stuttering. Similarly, the sufferer from acute stage fright is unable to speak. Many animals tend to stop vocalizing when frightened, and it is obvious that this tendency is adaptive in preventing them from attracting the attention of their enemies. In the light of this evidence one might suspect that the drive of fear has an innate tendency to elicit the response of stopping vocal behavior. –John Dollard and Neal E. Miller, *Personality and Psychotherapy* (McGraw-Hill Book Co. 1950), p. 203.

6. According to an advertisement for the Biorhythm Research Association published in *The Star* (December 27, 1983, p. 33), a Mrs. Audrey Sturm went to Las Vegas because her biorhythm analysis said she was having an eight-day "biorhythm hot streak." She won over $18,000 and attributed her success to her biorhythm hot streak.

7. Mean displacements of lines towards the less refrangible end of the spectrum are certainly revealed by statistical investigations of the fixed stars; but up to the present the examination of the available data does not allow of any definite decision being arrived at, as to whether or not these displacements are to be referred in reality to the effect of gravitation…. If the displacement of spectral lines towards the red by the gravitational potential does not exist, then the general theory of relativity will be untenable. On the other hand, if the cause of the displacement of spectral lines be definitely traced to the gravitational potential, then the study of this displacement will furnish us with important information as to the mass of the heavenly bodies. –Albert Einstein, *Relativity: The Special and General Theory* (Methuen & Co., 1916) (Source: Project Gutenberg).

8. While the earth revolves annually round the sun, it has a motion upon an axis which is inclined 28° 27′ from a perpendicular to the elliptic; and *this axis continually points in the same direction.* [This results in]

the succession of seasons. In June, when the north pole of the earth inclines toward the sun, the greater portion of the northern hemisphere is enlightened, and the greater portion of the southern hemisphere is dark.... The reverse is true in the southern hemisphere; but on the equator, the days and nights are equal. –Elias Loomis, *A Treatise on Astronomy* (Harper, 1870).

9. The history of the world informs us that there have been many civilizations which, in some respects, equaled our own. These races of people have all achieved a certain success, and have then passed entirely out of existence. Why? And are we destined to extinction in the same way? We [can infer] that the cause of the decline and ultimate extinction of all past civilizations was due primarily to the moral decadence of their people. Disease and vice gradually sapped their vitality, and their continuance was impossible. –Grant Hague, M.D., *The Eugenic Marriage* (The Review of Reviews Company, 1916).

10. [Let us consider] the case contemplated in the first law of motion, *viz.* that all bodies in motion continue to move in a straight line with uniform velocity until acted upon by some new force. This assertion is in open opposition to first appearances; all terrestrial objects, when in motion, gradually abate their velocity and at last stop; which accordingly the ancients, with their *inductio per enumerationem simplicem,* imagined to be law. Every moving body, however, encounters various obstacles, as friction, the resistance of the atmosphere, etc., which we know by daily experience to be causes capable of destroying motion. It was suggested that the whole of the retardation might be owing to these causes. How was this inquired into? ... It was found that every diminution of the obstacles diminished the retardation of the motion; and inasmuch as in this case (unlike the case of heat) the total quantities both of the antecedent and of the consequent were known, it was practicable to estimate, with an approach to accuracy, both the amount of the retardation and the amount of the retarding causes or resistances, and to judge how near they both were to being exhausted; and it appeared that the effect dwindled as rapidly, and at each step was as far on the road towards annihilation, as the cause was. The simple oscillation of a weight suspended from a fixed point, and moved a little out of the perpendicular, which in ordinary circumstances lasts but a few minutes, was prolonged in Borda's experiments to more than thirty hours, by diminishing as much as possible the friction at the point of suspension, and by making the body oscillate in a space exhausted as nearly as possible of its air. There could therefore be no hesitation in assigning the whole of the retardation of motion to the influence of the obstacles; and since, after subducting this retardation from the total phenomenon, the remainder was a uniform velocity, the result was the proposition known as the first law of motion. –John Stuart Mill, *A System of Logic* (Longmans, 1961 [1884]), p. 265.

11. So it was [Grassi] cleared a dozen or twenty different mosquitoes of the suspicion of the crime of malaria—he was always finding these beasts in places where there was no malaria. –Paul De Kruif, *Microbe Hunters*, p. 283.

12. Grassi went more than two-thirds of the way to solving this puzzle of how malaria gets from sick men to healthy ones before he had ever made a single experiment in his laboratory! For, everywhere where there was malaria, there *were* mosquitoes. And *such* mosquitoes! They were certainly a very special definite sort of blood-sucking mosquito Grassi found....

That was zanzarone, and the naturalists had given her the name *Anopheles claviger* many years before.... Always, where the "zan-za-ro-ne" buzzed, there Grassi found deep flushed faces on rumpled beds, or faces with chattering teeth going towards those beds... . Then Grassi went back to Rome to his lectures, and on September 28 of 1898, before ever he had done a single serious experiment, he read his paper before the famous and ancient Academy of the Lincei: "It is the anopheles mosquito that carries malaria if any mosquito carries malaria...." –Paul De Kruif, *Microbe Hunters*, pp. 284-85.

13. A study of prospect attitudes made in 1954 revealed that State Farm was thought to provide inferior claim service and that it was too small, with insufficient resources to cover policyholder claims. A multipage insert was run in *Life* magazine telling the full story of the company's history, size, record with claims, and so forth…. A consumer probe conducted three years later showed that there was no longer any doubt about the size of the company and its resources. Advertising had done its job.[9]

14. In *The Evil Eye* (London, 1895), Frederick Elworthy tells us of the *jettatore*, a man cursed with eyes which, by some natural, inherent force, cause misfortune to those around him. Examples abound. Consider one "man [who is the] godfather to three children all of whom die…. It is his fate, he cannot help it. Pio Nono was a renowned *jettatore*. In Théophile Gautier's romance, 'Jettature,' the *jettatore* ruins everyone whom he loves, and finally, but too late, plucks out his own eyes." Such stories occur throughout European lore (especially in Italy). It is inevitable that the *jettatore*, due to his curse, involuntarily brings about much undue misfortune.

15. On the day of conditioning, the rat is placed in the box as usual. The lever is present, and for the first time in the history of the rat its movement downward will operate the magazine [which dispenses a food pellet, called "the reinforcement"]. Figure 3 gives a record of the resulting change in behavior…. On the day of conditioning a first response was made five minutes after release. The reinforcement had no observable effect upon the behavior. A second response was made 51 ½ minutes later, also without effect. A third was made 47 ½ minutes later and a fourth 25 minutes after that. The fourth response was followed by an appreciable increase in rate showing a swift acceleration to a maximum. The intervals elapsing before the fifth, sixth, and following responses were 43, 21, 28, 10, 10, and 15 seconds respectively. From that point on the rat responded at an essentially constant rate…. –B. F. Skinner, *The Behavior of Organisms* (Appleton-Century-Crofts, 1938), p. 68.

16. This example [see exercise 15] is unusual in that conditioning does not take place until the fourth reinforcement. Five records showing a quicker effect are given in Figure 4, where conditioning occurs with the first or second reinforcement, although the rate is not immediately maximal. In the optimal case the first reinforcement produces complete and maximal change, as shown in the four records in Figure 5…. Twenty cases [out of 78] gave the instantaneous result shown in Figure 5, and the remaining cases were similar to those in Figure 4.

    I think it may be concluded from the high frequency of occurrence of the instantaneous change that a single reinforcement is capable of raising the strength of the operant to essentially a maximal value. –B. F. Skinner, *The Behavior of Organisms,* pp. 68-69.

17. Never was there a more conscientious searcher than this Loeffler…. He sat himself down; he wrote a careful scientific paper…. It was a most unlawyer-like report reciting all of the fors and againsts on the question of whether or no this new bacillus was the cause of diphtheria. He leaned over backward to be honest—he put last the facts that were against it! "This microbe *may* be the cause," you can hear him mumbling as he wrote, "but in a few children dead of diphtheria I could not find these germs. None of my inoculated animals get paralysis as children do. What is most against me is that I've discovered this same microbe—it was vicious against guinea pigs and rabbits too!—in the throat of a child with never a sign of diphtheria." –Paul De Kruif, *Microbe Hunters,* p. 176.

18. When I started out twelve years ago, just after I saw the first terrifying "swelling and sags" begin to appear on my hips, I probably tried every exercise, and made every mistake, in the book…. But then

[9] Based on Blair Vedder, "Like a Good Neighbor, Research Was There," 1975 *ARF Midyear Conference Proceedings.* Copyright 1975 by the Advertising Research Foundation.

The Break-Through Came! I Found What I Call an "Exercise-Magnifier." That Lets MY BODY Get as Much Firming Effect from Four Minutes as I Used to Get from Twenty to Forty....

So I Threw Away My Old Exercises. And I Use This Little Device—and Only This Little Device—to Exercise with for Four Minutes Every Day. AND MY BODY LOOKS LIKE *THIS* AT 47 YEARS AND 6 MONTHS. ["This" refers to a picture of a gorgeous model, clad in scanty running shorts, who does not look a day over 30.]

So that's my offer. I want you to give me 4 to 8 minutes a day of your time, and I want to borrow some of your money. In return I promise to give you a new figure—just as I've given one to myself, and kept it. –Oleda Baker, advertisement in *The Globe* (December 27, 1983), p. 48.

19. A study done by the Tufts University School of Veterinary Medicine tested the effects of secondhand smoke (also known as passive smoke) on domestic cats. Researchers observed cats that lived with smokers and found that they were twice as likely to acquire feline lymphoma as cats that lived with non-smokers and thus were not exposed to second-hand smoke. Cats that lived with smokers for 5 years were three times as likely to develop cancer as those that were not exposed. And if there were two smokers in the home, the risk of cats developing cancer was quadruple that of non-exposed cats. These results provide additional support for the connection between secondhand smoke and cancer, specifically, feline lymphoma.

20. For weeks they waited—hair graying again—for signs of rabies in these animals, but none ever came.... Their clumsy terrible fourteen vaccinations had not hurt the dogs—but were they immune?

Pasteur dreaded it.... But the test had to be made. Would the dogs stand an injection of the most deadly rabid virus—right into their brains—a business that killed an ordinary dog one hundred times out of one hundred? Then one day Roux bored little holes through the skulls of two vaccinated dogs—and two not-vaccinated ones: and into all four went a heavy dose of the most virulent virus.

One month later, Pasteur and his men, at the end of three years' work, knew that victory over hydrophobia was in their hands. For, while the two vaccinated dogs romped and sniffed about their cages with never a sign of anything ailing them—the two that had not received the fourteen protective doses of dried rabbit's brain—these two had howled their last howls and died of rabies. –Paul De Kruif, *Microbe Hunters,* pp. 167-68.

21. Careful studies have been made of the incidence of leukemia in the survivors of the atomic bombs burst over Hiroshima and Nagasaki. These survivors received exposures ranging from a few roentgens to 1,000 roentgens or more. They are divided into four groups.... The first group, A, consists of the estimated 1,870 survivors who were within 1 kilometer of the hypocenter (the point on the surface of the earth directly below the bomb when it exploded). There were very few survivors in this zone, and they received a large amount of radiation. The second group, B, consists of the 13,730 survivors between 1.0 and 1.5 kilometers from the hypocenter; the third, C, of the 23,060 between 1.5 and 2.0 kilometers; and the fourth, D, of the 156,400 over 2.0 kilometers from the hypocenter.

The survivors of zones A, B, and C have been dying of leukemia during the period of careful study, the eight years from 1948 to 1955, at an average rate of about 9 per year.... Many more cases of leukemia occurred in the 15,600 survivors of zones A and B than in the 156,400 survivors of zone D, who received much less radiation. There is no doubt that the increased incidence is to be attributed to the exposure to radiation.

... The survivors of zone A received an estimated average of 650 roentgens; those of zone B, 250; those of zone C, 25; and of zone D, 2.5.... To within the reliability of the numbers, the incidence of leukemia in the three populations A, B, and C is proportional to the estimated dose of radiation, even for class C, in which the estimated dose is only 25 roentgens. –Linus Pauling, *No More War!* (Dodd, Mead & Company, 1962), pp. 86-87.

22. The effect of motivation upon performance has been the subject of a large amount of research…. It provides a particularly clear example of the method of separating learning from performance variables by the factorial experiment. The study of Hillman, Hunter, and Kimble (1953) is typical. Two groups of rats were trained on a complex maze for water reward, initially under 2 and 22 hours of water deprivation. After 15 initial trials [during which the running time of both groups at first improved rapidly, but later leveled off, with the 22-hour deprivation group reaching the fastest level], the groups were subdivided. Half of the animals in each group continued under the original deprivation condition; the other half were switched to the alternative condition…. The important point is that the switch in deprivation produced a rapid shift in performance to the level characteristic of the group which had been on the same drive from the beginning. –Gregory A. Kimble, *Hilgard and Marquis' Conditioning and Learning* (Appleton-Century-Crofts, 1961), p. 122.

23. The change in the outlook towards the universe of Western man in the seventeenth century a change from a medieval, religious and teleological outlook to a modern, scientific and mechanistic one, has largely fashioned our present culture. What were the fundamental causes of this far-reaching change?… The Marxist historical materialists … maintain that the creation of modern science was the result of economic changes. We will examine, in a little detail, the arguments in favor of this view. The growth of trade and the beginnings of capitalism can be traced throughout the later Middle Ages; there was, however, a pronounced economic and industrial surge forward in the sixteenth and seventeenth centuries, coinciding with the modern scientific movement. –A. E. E. McKenzie, *The Major Achievements of Science.* vol. I, p. 79.

24. On 1 August 1774, Priestley, recently the possessor of a new and powerful burning glass of 12 in. diameter and 20 in. focal length, which provided a more intense heat than a flame, heated red calx of mercury (mercuric oxide, HgO), and discovered that gas was driven off and the calx changed to mercury. This was one of a series of experiments he had planned to find the effect of heating various substances by the burning glass. –A. E. E. McKenzie, *The Major Achievements of Science*, vol. I, p. 98.

25. There was yet another optical phenomenon to be accounted for, what is now called polarization. This can be most simply demonstrated by passing a beam of light through two crystals of tourmaline in turn. If the second crystal is rotated, the intensity of the light emerging from it varies; when the axes of the two crystals are perpendicular to each other, no light emerges from the second crystal; when the axes of the crystals are parallel, the emergent light has its maximum intensity. Newton saw in this phenomenon an indication that light has different properties in the two perpendicular directions. –A. E. E. McKenzie, *The Major Achievements of Science,* vol. I, p. 152.

26. Pasteur was urged by Napoleon to investigate the diseases of wines. Each variety of wine had its own peculiar maladies; champagnes were apt to become ropy, burgundies to become bitter, and clarets turbid and flat. Pasteur turned his microscope onto the diseased wines. He saw that, in addition to the wild yeasts originally present on the skins of grapes and responsible for the healthy fermentation of the grape sugar, there were other microorganisms, and he was convinced that these gave rise to the products causing the bad flavor. –A. E. E. McKenzie, *The Major Achievements of Science,* vol I, p. 226.

27. [Pasteur] first tried to kill the contaminating microorganisms by antiseptics, but eventually found that heating to 55°C would do so without destroying the flavor and bouquet of the wine. This heating process, now called pasteurization, was tested by a commission. Five hundred liters of wine half of it heated and

half unheated, were put aboard a ship at Brest and taken on a ten months' cruise. At the end of the cruise the heated wine had an excellent flavor, while the unheated wine was acid and sour. –A. E. E. McKenzie, *The Major Achievements* of *Science*. vol. I, p. 226.

28. In the October 1907 issue of the *Journal of the American Medical Association*, Dr. Robert Weir describes various cases of 'trigger fingers' as well as the history of the disease. In cases of 'trigger finger,' once a patient's fingers are flexed, it becomes difficult or painful for the patient to extend them. During attempts to extend the finger, it is not uncommon for the finger to suddenly 'pop' back into the extended position very quickly, as if releasing a trigger on a gun. Weir observed that in such patients there is usually an obstruction on the tendon or its sheath (the protective covering around the tendon). Furthermore, when such obstructions were surgically removed, normal functioning of the finger resumed. Dr. Weir's studies suggest that the trigger finger pathology results from such tendon obstructions.

LSAT Prep Questions

1. Physician: Heart disease generally affects men at an earlier age than it does women, who tend to experience heart disease after menopause. Both sexes have the hormones estrogen and testosterone, but when they are relatively young, men have ten times as much testosterone as women, and women abruptly lose estrogen after menopause. We can conclude, then, that testosterone tends to promote, and estrogen tends to inhibit, heart disease.

   The physician's argument is questionable because it presumes which one of the following without providing sufficient justification?

   (a) Hormones are the primary factors that account for the differences in age-related heart disease risks between women and men.

   (b) Estrogen and testosterone are the only hormones that promote or inhibit heart disease.

   (c) Men with high testosterone levels have a greater risk for heart disease than do postmenopausal women.

   (d) Because hormone levels are correlated with heart disease they influence heart disease.

   (e) Hormone levels do not vary from person to person, especially among those of the same age and gender.

   Preptest 30, Section 2, Question 25

2. During the recent economic downturn, banks contributed to the decline by loaning less money. Prior to the downturn, regulatory standards for loanmaking by banks were tightened. Clearly, therefore, banks will lend more money if those standards are relaxed.

   The argument assumes that

   (a) the downturn did not cause a significant decrease in the total amount of money on deposit with banks which is the source of funds for banks to lend.

   (b) the imposition of the tighter regulatory standards was not a cause of the economic downturn.

   (c) the reason for tightening the regulatory standards was not arbitrary.

(d) no economic downturn is accompanied by a significant decrease in the amount of money loaned out by banks to individual borrowers and to businesses.

(e) no relaxation of standards for loanmaking by banks would compensate for the effects of the downturn.

Preptest 30, Section 2, Question 15

3. Commissioner: Budget forecasters project a revenue shortfall of a billion dollars in the coming fiscal year. Since there is no feasible way to increase the available funds, our only choice is to decrease expenditures. The plan before you outlines feasible cuts that would yield savings of a billion dollars over the coming fiscal year. We will be able to solve the problem we face, therefore, only if we adopt this plan.

The reasoning in the commissioner's argument is flawed because this argument

(a) relies on information that is far from certain.

(b) confuses being an adequate solution with being a required solution.

(c) inappropriately relies on the opinions of experts.

(d) inappropriately employs language that is vague.

(e) takes for granted that there is no way to increase available funds.

Preptest 30, Section 4, Question 6

4. In a recent study, a group of subjects had their normal daily caloric intake increased by 25 percent. This increase was entirely in the form of alcohol. Another group of similar subjects had alcohol replace nonalcoholic sources of 25 percent of their normal daily caloric intake. All subjects gained body fat over the course of the study, and the amount of body fat gained was the same for both groups.

Which one of the following is most strongly supported by the information above?

(a) Alcohol is metabolized more quickly by the body than are other foods or drinks.

(b) In the general population, alcohol is the primary cause of gains in body fat.

(c) An increased amount of body fat does not necessarily imply a weight gain.

(d) Body fat gain is not dependent solely on the number of calories one consumes.

(e) The proportion of calories from alcohol in a diet is more significant for body fat gain than are the total calories from alcohol.

Preptest 30, Section 4, Question 22

5. In Debbie's magic act, a volunteer supposedly selects a card in a random fashion, looks at it without showing it to her, and replaces it in the deck. After several shuffles, Debbie cuts the deck and supposedly reveals the same selected card. A skeptic conducted three trials. In the first, Debbie was videotaped, and no sleight of hand was found. In the second, the skeptic instead supplied a standard deck of cards. For the third trial, the skeptic selected the card. Each time, Debbie apparently revealed the selected card. The skeptic concluded that Debbie uses neither sleight of hand, nor a trick deck, nor a planted "volunteer" to achieve her effect.

Which one of the following most accurately describes a flaw in the skeptic's reasoning?

(a) The skeptic failed to consider the possibility that Debbie did not always use the same method to achieve her effect.

(b) The skeptic failed to consider the possibility that sleight of hand could also be detected by some means other than videotaping.

(c) The skeptic failed to consider the possibility that Debbie requires both sleight of hand and a trick deck to achieve her effect.

(d) The skeptic failed to consider the possibility that Debbie used something other than sleight of hand, a trick deck, or a planted "volunteer" to achieve her effect.

(e) The skeptic failed to consider the possibility that Debbie's success in the three trials was something other than a coincidence.

Preptest 29, Section 1, Question 7

6. Twelve healthy volunteers with the Apo-A-IV-l gene and twelve healthy volunteers who instead have the Apo-A-IV-2 gene each consumed a standard diet supplemented daily by a high-cholesterol food. A high level of cholesterol in the blood is associated with an increased risk of heart disease. After three weeks, the blood cholesterol levels of the subjects in the second group were unchanged, whereas the blood cholesterol levels of those with the Apo-A-IV-I gene rose 20 percent.

Which one of the following is most strongly supported by the information above?

(a) Approximately half the population carries a gene that lowers cholesterol levels.

(b) Most of those at risk of heart disease may be able to reduce their risk by adopting a low-cholesterol diet.

(c) The bodies of those who have the Apo-A-IV-2 genes excrete cholesterol when blood cholesterol reaches a certain level.

(d) The presence of the Apo-A-IV-l gene seems to indicate that a person has a lower risk of heart disease.

(e) The presence of the Apo-A-IV-2 gene may inhibit the elevation of blood cholesterol.

Preptest 30, Section 4, Question 10

7. These days, drug companies and health professionals alike are focusing their attention on cholesterol in the blood. The more cholesterol we have in our blood, the higher the risk that we shall die of a heart attack. The issue is pertinent since heart disease kills more North Americans every year than any other single cause. At least three factors – smoking, drinking, and exercise – can each influence levels of cholesterol in the blood.

Which one of the following can be properly concluded from the passage?

(a) If a person has low blood cholesterol, then that person's risk of fatal heart disease is low.

(b) Smoking in moderation can entail as great a risk of fatal heart disease as does heavy smoking.

(c) A high-cholesterol diet is the principal cause of death in North America.

(d) The only way that smoking increases one's risk of fatal heart disease is by influencing the levels of cholesterol in the blood.

(e) The risk of fatal heart disease can be altered by certain changes in lifestyle.

Preptest 29, Section 1, Question 6

8. Many people claim that simple carbohydrates are a reasonable caloric replacement for the fatty foods forbidden to those on low-fat diets. This is now in doubt. New studies show that, for many people, a high intake of simple carbohydrates stimulates an overproduction of insulin, a hormone that is involved in processing sugars and starches to create energy when the body requires energy, or, when energy is not required, to store the resulting by-products as fat.

Which one of the following is most strongly supported by the nutritionist's statements?

(a) People on low-fat diets should avoid consumption of simple carbohydrates if they wish to maintain the energy that their bodies require.

(b) People who produce enough insulin to process their intake of simple carbohydrates should not feel compelled to adopt low-fat diets.

(c) People who consume simple carbohydrates should limit their intake of foods high in fat.

(d) People who wish to avoid gaining body fat should limit their intake of foods high in simple carbohydrates.

(e) People who do not produce an excessive amount of insulin when they consume foods high in simple carbohydrates will not lose weight if they restrict only their intake of these foods.

Preptest 29, Section 1, Question 8

4.2 Hypothetical Induction

Atomic Theory. All scientific knowledge is based on observation. The natural scientist's basic data is provided by looking, listening, feeling, tasting, and smelling. This does not mean, however, that science cannot concern itself with unobserved or even unobservable objects. For example, philosophers and scientists had speculated at least since Democritus (c. 428 B.C.) that all matter is composed of imperceptibly small particles called atoms. This was finally confirmed in the nineteenth century, largely as a result of John Dalton's labors. How? Not by observation alone, since atoms were too small to be seen even through the most powerful microscopes available at the time. Nor through observation supplemented only by causal or analogical inferences: for such an approach would have required knowing in advance of establishing their existence and nature that atoms are related in certain ways to observable objects. A more indirect method was necessary.

Dalton hypothesized in 1805 that elements like oxygen, hydrogen, and chlorine are composed of atoms of different weights, and that these atoms combine in fixed ways to form chemical compounds like water, hydrogen peroxide, and hydrochloric acid. Dalton inferred that his hypothesis was true from the fact that it explained two generalizations about chemical compounds established on the basis of careful observations: the law of conservation of matter, stated by Lavoisier in 1789, and the law of constant composition, stated by Proust in 1799. The law of conservation of matter states that matter is neither created nor destroyed in a chemical reaction. For example, if eight grams of oxygen combine with one gram of hydrogen to produce water, there will be nine grams of water. The law of constant composition states that all specimens of any particular compound possess the same composition by weight. Thus in any sample of water, there are eight grams of oxygen for every gram of hydrogen. Dalton's theory was confirmed when two further consequences of the theory, the laws of multiple and reciprocal proportions, were established, chiefly by Berzelius, who analyzed over two thousand chemical compounds between 1810 and 1820. The law of multiple proportions states that if two elements combine together to form more than one compound, then the weights of one element that combine with a fixed weight of the other element are in a simple multiple ratio to one another. For example, one gram of hydrogen combines with eight grams of oxygen to form water, while one gram of hydrogen combines with sixteen grams of oxygen to form peroxide. The ratio of the weights of oxygen combining with unit weights of hydrogen here is 1:2. Nitrogen and oxygen form five different compounds; the weights of oxygen combining with a unit weight of nitrogen stand in the ratio 1:2:3:4:5. The law of reciprocal proportions, finally, says that if x parts by weight of element A combine with y parts of B, and x parts of A combine with z parts of C, then y parts of B combine with z parts of C. Opposing theories, such as the Aristotelian view that matter is continuous, or the Cartesian view that particles of a given substance could have different sizes, shapes, and weights, were compatible with these laws, but could not explain them.[10]

The details of this case are complicated. But the pattern of inference is simple: from the fact that a hypothesis would explain the data, it was inferred that the theory is true. The same pattern is used widely outside of science as well. It is common in detective work, for example, where theories are developed to explain circumstantial evidence. Outstanding detectives, like Allan Pinkerton in real life and Sherlock Holmes in fiction, are superior not only at observing and gathering clues, but also at reasoning and figuring out what explains them.

The Edgewood Mystery. Let us examine a case from the Pinkerton files.[11] On March 14, 1869, a man was found dead in Edgewood, New Jersey. The man had been dead for several days as a result of heavy blows to the head by a blunt instrument. He had been stripped of his outer clothing, being clad only in vest, shirt, drawers, stockings, shoes, and a white hat (now stained with blood). He had thirty-five dollars in his pockets. The man appeared to be about twenty-eight, of German extraction, and well-to-do. His identity was completely unknown to the townspeople. The only evidence as to the identity of the murderer were footprints to and from the nearby woods; but these were quickly destroyed by the press of curious townspeople. Local authorities were stymied, so the Pinkerton agency was called in. The only clue as to the identity of the victim were the letters "A.B." embroidered on his shirt. An "Information Wanted" ad in the New York City papers produced the victim's landlord, a Mr. Kuenzle, who subsequently identified the victim as Adolph Bohner, an artist who had emigrated from Germany a year before. Kuenzle recognized the clothing found, except for the hat. He admitted the detectives to Bohner's room, which led them to his diary. The last line read: "Tomorrow will go to Edgewood, N.J., to meet August Franssen, who promises to pay his indebtedness to me." The landlord said that Franssen was a "wild, bad fellow," and had come over from Germany with Bohner. The diary indicated that Franssen was jealous because he had been rejected by a girl back home named Rosa in favor of Bohner.

The detectives now had a suspect, so they set out to obtain evidence that would place beyond doubt their theory that Franssen was the murderer, or was at least involved in the murder. Franssen was soon located working as a shoemaker. One detective, Mendelsohn, went under cover and secured

---

[10] From A. E. E McKenzie, *The Major Achievements of Science.* vol. 1 ch. 11; F. Greenaway, *John Dalton and the Atom* (Cornell University Press, 1966); "Atomic Structure," and "Atomic Weight" in *Encyclopaedia Britannica,* 15th ed., vol. 2 ('Encyclopaedia Britannica inc., 1980), pp. 330-45; and C. H. Yoder, F. H. Sydam. and F. A, Snavely, *Chemistry* (Harcourt Brace Jovanovich, 1975), ch. 2.

[11] Allan Pinkerton, "The Edgewood Mystery and the Detective," in *Professional Thieves and the Detective* (AMS Press Inc., 1973), pp. 287-394.

employment at the same shop, and even took a room with the suspect. Another detective pursued his investigations in Edgewood as a house painter. Together they turned up the following. One night, Franssen had a terrible nightmare in which he was talking to Rosa, and said things like "I see him now lying upon the snow." Franssen recently purchased the hat found on Bohner's body, but now had the hat Bohner was seen wearing. Franssen recently gave a girl a pair of fine leather gloves with the initials "A.B." marked on the inside. When Franssen received a letter from his father informing him of the death of his friend, which revealed that the victim had been identified, Franssen became agitated and later attempted to commit suicide. Sometime after the murder, Franssen, who was chronically borrowing money, had a considerable sum, including a twenty-franc gold piece, which the landlord had seen in Bohner's possession. After announcing his intention to go out west, Franssen borrowed five dollars from Mendelsohn and offered as security a pawn ticket; the ticket was dated March 13 and was for a coat and a pair of pants, which Kuenzle recognized as having been worn by Bohner when he left for Edgewood. At this point, the Pinkerton agency thought it had sufficient evidence to arrest and convict Franssen. Franssen was apprehended as he was about to board a train for Buffalo, and was subsequently convicted. Throughout the trial, Franssen maintained his innocence. But his credibility was severely weakened when he denied ever having known Bohner. Franssen was subsequently overheard in his cell talking in a crazed state to Bohner as he was killing him.

The evidence in this case was entirely circumstantial. No one had seen Franssen commit the murder, and Franssen himself did not confess. Franssen's nightmares and crazed utterances could not be considered reliable testimony. The case against Franssen was nonetheless thought to be conclusive, since his involvement provided far and away the best explanation of the evidence.

Hypothetical Induction. This pattern of inference has been given a variety of names, such as "abduction," "inverse induction," "hypothetical inductive inference," and "inference to the best explanation," but none has become standard. We shall call it *hypothetical induction.*

Hypothetical Induction
d is true.
h would explain *d*.
∴ *h* is true.
CONDITION OF VALIDITY: **No competing hypothesis explains *d* as well as *h*.**

The symbol *h* represents a **hypothesis**, or **theory**. There is no sharp distinction in common usage between hypotheses and theories, although there is some tendency to use "hypothesis" when referring to a single proposition, and "theory' when referring to a complex system of propositions. We shall use the terms interchangeably to denote *any statement or set of statements considered as an explanation of a body of data*. Both "hypothesis" and "theory" commonly connote lack of proof. Indeed, to describe something as a "*mere* theory" is to dismiss it as a groundless speculation. Nothing of the sort is intended here, of course, since we are trying to show the methods by which hypotheses and theories can be proven. Atomic theory and Dalton's hypotheses are no longer mere speculations.

The symbol *d* represents the **data**, the facts that are given. The symbol *d* stands for one or more propositions whose truth is accepted as having already been established. The data could consist of simple observational facts, as in the Pinkerton example, or generalizations based inductively on observation, as in the Dalton example. The data could also consist of theories previously established using hypothetical induction. Of course, we often *think* we know something when we do not. So what is *accepted* as true may not in fact be true. If so, our data is faulty or inaccurate. Our application of hypothetical induction is then fallacious, since its first premise is false.

Hypothetical induction is often characterized as ***indirect reasoning***. For in order to establish the truth of a hypothesis by this method, you assume it to be true and then see if you can explain the data better than if you assumed any other hypothesis to be true. Another method of indirect reasoning, which we will study in §8.5, is known as indirect proof, or proof by *reductio ad absurdum*. Using indirect proof, a hypothesis is proven to be true by showing that a contradiction can be derived if the hypothesis is assumed to be false. Whereas hypothetical induction is indirect inductive reasoning, proof by re*ductio ad absurdum* is indirect deductive reasoning. The other inductive arguments we have studied (the argument from authority, the argument from analogy, enumerative induction, statistical syllogism, causal induction, and causal elimination), and the other deductive arguments we shall study later, are in contrast characterized as ***direct reasoning,*** since they involve making no assumption about the truth or falsity of the conclusion.

Affirming the Consequent. Hypothetical induction bears a superficial resemblance to a fallacy known as ***affirming the consequent***, in which the truth of a proposition is inferred from the fact that it implies something that is true:

Affirming the Consequent

d is true.
If h is true, then d is true,
∴ h is true.

A compound statement of the form "If h is true, then d is true" is called a *conditional,* or *hypothetical, statement.* Component h is called the *antecedent* while d is called the *consequent.* In this fallacy, then, one of the premises affirms the consequent of the other, from which it is inferred that the antecedent is true. That affirming the consequent is a fallacy can be seen by letting d be "The earth has a moon" and letting h be "The earth has rings like Saturn as well as a moon." It is true that the earth has a moon, and it is also true that *if* the earth has rings as well as a moon, then the earth has a moon; but it hardly follows that the earth has rings as well as a moon. The fallacy of affirming the consequent will be discussed further in §7.7.

Conditions of Validity. How does hypothetical induction differ from affirming the consequent? In two ways. First, to infer that h is true by hypothetical induction, h must not merely *imply d,* it must *explain d.* The hypothesis that the earth has rings as well as a moon certainly implies that the earth has a moon; but the hypothesis would not explain *why* the earth has a moon even if it were true. Second, while the fact that h explains d will always provide some support for h, there will not be sufficient reason to infer h unless h is *unique* in enabling the *best* explanation of d. There will generally be many hypotheses capable of accounting for the data. Suppose we observe a broken window. The following hypotheses are all possible explanations of why it broke: Johnny threw a rock through it; Mary threw a rock through it; Bill put his fist through it; Joe fired a howitzer through it; and so on. We cannot infer any one of these hypotheses to be true merely from the fact that if it were true it would explain why the window broke; for all the hypotheses would have as much claim to be selected. We cannot accept one of these hypotheses instead of the others unless it can claim to be the best explanation of the broken window. Thus we have a condition of validity on hypothetical induction: *There must be no competing hypothesis that would explain d as well as h.* In other words, h must provide the ***best explanation*** of d, one that is better than *any* competing hypothesis. ***Competing hypotheses*** are those which are incompatible with each other; since at most one can be true, we have to choose between them. The criteria for evaluating explanations include consistency, completeness, simplicity, direct support, and confirmability; we will discuss these at length later. It will then be clear that the *best* explanation of the data is not necessarily the *true* explanation of the data. Hypothetical induction is therefore inductively, not deductively, valid. The best explanation is probably, but not necessarily, true.

In applications of hypothetical induction, the hypothesis need not, and generally will not, explain the data all by itself: it may be only *part* of the best complete explanation of the data. Thus the hypothesis that there are atoms only partly explains the chemical generalizations mentioned earlier. The full explanation also requires Dalton's hypothesis that atoms of different elements have different weights. Similarly, while the hypothesis that Franssen was involved in Bohner's murder provides the key to why he attempted suicide, a full explanation would specify in addition that he was aware of his involvement, and that he felt remorse or perhaps fear. Now, completeness is one criterion for evaluating explanations: the more complete an explanation is, the better. So the full explanation is better than any of its parts. However, the full explanation and its parts are not *competing* explanations of the data. Indeed, the full explanation implies its parts. Since the condition of validity only requires that *h* be the best of all *competing* explanations, *h* can be inferred as long as it is even part of the best complete explanation.

Hypothetical induction is also subject to the general condition of validity: there must be no undermining evidence, otherwise the fallacy of exclusion is committed. With hypothetical induction, undermining evidence typically consists of data excluded from *d* that cannot be explained by *h*. Thus Pinkerton's argument that Franssen killed Bohner would have committed the fallacy of exclusion if the murder weapon had been found, with fingerprints of an unknown individual but none of Franssen's and with no sign that any prints had been wiped clean or smudged by gloves.

Factors Influencing Strength. Like all other inductive arguments, hypothetical inductions vary in strength. The determining factors are *the quantity of data included in d* and *the quality of the explanation provided by h.* Other things equal (such as the quality of the explanation), the greater the amount of data included in *d,* the more likely it is that *h* is true. Thus, atomic theory was strengthened by Berzelius's analysis. And Pinkerton's theory was stronger with the evidence about Franssen's attempted suicide than without it. Holding constant the quantity of data, the likelihood of *h* depends on how well it explains *d*. The more consistent, complete, simple, and directly supported the explanation is, the stronger the hypothetical induction. Franssen's guilt would have been even more probable if there had been some direct evidence—for example, a witness who saw Franssen and Bohner arguing the night of the murder. Since a hypothetical induction involves a comparison among hypotheses, its strength depends primarily on *relative* quality. That is, the likelihood of *h* depends on how much *better* it explains the data than competing hypotheses. At one point, Pinkerton had a second hypothesis under consideration—namely, that Franssen was merely involved in the murder. Indeed, here is a theory that explains all the data Pinkerton had before the trial: someone else clubbed Bohner to death and left his body in the woods; Franssen found Bohner already dead, stripped him of his clothes and money, switched hats, and then dragged his body out from the woods, leaving it where it was subsequently found. This theory is not as simple as Pinkerton's, since two agents are involved rather than just one. But Pinkerton's theory is not that much better. The justice of the guilty verdict is therefore questionable, since murder must be proven beyond a reasonable doubt. There was no close competitor to the theory that Franssen was somehow involved in the murder, so that weaker conclusion was conclusively established. We will discuss the criteria determining the quality of explanations at length in §4.4.

The conclusion of a hypothetical induction may be strengthened or weakened in the usual ways, to "*h* must be true," "*h* might be true," and so on. And as always, the weaker the conclusion, the stronger the argument. The conclusion that *h must be* true is warranted only when *h* is not merely the best explanation of *d*, but the *only* explanation. Indeed, such a conclusion in a hypothetical induction has the force "*h* must be true, *otherwise d would be inexplicable.*"

The soundness of a hypothetical induction does not depend on the chronological order of inquiry. That is, it does not matter whether the data was gathered first and then the hypothesis formulated to explain it, or whether the hypothesis was formulated first and then the data gathered to support it. All that matters is that when hypothetical induction is used, the supporting data has been gathered and the explanatory hypothesis formulated. Dalton was generally led by preconceived hypotheses to supporting data, while Newton was led by preexisting data to explanatory hypotheses. Both were model scientists. The psychological genesis of a hypothesis is similarly irrelevant to its truth. Indeed, some of the most fruitful hypotheses originate in the strangest ways. August Kekulé was struggling with the problem of how organic molecules consisting of the same number and types of atoms could have radically different chemical properties. "The idea of the linking of carbon atoms into chains came to him when he was traveling on the open top of a London horse bus. It was the last bus on a fine summer evening, and, as he traveled from Islington to Clapham, the streets were deserted. He fell into a reverie; the atoms seemed to gambol before his eyes, whirling as in a dance, until they formed themselves into a chain."[12] The result was a revolution in organic chemistry.

The Hypothetico-Deductive Method. A theory is no more than speculation, of course, until supporting evidence is gathered. And scientists continue to *test* hypotheses even after they have been accepted on considerable evidence. As explained in the previous chapter, dogmatic acceptance is inappropriate in science, since its methods are inductive. Hypothetical induction is the basis for a method of testing hypotheses called the ***hypothetico-deductive method.*** Once a hypothesis has been formulated, it can be tested by deducing a prediction, and then determining whether the prediction is correct. The prediction must be new, something not already part of the data explained by the hypothesis. If the prediction is verified, the hypothesis is confirmed. It has more support than before, because it explains the new data as well as the old. If the prediction fails, the hypothesis (or auxiliary assumptions) must be rejected and either replaced or modified. The entire process can be repeated indefinitely. If a hypothesis survives one test, it can be retested; if a hypothesis is replaced or modified, the new hypothesis can be tested. The goal is to find a hypothesis that survives all subsequent tests. The hypothetico-deductive method can also be used to decide between two or more theories if they predict different results from a given experiment. The theory predicting the actual results is confirmed and the others can be rejected. Such a test is called a *crucial experiment.* Note the interconnected role of deduction and induction here. Predictions are derived deductively from a hypothesis; the hypothesis is then supported inductively by the success of those predictions, or refuted deductively by their failure. Note also the interplay of theory and experiment. The formulation of explanatory hypotheses and the derivation of predictions are theoretical activities; determining whether the predictions are correct requires observation and experiment.Some of the most famous examples of the hypothetico-deductive method surrounded the Michelson-Morley experiment in 1887. Physicists at the time believed that light was propagated in an imperceptible medium called aether, in much the same way waves are propagated in water and sound in air. They also believed that the aether was at rest in the otherwise empty spaces between planets and other material objects. Consequently, the earth was thought to be moving around the sun through the stationary aether. Using this hypothesis Michelson and Morley calculated that light should take more time to traverse a given distance and back in the direction of the earth's movement than to traverse the same distance and back in a direction perpendicular to the earth's movement. Figure 4-1 depicts the envisaged motions.

[12] A. E. E. McKenzie, *The Major Achievements of Science,* vol. I p. 195.

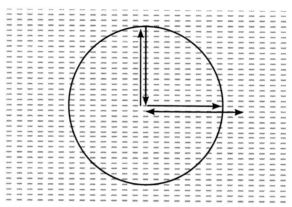

FIGURE 4-1: THE MICHELSON-MORLEY EXPERIMENT

Michelson and Morley devised an instrument sensitive enough to verify this prediction, but found the velocity of light exactly the same in both directions. To explain this result, Michelson and Morley modified the aether hypothesis slightly, adding that because of gravity, the earth carried some aether around the sun with it. From this revised hypothesis they predicted that directional differences in the velocity of light would show up at higher elevations, where gravity is less. None did.

Einstein completely rejected the aether hypothesis, replacing it with his now-famous theory of relativity, which holds that the velocity of light in a vacuum is a constant and that all motion is relative. From his theory, Einstein deduced two startling predictions. First, he predicted that an object's mass would increase as its velocity did; the change would be negligible at low velocities, but substantial near the speed of light. Second, he predicted that light rays would bend in a gravitational field; again, the deviation from a straight line would be noticeable only in an extremely strong gravitational field. Both predictions were verified. The increase of mass was observed in particle accelerators, where electrons and other particles approach the speed of light. The bending of light was observed during a solar eclipse. The relative positions of the stars photographed near the sun during the eclipse differed slightly from the positions recorded when the light from the stars did not pass near the sun. The successful outcomes of these tests led to the universal acceptance of Einstein's theory.[13]

In the cases just examined, the reasoning necessary to derive the predictions from the theories was complex and mathematical. In other cases it is very simple. After spending years poring over Tycho Brahe's observations, Kepler determined that the orbit of Mars was an ellipse, not a circle as had been thought since antiquity. Kepler inferred that all planets have elliptical orbits, whence it is not difficult to deduce that Venus must have an elliptical orbit. This prediction was subsequently verified, confirming Kepler's hypothesis.

Auxiliary Assumptions. In most applications of hypothetico-deductive method, the predictions are not deduced exclusively from the hypothesis being tested. Previously established principles, subsidiary hypotheses—and sometimes even unnoticed assumptions—are also used; we shall call these *auxiliary assumptions.* Auxiliary assumptions cause no problem if the prediction is successful: the hypothesis is still confirmed. For as long as the hypothesis is even part of the best complete explanation, it is supported by the data. However, if the prediction is not borne out, we cannot automatically reject the hypothesis. All we can infer is that the hypothesis *or* one of the auxiliary assumptions is false. For example, Michelson and Morley set out to test the hypothesis that the earth was moving through stationary aether.

[13] See A.E.E. McKenzie, *The Major Achievements of Science*, vol. I, ch. 21

But in calculating what their instrument would show, they made the seemingly innocent assumption that motion does not change the length of an object. This left an escape route for a diehard adherent of the aether hypothesis like Fitzgerald, who explained away the negative result of the Michelson-Morley experiment by postulating that all bodies contract in the direction they are moving, the contraction being proportional to the velocity. Fitzgerald attributed this contraction to the pressure of the aether against the object. The contraction would be unobservable, since our measuring rod would shorten similarly. The negative result of the Michelson-Morley experiment could then be attributed to the fact that their instrument shrank in the direction of the earth's movement but not in the perpendicular direction; consequently the light traveled a shorter distance in the direction of the movement, compensating for the predicted slower velocity. As it turns out, Einstein's theory predicted the same contraction, without postulating aether.

Glossary

Hypothetical induction: the argument in which the conclusion is drawn that a hypothesis or theory is true from the premise that it would explain the data; to be valid, the hypothesis must provide the best explanation.

Hypothesis: any statement or set of statements considered as an explanation of a body of data.

Theory: a hypothesis.

Data: the given facts, represented by propositions accepted as having already been established.

Best explanation: an explanation that is better than all competing explanations; the quality of an explanation is determined by its consistency, completeness, simplicity, direct support, and confirmability.

Competing hypotheses: hypotheses that are incompatible with each other (or with a given hypothesis), so that at most one can be true.

Hypothetico-deductive method: testing hypotheses by deducing something new and then determining whether the prediction is correct; if the prediction is verified, the hypothesis is confirmed; otherwise, the hypothesis or auxiliary assumptions must be rejected or modified.

Auxiliary assumptions: previously established principles, subsidiary hypotheses, or other statements assumed to be true when deriving predictions from the hypothesis being tested.

Indirect reasoning: reasoning based on the consequences of assuming the conclusion to be true or false.

Direct reasoning: reasoning that is not indirect.

Affirming the consequent: the fallacy of concluding that a statement is true merely from the premise that it implies something true.

Exercises

The following passages contain applications of hypothetical induction. In each, identify the data, the hypothesis, and any competing hypotheses. If any of the theories were tested by the hypothetico-deductive method, explain how.

1. Every naturalist admits that there is a general tendency in animals and plants to vary; but it is usually taken for granted, though he have no means of proving the assumption to be true, that there are certain limits beyond which each species cannot pass under any circumstances or in any number of generations. Mr. Darwin and Mr. Wallace say that the opposite hypothesis, which assumes that every species is capable of varying indefinitely from its original type, is not a whit more arbitrary, and has this manifest claim to be preferred, that it will account for a multitude of phenomena which the ordinary theory is incapable of explaining. –Charles Lyell, *The Antiquity of Man.*

2. He who believes in separate and innumerable acts of creation may say, that in these cases it has pleased the Creator to cause a being of one type to take the place of one belonging to another type; but this seems to me only restating the fact in dignified language. He who believes in the struggle for existence and in the principle of natural selection, will acknowledge that every organic being is constantly endeavoring to increase in numbers; and that if any one being varies ever so little, either in habits or structure, and thus gains an advantage over some other inhabitant of the same country, it will seize on the place of that inhabitant, however different that may be from its own place. Hence it will cause him no surprise that there should be geese and frigate-birds with webbed feet, living on the dry land and rarely alighting on the water, that there should be long-toed corncrakes, living in meadows instead of in swamps; that there should be woodpeckers where hardly a tree grows; that there should be diving thrushes and diving Hymenoptera, and petrels with the habits of auks. –Charles Darwin, *On The Origin of Species*, 6th Ed.

3. Now, there was a difficulty in the movement of the planet Mercury which could not be solved. Even after all the disturbances caused by the attraction of other planets had been taken into account, there remained an inexplicable phenomenon—i.e., an extremely slow turning of the ellipsis described by Mercury on its own plane; Leverrier had found that it amounted to forty-three seconds a century. Einstein found that, according to his formulas, this movement must really amount to just that much. Thus with a single blow he solved one of the greatest puzzles of astronomy. –H.A. Lorentz, *The Einstein Theory of Relativity.*

4. The fourth and last great division of rocks are the crystalline strata and slates, or schists, called gneiss, mica-schist, clay-slate, chlorite-schist, marble, and the like, the origin of which is more doubtful than that of the other three classes. They contain no pebbles, or sand, or scoriae, or angular pieces of imbedded stone, and no traces of organic bodies, and they are often as crystalline as granite, yet are divided into beds, corresponding in form and arrangement to those of sedimentary formations, and are therefore said to be stratified. The beds sometimes consist of an alternation of substances varying in colour, composition, and thickness, precisely as we see in stratified fossiliferous deposits. According to the Huttonian theory, which I adopt as the most probable, and which will be afterwards more fully explained, the materials of these strata were originally deposited from water in the usual form of sediment, but they were subsequently so altered by subterranean heat, as to assume a new texture. –Charles Lyell, *The Student's Elements of Geology.*

5. On the principle of successive slight variations, not necessarily or generally supervening at a very early period of life, and being inherited at a corresponding period, we can understand the leading facts in embryology; namely, the close resemblance in the individual embryo of the parts which are homologous, and which when matured become widely different in structure and function; and the resemblance of the

homologous parts or organs in allied though distinct species, though fitted in the adult state for habits as different as is possible. –Charles Darwin, *On the Origin of Species*, 6th Ed.

6. In April 1774 Lavoisier submitted to the *Académie* a memoir on his work concerning the calcination of metals in sealed vessels. [Some metals, such as lead, when heated until they are molten, leave a dross on the surface, called a calx, the process being known as calcination.] Boyle had heated tin and lead in sealed vessels, unsealing the vessels after cooling, and found an increase in weight, which he ascribed to absorption of igneous particles from the furnace. Lavoisier realized that, if the increase in weight of the calx was derived, as he believed, from the absorption from the air in the vessel, the total weight of the vessel after heating, but before unsealing, should be the same as before heating. Boyle had not weighed the vessel before unsealing. Lavoisier therefore repeated Boyle's experiment, heating lead in a sealed retort on a charcoal furnace, until no further calcination took place. He cooled the retort and found that its weight was unchanged. When he broke the seal he heard a whistling noise as air rushed into the retort. The increase in the total weight of the unsealed retort and its contents was equal to the increase in weight of the calx. –A. E. E. McKenzie, *The Major Achievements of Science* vol. I, pp. 95-96.

7. Our right to assume the existence of something mental that is unconscious and to employ that assumption for the purposes of scientific work is disputed in many quarters. To this we can reply that our assumption of the unconscious is *necessary* and *legitimate,* and that we possess numerous proofs of its existence.

    It is *necessary* because the data of consciousness have a very large number of gaps in them; both in healthy and in sick people physical acts often occur which can be explained only by presupposing other acts, of which, nevertheless, consciousness affords no evidence. These not only include parapraxes [like slips of the tongue] and dreams in healthy people, and everything described as a psychical symptom or an obsession in the sick: our most personal daily experience acquaints us with ideas that come into our head that we do not know from where, and with intellectual conclusions arrived at we do not know how. All these conscious acts remain disconnected and unintelligible if we insist upon claiming that every mental act that occurs in us must also necessarily be experienced by us through consciousness; on the other hand, they fall into a demonstrable connection if we interpolate between them the unconscious acts which we have inferred. A gain in meaning is a perfectly justifiable ground for going beyond the limits of direct experience. When, in addition, it turns out that the assumption of there being an unconscious enables us to construct a successful procedure by which we can exert an effective influence upon the course of conscious processes, this success will have given us an incontrovertible proof of the existence of what we have assumed. –Sigmund Freud, "The Unconscious," *The Complete Psychological Works of Sigmund Freud*, vol. XIV (Hogarth Press, 1957), pp. 186-7.

8. The chief founder of the wave theory of light was the Dutchman, Christiaan Huygens (1629-95)…. Huygens's most original contribution to the wave theory was a geometrical method of determining the positions of successive waves, known as Huygens's principle…. The principle was applied in a satisfying manner to account for the laws of reflection and refraction…. The weakness of the principle was its failure to account for the fact that light travels in straight lines. [If Huygens's principle were true] light, like sound, should spread round corners. This was the decisive objection which led Newton to reject the wave theory….

    Newton regarded light as consisting of tiny corpuscles emitted at great speed from shining bodies. Corpuscles travel naturally in straight lines, unless acted upon by a force, and hence the rectilinear propagation of light is accounted for. Reflection consists of the bouncing of these particles from a reflecting surface; refraction is explained by their attraction by the surface of a medium, such as glass or water, when they approach very closely to it. –A. E. E. McKenzie, *The Major Achievements of Science* vol. I, pp. 146-49.

9.   There was yet another optical phenomenon to be accounted for, what is now called polarization. This can be most simply demonstrated by passing a beam of light through two crystals of tourmaline in turn…. If the second crystal is rotated, the intensity of the light emerging from it varies; when the axes of the two crystals are perpendicular to each other, no light emerges from the second crystal; when the axes of the crystals are parallel, the emergent light has its maximum intensity…. [Newton] could find no explanation for this on a wave theory, the waves being regarded as pulses or compressions traveling through the aether…. He was able to account for the phenomenon on his own theory by assuming that the corpuscles of light had a kind of asymmetry, with different properties in two perpendicular directions. –A. E. E. McKenzie, *The Major Achievements of Science, vol. I. p. 152.*

10. [As a result of developments by Thomas Young and Augustin Fresnel, the] theory that light consists of transverse waves in the aether provided a satisfying explanation of all known optical phenomena. Newton and the supporters of the corpuscular theory had been obliged to invent arbitrary, unconnected hypotheses to account for several phenomena: fits of easy transmission and reflection to explain the colors of thin films, attraction and repulsion of the corpuscles by a variation in the density of the aether at the edge of a body to explain diffraction, and a two-sided property of the corpuscles to explain polarization. The wave theory provided a single common principle by which all these diverse phenomena became intelligible and interconnected. As Sir John Herschel wrote: it is "a theory which, if not founded in Nature, is certainly one of the happiest fictions that the genius of man ever invented to grasp together natural phenomena…." –A. E. E. McKenzie, *The Major Achievements of Science*, vol. I pp. 160-61.

11. A remarkable fact of fundamental significance emerged. Two or more substances, with quite different chemical properties, were found to have identical compositions. Silver fulminate (CNOAg), analyzed by Liebig in 1823, had the same composition as silver cyanate, analyzed by Wöhler. At first it was thought that an error must have been made, but it was then found that the same applied to other substances…. Berzelius coined the word isomerism (Gk. *isos*, equal; *meros*, part) to describe the phenomenon of several substances of different chemical properties having the same composition, and it was realized that the arrangement of the atoms in a molecule must have an importance comparable with the number and nature of the atoms. –A. E. E. McKenzie, *The Major Achievements of Science, vol. I, p. 192.*

12. [Mendel's] most important experiments were conducted with plants of the edible pea. He obtained a considerable number of varieties from seedsmen and, after a two years' trial to find which of them bred true when self-fertilized, he chose twenty-two varieties for his investigations. His object was to find the effect of cross-fertilization on seven pairs of contrasting characters, such as tallness and dwarfness, yellow and green seeds, and round and wrinkled seeds.

In one series of experiments he crossed peas about 6 to 7 feet high with peas ¾ to 1½ feet high…. The first hybrid generation, F_1, were all tall—as tall as the tall parents…. Mendel then self-fertilized this first generation and obtained a second generation, F_2, some of whom were tall and some dwarf. He counted the two varieties of plants, and found that the tall ones were about three times as numerous as the dwarf….

This fundamental conception is known as Mendel's *law of segregation,* and it may be stated generally as follows: there are pairs of corresponding hereditary factors, which retain their identity from one generation to another; the factors in each pair are separated, or segregated, during the mechanism of reproduction.

The first generation, F_1, obtains factors T ["tall"] and t ["dwarf'] from its parents and, since the plants are all tall, T is said to be *dominant* and *t recessive*.... The second generation, F_2, obtained by self-fertilization of F_1, springs from the union of male and female germ cells, which may carry the factors T or t. Mendel's numerical results showed that the union occurs according to the taws of chance. Male germ cells carrying factors T or t, and female germ cells carrying factors T or t, will give rise with equal probability to offspring having factors TT, Tt, tT, or tt. The first three offspring are tall, because T is dominant, and the fourth is dwarf. Hence the Mendelian ratio 3:1 is given a simple and satisfying explanation. –A. E. E. McKenzie, *The Major Achievements of Science,* vol. I, pp. 258-60.

13. When Emile Roux went to the Hospital for Sick Children to find the cause of diphtheria, he found the same bacillus Loeffler had found [see §4.1, exercise 17]. Roux grew the bacillus in flasks of broth, and then shot this "diphtheria soup" into laboratory animals. The animals subsequently developed diphtheria and died, confirming that the bacillus was somehow involved in the disease. However, Roux could find none of the bacilli in the dead animals. Roux then recalled Loeffler's conclusion that the bacillus must secrete a poison, which causes the diphtheria. To test this idea, Roux constructed a filtering apparatus that would pass the broth containing the suspected toxin, but not the bacillus. Animals receiving injections of the filtered broth did indeed die of diphtheria, leading Roux to conclude that he had finally discovered the cause of diphtheria. (Based on Paul De Kruif, *Microbe Hunters,* pp. 178-81.)

14. The German investigators were unanimously opposed to the view of Crookes that the cathode rays were particles; they considered them to be aether waves, rather like the electromagnetic waves discovered by Hertz in 1887. This belief was strengthened by the further discovery of Hertz that the cathode rays could penetrate gold leaf.

   If cathode rays consist of negatively charged particles they should be deflected by an electric field. Hertz tried to detect such an effect without any success. This to his mind, was decisive evidence against the negative particle theory.

   There was a feeling among German physicists that corpuscular theories were an archaic survival from the seventeenth and eighteenth centuries, and were alien to the science of their day. –A. E. E. McKenzie, *The Major Achievements of Science,* vol. I, p. 278.

15. Thomson became convinced that the cathode rays in a discharge tube were negative gaseous ions. He had no suspicion that they were other than negatively charged atoms until he measured their deflection in a magnetic field, an experiment already performed by Sir Arthur Schuster ten years earlier. The deflection was much greater than Thomson expected and suggested that the particles were lighter than atoms, although the evidence was by no means decisive. The large deflection was accounted for by Schuster, not by the small mass of the particles, but by their comparatively low velocity. Thomson believed that the sharp outlines of his beam of cathode rays indicated that the rays were traveling at a much higher velocity than Schuster imagined.

   The obvious next step was to devise a method of measuring their velocity. The heat produced by the cathode rays was measured by causing them to strike an instrument (a thermopile) inside the discharge tube, and the total charge was also measured. By this means Thomson confirmed that the velocity was as high as he suspected. The experiment, together with the deflection of the rays by a magnetic field, enabled him to estimate the ratio of the charge e to mass m of the cathode ray particles. His value for e/m was about 10^7, whereas the corresponding ratio for the lightest known atom, hydrogen, was 10^4. He was inclined to infer that the cathode ray particles were 1,000 times lighter than the hydrogen atom.

Among the considerations which persuaded Thomson that the cathode ray particles were much smaller than atoms were the experiments of Hertz and Lenard showing that cathode rays could penetrate gold leaf or an aluminum window. No atom could do this; the particles must be much smaller. Also, Thomson's own experiments showed that the deflection of cathode rays by a magnetic field was independent of the nature of the gas in the discharge tube. This implied that the cathode rays could not be charged atoms of the gas because otherwise a different deflection would be expected for each gas. –A. E. E. McKenzie, *The Major Achievements of Science*, vol. I pp. 382-80.

16. The unraveling of the complicated processes of radioactivity, and their explanation by a theory, supported and checked at every point by careful experiment, was primarily the work of Ernest Rutherford (1871-1937).…. He examined the radiations from uranium salts by means of their effect in ionizing a gas—that is, by their generation of positively and negatively charged gaseous particles, or ions, thereby making the gas an electrical conductor. He discovered that the intensities of ionization, measured by the rate of leak of a charged electroscope, near to the surface of the uranium salt was very much greater than that a few centimeters away. With his typical flair for seizing upon the implications of a small but significant fact, he deduced that the radiations were complex and consisted of at least two different types. The less penetrating he called alpha radiation and the more penetrating beta radiation. –A. E. E. McKenzie, *The Major Achievements of Science,* vol. I pp. 288-90.

17. Rutherford perceived that the scattering of alpha particles was worth further investigation, and he allotted this task to Geiger and Marsden. They shot alpha particles from a preparation of radium at a thin sheet of gold foil and determined the directions of scatter by the scintillation method. They found that the majority of the alpha particles were scattered through only a few degrees, but about 1 in 10,000 actually bounced back from the gold foil. The model of the atom then generally accepted [the Thomson model] was a diffuse sphere of positive electricity in which electrons were embedded. Rutherford said that the bouncing back of an alpha particle from such an atom was "as incredible as if you had fired a fifteen-inch shell at a sheet of tissue paper and it came back and hit you."

He pondered over these results for a year and then one day, just before Christmas in 1910 as Geiger related, "he came into my room obviously in the best of tempers, and told me that now he knew what the atom looked like and what the strong scattering signified." The atom had a tiny, massive, positively charged nucleus, with negative electrons circling round it—a kind of miniature solar system. It was possible to work out mathematically, assuming an inverse square law of repulsion between nucleus and alpha particle, the probability of scattering through various angles; for example, eight times as many particles should be scattered between 60° and 120° as between 120° and 180° During the next twelve months, by accurate experiments, Geiger and Marsden confirmed that the scattering did, in fact, conform with this theory. This was a beautiful example of a revolutionary discovery made by simple but ineluctable reasoning, based on experimental facts. –A. E. E. McKenzie, *The Major Achievements of Science,* vol. I, p. 293.

18. In one of the most notable of these attempts Michelson devised a method which appears as though it must be decisive. Imagine two mirrors so arranged on a rigid body that the reflecting surfaces face each other. A ray of light requires a perfectly definite time T to pass from one mirror to the other and back again, if the whole system be at rest with respect to the æther. It is found by calculation, however, that a slightly different time T1 is required for this process, if the body, together with the mirrors, be moving relatively to the æther. And yet another point: it is shown by calculation that for a given velocity v with reference to the æther, this time T1 is different when the body is moving perpendicularly to the planes of the mirrors from that resulting when the motion is parallel to these planes. Although the estimated difference between these two times is exceedingly small, Michelson and Morley performed an

experiment involving interference in which this difference should have been clearly detectable. But the experiment gave a negative result—a fact very perplexing to physicists. Lorentz and FitzGerald rescued the theory from this difficulty by assuming that the motion of the body relative to the æther produces a contraction of the body in the direction of motion, the amount of contraction being just sufficient to compensate for the difference in time mentioned above.... From the standpoint of the theory of relativity this solution of the difficulty was the right one. But on the basis of the theory of relativity the method of interpretation is incomparably more satisfactory. According to this theory there is no such thing as a "specially favoured" (unique) co-ordinate system to occasion the introduction of the æther-idea, and hence there can be no æther-drift, nor any experiment with which to demonstrate it. –Albert Einstein, *Relativity*, Chapter 16.

19. Muller was thus led carefully to examine the apparatus in the air-breathing species [of crustacean]; and he found it to differ in each in several important points, as in the position of the orifices, in the manner in which they are opened and closed, and in some accessory details. Now such differences are intelligible, and might even have been expected, on the supposition that species belonging to distinct families had slowly become adapted to live more and more out of water, and to breathe the air. For these species, from belonging to distinct families, would have differed to a certain extent, and in accordance with the principle that the nature of each variation depends on two factors, viz., the nature of the organism and that the surrounding conditions, their variability assuredly would not have been exactly the same. Consequently natural selection would have had different materials or variations to work on, in order to arrive at the same functional result; and the structures thus acquired would almost necessarily have differed. –Charles Darwin, *On the Origin of Species, 6th ed.*

20. The main conclusion here arrived at, and now held by many naturalists who are well competent to form a sound judgment, is that man is descended from some less highly organized form. The grounds upon which this conclusion rests will never be shaken, for the close similarity between man and the lower animals in embryonic development, as well as in innumerable points of structure and constitution, both of high and of the most trifling importance,—the rudiments which he retains, and the abnormal reversions to which he is occasionally liable,—are facts which cannot be disputed. They have long been known, but until recently they told us nothing with respect to the origin of man. Now when viewed by the light of our knowledge of the whole organic world, their meaning is unmistakable. The great principle of evolution stands up clear and firm, when these groups or facts are considered in connection with others, such as the mutual affinities of the members of the same group, their geographical distribution in past and present times, and their geological succession. It is incredible that all these facts should speak falsely. He who is not content to look, like a savage, at the phenomena of nature as disconnected, cannot any longer believe that man is the work of a separate act of creation. He will be forced to admit that the close resemblance of the embryo of man to that, for instance, of a dog—the construction of his skull, limbs and whole frame on the same plan with that of other mammals, independently of the uses to which the parts may be put—the occasional reappearance of various structures, for instance of several muscles, which man does not normally possess, but which are common to the Quadrumana—and a crowd of analogous facts—all point in the plainest manner to the conclusion that man is the co-descendant with other mammals of a common progenitor. –Charles Darwin, *The Descent of Man.*

LSAT Prep Questions

1. An antidote for chicken pox has been developed, but researchers warn that its widespread use could be dangerous, despite the fact that this drug has no serious side effects and is currently very effective at limiting the duration and severity of chicken pox.

   Which one of the following, if true, helps most to reconcile the apparent discrepancy indicated above?

   (a) The drug is extremely expensive and would be difficult to make widely available.

   (b) The drug has to be administered several times a day, so patient compliance is likely to be low.

   (c) The drug does not prevent the spread of chicken pox from one person to another, even when the drug eventually cures the disease in the first person.

   (d) When misused by taking larger-than-prescribed doses, the drug can be fatal.

   (e) Use of the drug contributes to the development of deadlier forms of chicken pox that are resistant to the drug.

   Preptest 32, Section 4, Question 17

2. North American eastern white cedars grow both on cliff faces and in forests. Cedars growing on exposed cliff faces receive very few nutrients, and rarely grow bigger than one-tenth the height of cedars growing in forests, where they benefit from moisture and good soil. Yet few eastern white cedars found in forests are as old as four hundred years, while many on cliff faces are more than five hundred years old.

   Which one of the following, if true, most helps to explain the difference in the ages of the cedars on cliff faces and those in forests?

   (a) The conditions on cliff faces are similar to those in most other places where there are few tall trees.

   (b) In areas where white cedars grow, forest fires are relatively frequent, but fires cannot reach cliff faces.

   (c) Trees that are older than a few hundred years start to lose the protective outer layer of their bark.

   (d) The roots of cedars on cliff faces lodge in cracks in the cliff, and once the roots are so large that they fill a crack, the tree is unable to grow any taller.

   (e) Eastern white cedar wood is too soft to be used for firewood for modern buildings, but it is occasionally used to make furniture.

   Preptest 33, Section 3, Question 1

3. Some people claim that the reason herbs are not prescribed as drugs by licensed physicians is that the medical effectiveness of herbs is seriously in doubt. No drug can be offered for sale, however, unless it has regulatory-agency approval for medicinal use in specific illnesses or conditions. It costs about $200 million to get regulatory-agency approval for a drug, and only the holder of a patent can expect to recover such large expenses. Although methods of extracting particular substances from

herbs can be patented, herbs themselves and their medicinal uses cannot be. Therefore, under the current system licensed physicians cannot recommend the medicinal use of herbs.

Which one of the following most accurately describes the argumentative technique used in the argument?

(a) questioning a claim about why something is the case by supplying an alternative explanation

(b) attacking the validity of the data on which a competing claim is based.

(c) revealing an inconsistency in the reasoning used to develop an opposing position

(d) identifying all plausible explanations for why something is the case and arguing that all but one of them can be eliminated

(e) testing a theory by determining the degree to which a specific situation conforms to the predictions of that theory

Preptest 33, Section 3, Question 12

4.3 Scientific Case Studies

Before detailing the criteria for a good explanation, let us examine further scientific applications of hypothetical induction. The abstract description of this form of reasoning is not as helpful as the study of paradigm cases.

The Circulation of the Blood. Anatomy can be studied observationally. An animal's parts can be seen and touched. The study is difficult chiefly because some parts are hidden behind others, and many are too small to be seen by the naked eye. Galen (A.D. 131-201) achieved a basic understanding of human anatomy despite his lack of a microscope and the taboo of his time against human dissection. Given the taboo, Galen was forced to draw analogical conclusions about human anatomy from his dissections of apes, dogs, and pigs. Many of Galen's errors were eliminated, notably by Vesalius (1514-1564), once human dissection became common. The finer structure became known when Malpighi (1628-1694) and Leeuwenhoek (1632-1723) began their microscopic studies. Physiology is more difficult. An organ's function is usually imperceptible. Consider one of the easier cases, namely, the flow of the blood. You cannot just "look and see" how the blood flows, since arteries and veins are opaque. And if you cut them open to see inside, the system ceases to function normally. Indirect methods are therefore necessary. The discovery by William Harvey (1578-1657) of the circulation of the blood, one of the events constituting the Scientific Revolution, provides a good example.

The minute capillaries connecting arteries and veins were not discovered by Malpighi until after Harvey died. So the circulation of the blood could not simply be inferred from the anatomical fact that the blood vessels form a closed loop. Galen theorized that there are two separate systems—the venous carrying bluish blood and the arterial carrying red blood—connected only by a wall (the septum) in the heart. The blood "ebbs and flows" through these systems, powered by the simultaneous contractions of the heart and the arteries, observed as the heart beat and pulse respectively. Galen thought that blood is manufactured in the venous system by the liver from ingested food, that it seeps slowly from the venous side of the heart to the arterial, and that it is absorbed by the tissues. Galen's theory was not questioned until the sixteenth century. Vesalius could not see how blood could seep through the thick septum. Others wondered how blood could flow from the heart to the arteries if both contracted at the same time. The apparently one-way valves in the heart and veins also needed explanation.

Harvey made careful observations of the actions of the heart and arteries, and conducted numerous experiments, to determine how the blood flows. He concluded that the blood is pumped by the contractions of the heart into the arteries, flowing through the arteries to the veins, and through the veins back to the heart. His theory was based on the following data, which it easily explains: (1) If either a vein or an artery is cut, all the blood can be drained rapidly, in about half an hour. This would be impossible if the arterial and venous systems were connected only by the septum. (2) Much more blood passes from the heart to the arteries in a day than could be produced from ingested food. This would be hard to explain on Galen's hypothesis that blood is produced on one end of the system, consumed on the other. (3) The walls of the arteries are thicker than those of the veins, and are thicker closer to the heart. This suggests that the arteries are reinforced to sustain the greater pressure nearer the heart. (4) When the heart contracts, it strikes the chest, causing the audible beat. The pulse, however, is produced by the expansion of the arteries. The fact that the heart beat and pulse are synchronous therefore contradicts Galen's idea that the heart and arteries contract simultaneously, and suggests instead that the blood is pumped from the heart through the arteries. (5) If the arteries coming from the heart are cut, the blood spurts when the heart contracts. This confirms that the blood is pumped from the heart to the arteries. (6) If a ligature around the arm is applied tightly enough, the pulse stops and the veins in the arm empty. If the ligature is loosened just enough to let the pulse resume, the veins below the ligature swell up, while those above remain empty. This indicates that the blood normally travels under pressure from the arteries to the veins. (7) With the loosened ligature, the valves in the veins look like knots. Blood in the veins can be streaked with the finger toward the heart, but not in the other direction. This indicates that the function of the valves is to ensure that the blood flows through the veins in only one direction, toward the heart. (8) If the veins entering the heart are pinched, the heart soon empties. If the arteries leaving the heart are pinched, the heart becomes engorged. This indicates that the blood enters the heart from the veins, to be pumped out through the arteries.

Historically, Harvey was apparently led to the circulation hypothesis to explain how so much blood could pass through the heart. He then thoroughly tested and confirmed his theory by conducting the ligature experiments. His prediction that there are "pores in the flesh" connecting the arteries and veins remained unverified, however, until four years after his death.[14]

The Movement of the Earth. Since the Babylonians, men have observed the heavens and recorded the apparent motions of the stars, the five planets Mercury, Venus, Mars, Jupiter, and Saturn, and the sun and the moon. The stars seem fixed in relation to each other; the Big Dipper, for example, and the constellations of the zodiac, are permanent features of the sky. They all form a sphere that revolves around the earth once a day. The motion of the sun is more complicated. It too moves around the earth once a day with the heavenly sphere. But it also moves in relation to the stars. It moves around the twelve signs of the zodiac once a year, rising with Virgo for a month, then rising with Leo, and so on. This circular path traced out by the sun in the heavenly sphere is called the *ecliptic*. The moon's motion resembles the sun's, except the moon traverses the heavenly sphere once a month. The planets have a much more complicated movement. Mars, for example, revolves around the earth with the heavenly sphere once a day. It also travels around the ecliptic about once every two years. But its motion around the ecliptic does not seem uniform Most of the time it travels in one direction like the sun. But every now and then it seems to stop and move backwards.

---

[14] From William Harvey, *Anatomical Studies of the Motion of the Heart and Blood,* trans. C. D. Leake; Charles C. Thomas, 1970): A. E. E. McKenzie. *The Major Achievements of Science,* vol. I, ch. 4; Jerome J. Bylebyl, "Harvey," *Dictionary of Scientific Biographies,* vol. VI (Charles Scribner's Sons, 1972), pp. 152-58; "William Harvey," *Encyclopaedia Britannica* 15th ed., vol. 8, pp. 660-63.

The ancient Greeks—notably Pythagoras, Plato, and Aristotle—believed for philosophical reasons that the heavenly bodies had to move uniformly in perfect circles. The planets therefore posed a serious theoretical problem. One solution hypothesized something called an *epicycle*. It was proposed that Mars moves around a small circle lying in the plane of the ecliptic several times per year. The center of this circle in turn travels around the ecliptic once a year. The large circle is called a cycle, the small circle an epicycle. Each planet has both a cycle and an epicycle, which accounts for the occasional backward motions of the planets. This, in brief, is the geocentric (earth-centered) system postulated by the ancient Greeks and refined by Ptolemy in the second century A.D. It is depicted in Figure 4-2. The geocentric system enabled astronomers to predict the positions of the heavenly bodies tolerably well, but not exactly. The details of the system were continually revised to improve its accuracy.

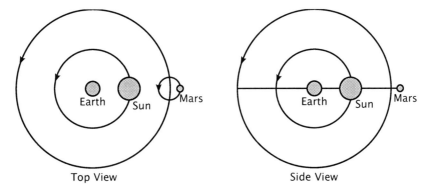

FIGURE 4-2: THE GEOCENTRIC OR PTOLEMAIC SYSTEM

Copernicus (1473-1543) proposed a revolutionary simplification. First, he accounted for the apparent daily revolution of the entire heavenly sphere by postulating that the earth revolved around its axis daily, the stars remaining fixed. This was more plausible, he thought, than that all the stars whipped around the earth at incredible velocities. He explained away our failure to notice the rotation of the earth by supposing that we and the atmosphere are carried around with it. Second, Copernicus accounted for the motion of the sun and the moon by supposing that the earth revolves around the sun once a year, and the moon around the earth once a month. The planets also move around the sun, he postulated. Mars appears to move backwards when it is nearest the earth, because the earth is revolving faster. Copernicus was thus able to dispense with the epicycles of Ptolemy. Copernicus's heliocentric (sun-centered) system also accounted for something unexplained by the geocentric system—namely, the significant changes in apparent brightness of the planets.

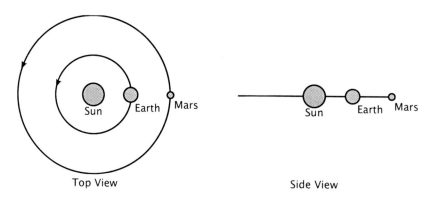

Top View   Side View

FIGURE 4-3: THE HELIOCENTRIC OR COPERNICAN SYSTEM

Mars is brightest when closest to the earth, dimmest when on the opposite side of the sun. The heliocentric system is depicted in Figure 4-3.

Copernicus was never able to account well for the exact positions of the planets without resorting to epicycles or similar devices himself. It was left to Kepler (1571-1630) to refine the system. Copernicus had assumed, like the Greeks, that the planets move uniformly in circular orbits. Kepler showed that the position of Mars could be accounted for within the limits of accuracy of the available observations by assuming that its orbit is elliptical instead of circular.[15]

Gravitation and Neptune. Ptolemy and Copernicus sought to explain the apparent motions of the heavenly bodies by constructing hypotheses about their actual motions. Neither tried to explain the actual motions, however. Kepler thought that the sun caused the motion, but it was Isaac Newton (1642-1727) who postulated that the planets move because of the gravitational force of the sun, the same force that makes apples fall on earth. Newton was able to deduce Kepler's law that the planets have approximately elliptical orbits from his own law of universal gravitation, which states that all objects attract each other with a gravitational force proportional to their masses and inversely proportional to the square of the distance between them. Newton's law also predicted, though, that the orbit of a planet would be perfectly elliptical only if the sun were the only gravitational force acting on it. Since planets act on each other, their orbits should deviate slightly from perfect ellipses. Such deviations are called *perturbations*. Advances after Kepler, notably the telescope, enabled astronomers to detect these perturbations. The fact that the law of gravitation explained Kepler's generalization and the observed perturbations of the planets better than any other theory constituted a significant part of the inductive support for Newton's theory. Support also came from the theory's ability to explain Galileo's generalization that objects fall at the surface of the earth with an acceleration of 32 feet per second squared.

In 1781, William Herschel discovered a seventh planet, Uranus. Astronomers immediately began to calculate its orbit, a difficult task since Uranus takes 84 years to revolve around the sun. By 1840 it was clear that the perturbations of Uranus's orbit significantly exceeded what could be accounted for by the actions of Saturn and Jupiter in accordance with the law of gravitation. Numerous hypotheses were advanced to explain the perturbations of Uranus. Some proposed that the law of gravitation broke down at such distances from the sun; but Newton's theory had so much support that this idea was not taken very seriously. Others suggested that Uranus had a massive undiscovered satellite; but it was

[15] From A.E.E. McKenzie, *The Major Achievements of Science*, vol. I ch. 2; J. L. E. Dreyer, *A History of Astronomy from Thales to Kepler*, 2nd ed. (Denver 1953), chs. VII, IX, XII-XVI.

shown that such a satellite would cause perturbations quite different from those observed. Scientists and mathematicians concentrated on a third theory, that there was an unknown planet acting on Uranus. Within a few years, the theory was established as probable when John Couch Adams and Urbain Le Verrier showed independently that, given reasonable assumptions about its mass and orbit, an eighth planet would account quite accurately for the perturbations of Uranus. Both predicted where this planet could be observed in the heavens, and how it would appear in a telescope. In 1846, Le Verrier persuaded Johann Galle to search for the planet. On the first night, Galle observed a moving object remarkably close in position and appearance to that predicted by Adams and Le Verrier, and the theory was conclusively established. The new planet was named Neptune.[16]

Continental Drift. Our next example comes from geology. There are two opposing theories about the evolution of the earth's crust. The traditional view was that the continents are at rest relative to one another, and that they developed in their current positions. This seems the obvious theory, since the continents do not appear to move, and since it is hard to imagine forces great enough to move such massive objects resting on material as hard as the mantle. In 1912, however, Alfred Wegener proposed that the continents were originally joined together, and began drifting apart hundreds of millions of years ago. Their apparent lack of motion could be explained away, since movement as slight as a few centimeters a year over so many years would account for the current positions of the continents, and would be imperceptible. Moreover, the continental drift theory easily explained an amazing variety of data difficult to explain on the opposing continental fixity theory.

Here is but a small sampling of the evidence for continental drift: (1) There is a remarkable fit between the shorelines of eastern South America and southwestern Africa, and a similar fit between the continental shelves of eastern North America and northwestern Africa and Europe. The map that results when the continents are fit together in this way is called the *predrift map*. (2) Massive two-billion-year-old rock formations in eastern South America and southwestern Africa have the same mineral composition, and fit together on the predrift map to form one continuous formation. Similarly, the Appalachian Mountains of the United States, formed over 250 million years ago, form a continuous folded chain on the predrift map with the mountains of Scotland and Scandinavia, which are of the same age and geological type. (3) Fossils of a reptile called Mesosaurus are found only in similar South American and African rock formations, adjoining on the predrift map but currently separated by 3,000 miles of ocean. Mesosaurus was adapted to shallow inland waters, not the deep sea. In general, the fossil record shows that the land animals of South America and Africa, once very similar, have been diverging over the last 100 million years or so. (4) While some rocks in South America and Africa are billions of years old, the oldest marine sediments and rocks from the Atlantic floor are only about 200 million years old. Furthermore, the age of these sediments and rocks increases as their distance from the mid-Atlantic ridge increases. This suggests that new sea floor is being created at the ridge as the older sea floor and the continents spread apart. (5) It is known that when molten rock cools, it records the polarity of the earth's magnetic field. It is also known that the polarity of the earth's field has reversed several times in the last 4 million years. When the polarity recorded in the Atlantic sea floor is mapped, a striped pattern emerges paralleling the ridge, which also indicates sea floor spreading. (6) The western edge of North and South America, which would be colliding with the crustal plate under the eastern Pacific, is bounded by a continuous folded mountain range formed less than 200 million years ago, and is a zone of frequent earthquakes and vulcanism. There is a similar chain of mountains in southern Europe, where Africa and Europe would be colliding.

---

[16] From A. E. E. McKenzie, The Major Achievements of Science, vol. 1, ch. 3; M. Grosser, *The Discovery of Neptune* (Harvard University Press, 1962); W. G. Hoyt, *Planets X and Pluto* (University of Arizona Press, 1980), chs. 1-2.

Since the opposing theory cannot explain facts like these nearly as well, the continental drift hypothesis is today generally accepted as true.[17]

Evolution. Hypothetical induction has also been used to determine the origin of animal species. In 1859, Charles Darwin published *On the Origin of Species,* in which he argued that animal species evolved by natural selection. Darwin's hypothesis had two principal competitors. Lamarck had earlier proposed that complex animals evolved from primitive organisms, but by a different mechanism. According to Lamarck a living being acquires many characteristics as it adapts to its environment; it then passes these characteristics on to its offspring. Lamarck's theory was soon dismissed because acquired traits (like a weight lifter's muscles or a soprano's ability to sing the "The Star Spangled Banner") are not inherited. Darwin's major competitor was the theory of special creation, which had the weight of tradition, religion, and strong social sanctions on its side. According to special creation, the species did not evolve. Rather, a divine being created all species as they are found today.

The theory of special creation provided the simplest explanation of why cats and dogs and other living beings had not been observed to evolve over the long period of human history. But the theory of evolution could also explain the failure to observe evolution, since the changes it postulated occurred ever so slowly over millions or even billions of years. Both theories could account for the remarkable adaptation of living things to their environments. Examples of such adaptation include the fact that freshwater fish are generally incapable of surviving in salt water, while saltwater fish perish in fresh water. On a smaller scale, the ears of carnivorous animals like wolves face forward, while those of rabbits and the other herbivorous animals they pursue face backward. According to the theory of special creation, such adaptation exists because the creator knew the environment the species was intended for, and designed the species to survive there. According to the theory of evolution by natural selection, the species we observe are adapted to their environments simply because species that were not adapted died out. Within any species, many more offspring are born than live to reproduce, so there is a constant natural selection of survivors. Evolution occurs because there is a natural variation in inherited traits, even within a single species. Traits that enable organisms to leave more offspring become more common. Variation is now known to result from mutation and the shuffling of genes involved in sexual reproduction.

There are many facts that only the theory of evolution by natural selection can account for. For one, there is the occurrence of homologous and analogous organs. *Homologous organs* have essentially the same internal structure but radically different functions. For example, the arm of a man, the wing of a bat, the front leg of a horse, and the paddle of a porpoise are made up of similar bones in the same relative positions. *Analogous organs* have essentially the same function, but radically different internal structures. The wing of a bat is very different internally from that of an insect, yet both enable flight. The theory of evolution can explain homologous organs as resulting from a common ancestor evolving in different environments. Analogous organs would result from different ancestors evolving in a common environment. It is hard to understand, on the other hand, why a divine creator would use the same structure for different functions in some cases, and different structures for the same function in others.

The theory of special creation also fails to explain the existence of extinct species or degenerate organs. Fossils show that the number of extinct species is about 100 times greater than the number of surviving species. But if all species have been designed to survive, why have so many died out? Extinction is expected on the theory of evolution when the environment changes significantly or when other species evolve more successfully. Degenerate organs, like the wing of the flightless ostrich, are

[17] From "Continental Drift," *Encyclopaedia Britannica,* 15th ed.. vol. 5, pp. 108-14; J. Tuzo Wilson, ed., *Continents Adrift and Continents Aground: Readings from "Scientific American"* (W. H. Freeman and Co., 1976).

also harder to explain if each species has been designed and created than if species with degenerate organs have evolved from species in which those organs were functional.

The most important evidence for evolution is the fossil record, which contains many series of species ancestral to existing species, as well as many series terminating in extinction. One series of fossils, for example, shows the development of the elephant's trunk. Another shows the development of the horse. Of particular significance is the fact that structural differences in ancestral species are correlated with environmental differences. About 65 million years ago, for example, the ancestors of today's horses lived in a swampy environment, with abundant vegetation and leafy plants. These ancestors (Hyracotherium) had feet with four toes (less likely to sink in mud than the hooves of modern horses) and short teeth (adequate for eating soft leaves). By 20 million years ago, the climate had become much drier. The vegetation was now largely grass, which is abrasive to teeth The horse's ancestors (Merychippus) at this time developed long, high-crowned teeth, which grew continuously. The toes in the feet were gradually replaced by a hoof, better suited to running on hard dry ground.[18] Finally, fossils show the general order of evolution: invertebrates appear hundreds of millions of years before fish, which are followed by amphibians, reptiles, birds, and mammals in that order.[19]

4.4 Criteria For Evaluating Explanations

Hypothetical induction concludes that a hypothesis is true given that it is part of the best explanation of the data. The strength of such an argument depends on how good the explanation is and how much better it is than competing explanations. The principle difficulty in applying the method lies in evaluating explanations. Part of the problem is practical: massive amounts of data and complex mathematical hypotheses must often be manipulated. But the main problem is theoretical: there are no known rules or formulas that can be mechanically applied to select the best explanation. The evaluation of explanations is still largely an art, whose finest practitioners are scientists and detectives. We can, however, isolate several criteria for evaluating explanations. We shall focus on **consistency, completeness, simplicity, direct support,** and **confirmability.** Each criterion is complex, comprising two or more closely related factors. All vary quantitatively, and the quality of an explanation is directly related to each of them. Other things equal, the more consistent, complete, simple, directly supported, or confirmable an explanation is, the better it is.

Consistency. Two kinds of consistency are important for evaluating hypotheses: *internal consistency* and *consistency with previously established facts.* A theory is internally consistent if it is not self-contradictory. A self-contradictory theory cannot possibly be true and must therefore be dismissed. The Pinkerton agency, for example, provided strong evidence that Franssen murdered Bohner. But the jury also had some evidence that Franssen did not kill Bohner—namely, Franssen's own claim of innocence. The jury undoubtedly gave little consideration to the hypothesis that Franssen both did and did not kill Bohner. Any consistent hypothesis would better explain the data than this impossibility. Hypotheses so obviously inconsistent never get proposed, fortunately. But occasionally a complex and mathematically intricate theory is shown to entail a contradiction, and thereby suffers the worst form of refutation. We will study the concept of self-contradiction in the chapters on deduction.

A good explanation must also be consistent with established facts, which means that it must not contradict them. *Established facts* should be understood as including proven theories as well as observational evidence. A theory inconsistent with known facts of any kind must also be dismissed as

[18] "Evolution," *Encyclopaedia Britannica,* 15th ed., vol. 7, p. 13.
[19] From A. E. E. McKenzie, *The Major Achievements* of *Science,* vol. I chs. 16 and 19; G. G. Simpson, *The Meaning of Evolution (*Yale University Press, 1967); "Evolution," *Encyclopaedia Britannica,* 15th ed., vol. 7, pp. 7-23.

false. Aristotle's principle that heavenly bodies are unchangeable was consistent with known facts until Galileo observed the eruption of sunspots. Galen's theory of the flow of blood was contradicted when it was found that the heart and the arteries did not contract simultaneously. Hegel's principle that there can at most be seven planets became incompatible with known facts when Neptune, the eighth planet, was discovered. Lamarck's theory of evolution was inconsistent with the fact that traits acquired as a result of use or disuse are not passed on to offspring. These theories all took their place on the scientific scrap heap.

Consistency is the only one of our five criteria that is *essential* for a good explanation. A good explanation may be incomplete, complex, lacking in direct support, or unconfirmable, but it must not be inconsistent. One theory may be better than another because it is more consistent, containing fewer internal contradictions or contradicting fewer known facts; but even the slightest inconsistency means the explanation is inadequate.

There are two complications: First, special care must be taken with numerical data. It is a well-known fact that measuring devices and procedures are inaccurate to some extent. The numbers recording the results of measurement must therefore always be interpreted as approximations or intervals. Suppose a theory predicts that a certain object should weigh 29.61 pounds, say. But the scale reads 29.63 pounds. We must not yet conclude that the theory is incompatible with the data. If the scale is only accurate to one-tenth of a pound, then the theory is quite consistent with the data. For 29.63 and 29.61 differ by considerably less than a tenth. On the other hand, if the scale is accurate to one-hundredth of a pound, then the theory must be rejected.

Second, recall that the data is what is accepted as previously established fact. If a theory is inconsistent with the data, then we know that they cannot both be true. In that case, the theory is usually rejected. There is always the possibility, however, that mistakes were made in gathering the data, so that what is thought to have been established as fact really is not a fact at all. So occasionally when a theory is incompatible with the data, the data should be rejected and not the theory. For example, in 1666 Newton tested his theory of gravitation by examining the orbit of the moon. From the orbit, he calculated that the moon "falls" toward the earth about 16 feet in a minute. In order to derive the moon's fall from his law of gravitation, Newton needed the circumference of the earth. He used the figure available at the time, about 20,500 miles. The derivation then produced a fall of about 13 feet in a minute, a substantial discrepancy. Newton tentatively concluded that some other force must be acting on the moon in addition to gravity, and he set aside his theory for about twenty years. A considerably more accurate estimate of about 23,700 miles was by then available for the earth's circumference, which produced a satisfactory figure for the fall of the moon.[20] (The actual circumference is now known to be about 24,900 miles.) When a theory becomes firmly established, it can actually be used as a test of the data. Newton had just discovered the law of gravitation in 1666, so he did not yet have much confidence in it. Today, the law is so firmly established it is used to check the accuracy of past astronomical observations. The actual positions of the heavenly bodies are calculated using the law, and then compared to the reported positions.

Completeness (Explanatory Power). While consistency is essential for an adequate explanation, it is hardly sufficient. The hypothesis that there are amoebas in other solar systems is fully consistent both internally and with all known facts. But it is obviously not an adequate explanation, say, of the perturbations of Neptune. Adequate explanations must be *relevant*. They must also be *noncircular*. The hypothesis that opium has the dormitive virtue is consistent with the fact that opium produces sleep. But that hypothesis does not explain *why* opium produces sleep, since it merely restates the

---

[20] This account is based on John Herival's *The Background to Newton's "Principia"* (Oxford, 1965), ch. 4.

data to be explained: "has the dormitive virtue" is an inflated way of saying "produces sleep." "Opium produces sleep because it has the dormitive virtue" is therefore a circular explanation. Neither irrelevant hypotheses nor restatements of the data have any explanatory power.

Next to consistency, the most important criterion for evaluating a hypothesis is how much explanatory power it has, or equivalently, how completely it explains the data. Completeness depends on two independent variables: First, an explanation may explain all or only part of the data. We shall refer to this variable as **breadth of scope**. An explanation is said to have within its scope the data it explains. The greater the amount of data it explains, the broader its scope is said to be. Suppose John has a fever, a sore throat, and a stuffy nose. Then consider the following hypotheses: he has a cold; he has strep throat; he has high blood pressure. The cold hypothesis explains all three symptoms, and is therefore complete in scope. The strep throat hypothesis fails to explain the stuffy nose, so its scope is narrower. The high blood pressure hypothesis explains none of the symptoms, so it has no scope at all. Second, an explanation may state all of the factors needed to explain the data, or only some of them. This variable we shall call **depth**. None of our three hypotheses explains any of John's symptoms in complete depth. A cold, for example, does not invariably produce a fever. So some additional factors would be necessary to completely account for John's fever. As long as we are ignorant of those factors, we will wonder why John has a fever this time while with other colds he did not have a fever. A complete explanation must explain all the data and state all the explanatory factors: it must be complete in breadth of scope and in depth. The more complete an explanation is in either respect, the better it is.

Suppose a pot of water boils because, we are told, it was heated to 212°F. This may be the correct explanation, but it is not complete in depth. There are several other explanatory factors, including the fact that the water was at sea level, that the water was pure, and that the boiling point of pure water at sea level is 212°F. So a more complete explanation would be that the water boiled because of all these facts. In everyday life, we seldom if ever give complete explanations. Even in science, we find a gradient of completeness. Explanations in the natural sciences like physics and chemistry tend to be more complete than those in the social sciences like psychology and sociology. Explanations in biology and economics fall somewhere in between. The ability to give complete explanations depends on knowledge of general laws specifying verifiable conditions under which the phenomena to be explained invariably occur. Such laws are common in physics, rare in psychology.

While the completeness, and therefore the quality, of an explanation depend on it, depth is generally not important in applications of hypothetical induction. For to infer by hypothetical induction that h is true, all we need to know is that h is *part of* the best complete explanation of the data. The condition of validity requires that h be the best of all *competing* explanations; but a complete explanation does not compete with its parts. Consequently, we can infer that h is true without considering depth as long as the explanation provided by h can in principle be completed to at least the same depth as competing explanations. If this assumption is dubious, it will also be dubious that h even partly explains the data. Note that it is possible to establish that h is part of the best complete explanation of the data without knowing precisely what the best complete explanation is. The hypothesis of a planet beyond Uranus, for example, does not all by itself completely explain the perturbations of Uranus. The distance of the postulated planet from the sun and its mass must also be known. Both Adams and Le Verrier selected a most likely mass and distance, but their calculations showed that within certain limits, a greater mass could be hypothesized as long as an appropriately greater distance was assumed.

Breadth of scope is therefore the relevant aspect of completeness for hypothetical induction. Irrelevant hypotheses and circular explanations have no scope, and therefore will never provide the best explanation of the data. A theory inconsistent with part of the data is necessarily limited in scope, for the theory fails to explain that part of the data it contradicts. But unlike inconsistency with previously established facts, mere failure to explain part of the data is not a fatal defect. A theory with limited scope might still be the best explanation of the data, because it explains more than its competitors.

Harvey's theory of the blood flow was superior to Galen's primarily in explanatory power. Both Galen's theory and Harvey's explained the simultaneity of the heart beat and the pulse, and the fact that both the venous and the arterial systems could be drained by cutting a vessel in either system. But only Harvey's theory could explain how quickly both systems could be drained, how the blood flowed from the heart to the arteries, how so much blood could pass through the heart each day, how the valves functioned, and so on. The chief strength of Newton's theory of universal gravitation was its amazing breadth. The theory explained Kepler's laws of planetary motion, Galileo's law of free fall on earth, the orbit of the moon, the paths of comets, the action of the tides, the flattened shape of the earth, and the wobble of the earth's axis. (It is hard for us in the twentieth century to appreciate Newton's achievement; for as a result of his influence, these phenomena seem much more closely related than they did to Newton's predecessors.) The only real competitor was Descartes' theory that the planets moved because of vortices in the aether. But as Newton showed, this theory did not even adequately explain Kepler's laws. We saw that continental drift is accepted because it explains a broad range of data difficult to explain assuming fixity, such as the fit of the shorelines, rock formations, and fossils of eastern South America and western Africa, the relatively young age of sediments on the Atlantic floor, the striped pattern of magnetic polarity in the Atlantic floor, and the mountains and earthquakes on the west coast of the Americas. Darwin's theory of evolution by natural selection is superior in breadth of scope to the competing theory of special creation. Both theories explain the failure to observe evolution and the adaptation of species to their environments. But only evolution explains homologous and analogous organs, extinct species, and, most important, the fossil record.

Simplicity. Theories comparable in explanatory power often differ markedly in simplicity. The simplest theory postulates the fewest number of things and principles and the least amount of difference and variation. Simplicity, therefore, requires *economy* and *uniformity*. Suppose a cat walks into the shed, and a few seconds later an apparently identical cat walks out. There are two hypotheses to consider: the same cat walked out of the shed; a different but indistinguishable cat walked out. Both hypotheses are consistent, and both account for what was observed. But the first is simpler. It is more economical because it postulates one cat rather than two, and more uniform because it postulates that the similar appearances were of the same cat rather than different cats. Other things equal, the simplest theory is the best. So without further evidence, we should infer that the same cat walked out as walked in.

When other things are not equal, the more complex theory may be better. For example, Dalton hypothesized that all atoms of the same element have the same weight. Another hypothesis, however, explained the same data—namely, that atoms of the same element differ slightly but have the same *average* weight in any sample. Dalton's simpler hypothesis was accepted until 1912, when J. J. Thomson discovered isotopes. One experiment showed that while most neon atoms have an atomic weight of 20, some have a weight of 22. The chemically established weight of 20.2 proved to be the average weight of neon atoms in any sample.

The principle that, other things equal, the simplest theory is to be preferred to more complex theories has come to be known as *Ockham's razor,* after the fourteenth-century British philosopher William of Ockham, who made frequent use of it to eliminate pseudoexplanatory entities. One formulation of Ockham's razor says, "Entities are not to be multiplied beyond necessity." Another says, "Plurality is not to be assumed without necessity." Newton formulated similar "rules of reasoning" in his *Principia,* the great work which presented the law of gravitation and revolutionized physics. Rule I is a principle of economy: "We are to admit no more causes of natural things than such as are both true and sufficient to explain their appearances." Rule II is a principle of uniformity: To the same natural effects we must, as far as possible, assign the same causes. His other rules basically formulate enumerative induction.

Economy contributes to uniformity. That is, a theory postulating three different things rather than four, say, or two different principles rather than three, ascribes less difference and variation to the world.

So the simplicity criterion essentially says that wherever possible we should *select that theory which attributes the greatest uniformity to nature*. Indeed, the simplicity criterion represents a generalization of the argument from analogy and enumerative induction. These lead us to infer that unobserved objects are like observed objects, which postulates greater uniformity than the hypothesis that unobserved objects are different from observed objects.

Hypothetical induction allows us to infer that the best explanation of the data is true. The simplicity criterion guarantees that the best explanation has only *essential* parts. This is important; for consider the rather bizarre theory that there is a planet beyond Uranus *and* some amoebas in other solar systems, This does explain the perturbations of Uranus, so you might think we could infer that there are amoebas in other solar systems. That would make quite a mockery of hypothetical induction! Fortunately, there is a better explanation of the Uranian perturbations—the hypothesis that there is a planet beyond Uranus *simpliciter.* Dropping inessential parts will always simplify a theory and produce a better explanation.

Simplicity guides the process of curve fitting. Suppose an engineer has developed a new treatment for hardening steel, which can be applied for any amount of time. The engineer will naturally want to know how the hardness of the treated steel is related to the length of time the treatment is applied. This will enable him to select a treatment period that is optimal, considering both cost and performance. The engineer will select a range of treatment times for testing—say, 5, 10, 15, and 20 minutes. Suppose steel treated for these periods has a hardness of 1, 2, 3, and 4, respectively, on an appropriate scale of hardness. Graphing these results, we get Figure 4-4.

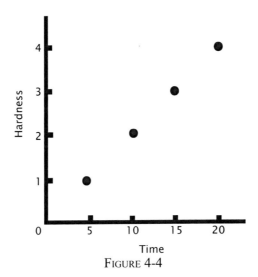

FIGURE 4-4

The engineer, of course, will generalize this limited data. He will draw a curve representing the general relationship between hardness and treatment time. Assuming the measurements have been made with perfect accuracy, the curve must be drawn through the four data points obtained, otherwise the hypothesis will not explain the data. But infinitely many curves can be drawn through these four points. Two are graphed in Figure 4-5.

Which curve is the engineer to choose? The simplest one, which in this case is the straight line. More data may confirm or disconfirm this choice, but no matter how many experiments are performed, there will always be a choice of curves. For a finite number of points can always be connected by an infinite number of curves. In general, scientists try to select a smooth curve as close as possible to a straight line. Such a curve represents the least amount of difference and variation, and is therefore the simplest.

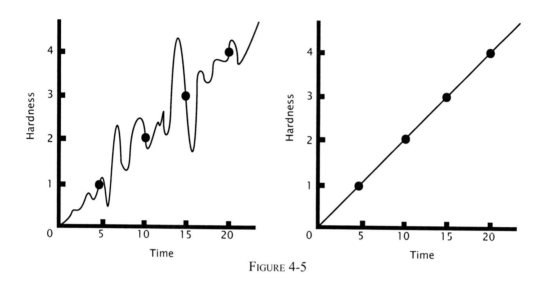

FIGURE 4-5

Actually, the curve selected does not even have to pass through the data points. For as noted earlier, all measurement is inaccurate to some extent. So it is proper to attribute some of the variation in the data points to measurement error. Suppose our engineer conducts many more experiments, obtaining the data points plotted in Figure 4-6. The engineer may still draw a straight line through the points. He would then be explaining the data in terms of two hypotheses: first, that hardness is linearly related to time; and second, that the measurements were inaccurate to a certain extent. This explanation would still be simpler than that represented by a very rough line drawn through all the data points. A variety of statistical techniques exist for selecting the best-fitting line in such cases. One is the method of least squares.

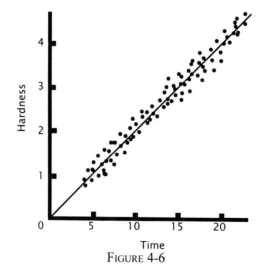

FIGURE 4-6

Simplicity was a major advantage of the Copernican system over the Ptolemaic. The Copernican system did have slightly greater explanatory power, since it accounted for the changes in apparent brightness of the planets. But it was far more economical and uniform to have the earth revolve around its axis once a day than to have all the heavenly bodies revolve around the earth once a day. And by having the earth move around the sun like the planets, the Copernican system (perfected by Kepler) could dispense with the epicycles that complicated the Ptolemaic system.

Explanatory power is the major advantage of continental drift theory, but simplicity favors it too. Some of the strongest pieces of evidence are rock formations called the Gondwana tillites.

> The name comes from the typical locality in peninsular India of a highly distinctive series of flat-lying strata, about 20,000 feet thick, ranging in age from Late Pennsylvanian to Early Cretaceous (about 290,000,000 to 130,000,000 years old). The basal bed of the series is a thick tillite, indicating extensive and prolonged continental glaciation. Overlying the tillite are thousands of feet of sandstone, shales, and clay ironstones of predominantly continental origin, interbedded with minor marine deposits and thick seams of coal. Capping the sediments are massive flows of basalt. This succession, the Gondwana System, has counterparts in six landmasses of the Southern Hemisphere: Africa, South America, the Falkland Islands, Madagascar, Antarctica, and Australia…. The overall resemblances of the Gondwana-type sediments demonstrate clearly that seven landmasses, new separated by oceans and distributed over 120' of latitude, had remarkably similar histories from the Late Paleozoic into the Cretaceous. Nothing resembling the Gondwana record has been found in the Northern Hemisphere except in India. While glacial tillites were being deposited at sea level on lands now straddling the equator, the northern continents were free of continental ice caps. This pattern is so unlikely as to force a choice between continental fixity with extreme irregularity of climate and continental drift with climatic zoning based on latitude. The latter choice seems the more reasonable.[21]

The argument here is based primarily on uniformity. The drift theory postulates that one series of geological events caused all the Gondwana tillites which are now widely scattered. The fixity theory must postulate separate though similar causes for the tillites in India, the Falkland Islands, and the rest.

We saw above that the drift theory was more complete because it could explain how fossils of Mesosaurus, which inhabited inland waters, could be found in South American and African rock formations currently separated by 3,000 miles of ocean. The fixity theory could explain this, we may now note, but only if it is complicated by additional hypotheses. Many fixity theorists, for example, postulated land bridges rising from and then sinking back into the oceans. An incomplete theory can often be completed by adding a patch-work of subsidiary hypotheses. But the gain in completeness may be offset by the loss of simplicity.

Direct Support. In §4.2 we said that hypothetical induction is indirect reasoning, whereas the argument from authority, the argument from analogy, enumerative induction, causal induction, and deductive arguments generally, are direct. We shall say that the conclusion of a direct argument is *directly supported* by the premises, and that the conclusion of an indirect argument is *indirectly supported* by the premises, as long as the premises in either case provide at least some reason to believe the conclusion. Thus the fact that all observed emeralds are green directly supports the conclusion that all emeralds are green, while the fact that all specimens of any compound possess the same composition by weight is indirect support for the conclusion that there are atoms. Note that whereas the premises of an argument *establish* the conclusion (i.e., the argument is sound) only if they provide *sufficient* reason to believe it, the premises of an argument may be said to *support* the conclusion as long as they provide *some* reason to believe it. Thus the premise of a hasty generalization or a *post hoc* argument supports the conclusion even though the argument is fallacious due to insufficient evidence.

---

[21] "Continental Drift," *Encyclopaedia Britannica*, 15th ed., vol. 5, p 111.

Since a given proposition may be a premise in more than one argument, it may support a conclusion both directly and indirectly. Suppose an object looks green. You might think we could infer that the object is green without any further premise, but several possibilities need to be ruled out. Are we looking at a white object through green sunglasses? or in green light? or do we have an unusual form of color blindness in which everything looks light or dark green? We might therefore reason by analogy: "This object looks green. All other objects that look green in these circumstances are green. Therefore, this object is green." But we might equally well reason indirectly: "This object looks green. The hypothesis that this object is green would best explain why it looks green. Therefore, this object is green." Assuming both arguments are sound, the premise that this object looks green supports the conclusion that it is green both directly and indirectly.

We are discussing the criteria that determine which of all competing explanations is the best. Besides consistency, completeness, and simplicity, the quality of an explanation depends on how much direct support it has. The more direct support there is for the *truth* of a given explanation, the more *plausible* it is, and therefore the better it is. The Golden Age of Geology occurred when geologists accepted a principle called *uniformitarianism* advocated by James Hutton (1726-1797) and Charles Lyell (1797-1875). "No powers are to be employed," Hutton said, "that are not natural to the globe, no action to be admitted to except those of which we know the principle, and no extraordinary events to be alleged in order to explain a common appearance." This was in part a principle of uniformity; but it was mainly a principle of direct support, for it requires that the causes invoked to explain past events should as far as possible be causes known to operate in the present. In the early 1880s, geologists were puzzled by huge boulders found high in the Jura Mountains; they were formed of rock similar to that in the Alps but unlike that in the Jura. These boulders were explained by one eminent geologist as the result of a "frightful convulsion" in the Alps, which hurled the boulders across the Geneva valley. This explanation had no direct support, for no such convulsion had ever been observed. An alternative explanation compatible with uniformitarianism was provided by an Alpine hunter, who suggested that the Jura boulders had been transported by glaciers extending down from the Alps. He had noticed large boulders being transported by existing glaciers in the Alps, which provided direct support for his theory.[22]

Direct support may be *authoritative, analogical, correlational, observational,* or *theoretical.* That is, the elements of an explanation may be directly supported by deduction from observations or previously established theories or by induction from similar phenomena, correlations, or authoritative testimony. What is to be supported, more precisely, is the claim that h is part of the correct explanation of d. This can be accomplished by supporting the truth of h itself, or the claim that h would, if true, explain d. It can also be accomplished by supporting the components of h if h is a complex theory consisting of a number of different hypotheses, or by supporting auxiliary hypotheses if h is only part of the proposed explanation of d. Direct support may be *negative* as well as *positive.* That is, there may be direct support *against* the elements of an explanation as well as *for* them. A piece of evidence provides support against an explanation if it provides support for a competing explanation. Naturally, as negative support increases, the plausibility of an explanation decreases. Note that inconsistency with previously established facts is a special case of negative support. It is conclusive observational or theoretical support against the theory. Always remember that evidence may support a hypothesis even though the evidence is not sufficient on its own to establish the hypothesis.

Let us return to the Edgewood mystery. Pinkerton's detectives hypothesized that Franssen was Bohner's murderer in order to explain a large body of circumstantial evidence, such as the clothing Franssen had in his possession. The explanation would have been even more plausible if the Pinkertons had had some direct evidence. There would have been observational support for the hypothesis if someone had seen Franssen strike and kill Bohner. Franssen's confession would have been authoritative

---

[22] A. E. E. McKenzie, *The Major Achievements of Science,* vol. I pp. 111-21.

support; his denials were negative support. Analogical support would have existed if Franssen had killed several other people with a blunt instrument and then taken their clothes. The theory would have had theoretical support if the detectives had had reason to believe that Franssen would kill anyone he was jealous of. Absence of motive or opportunity would have been negative support.

In the previous illustration, the explanation of *d* by *h* was made more plausible by supporting *h*. The explanation's plausibility can also be increased by supporting the claim that *h* would explain *d* if *h* were true. Both *h* and *d* may be true even though *h* does not explain *d*, as our previous discussion of *post hoc* reasoning should make us realize. So the plausibility of *h* as an explanation of *d* does not depend solely on the plausibility of *h*. Thus, many were skeptical of Harvey's claim that the pulse of the arteries was due to the contraction of the heart. So he supported this claim analogically, by blowing into a glove, whereupon the fingers all expanded simultaneously.

As noted earlier, an explanation complete in depth generally involves numerous explanatory factors. An explanation can be made more plausible by finding direct support for any of them. For example, the hypothesis of a planet beyond Uranus did not in itself completely explain the perturbations of Uranus. Additional hypotheses were required concerning the orbit and mass of the transuranian planet. There was little direct support for the existence of the transuranian planet until it was observed by Galle. There was considerable direct support, however, for the subsidiary hypotheses. Both Le Verrier and Adams assumed that the orbit of the hypothesized planet would be elliptical. This had conclusive theoretical support, since it followed from Newton's law of gravitation. Both also postulated that the plane of the new planet's orbit would be about the same as that of all the other planets. The orbital planes of the other planets, therefore, provided analogical support for the hypothesized plane of the new planet. Adams and Le Verrier postulated in addition that the new planet would be about twice as far from the sun as Uranus. This was supported by Bode's law (discussed in §3.3). Adams went so far as to derive the orbit of the new planet exclusively from the observed perturbations of Uranus and the law of gravitation, proving that the hypothesized orbit had a strong combination of theoretical and observational support. Note that the hypothesized orbit was directly supported by the data because the orbit could be deduced from the data. In contrast the hypothesized orbit was indirectly supported by the data because the data could be deduced from the hypothesized orbit.

When Darwin first proposed the theory of evolution, little direct evidence existed for either natural selection or divine creation. The word of the Bible was often cited in favor of divine creation. But the authority of the Bible in a scientific matter was questionable. The unknown individuals who originally formulated the Biblical account of the origin of the species were not biologists, nor were they eyewitnesses to creation. Moreover, there was no objective reason to think that they were in a better position to know about the origin of the species than the authors of, say, the Greek myths. There was some direct support for the theory of special creation, though—namely, the strong resemblance between living things and man-made objects. Both horses and locomotives, for example, are capable of functioning in their environments; and both are complex objects whose parts have a function, and a structure enabling them to fulfill that function. Since man-made objects were created, there is analogical support for the claim that living beings were created too. But counterbalancing this, Darwin could point to the analogy of artificial selection. Animal breeders had known for centuries that new breeds, like the Clydesdale horses, could be developed by selecting which animals would leave offspring. Natural selection operates similarly, except that nature, as it were, does the selecting. Since artificial selection produces new breeds, there is analogical support for the claim that natural selection produces new species.

When Darwin wrote, no one had ever observed either divine creation or evolution by natural selection. Once scientists knew what to look for, however, evolution was observed. For example, a species of light moths living in England evolved into a species of dark moths in many industrial areas as the trees became blackened with soot. Black moths occasionally resulted from a mutation, but were quickly suppressed in unpolluted areas, where observation of feeding birds has shown the survival rate of the conspicuous black moths to be 17 percent worse than grey moths. But in polluted areas, where black moths are inconspicuous, the grey moths have a 10 percent worse survival rate, and eventually disappear. "Industrial melanism," as such evolution is called, has been observed in nearly 100 species of insects and spiders. The use of pesticides and antibiotics has resulted in similar evolutionary changes. New strains of DDT-resistant mosquitoes have evolved, as well as penicillin-resistant streptococci. The number of species in which evolution has been observed may be relatively small, and the changes observed slight, but such observations do constitute direct support for the theory of evolution by natural selection.

Confirmability. A theory or hypothesis need not have direct support in order to provide a good explanation of the data. Atomic theory, for example provided the best explanation of several chemical generalizations, even though there was no direct evidence for the existence of atoms. A theory without direct support is suspect, however, unless it is *confirmable*. A theory is confirmable if it can be used to explain known facts other than the data the theory was designed to explain, or to predict the results of future investigations. Confirmability, therefore, depends on how much explanatory or predictive power the theory has beyond what is needed to explain the original data.

Atomic theory was confirmable since it could be used to explain or predict a wide variety of phenomena beyond what it was designed to explain. Dalton postulated that the elements consist of atoms of different weights that combine to form chemical compounds, in order to explain the laws of conservation and constant composition. These laws had previously been established, however, only for a limited number of compounds, chiefly oxides. Dalton's theory correctly predicted that conservation and constant composition would be found to hold for all other compounds. More significantly, Dalton's theory predicted completely new laws, those of multiple and reciprocal proportions, which were also verified. Furthermore, Avogadro used Dalton's theory, together with the hypothesis that equal volumes of a gas contain equal numbers of molecules, to explain Gay-Lussacs law of simple proportions, which states that gases combine in simple proportions by volume (for example, two liters of hydrogen and one liter of oxygen produce two liters of steam). And later theorists used Dalton's theory, together with the hypothesis that the molecules in a gas are in rapid motion, to explain why gases exert pressure on things and diffuse thoroughly when mixed. Since the molecules in mixtures of gases do not combine chemically to form larger molecules, and since gases are mostly empty space, atomic theory predicted that the total pressure exerted by a mixture of gases should equal the sum of the pressures exerted by its component gases. This prediction was verified and is known as Dalton's law of partial pressure.

A theory that is neither directly supported nor confirmable is described pejoratively as an *ad hoc hypothesis*. The scientists struggling to explain the perturbations of Uranus would have rejected as *ad hoc* the hypothesis that God simply wanted the orbit to be perturbed in just the ways astronomers had observed. There was no direct support for such a divine desire, and the hypothesis predicted nothing beyond the data at hand. Even Fitzgerald's contraction hypothesis was rejected as *ad hoc* before Einstein. For there was no direct support for the claim that all objects contract in the direction of their motion until it was deduced from Einstein's theory of relativity, and there was no way to test the hypothesis since all measuring rods would contract proportionately. *Ad hoc* hypotheses are often described as "contrived." Their success in explaining the data is considered more a reflection of the theorist's ingenuity than of the theory's truth.

Hypotheses are not *ad hoc* unless they lack *both* direct support and confirmability. Atomic theory was a confirmable hypothesis that lacked direct support. Unconfirmable hypotheses with direct support may also be acceptable. Suppose we hear Bob singing in the shower, and wonder why. When we ask him, he says he just had an urge to sing. The hypothesized urge to sing explains his singing, but predicts nothing further about Bob's behavior. Nevertheless, the hypothesis is not *ad hoc,* because Bob's affirmation of the hypothesis constitutes authoritative, and therefore direct, support. Similarly, suppose the astronauts on the Space Shuttle launch a satellite that suddenly goes out of orbit and disintegrates in the atmosphere. One astronaut aboard reports seeing a small meteorite collide with it. The hypothesis that the satellite was hit by a meteorite explains why it went out of orbit; but assuming that no cameras or high-powered telescopes happened to be trained on the satellite, there is no way to test the hypothesis. It is not *ad hoc,* however, because it is supported by the astronaut's observational report.

Difficulties in Application. We have been discussing five criteria for evaluating explanations. An explanation better in one or more of these respects, and at least as good in the others, is the better explanation. I mentioned above that the evaluation of explanations is still largely an art. There are two reasons for this: First, it is often difficult to decide whether one explanation is better than another in even one of these criteria. Suppose we have a number of data points that both a parabolic and a hyperbolic curve fit fairly well. It is hard to say whether one curve is simpler than the other, or whether they are equally simple. Second, it is difficult to decide whether an explanation is better when it is superior in some respects but inferior in others. Scientists often have to "trade off" completeness and simplicity, for example, as when choosing between a slightly wavy curve, which fits the data better, and a straight line, which is simpler. But there are no rules as yet for doing so.

Glossary

Consistency: absence of contradiction; a theory is internally consistent if it is not self-contradictory, and is consistent with previously established facts if it does not contradict them.

Completeness: explaining all the data and stating all the explanatory factors.

Breadth of scope: how much of the data a theory explains.

Depth: how many of the explanatory factors a theory specifies.

Simplicity: how economical and uniform an explanation is.

Economy: postulating a small number of things and principles.

Uniformity: postulating a small amount of difference and variation.

Ockham's razor: a methodological principle stating that, other things equal, the simplest theory is better than more complex theories.

Direct support: support provided by direct reasoning (arguments from authority, analogical arguments, and so on).

Confirmability: the ability of a theory to explain known facts other than those the theory was designed to explain, or to predict the results of future investigations.

Ad hoc hypothesis: a hypothesis that is neither directly supported nor confirmable, and is therefore suspect.

Exercises

Many of the exercises in §4.2 involve a comparison between two or more explanations. Identify the criteria in virtue of which the preferred explanations were thought to be superior to the competing explanations.

LSAT Prep Questions

1. Several thousand years ago, people in what is now North America began to grow corn, which grows faster and produces more food per unit of land than do the grains these people had grown previously. Corn is less nutritious than those other grains, however, and soon after these people established corn as their staple grain crop, they began having nutrition-related health problems. Yet the people continued to grow corn as their staple grain, although they could have returned to growing the more nutritious grains.

    Which one of the following, if true, most helps to explain why the people mentioned continued to grow corn as their staple grain crop?

    (a) The variety of corn that the people relied on as their staple grain produced more food than did the ancestors of that variety.

    (b) Modern varieties of corn are more nutritious than were the varieties grown by people in North America several thousand years ago.

    (c) The people did not domesticate large animals for meat or milk; either of which could supply nutrients not provided by corn.

    (d) Some of the grain crops that could have been planted instead of corn required less fertile soil in order to flourish than corn required.

    (e) The people discovered some years after adopting corn as their staple grain that a diet that supplemented corn with certain readily available nongrain foods significantly improved their health.

    Preptest 31, Section 2, Question 11

2. Studies have shown that, contrary to popular belief, middle-aged people have more fear of dying than do elderly people.

    Each of the following, if true, contributes to an explanation of the phenomenon shown by the studies EXCEPT:

    (a) The longer one lives, the more likely it is that one has come to terms with dying.

    (b) Middle-aged people have more people dependent upon them than people of any other age group.

    (c) Many people who suffer from depression first become depressed in middle age.

    (d) The longer one lives, the more imperturbable one becomes.

    (e) Middle-aged people have a more acute sense of their own mortality than do people of any other age group.

    Preptest 31, Section 2, Question 13

3. A running track with a hard surface makes for greater running speed than a soft one, at least under dry conditions, because even though step length is shorter on a hard surface, the time the runner's foot remains in contact with the running surface is less with a hard surface.

    Which one of the following, if true, is evidence that the explanation given above is only a partial one?

    (a) Dry running conditions can be guaranteed for indoor track races only.

    (b) In general, taller runners have greater average step length than shorter runners do.

    (c) Hard tracks enhance a runner's speed by making it easier for the runner to maintain a posture that minimizes wind resistance.

    (d) The tracks at which the world's fastest running times have been recorded are located well above sea level, where the air is relatively thin.

    (e) To remain in top condition, a soft track surface requires different maintenance procedures than does a hard one.

    Preptest 30, Section 2, Question 9

CHAPTER FIVE

Syllogistic Logic: Aristotle

5.1 General Categorical Propositions

The remainder of the book will be devoted to deductive logic. The principles and methods presented in this chapter were first formulated by Aristotle (384-322 B.C.), who was to logic what Euclid (*c*. 300 B. C.) was to geometry. We begin by studying propositions like the following:

> Every man is an animal, every cat is a plant,…
> No man is an animal, no cat is a plant,…
> Some man is an animal, some cat is a plant,…
> Some man is not an animal, some cat is not a plant,…

Such propositions each contain two *terms*: a *subject* ("man," "cat"), and a *predicate* ("animal," "plant"). Hence they are called subject-predicate propositions. The above propositions are simple, in contrast to "Every man is an animal and every cat is an animal," "If every lizard is a reptile then no lizard is an amphibian," and the like, which are compound. Simple subject-predicate propositions are called *categorical propositions*. The examples above are general, in contrast to "John is an animal" and "John is not an animal," which is singular. Singular categorical propositions will be discussed in §5.7, compound propositions in Chapters 7 and 8. Note that the terms "subject" and "predicate" have a meaning in logic that is slightly different from their meaning in grammar. One of the grammatical subjects above is "every man"; the logical subject is expressed by "man." The grammatical predicate of the same sentence is "is an animal" while the logical predicate is expressed simply by "animal." Another difference between logical and grammatical subjects and predicates will emerge below.

General categorical propositions also contain a *quantifier* and a *copula*, which together determine the logical properties of the proposition. We shall focus on three quantifiers: *every, no*, and *some,* and two copulas: *is* and *is not*. We will therefore examine categorical propositions with the following four forms:

A Every S is a P.
E No S is a P.
I Some S is a P.
O Some S is not a P.

The letters **A**, **E**, **I**, and **O** are the convenient traditional names for the forms. Each form represents the logical structure of an unlimited number of propositions. The variables S and P represent *any* term—not only "man," "animal," "cat," and "plant," but also "dog," "lion," "cow," and so on. Furthermore, common nouns are not the only terms. S and P also stand for noun phrases of any degree of complexity: "tall man," "red-haired, tall man," "red-haired, tall, handsome man," "red-haired, tall, handsome man who cheated on his income taxes in 1981 and drinks either beer or bourbon," and so on.

Every general categorical proposition has a *quantity* and a *quality*. The quality is either *affirmative* or *negative*, depending on whether the predicate is affirmed or denied of the subject. Thus "Every man is an animal" is affirmative because it affirms that men are animals. "No man is an animal" is negative, because it denies that men are animals. The **A** and the **I** propositions are affirmative, while the **E** and the **O** are negative. The letter names, in fact, probably come from the Latin words "AffIrmo" and "nEgO," which mean "I affirm" and "I deny," respectively. The quantity is *universal* or *particular*, depending on the quantifier. The **A** and **E** propositions are universal, because they affirm or deny the predicate of the entire set of things to which the subject applies. The **I** and the **O** are particular, because they affirm or deny the predicate of only part of the set denoted by the subject. Particular propositions are often described as *existential* because they say that *there is* at least one thing, among those described by the subject, to which the predicate either does or does not apply. Note now that the logical form of a categorical preposition is completely specified by its quantity and quality:

A universal and affirmative
E universal and negative
I particular and affirmative
O particular and negative

Simplicity and symmetry suggest that there are really only two quantifiers, "every" and "some," and that "No Republican is a libertarian" should be replaced by "Every Republican is not a libertarian." This idea has considerable merit, as we will see in Chapter 9. Unfortunately, while "Every Republican is not a libertarian" *can* be interpreted as meaning "No Republican is a libertarian," it is most naturally interpreted as meaning "Not every Republican is a libertarian," which is equivalent to "Some Republican is not a libertarian." Consequently, the replacement of "No S is a P" by "Every S is not a P" would lead to confusion.

Grammatical Irrelevancies. We shall ignore the purely grammatical details of the linguistic vehicles used to represent logical form. The following sentences, for example, while very different grammatically have exactly the same meaning:

Every senator is a congressman.
All senators are congressmen.
Each of the senators is a congressman.

All three sentences express the same universal affirmative proposition whose subject can be expressed by either "senator" or "senators," and whose predicate can be expressed by either "congressman" or "congressmen." In other words, "All S are P" and "Each of the S is a P" represent the logical form of an **A** proposition just as well as "Every S is a P" does. We will similarly ignore the grammatical differences between "No birds are reptiles," "None of the birds are reptiles," and "No bird is a reptile"; between "Some organic compounds are proteins," "Some of the organic compounds are proteins," and "Some organic compound is a protein"; and so on.

The grammatical distinction between noun, adjective, and verb is also irrelevant in logic. Compare:

> Every American is a coffee lover.
> Every American loves coffee.

Since these sentences are synonymous, both express the **A** proposition whose subject is "American" and whose predicate can be expressed as either "coffee lover" or "loves coffee." 'Every rose is red' and "Every rose is a red thing" similarly express the **A** proposition whose subject is "rose" and whose predicate is "red thing" or "red." "Do" and "do not" often express the copula when the predicate is expressed by a verb, as in:

> Some Americans do love coffee.
> Some Americans do not love coffee.

Sometimes the word expressing the subject is combined with the quantifier. Thus in "Everything is a man or a nonman," the subject is "thing" in the most general sense of "being" or "existent." And in "Everyone born in the United States is a citizen," the subject is "one born in the United States," where "one" means "person." The tendency of language toward economy of expression is particularly evident in a sentence like "Whenever it rains the streets get wet," which expresses the **A** proposition "Every time when it rains is a time when the streets get wet," whose subject is "time when it rains" and whose predicate is "time when the streets get wet." "Wherever there's smoke there's fire" similarly means "Every place where there is smoke is a place where there is fire."

Sometimes the quantifier is deleted altogether, and we have to figure out for ourselves which was intended. Thus "A man is an animal" would normally mean "Every man is an animal." But "A man is waiting to see you" would undoubtedly mean "Some man is waiting to see you." Worse yet, quantifier-free sentences often are neither **A** nor **I** propositions. For example, "A basketball player is tall" means something weaker than "All basketball players are tall" but something stronger than "Some basketball players are tall." There are many quantifiers we shall not study: "nearly all," "most all," "exactly half of all," "at least half of all," "one," "two," "three," "lots of," "few of," and so on.

Sentences vs. Propositions. An important distinction exists between *sentences* and *propositions*. Sentences are made up of words; propositions are more abstract. Sentences are used to *express* propositions, and parts of sentences are used to express parts of propositions. One proposition may be expressed by many different sentences: all sentences that are perfectly *synonymous* in one language, and all exact *translations* in other languages, express the same proposition. Thus "Every man is an animal" and "All men are animals" are different sentences (no two words are the same) that express the same proposition. The subject of the proposition is expressed by "man" in the one sentence, and by "men" in the other. *Nondeclarative sentences* like "Are you going to the store?" and "Go to the store!" do not express propositions. *Ambiguous sentences* express many different propositions. "Flying planes can be dangerous," for example, can mean either "The act of flying planes can be dangerous" or "Planes that are flying can be dangerous." On any given occasion, however, an ambiguous sentence is used to express only one proposition. The term *statement* is also commonly used to denote propositions, as in Chapter 1. Later we shall reserve the term "statement" for a special type of proposition.

In classifying a proposition as **A, E, I,** or **O,** and in identifying its subject and predicate, we must be guided by the *meaning* of the sentence expressing the proposition; we cannot go entirely by the grammatical structure. We have selected a set of *standard forms,* those listed after **A, E, I,** and **O** above. The terms expressing the subjects and predicates of propositions in standard form can be identified easily by their grammatical position. But to identify subjects and predicates of propositions not in standard form, we may first have to reexpress them by finding a synonymous sentence in standard form. The ability to reexpress propositions in standard form is not a mere academic exercise: it is a test of whether you fully understand the proposition given.

Other Tenses and Modalities. The two copulas we will be studying have the present tense. Other copulas have different tenses.

> Each demonstrator is a prisoner.
> Each demonstrator was a prisoner.
> Each demonstrator will be a prisoner.

These sentences are obviously not equivalent and do not express the same proposition. Nevertheless, categorical propositions have the same *logical* properties, no matter what the tense of the copula. Consequently, everything we say about present-tense categorical propositions will hold, when appropriate changes have been made, for all other categorical propositions. In Chapter 9, a more general method of representing form will be developed that enables us to handle all tenses simultaneously. Similarly, our two copulas express actuality, as discussed in §2.2. Other copulas express different modalities:

> Each demonstrator is a prisoner.
> Each demonstrator must be a prisoner.
> Each demonstrator might be a prisoner.

These propositions, while not equivalent, do have many of the same logical properties. Their relationships will be studied in Chapter 10. For now we shall focus on categorical propositions with the modality of actuality.

Glossary

Categorical propositions: simple subject-predicate propositions like "Every man is an animal," "Some man is not an animal," and "Fido is an animal."

Subject: one of the terms in a categorical proposition, represented by S in the forms "Every S is a P," "No S is a P," "Some S is a P," and "Some S is not a P" (or by s in "s is a P" and "s is not a P" §5.7.)

Predicate: one of the terms in a categorical proposition, represented by P in the forms "Every S is a P," "No S is a P," "Some S is a P," and 'Some S not a P" (or in "s is a P," and "s is not a P")

Term: a subject or predicate.

Copula: the part of a categorical proposition expressed by "is" or "is not," or smilar expressions.

Quantifier: the part of a categorical proposition expressed by "every," "no," "some" or similar words.

Sentence: a sequence of words used to express a proposition, give a command, raise a question, and so on.

Proposition: what is expressed by a declarative sentence. The same proposition is expressed by all sentences with the same meaning.

A, E, I, O: forms of categorical propositions, respectively: "Every S is a P"; "No S is a P"; "Some S is a P"; and "Some S is not a P."

Quality—affirmative or negative: The quality of a proposition is affirmative or negative, depending on whether the predicate is affirmed or denied of the subject.

> **Quantity—universal or particular:** When the subject is a general term, the quantity of a categorical proposition is universal if the predicate is affirmed or denied of everything denoted by the subject, particular if the predicate is affirmed or denied of something denoted by the subject.

Exercises

A. For each of the following categorical propositions, identify its form (**A, E, I, O**), its quantity and quality, and its subject and predicate.

1. Every mammal is a vertebrate.

2. Some mammal is not a vertebrate.

3. No businessman is a politician.

4. All Democrats are liberals.

5. Some Republicans are not liberals.

6. Some Republicans are liberals.

7. Each senator is a congressman.

8. Some women are geniuses.

9. Any woman is a female.

10. No man is a genius.

B. Identify each of the following, according to the directions for Set A.

1. All behavior springs from desire.

2. Some politicians are downright evil.

3. Some politicians are very fine people.

4. Each man owns his own life.

5. No society operates entirely on the command principle.

6. Every living thing has parents.

7. Some animals we find and kill.

8. Each and every true patriot votes Republican.

9. Some elements are solids at room temperature.

10. Some elements at room temperature are not solids.

11. Each variety of wine has its own peculiar maladies,

12. All governments restrain and rule people.

13. All governments are totalitarian and authoritarian to one extent or another.

14. Some humans are still oppressed by the idea that the universe is a marionette whose strings are pulled by a god or gods.

15. All technological developments derive from common basic scientific knowledge.

16. Some moons are so close that their planet looms high in the heavens, covering half the sky.

17. Every social phenomenon is a fluid product of human history.

18. No mountains or sediments are preserved to give any hint of the products of the earth's dynamics in early days.

19. All bodies in motion continue to move in a straight line with uniform velocity until acted upon by some new force.

20. All terrestrial objects, when in motion, gradually abate their velocity and at last stop.

21. Man's beneficent ideals are all rationalizations of the great primordial forces of lust and terror, of blind striving for survival, which we believe to be the basic impulses of nature.

22. Some historians raise the question as to whether World War II might not have ended sooner if the Tokyo government had been assured earlier that the emperor would be left on the throne.

23. Some students are not able to get through school without either cheating or plagiarizing and without causing teachers and deans untold amounts of grief.

C. For each of the following categorical propositions, identify its form, and its subject and predicate. It may be necessary first to reexpress the proposition in standard form.

1. Atheists are all hedonists.

2. Atheists are not all hedonists.

3. Atheists are all not hedonists.

4. All scientists are not atheists.

5. Unborn babies have the right to life.

6. Educated people do not believe in God.

7. Expectant mothers have the right to choose an abortion.

8. An experiment by Needham shows that life can come spontaneously from dead stuff.

9. A comet is made mostly of ice.

10. An error is responsible for the discrepancy.

11. Insecticides remain in the soil for years.

12. Measures to provide health care for the aged under Social Security will be undertaken this year.

13. Some of the most necessary laws are considered by some to be a challenge and an intrusion.

14. Psychotic mothers sometimes kill their children in attempts to exorcise devils.

15. Not all payroll savings plans are to be sniffed at.

16. The alternatives to deterrence that have been proposed are no more moral or rational.

17. An individual in prison does not lose the right to have rights.

18. These voluntary market elements flourish in China despite their inconsistency with official Marxist ideology.

19. Transactions in a free-trade world take place among private entities.

20. In a free-trade world, any transaction takes place at terms that are agreed on by all the parties to that transaction.

21. A politician's decisions and actions flow naturally from his mental convictions.

22. Living things exist that are able to stand boiling water and still live.

23. Not a single one of all my dogs is dead as a result of the vaccine.

24. Everywhere there is malaria, there are mosquitoes.

25. Always, where the zanzarone mosquito buzzes, there is malaria.

26. None of my inoculated animals gets paralysis as children do.

27. Tests conducted by Pasteur show that the rabies vaccine is effective.

28. Not all the eight attributes characterizing excellent companies are present or conspicuous in all excellent companies.

29. The craters on the moon are depressions rather than mounds.

30. The German investigators are unanimously opposed to Crookes' view that cathode rays are particles.

31. A giant fireball is moving rapidly across the sky.

32. Cathode ray particles are much smaller than atoms.

33. Feelings are created by what you put into your own mind.

34. Not one of the worlds in the billions of planetary systems in the galaxy is like earth.

35. In all those other worlds in space there are events in progress that will determine their futures.

36. Anyone who believes in majority rule in fact believes in slavery.

37. An earthquake is always followed by aftershocks.

38. Whenever a president runs for reelection, he uses his control over various appropriations to buy support.

39. He who lives by the sword dies by the sword.

40. Acorns never grow into pine trees.

41. All these things—a good education, friends, love, children, a sufficient income, good health, and work—depend upon the community and are helped or hindered by political events.

5.2 Opposition

Different categorical propositions that have the same subject and predicate are said to be ***opposed.*** Opposing propositions differ only in quality or quantity. Thus "Every man is an animal" and "No man is an animal" are opposed because both have the subject "man" and the predicate "animal." The two propositions differ in quality, the first being affirmative, the second negative. "Every man is an animal" and "Every man is a plant" are not opposed, in our technical sense of the term, because their predicates are different. The two propositions do not differ in quality or quantity. The way in which categorical propositions are opposed determines the logical relationship between them.

Opposing propositions that differ in both quantity and quality are **contradictory**. Two propositions are contradictory if one affirms precisely what the other denies. Consequently, *contradictories cannot both be true and cannot both be false.* In other words, contradictory statements are both incompatible and complementary. ***Incompatible*** means *mutually exclusive:* if one proposition is true, then the other must be false; hence both cannot be true. ***Complementary*** means *jointly exhaustive:* if one proposition is false, the other must be true; hence both cannot be false. Opposing **A** and **O** propositions, such as "Every man is a chauvinist" and "Some man is not a chauvinist," differ in both quantity and quality, and therefore contradict one another. So do opposing **E** and **I** propositions, such as "No man is a chauvinist" and "Some man is a chauvinist." If "No man is a chauvinist" is true, then "Some man is a chauvinist" mast be false. And, if "No man is a chauvinist" is false, "Some man is a chauvinist" must be true.

Opposing **A** and **E** propositions, such as "Every man a genius" and "No man is a genius," differ only in quality. These are not contradictory, for both propositions are false. The two nevertheless are *incompatible*—that is, mutually exclusive. If one were true, the other would have to be false. Incompatible but noncomplementary statements about the same subject are **contrary**. Opposing **A** and **E** propositions, then, are contrary but not contradictory. The key fact to remember is this, *contraries cannot both be true but may both be false.*

Opposing **I** and **O** propositions, such as "Some woman is a musician" and "Some woman is not a musician," also differ in quality alone. These are not contradictory or even contrary, for both are true. Note carefully that opposition in our technical sense does not require any sort of incompatibility. Indeed, opposing **I** and **O** propositions are *complementary*—that is, jointly exhaustive. If one is false, the other must be true. Complementary but not incompatible statements about the same subject are said to be **subcontrary**. *Subcontraries cannot both be false but may both be true.*

We have looked at opposing propositions differing in both quality and quantity, and those differing in quality alone. The remaining case involves opposing propositions that differ in quantity alone, which we shall call **alterns**. Opposing **A** and **I** propositions are alterns, as are opposing **E** and **O** propositions. Alterns are neither incompatible nor complementary. What we find instead is that the universal altern implies the particular. Thus "Every emerald is green" implies "Some emerald is green." And "No composer is a pianist" implies "Some composer is not a pianist." The universal altern is called the **superaltern**, the particular the **subaltern**. We have then the following principle: *The truth of the superaltern implies the truth of the subaltern.* The converse does not hold. From the truth of the subaltern, we cannot infer the truth of the superaltern. The fact that some men are not geniuses fortunately does not prove that no men are geniuses. The principle governing alternation can, though, be reformulated as follows: *the falsity of the subaltern implies the falsity of the superaltern.* Since it is false that some men are reptiles, the stronger statement that all men are reptiles must also be false. From the falsity of the superaltern, however, nothing follows about the falsity of the subaltern.

It is often thought that alterns are incompatible, and that subcontraries imply one another. There are two reasons for this inversion of the truth. First, there is a general tendency in speech and writing to avoid understatement. A speaker will typically not make a statement about some objects of a certain sort when he could just as truthfully say the same about all. Thus, if a professor walked into class after grading exams and announced "Someone passed," fear could be justified. For in that context, the professor's statement would suggest that some students did not pass. If everyone passed, the students might reason, wouldn't he have said so? Nevertheless, the professor's statement would be true as long as *at least one* student passed. The fact that every student passed guarantees that at least one did, and rules out the possibility that even one did not. The second reason for thinking that alterns are incompatible is that *"Some S are P"* is confused with *"Only some S are P."* The latter entails "Some S are not P," which contradicts "All S are P." But the former does not. "Only some students passed" says that some *but not all* students passed.

These logical relationships are conveniently represented by a diagram called a ***square of opposition***, presented in Figure 5-1. This square of opposition, which represents the logical principles formulated by Aristotle, is called the Aristotelian square, to distinguish it from the related square based on the principles formulated by Boole and Venn discussed in the next chapter.

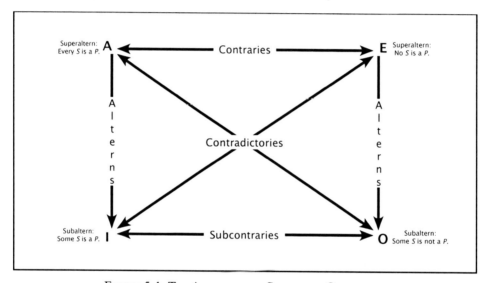

FIGURE 5-1. THE ARISTOTELIAN SQUARE OF OPPOSITION

Given the truth or falsity of one categorical proposition, the square of opposition can be used in many cases to determine the truth or falsity of opposing propositions. Thus, given that an **A** proposition is *true*, we can infer the following: the opposing **E** proposition is false (contraries cannot both be true); the opposing **O** proposition is false (contradictories cannot both be true); and the opposing is **I** true (if the superaltern is true, the subaltern is true). Given that an **A** proposition is *false*, we can infer that the opposing **O** is true (contradictories cannot both be false); however, nothing can be inferred about the opposing **E** or the **I** so we say they are *undetermined*. The square of opposition therefore enables us to classify as valid or invalid all arguments involving a single categorical proposition as premise and an opposing proposition as conclusion. For example, "All men are animals, therefore some men are animals" is valid: the premise and conclusion are alterns, and the truth of the subaltern follows from the truth of the superaltern. On the other hand, "Some carpenters are men, hence some carpenters are not men" is invalid: the premise and conclusion are subcontraries and the truth of a proposition does not follow from the truth of its subcontrary. Any argument classified as valid, using the square of opposition in this way, is deductively and formally valid. An argument similarly classified as invalid is not even inductively valid.

Glossary

Opposition: the relationship between different categorical propositions that have the same subject and predicate, and that consequently differ only in quantity or quality.

Contradictories: opposing general categorical propositions that differ in both quantity and quality (and opposing singular categorical propositions that differ in quality). In general, two propositions are contradictory if one asserts what the other denies, so that the statements cannot both be true nor both false.

Contraries: opposing categorical propositions that differ in quality and are both universal. In general, two propositions are contrary if they make incompatible but not complementary claims about the same subject, so that both cannot be true although both may be false.

Subcontraries: opposing categorical propositions that differ in quality and are both particular. In general, two propositions are subcontrary if they make complementary but not incompatible claims about the same subject, so that both cannot be false although both may be true.

Alterns, super- and sub-: opposing categorical propositions that differ only in quantity. The universal altern is the superaltern, the particular the subaltern. The superaltern implies the subaltern.

Square of opposition: a diagram representing the logical relationships between opposing propositions.

Compatible: not incompatible.

Incompatible: Two propositions are incompatible provided that if either one is true the other must be false, so that they cannot both be true; mutually exclusive.

Complementary: Two propositions are complementary provided that if either one is false the other must be true, so that they cannot both be false; jointly exhaustive.

Exercises

A. Assume that the numbered propositions are true, and then determine whether the lettered ones under them are true, false, or undetermined, and explain why. For example, if (1) is assumed to be true, then (a) must be false, because they are contraries and contraries cannot both be true.

1. Every mammal is a vertebrate.
    - (a) No mammal is a vertebrate.
    - (b) Some mammal is a vertebrate.
    - (c) Some mammal is not a vertebrate.

2. No governments are totalitarian and authoritarian.
    - (a) Some governments are totalitarian and authoritarian.
    - (b) Some governments are not totalitarian and authoritarian.
    - (c) All governments are totalitarian and authoritarian.

3. Some educated people believe in God.
    - (a) Some educated people do not believe in God.

    (b) All educated people believe in God.
    (c) No educated people believe in God.

4. Some of my dogs are not immune to rabies.
    (a) All of my dogs are immune to rabies.
    (b) Not a single one of my dogs is immune to rabies.
    (c) Some of my dogs are immune to rabies.

B. Assuming now that the numbered propositions in Set A are false, determine whether the lettered ones are true, false, or undetermined, and explain why.

C. Determine whether the following arguments are valid or invalid, and explain why in terms of the square of opposition.

1. All widgeons are ducks, so some widgeons are ducks.

2. Some widgeons are ducks, so all widgeons are ducks.

3. Some widgeons are ducks, so some widgeons are not ducks.

4. No ducks are widgeons, so some ducks are not widgeons.

5. Some ducks are not widgeons, so no ducks are widgeons.

6. All ducks are widgeons, so no ducks are widgeons.

7. Some ducks are widgeons, so it is not the case that no ducks are widgeons.

8. Some ducks are not widgeons, so it is not the case that all ducks are widgeons.

9. All widgeons are ducks, so it is not the case that no widgeons are ducks.

10. Some widgeons are ducks, so it is not the case that all widgeons are ducks.

D. Contradictories, contraries, subcontraries, and alterns can be found among propositions other than **A**, **E**, **I**, and **O** propositions. Study the general definitions of these terms, and then determine which apply to the following pairs.

1. Most cars are red; most cars are not red.

2. My car is red; my car is not red.

3. Most cars are red; some cars are red.

4. No mammals are reptiles; most mammals are not reptiles.

5. More than ten women are geniuses; less than twenty women are geniuses.

6. All men are good-looking; all men are ugly.

7. All birds are crows; only some birds are crows.

8. It will probably rain; it will probably not rain.

9. Rain is probable; rain is not probable.

10. My birthday is in the fall, spring, or summer; my birthday is in spring, summer, or winter.

11. There is at least one god; there is at most one god.

12. There are many gods; there are not many gods.

13. The statements in (1) above are contradictory; they are contrary.

14. The statements in (1) above are contrary; they are subcontrary.

5.3 Conversion, Obversion, and Contraposition

By definition, categorical propositions with different subject or predicate terms are not opposed. Nevertheless, they may still stand in important logical relationships. Many pairs of categorical propositions are *transformationally related,* meaning that one can be transformed into the other by specific formal operations. We shall study three transformations: conversion, obversion, and contraposition. We are interested in when these transformations produce equivalent propositions.

Conversion. To *convert* a categorical proposition is to interchange its subject and predicate. The result of converting a proposition is called its **converse.** Thus if we convert the **A** proposition "Every man is an animal," we produce "Every animal is a man," another **A** proposition. If we then convert "Every animal is a man," we end up back at "Every man is an animal." Since one is the converse of the other, the two propositions are said to be converses. The converse of "Some athletes are not baseball players" is "Some baseball players are not athletes." In general, conversion produces the following results:

Converses
Every S is a $P \neq$ Every P is an S.
No S is a $P =$ No P is an S.
Some S is a $P =$ Some P is an S.
Some S is not a $P \neq$ Some P is not an S.

Note that converses are not opposed, since their subjects and predicates differ. Moreover, converses do not differ in quality or quantity.

The equals sign (=) expresses equivalence, while ≠ expresses lack of equivalence. Two propositions are **equivalent** if they imply each other. One proposition **implies** another provided that if the former is true then so is the latter. The examples used in the preceding paragraph show that converses are not always equivalent. While "Every man is an animal" is true, its converse "Every animal is a man" is false. And while "Some athletes are not baseball players" is true, "Some baseball players are not athletes" is false. However, *the converses of E and I propositions are equivalent,* except in one special case. Thus "Some athletes are baseball players" is equivalent to "Some baseball players are athletes," and "No man is a reptile" is equivalent to "No reptile is a man." **E** and **I** propositions, we shall say, are *convertible.* **A** and **O** propositions are not convertible. The only time **E** and **I** converses fail to be equivalent is when one of their terms fails to apply to anything, like "1984 Edsel" or "winged earthworms." This case arises infrequently in practice, and we shall ignore it until §6.4.

Complements. Before we can describe the operations of obversion and contraposition, we need to introduce the notion of complementary terms. The **complement** of a term is formed by adding or subtracting the prefix *non,* or by some equivalent operation. Thus "nonman" is the complement of "man," and "man" is the complement of" "nonman." "Man" is said to be the *positive complement,* "nonman" the *negative complement.* Complementary terms are mutually exclusive and jointly exhaustive: non-*T* applies to an object if and only if *T* does not apply. Hence complementary terms are often called contradictory terms. Be careful not to confuse them with mere contrary terms. "Man-woman," "introvert-extrovert," and "winner-loser" are contrary but not complementary pairs. The complement of "man," for example, applies to everything that is not a man, not just women. Note that a negative term like "non-man" has *two* complements: both "man" and "nonnonman." These two complements are equivalent, of course, by the *double negation* rule, which says in general that any term *T* and nonnon-*T* are equivalent. Two negatives, in other words, make a positive. We will generally avoid double negatives of this sort. So by the complement of "nonman" we will generally mean "man."

The complements of complex terms cannot be formed in plain English simply by prefixing "non." For example, the complement of "tall, dark, and handsome man" is not the contrary term "nontall, dark, and handsome man." For the complement should apply to fair men, ugly men, women, frogs, and everything else that is not a tall, dark, and handsome man. Hence the complement must be something like "thing that is not a tall, dark, and handsome man" or "thing other than a tall, dark, and handsome man." Similarly, the complement of "thing weighing more than fifty pounds" is not "nonthing weighing more than fifty pounds," for that term applies to nothing at all (nothing is a nonthing). Rather, the complement is "thing that is not a thing weighing more than fifty pounds," or more simply "thing not weighing more than fifty pounds." A simple and uniform method for forming the complements of complex terms employs parentheses as they are used in mathematics. First, put the term in parentheses. Then prefix "non." Thus, we can express the complement of "tall, dark, and handsome man" as "non(tall, dark, and handsome man)," and the complement of "thing weighing more than fifty pounds" as "non(thing weighing more than fifty pounds) " The parentheses tell us that the "non" applies to the whole phrase within, not just to the first word of the phrase. We will always strive, though, to express complements in standard English that is as unstilted as possible.

Obversion. To *obvert* a proposition is to change its quality and replace the predicate with its complement. The resulting proposition is its ***obverse***. If we start with "Every man is an animal" and change its quality, we get "No man is an animal." If we then replace the predicate with its complement, we get "No man is a nonanimal." In general, obversion produces the following results.

Obverses
Every *S* is a *P* = No *S* is a non-*P*.
No *S* is a *P* = Every *S* is a non-*P*.
Some *S* is a *P* = Some *S* is not a non-*P*.
Some *S* is not a *P* = Some *S* is a non-*P*.

When the predicate is expressed by a verb it will be more natural to reexpress the obverse by using a noun phrase. The obverse of "Some women smoke" could be given as "Some women do not nonsmoke," but your English teacher will be less offended if you say instead "Some women are not non-smokers." As should be evident on reflection, *the obverses of all categorical propositions are equivalent.* This means that a negative proposition with a positive predicate is equivalent (other things equal) to an affirmative proposition with a negative predicate, and that a negative proposition with a negative is equivalent to an affirmative proposition with a positive predicate. Note that we are not avoiding double negatives of the form "not a non-*P*," for "not" and "non" occupy different roles in the structure of the proposition: "not" is part of the copula, while "non" is part of the predicate. Verify that by obverting twice you will always end up where you started (if you avoid double negatives of the form "nonnon-*T*"). There are no exceptions to the rule that categorical propositions are equivalent to their obverses.

Contraposition. To *contrapose* a categorical proposition is to replace the subject with the complement of the predicate and the predicate with the complement of the subject. The resulting proposition is its *contrapositive*. Thus the contrapositive of "Every man is an animal" is "Every nonanimal is a nonman." Special care must be taken with **O** propositions to leave the "not" in the copula. The contrapositive of "Some man is not a genius" is "Some nongenius is not a nonman." not the equivalent 'Some nongenius is a man."

Contrapositives
Every *S* is a *P* = Every non-*P* is a non-*S*.
No *S* is a *P* ≠ No non-*P* is a non-*S*.
Some *S* is a *P* ≠ Some non-*P* is a non-*S*.
Some *S* is not a *P* = Some non-*P* is not a non-*S*.

The contrapositives of A and O propositions are equivalent, except in the special case in which one of the terms fails to refer to anything. **E** and **I** propositions are not contraposable. "No cat is a reptile" is true, but its contrapositive "No nonreptile is a noncat" is false (birds are nonreptiles that arc noncats). And "Some noncat is an animal" is true, but its contrapositive "Some nonanimal is a cat" is false. Note that when *S* is "noncat," non-*S* is "cat" due to our rule against double negatives.

"Only." An important type of categorical proposition that does not have one of our four standard forms is *"Only S are P."* It is often thought that "only" here simply means "all." This is a mistake. "Only men are members," for example, means "All members are men" and not "All men are members." In general,

Only *S* are *P* = All *P* are *S*.

Now "All *P* are *S*" is equivalent by contraposition to "All non-*S* are non-*P*," which is equivalent to "No non-*S* are *P*" by obversion, which is in turn equivalent to "No *P* are non-*S*" by conversion. Hence "Only men are members" is equivalent to "All nonmen are nonmembers," "No nonmen are members," and "No members are nonmen." Since "Only *S* are *P*" is equivalent to "All *P* are *S*," it is contraposable but not convertible. Thus "Only men are members" is equivalent to "Only nonmembers are nonmen," but not to "Only members are men."

"Only" also appears in the compound quantifier *only some,* as in "Only some birds are crows." This means neither "Only birds are crows" nor "Some birds are crows." What it does mean is *"Some but not all* birds are crows," a compound proposition formed by conjoining an **I** and the negation of the opposing **A**, or equivalently, by conjoining an **I** and the opposing **O**.

Only some *S* are *P* = Some but not all *S* are *P*.

Finally, "only" appears as part of *the only,* as in "The only egg-laying mammals are marsupials," or equivalently "Marsupials are the only egg-laying mammals," which simply means "All egg-laying mammals are marsupials." In general,

The only *S* are *P* = All *S* are *P*.

Summary. To summarize the results of this section: **E** and **I** propositions are convertible, **A** and **O** propositions are contraposable, and all categorical propositions are obvertible. Glancing back at the square of opposition, note that the convertible propositions are contradictories, and that the contraposable propositions are the other contradictories.[1] These rules enable us to classify many simple arguments as valid or invalid. Thus "Every weasel is a carnivore, therefore every noncarnivore is a nonweasel" is valid, since the conclusion is equivalent to the premise by contraposition. On the other hand, "Every businessman is a millionaire, therefore every millionaire is a businessman" is invalid, since **A** propositions are not convertible. Arguments classified as valid in this way are deductively and formally valid; those classified as invalid are not even inductively valid. In §5 6, we will use the same rules in more complex ways to validate arguments.

Glossary

Converse: the result of exchanging the subject and predicate of a categorical proposition.

Obverse: the result of changing the quality of a proposition and exchanging the predicate for its complement.

Contrapositive: the result of replacing the subject of a categorical proposition with the complement of its predicate, and the predicate with the complement of its subject.

Complementary terms: The complement of a term is formed by adding or subtracting "non," or by some equivalent operation; the complement of a term applies to an object if and only if the term does not.

Implication: One proposition implies another provided that if the former is true then the latter is true.

Equivalence: Two propositions are equivalent provided the first implies the second and the second implies the first.

Exercises

Produce the converse, obverse, and contrapositive of each of the following propositions, expressing them in standard English.

A. 1. Every mammal is a vertebrate.
2. No businessman is a politician.
3. Some Republicans are liberals.
4. Some women are not geniuses.

B. 1. Every politician is corrupt.
2. No metal is soft,.
3. Some women are beautiful.
4. Some men are not handsome.

C. 1. Every soprano sings.
2. No athlete smokes.
3. Some people lie.

---

[1] If you like mnemonics this may help: convErsIon holds for **E** and **I** while contrApOsition holds for **A** and **O**.

4. Some machines do not work.

D.   1. Every true patriot votes Republican.
2. No society operates entirely on the command principle.
3. Some elements at room temperature are solids.
4. Some elements are not liquid at room temperature.

E.   1. All behavior springs from desire.
2. Every living thing has parents.
3. Each variety of wine has its own peculiar maladies.
4. No mountains or sediments are preserved to give any idea of the products of the earth's dynamics in the early days.
5. No terrestrial objects continue moving indefinitely.
6. Not a single one of my dogs is dead as a result of the vaccine.
7. Some humans are still oppressed by the idea that the universe is a marionette whose strings are pulled by a god or gods.
8. Some moons are so close that their planet looms high in the heavens, overing half the sky.
9. Some students are not able to get through school without cheating and plagiarizing.
10. Living things exist that are not able to withstand boiling water.
11. Everywhere there is malaria, there are mosquitoes.
12. Anyone who believes in majority rule in fact believes in slavery.

F. Assuming that the numbered propositions below are true, determine whether the lettered ones are true, false, or undetermined, and explain why.

1.   Every mammal is a vertebrate.

 (a) Every vertebrate is a mammal.

 (b) No mammal is a nonvertebrate.

 (c) Every nonvertebrate is a nonmammal.

 (d) No mammal is a vertebrate.

 (e) Some mammal is a vertebrate.

2.   No men are women.

 (a) No nonwomen are nonmen.

 (b) All men are nonwomen.

 (c) No women are men.

 (d) All men are women.

 (e) Some men are not women.

3. Some Republicans are liberal.

 (a) All Republicans are liberal.

 (b) Some liberals are Republican.

(c) Some Republicans are not nonliberal.

(d) Some Republicans are not liberal.

(e) Some nonliberals are non-Republicans.

4. Some mammal is not a marsupial.

(a) No mammal is a marsupial.

(b) Some marsupial is not a mammal.

(c) Some mammal is a nonmarsupial.

(d) Some nonmarsupial is not a nonmammal.

(e) Some mammal is a marsupial.

5. No society operates entirely on the command principle.

(a) Nothing operating entirely on the command principle is a society.

(b) Every society operates not entirely on the command principle.

(c) Nothing not operating entirely on the command principle is a nonsociety.

(d) Some society does operate entirely on the command principle.

(e) Some society does not operate entirely on the command principle.

6. Some politicians are very fine people.

(a) Some politicians are not very fine people.

(b) Some very fine people are politicians.

(c) Some beings that are not very fine people are nonpoliticians.

(d) Some politicians are not beings that are not very fine people.

(e) All politicians are very fine people.

G. Assume that the numbered propositions in Set F are false, and then determine whether the lettered ones are true, false, or undetermined.

H. Determine whether the following arguments are valid or invalid, and explain why.

1. All widgeons are ducks, so all ducks are widgeons.

2. All widgeons are ducks, so some widgeons are ducks.

3. All widgeons are ducks, so all nonducks are nonwidgeons.

4. All widgeons are ducks, so no widgeons are nonducks.

5. Some ducks are widgeons, so some widgeons are ducks.

6. Some ducks are not widgeons, so some widgeons are not ducks,

7.   Some ducks are not widgeons, so some ducks are widgeons.

8.   Some ducks are widgeons, so some ducks are not nonwidgeons.

9.   Some ducks are not widgeons, so some nonwidgeons are not nonducks.

10. No widgeons are ducks, so no ducks are widgeons.

11. No widgeons are ducks, so all widgeons are nonducks.

12. No widgeons are ducks, so some widgeons are ducks.

13. No widgeons are ducks, so no nonducks are nonwidgeons.

14. No widgeons are ducks, so some widgeons are not ducks.

15. All widgeons are ducks, so it is not the case that all ducks are widgeons.

16. No widgeons are ducks, so it is not the case that no ducks are widgeons.

I.   Reexpress the following propositions using standard form categorical propositions.

1.   The only students who pass are those who study.

2.   Only students who pass study.

3.   Only some students who pass study.

4.   Only some students who study pass.

5.   Only students who study pass.

6.   Only amateurs are eligible for the Olympics.

7.   Only some amateurs are eligible for the Olympics.

8.   The only athletes eligible for the Olympics are amateurs.

9.   All and only triangles are three-sided figures.

10. Only some three-sided figures are triangles.

11. Only triangles are three-sided figures.

12. Triangles are the only three-sided figures.

5.4 Categorical Syllogisms

We shall now examine a class of more complex arguments containing categorical propositions, called *categorical syllogisms.* These are defined as arguments consisting of three categorical propositions containing three different terms, each of which occurs in two of the propositions. An example would be:

            Every mammal is an animal.
            Every cat is a mammal.
            ∴ Every cat is an animal.

The simple arguments discussed in the last two sections are not categorical syllogisms because they have only one premise:

Every cat is a mammal.   No cat is a reptile.
∴ Some cat is a mammal.   ∴ No reptile is a cat.

The term *syllogism* by itself is often used more broadly to denote any simple argument with two premises, including:

If today is Sunday, then pro football will be played.
If pro football will be played, then it will be televised.
∴ If today is Sunday, then pro football will be televised.

Every man is an animal.
Every woman is an animal.
∴ Every human is an animal.

The syllogism about football is not categorical because the premises and conclusion are hypothetical propositions. The syllogism about humans is not categorical because it contains four terms, and one term occurs in all three propositions. In this chapter, for convenience, we shall use "syllogism" as short for "categorical syllogism."

Every categorical syllogism contains exactly three terms. The predicate of the conclusion is called the *major term.* The subject of the conclusion is called the *minor term.* The other term, which occurs in both the premises, is called the *middle term.* The premise containing the major term is called the *major premise.* The remaining premise, which contains the minor term, is the *minor premise.* In the sample categorical syllogism above, "animal" is the major term, "cat" the minor term, and "mammal" the middle term. The major premise is "Every mammal is an animal" and the minor premise is "Every cat is a mammal." In general, every syllogism tries to infer a link between the major and minor term by linking them in the premises to the middle term. Note that the major and minor premises are defined by their formal relationship to the conclusion. The order in which the premises are stated is irrelevant.

The form of a categorical syllogism is determined by two factors: the type of categorical propositions in the premises and conclusion, and the order of the terms in the premises. The first factor is called the *mood* of the syllogism, the second its *figure.* The mood of a syllogism can be specified very simply by an ordered triple of the letter names of the propositions. The mood of our sample is **AAA**, since it contains nothing but **A** propositions. We shall stipulate that the first letter designates the major premise, the second the minor premise, and the third the conclusion. Thus **AEO** and **EOA** are very different moods.

Every man is a mammal.   Some reptile is not a man.
No mammal is a reptile.   No mammal is a reptile.
∴ Some reptile is not a man.   ∴ Every man is a mammal.
AEO   **EOA**

Note that even though stated second, "No mammal is a reptile" is the major premise of the argument on the right, since it contains the predicate of the conclusion. That is why its mood is **EOA** rather than **OEA**.

The figure of a syllogism is determined by the position of the middle term in the premises. There are four possibilities, which are named simply "First Figure," "Second Figure," and so on. *First Figure:* the middle term is the subject of the major premise, predicate of the minor. *Second Figure:* the middle term is the predicate of both premises. *Third Figure:* the middle term is the subject of both premises. *Fourth Figure:* the middle term is the predicate of the major premise, subject of the minor. The four figures are schematized in Table 5-1 by ignoring mood altogether.[2] We can completely specify the form of a categorical syllogism, then, by adding a numeral indicating figure to the three letters indicating mood. For example:

All mammals are animals.	All mammals are animals.
All cats are mammals.	All mammals are animals.
∴ All cats are animals.	∴ All animals are cats.
AAA1	**AAA4**

1st Figure	2nd Figure	3rd Figure	4th Figure
M–P	*P–M*	*M–P*	*P–M*
S–M	*S–M*	*M–S*	*M–S*
∴ S–P	*∴ S–P*	*∴ S–P*	*∴ S–P*

TABLE 5-1. THE FIGURES

There are infinitely many categorical syllogisms, since there is an unlimited number of possible terms. The number of *forms* all these syllogisms possess, however, is limited. Given the four forms of categorical proposition we have studied, there are 4 x 4 x 4 = 64 different moods. Given that there are four figures, we have 64 x 4 = 256 different syllogistic forms (for a complete listing, see Table 5-2 on page 226). Relatively few of the forms are valid, however. Our goal in the next two sections will be to devise methods that enable us to distinguish the valid forms from the invalid.

Glossary

Categorical syllogism: an argument consisting of three categorical propositions containing three different terms, each of which occurs in two of the propositions.

Major term: the predicate in the conclusion of a categorical syllogism.

Minor term: the subject in the conclusion of a categorical syllogism.

Middle term: the term that occurs in both premises of a categorical syllogism.

Major premise: the premise that contains the major term.

Minor premise: the premise that contains the minor term.

Mood: one of two factors defining the form of a categorical syllogism, determined by which form of categorical proposition occurs in the major premise, the minor premise and the conclusion.

---

[2] A mnemonic may help you to remember the *figures*. Arrange the numerals 1, 2, 3, and 4 in a square as follows, and imagine drawing a line from 1 to 2 to 3 and finally to 4.

The middle terms of the first figure line up on the upper left to lower right diagonal, while the middle terms of the fourth figure line up on the lower left to upper right diagonal. The middle terms of the third figure line up on the left side, while the middle terms of the second figure line up on the right side.

Figure: the other factor defining the form of a categorical syllogism, determined by whether the middle term is the subject or predicate in the premises.

Exercises

Identify the mood and figure of the following syllogisms.

1. All widgeons are ducks and some pigeons and widgeons, so some pigeons are not ducks.

2. Some lemurs are animals, for all lemurs are mammals and some animals are mammals.

3. Some primates are animals, for some mammals are animals and all primates are mammals.

4. Every maggot is a living thing. Every living thing has parents. Therefore, every maggot has parents.

5. Some elements are solids at room temperature. All metals are solids at room temperature. Therefore, some elements are metals.

6. No dogs are dead as a result of the vaccine. Some things which are dead as a result of the vaccine are rabbits. Therefore, some rabbits are dogs.

7. No monotheists are polytheists, for no atheists are polytheists and no atheists are monotheists.

8. Some viruses are not living things, for no viruses are able to stand boiling water but some living things are.

9. Every action springs from desire. No belief is an action, so some beliefs do not spring from desire.

10. All dictatorships are authoritarian and totalitarian societies. Some dictatorships are not prosperous. Therefore, some authoritarian and totalitarian societies are not prosperous.

5.5 Refutation By Counterinstance

As we said in §2.5, an argument is formally valid only if every argument with the same logical form is valid. Now any argument must be deductively invalid if it has true premises and a false conclusion. There is, then, a simple way of proving that an argument is formally invalid: find a *counterinstance*—that is, find another argument with the same form that has true premises and a false conclusion. This procedure will be called *refutation by counterinstance*. Suppose a friend of yours proposes this syllogism:

> Every Brahms quartet is a romantic work.
> No atonal composition is a Brahms quartet.
> ∴ No atonal composition is a romantic work.

You may realize on an intuitive basis that this is an invalid argument, that the conclusion does not follow from the premises. You cannot, however, refute your friend with the simple assertion that the argument is obviously invalid. Since your friend offered the argument, he undoubtedly thought it was valid. A shouting match in which one party proclaims "It's valid!" while the other party declares with equal fervor "It's not!" is not a proof of validity or invalidity. You could, though, legitimately establish that the argument was invalid by showing that the conclusion is in fact false even though the premises are true. But this method will be of no use if you know little about classical music while your friend is an expert.

The method of refutation by counterinstance enables you to get around ignorance of the specific subject matter of the argument. All you need to do is find another argument, about more familiar topics, that has the same form with true premises and a false conclusion. You can then refute your friend by saying, "But that is like arguing:

> Every cat is an animal.
> No dog is a cat
> ∴ No dog is an animal!"

Your argument is logically analogous to your friend's—that is, both have the same form: **AEE1**. Your argument has true premises and a false conclusion, as any child will realize. It is therefore a counterinstance of your friend's argument, proving that your friend's argument is not formally valid. Since refutation by counterinstance proceeds by finding a logically analogous argument with true premises and a false conclusion, it is often called "refutation by logical analogy." It is best to find a counterinstance in which it is *common knowledge* that the premises are true and the conclusion false. That way you foreclose further debate.

A certain amount of care and ingenuity is needed to refute an argument by the method of counterinstance. Care is required to make sure you end up with another argument of the same form. Ingenuity is required to find an analogy with true premises and a false conclusion. The procedure can be facilitated by following a systematic routine. Suppose you are given an argument, say:

> Every tree is a plant, for every oak is a plant and every oak is a tree.

First abstract form of the argument:

> Every M is a P.
> Every M is an S.
> ∴ Every S is a P.

The order of the premises and conclusion is irrelevant here. Just make sure you do not confuse premises and conclusions. Once the form is abstracted, the task is simply to think of three terms to put in the place of *M*, *S*, and *P* that will make the premises true and the conclusion false. It is always easy to make two of the choices: simply pick an *S* and a *P* that will make the conclusion false, say "animal" and "mammal":

> Every M is a mammal.
> Every M is an animal.
> F ∴ Every animal is a mammal.

Now all you have to do is think of one term for *M* that will make both premises true. "Tree" makes both premises false, so that won't work. "Snake" is no good either because it makes the first premise false. "Cat," however, makes both premises true. So here is your refutation:

> T   Every cat is a mammal.
> T   Every cat is an animal.
> F   ∴ Every animal is a mammal.

If one argument is formally invalid, then all other arguments with the same form are formally invalid. The same counterinstance refutes them all. We say that the counterinstance is a *counterinstance of the form* and that *the form itself is invalid*. We shall define a **valid argument form** as an argument form all of whose instances are valid. Thus **AEE1** is an invalid argument form. **AAAl**, on the other hand, is a valid form: no **AAA1** argument is invalid. Thus we can refute both arguments and argument forms by the method of counterinstance. Refuting an argument form is one step easier than refuting an argument, since we do not first have to abstract its form.

The method of counterinstance can be applied to *any* kind of argument, not just syllogisms. Suppose a philosophy major argues that every a priori truth is an analytic truth, since every analytic truth is an a priori truth. You may not even know what the terms "a priori" or "analytic" mean, but you can still prove that the argument is formally invalid by pointing out that "Every animal is a man, since every man is an animal" has the same form, a true premise, and a false conclusion, We used just this method in §5.3 to show that **A** and **O** propositions are not convertible, while **E** and **I** propositions are not contraposable.

Limitations. The method of counterinstance only provides a method for proving *invalidity*. We could theoretically prove that an argument is formally valid by examining *all* arguments with the same form, and finding in each case that the conclusion is true if the premises are. But such a procedure is impracticable, since there are infinitely many such arguments, and our time and knowledge are limited. One example with true premises and a false conclusion suffices to prove formal invalidity, but even a thousand examples in which the conclusion is true if the premises are would not suffice to prove validity. After the thousand examples, we would not be able to decide whether our failure to refute the argument was due to its validity or only to our lack of ingenuity. In the next section we will learn a method for proving validity.

Refutation by counterinstance shows that an argument is not *formally* valid. We observed in §2.5, however, that some valid arguments are not formally valid. Consider, for example, the following asyllogistic argument:

> Every Saturday is a football day.
> Every Sunday is a football day.
> ∴ Every weekend day is a football day.

It is easy to show that this argument is not formally valid by the method of counterinstance:

> Every pine is a tree.
> Every oak is a tree.
> ∴ Every daisy is a tree.

However, the original argument can still be defended as valid by observing that in fact every weekend day is either a Saturday or a Sunday. When this is added to the original argument as a suppressed premise, we obtain an argument that is formally valid. The same example will not refute it, because the analogous suppressed premise "Every daisy is either a pine or an oak" is false.

In general, then, a refutation by counterinstance conclusively proves that an argument is not formally valid. It also provides a *presumption* that the argument is invalid, which must be countered. To defend the argument against the refutation, one must show that there are certain facts which, when added as suppressed premises, result in a formally valid argument.

Glossary

Valid argument form: an argument form all of whose instances are valid.

Counterinstance: an argument possessing a given form that has true premises and a false conclusion is a counterinstance of that form, and of any other argument having that form.

Refutation by counterinstance: proving that an argument form is invalid, or that an argument is formally invalid, by producing a counterinstance.

Exercises

A. Refute the following arguments by finding a counterinstance.

1. All widgeons are ducks and some pigeons are widgeons, so some pigeons are not ducks.

2. Some lemurs are animals, for all lemurs are mammals and some animals are mammals.

3. Some primates are animals, for some mammals are animals and all primates are mammals.

4. Every maggot is a living thing, for every maggot has parents and every living thing has parents.

5. Some elements are solids at room temperature. All metals are solids at room temperature. Therefore, some elements are metals.

6. No dogs are dead as a result of the vaccine. Some things that are dead as a result of the vaccine are rabbits. Therefore, some rabbits are dogs.

7. No monotheists are polytheists, for no atheists are polytheists and no atheists are monotheists.

8. Some viruses are not living things, for no viruses are able to stand boiling water, but some living things are.

9. Every action springs from desire. No belief is an action, so some beliefs do not spring from desire.

10. All authoritarian and totalitarian societies are dictatorships. Some dictatorships are not prosperous. Therefore, some authoritarian and totalitarian societies are not prosperous.

B. Show that the following argument forms are invalid by finding a counterinstance.

1. AAA2	6. AAE2	11. EIA3	16. IIO2
2. AEE 1	7. AAE3	12. EIA4	17. AIO1
3. EII3	8. AEO1	13. IIA3	18. AIO2
4. OAA4	9. EIA1	14. IEO4	19. OAA2
5. AAA3	10. EIA2	15. IEE1	20. III1

C. Show that the following argument forms are invalid by finding a counterinstance.

1. Some *S* are *P*, therefore all *S* are *P*.

2. Some *S* are *P*, therefore some *S* are not *P*.

3. Some *S* are not *P*, therefore no *S* are *P*.

4. No *S* are *P*, therefore all *S* are *P*.

5. All *S* are *P*, therefore no *S* are *P*.

6. Every *S* is a *P*, therefore every *P* is an *S*.

7. No *S* is a *P*, therefore no non-*P* is a non-*S*.

8. Some *S* are *P*, therefore some non-*P* are non-*S*.

9. Some *S* are not *P*, therefore some *P* are not *S*.

10. Only *S* are *P*, therefore all *S* are *P*.

11. Some *S* are *P*, therefore only some *S* are *P*.

12. No *S* are *P*, therefore no non-*S* are *P*.

13. All *S* are *P*, therefore all non-*S* are non-*P*.

14. All *P* are *M*, all *M* are *N*, all *N* are *S*, therefore all *S* are *P*.

15. Some *S* are *M* some *M* are *N*, some *N* are *P*, therefore some *S* are *P*

16. All *M* are *P*, all *S* are *N*, therefore all *S* are *P*.

17. Some *M* are *P*, no *S* are non-*M*, therefore some *S* are *P*.

5.6 Proof By Deduction

Rules of Inference. We have a method for proving that syllogisms and other arguments are formally invalid. How can we prove that an argument is valid? One way is to show that the conclusion can be derived from the premises, using argument forms that are already known to be valid. To take a very simple example, we can prove the validity of "Every human is an animal, therefore some animal is a human" by observing that from the premise "Every human is an animal" we can infer "Some human is an animal" by subalternation, and from "Some human is an animal" we can infer the conclusion by conversion. Such a derivation is known as a *deduction,* and the argument forms used in the derivation are called *rules of inference.* A specific set of rules of inference defines a *system of deduction.* There is substantial freedom in choosing a system of deduction, for many different systems enable us to prove the validity of the same arguments. The list of inference rules should be short, to make the system easy to learn and to make deductions easy to check. But the list should be long enough to facilitate the construction of proofs. These general considerations provide some guidelines for selecting a system of deduction, but do not narrow the choice to one system.

We shall select the first five rules of our system from sections 5.2 and 5.3. They are **subalternation***:* from an **A** or an **E** proposition, we can infer its subaltern; *conversion:* from an **E** or an **I** proposition, we can infer its converse; *contraposition:* from an **A** or an **O** proposition, we can infer its contrapositive; **obversion***:* from any categorical proposition, we can infer its obverse; and finally *double negation:* we can infer the result of replacing any general term *T* with nonnon-*T*, or nonnon-*T* with *T*, wherever it occurs. (Conversion and contraposition must be restricted slightly to allow for the exception discussed in §6.4; we will ignore the restrictions until then.) We complete our system by selecting as rules of inference two syllogisms whose validity is self-evident-namely, **AAA1** and **AII1**, which we shall call collectively *general categorical syllogism.* General categorical syllogism consists of two valid categorical syllogisms containing only general propositions that we will use to prove the validity of all other valid general categorical syllogisms. We cannot, of course, use this system of deduction to prove the validity of the rules it consists of. Indeed, it is impossible in principle to prove the validity of *every* valid argument form, for some rules of inference must be used in any proof. Fortunately, some rules, such as the ones we have selected, are self-evidently valid and do not need to be proven valid. For easy reference and comparison, our rules of inference are written out below, along with representative argument forms.

Using the Rules. How do we go about using these rules to prove the validity of syllogisms? Suppose we are to validate the following argument:

Every bat is a mammal.
Every mammal is an animal.
∴ Some animal is a bat.

First note that this is an **AAI4** syllogism; so it is not valid directly by general categorical syllogism. But from the two premises we can infer "Every bat is an animal" by general categorical syllogism (specifically by **AAA1**). From "Every bat is an animal" we can infer "Some bat is an animal" by subalternation. And from "Some bat is an animal" we can infer "Some animal is a bat" by conversion. Since "Some animal is a bat" is the conclusion of the argument we are trying to validate, our deduction is complete. We have shown that the conclusion follows from the premises by a chain of valid inferences. So the argument must be valid.

Rules Of Inference

Subalternation (Sub): From an **A** or an **E** proposition, infer its subaltern.

Every S is a P.	No S is a P.
∴ Some S is a P.	∴ Some S is not a P.

Conversion (Conv): From an **E** or an **I** proposition, infer its converse.

No S is a P.	Some S is a P.
∴ No P is an S.	∴ Some P is an S,

Contraposition (Contr): From an **A** or an **O** proposition, infer its contrapositive.

Every S is a P.	Some S is not a P.
∴ Every non-P is a non-S.	∴ Some non-P is not a non-S.

Obversion (Obv): From any categorical proposition, infer its obverse.

Every S is a P.	No S is a P.
∴ No S is a non-P.	∴ Every S is a non-P.

Some S is a P.	Some S is not a P.
∴ Some S is not a non-P.	∴ Some S is a non-P.

General Categorical Syllogism (GCS): Infer any proposition that follows by an **AAA1** or **AII1** syllogism.

Every *S* is an *M*.	Some *S* is an *M*.
Every *M* is a *P*.	Every *M* is a *P*.
∴ Every *S* is a *P*.	∴ Some *S* is a *P*.

Double Negation (DN): Infer any proposition that results from replacing any general term *T* with nonnon-*T*, or nonnon-*T* with *T*, wherever it occurs.

$$T = \text{nonnon-}T$$

We write out our deductions as numbered and annotated sequences of steps.

1. Every bat is a mammal.
2. Every mammal is an animal.   / ∴ Some animal is a bat.
3. Every bat is an animal.   1,2 GCS
4. Some bat is an animal.   3 Sub
5. Some animal is a bat.   4 Conv

We place the conclusion off to one side, separated by a slash from the last premise, so that we can use it to guide our proof without being tempted to use it as a premise. Lines are numbered for easy reference. Each line that is not a premise must be *justified* by citing the rule of inference according to which, and the previous lines of the proof from which, the line in question follows. Thus the notation "1,2 GCS" after line 3 means that line 3 follows from lines 1 and 2 by general categorical syllogism. This can easily be verified by observing that

> 1. Every bat is a mammal.
> 2. Every mammal is an animal.
> 3. ∴ Every bat is an animal.

is an AAAl argument, and so has one of the forms comprising general categorical syllogism. It does not matter whether "Every bat is a mammal" appears before or after "Every mammal is an animal." The validity of an argument does not depend on the order of its premises. Thus the following deduction is just as correct as the one above:

> 1. Every mammal is an animal.
> 2. Every bat is a mammal,   /∴ Some animal is a bat.
> 3. Every bat is an animal.   1,2 GCS
> 4. Some bat is an animal.   3 Sub
> 5. Some animal is a bat.   4 Conv

The justification of line 3 in both deductions could be written either "1,2 GCS" or "2,1 GCS." Putting the conclusion on the line of the last premise indicates that only subsequent lines need to be justified.

Variants. To keep the list of forms manageable, only some of the patterns of inference sanctioned by obversion and contraposition were listed with the rules. For example, the rule of obversion says in general that *from any categorical proposition we can infer its obverse*. This means that both of the following forms of inference are sanctioned by the rule of obversion, since in both, the conclusion is the obverse of the premise:

> A. Some *S* is a *P*.   B. Some *S* is a non-*P*.
> ∴ Some *S* is not a non-*P*.   ∴ Some *S* is not a *P*.

Even though form B was not listed with the rules, it is still a pattern of inference justified by obversion. Thus the fifth step of the following deduction is correct:

> 1. No whales are fish.
> 2. Some mammals are whales.   /∴ Some mammals are not fish.
> 3. All whales are nonfish.   1 Obv
> 4. Some mammals are nonfish.   2,3 GCS
> 5. Some mammals are not fish.   4 Obv

The two forms of obversion for **I** propositions are equivalent, so we shall call them *variants* of each other. One form can be derived from the other using double negation. To derive form B from A, suppose we are given "Some *S* is a non-*P*"; by form A of obversion we can derive "Some *S* is not a nonnon-*P*," which is equivalent to "Some *S* is not a *P*" by double negation. To derive form A from B, suppose we are given "Some *S* is a *P*"; by double negation we can infer "Some *S* is a nonnon-*P*," which yields "Some *S* is not a non-*P*" by form B of obversion. Each of the forms listed with the rules is intended to represent all of its variants. But in case you fail to recognize a variant, or are unsure whether you have one or not, you can use double negation to get the same result. Thus the following deduction is also legitimate:

> 1. No whales are fish.
> 2. Some mammals are whales.   /∴ Some mammals are not fish.
> 3. All whales are nonfish.   1 Obv

4. Some mammals are nonfish.	2,3 GCS
5. Some mammals are not nonnonfish.	4 Obv
6. Some mammals are not fish.	5 DN

If you recognize variants of the forms listed, you can save steps in your deductions. If you overlook a variant, you will still be able to solve the problems by using double negation.

Each of the four patterns of inference listed with obversion has a single variant. The two forms listed with contraposition both have four variants. All of the following forms, for example, are equivalent to one another by double negation:

Every *S* is a *P*.	Every non-*S* is a non-*P*.
∴ Every non-*P* is a non-*S*.	∴ Every *P* is an *S*.
Every *S* is a non-*P*.	Every non-*S* is a *P*.
∴ Every *P* is a non-*S*.	∴ Every non-*P* is an *S*.

In each one of these forms, the conclusion is the contrapositive of the premise, so all steps having any one of these four forms can be justified by contraposition. If you overlook a variant, though, you can still solve the problems using the forms listed with the rules together with double negation.

Note finally that the order of the premises in any argument is logically irrelevant. It does not matter, therefore, whether the syllogisms in applications of GCS are in "standard form" or not. Indeed, the argument forms illustrating GCS are in "reverse" order because most people find that order most intuitive.

Proving the Validity of Nonsyllogisms. Our six rules of inference suffice to prove the validity of all valid categorical syllogisms that contain only general propositions. The rules have considerably more power, however, for they enable us to validate arguments that are not syllogisms just as easily. As an example, we have already proven the validity of "Every human is an animal, so some animal is a human."

1. Every human is an animal.	/∴ Some animal is a human.
2. Some human is an animal.	1 Sub
3. Some animal is a human.	2 Conv

Consider also "No nonanimals are mammals, and all nonmammals are non-bears, so all bears are animals." This is not a categorical syllogism, since there are six terms instead of three: "animals," "nonanimals," "mammals," "non-mammals," "bears," and "nonbears." Nevertheless, its validity can be proven using the same rules:

1. No nonanimals are mammals.	
2. All nonmammals are nonbears.	/∴ All bears are animals.
3. All nonanimals are nonmammals.	1 Obv
4. All nonanimals are nonbears.	2,3 GCS
5. All bears are animals.	4 Contr

We have proven the validity of arguments with one or two premises. But we have still used only a fraction of our system's power. for the five rules of inference can be used with *any* number of premises. For example:

1. Every tiger is a cat.	
2. Every cat is a carnivore.	
3. Every carnivore is a mammal.	
4. Every mammal is a vertebrate.	
5. Every vertebrate is a chordate.	
6. Every chordate is an animal.	/∴ Every tiger is an animal.

7. Every tiger is a carnivore.	2,1 GCS
8. Every tiger is a mammal.	3,7 GCS
9. Every tiger is a vertebrate.	4,8 GCS
l0. Every tiger is a chordate.	5,9. GCS
11.Every tiger is an animal.	6,10 GCS

The same argument can be used to show that there may well be several equally legitimate ways to prove the validity of one argument:

7′. Every tiger is a carnivore.	2,1 GCS
8′. Every carnivore is a vertebrate.	4,3 GCS
9′. Every vertebrate is an animal.	6,5 GCS
10′. Every tiger is a vertebrate	8′,7′ GCS
11′. Every tiger is an animal.	9′,10′ GCS

Constants. When the terms involved in an argument are long and complex, abbreviating them will greatly facilitate deduction. This saves a lot of writing and makes the forms of the propositions easier to see. Suppose we want to validate the following:

No tall, dark, and handsome man is a bachelor who is not dating beautiful women. Every male member of the Johnson family over the age of 20 is a tall dark and handsome man. Therefore, no male member of the Johnson family over the age of 20 is a bachelor who is not dating beautiful women.

Our first step will be to symbolize the argument. Let T abbreviate "tall, dark, and handsome man," let B abbreviate "bachelor who is not dating beautiful women," and let J abbreviate "male member of the Johnson family over the age of 20." Then we can abbreviate the whole argument and prove its validity as follows:

1. No T is a B.	
2. Every J is a T.	/∴ No J is a B.
3. Every T is a non-B.	1 Obv
4. Every J is a non-B.	3,2 GCS
5. No J is a B.	4 Obv

To appreciate the value of the symbols, try writing out this simple deduction without them.

The letters T, J, and B are here functioning as **constants**: they abbreviate *particular* terms. You may use any capital letters you like as constants. We have been using S, M, and P as **variables**, which hold places in statement and argument forms for any term or abbreviation thereof. Note that when applying general categorical syllogism to derive line 8 of the deduction concerning tigers, we had to think of "mammal"' as P, "carnivore" as M, and "tiger" as S. But when we applied general categorical syllogism again to derive line 9, we had to think of "vertebrate " as P, "mammal" as M, and "tiger" again as S. To avoid confusion, it is best not to use S, P, or M as constants. When symbolizing an argument, use the same constant to abbreviate synonyms, since they express the same term. Thus, if R is used to symbolize "rich." it should also be used to symbolize "wealthy." Also, if two terms are complementary, be sure to represent that fact. Thus if H is used to abbreviate "human," non-H should be used to abbreviate "nonhuman."

Independence, Completeness, and Soundness. One of our rules of inference, namely, contraposition, is redundant, for its validity can be proven using two of the other rules: obversion and conversion.

1. Every S is a P.	/∴ Every non-P is a non-S.
2. No S is a non-P.	1 Obv
3. No non-P is an S.	2 Conn
4. Every non-P is a non-S.	3 Obv

The same sequence of inferences (Obv, Conv, Obv) can be used to validate contraposition for **O** propositions, as you should verify for yourself. (For future reference, note that conversion for **E** and contraposition for **A** both have a condition of validity, and that conversion for **I** and contraposition for **O** are both valid under all conditions.) While the elimination of contraposition would shorten our list of inference rules, it would also lengthen many of our deductions, and hinder their construction. The other rules of our system are *independent,* meaning that their validity cannot be proven using the other rules of the system.

Ideally, a system of deduction should be *complete* and *sound.* A system of deduction is said to be sound if all arguments that can be proven valid using the system are valid. A system is complete for a defined class of arguments if every valid argument in that class can be proven valid using the system. The system we are using is sound (when the conversion and contraposition rules are restricted as in §6.4), and it is complete for the class of general categorical syllogisms. The power of the system extends beyond categorical syllogisms, as we have seen. But there are many valid arguments that cannot be proven valid using the present rules. A vastly more complete system will be developed in Chapter 9. One of the difficult tasks taken up in advanced logic courses is to prove whether or not any given system is sound and complete. The completeness of our system for general categorical syllogisms is relatively easy to verify, since only a finite number of forms—256—are possible (see Table 5-2 in Set I of the exercises for this section). Proofs of completeness can be very difficult, however, when these are an unlimited number of possible forms, which is the typical case.

Glossary

Proof by deduction: proving that an argument is valid by deducing intermediate conclusions from the premises, and the conclusion from the intermediate conclusions, using argument forms already known to be valid.

System of deduction: a set of inference rules used to prove validity by the method of deduction.

Rule of inference: an argument form used to prove the validity of other arguments by the method of deduction.

General categorical syllogism: the rule that you can infer any proposition that follows by an **AAA1** or **AII1** syllogism.

Subalternation: the rule that from an **A** or an **E** proposition you can infer its subaltern.

Conversion: the rule that from an **E** or an **I** proposition you can infer its converse.

Obversion: the rule that from any categorical proposition you can infer its obverse.

Contraposition: the rule that from an **A** or an **O** proposition you can infer its contrapositive.

Double negation: the rule that you can infer the result of replacing any general term *T* with nonnon-*T*, or nonnon-*T* with *T*, wherever it occurs.

Variants: equivalent but different argument forms sanctioned by the same rule of inference.

> **Constant:** a symbol used to abbreviate a particular term.
>
> **Variable:** a symbol used to represent form by holding a place for any term or constant.

Exercises

A. For each of the following arguments, state the rule of inference by which the conclusion follows from its premise or premises.

1. Every man is an animal.
    ∴ Some man is an animal.

2. All cats are mammals.
    ∴ All nonmammals are noncats.

3. No Democrat is a Republican.
    ∴ No Republican is a Democrat.

4. No Democrats are Republicans.
    ∴ All Democrats are non-Republicans.

5. Every senator is a member of Congress.
    Every member of Congress is a politician.
    ∴ Every senator is a politician.

6. Ever senator is a nonnonpolitician.
    ∴ Every senator is a politician.

7. Every senator is a member of Congress.
    Some priest is a senator.
    ∴ Some priest is a member of Congress.

8. Some planets are larger than the earth.
    ∴ Some things larger than the earth are planets

9. Some planets are larger than the earth.
    ∴ Some nonnonplanets are larger than the earth.

10. Every planet beyond Mars is larger than the earth.
    ∴ No planet beyond Mars is an object not larger than the earth.

11. Every cat is a mammal.
    Every mammal is an animal.
    ∴ Every cat is an animal.

12. Some mammals are marsupials.
    All marsupials live in Australia.
    ∴ Some mammals live in Australia.

B. State the rule of inference for each of the following arguments.

1. Every A is a B.
    ∴ Every non-B is a non-A.

2. No *F* is a *G*.
   ∴ Some *F* is not a *G*.

3. All *P* are *Q*.
   All *Q* are *R*.
   ∴ All *P* are *R*.

4. Some *A* is a *B*.
   ∴ Some *A* is a nonnon-*B*.

5. Some *A* is a *B*.
   ∴ Some *A* is not a non-*B*.

6. Some *A* is not a non-*B*.
   ∴ Some *B* is not a non-*A*.

7. Every *R* is a *T*.
   ∴ Some *R* is a *T*.

8. Some R is a T.
   ∴ Some *T* is an R.

9. Some *T* is an *R*.
   ∴ Some *T* is not a non-*R*.

10. Some nonnon-*T* is an *R*.
    ∴ Some *T* is an *R*.

11. Some *T* is a *Q*.
    Every *Q* is an *R*.
    ∴ Some *T* is an *R*.

12. No *A* are *B*.
    ∴ All *A* are non-*B*.

C. For the following deductions, justify each line that is not a premise.

1. 1. No cat is a dog.　　　　/∴ Some dog is a noncat.
   2. Every cat is a nondog.
   3. Every dog is a noncat.
   4. Some dog is a noncat.

2. 1. Some saints are martyrs.　　/∴ Some martyrs are not nonsaints.
   2. Some martyrs are saints.
   3. Some martyrs are not nonsaints

3. 1. No salt is a metal　　　　/∴ Some nonmetal is a salt.
   2.Some salt is not a metal.
   3. Some salt is a nonmetal.
   4. Some nonmetal is a salt.

4. 1. Every primate is a mammal.
   2. Every ape is a primate.　　　/∴ Some ape is a mammal.
   3. Every ape is a mammal.

4. Some ape is a mammal.

5.   1. No women are men.
      2. Some doctors are women. /∴ Some doctors are not men.
      3. All women are nonmen.
      4. Some doctors are nonmen.
      5. Some doctors are not men.

6.   1. No nonresident is a citizen.
      2. All noncitizens are nonvoters.   /∴ Every voter is a resident.
      3. All voters are citizens.
      4. No citizen is a nonresident.
      5. Every citizen is a nonnonresident
      6. Every citizen is a resident.
      7. Every voter is a resident.

7.   1. All primates are mammals.
      2. No lizards are mammals.   /∴ All lizards are nonprimates.
      3. No mammals are lizards.
      4. All mammals are nonlizards.
      5. All primates are nonlizards.
      6. All lizards are nonprimates.

D. For the following deductions, justify each line that is not a premise.

1.   1. Some L is a K.
      2. Each K is a J.   /∴ Some J is an L.
      3. Some L is a J.
      4. Some J is a L.

2.   1. Every B is an A.
      2. Some O is not an A.   /∴ Some O is a non-B.
      3. Some O is a non-A.
      4. Every non-A is a non-B.
      5. Some O is a non-B.

3.   1. All non-I are T.
      2. All V are non-T.   /∴ No V are non-I.
      3. All T are non-V.
      4. All non-I are non-V.
      5. No non-I are V.
      6. No V are non-I

4.   1. No C is a B.
      2. Some C is an A.   /∴ Some A is not a B.
      3. Some A is a C.
      4. Every C is a non-B.
      5. Some A is a non-B.
      6. Some A is not a B.

5.   1. Some H are not G.
      2. All H are F.   /∴ Some F are not G.

    3. Some *H* are non-*G*.
    4. Some non-*G* are *H*.
    5. Some non-*G* are *F*.
    6. Some *F* are non-*G*.
    7. Some *F* are not nonnon-*G*.
    8. Some *F* are not *G*.

6.   1. All *B* are *I*.
    2. No *C* are *D*.
    3. All *I* are *D*.   /∴ No *B* are *C*.
    4. All *B* are *D*.
    5. All *C* are non-*D*.
    6. All non-*D* are non-*B*.
    7. All *C* are non-*B*.
    8. No *C* are *B*.
    9. No *B* are *C*.

7.   1. Every non-*R* is a non-*H*.
    2. Every *B* is a *W*.
    3. Every *N* is an *H*.
    4. Every non-*B* is a non-*R*.   /∴ Every *N* is a *W*.
    5. Every non-*B* is a non-*H*.
    6. Every *H* is a *B*.
    7. Every *H* is a *W*.
    8. Every *N* is a *W*.

8.   1. All *B* are *W*.
    2. All *A* are *N*.
    3. All *C* are *B*.
    4. No *N* are *W*.   /∴ No *A* are *C*.
    5. All *N* are non-*W*.
    6. All *A* are non-*W*.
    7. All non-*W* are non-*B*.
    8. All *A* are non-*B*.
    9. All non *B* are non-*C*.
    10. All *A* are non-*C*.
    11. No *A* are *C*.

E. Construct a proof of validity for the following arguments.

1. All men are animals, so some animals are men.

2. All socialists are pacifists, so no nonpacifists are socialists.

3. No scientist is a philosopher, so some nonphilosopher is not a nonscientist.

4. Every steel is a metal, so no nonmetal is a steel.

5. Some fish are not sharks, so some nonsharks are fish.

6. Some saints are martyrs, so some martyrs are not nonsaints.

7. No apple is a vegetable, so some nonvegetable is an apple.

8. All chemicals are nonpoisons, so some poisons are not chemicals.

9. Every nonathlete is a bookworm, so some nonbookworm is not a nonathlete.

10. No nonathlete is a nonbookworm, so some nonbookworm is an athlete.

F. Construct a proof of validity for the following arguments.

1. All flowers are plants. All roses are flowers. Therefore, some roses are plants.

2. Some plants are roses. All roses are flowers. Therefore, some flowers are plants.

3. Every flower is a plant. Some flower is a rose. Therefore, some rose is a plant.

4. All whales are mammals. All mammals are animals. Therefore, some animals are whales.

5. Every ape is a primate. Every ape is a mammal. Therefore, some mammal is a primate.

6. No whales are fish. Some mammals are whales. Therefore, some mammals are not fish.

7. Some parents are understanding people. No parents are nonadults. Therefore, some adults are understanding people.

8. Every television is an electronic instrument. No model F21 is an electronic instrument. Therefore, no model F21 is a television.

9. No nonbirds are ducks. All nonducks are nonmallards. Therefore, all mallards are birds.

10. Some Americans are not Democrats. All Americans are taxpayers. Therefore, some taxpayers are not Democrats.

G. Symbolize the following arguments using constants to abbreviate terms. Then prove the validity of the arguments by the method of deduction.

1. Some member of the House of Representatives who has served on the armed forces subcommittee for many years is a Republican from the Finger Lakes region of upstate New York. Every member of the House of Representatives who has served on the armed forces subcommittee for many years is a congressman with enormous political clout in matters concerning military procurement. Therefore, some congressman with enormous political clout in matters concerning military procurement is a Republican from the Finger Lakes region of upstate New York.

2. No executive at the rank of vice-president or above at one of the Fortune 500 companies is paid less than $300,000 a year. Some alumnus of our school who majored in philosophy is an executive at the rank of vice-president or above at one of the Fortune 500 companies. Therefore, some alumnus of our school who majored in philosophy is not paid less than $300,000 a year.

3. Every left-handed tennis player who has ever won at Wimbledon is an individual who has a good chance of making it into the tennis Hall of Fame. No individual who has a good chance of making it into the tennis Hall of Fame is a football player, a hockey player, or a professor. Therefore, no football player, hockey player, or professor is a left-handed tennis player who has ever won at Wimbledon.

4. All Jettas manufactured by Volkswagon between 2000 and 2005 have numerous defects in the brake and transmission systems. Some cars manufactured at Volkswagon's Wolfsburg assembly plant do not

have numerous defects in the brake and transmission systems. Therefore, some cars manufactured at Volkswagon's Wolfsburg assembly plant are not Jetta's manufactured by Volkswagon between 2000 and 2005.

5. No one who has carefully studied the problem of hunger in the United States holds that the problem is negligible. Every member of the committee appointed by President Reagan to study hunger in America holds that the problem is negligible. Therefore, no member of the committee appointed by President Reagan to study hunger in America has carefully studied the problem.

6. Babies are illogical. Nobody is despised who is able to manage a crocodile. Illogical persons are despised. Therefore babies are unable to manage a crocodile.[3]

7. Everyone who is sane is able to do logic. Only one who is sane is fit to serve on a jury. None of *your* sons is able to do logic. Therefore, none of your sons is fit to serve on a jury.

8. No one takes in the *Times* who is not well-educated. No hedgehogs are able to read. Those who are unable to read are not well-educated. Therefore, no hedgehogs take in the *Times*.

H. Construct proofs of validity for the following arguments.

1. Some N is an S.
    Every V is a T.
    No S is a non-V.
    ∴Some N is a T.

2. Every Q is an N.
    Every D is a Q.
    No N is a W.
    ∴No D is a W.

3. All T are W.
    No H are R.
    All W are R.
    ∴No H are T.

4. No B is a non-T.
    Some G is an I.
    No I is a T.
    ∴Some G is a non-B.

5. No T is a W.
    No non-W is a C.
    Each K is a T.
    ∴ No K is a C.

6. All C are T.
    No non-O are L.
    No O are non-C.
    ∴ All L are T.

7. No T is a non-W.
    No H is an R.
    Every non-R is a non-W.
    ∴Some H is not a T.

8. All non-R are N.
    No T are D.
    All R are U.
    All N are D.
    ∴ All T are U.

9. All F are non-R.
    No A are non-T.
    All W are R.
    All T are F.
    ∴ No W are A.

10. Every E is a C.
    Every D is a T.
    No C is an R
    Every F is an E.
    Every T is an R.
    ∴ No F is a D.

I. Fill in Table 5-2, which represents all possible forms of general categorical syllogisms. There are 64 different moods, and each mood occurs in 4 different figures. Prove validity by the method of deduction, and invalidity by the method of counterinstance. Enter "V" for valid, and "1" for

---

[3] Exercises 6 to 8 are adapted from Lewis Carroll's *Symbolic Logic* (Dover, 1958 [1896]), pp. 112-13.

invalid. **AAA1** and **AII1** are already listed as valid, since they are rules of inference in our system of deduction. **AEE1** is listed as invalid, since it is refuted by the counterinstance presented in §5.5.

	1	2	3	4		1	2	3	4		1	2	3	4		1	2	3	4
AAA	V	_	_	_	EAA	_	_	_	_	IAA	_	_	_	_	OAA	_	_	_	_
AAE	_	_	_	_	EAE	_	_	_	_	IAE	_	_	_	_	OAE	_	_	_	_
AAI					RAI					IAI					OAI				
AAO	_	_	_	_	EAO	_	_	_	_	IAO	_	_	_	_	OAO	_	_	_	_
AEA					EEA					IEA					OEA				
AEE	I	_	_	_	EEE	_	_	_	_	IEE	_	_	_	_	OEE	_	_	_	_
AEI					EEI					IEI					OEI				
AEO	_	_	_	_	EEO	_	_	_	_	IEO	_	_	_	_	OEO	_	_	_	_
AIA					EIA					IIA					OIA				
AIE	_	_	_	_	EIE	_	_	_	_	IIE	_	_	_	_	OIE	_	_	_	_
AII	V	_	_	_	EII					III					OII				
AIO	_	_	_	_	EIO	_	_	_	_	IIO	_	_	_	_	OIO	_	_	_	_
AOA					EOA					IOA					EOA				
AOE	_	_	_	_	EOE	_	_	_	_	IOE	_	_	_	_	EOE	_	_	_	_
AOI					EOI					IOI					EOI				
AOO	_	_	_	_	EOO	_	_	_	_	IOO	_	_	_	_	EOO	_	_	_	_

TABLE 5-2

5.7 Singular Categorical Propositions

We have confined our attention to **general categorical propositions**, whose subject and predicate terms are called **general terms**. The class of general terms includes common nouns like "man," "animal," and "reptile." It also includes complex noun phrases like "tall, dark, and handsome man," and "man who failed to pay his taxes in 2006." General terms are those that can occur grammatically after quantifiers and articles, and can therefore occupy the place of S and P in the forms we have designated **A**, **E**, **I**, and **O**. There is also a very different category of terms called **singular terms**. These include proper names like "John F. Kennedy," "America," and "earth," pronouns like "you," "me," and "this," and complex noun phrases like "the thirty-fifth president of the United States," "my country," and "this book." A singular term is a noun or noun phrase used to refer to a single, definite thing. Singular terms as such cannot occur after quantifiers or articles. Several complications must be mentioned. First, proper names often function as general terms, as in "He is a Kennedy," which might mean that he is a person like Kennedy, or that he is a member of the Kennedy family, or even that he is a person named Kennedy. Second, pronouns like "he" and common proper names like "John Smith," are used on different occasions to refer to different individuals; but on any one occasion they denote a single individual. Finally, the pronoun "you" does not always function as a singular term: it occasionally refers to a number of people collectively, as in "All of you did well."

   Singular categorical propositions have general terms as their predicates, but have singular terms as their subjects. Such propositions accordingly lack a quantifier. Examples are "George W. Bush is a man," and "The president is not a Democrat." Whereas we have been using capital letters to represent general terms, we will use lower-case letters to represent singular terms. There are two forms of singular categorical proposition, which we represent as follows.

U *s* is a *P*.
Y *s* is not a *P*.

Although this is not traditional, we will use the remaining two vowels to name these forms. We will refer to *s* as the *subject*. Like their general counterparts, singular categorical propositions differ in *quality*. **U** propositions are *affirmative,* **Y** propositions *negative*. We shall say that the **quantity** *of* a **U** or a **Y** proposition is *singular.* Thus the logical form of singular categorical propositions can be specified as follows:

U singular and affirmative
Y singular and negative

Opposing **U** and **Y** propositions are contradictory, "Socrates is a philosopher" contradicts "Socrates is not a philosopher." If one is true, the other must be false.

U ← contradictories → **Y**

Singular and general categorical propositions are not opposed, since their subjects necessarily differ. Hence no arrows are needed to connect the above line to the square of opposition presented earlier.

Singular propositions cannot be converted or contraposed, for several reasons. First, a singular term cannot occur in the predicate after "a" or "an." Second, a general term cannot be the subject of a singular proposition. And third, a singular term does not have a complement. Singular propositions can, however, be obverted. As usual, you obvert a singular proposition by changing its quality and replacing the predicate with its complement.

Obverses
s is a *P* = *s* is not a non-*P*.
s is not a *P* = *s* is a non-*P*.

As with general categorical propositions, the obverses of singular categorical propositions are equivalent.

Categorical syllogisms may contain singular propositions as well as general. Consider for example:

Every Republican is a conservative.
George W. Bush is a Republican.
∴ George W. Bush is a conservative.

We can specify the mood and figure of such syllogisms in the customary way, by making use of our two new letter names in specifying mood. The example is an **AUU1** syllogism. Every syllogism containing singular propositions has a specifiable mood and figure, but not every combination of mood and figure is possible with singular propositions. For example, there are no **UUU4** syllogisms, for the middle term would have to be a general term in the major premise and a singular term in the minor, which is impossible. For a complete tabulation, see Table 5-3 in Set H of the exercises for this section.

We can prove the invalidity of syllogisms and other arguments with singular propositions by the method of counterinstance. Thus we can refute an argument like

Every mammal is a warm-blooded animal.
Fido is a warm-blooded animal.
∴ Fido is a mammal.

by observing that at least one other argument with the same form has true premises and a false conclusion, such as:

> Every senator is a politician.
> The president is a politician.
> ∴ The president is a senator.

This counterinstance shows that **AUU2** is an invalid argument form.

Arguments with singular propositions can be proven valid by the method of deduction. We must, however, expand our system of deduction by including rules that apply to singular propositions. We will allow obversion of singular propositions, and we will add **AUU1** and **UUI3** to our list of basic syllogisms, under the heading *singular categorical syllogism.*

Rules Of Inference

Obversion (Obv): From any categorical proposition, infer its obverse.

s is a *P*.	*s* is not a *P*.
∴ *s* is not a non-*P*.	∴ *s* is a non-*P*.

Singular Categorical Syllogism (SCS): infer any proposition that follows by an **AUU1** or **UUI3** syllogism.

s is an *M*.	*m* is an *S*.
Every *M* is a *P*.	*m* is a *P*.
∴ *s* is a *P*.	∴ Some *S* is a *P*.

Suppose we are asked to prove the validity of

> Every dog is carnivore.
> Tweety is not a carnivore.
> ∴ Tweety is not a dog.

We do not have to abbreviate the terms here; but if we do, the proof looks like this:

1. Every *D* is a *C*.	
2. *t* is not a *C*.	/∴ *t* is not a *D*.
3. *t* is a non-*C*.	2 Obv
4. Every non-*C* is a non-*D*.	1 Contr
5. *t* is a non-*D*.	4,3 SCS
6. *t* is not a *D*.	5 Obv

Categorical Propositions with Singular Predicates. In all the categorical propositions we have studied, both singular and general, the predicates are general terms. There are categorical propositions, nonetheless, in which the predicates are singular terms:

> Every man is the president.
> No man is the president.
> Some man is the president.
> Some man is not the president.
> Bush is the president.
> Bush is not the president.

These share many logical properties with the categorical propositions we have studied. For example, the relationships represented by the square of opposition all hold. Thus "No man is the president" implies "Some man is not the president," and contradicts "Some man is the president." There are also valid syllogisms like "Bush is the president, and the president is a former cheerleader, therefore Bush is a former cheerleader," which resembles the **AAA1**, **AII1**, and **AUU1** syllogisms in GCS and SCS. There are differences, however. For example, conversion is not even a possible transformation with the first four propositions above, but it is both possible and valid for the last two. Now we could study the logic of categorical propositions with singular predicates in the same way we have studied other categorical propositions, by introducing and naming additional standard forms, adding to our rules of inference, and so on. However, all categorical propositions are handled uniformly and efficiently by quantification theory, introduced in Chapter 9. So we will defer study of categorical propositions with singular predicates until then.

Glossary

General term: a term like "cow" or "big brown cow," which is not used to refer to a single definite thing, and which can occur after quantifiers and articles.

Singular term: a term like "America" or "the nation," which is used to refer to a single definite thing, and which cannot occur after quantifiers or articles.

General categorical proposition: a categorical proposition whose subject and predicate are general terms.

Singular categorical proposition: a categorical proposition whose subject is a singular term and whose predicate is a general term.

U, Y: forms of singular categorical propositions, respectively: "*s* is a *P*" and "*s* is not a *P*."

Quantity-singular: the quantity of a singular categorical proposition is singular.

Singular categorical syllogism: the rule that you can infer any proposition that follows by an **AUUI** or **UUI3** syllogism.

Exercises

A. For each of the following categorical propositions, identify its form (**A, E, O, U, Y**), its quantity and quality, and its subject and predicate.

1. Ted Kennedy is a Democrat.

2. The prime minister of England is not a woman.

3. Taxpayers are advised to read the IRS manual carefully.

4. Billy Mitchell holds a record Pac-Man score of 3,333,360.

5. Steffi Graf is not left-handed.

6. No city in Turkey has a population of 3 million.

7. Arabic is spoken in Syria.

8. Catholicism is not a major religion in Greece.

9. The Nile is longer than any other river.

10. Some forests in California are treeless.

B. Produce the obverse of each proposition in Set A.

C. Identify the mood and figure of the following syllogisms.

1. Every senator is a member of Congress. Pat Roberts is not a senator. Therefore Pat Roberts is not a member of Congress.

2. No representative is a senator. John Conyers is a representative. Therefore John Conyers is not a senator.

3. Mt. Everest is a river. No river is a lake. Therefore, Mt. Everest is a lake.

4. The Statue of Liberty is not in Newark. Nothing in Newark is far from Manhattan. Therefore, the Statue of Liberty is not far from Manhattan.

5. Mick Jagger is a singer. Mick Jagger is not a pianist. Therefore, some singers are not pianists.

6. Queen Elizabeth II is not a musician. All rock singers are musicians. Therefore Queen Elizabeth II is not a rock singer.

7. Lee R. Raymond is an Exxon executive. Some Exxon executives make $6 million a year. Therefore, Lee R. Raymond makes $6 million a year.

8. All objects revolving around the sun have elliptical orbits. The moon has an elliptical orbit. Therefore, the moon revolves around the sun.

9. Zinc is a metal. No organic compound is a metal. Therefore zinc is not an organic compound.

10. Some politicians are not former athletes. The president is a politician. Therefore, he is not a former athlete.

D. For each of the following arguments, state the rule of inference by which the conclusion follows from its premise or premises.

1. Every senator is a member of Congress.
    Pat Roberts is a senator.
    ∴ Pat Roberts is a member of Congress.

2. Rostropovich is a cellist.
    Rostropovich is a conductor.
    ∴ Some cellists are conductors.

3. Mick Jagger is not a pianist.
    ∴ Mick Jagger is a nonpianist.

4. Every executive is hard-driving.
    Some woman is an executive.
    ∴ Some woman is hard-driving.

5. Henry Kissinger is a famous American.
    Every famous American is wealthy.
    ∴ Henry Kissinger is wealthy.

6. Sulfur is nonmetallic.

∴ It is not metallic.

7. Jacques Chirac is a non-American.
    Jacques Chirac is famous.
    ∴ Some non-American is famous.

8. Some metal is not an alloy.
    ∴ Some metal is a nonalloy.

9. All bachelors are unmarried.
    Brad Pitt is a bachelor.
    ∴ Brad Pitt is unmarried.

10. Brad Pitt is unmarried.
    ∴ Brad Pitt is not married.

E. Determine whether the arguments in Set C are valid or invalid, using the method of deduction or the method of counterinstance.

F. Prove the validity of the following arguments, using the method of deduction. (Assume that the conditions of validity on contraposition and conversion are satisfied.)

1. k is not an A.
    All non-A are B.
    ∴ k is a B.

2. c is a J.
    c is a K.
    Every K is an L.
    ∴ Some J is an L.

3. d is an A.
    No A is a B.
    d is a C.
    ∴ Some C is a non-B.

4. f is an X.
    Every Y is a non-X.
    ∴ f is not a Y.

5. c is not an H.
    Every non-G is an H.
    ∴ c is a G.

6. All C are D.
    i is not a non-G.
    No G are non-C.
    ∴ i is a D.

7. b is an F.
    Every F is a G.
    No G is an H.
    ∴ b is not an H.

8. All A are B.
    No C are D.
    All B are D.
    k is a C.
    ∴ k is not an A.

9. No T is a W.
    No non-W is a C.
    Every K is a T.
    b is a K.
    ∴ b not a C.

10. Every C is a T.
    Every L is an O.
    No 0 is a non-C.
    b is not a T.
    ∴ b is not an L.

G. Symbolize the following arguments, then prove them valid using the method of deduction.

1. Liechtenstein is a country in which taxes are low. No country in which taxes are low fails to attract the headquarters of many international corporations. Therefore Liechtenstein attracts the headquarters of many international corporations.

2. The United Arab Emirates is a small Arab state located on the Persian Gulf. All small Arab Persian Gulf' states are nations that have become very wealthy by exploiting their enormous reserves of petroleum. No nation that has become very wealthy by exploiting its enormous oil reserves has failed to suffer from the changing values that accompany rapid industrial development. Therefore, the United Arab Emirates has not failed to suffer from the changing values that accompany rapid industrialization.

3. The Sacramento-San Joaquin Valley system is located in central California. Anything located in central California is located in California. Anything located in California is located in the United States of America. Anything located in the United States of America is safe from foreign invasion. Therefore, the Sacramento-San Joaquin Valley system is safe from foreign invasion.

4. No experienced person is other than competent. Jenkins is always blundering. Nothing competent is always blundering. Therefore, Jenkins is not an experienced person.[4]

5. My gardener is well worth listening to on military subjects. Nothing that is not very old is able to remember the battle of Waterloo. Nothing that is unable to remember the battle of Waterloo is really worth listening to on military subjects. Therefore, my gardener is very old.

H. Continue to fill in Table 5-3, which represents all possible forms of singular categorical syllogisms. Use the method of deduction to prove validity and the method of counter-instance to prove invalidity.

	1	2				3
AUU	V	__	__	UUA	__	
EUU	__	__	__	UUE	__	
IUU	__	__	__	UUI	V	
OUU	__	__	__	UUO	__	
AUY	__	__	__	UYA	__	
EUY	__	__	__	UYE	__	
IUY	__	__	__	UYI	__	
OUY	__	__	__	UYO	__	
AYU	__	__	__	YUA	__	
EYU	__	__	__	YUE	__	
IYU	__	__	__	YUI	__	
OYU	__	__	__	YUO	__	
AYY	__	__	__	YYA	__	
EYY	__	__	__	YYE	__	
IYY	__	__	__	YYI	__	
OYY	__	__	__	YYO	__	

TABLE 5-3

[4] Exercises 4 and 5 are adapted from Lewis Carroll's *Symbolic Logic*, p. 113.

LSAT Prep Questions

1. Manuscripts written by first-time authors generally do not get serious attention by publishers except when these authors happen to be celebrities. My manuscript is unlikely to be taken seriously by publishers for I am a first-time author who is not a celebrity.

   The structure of which of the following arguments is most similar to the structure of the argument above?

   (a) Challengers generally do not win elections unless the incumbent has become very unpopular. The incumbent in this election has become very unpopular. Therefore, the challenger may win.

   (b) Fruit salad that contains bananas is ordinarily a boring dish unless it contains two or more exotic fruits. This fruit salad has bananas in it, and the only exotic fruit it has is guava. Thus, it will probably be boring.

   (c) Thursday's city counsel meeting is likely to be poorly attended. Traditionally, council meetings are sparsely attended if zoning issues are the only ones on the agenda. The agenda for Thursday is exclesively devoted to zoning.

   (d) The bulk of an estate generally goes to the spouse, if surviving, and otherwise goes to the surviving children. In this case there is no surviving spouse; hence the bulk of the estate is likely to go to the surviving children.

   (e) Normally about 40 percent of the deer population will die over the winter unless it is extremely mild. The percentage of the deer population that died over the recent winter was the normal 40 percent. I conclude that the recent winter was not unusually mild.

   Preptest 30, Section 4, Question 9

5.8 Suppressed Premises

We observed in §1.3 that it is common for obvious premises to be omitted. The speaker assumes that the deleted premises will be "understood" by the audience. Such implicit premises are said to be ***suppressed.***[5] The use of suppressed premises not only saves time and effort, it also may increase comprehension by focusing the audience's attention on the crucial links of the argument. However, before we can prove the validity of such elliptical arguments using the logical tools we have developed so far, it may be necessary to supply the missing premises. Consider, for example:

> All dogs are mammals.
> ∴ All terriers are mammals.

We cannot deduce the conclusion from the one explicit premise using any or all of the rules of syllogistic logic. Indeed, counterinstances arise by the thousands (just change "terriers" to almost any other term like "trees"). Yet it would be a mistake to classify this argument as a fallacy. For it is most reasonable to assume that "All terriers are dogs" is functioning as a suppressed premise. It is a piece of common knowledge whose relevance will be obvious to all. When it is supplied, the argument is easily seen to be valid.

---

[5] An argument with a premise or even the conclusion suppressed is traditionally called an enthymeme, from the Greek for "to have in mind."

> [All terriers are dogs.]
> All dogs are mammals.
> ∴ All terriers are mammals.

The conclusion now follows in one step, by GCS. The deduction will not always be so easy, of course. Consider:

> Bill's cars are all Chevies.
> ∴ None of them are Fords.

The suppressed premise this time is "No Chevies are Fords," or equivalently, "No Fords are Chevies." When either proposition is added to the premises, the resulting argument is easy to prove valid. We shall symbolize the propositions first.

> 1. [No C are F.]
> 2. All B are C.   /∴ No B are F.
> 3. All C are non-F.   1 Obv
> 4. All B are non-F.   2,3 GCS
> 5. No B are F.   4 Obv

What do we look for when we need to supply suppressed premises? When using the rules of syllogistic logic to prove validity, we should look for categorical propositions that relate two terms not already connected in the conclusion or in any of the explicit premises. The suppressed premises may be affirmative, as in the dog example, or negative, as in the car example. In both examples, the suppressed premises were universal; but particular and singular premises may also be suppressed. Arguments may, of course, contain suppressed premises that are not categorical propositions. But we do not yet have the means for dealing with them. It is often helpful to try proving the validity of the argument as it stands first, to see what additional premises are necessary to complete the proof. In both our examples, adding one suppressed premise enabled us to prove the argument's validity. In other cases, it may be necessary to add more than one. There is no theoretical limit on the number of possible suppressed premises.

Can a suppressed premise be false? Yes. The speaker may have been mistaken about the facts, and may have assumed that everyone shares his or her opinion. You, nevertheless, may know more. An argument with a false premise, whether suppressed or explicit, is unsound. Be careful, though, about imputing false suppressed premises. the speaker may know more than you think! The principle of charity, one of our guides to good interpretation, advises us as a general rule to assume that the speaker is as knowledgeable as we are. Can an argument with a suppressed premise be invalid? Again, the answer is yes. The supplying of suppressed premises is not an "anything goes" procedure designed to preserve validity at all costs. If proving an argument's validity required supplying a premise like "All animals are men," we should judge the argument invalid. It is just too unlikely that anyone would intend such a premise.

Glossary

Suppressed premise: a proposition that is intended as a premise but was omitted because it is obvious.

Exercises

Prove the validity of the following arguments, supplying suppressed premises as needed. Reexpress any premises or conclusions that are not in standard form.

1. Some mammals are aquatic, for whales are.

2. No star revolves around the sun, so Neptune is not a star.

3. Only four-cylinder cars are allowed to race. Hence Mustangs are not allowed to race, because they are six-cylinder cars.

4. Only women are qualified for the job. So no men should apply.

5. Pregnant women should avoid alcohol and therefore should not drink martinis.

6. All libertarians oppose the draft. Conservatives favor the draft, so libertarians are not conservatives.

7. Some blue whales are 115 feet long. So some whales are over 100 feet long.

8. Anything containing refined sugar is unhealthy. Thus candy should not be eaten by children.

9. A comet's tail streams away from the sun. Hence the tail of Halley 's comet does not stream toward the sun.

10. No one who gets at least a C on the final fails the course. Mary got an A on the final, so she passed the course.

LSAT Prep Questions

1. Some people take their moral cues from governmental codes of law; for them, it is inconceivable that something that is legally permissible could be immoral.

    Those whose view is described above hold inconsistent beliefs if they also believe that

    (a) law does not cover all circumstances in which one person morally wrongs another

    (b) a legally impermissible action is never morally excusable

    (c) governmental officials sometimes behave illegally

    (d) the moral consensus of a society is expressed in its laws

    (e) some governmental regulations are so detailed that they are burdensome to the economy

    Preptest 9, Section 2, Question 16

2. No chordates are tracheophytes, and all members of Pteropsida are tracheophytes. So no members of Pteropsida belong to the family Hominidae.

    The conclusion above follows logically if which one of the following is assumed?

    (a) All members of the family Hominidae are tracheophytes.

    (b) All members of the family Hominidae are chordates.

    (c) All tracheophytes are members of Pteropsida.

    (d) No members of the family Hominidae are chordates.

    (e) No chordates are members of Pteropsida.

    Preptest 35, Section 1, Question 22

3. Several critics have claimed that any contemporary poet who writes formal poetry—poetry that is rhymed and metered—is performing a politically conservative act. This is plainly false. Consider Molly Peacock and Marilyn Hacker, two contemporary poets whose poetry is almost exclusively formal and yet who are themselves politically progressive feminists.

The conclusion drawn above follows logically if which of the following is assumed?

(a) No one who is a feminist is also politically conservative.

(b) No poet who writes unrhymed or unmetered poetry is politically conservative.

(c) No one who is politically progressive is capable of performing a politically conservative act.

(d) Anyone who sometimes writes poetry that is not politically conservative never writes poetry that is politically conservative.

(e) The content of a poet's work, not the work's form, is the most decisive factor in determining what political consequences, if any, the work will have.

Preptest 35, Section 4, Question 19

4. People who do not believe that others distrust them are confident in their own abilities, so people who tend to trust others think of a difficult task as a challenge rather than a threat, since this is precisely how people who are confident in their own abilities regard such tasks.

The conclusion above follows logically if which of the following is assumed?

(a) People who believe that others distrust them tend to trust others.

(b) Confidence in one's own abilities gives one confidence in the trustworthiness of others.

(c) eople who tend to trust others do not believe that others distrust them.

(d) People who are not threatened by difficult tasks tend to find such tasks challenging.

(e) People tend to distrust those who they believe lack self–confidence.

Preptest 38, Section 4, Question 16

5. Some of the world's most beautiful cats are Persian cats. However, it must be acknowledged that all Persian cats are pompous, and pompous cats are invariably irritating.

If the statements above are true, each of the following must also be true on the basis of them EXCEPT:

(a) Some of the world's most beautiful cats are irritating.

(b) Some irritating cats are among the world's most beautiful cats.

(c) Any cat that is not irritating is not a Persian cat.

(d) Some pompous cats are among the world's most beautiful cats.

(e) Some irritating and beautiful cats are not Persian cats.

Preptest 13, Section 4, Question 14

6. There is no genuinely altruistic behavior. Everyone needs to have a sufficient amount of self-esteem, which crucially depends on believing oneself to be useful and needed. Behavior that appears to be altruistic can be understood as being motivated by the desire to reinforce that belief, a clearly self-interested motivation.

A flaw in the argument is that it

(a) presupposes that anyone who is acting out of self-interest is being altruistic

(b) illicitly infers that behavior is altruistic merely because it seems altruistic

(c) fails to consider that self-esteem also depends on maintaining an awareness of one's own value

(d) presumes, without providing justification, that if one does not hold oneself in sufficient self-esteem one cannot be useful or needed

(e) takes for granted that any behavior that can be interpreted as self-interested is in fact self-interested

Preptest 32, Section 1, Question 19

CHAPTER SIX

Syllogistic Logic: Venn

6.1 Venn Categoricals

The last half of the nineteenth century saw many developments in logical theory. The main figures in this activity were Augustus De Morgan (1806-1871), George Boole (1815-1864), and John Venn (1834-1923). One result was a remarkably easy and general method for proving both validity and invalidity. Boole was perhaps the major innovator, but Venn gave the developments a simple and clear formulation that has subsequently become standard.

Venn studied the logical properties of four forms related to Aristotelian categorical propositions by a simple transformation. Under this transformation, an **E** proposition like "No man is a reptile" becomes "Nothing is a man and a reptile." The **I** proposition "Some man is a genius" becomes "Something is a man and a genius." The transformation for **E** and **I** propositions involves conjoining the subject with the predicate and replacing the subject with "thing" combined with the quantifier. The transformation for **A** and **O** propositions is more complex. **A** and **O** propositions are first obverted to produce **E** and **I** propositions, which are transformed as above; then "non" is changed to "not." Thus "Every man is an animal," equivalent to "No man is a nonanimal" by obversion, becomes "Nothing is a man and not an animal." Similarly, "Some man is not a genius," equivalent by obversion to "Some man is a nongenius," becomes "Something is a man and not a genius." We will refer to this procedure for transforming general categorical propositions as the ***Venn transformation***. We will subsequently refer to **A, E, I,** and **O** propositions as ***Aristotelian categoricals*** and to their Venn transforms as ***Venn categoricals***. We will name the forms of the Venn categoricals **A***, **E***, **I***, and **O***. Henceforth, we will drop the logically meaningless articles "a" and "an" from our standard forms.

Aristotelian categoricals		Venn categoricals	
A	Every *S* is *P*.	A*	Nothing is *S* and not *P*.
E	No *S* is *P*.	E*	Nothing is *S* and *P*.
I	Some *S* is *P*.	I*	Something is *S* and *P*.
O	Some *S* is not *P*.	O*	Something is *S* and not *P*.

An Aristotelian categorical and its Venn transform are equivalent, except in one special case discussed in §6.4. Until then, we will focus on Venn categoricals, and on the respects in which they resemble Aristotelian categoricals.

A Venn categorical can be viewed as a special type of Aristotelian categorical. For example, the **A*** proposition "Nothing is a man and not an animal" can be treated as an **E** proposition whose subject is "thing" combined with the quantifier "No," and whose predicate is the term "a man and not an animal." However, we will analyze Venn categoricals differently in order to highlight the similarities between an Aristotelian categorical and its Venn transform. We will classify *nothing* and *something* as the *quantifiers.* And we'll call *S* the *subject* and *P* the *predicate.* So "Nothing is a man and not an animal" is the Venn categorical in which the quantifier is "nothing," the subject is "man," and the predicate is "animal." We will continue to say that **A*** and **E*** propositions are *universal* in quantity, while **I*** and **O*** propositions are *particular.* Furthermore, we will say that **A*** and **I*** propositions are *affirmative* in quality, while **E*** and **O*** propositions are *negative.* If it seems forced to say that an **A*** proposition is affirmative, it should help to think of the two negatives "nothing" and "not" as canceling out.

Given this analysis, the definitions of conversion, obversion, and contraposition apply to Venn categoricals as well as their Aristotelian counterparts, and the same logical relationships hold. We convert a categorical proposition by interchanging its subject and predicate terms. Thus the converse of "Nothing is a man and a reptile" is "Nothing is a reptile and a man."

Converses
Nothing is *S* and not *P* ≠ Nothing is P and not S.
Nothing is *S* and *P* = Nothing is *P* and *S*.
Something is *S* and *P* = Something is *P* and *S*.
Something is *S* and not *P* ≠ Something is *P* and not *S*.

The converses of E* and I* propositions are equivalent, but A* and O* propositions are not convertible. There are no exceptions to this rule. We obvert a categorical proposition by changing its quality and replacing the predicate with its complement. The obverse of "Nothing is a man and not an animal" is "Nothing is a man and a nonanimal." The obverse of "Nothing is a man and a reptile" is "Nothing is a man and not a nonreptile."

Obverses
Nothing is *S* and not *P* = Nothing is *S* and non-*P*.
Nothing is *S* and *P* = Nothing is *S* and not non-*P*.
Something is *S* and *P* = Something is *S* and not non-*P*.
Something is *S* and not *P* = Something is *S* and non-*P*.

The obverses of all Venn categoricals are equivalent. Finally, the contrapositive of a categorical proposition is obtained by replacing the subject with the complement of the predicate, and the predicate with the complement of the subject. Do not touch the "not" in **A*** and **O*** propositions. The contrapositive of "Nothing is a man and not an animal" is "Nothing is a nonanimal and not a nonman."

Contrapositives
Nothing is S and not P = Nothing is non-P and not non-S.
Nothing is S and P ≠ Nothing is non-P and non-S.
Something is S and P ≠ Something is non-P and non-S.
Something is S and not P = Something is non-P and not non-S.

The contrapositives of **A*** *and* **O*** *propositions are equivalent while* **E*** *and* **I*** *propositions are not contraposable.* There are also no exceptions to the contraposability of **A*** and **O*** propositions.

With respect to conversion, obversion, and contraposition, the Venn transformation is what is known in mathematics as an *isomorphism*: the Venn transform of the converse of an Aristotelian categorical is the converse of its Venn transform; the Venn transform of the obverse of an Aristotelian categorical is the obverse of its Venn transform; and so on. Consider, for example, "Every man is an animal." Obversion yields "No man is a nonanimal," whose Venn transform is "Nothing is a man and a nonanimal." Reversing the order of the transformations yields the same result. The Venn transform of "Every man is an animal" is "Nothing is a man and not an animal," whose obverse is "Nothing is a man and a nonanimal." You should verify for yourself that the isomorphism holds for all the relationships mentioned.

Venn categoricals occur in syllogisms, and the structure of Venn categorical syllogisms is similar to that of Aristotelian categorical syllogisms. The form of a Venn syllogism can even be specified in terms of mood and figure. Consider:

> Nothing is a mammal and not an animal.
> Nothing is a cat and not a mammal.
> ∴ Nothing is a cat and not an animal.

This is an **A*A*A*I** syllogism and, like its Aristotelian counterpart, it is valid.

Glossary
Aristotelian categorical: a proposition of the form A "Every S is P," E "No S is P," I "Some S is P," or O "Some S is not P."
Venn categorical: a proposition of the form A* "Nothing is S and not P," E* "Nothing is S and P," I* "Something is S and P," or O* "Something is S and not P."
Venn transformation: the operation that transforms an Aristotelian categorical into a Venn categorical having the same letter name.
Venn transform: the Venn categorical that results when the Venn transformation is applied to a given Aristotelian categorical.

Exercises

A. Identify the form (**A***, **E***, **I***, or **O***) of the following Venn categoricals.

1. Nothing is a skunk and not a mammal.

2. Nothing is a mouse and a reptile.

3. Something is a mouse and a rodent.

4. Something is a rodent and not a mouse.

5. Something is an even-toed hoofed mammal and a rhinoceros.

6. Nothing is an even-toed hoofed mammal and a hippopotamus.

7. Nothing is both a rhinoceros and a hippopotamus.

8. Nothing is a black-footed ferret and not a member of the weasel family.

9. Something is an aggressive, bloodthirsty predator and a wolverine.

10. Nothing is a member of the weasel family and not an aggressive bloodthirsty predator.

B. Produce the Venn transform of the following Aristotelian categoricals.

1. Every mammal is a vertebrate.

2. Some mammal is not a vertebrate.

3. No businessman is a politician.

4. All Democrats are liberals.

5. Some Republicans are not liberals.

6. Some Republicans are liberals.

7. Each senator is a congressman.

8. Some women are geniuses.

9.   Any woman is a female.

10. No man is a genius.

C.   Produce the Venn transform of the following Aristotelian categoricals.

1. Some politicians are downright evil.

2. Each man owns his own life.

3. No society operates entirely on the command principle.

4. Each and every true Christian is a member of the Moral Majority.

5. Some elements at room temperature are solids.

6. All governments restrain and rule people.

7.   Some moons are so close that their planet covers half the sky.

8. Some payroll savings plans are not to be sniffed at.

9. Free transactions take place among private entities.

10. An experiment by Needham shows that life can come spontaneously from dead stuff.

D. Identify the relationships between the following pairs of Venn categoricals. Determine whether they are converses, obverses, or contrapositives, and whether or not they are equivalent.

1.   (a) Nothing is a skunk and not a mammal. (b) Nothing is a skunk and a nonmammal.

2.   (a) Something is a rodent and a mouse. (b) Something is a mouse and a rodent.

3.   (a) Something is a hoofed mammal and a rhinoceros (b) Something is a hoofed mammal and not a nonrhinoceros.

4.   (a) Nothing is a sandpiper and not a shorebird. (b) Nothing is a nonshorebird and not a nonsandpiper.

5.   (a) Nothing is a sandpiper and a nonshorebird. (b) Nothing is a nonshorebird and a sandpiper.

6.   (a) Nothing is an eagle and not a hawk. (b) Nothing is a hawk and not an eagle.

7.   (a) Something is a hawk and an osprey. (b) Something is a non-osprey and a nonhawk.

8.   (a) Nothing is a shorebird and a hawk. (b) Nothing is a shorebird and not a nonhawk.

9.   (a) Something is an aquatic carnivore and not a walrus. (b) Something is a walrus and not an aquatic carnivore.

10. (a) Nothing is a lynx and a bobcat. (b) Nothing is a bobcat and a lynx.

E.   Identify the mood and figure of the following Venn categorical syllogisms.

1.   Nothing is a widgeon and not a duck, and something is a pigeon and a widgeon, so something is a pigeon and not a duck.

2.   Something is a lemur and an animal, for nothing is a lemur and not a mammal and something is an animal and a mammal.

3.   Something is a primate and an animal, for something is a mammal and an animal, and nothing is a primate and not a mammal.

4.   Nothing is a maggot and not a living thing. Nothing is a living thing and not a thing with parents. Therefore, nothing is a maggot and not a thing with parents.

5.   Nothing is an atheist and a polytheist, for nothing is a monotheist and a polytheist, and nothing is a monotheist and an atheist.

6.   Something is a virus and not a living thing, for nothing is a virus and not a thing that is able to stand boiling water, while something is a both living and able to stand boiling water.

7.   Something is a lynx and a mammal. Nothing is a mammal and a reptile. Therefore, something is a reptile and not a lynx.

8.   Nothing is a hawk and a duck. Something is a hawk and an eagle. Therefore, nothing is an eagle and not a duck.

9.   Nothing is a member of the cat family and not a carnivore. Something is a jaguar and a member of the cat family. Therefore, something is a jaguar and a carnivore.

10. Nothing is an element and a synthetic material. Nothing is a plastic and not a synthetic material. Therefore, nothing is a plastic and an element.

6.2 Sets and Venn Diagrams

Empty and Nonempty Sets. Boole was a pioneer in the development of the mathematical theory of sets or classes. A *set* consists of any number of objects considered as a single group or collection. Corresponding to every general term in a categorical proposition, there is a unique set of objects, the set of all things the term applies to. Corresponding to the term "man" there is the set of all men. Corresponding to the term "animal" there is the set of all animals. Corresponding to the term "tall, dark, and handsome men" there is the set of all tall, dark, and handsome men. A convenient, short way to refer to the set of all objects denoted by a term is to enclose the term in braces: $\{T\}$ means the set of all T.

Sets generally have *members*. This book is a member of the set of all logic books. The symbol $\in$ means "is a member of." Thus $b \in \{logic\ books\}$ says that b (this book) is a member of the set of all logic books. Now it is somewhat paradoxical to think of a set with *no* members. After all, you might wonder, how can a set of objects contain no objects? Nevertheless, in both mathematics and logic it is highly useful to allow that a set might not have members. We only need one such set, which is appropriately called the *empty set*. The empty set is no stranger than zero, which is the number of objects in the empty set. The set of all unicorns is the empty set, since there are no unicorns. The set of all griffins is also the empty set, as is the set of all planets between Mercury and Venus, and the set of all even prime numbers greater than 2. We use the symbol "$\varnothing$" to represent the empty set. Then an equation like "$\{unicorns\} = \varnothing$" means that the set of unicorns is the empty set—that is, it has no members. "$\{Men\} \neq \varnothing$," on the other hand, means that the set of all men is not the empty set—that is, the set does have members: there are men.

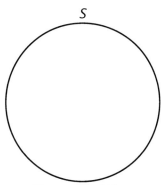

FIGURE 6-1. $\{S\}$.

Venn developed a technique for proving validity and invalidity that is especially easy because it employs simple diagrams—called *Venn diagrams*—of all the sets and propositions involved in a syllogism. Sets of objects are represented geometrically by regions in a plane. For example, the set $\{S\}$ can be represented by the area within a circle (see Figure 6-1).

A circle or other region, with no further marking, simply represents the set without making any statement about it. To represent the fact that a set is empty, we *shade out* the circle (or other region). To represent the fact that a set is not empty—that is, that it has at least one member—we put an x (or later, any other letter) in the circle (See Figures 6-2 and 6-3). Of course, to say that $\{centaurs\}$ is empty is to say that there are no centaurs. So shading out the S circle represents the proposition "Nothing is S." Similarly, to say that $\{men\}$ is not the empty set is to say that there are men. So putting an x in the S circle represents "Something is S."

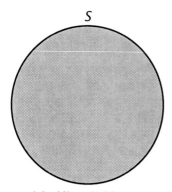

FIGURE 6-2. {*S*} = ∅. NOTHING IS *S*.

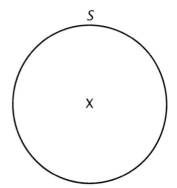

FIGURE 6-3. {*S*} ≠ ∅. SOMETHING IS *S*.

Complements. The *complement of a set* is defined as the unique set containing everything that is *not* in the original set. The prime mark (′) signifies the complement of a set. For example, {men}′ is the complement of {men}, and is the set containing everything that is not a man. The complement of the set of men, it should be clear, is the set of all nonmen. In general, {*S*}′ = {non-*S*}. Graphically, the complement of a set is represented by the region outside the region representing the set. If {*S*} is represented by the area within a circle, {*S*}′ is represented by the area outside the circle. The area outside a circle may be marked as appropriate (see Figures 6-4 and 6-5). Verify for yourself that the complement of the complement of a set is the set itself: {*S*}″ = {S}. The complement of the empty set is called the *universal set,* since it is the set containing everything: ∅′ = *U*.

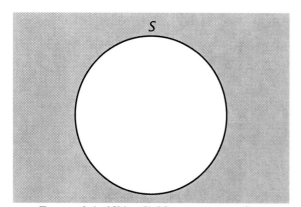

FIGURE 6-4. {*S*}′ = ∅. NOTHING IS NON-*S*.

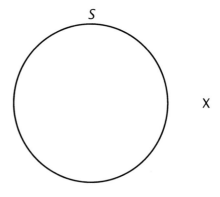

FIGURE 6-5. {*S*}′ ≠ ∅. SOMETHING IS NON-*S*.

Intersections. The *intersection* of two sets is defined as the unique set containing every object that is a member of *both* sets. Intersections are symbolized by ∩. Thus, {violinists} ∩ {pianists} is the intersection of {violinists} and {pianists}, and is the set consisting of everything that is both a violinist and a pianist. We diagram the intersection of two sets by making sure that the regions representing the two sets have some overlap. The overlapping region can then be marked to indicate whether or not it is empty (as in Figures 6-6 and 6-7).

Every Venn categorical is equivalent to a statement about the intersection of two sets. **E*** states that {*S*} ∩ {*P*} is empty, and is therefore represented by Figure 6-6. **I*** states that {*S*} ∩ {*P*} is not empty, and is represented by Figure 6-7. The other two Venn categoricals describe the intersection of $\{S\}$ and $\{P\}'$.

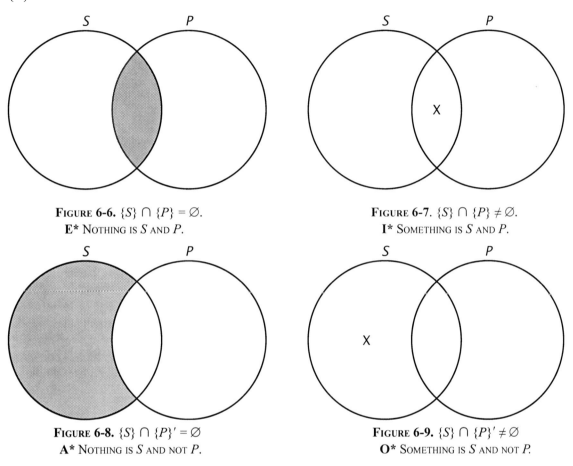

FIGURE 6-6. $\{S\} \cap \{P\} = \varnothing$.
E* NOTHING IS S AND P.

FIGURE 6-7. $\{S\} \cap \{P\} \neq \varnothing$.
I* SOMETHING IS S AND P.

FIGURE 6-8. $\{S\} \cap \{P\}' = \varnothing$
A* NOTHING IS S AND NOT P.

FIGURE 6-9. $\{S\} \cap \{P\}' \neq \varnothing$
O* SOMETHING IS S AND NOT P.

A* says that $\{S\} \cap \{P\}'$ is empty, while **O*** says that $\{S\} \cap \{P\}'$ is not empty. $\{S\} \cap \{P\}'$ is represented geometrically by the region outside $\{P\}$ but inside $\{S\}$. (See Figures 6-8 and 6-9).

How should we diagram a proposition like "Nothing is a tern and a non-bird"? There are two equivalent ways to do so (see Figures 6-10 and 6-11). For the sake of uniformity, we shall use the diagram in Figure 6-10. For "Nothing is a tern and a nonbird" is an **E*** proposition whose predicate term is "nonbird." It will facilitate our work greatly if we diagram all **E*** propositions the same way, as in Figure 6-6. We should diagram all other Venn categoricals uniformly as well, so that every **I*** proposition is diagrammed as in Figure 6-7, and so on.

Subsets and Unions. When $\{S\} \cap \{P\}' = \varnothing$, $\{S\}$ is said to be a ***subset*** of $\{P\}$, which is symbolized $\{S\} \subseteq \{P\}$. So the **A*** proposition says that $\{S\}$ is a subset of $\{P\}$. Since nothing is a man and not an animal, the set of men is a subset of the set of animals. The fact that $\{S\}$ is a subset of $\{P\}$ is represented in our diagrams by shading out every portion of the S circle lying outside the P circle; consequently, any unshaded portion of the S circle, or any portion marked with an x, must lie entirely within the P circle. The **O*** proposition says that $\{S\}$ is *not* a subset of $\{P\}$, which is symbolized $\{S\} \not\subseteq \{P\}$. The set of animals is not a subset of the set of men, since something is an animal and not a man. In our diagrams, the fact that $\{S\}$ is not a subset of $\{P\}$ is represented by putting an x in some portion of the S circle outside the P circle. Similarly, the **E*** proposition "Nothing is an S and a P" says that $\{S\}$ is a subset of $\{P\}'$, and the P proposition "Something is an S and a P" says that $\{S\}$ is not a subset of $\{P\}'$.

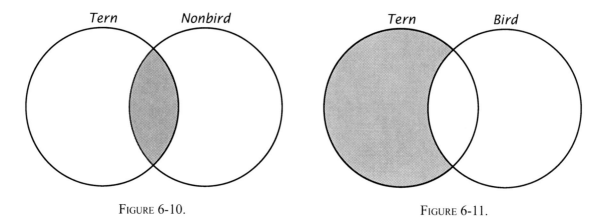

FIGURE 6-10.   FIGURE 6-11.

The mathematical theory describing the basic relationships among sets and their members, complements, intersections, and subsets has come to be known as *Boolean algebra*. One further important idea in Boolean algebra is the ***union*** of two sets, defined as the unique set containing everything that is in one or the other or both sets. Unions are represented by the symbol ∪ Thus {violinists} ∪ {pianists} is the union of {violinists} and {pianists}, and contains every individual who plays either the violin or the piano or both instruments. The union of two sets is represented by the sum of the regions representing the two sets, rather than just the overlap. Unions will play no role in our study of logic. But it is important not to confuse them with intersections. We will not use subsets either, since we can do everything we need to do with intersections and complements.

Glossary

Set or class: a number of objects considered as a single group or collection; for any term T, $\{T\}$ symbolizes the set of all T.

Member: an object in a set; the statement that x is member of $\{T\}$ is symbolized: $x \in \{T\}$.

Empty set: the set that has no members; symbolized $\varnothing$.

Complement: the complement of a set is the set containing everything that is not in the set; $\{T\}'$ symbolizes the complement of $\{T\}$ and is equal to {non-T}.

Universal set: the set containing everything; symbolized U.

Intersection: the intersection of two sets is the set containing everything that is in both sets; $\{S\} \cap \{P\}$ symbolizes the intersection of $\{S\}$ and $\{P\}$.

Union: the union of two sets is the set containing everything that is in either or both sets; $\{S\} \cup \{P\}$ symbolizes the union of $\{S\}$ and $\{P\}$.

Subset: $\{S\}$ is a subset of $\{P\}$, symbolized $\{S\} \subseteq \{P\}$, when the intersection of $\{S\}$ and the complement of $\{P\}$ is the empty set.

> **Venn diagram:** a graphic representation of a statement about sets or any equivalent proposition. A set is represented by a circle or other region; the complement of a set is represented by the region outside the region representing the set; the intersection of two sets is represented by the overlap of the regions representing the two sets. The fact that a set is empty is represented by shading out the region representing it; the fact that a set is not empty is represented by putting an x (or other letter) in the region representing the set.

Exercises

A. Reexpress each of the following propositions as a statement about sets, and represent it geometrically by a Venn diagram. If the proposition is a Venn categorical, identify its form.

1. There are no twenty-toed mammals.

2. There are some even-toed hoofed mammals.

3. Nothing is a nonmaterial object.

4. There is an honest politician.

5. There is no such thing as a free lunch.

6. Something is an aggressive, bloodthirsty predator.

7. Nothing is a skunk and not a mammal.

8. Nothing is a mouse and a reptile.

9. Something is a mouse and a rodent.

10. Something is an even-toed hoofed mammal and a hippopotamus.

11. Nothing is both a rhinoceros and a hippopotamus.

12. Something is an aggressive, bloodthirsty predator and a wolverine.

13. Nothing is a member of the weasel family and not an aggressive, bloodthirsty predator.

14. Nothing is a black-footed ferret and not a member of the weasel family.

15. Nothing is an eagle and not a hawk.

16. Nothing is a nonhawk and an eagle.

17. Nothing is a nonhawk and not a noneagle.

18. Something is a hawk and an osprey.

19. Something is a hawk and not a non-osprey.

20. Something is a non-osprey and a nonhawk.

21. Nothing is a hard rock group and a musical group.

22. Nothing is a hard rock group and not a musical group.

23. Something is a rock group and a country music group.

24. Nothing is both an avant-garde composition and a piece of music containing pretty melodies and sweet harmonies.

25. Nothing is a violation of property rights and not a violation of human rights.

26. Something is a violation of property rights and not a violation of human rights.

27. Something is a violation of human rights and not a violation of property rights.

28. Nothing is a violation of human rights and a violation of property rights.

29. Nothing is a government and not something that rules and constrains people.

30. Nothing is a government and something that does not rule and constrain people.

B.   Which of the following are correct?

1.   The intersection of the empty set and the universal set is: (a) the empty set; (b) the universal set; (c) neither of the above.

2.   The union of the empty set and the universal set is: (a) the empty set; (b) the universal set; (c) neither of the above.

3.   The intersection of any set and its complement is: (a) the empty set; (b) the universal set, (c) neither of the above.

4.   The union of any set and its complement is: (a) the empty set: (b) the universal set; (c) neither of the above.

5.   (a) The empty set is a subset of the universal set: (b) the universal set is a subset of the empty set; (c) neither of the above.

6.   The intersection of any set $\{S\}$ and itself is: (a) $\{S\}$; (b) the empty set; (c) the universal set; (d) none of the above.

7.   The union of any set $\{S\}$ and itself is: (a) $\{S\}$; (b) the empty set; (c) the universal set; (d) none of the above.

8.   The intersection of any set $\{S\}$ and the empty set is: (a) $\{S\}$; (b) the empty set; (c) the universal set; (d) none of the above.

9.   The union of any set $\{S\}$ and the empty set is: (a) $\{S\}$; (b) the empty set; (c) the universal set; (d) none of the above.

10.   The intersection of any set $\{S\}$ and the universal set is: (a) $\{S\}$; (b) the empty set; (c) the universal set; (d) none of the above.

11.   The union of any set $\{S\}$ and the universal set is: (a) $\{S\}$; (b) the empty set; (c) the universal set; (d) none of the above.

12.   The intersection of $\{men\}$ and $\{women\}$ is: (a) the empty set; (b) the universal set; (c) neither of the above.

13.   The union of $\{men\}$ and $\{women\}$ is: (a) the empty set; (b) the universal set; (c) neither of the above.

14. The intersection of the set of women and the set of mothers is: (a) the set of women; (b) the set of mothers; (c) neither of the above.

15. The union of the set of women and the set of mothers is: (a) the set of women; (b) the set of mothers; (c) neither of the above.

16. The union of the set of mothers and the set of fathers is: (a) the set of parents; (b) the empty set; (c) the universal set; (d) none of the above.

17. The intersection of the set of mothers and the set of fathers is: (a) the set of parents; (b) the empty set; (c) the universal set; (d) none of the above.

18. The intersection of the set of women and the complement of the set of fathers is: (a) the set of women; (b) the empty set; (c) the universal set; (d) none of the above.

19. The union of the set of women and the complement of the set of fathers is: (a) the set of women; (b) the empty set; (c) the universal set; (d) none of the above.

20. (a) The set of women is a subset of the complement of the set of fathers. (b) The complement of the set of fathers is a subset of the set of women. (c) Both of the above. (d) None of the above.

6.3 The Venn Diagram Test of Validity

Venn diagrams represent the *form* of a statement. Every **A*** proposition, for example, is diagrammed in exactly the same way. Now an argument is formally valid provided its form guarantees that the conclusion follows from the premises with necessity. Expressed in geometric terms, to say that an argument is formally valid is to say that if the premises are diagrammed then the conclusion is diagrammed. This provides the basis for the **Venn diagram test of validity**: first, diagram the premises of the argument; then check to see if the conclusion of the argument is already diagrammed; if it is, the argument is formally valid; if the conclusion is not diagrammed, the argument is formally invalid.

Arguments with Two Terms. Up to this point, we only know how to diagram Venn categoricals. So for now, we can only apply the Venn diagram test to arguments whose premises and conclusions are Venn categoricals. Let us begin by examining arguments in which there are a total of two terms, such as:

> Nothing is a man and a reptile.
> ∴ Nothing is a reptile and a man.

The first step in applying the Venn diagram test is to diagram the premise of this argument (see Figure 6-12). The circle labeled *M* represents the set of men, and the circle labeled *R* represents the set of reptiles. We diagram the premise by shading out the overlapping region of the two circles. Now observe that the conclusion of the argument is already diagrammed. We do not need to do anything more to represent the conclusion. Nothing we could add to the diagram would make the conclusion false. Consequently, the argument is formally valid. We have therefore proved that conversion is valid for **E*** propositions.

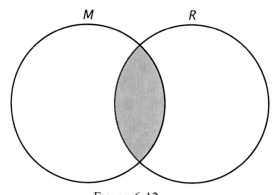

FIGURE 6-12.

As a contrast, consider an invalid argument containing just two terms:

Nothing is a man and not an animal.
∴Nothing is an animal and not a man.

We diagram the premise as in Figure 6-13, letting the *M* circle represent the set of men and the *A* circle represent the set of animals. When we check the conclusion, we see that it is not diagrammed. To diagram the conclusion, we would have to shade out the portion of the *A* circle that is outside the *M* circle. Diagramming the premise, we see, is not enough to exclude the possibility of an *x* in that portion of the *A* circle outside the *M* circle, which would represent the falsity of the conclusion. Since the conclusion is not already diagrammed once we diagram the premise, the argument is formally invalid. We have therefore shown that conversion is invalid for **A*** propositions.

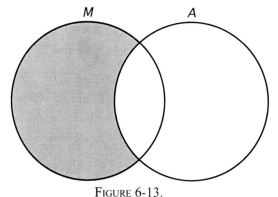

FIGURE 6-13.

In general, the diagram for an **A*** or an **O*** proposition is also a diagram for its obverse and contrapositive but not its converse, while the diagram for an **E*** or an **I*** proposition is also a diagram for its obverse and converse but not its contrapositive, which proves the rules discussed above. As an exercise, examine the diagrams for Venn categoricals and verify these points for yourself.

Arguments with Three Terms. Before we can apply the Venn diagram test to arguments involving three terms, such as syllogisms, we need to devise a method of representing geometrically all possible relationships that might exist among three sets. We must have three circles that overlap in such a way that the intersection of each pair of circles is represented, as well as the intersection of all three circles. This can be done by arranging the circles as in Figure 6-14.

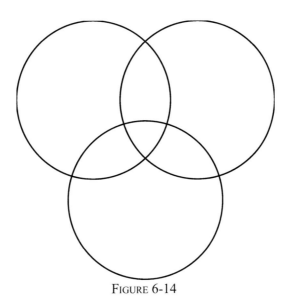

FIGURE 6-14

Consider now an **A*A*A*1** syllogism:

> Nothing is a mammal and not an animal.
> Nothing is a cat and not a mammal.
> ∴ Nothing is a cat and not an animal.

To apply the Venn diagram test, we will need three overlapping circles labeled *M*, *A*, and *C*. The first step is to diagram the premises. To diagram the first premise, we focus on the *M* and *A* circles, ignoring the *C* circle (see Figure 6-15).

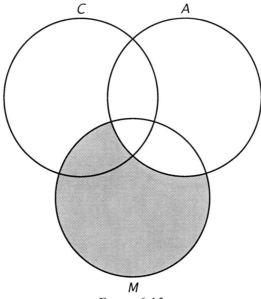

FIGURE 6-15

To diagram the second premise, we ignore the *A* circle (see Figure 6-16). Since both premises have now been diagrammed, we need to see whether the conclusion is already diagrammed. It is. In Figure 6-16, the entire portion of the *C* circle outside the *A* circle has been shaded out, which means that nothing is a cat and not an animal. The argument is therefore formally valid, and we have verified that **A*A*A*1** is a valid argument form.

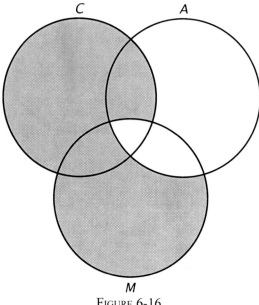

FIGURE 6-16

In contrast, consider the **A*A*A*4** syllogism:

Nothing is *P* and not *M*.
Nothing is *M* and not *S*.
∴ Nothing is *S* and not *P*.

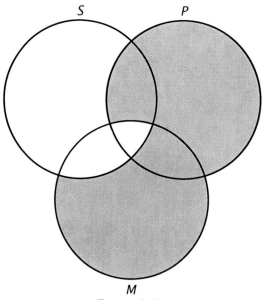

FIGURE 6-17

When we diagram the premises, we get Figure 6-17. We now check whether the conclusion is represented in the diagram. For the conclusion to be diagrammed, the entire part of the *S* circle lying outside the

P circle would have to be shaded out. None of that region is shaded. **A*A*A*4** is therefore an invalid argument form.

Putting an "x" on the Line. One complication remains to be explained. Suppose we try to test the validity of the **I*I*I*3** syllogism:

> Something is *M* and *P*.
> Something is *M* and *S*.
> ∴ Something is *S* and *P*.

First we draw the usual three overlapping circles (figure 6-18).

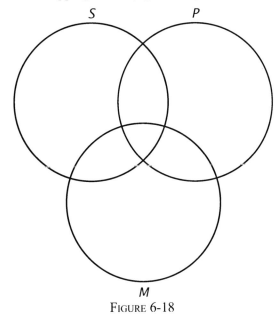

FIGURE 6-18

Then we isolate the *M* and *P* circles in order to diagram the first premise. We need to put an *x* inside the intersection of the *M* and *P* circles. But we have a problem. The intersection of the *M* and *P* circles is cut by the line representing the border of the *S* circle. Which side of the line do we put the *x* on? We cannot put it on either side. For the first premise does not tell us whether the object that is *M* and *P* is, or is not, *S*. When diagramming premises, we must not represent any information that is not contained in those premises. The only thing we can do, then, is *put the "x" on the line*. We stipulate *an "x" on a line represents an object that could be on either side of the line*. When both premises are diagrammed in this way, we get Figure 6-19.

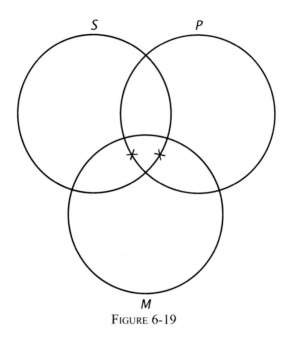

FIGURE 6-19

Now it is time to see whether the conclusion is diagrammed. For the conclusion to be diagrammed, there would have to be an *x* inside the intersection of the *S* and *P* circles. There is no *x* inside that intersection, so the argument form is invalid. There are two *x*'s on the *border* of the intersection. But they are not *inside* the intersection. Since an *x* on a line represents an object that could be on either side of the line, Figure 6-19 shows that the information in the premises of an **I*I*I*3** argument does not enable us to conclude that something is both *S* and *P*. The premises do not rule out the possibility that nothing is both *S* and *P*.

Let us work out another case, the **E*I*O*1** syllogism.

> Nothing is *M* and *P*.
> Something is *S* and *M*.
> ∴ Something is *S* and not *P*.

We already know how to diagram the first premise (Figure 6-20). Given our discussion of the **I*I*I*3** syllogism, you might diagram the second premise of the **E*I*O*1** syllogism by putting an *x* in the intersection of the *S* and *M* circles on the line marking the *P* circle. This would mean that the object represented by *x* could be on either side of the line. But this way of diagramming the second premise would ignore some information contained in the first premise and already represented in the diagram; nothing is in the intersection of all three circles, since nothing is both *M* and *P*. To determine whether an argument is valid, we must consider *all* the information contained in the premises. So we should diagram the second premise by putting the *x* in the *unshaded* portion of the intersection of the *S* and *M* circles.

Now, is the **E*I*O*1** syllogism valid? We need to see whether the conclusion is diagrammed. It is. There is an *x* inside the *S* circle and outside the *P* circle, which means that something is *S* and not *P*. Note that if we ignored the information contained in the universal premise and put the *x* on the line, we would mistakenly conclude that **E*I*O*1** is an invalid argument form. For then the *x* would not be outside the *P* circle. Reflection on this example will show that *universal premises should always be diagrammed before nonuniversal premises.* Any premise requiring shading out a region should be diagrammed before one requiring marking in letters. If we diagrammed "Something is *S* and *M*" first, we would have to put the x on the line. Then when we diagrammed "Nothing is M and P," we would have to move the x. It is cumbersome and messy to move an x, and easily forgotten.

The Venn diagram test of validity can be extended to cover arguments in which there are more than three terms. However, the diagrams in such cases become quite complex (see the solution to section 6.6, LSAT problem 4). We shall stop with three terms.

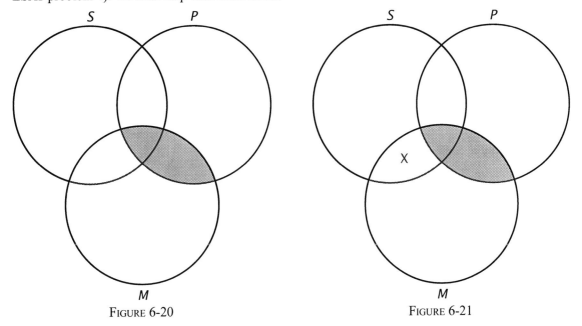

FIGURE 6-20   FIGURE 6-21

Glossary

    Venn diagram test of validity: proving the formal validity or invalidity of an argument by diagramming its premises and then checking to see if its conclusion is already diagrammed; if the conclusion is already diagrammed, the argument is formally valid; otherwise it is formally invalid.

Exercises

A. Determine whether each proposition below is diagrammed by the Venn diagram accompanying it.

1. Figure 6-22.

    (a) Nothing is *P* and *M*.

    (b) Nothing is *M* and *S*.

    (c) Something is *S* and *P*.

    (d) Nothing is *S* and not *P*.

    (e) Nothing is *S* and not *M*.

    (f) Nothing is *S* and *P*.

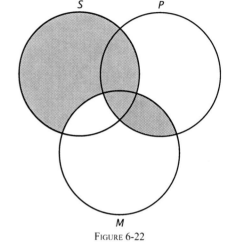

FIGURE 6-22

2. Figure 6-23.

    (a) Something is *S* and *M*.

    (b) Something is *S* and *P*.

    (c) Something is *M* and not *P*.

    (d) Something is *P* and not *M*.

    (e) Something is *P* and not *S*.

    (f) Nothing is *P* and *M*.

FIGURE 6-23

3. Figure 6-24.

    (a) Something is *S* and not *M*.

    (b) Something is *S* and *M*.

    (c) Nothing is *S* and *M*.

    (d) Nothing is *S* and *P*.

    (e) Something is *S* and *P*.

    (f) Nothing is *M* and *P*.

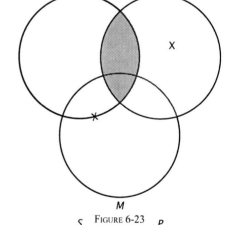

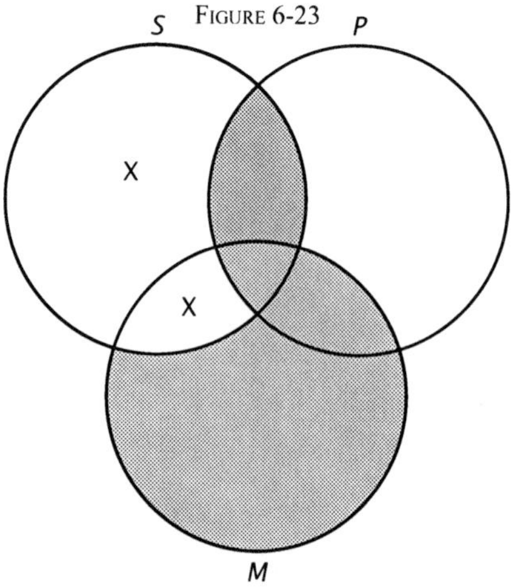

FIGURE 6-24

4. Figure 6-25.

   (a) Nothing is S and P.

   (b) Nothing is S and M.

   (c) Something is P and M.

   (d) Nothing is M and not S.

   (e) Nothing is S and not M.

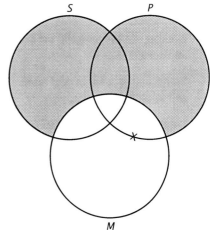

FIGURE 6-24

B. Test the following arguments for validity, using Venn diagrams.

1. Something is a rodent and a mouse. Therefore, something is a mouse and a rodent.

2. Nothing is a mouse and not a rodent. Therefore, nothing is a rodent and not a mouse.

3. Nothing is a mouse and a cat. Therefore, nothing is a cat and a mouse.

4. Something is an aquatic carnivore and not a walrus. Therefore, something is a walrus and not an aquatic carnivore.

5. Nothing is a skunk and not a mammal. Therefore, nothing is a skunk and a mammal.

6. Nothing is a skunk and not a mammal. Therefore, something is a skunk and a mammal.

7. Something is a man and a carpenter. Therefore, something is a man and not a carpenter.

8. Nothing is a sandpiper and a mammal. Therefore, something is a sandpiper and not a mammal.

9. Nothing is a lynx and a bobcat. Therefore, nothing is a lynx.

10. Something is a lynx and a mammal. Therefore, something is a lynx.

11. Something is a lynx and a mammal. Therefore, something is a mammal.

12. Nothing is a skunk and not a mammal. Therefore, nothing is a skunk and a nonmammal.

13. Nothing is a skunk and not a mammal. Therefore, something is a skunk,

14. Something is a hoofed mammal and a rhinoceros. Therefore, something is a hoofed mammal and not a nonrhinoceros.

15. Nothing is a sandpiper and not a shorebird. Therefore, nothing is a nonshorebird and not a nonsandpiper.

16. Nothing is a sandpiper and a nonshorebird. Therefore, nothing is a nonshorebird and a sandpiper.

17. Something is a hawk and an osprey. Therefore, something is a non-osprey and a nonhawk.

18. Nothing is a hawk and an osprey. Therefore, nothing is an osprey and not a nonhawk.

C. Test the validity of the following syllogisms using Venn diagrams.

1. Nothing is a widgeon and not a duck, and something is a pigeon and a widgeon, so something is a pigeon and not a duck.

2. Something is a lemur and an animal, for nothing is a lemur and not a mammal and something is an animal and a mammal.

3. Something is a primate and an animal, for something is a mammal and an animal, and nothing is a primate and not a mammal.

4. Nothing is a maggot and not a living thing. Nothing is a living thing and not a thing with parents. Therefore, nothing is a maggot and not a thing with parents.

5. Nothing is an atheist and a polytheist, for nothing is a monotheist and a polytheist, and nothing is a monotheist and an atheist.

6. Something is a virus and not a living thing, for nothing is a virus and not a thing that is able to stand boiling water, while something is both living and able to stand boiling water.

7. Something is a lynx and a mammal. Nothing is a mammal and a reptile. Therefore, something is a lynx and not a reptile.

8. Nothing is a hawk and a duck. Something is a hawk and an eagle. Therefore, nothing is an eagle and not a duck.

9. Nothing is a member of the cat family and not a carnivore. Something is a jaguar and a member of the cat family. Therefore, something is a jaguar and a carnivore.

10. Nothing is an element and a synthetic material. Nothing is a plastic and not a synthetic material. Therefore, nothing is a plastic and an element.

D. Test the validity of the following syllogistic forms, using Venn diagrams.

1. A*A*A*3	7. E*A*E*3	13. E*I*O*2	19. E*A*O*4
2. E*A*E*1	8. E*I*O*1	14. A*E*O*4	20. E*I*O*4
3. A*A*I*1	9. I*A*I*3	15. A*O*O*4	21. I*I*I*1
4. A*A*I*2	10. O*A*O*3	16. A*E*O*2	22. I*I*I*2
5. I*A*I*4	11. O*O*O*1	17. E*I*O*3	
6. A*A*I*3	12. A*O*O*2	18. E*A*O*3	

6.4 Aristotelian Categoricals and Their Presuppositions

Presuppositions. We said earlier that corresponding Aristotelian and Venn categoricals are equivalent except in one special case. The difference between them is small, but large enough, nonetheless, to produce different squares of opposition, as we shall see. The differences are due entirely to the following fact: *Aristotelian categoricals presuppose that there is an S—i.e., that there is at least one thing to which their subjects apply; Venn categoricals do not.* The notion of a presupposition is best introduced in connection with questions. Consider a famous "loaded question," and think seriously about how you would answer it:

> Have you stopped beating your wife?

This question presupposes that you have a wife and that you have been beating her. If either of these presuppositions is false (and I trust that at least one is), you cannot answer the question. You cannot say "Yes, I have stopped beating my wife" or "No, I have not stopped beating her." The question has no answer. It is simply out of place. All you can do is point out its incorrect presuppositions by saying "I don't have a wife" or "I've never beaten her" or something to that effect. As this example illustrates, the presuppositions of a question are things that must be true for the question to have an answer. The problem with the above question is not simply that, due to lack of information, you do not know the answer. The response "I don't know" would be just as damaging as "Yes" or "No." In contrast, the question "Is there any extraterrestrial life?" has an answer even though we happen to be ignorant of it. Propositions also have presuppositions. *The **presuppositions** of a proposition are things that must be true for the proposition to be either true or false.* Truth and falsity are referred to as the two **truth values.** So presuppositions are things that must be true for a proposition to have a truth value. Consider:

> Your dodo is big.

This statement presupposes that you have a dodo. Since you do not (dodos became extinct in the seventeenth century), we cannot say whether this statement is true or false. The problem is not just lack of information. Since you do not have a dodo, there is nothing for us to have information about. The proposition simply has no truth value. It is not only undetermined, but *undeterminable*. Note that when the proposition is transformed into the question "Is your dodo big?" the presupposition remains; as a result, the question is unanswerable because it has no answer.

The presuppositions of a statement are not part of what it asserts. They are unstated assumptions representing background information that should be secured before the statement is made. Contrast:

> You have a big dodo.

This asserts in part that you have a dodo. The proposition that you have a big dodo is therefore false since you do not have any dodo. Being false, the statement has a truth value. The corresponding question "Do you have a big dodo?" must be answered "No." In general, if a proposition asserts anything false, then it is false (and therefore not true). But if a proposition presupposes something false, then it is neither true nor false. You should have an intuitive "feel" for the fact that the first statement simply takes for granted something that the second forthrightly asserts.

Presupposition is a special kind of *implication*. Anything that must be true for a proposition to be true is an implication of that proposition. A presupposition, however, is something that must be true both for a proposition to be true and for it to be false. Both statements we have been examining imply that you have a dodo. Consequently, neither statement is true, since you do not have one. But only the first presupposes that you have a dodo. So given that you do not have a dodo, the second is not true because it is false while the first is neither true nor false. This suggests a simple "thought experiment" that might help you determine whether an implication of a given proposition is a presupposition or not. Imagine that the implication is false. Then see whether in the case imagined the given proposition is false, or undeterminable. If the falsity of the implication makes the given proposition neither true nor false, then the implication is a presupposition. If the falsity of the implication makes the given proposition false, then the implication is not a presupposition.

Aristotelian vs. Venn Categoricals. Aristotelian categoricals presuppose that their subjects apply to something. When this presupposition is false, every Aristotelian categorical with that subject is neither true or false. Consider the following opposing propositions, for example:

Every 2006 Edsel is a four-door.	*Neither T nor F*
No 2006 Edsel is a four-door.	*Neither T nor F*
Some 2006 Edsel is a four-door.	*Neither T nor F*
Some 2006 Edsel is not a four-door.	*Neither T nor F*

These all presuppose that there is at least one 2006 Edsel. There isn't. The last Edsel was produced in 1959. None of the propositions, therefore, has a truth value. They can only be described as "odd." Do Aristotelian categoricals presuppose that their *predicates* apply to something? No. Consider "No car is a 2006 Edsel." This is *true:* no car produced in 2006 is an Edsel, and none of the Edsels still around were made in 2006. Since "No car is a 2006 Edsel" is true, it's subaltern "Some car is not a 2006 Edsel" is also true, while it's contradictory "Some car is a 2006 Edsel" and its contrary "All cars are 2006 Edsels" are both false. So an Aristotelian categorical presupposes that its subject applies to something, but not it's predicate.

Venn categoricals, on the other hand, do not even presuppose that their subjects apply to something. Consequently, Venn categoricals all have definite truth values, even when there is no *S*. Consider the Venn transforms of the above Aristotelian categoricals:

Nothing is a 2006 Edsel and not a four-door.	T
Nothing is a 2006 Edsel and a four-door.	T
Something is a 2006 Edsel and a four-door.	F
Something is a 2006 Edsel and not a four-door.	F

The **A*** and **E*** propositions here are true: since nothing is a 2006 Edsel, nothing is both a 2006 Edsel and either a four-door or a nonfour-door. The intersection of the empty set with the set of four-doors or with the set of nonfour-doors is empty. Since nothing whatsoever is in the empty set, nothing is simultaneously in the empty set and any other set. The **I*** and **O*** propositions are false, however, because both assert in part that something is a 2006 Edsel which is false. The **I*** and **O*** propositions imply, but do not presuppose, that there are 2006 Edsels. The **A*** and **E*** propositions do not imply in any way that there are.

The presuppositions of *any* categorical proposition are introduced by its *grammatical* subject. The term introduced by the grammatical subject of an Aristotelian categorical is the subject term, so an Aristotelian categorical presupposes that its subject applies to something. The subject term of a Venn categorical, however is expressed in the grammatical predicate, so there is no presupposition involving it. Thus "Nothing is a 2006 Edsel and a four-door" does not presuppose that there is a 2006 Edsel, since "2006 Edsel" appears in the grammatical predicate. In contrast, "No 2006 Edsel is a four-door" does presuppose that there is a 2006 Edsel, since "2006 Edsel" appears in the grammatical subject.

We observed above that Venn categoricals could also be analyzed as Aristotelian categoricals. For example, both "Something is a 2006 Edsel and a four-door" and "Nothing is a 2006 Edsel and a four-door" can be analyzed as having the term "thing" as subject and "2006 Edsel and a four-door" as predicate. So Venn categoricals do have a presupposition, but it is simply that *there is at least one thing.* Since satisfaction of this presupposition is guaranteed as long as we are alive and thinking, it can safely be ignored. Note that a Venn categorical's presupposition is also introduced by its grammatical subject.

Aristotelian categoricals and their Venn transforms have the same truth values as long as there is something to which their subjects apply. So we may state the following rule:

Venn Transforms
Provided there is an *S*:

Every *S* is *P* = Nothing is *S* and not *P*,

No *S* is *P* = Nothing is *S* and *P*,

Some *S* is *P* = Something is *S* and *P*, and

Some *S* is not *P* = Something is *S* and not *P*.

When there is no *S*, however, then any **A**, **E**, **I**, or **O** proposition whose subject is *S* is neither true nor false; any **A*** or **E*** proposition with subject *S* is true; and any **I*** or **O*** proposition with subject *S* is false. The exceptional case where Aristotelian categoricals and their Venn transforms are not equivalent is illustrated by the Edsel example.

The Edsel example also shows that the Venn square of opposition (see Figure 6-26) must be weaker than the Aristotelian.

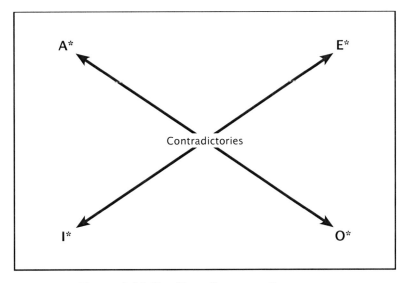

FIGURE 6-26. THE VENN SQUARE OF OPPOSITION.

Opposing **A*** and **O*** propositions are still contradictory, as are opposing **E*** and **I*** propositions. For example, "Nothing is a 2006 Edsel and not a four-door" denies precisely what "Something is a 2006 Edsel and not a four-door" asserts. Necessarily, one of these propositions is true (the first in this case), and the other false. Similarly, "Nothing is a 2006 Edsel and a four-door" contradicts "Something is a 2006 Edsel and a four-door"; the former is true, the latter false. However, opposing **A*** and **E*** propositions are not contrary, because both are true when there is no *S*, as in the Edsel example. Opposing **I*** and **O*** propositions are not subcontraries because both are false in the same case. Opposing **A*** and **I*** propositions are not alterns, for the **A*** is true and the **I*** false when there is no *S*. Opposing **E*** and **O*** propositions are not alterns for the same reason. Subalternation, therefore, is not a valid rule of inference for Venn categoricals.

Fictitious Subjects. Statements about mythical or fictitious objects may appear to be exceptions to the rule that Aristotelian categoricals have no truth value when there is nothing to which their subject terms apply. For example, we would without hesitation affirm that "Every unicorn has a horn" is true, and that "Every unicorn has an elephant's trunk" is false, even though we fully realize that there are no unicorns. Now the fact that we would count "Every unicorn has a horn" as true might even incline you to think that Aristotelian categoricals are completely equivalent to their Venn transforms, since "Nothing is a unicorn and not a thing with a horn" is true. But this inclination should evaporate once you realize that if Aristotelian categoricals *were* completely equivalent to their Venn transforms, then "Every unicorn has an elephant's trunk" and "No unicorn has a horn" would be just as true as "Every unicorn has a horn," while "Some unicorn has a horn" and "Some unicorn does not have an elephant's trunk" would be perfectly false.

Well then, why *do* we count "Every unicorn has a horn" as true, and "Every unicorn has an elephant's trunk" as false? Because we understand these as *elliptical statements about myths.* That is, we automatically interpret "Every unicorn has a horn" to mean something like *"The myth says* that every unicorn has a horn." Such a statement presupposes that a myth of the unicorn exists, but not that unicorns exist. There is such a myth, and it does say that unicorns have horns, so the statement is true. The myth does not describe unicorns as having trunks, so "The myth says that unicorns have trunks" is false. Note that "The myth says that every unicorn has a horn" is a singular categorical proposition whose subject is "The myth" and whose predicate is "says that every unicorn has a horn." Similarly, we interpret "Sherlock Holmes is a detective" as an elliptical statement about a body of fiction—namely, Arthur Conan Doyle's *The Adventures of Sherlock Holmes.* The statement presupposes that *The Adventures of Sherlock Holmes* exists, but not that Sherlock Holmes exists.

Conversion and Contraposition. In §5.3, we said that the conversion and contraposition rules for Aristotelian categoricals had an exception. The exception arises because of the existential presupposition of Aristotelian categoricals. The converses of **E** and **I** propositions are equivalent *except* when one of the terms applies to nothing. For example, "No four-door is a 2006 Edsel" is true; but its converse "No 2006 Edsel is a four-door" is neither true nor false. Similarly, "Some four-door is a 2006 Edsel" is false, while its converse "Some 2006 Edsel is a four-door" is neither true nor false. The presuppositions of these converses differ because they have different subjects. It remains true that the converse of a false **E** is always false, while the converse of a true **I** is always true. However, the converse of a true **E** or a false **I** is sometimes neither true nor false.

Similarly, the contrapositives of **A** and **O** propositions are equivalent *except* when one of the terms applies to nothing. For instance, "Every canary is a nondodo" is true, but its contrapositive "Every dodo is a noncanary" is neither true nor false. Similarly, "Some canary is not a nondodo" is false, while "Some dodo is not a noncanary" is neither true nor false. It remains true that the contrapositive of a false **A** is always false, and that the contrapositive of a true **O** is always true. However, the contrapositive of a true **A** or a false **O** is sometimes neither true nor false. The reason for these failures of equivalence is that contraposition alters the subject of a proposition, which changes its presuppositions. Note that there are no exceptions to the rule that obverses are equivalent; obversion does not change the subject of a proposition, so obversion does not change any presuppositions.

It will never be the case that an **E** or an **I** proposition is true while its converse is false, or that an **A** or an **O** proposition is true while its contrapositive is false. Failures of equivalence occur only when one of the propositions is neither true nor false. No matter how unusual, the existence of any failures of equivalence means that the conversion and contraposition rules used in Chapter 5 must be restricted by a condition of validity.

Conversion	
No *S* is *P*.	Some *S* is *P*.
∴ No *P* is *S*.	∴ Some *P* is *S*.
CV: *There is a P.*	
Contraposition	
Every *S* is *P*.	Some *S* is not *P*.
∴ Every non-*P* is non-*S*.	∴ Some non-*P* is not non-*S*.
CV: *There is a non-P.*	

("CV" here abbreviates "condition of validity.") The conversion rule for **E** propositions must be restricted, because the truth of "No *P* is *S*" follows from "No *S* is *P*" only on the condition that there is a *P*. The converse of a true **E** is never false, but it is not always true. No similar condition is needed on the conversion rule for **I** propositions. It is impossible for "Some *S* is *P*" to be true without "Some *P* is *S*" also being true. The converse of a true **I** is always true. For similar reasons, a condition of validity is needed on the contraposition rule for the **A** proposition but not for the **O**. "Every non-*P* is non-*S*" follows from "Every *S* is *P*" only on the condition that there is a non-*P*, while "Some non-*P* is not non-*S*" follows from "Some *S* is not *P*" under all conditions.

An argument form is *valid,* provided *all* arguments possessing the form are valid. Let us say that an argument form is ***conditionally valid*** if arguments possessing the form are valid *only under certain conditions.* For purposes of emphasis and contrast, we may say that a valid argument form is ***unconditionally valid,*** since there are no conditions on the validity of arguments possessing the form. Thus "Some *S* is *P*, ∴ Some *P* is *S*" is unconditionally valid, while "No *S* is *P*, ∴ No *P* is *S*" is conditionally valid. If a conditionally valid rule of inference is used to prove the validity of an argument, you must check to be sure that the conditions of validity are satisfied each time the rule is used. If conversion or contraposition is used to prove the validity of an argument *form,* its conditions of validity cannot be checked: you have to know what *P* or non-*P* is in order to determine whether or not there is a *P* or a non-*P*. Consequently, if an **E** proposition is converted or an **A** proposition contraposed in the proof of an argument form, all that is proved is the conditional validity of that argument form. Now it is not very informative to be told simply that an argument form is conditionally valid. What is important is to know—and remember—the *specific* conditions under which its instances are valid.

Glossary

Presuppositions: things that must he true for a proposition to be either true or false. Aristotelian categoricals (and singular categoricals) presuppose that there is something to which their subject terms apply; Venn categoricals have no such presupposition.

Truth value: The truth value of a proposition is its truth or falsity. That is, the truth value of a true proposition is truth, while the truth value of a false proposition is falsity. Propositions that are neither true nor false have no truth value.

Conditionally valid argument form: an argument form such that arguments possessing the form are valid only under certain conditions.

Unconditionally valid argument form: an argument form such that all arguments possessing the form are valid.

Exercises

A. What are the presuppositions of the following propositions?

1. Every mammal is a vertebrate.

2. No businessman is a politician.

3. Some Republicans are liberals.

4. Some women are not geniuses.

5. Nothing is a skunk and not a mammal.

6. Something is a mouse and a rodent.

7. The United States is a free country.

8. The present king of France is bald.

9. All male vixens are overweight.

10. Some elements at room temperature are solids.

B. Are the following propositions true, false, or neither?

1. All roses growing on the moon are red.

2. No roses growing on the moon are red.

3. Nothing is a rose growing on the moon and not red.

4. Something is a rose growing on the moon and red.

5. Some men who are over 300 years old drink coffee.

6. No men who are over 300 years old drink coffee.

7. Something is a male vixen and overweight.

8. Something is a male vixen and not overweight.

9. The present king of France is bald.

10. The present king of France is not bald.

C. Identify which, if any, lines in the following deductions violate the conditions of validity on the rules used.

1. 1. All men are nonunicorns.   /∴ No unicorns are men.
    2. All unicorns are nonmen.   1 Contr
    3. No unicorns are men.   2 Obv

2. 1. No cat is a centaur.   /∴ Some centaur is a noncat.
    2. Every cat is a noncentaur.   1 Obv

      3. Every centaur is a noncat.   2 Contr
      4. Some centaur is a noncat.   3 Sub

3.   1. No nonhorse is a centaur.
      2. All noncentaurs are nonunicorns.   /∴ Every unicorn is a horse.
      3. All unicorns are centaurs.   2 Contr
      4. No centaur is a nonhorse.   1 Conv
      5. Every centaur is a horse.   4 Obv
      6. Every unicorn is a horse.   3,5 GCS

4.   1. No nonlion is a griffin.   /∴ Some lion is a griffin.
      2. No griffin is a nonlion.   1 Conv·
      3. Some griffin is not a nonlion.   2 Sub
      4. Some griffin is a lion.   3 Obv
      5. Some lion is a griffin.   4 Conv

5.   1. All stallions are flying horses.   /∴ Some flying horses are stallions.
      2. Some stallions are flying horses.   1 Sub
      3. Some flying horses are stallions.   2 Conv

6.   1. All men are satyrs.   /∴ No men are nonsatyrs.
      2. All nonsatyrs are nonmen.   1 Contr
      3. No nonsatyrs are men.   2 Obv
      4. No men are nonsatyrs.   3 Conv

6.5 Diagramming Aristotelian Categoricals

In §6.3, the Venn diagram test of validity was developed for arguments whose premises and conclusions are Venn categoricals. We diagram the premises and then see whether or not the conclusion is already diagrammed. We shall now extend the Venn diagram test to arguments involving Aristotelian categoricals.

As we saw in the previous section, an Aristotelian categorical differs from its Venn transform only in having an existential presupposition. When that presupposition is true, the Aristotelian categorical and its Venn transform have the same truth value. When the presupposition is false, the Aristotelian categorical is neither true nor false. We wish to prove that if the premises of an Aristotelian argument are true then the conclusion must be true. The premises are true only if both their presuppositions and their Venn transforms are true; the conclusion is not true if either its presupposition or its Venn transform is false. It follows that an argument involving Aristotelian categoricals is valid, provided that if both the presuppositions and the Venn transforms of the premises are diagrammed, then both the presupposition and the Venn transform of the conclusion are also diagrammed. We know how to diagram both the presuppositions and the Venn transforms of Aristotelian categoricals. The presupposition of an Aristotelian categorical will always be a statement of the form "There is an S," which we diagram by putting an x anywhere in the S circle. So we have an effective Venn diagram test for arguments whose premises and conclusions are Aristotelian categoricals: first, diagram both the presuppositions and the Venn transforms of the premises; then check to see if the presupposition and Venn transform of the conclusion are both diagrammed; if they are, the argument is valid; if either the presupposition or the Venn transform of the conclusion is not diagrammed, the argument is invalid.

If both the Venn transforms and presuppositions of the universal Aristotelian categoricals are diagrammed, we get the Venn diagrams in Figures 6-27 and 6-28. In constructing both diagrams, we do the Venn transform (VT) before the presupposition (PS), since the Venn transform is universal.

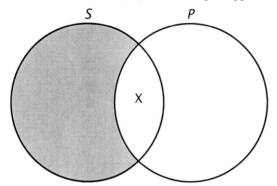

FIGURE 6-27. A: EVERY *S* IS *P*.
VT: NOTHING IS *S* AND NOT *P*.
PS: SOMETHING IS *S*.

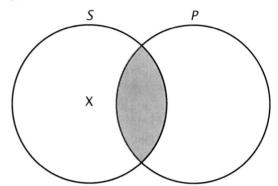

FIGURE 6-28. E: NO *S* IS *P*.
VT: NOTHING IS *S* AND *P*.
PS: SOMETHING IS *S*.

If the Venn transforms and presuppositions of the particular Aristotelian categoricals are diagrammed, we get Figures 6-29 and 6-30. In constructing both diagrams, one mark suffices for both the Venn transform and the presupposition. Even though the Venn transforms in these cases are particular, we should still diagram them before the presuppositions. If we diagrammed the presuppositions first, we would not know which side of the P line to put the x on in the S circle. We would have to put it on the line, and then move it when we diagrammed the Venn transform, or add a second x. So in general: diagram Venn transforms before diagramming presuppositions.

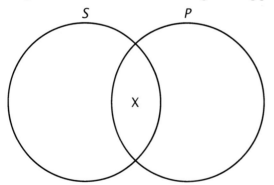

FIGURE 6-29. I: SOME *S* IS *P*.
VT: SOMETHING IS *S* AND *P*.
PS: SOMETHING IS *S*.

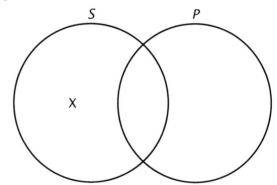

FIGURE 6-30. O: SOME *S* IS NOT *P*.
VT: SOMETHING IS *S* AND NOT *P*.
PS: SOMETHING IS *S*.

Arguments with Two Terms. Let us begin with an argument involving two terms, namely subalternation:

      A.   All men are animals.
             ∴ Some men are animals.

First, we diagram "Nothing is a man and not an animal," which is the Venn transform of the premise, by shading out that portion of the man circle that is outside the animal circle. Then we diagram "There is a man," which is the presupposition of the premise, by putting an x in the unshaded portion of the man circle (see Figure 6-31).

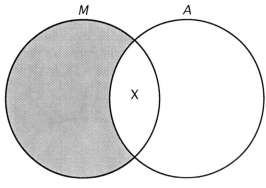

FIGURE 6-31

Both the Venn transform and the presupposition of the conclusion are diagrammed, so subalternation is valid for Aristotelian categoricals. In contrast, subalternation fails for Venn categoricals because they have no existential presupposition. Let us apply the Venn diagram test to B (see Figure 6-32).

> B.   Nothing is a man and not an animal.
> ∴ Something is a man and an animal.

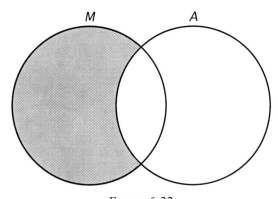

FIGURE 6-32

The diagram for the premise does not require marking an x. but the diagram for the conclusion does. The test therefore shows that the argument is invalid. Note that in constructing Figure 6-31, we are directly testing argument C for validity, using the Venn diagram test for arguments involving Venn categoricals:

> C.   There is a man, but nothing is a man and not an animal.
> ∴ There is a man, and something is a man and an animal.

We diagrammed the premise of argument C, and then determined that the conclusion was already diagrammed. The premise and conclusion of argument C are not equivalent to those of argument A, as we saw in §6.4. Nevertheless, argument A is valid (and even sound) if and only if C is. Hence we can prove the validity of A indirectly by proving the validity of C.

We get a negative result if we apply the Venn diagram test to arguments involving Aristotelian categoricals in which the superaltern is inferred from the subaltern, such as:

> Some men are not geniuses.
> ∴ No men are geniuses.

First we diagram "Something is a man and not a genius," the premise's Venn transform, by putting an *x* in the man circle outside the genius circle. Since this puts an *x* in the man circle, we do not have to do anything more to diagram "Something is a man," the premise's presupposition (see Figure 6-33). The conclusion's presupposition is diagrammed in Figure 6-33, but its Venn transform is not; so the argument is invalid.

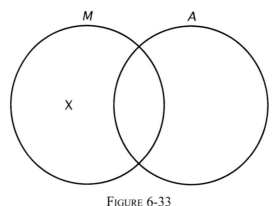

FIGURE 6-33

The Venn diagram test shows that conversion is always valid for an **E*** proposition, while valid for an **E** only under certain conditions (see Figures 6-34 and 6-35).

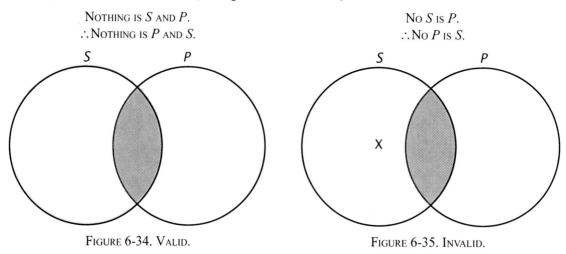

NOTHING IS *S* AND *P*.
∴NOTHING IS *P* AND *S*.

No *S* IS *P*.
∴No *P* IS *S*.

FIGURE 6-34. VALID.   FIGURE 6-35. INVALID.

The argument diagrammed in Figure 6-35 is invalid because, while the Venn transform of the conclusion is diagrammed, its presupposition that there is a *P* is not diagrammed. The condition of validity on the conversion rule for an **E** is precisely that this presupposition be satisfied.

Arguments with Three Terms. Moving up a term, let us work through the **AAA1** syllogism.

All *M* are *P*.
All *S* are *M*.
∴ All *S* are *P*.

Diagram the Venn transforms of the premises first and then their presuppositions. One *x* is sufficient in this case to diagram both the existential presuppositions (see Figure 6-36). We see that the **AAA1** syllogism is valid, since both the presupposition and the Venn transform of the conclusion are diagrammed. Note that diagramming the presuppositions of the premises only served to ensure that the presupposition of the conclusion was diagrammed, and that diagramming the Venn transforms of the premises sufficed to diagram the Venn transform of the conclusion. Consequently, the **A*A*A*1** syllogism is valid too.

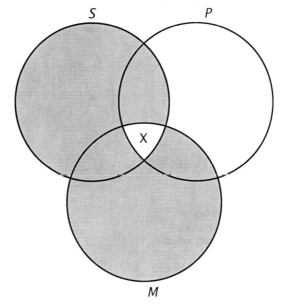

FIGURE 6-36. VALID.

Diagramming the existential presuppositions of the premises in a valid Aristotelian syllogism sometimes does help to diagram the Venn transform of the conclusion, however—in which case the corresponding Venn syllogism will not be valid. For example, while the **EAO1** syllogism is valid, the corresponding Venn syllogism **E*A*O*1** is not, as the following examples and diagrams make clear:

E*A*O*1:
Nothing is a mammal and a reptile.
Nothing is a lemur and not a mammal.
∴ Something is a lemur and not a reptile.

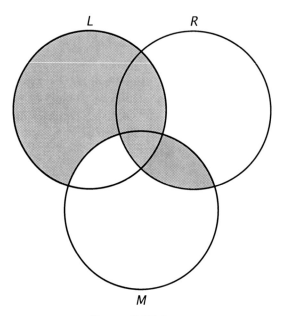

FIGURE 6-37. INVALID.

EAO1:
No mammal is a reptile.
Every lemur is a mammal.
∴ Some lemur is not a reptile.

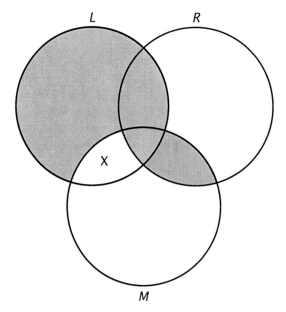

FIGURE 6-38. VALID.

Note that Figure 6-38 can be obtained from Figure 6-37 simply by diagramming the presuppositions of the Aristotelian syllogism's premises. Once again, both presuppositions can be diagrammed by the same x.

EAO1 arguments should seem intuitively valid. You should also find it impossible to refute them by the method of counterinstance, that is, by finding another argument with the same form that has true premises and a false conclusion. **E*A*O*1** arguments should seem invalid, though, at least after realizing that the conclusion asserts existence while the premises deny it. It is easy to find a counterinstance.

> Nothing is a car and a tree.
> Nothing is a 2006 Edsel and not a car.
> ∴ Something is a 2006 Edsel and not a tree.

The minor premise is true and the conclusion false because nothing is a 2006 Edsel. The corresponding Aristotelian categoricals are neither true nor false, for the same reason. So the three terms that refute **E*A*O*1** do not refute **EAO1**.

Mixed Arguments. We have concentrated on arguments that are "pure" in the sense of involving either all Aristotelian or all Venn categoricals. "Mixed" arguments are perfectly legitimate, however, and Venn diagrams enable us to test their validity in the same way. Consider the **E*AI*1** syllogism:

> Nothing is *M* and *P*.
> Every *S* is *M*.
> ∴ Something is *S* and not *P*.

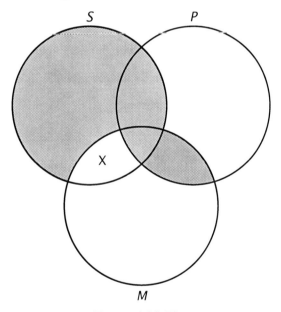

FIGURE 6-39. VALID.

"Every *S* is *M*" is an Aristotelian categorical, so we need to diagram both its Venn transform and its presupposition. We diagram its Venn transform by shading out that portion of the *S* circle lying outside the *M* circle. "Nothing is *M* and *P*" is a Venn categorical, which we diagram by shading out the intersection of the *M* and *P* circles. Finally, we diagram the presupposition of "Every *S* is *P*" by putting an *x* in the portion of the *S* circle that remains unshaded (see Figure 6-39). Now we check to see if the conclusion is diagrammed. It is, since there is an *x* in a portion of the *S* circle lying outside the *P* circle. So the argument is valid.

Exercises

A. Diagram both the Venn transform and the presupposition of the following Aristotelian categoricals.

1. All skunks are mammals.

2. Some rodents are not mice.

3. Some even-toed hoofed mammals are rhinoceroses.

4. No rhinoceros is a hippopotamus.

5. Every black-footed ferret is a member of the weasel family.

6. Some aggressive, bloodthirsty predators are wolverines.

7. Any violet growing on the moon is blue.

8. No men over 300 years old drink gin.

9. Some foxes are not male vixens.

10. All governments restrain and rule people.

B. Determine whether the following arguments are formally valid, using Venn diagrams.

1. No scientist is a philosopher, so some scientist is not a philosopher.

2. Some men are carpenters, so some carpenters are men.

3. Some birds are terns, so some birds are not terns.

4. Some fish are not sharks, so some nonsharks are fish.

5. Some birds are not reptiles, so no birds are reptiles.

6. All mammals are vertebrates, so all vertebrates are mammals.

7. All robins are nongriffins, so all griffins are nonrobins.

8. No apple is a vegetable, so some nonvegetable is an apple.

9. All rodents are mice, so all nonrodents are nonmice.

10. No birds are reptiles, so some reptiles are not birds.

C. Follow the instructions for Set B.

1. All widgeons are ducks and some pigeons are widgeons, so some pigeons are not ducks.

2. All flowers are plants. All roses are flowers. Therefore, some roses are plants.

3. Some plants are roses. All roses are flowers. Therefore, some flowers are plants.

4. Some lemurs are animals, for all lemurs are mammals and some animals are mammals.

5. Some primates are animals, for some mammals are animals and all primates are mammals.

6. No whales are fish. Some mammals are whales. Therefore, some mammals are not fish.

7. Some Americans are not Democrats. All Americans are taxpayers. Therefore, some taxpayers are not Democrats.

8. Every maggot has parents. Every living thing has parents. Therefore, every maggot is a living thing.

9. Every ape is a primate. Every ape is a mammal. Therefore some mammal is a primate.

10. No monotheists are polytheists, for no atheists are polytheists and no atheists are monotheists.

D. Determine the validity or invalidity of the following argument forms by the Venn diagram test.

1. **AAI1**	2. **AAI2**
3. **AAA2**	4. **EAO3**
5. **EAO4**	6. **IAI3**
7. **OOO1**	8. **AOO2**
9. **AEO2**	10. **IEO4**

E. Determine the validity or invalidity of the following "mixed" argument forms by the Venn diagram test.

1. **AA*A*1**	2. **A*A*A1**
3. **AAI*1**	4. **A*A*I1**
5. **AI*I3**	6. **A*A*I3**
7. **EI*O4**	8. **A*E*O4**

F. For further practice with the Venn diagram test, check your entries in Table 5-2, which represents all possible forms of Aristotelian categorical syllogisms (see Set I of the exercises in §5.6). Use the results from Set D above.

6.6 Diagramming Singular Categoricals

We complete our study of syllogistic logic by developing a method for diagramming singular categorical propositions. We shall then be able to apply the Venn diagram test to arguments containing singular as well as general categorical propositions. Recall that singular categoricals have the following forms:

U	s is P.
Y	s is not P.

The subject s represents a singular term like "George W. Bush," "Paris" or "the tallest mountain." From a Boolean point of view, a statement like "George W. Bush is a conservative" asserts that George W. Bush is a member of the set of conservatives. Symbolically, $b \in \{C\}$, where b abbreviates "George W. Bush," C abbreviates "conservative," and $\in$ means "is a member (or element) of." This affirmative singular proposition can be diagrammed by putting the letter b rather than x inside the C circle. We have been using x as a variable standing for the name of some unspecified individual. In contrast, b is a constant that stands for the name of a particular individual, George W. Bush. "George W. Bush is not a pianist" similarly asserts that Bush is not a member of the set of pianists: $b \notin \{$pianists$\}$. We diagram this negative singular proposition by putting the letter b any place outside the P (for "pianist") circle. In general then, we use Figures 6-40 and 6-41 for singular categoricals.

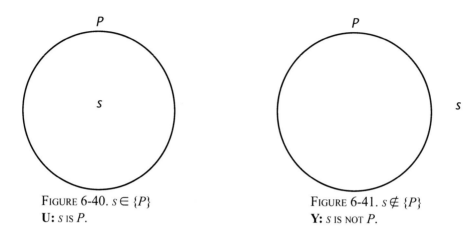

FIGURE 6-40. $s \in \{P\}$ FIGURE 6-41. $s \notin \{P\}$
U: s IS P.   **Y:** s IS NOT P.

Like an Aristotelian categorical, *a singular categorical presupposes that there is something to which its subject applies.* That is, a singular categorical presupposes that s exists. "George W. Bush is a conservative" presupposes that George W. Bush exists. "Your youngest grandchild is a girl" presupposes that there is something properly described as "your youngest grandchild"; and so on. If you have no grandchildren, for example, then "Your youngest grandchild is a girl" is neither true nor false. To diagram the proposition that s exists, it suffices to *place "s" anywhere in the Venn diagram.* Diagramming a singular premise will only require one mark, since whether s is put inside or outside the P circle, it will be somewhere in the diagram.

The Venn Diagram Test. This is all we need to apply the Venn diagram test to arguments containing singular categoricals. Let us validate the inference rule singular categorical syllogism; first, an **AUU1** syllogism:

> Every Republican is a conservative.
> Dick Cheney is a Republican.
> ∴ Dick Cheney is a conservative.

To test this, we draw only two overlapping circles since there are only two general terms, "Republican (R)" and "conservative (C)." *Only general terms represent sets.* We diagram the Venn transform of the major premise by shading out that portion of the R circle lying outside the C circle. We diagram the minor premise by placing the letter c for "Dick Cheney") in the unshaded portion of the R circle. Then we make sure the presupposition of the general premise is diagrammed, which requires that there is some letter in the R circle. There is, namely, the letter c. Note: *a set is nonempty as long as there is some letter—any letter—in the circle representing that set.* It does not matter whether the letter is the variable x (representing an unspecified individual) or a constant (representing a particular individual). So the diagram in Figure 6-42 is complete:

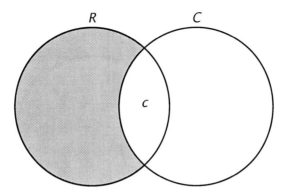

FIGURE 6-42. VALID.

Now we determine whether the conclusion is diagrammed. It is. There is a *c* somewhere inside the *C* circle, which means that *c* is a *C*—i.e., Cheney is a conservative. Consider next a **UUI3** syllogism:

> Bush is a conservative.
> Bush is a Republican.
> ∴ Some Republican is a conservative.

Again we need only two circles labeled *R* and *C*. We diagram the Venn transform of the major premise by putting the letter *b* (for "Bush") somewhere inside the *C* circle. We do not know which side of the *R* line to put the *b* on until we examine the minor premise, which requires that the *b* be inside the *R* circle. Note: *whereas the variable x can appear more than once in a diagram, representing different individuals each time, a constant can appear at most once in any given diagram.* If, for example, we had put one *b* (representing Bush) in the *R* circle, and another *b* (also representing Bush) outside the *R* circle, we would have diagrammed a contradiction, namely, "Bush both is and is not a Republican (see Figure 6-43). The conclusion, which requires that some letter be in the intersection of the two circles, is already diagrammed, so the argument is valid.

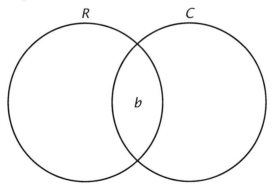

FIGURE 6-43. VALID.

For an invalid example, consider an **AYY1** argument:

> All *A* are *B*.
> *c* is not *A*.
> ∴ *c* is not *B*.

We need two circles, one labeled *A*, the other *B*. To diagram the Venn transform of "All *A* are *B*," we shade out the *A* circle outside the *B* circle (see Figure 6-44).

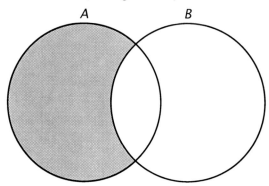

FIGURE 6-44

To diagram "*c* is not *A*." we need to mark a *c* somewhere outside the *A* circle. But we face a choice: should it go inside or outside that portion of the *B* circle lying outside of the *A* circle? We do not know which side of the *B* line to put the *c* on, so we must put it on the line. To finish, we need to diagram the presupposition of "All *A* are *B*," so we put an *x* in the remaining portion of the *A* circle (see Figure 6-45). Now we check to see whether the conclusion is diagrammed. It is not. There is no *c* outside the *B* circle; all we have is one on the line. So **AYY1** is an invalid argument form.

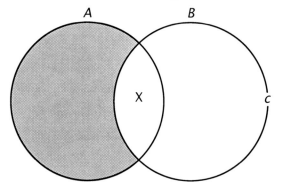

FIGURE 6-45. INVALID.

Consider finally an **AYY2** argument:

> Every *A* is *B*.
> *c* is not *B*.
> ∴ *c* is not *A*.

First we diagram the Venn transform of "Every *A* is *B*" by shading out the *A* circle outside the *B* circle (see Figure 6-46).

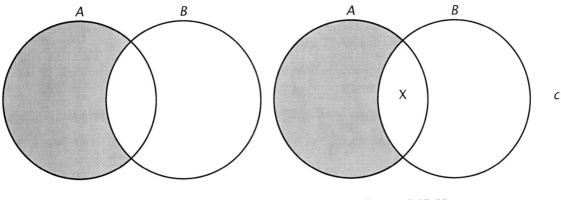

FIGURE 6-46   FIGURE 6-47. VALID.

To diagram "*c* is not *B*," we need to put a *c* somewhere outside the *B* circle. This time we have no choice. The *c* cannot go in that part of the *A* circle lying outside the *B* circle, because it is shaded out. So we have to put the *c* outside *both* circles: anywhere will do. Finally, we diagram the presupposition of the first premise by putting an *x* in the remaining portion of the *A* circle (see Figure 6-47). This time the conclusion is diagrammed. There is a *c* outside the *B* circle. So **AYY2** is valid.

Exercises

A. Reexpress each of the following propositions as a statement about sets, and represent it geometrically by a Venn diagram.

1. Ted Kennedy is a Democrat.

2. The prime minister of England is not a man.

3. Something is a slime mold.

4. Billy Mitchell holds the record Pac-Man score.

5. Maria Sharapova is not right-handed.

6. French is a beautiful language.

7. English is not a beautiful language.

8. Catholicism is not a major religion in Greece.

9. Catholicism is a major religion in Italy.

10. Something is able to penetrate gold foil.

B. Use the Venn diagram test to determine whether or not the following arguments are formally valid.

1. Every senator is a member of Congress. Arnold Schwarzenegger is not a senator. Therefore Arnold Schwarzenegger is not a member of Congress.

2. No representative is a senator. John Conyers is a representative. Therefore John Conyers is not a senator.

3. Mt. Everest is a river. No river is a lake. Therefore, Mt. Everest is a lake.

4. The Statue of Liberty is not in Newark. Nothing in Newark is far from Manhattan. Therefore, the Statue of Liberty is not far from Manhattan.

5. Mick Jagger is a singer. Mick Jagger is not a pianist. Therefore, some singers are not pianists.

6. Queen Elizabeth II is not a musician. All rock singers are musicians. Therefore Queen Elizabeth II is not a rock singer.

7. Lee R. Raymond is an Exxon executive. Some Exxon executives make six million dollars a year. Therefore, Lee R. Raymond makes six million dollars a year.

8. All objects revolving around the sun have elliptical orbits. The moon has an elliptical orbit. Therefore, the moon revolves around the sun.

9. Zinc is a metal. No organic compound is a metal. Therefore zinc is not an organic compound.

10. Some politicians are not former athletes. The president is a politician. Therefore, he is not a former athlete.

C. Check your entries in Table 5-3, which represents all possible forms of singular categorical syllogisms (see Set H of the exercises in §5.7).

LSAT Prep Questions

1. Some planning committee members—those representing the construction industry—have significant financial interests in the committee's decisions. No one who is on the planning committee lives in the suburbs, although many of them work there.

    If the statements above are true, which one of the following must also be true?

    (a) No persons with significant financial interests in the planning committee's decisions are not in the construction industry.

    (b) No person who has a significant financial interest in the planning committee's decisions lives in the suburbs.

    (c) Some persons with significant financial interests in the planning committee's decisions work in the suburbs.

    (d) Some planning committee members who represent the construction industry do not work in the suburbs.

    (e) Some persons with significant financial interests in the planning committee's decisions do not live in the suburbs.

    Preptest 29, Section 1, Question 18.

2. Since anyone who supports the new tax plan has no chance of being elected, and anyone who truly understands economics would not support the tax plan, only someone who truly understands economics would have any chance of being elected.

   The reasoning in the argument is flawed because the argument ignores the possibility that some people who

   (a) truly understand economics do not support the tax plan

   (b) truly understand economics have no chance of being elected

   (c) do not support the tax plan have no chance of being elected

   (d) do not support the tax plan do not truly understand economics

   (e) have no chance of being elected do not truly understand economics

   Preptest 14, Section 4, Question 9

3. Only an expert in some branch of psychology could understand why Patrick is behaving irrationally. But no expert is certain of being able to solve someone else's problem. Patrick wants to devise a solution to his own behavioral problem.

   Which of the following conclusions can be validly drawn from this passage?

   (a) Patrick does not understand why he is behaving in this way.

   (b) Patrick is not an expert in psychology.

   (c) Patrick is not certain of being able to devise a solution to his own behavioral problem.

   (d) Unless Charles is an expert in some branch of psychology, Charles should not offer a solution to Patrick's behavioral problem.

   (e) If Charles is certain of being able to solve Patrick's behavioral problem, then Charles does not understand why Patrick is behaving in this way.

   Preptest 10, Section 4, Question 22

4. All actors are exuberant people, and all exuberant people are extroverts, but nevertheless it is true that some shy people are actors.

   (a) If the statements above are true, each of the following must be true EXCEPT:

   (b) Some shy people are extroverts.

   (c) Some shy people are not actors.

   (d) Some exuberant people who are actors are shy.

   (e) All people who are not extroverts are not actors.

   (f) Some extroverts are shy.

   Preptest 12, Section 1, Question 25

CHAPTER SEVEN

Propositional Logic: Truth Tables

7.1 Conjunctions, Disjunctions, and Negations

Conjunctions. We have confined our attention almost exclusively to propositions that are *simple* in the sense of not being composed of other propositions. We now turn to *compound* propositions, which do have other propositions as parts. Consider, for example, "All men are animals and all cats are animals." This proposition is compound, since it is formed from two other propositions: "All men are animals" and "All cats are animals." Such a compound proposition, which asserts that both of its components are true, is called in logic a ***conjunction***, and its components are called ***conjuncts***. We shall use the ampersand & (or "and" sign) to symbolize conjunctions. Let p and q be any two propositions; then p & q is the conjunction formed from them. The expression p & q may be read "p and q."

We will continue to refer to truth and falsity as ***truth values***. The truth value of a conjunction bears a very simple relationship to the truth values of its components. For a conjunction is true when, and only when, both of its conjuncts are true. If even one conjunct is false, the conjunction as a whole is false. Thus "All men are animals and all cats are animals" is true because "All men are animals" and "All cats are animals" are both true. But "All cats are animals and all men are geniuses" is false because "All men are geniuses" is false. This functional relationship between a conjunction and its conjuncts is summarized by Table 7-1, in which T and F abbreviate "true" and "false."

p	*q*	*p* & *q*
T	T	T
T	F	F
F	T	F
F	F	F

TABLE 7-1. THE TRUTH TABLE FOR CONJUNCTIONS

Given two statements *p* and *q*, there are just four possible pairs of truth values they can have. They might both be true, *p* might be true while *q* is false, and so on. The conjunction *p* & *q* has a unique truth value in each of these four cases, as displayed in the table. When *p* and *q* are both true, *p* & *q* is true. In the other three cases, *p* & *q* is false. Such a table, which relates the truth value of a compound to the truth values of its components in all possible cases, is called a **truth table**. Table 7-1 is therefore the truth table for conjunction.

Conjunctions are often abbreviated in English. When the conjuncts have the same subject, their conjunction is generally formed by putting "and" between the two predicate terms. Thus instead of the cumbersome "George Bush is a Republican and George Bush is a conservative," we would say "George Bush is a Republican and a conservative." The sentences are synonymous, and express the same conjunction *R* & *C*, where *R* is the proposition that Bush is a Republican and *C* the proposition that Bush is a conservative. Similarly, when the conjuncts have the same predicate, the conjunction is most naturally formed by putting "and" between the subject terms. Thus "George Bush and Dick Cheney are Republicans" would be preferred to "George Bush is a Republican and Dick Cheney is a Republican," but both express the same conjunction *R* & *N*, where *N* is the proposition that Cheney is a Republican.

While conjunctions are typically formed using "and," the word has other functions. The proposition "Bob and George are the same height" is not a conjunction. It is not a reduction of "Bob is the same height and George is the same height," which is nonsensical. And "Jack and Mary are husband and wife" is obviously not short for "Jack is a husband and Jack is a wife and Mary is a husband and Mary is a wife." "And" is used in these cases to state a *relationship* between two things. In still other contexts, "and" conveys the stronger sense of "and then," as in "John died and went to heaven." If this were a mere conjunction, it would be the equivalent of "John went to heaven and died." In these examples, "and" is most naturally interpreted as expressing *temporal succession* in addition to conjunction.

Furthermore, "and" is not the only word in English that expresses conjunction. For example, the statement "John went to the store but he did not buy anything" is true if and only if both of its components statements are true, so it expresses a conjunction. The word "but" is used instead of "and" to signal that the second conjunct is not what you might expect, given the first. "However," "although," "nevertheless," and "yet" would have the same force here as "but." We shall ignore the extra meaning of "but" because it has no influence on **truth conditions.** That is, the difference between "and" and "but" does not affect the truth or falsity of compounds containing them.

Negations. Another type of compound proposition is the **negation**, which can always be formed in English by prefixing the whole sentence with "It is not the case that," and can often be formed by inserting "not" within the sentence to be negated. Thus the negation of "The sky is blue" is "It is not the case that the sky is blue," or more simply "The sky is not blue." A negation has only one component. We use the negative sign – to express negation. The negation of any sentence *p* is written –*p*. The relationship between the truth value of a negation and that of the statement negated is very simple: the negation has the opposite truth value. If p is true, then $-p$ is false. If p is false, then $-p$ is true. (See Table 7-2.)

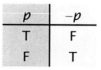

p	$-p$
T	F
F	T

TABLE 7-2. THE TRUTH TABLE FOR NEGATIONS

Negations, we see, are contradictory. Note that the **Y** proposition "s is not P" is the negation of the **U** proposition "s is P." Note also that the negation of the **A** proposition "Every S is P" is "Not every S is P," which is equivalent to "Some S is not P." "Every S is not P" is ambiguous, however; it most commonly means "Not every S is P," and therefore expresses the negation of "Every S is P." But "Every S is not P" could also mean "Every S is non-P." There is only one way to express the negation of the **E** proposition "No S is P"—namely, "It is not the case that no S is P." "Not no S is P" or "No S is not P" would be poor English. Note finally that the negation of "Some S is P" is not its subcontrary "Some S is not P," but rather "It is not the case that some S is P," which is equivalent to "No S is P."

Disjunctions. The *disjunction* (or *alternation*) of two propositions is formed with the word "or," as in "The US will attack North Korea or North Korea will attack the US." The two components of a disjunction are called *disjuncts* (or *alternatives*). Like conjunctions, disjunctions are generally abbreviated when their disjuncts have a common subject or predicate, as in "The president will visit France or Germany." A more important resemblance to conjunctions is that disjunctions too are false if both their components are false. The statement about the president, for example, would be false if the president spent all his time in England. Disjunctions differ from conjunctions, however, in not requiring that both components be true. Thus, the disjunction about the US and North Korea would be true if the US attacked but North Korea did not.

The English word "or" is ambiguous. For example, "The president will visit France or Germany" may be interpreted as allowing the possibility that he will visit both countries; but the disjunction may also be interpreted as ruling out that same possibility. To avoid this ambiguity, a disjunction in English must be supplemented with "or both" or "but not both." "The president will visit France or Germany *or both*" is true if the president visits both countries, while "The president will visit France or Germany *but not both*" is false if he visits both. "And/or" is often used to mean "or...or both," as in "The president will visit France and/or Germany." "And/or" is particularly common in legal contexts, where ambiguity is extremely undesirable. "Or else," on the other hand, implies "or...but not both," as in "The president will visit France or else Germany."

A disjunction that is intended to be true when both disjuncts are true is called an ***inclusive disjunction***, because the cases in which it is true include the case in which both its components are true. A disjunction that is intended to be false when both disjuncts are true is called an ***exclusive disjunction***, because that case is excluded. Since an exclusive disjunction implies an inclusive disjunction, but not vice versa, exclusive disjunction is often called *strong* disjunction, while inclusive disjunction is called *weak*. Because ambiguity is undesirable in logic, we use different symbols for the different disjunctions. We shall use the symbol v to symbolize inclusive disjunctions, counting any sentence p v q as true when either p or q or both are true. We shall use the symbol v to symbolize exclusive disjunctions, and count p v q as true when either p or q but not both are true. We therefore have the Table 7-3:

		Inclusive	Exclusive
p	*q*	*p* ∨ *q*	*p* ∀ *q*
T	T	T	F
T	F	T	T
F	T	T	T
F	F	F	F

TABLE 7-3. THE TRUTH TABLE FOR DISJUNCTIONS

Note that an inclusive disjunction is true whenever *at least one* disjunct is true, while an exclusive disjunction is true only when *exactly one* is true. Unlike English, Latin had distinct words for the two types of disjunction. *Vel* expressed inclusive disjunction, *aut* exclusive. We will therefore call the symbol ∨ "vel" and ∀ "aut."[1] When there is no need to be specific, both symbols may be read "or."

Since we have two symbols for disjunction, a problem arises as to how "or" should be symbolized. The following procedure has been found to work very well in practice, as judged by both the principle of fidelity and the principle of charity: *Always use ∨ to symbolize disjunctions.* When it is not perfectly clear from the context that an exclusive disjunction is intended (our exercises will usually not be clear), assume that an inclusive disjunction is intended. When "…but not both" is explicit or clearly implied, still use ∨, but symbolize the statement as a compound of compounds. That is, symbolize "*p* or *q*, but not both" quite literally as "(*p* ∨ *q*) & –(*p* & *q*)." This is equivalent to "*p* ∀ *q*," as can be seen by examining the truth tables for conjunction and disjunction (we will go over this below). Similarly, symbolize "*p* or *q*, or both" as "(*p* ∨ *q*) ∨ (*p* & *q*)," which is equivalent to "*p* ∨ *q*." We will subsequently devote most of our attention to inclusive disjunction.

Conjunctions and Disjunctions with More than Two Components. We will concentrate almost exclusively on conjunctions and disjunctions that have two conjuncts or disjuncts. However, a conjunction or disjunction can have any number of components. Thus "John kissed Alice, Betty, Cindy, and Diane" would be a conjunction with four conjuncts, symbolized *A* & *B* & *C* & *D*. And "John kissed Alice, Betty, Cindy, or Diane" would be a disjunction with four disjuncts, symbolized *A* ∨ *B* ∨ *C* ∨ *D*. In general, conjunctions are true provided *all* conjuncts are true; inclusive disjunctions are true provided *at least one* disjunct is true; and exclusive disjunctions are true provided *exactly one* disjunct is true.

Compounds of Compounds. Conjunctions, disjunctions, and negations may have any degree of complexity. There may be conjunctions whose conjuncts are disjunctions whose disjuncts are conjunctions whose conjuncts are negations, and so on. Unfortunately, when we start mixing the symbols &, ∨, and –, serious ambiguities can arise. Consider for example *A* ∨ *B* & *C*. This could either symbolize a conjunction whose left-hand conjunct is the disjunction *A* ∨ *B*, or a disjunction whose right-hand disjunct is *B* & *C*. The difference makes a difference. Suppose *A* and *B* are true, while *C* is false. Then on the first interpretation, *A* ∨ *B* & *C* is false (it is a conjunction, one of whose conjuncts is false—namely, *C*). But on the second interpretation, *A* ∨ *B* & *C* is true (it is a disjunction, one of whose disjuncts is true—namely, *A*). To resolve such ambiguities, we use *parentheses* ( ), *brackets* [ ], and *braces* { } just as they are used in mathematics. The two interpretations of *A* ∨ *B* & *C* are then (*A* ∨ *B*) & *C* and *A* ∨

---

[1] The vel is the standard symbol for inclusive disjunction, but it is commonly called the "wedge" or the "vee." There is no standard symbol for exclusive disjunction, which is usually symbolized (p ∨ q) & –(p & q).

(*B & C*). In the very same way, 2 + 3 x 4 is ambiguous, meaning either (2 + 3) x 4, which is 20, or 2 + (3 x 4), which is 14. Punctuation marks such as commas often play the same vital role in English. Thus "John will buy a plane or a car and a boat" could mean "John will buy a plane, or a car and a boat," or "John will buy a plane or a car, and a boat." The word "either" commonly functions in a similar way, as a left-hand parenthesis. "Mary will have a danish and coffee or tea" can mean "Mary will have either a danish and coffee or tea" or "Mary will have a danish and either coffee or tea."

Complex expressions often require so many parentheses and the like, that they are hard to read. To reduce the number of parentheses, we adopt the following convention: *the negation sign – applies to the smallest unit permitted by the explicit punctuation.* Thus –*A* v *B* means (–*A*) v *B* rather than –(*A* v *B*), since *A* is a smaller unit than *A* v *B*. This convention enables us to reduce – {–[(–*A*) & (–*B*)]} to the more manageable – –(–*A* & –*B*) A similar convention governs the negative sign in algebra. The expression –3 + 4 means (–3) + 4, which is 1, and not –(3 + 4), which is –7.

As noted above, "either" often functions as a parenthesis, punctuating the left side of a disjunction. "Either" also functions to give advance warning that a proposition is going to be one disjunct of a disjunction. When we hear "Bob will get married or he will become a priest," we do not know until the "or" arrives whether to interpret "Bob will get married" as presenting a simple statement, a conjunct of' a larger statement, a disjunct, or something else. It is therefore easier to understand "Either Bob will get married or he will become a priest." "Both" has a similar function, indicating that a conjunction is on the way, as in "Bob will both get married and have children." A common *misconception* is that "either" signals an exclusive disjunction. "Bush will visit either France or Germany" is just as ambiguous as "Bush will visit France or Germany." We will interpret both as inclusive without explicit evidence that an exclusive disjunction was intended.

We have seen that "either-or" is ambiguous, expressing either inclusive or exclusive disjunction. But "either-or" is ambiguous in another way as well. It sometimes expresses *conjunction* instead of disjunction! "Reagan is more conservative than either Kennedy or Carter" would most likely mean "Reagan is both more conservative than Kennedy and more conservative than Carter" rather than "Reagan is either more conservative than Kennedy or more conservative than Carter." This illustrates another important reason for using special symbols in logic. We use them not only to represent form and to abbreviate longer expressions, but also to avoid the vagueness and ambiguity inherent in nearly all expressions in "natural" languages like English. To the extent that an "artificial" language like that of logic avoids vagueness and ambiguity, it is easier to comprehend. The unfamiliarity of the symbols is a drawback, of course: their use has not been practiced since childhood. But the benefits far outweigh the cost.

"Neither-nor" can be symbolized as either the negation of a disjunction or as a conjunction of negations. For example, "Neither Kennedy nor Carter will run for president this year" is equivalent to "It is not the case that either Kennedy or Carter (or both) will run for president," which in turn is equivalent to "It is the case that both Kennedy and Carter will not run." In general, "neither *p* nor *q*" is true if and only if both *p* and *q* are false. Reflection on the truth tables for conjunction, inclusive disjunction, and negation will reveal that –(*p* v *q*) and –*p* & –*q* are also true if and only if *p* and *q* are both false (we shall return to this later). So we can symbolize "neither *p* nor *q*" as –(*p* v *q*) or equivalently as –*p* & –*q*.

Neither *p* nor *q* = (–*p* & –*q*) = –(*p* v *q*)

Be sure to use v and not ᵥ. "Or" generally must be interpreted as expressing inclusive disjunction after "not." Since "Bush will not visit Italy or Greece" would be false if Bush visited both countries, the statement must be symbolized –(*I* v *G*) rather than –(*I* ᵥ *G*). The latter would be true if both *I* and *G* were true, since *I* ᵥ *G* would be false.

Truth-Functional Compounds. Conjunctions, disjunctions, and negations are examples of *truth-functional compounds.* A truth-functional compound is one whose truth value is determined in every case by the truth values of its components. In mathematical terms, the truth value of the compound is a "function" of the truth values of the components. That is, for every possible assignment of truth values to the components, there is a unique truth value for the compound. For example, given that A and B are both true, the conjunction A & B is definitely true. The truth value of A & B is uniquely determined and does not depend on any other factors in addition to the joint truth of A and B. Since conjunctions, disjunctions, and negations are truth-functional, the symbols &, ∨, v, and – are called *truth-functional connectives*: they connect propositions together to form truth-functional compounds.

Not all compounds are truth-functional. Consider "John believes that it is raining." This is a compound proposition, since it contains the proposition "It is raining" as a component. Let us suppose now that it *is* raining, so that the component is true. Does it follow that the compound is true or that it is false? No. Given that it is raining, John may or may not believe that it is He may know that it is raining because he is standing outside getting soaked, or he may not realize that it is raining because he is inside. To determine whether "John believes that it is raining" is true, we need to know something about John; the truth value of "It is raining" is irrelevant. In §7.7 below, we will study a very important compound that is not truth-functional.

Calculating Truth Values. The truth value of any compound analyzable entirely into conjunctions, disjunctions, and negations can be calculated using the truth tables above if we are given the truth values of the simple components. This is possible no matter how complex the compound is. We start with the innermost components and work our way outward. Let A and B be true and let X and Y be false. Then we can calculate the truth value of a statement like $[(A \ \& \ B) \lor X] \ \& \ [-(-X \lor Y) \ \& -A]$ as follows. First, we assign truth values to the simple statements. When using pencil and paper, we simply write T or F directly underneath the statement constants.

1. $[(A \ \& \ B) \lor X] \ \& \ [-(-X \lor Y) \ \& -A]$
   T   T   F   F F   T

Since A and B are both true, their conjunction A & B is true. We can note this by putting a T underneath the &:

2. $[(A \ \& \ B) \lor X] \ \& \ [-(-X \lor Y) \ \& -A]$
   T **T** T   F   F F   T

Next, since A & B is true and X is false, their disjunction is true. We put a T underneath the disjunction sign.

3. $[(A \ \& \ B) \lor X] \ \& \ [-(-X \lor Y) \ \& -A]$
   T T T **T** F   F F   T

Turning to the brackets on the right, since X is false, its negation is true:

4. $[(A \ \& \ B) \lor X] \ \& \ [-(-X \lor Y) \ \& -A]$
   T T T T F   **T**F F   T

Since $-X$ is true and Y is false, their disjunction is true:

5. $[(A \ \& \ B) \lor X] \ \& \ [-(-X \lor Y) \ \& -A]$
   T T T T F   TF **T** F   T

Since $-X \lor Y$ is true, its negation is false:

6. $[(A \ \& \ B) \lor X] \ \& \ [-(-X \lor Y) \ \& -A]$
   T T T T F   **F** TF T F   T

Since A is true, its negation is false:

7. $[(A \& B) \vee X] \& [-(-X \vee Y) \& -A]$
     T   T   T   T   F   F TF T F   **F**T

Since $-A$ and $-(-X \vee Y)$ are both false, their conjunction is false:

8. $[(A \& B) \vee X] \& [-(-X \vee Y) \& -A]$
     T   T   T   T   F   F TF T   F   **F**   FT

Finally, since $[(A \& B) \vee X]$ is true while $[-(-X \vee Y) \& -A]$ is false, their conjunction, which is the entire statement, is false:

9. $[(A \& B) \vee X] \& [-(-X \vee Y) \& -A]$
     T   T   T   T   F   **F**   F TF T F   F   FT

Of course, when you work this with pencil and paper, you write $[(A \& B) \vee X] \& [-(-X \vee Y) \& -A]$ only once, and you gradually add T's and F's in the order indicated until you end up with line 9.

     Two shortcuts can save quite a bit of time in such calculations. First, we know that a conjunction is false if even one conjunct is false. So once you come upon a false conjunct, you do not need to evaluate the other conjunct. A lengthy proposition like the following can therefore be evaluated rather swiftly:

$X \& -\{A \vee -[(B \vee Y) \& X]\}$
F F

Since we do not need to know the truth value of the statement within the braces, we do not have to evaluate it. Second, we know that an inclusive disjunction is true if even one disjunct is true. Once you come upon a true disjunct, therefore, you do not need to evaluate the other one.

Glossary

Simple statement: a statement that is not composed of other statements.

Compound statement: a statement that is composed of other statements.

Conjunction: a compound statement of the form $p \& q$, which states that p *and* q are true.

Conjuncts: the statements conjoined in a conjunction.

Truth value: the truth or falsity of a statement.

Truth table: a table showing how the truth value of a compound statement is related to the truth values of its components.

Truth conditions: the conditions under which a statement is true.

Negation: a compound statement of the form $-p$, which states that p is *not* true.

Disjunction: a compound statement of the form $p \vee q$ or $p \veebar q$, asserting that p *or* q is true.

Inclusive disjunction: a disjunction of the form $p \vee q$, which asserts that p or q *or both* are true.

Excusive disjunction: a disjunction of the form $p \veebar q$, which states that p or q *but not both* are true.

Disjuncts: the statements disjoined in a disjunction.

Truth-functional compound: a compound statement whose truth value is determined in every case by the truth values of its components.

Exercises

A. Using capital letters to abbreviate simple statements, symbolize the following compound statements. Determine whether they are true or false.

1. Both Italy and Greece are on the Mediterranean.

2. Either Italy or Greece is on the Mediterranean.

3. It is not the case that England is on the Mediterranean.

4. Greece is not on the Mediterranean.

5. Italy is on the Mediterranean, but not Greece.

6. It is not the case that Monaco is not on the Mediterranean.

7. England is on the Mediterranean, and either Greece or Italy is on the Mediterranean.

8. Either England and Greece are on the Mediterranean, or Italy is on the Mediterranean.

9. Greece and England are not both on the Mediterranean.

10. Greece and England are both not on the Mediterranean.

11. Neither Greece nor England is on the Mediterranean.

12. Greece or England is on the Mediterranean, but not both.

13. Greece or England is on the Mediterranean, or both are.

14. Greece and/or England is on the Mediterranean.

15. It is not the case that Monaco is on the Mediterranean, and England is not on the Mediterranean either.

16. It is not the case that Monaco is on the Mediterranean, but Greece and Italy are both on the Mediterranean.

17. Monaco is on the Mediterranean, but Greece and Italy are not both on the Mediterranean.

18. Monaco is on the Mediterranean; however Greece and Italy are both not on the Mediterranean.

19. Monaco is on the Mediterranean, but neither Greece nor Italy is on the Mediterranean.

20. It is not the case that neither Greece nor Italy is on the Mediterranean.

21. Belgium and England are on the Mediterranean, but Greece and Italy are not.

22. It is not the case that both Greece and England are on the Mediterranean, but it is the case that both Greece and Italy are.

23. Either England or Belgium is on the Mediterranean, or England or Greece is.

24. Either England or Belgium is not on the Mediterranean, or neither Greece nor Italy is.

25. It is not the case either that England and France are both on the Mediterranean or that Belgium and Greece are both on the Mediterranean.

26. Either it is not the case that England and France are both on the Mediterranean, or Belgium and Greece are both on the Mediterranean.

27. Either England and Greece are both on the Mediterranean, or England is on the Mediterranean but Greece is not; furthermore, either Belgium and France are both on the Mediterranean, or France is while Belgium is not.

B. Let *F* be "Ford raised prices" and *G* "General Motors raised prices." Then reexpress the following statements in English, doing so as economically as possible.

1. $F \lor G$ 2. $F \& G$
3. $F \& -G$ 4. $-F \& -G$
5. $-(F \& G)$ 6. $-F \lor -G$
7. $(F \lor G) \& -(F \& G)$ 8. $(F \lor G) \lor (F \& G)$
9. $(F \& G) \lor (-F \& -G)$ 10. $G \lor -G$
11. $(F \& G) \lor (F \& -G)$ 12. $F \lor [(G \& -F) \lor (-G \& -F)]$

C. Assume that *A*, *B*, and *C* are true statements, and that *X*, *Y*, and *Z* are false. Then determine whether the following compound statements are true or false.

1. $-A \lor B$ 2. $-(A \lor B)$
3. $-Y \lor Z$ 4. $-(Y \lor Z)$
5. $-(Y \& Z)$ 6. $-Y \& -Z$
7. $-Y \lor -Z$ 8. $-(A \lor B)$
9. $A \veebar Z$ 10. $A \veebar B$
11. $A \lor B$ 12. $A \veebar -B$
13. $-(A \veebar C)$ 14. $(A \lor Z) \& -(A \& Z)$
15. $(A \lor B) \& -(A \& B)$ 16. $(A \lor B) \lor -(A \& B)$
17. $(A \lor B) \lor (A \veebar B)$ 18. $(A \lor B) \veebar (A \veebar Z)$
19. $-[-(A \lor B) \& (A \lor C)]$ 20. $-[(A \lor B) \& (X \lor Y)]$
21. $-[-(A \lor B) \& -(X \lor Y)]$ 22. $-[-(A \& C) \& -(A \lor C)] \& [(A \veebar Z) \& B]$
23. $(-\{[(A \lor C) \lor X] \lor Y\} \& C) \& A$ 24. $[X \lor (Y \& Z)] \lor -[(X \lor Y) \& (X \lor Z)]$
25. $-\{-[(B \& -C) \lor (Y \& -C)] \& [(-B \lor X) \lor (B \lor -Y)]\}$

D. Assume that *A* and *B* are true, that *X* and *Y* are false, and that *P* and *Q* are unknown. Are the following statements true, false, or undetermined?

1. $A \lor P$ 2. $X \& Q$
3. $X \lor P$ 4. $A \& P$
5. $-(A \lor Q)$ 6. $-(Y \& P)$
7. $-A \& P$ 8. $A \& -P$
9. $(X \& P) \lor (X \& Q)$ 10. $(A \lor P) \& (A \lor Q)$
11. $(A \lor P) \lor (A \& P)$ 12. $(A \lor P) \& -(A \& P)$
13. $P \lor -P$ 14. $P \& -P$
15. $(P \& Q) \lor -(P \& Q)$ 16. $(P \lor Q) \& -(P \lor Q)$

7.2 Arguments and Argument Forms

Statements. In Chapter 6, we saw that some propositions do not have a truth value—namely, those whose presuppositions are false. "Your dodo is big" is neither true nor false, for example, since you do not have a dodo. In a complete study of logic, we would have to consider what truth value if any to assign to a conjunction, disjunction, or negation that has one or more components without a truth value. In the remainder of this book, however, we shall concentrate on propositions that have a truth value. It will be convenient to define a ***statement*** as a proposition that is either true or false. We will therefore be using "statement" as a technical term, for in ordinary English, "statement" and "proposition" are synonymous. For us, any proposition without a truth value, such as "Your dodo is big," is by definition not a statement. Hereafter we shall discuss only propositions that are statements.

Constants vs. Variables. We have used symbols in two very different ways. A ***constant*** stands for a *particular* term or statement. Constants are used to abbreviate. We might let A stand for "All men who worked on the railroads in 2000 but were not represented by a union were underpaid." Then we could use the single letter A in place of that lengthy sentence, saving space and time. $-A$ would abbreviate its negation, $A \vee -A$ would abbreviate the disjunction of it with its negation, and so on. Abbreviating sentences in this way is especially economical when the sentence is complex. It also promotes comprehension by making the structure of the statement more visible. We will generally use capital letters from the beginning of the alphabet (A, B, C, ...) as ***simple statement constants,*** constants that abbreviate simple statements. We may view expressions like $-A$, $A \vee B$, $A \vee (-B \mathbin{\&} C)$, and so on as ***compound statement constants,*** since they abbreviate compound statements.

    Variables stand for *any* term or statement. They are used to represent form, holding a place where terms or statements (or constants abbreviating them) could appear. Variables have the same function as blanks, except that we have to substitute terms or statements for variables, whereas we write terms or statements on top of blanks. We shall use lower-case letters from the middle of the alphabet (p, q, r, ...) as ***statement variables,*** which hold a place for statements. Statement variables stand for compound statements as well as simple statements. Note the asymmetry of our conventions: A, B, C ... stand only for simple statements, while p, q, r, stand for compound statements as well.

Argument Forms. Consider the following argument:

>Alan or Bill will come to the party.
>Alan will not come.
>Therefore, Bill will come.

We could abbreviate this argument by letting A stand for "Alan will come to the party" and B stand for "Bill will come to the party":

>$A \vee B$
>$-A$
>$\therefore B$

The symbols $\vee$, $-$, and $\therefore$ are also constants, standing for certain logical terms. Hence they are called ***logical constants***. We could represent the form of the argument in a similar way:

>$p \vee q$
>$-p$
>$\therefore q$

This pattern of argument is called the **_disjunctive syllogism_**: "syllogism" because such arguments have two premises; "disjunctive" because one of the premises is a disjunction. Intrinsically, these two arrays of symbols differ very little. But their symbolic functions differ considerably.

Argument forms have **_substitution instances_**. We get substitution instances from argument forms by substituting statements (or statement constants) for variables, making sure to substitute the same statement for the same variable everywhere that variable occurs in the form. Thus "A v B, $-A$, $\therefore B$" is a substitution instance of the disjunctive syllogism. But the disjunctive syllogism has infinitely many other substitution instances, including:

B v A	C v D	$(A \& C)$ v $(B \& D)$	$(A \& D)$ v $-A$	$[E$ v $(F \& G)]$ v H
$-B$	$-C$	$-(A \& C)$	$-(A \& D)$	$-[E$ v $(F \& G)]$
$\therefore A$	$\therefore D$	$\therefore (B \& D)$	$\therefore -A$	$\therefore H$

The third argument in this sequence is obtained by substituting $A \& C$ for p, and $B \& D$ for q. The fourth is obtained by substituting $A \& D$ for p and $-A$ for q. An argument is said to have a given form if the argument is a substitution instance of that form. All the arguments in the above sequence, therefore, have the form called disjunctive syllogism. Note that arguments are said to have forms, while forms are said to have substitution instances.

Specific vs. Generic Forms. A given argument may have many different forms. Consider the fourth argument in the sequence above.

$(A \& D)$ v $-A$
$-(A \& D)$
$\therefore -A$

This argument has all of the following forms:

p v q	$(p \& q)$ v $-p$	p v q	p
$-p$	$-(p \& q)$	r	q
$\therefore q$	$\therefore -p$	$\therefore s$	$\therefore r$

We already know that the argument is a substitution instance of the disjunctive syllogism, which is the first form. The argument can be obtained from the second form by substituting A for p, and D for q. The argument can be obtained from the third form by substituting $A \& D$ for p, $-A$ for q, $-(A \& D)$ for r, and $-A$ for s. When substituting, we are not allowed to substitute different statements for the same variable, but we may substitute the same constant for different variables. Finally, the argument can be obtained from the fourth form by replacing p with the entire first premise $(A \& D)$ v $-A$, q with the second premise $-(A \& D)$, and r with the conclusion $-A$.

While the argument has all the forms listed, the second form is the most specific, representing the narrowest class of substitution instances, while the fourth is the most general, representing the broadest class of arguments. The second form represents more of the argument's structure than the fourth. The fourth form tells you only that the argument has two premises. The second tells you that the argument has a disjunctive premise whose left-hand disjunct is a conjunction, and whose right-hand disjunct is the negation of the first conjunct in the left-hand disjunct. We describe that form which represents *all* the logical structure of an argument as the **_specific form_** of the argument. We will generally refer to the specific form simply as "the form" of the argument, or as "its form." We call any form other than the specific form a **_generic form_**. Generic forms represent some, but not all, of the logical structure of an argument.

Formal Validity and Valid Forms. A *formally valid argument* is an argument whose specific form is such that every argument having that form is deductively valid (see §2.5). A *valid argument form* is an argument form all of whose substitution instances are deductively valid (see §5.5). Invalid arguments or forms are those which are not valid. It follows that an argument is formally valid if and only if its specific form is valid. Note carefully that the formal validity of an argument depends on the validity of its *specific* form, which represents all the logical structure of the argument. Generic forms of the argument, which fail to represent part of its structure, may be invalid. Thus an argument whose specific form is the disjunctive syllogism is valid, even though the generic form "$p, q \; \therefore r$," possessed by any two-premise argument, is invalid. Also note that while no substitution instances of a valid argument form can be invalid, some substitution instances of an invalid argument form may be valid.

Glossary

Statement: used in a technical sense, a proposition that is true or false.

Simple statement constants: symbols like A, B, and C used to abbreviate simple statements.

Logical constants: symbols used to abbreviate logical expressions, e.g. & ("and"), ∨ (inclusive "or"), – ("not"), etc.

Compound statement constants: complex symbols composed of simple statement constants and logical constants, used to abbreviate compound statements.

Statement variables: symbols like p, q, and r used to represent form by holding a place for any statement.

Disjunctive syllogism: the valid argument form "$p \lor q, -p, \; \therefore q$."

Substitution instance: any argument (or statement) that can be obtained from a form by substituting statements or statement constants for the statement variables in the form, where the same statement or constant replaces the same variable wherever it occurs. An argument (or statement) is said to *have* any form it is a substitution instance of.

Specific form: The specific form of an argument (or statement) is the form that represents all of its logical structure.

Generic form: A generic form of an argument (or statement) is one that represents some but not all of its logical structure.

Valid argument form: an argument form all of whose substitution instances are deductively valid.

Formally valid argument: an argument whose specific form is valid.

Exercises

A. For each argument form in Set A, determine which if any of the arguments in Set B are its substitution instances.

1. p
    $\therefore p \lor q$

2. $p \lor q$
    p
    $\therefore -q$

3. $p \& q$
   $\therefore p$

4. $p \lor q$
   $-p$
   $\therefore q$

5. $p \lor q$
   $\therefore p \lor (p \& q)$

6. $-p \lor q$
   $-q \lor r$
   $\therefore -p \lor r$

7. p
   $\therefore q$

8. $p \lor q$
   r
   $\therefore s$

9. $p \& q$
   $\therefore (p \& q) \lor r$

10. $(p \& q) \lor (r \& s)$
    $-(p \& q)$
    $\therefore r \& s$

B.   For each argument in Set B, determine which if any of the forms in Set A it possesses. Classify any form it has as its specific form or one of its generic forms (assume that the constants $A, B, C, \ldots, L$ represent simple statements with no logical structure).

a. $A \& B$
     $\therefore A$

b. C
     $\therefore C \lor D$

c. $E \lor F$
     $-E$
     $\therefore F$

d. $A \lor B$
     A
     $\therefore -B$

e. C
     D
     $\therefore C \& D$

f. $C \& D$
     $-C$
     $\therefore D$

g. $A \& B$
     $\therefore (A \& B) \lor C$

h. $(F \& G) \lor (H \& I)$
     $-(F \& G)$
     $\therefore H \& I$

i. $-J \lor K$
     $-K \lor L$
     $\therefore -J \lor L$

j. $(D \& E) \& F$
     $\therefore D \& E$

k. $-(A \lor B) \lor (C \& D)$
     $-(C \& D) \lor E$
     $\therefore -(A \lor B) \lor E$

l. $(F \lor G) \lor (H \& I)$
     $F \lor G$
     $\therefore -(H \& I)$

7.3 The Truth Table Test of Validity

To prove an argument form valid, we need to show that if any substitution instance of the form has true premises, then it must have a true conclusion. Since an argument form has infinitely many substitution instances, there is no humanly possible way to examine them one by one. Furthermore, because our knowledge is limited, we will not know in many cases whether the premises and conclusion are actually true or false. However, as long as we confine ourselves to argument forms whose premises and conclusions are truth-functional compounds, we can surmount these human limitations. For the truth or falsity of a truth-functional compound depends only on the truth values of its components, not on the specific content of the components. Consider the disjunctive syllogism.

$$p \vee q$$
$$-p$$
$$\therefore q$$

It contains two statement variables, p and q. Each variable stands for infinitely many statements. But since the premises of the disjunctive syllogism are truth-functional, their truth value depends only on the truth values of the statements substituted for p and q. It does not matter, for example, whether "2 + 2 = 4" or "The sky is blue" is substituted for p. In both cases, the first premise is true while the second is false. Consequently, even though the disjunctive syllogism has infinitely many substitution instances, they represent only four different cases: (1) the statements substituted for both p and q are true; (2) the statement substituted for p is true while that substituted for q is false; (3) the statement substituted for p is false while that substituted for q is true; and finally (4) the statements substituted for both p and q are false. It is easy to see that in the first case, the first premise will be true, the second false, and the conclusion true. In the second case, the first premise will be true, the second false, and the conclusion false. In the third case, the first premise will be true, the second true, and the conclusion true. And in the fourth case, the first premise will be false, the second true, and the conclusion true. Observe that the conclusion is true in that case in which both premises are true. So we have shown that the disjunctive syllogism is a valid argument form.

The demonstration can be conveniently summarized by means of a truth table with a row for the four possible cases, and a column for the conclusion and each of the premises (see Table 7-4).

p	q	$p \vee q$	$-p$	$\therefore q$
T	T	T	F	T
T	F	T	F	F
F	T	T	T	T
F	F	F	T	F

TABLE 7-4. VALID

The first two columns represent all the possible cases, which consist of all possible assignments of truth values to the two variables. The second two columns represent the truth values of the premises in each of the possible cases, and the last column represents the truth value of the conclusion in each case. The validity of the argument form is shown by the fact that there is no row with both premises true and the conclusion false.

The disjunctive syllogism's validity depends on the fact that the second premise *denies* one of the disjuncts of the first premise. If the second premise *affirmed* that disjunct, the argument would be invalid. That is, the following relative of the disjunctive syllogism is invalid:

$$p \vee q$$
$$p$$
$$\therefore q$$

The invalidity of this form can be shown by a truth table. Instead of reasoning out the demonstration verbally, and then summarizing the results with a table, the most efficient procedure is to do the demonstration by constructing the table. First, make a column for each of the variables. Again we have only two: p and q.

p	q	p ∨ q	p	∴ q
T	T	T	T	T
T	F	T	T	F
F	T	T	F	T
F	F	F	F	F

TABLE 7-5. INVALID

Second, make a row for each of the possible cases. There will be the same four. Third, make a column for each premise and one for the conclusion, and then evaluate them in every possible case. The result is Table 7-5. Having constructed the table, we see if in any row the premises are true while the conclusion is false. We do find such a row here: the second. So the argument form is invalid.

In general, then, the **truth table test of validity** for a given argument form goes as follows: First construct a table by making a row representing all possible assignments of truth values to the statement variables contained in the argument form and by evaluating the premises and the conclusion in each row. Then see if there are any rows in which all the premises are true while the conclusion is false. If there are, the argument form is invalid. If there are no such rows, the form is valid (except in a special case to be discussed in §7.4).

More than Two Variables. If an argument form contains more than two statement variables, there will be more than four possible cases to consider, but otherwise the procedure is exactly the same. Consider an argument form with three variables:

$$p \lor q$$
$$q \lor r$$
$$\therefore p \lor r$$

There are eight possible cases, so our truth table will have to contain eight rows (see Table 7-6).

p	q	r	p ∨ q	q ∨ r	∴ p ∨ r
T	T	T	T	T	T
T	T	F	T	T	T
T	F	T	T	T	T
T	F	F	T	F	T
F	T	T	T	T	T
F	T	F	T	T	F
F	F	T	F	T	T
F	F	F	F	F	F

TABLE 7-6. INVALID

In the sixth row, both $p \lor q$ and $q \lor r$ are true, while $p \lor r$ is false, so the argument form is invalid. Its invalidity shows that disjunction is not a *transitive* connective. From the truth of $p \lor q$ and $q \lor r$, we cannot infer $p \lor r$. A similar pattern of argument, however, is valid:

$p \lor q$
$-q \lor r$
$\therefore p \lor r$

This is proven valid by Table 7-7.

p	q	r	$p \lor q$	$-q \lor r$	$\therefore p \lor r$
T	T	T	T	T	T
T	T	F	T	F	T
T	F	T	T	T	T
T	F	F	T	T	T
F	T	T	T	T	T
F	T	F	T	F	F
F	F	T	F	T	T
F	F	F	F	T	F

TABLE 7-7. VALID

No row in this table has both premises true and the conclusion false. In the sixth row, $-q \lor r$ is false, whereas $q \lor r$ would be true. We shall refer to the argument form "$p \lor q, -q \lor r, \therefore p \lor r$" as *disjunctive transitivity*, because it formulates something resembling a transitive property for disjunction.

When the premises and conclusion are complex, you may find it easier to work through an expanded truth table, which has extra columns for the subcomponents of the premises and conclusion. Suppose, for example, we wished to prove the validity of the following argument:

$(-p \lor q) \& (-q \lor p)$
$\therefore (p \& q) \lor (-p \& -q)$

An expanded table would have six extra columns (see Table 7-8).

p	q	$-p$	$-q$	$p \& q$	$-p \& -q$	$-p \lor q$	$-q \lor p$	$(-p \lor q) \&$ $(-q \lor p)$	$\therefore (p \& q) \lor$ $(-p \& -q)$
T	T	F	F	T	F	T	T	T	T
T	F	F	T	F	F	F	T	F	F
F	T	T	F	F	F	T	F	F	F
F	F	T	T	F	T	T	T	T	T
1	2	3	4	5	6	7	8	9	10

TABLE 7-8. VALID

The third column in Table 7-8 is evaluated by negating the first. The fifth column is evaluated by conjoining the first two. The sixth column is evaluated by conjoining the third and fourth columns. The ninth column is obtained by conjoining the seventh and eighth. And finally the tenth column is obtained by disjoining the fifth and sixth. The argument form is valid, since the two rows with the premise true have the conclusion true. You have to decide for yourself whether you prefer a shorter table with harder calculations, or a longer table with easier calculations. Just be sure you do not treat subcomponents as premises.

The success of the truth table test depends on representing all possible cases. If even one is overlooked, the results may be inconclusive. With only two statement variables, it is easy to memorize the four possible cases. Memorizing is more difficult, but still feasible, with three variables and eight cases. But with more than three variables, brute memorization is out of the question. Fortunately, a simple mechanical procedure exists for constructing all possible cases. As we have seen, if there is only 1 variable (as in the table for negation), there are just 2 cases. With 2 variables (as in Tables 7-4 or 7-5), there are $4 = 2 \times 2 = 2^2$ cases. With 3 variables (as in Tables 7-6 or 7-7), there are $8 = 2 \times 2 \times 2 = 2^3$ cases. With 4 variables, there are $16 = 2 \times 2 \times 2 \times 2 = 2^4$ cases. In general, if there are n variables, there must be 2^n cases. We construct a table with only 1 variable (see Table 7-2) by having one T followed by one F under the one variable. We construct a table with 2 variables (see Table 7-4) by having 2 T's followed by 2 F's in the first column, and then alternating T's and F's by ones in the second column. We construct a table with 3 variables (see Table 7-6) by having 4 T's followed by 4 F's in the first column, and then alternating T's and F's by twos in the second column and alternating by ones in the third column. In a table with 4 variables, there would be 8 T's followed by 8 F's in the first column, and in succeeding columns we would alternate by fours, twos, and ones. In a table with 5 variables, the first column would have 16 T's followed by 16 F's, the second would alternate by eights, and so on. All of this can be summarized by three mathematical progressions:

Number of variables:	1	2	3	4	5	...n
Number of cases:	2	4	8	16	32	...2^n
Alternate first by:	1	2	4	8	16	...$2^n/2$

Suppose you have 7 variables. Proceed systematically as follows: First make a column for each of the variables. Then write "1" over the last variable, "2" over the second from last, "4" over the third from last, and so on:

$$64\ 32\ 16\ 8\ 4\ 2\ 1$$
$$p\quad q\quad r\ s\ t\ u\ v$$

Now you know to construct the first column by writing 64 T's followed by 64 F's, producing 128 rows. In the second column, you alternate T's and Fs by 32 (until you have 128 entries). And so on.

It is generally more efficient to evaluate one row at a time rather than one column at a time (i.e., to go across rather than down). For then you can use three shortcuts, which are especially welcome with lengthy tables. First, once you come upon a row in which all the premises are true and the conclusion is false, you have proven the argument form to be invalid. There is therefore no reason to finish the table. One row proves invalidity. Second, if you come upon a false premise in any row, you need not finish the row. A row with a false premise is not a row in which all the premises are true while the conclusion is false. Third, if you find that the conclusion is true in any row, you do not need to evaluate the premises in that row. For again, that row will not be one with the premises true and the conclusion false.

Limitations. The truth table test is effective only for *truth-functional* argument forms, argument forms containing nothing but statement variables and truth-functional connectives like &, v, and –. If an argument contains a premise or conclusion that is not truth-functional, we will generally be unable to evaluate it in all of the rows. For the truth value of that premise or conclusion will not be completely determined by the truth values of its simple components. We shall examine this point at greater length in §7.7. Furthermore, the truth table test proves invalidity only for argument *forms*. Of course, if an argument form is valid, then all its substitution instances are valid. So we can prove that an argument is valid by using truth tables to show that its truth-functional form is valid. However, an argument may be formally valid even though its truth-functional form is invalid. Consider an **AAA1** syllogism, such as:

> All mammals are animals.
> All cats are mammals.
> ∴ All cats are animals.

This is a formally valid argument, as we saw in Chapters 5 and 6. However, its premises and conclusion are *simple* statements, so its truth-functional form is just:

> p
> q
> ∴ r

This argument form is obviously invalid. But that does not mean that **AAA1** syllogisms are invalid. For "$p, q, \therefore r$" is not the *specific* form of an **AAA1** syllogism. Indeed, "$p, q, \therefore r$" is a form shared by *all* syllogisms. In short, the method of truth tables could be used to establish the deductive invalidity of an argument only if its logical structure could be completely represented in terms of truth-functional compounds like conjunctions, disjunctions, and negations. But an argument will always have more structure.

Truth-Functional Validity. Let us now define the *specific truth-functional form* of an argument as that form which represents its logical structure completely insofar as it is composed of simple statements and truth-functional compounds of simple statements. And let us say that an argument is *truth-functionally valid* if its specific truth-functional form is valid, and *truth-functionally invalid* if its specific truth-functional form is invalid. Then what the truth table test can show in general is whether an argument is truth-functionally valid or invalid. Any truth-functionally valid argument is formally valid. But a truth-functionally invalid argument may still be formally valid, depending on the internal structure of its simple statements.

Now suppose we are given an argument to evaluate by the truth table test, say:

> It is going to be rainy. Therefore, it is going to be either rainy and hot or rainy and not hot.

The first step is to represent its truth-functional form. There are two simple statements, "It is going to be rainy" and "It is going to be hot," so we need two statement variables. The truth-functional form is:

> p
> ∴ $(p \mathbin{\&} q) \lor (p \mathbin{\&} {-}q)$

The truth table will have four rows (see Table 7-9).

p	q	p	$\therefore (p \mathbin{\&} q) \lor (p \mathbin{\&} {-}q)$
T	T	T	T
T	F	T	T
F	T	F	F
F	F	F	F

TABLE 7-9

There is no row in which the premise is true and the conclusion false, so we have shown that the given argument is truth-functionally valid, and therefore formally valid. We have also shown that its truth-functional form is valid. Now consider:

> Either no men are geniuses, or some are.
> Some men are geniuses.
> Therefore, it is not the case that no men are geniuses.

There are again two simple statements: "No men are geniuses" and "Some men are geniuses." Hence we need two variables to represent the argument's truth-functional form, which is:

$$p \lor q$$
$$q$$
$$\therefore -p$$

Table 7-10 is the truth table for this argument form.

p	q	p ∨ q	q	∴-p
T	T	T	T	F
T	F	T	F	F
F	T	T	T	T
F	F	F	F	T

TABLE 7-10

Because the first row has both premises true and the conclusion false, we have shown that the given argument is truth-functionally invalid, and that its truth-functional form is invalid. We cannot conclude, however, that the argument is invalid, for it has considerable structure in addition to its truth-functional structure. Indeed, the argument is valid because the two simple statements involved are contradictory.

We may want to apply the truth table test to an argument that has already been symbolized using constants, for example:

$$-A \lor -B$$
$$\therefore -(A \lor B)$$

Since the truth-functional form of the argument is already clearly represented, there is no need to re-represent it using variables. We simply treat the constants as if they were variables, making a row for every possible assignment of truth values to the simple statement constants, evaluating the premises in each row, and so on. The result is Table 7-11.

A	B	-A ∨ -B	∴-(A ∨ B)
T	T	F	F
T	F	T	F
F	T	T	F
F	F	T	T

TABLE 7-11

There are two rows in which the premise is true and the conclusion false. So the argument is not truth-functionally valid. We have not shown that the argument is invalid, however, since there may be important logical relationships between A and B that have not been represented.

Glossary

Truth table test of validity: determining whether an argument form is valid or invalid by constructing a table with a row representing each possible assignment of truth values to the statement variables in the form, and a column for the conclusion and each premise representing its truth or falsity in each of the possible cases; the argument form is invalid if there is a row in which the premises are all true and the conclusion false; the form is valid if there is no such row (except possibly when the conclusion is logically true or the conjunction of the premises logically false, as discussed in §7.4 below). An argument can be shown to be truth-functionally valid or invalid by testing its specific truth functional form for validity.

Disjunctive transitivity: the valid argument form "$p \lor q$, $-q \lor r$, $\therefore$ $p \lor r$."

Specific truth-functional form: that form which represents the logical structure of a statement or argument completely insofar as it is composed of simple statements and truth-functional compounds.

Truth-functionally valid: an argument is truth-functionally valid if its specific truth-functional form is valid; otherwise it is truth-functionally invalid.

Exercises

A. Prove the validity or invalidity of the following argument forms using the truth table test.

1. p
   $\therefore p \lor q$

2. p
   $\therefore p \& q$

3. $p \& q$
   $\therefore p$

4. $-p \lor -q$
   $\therefore -(p \& q)$

5. $-p \& -q$
   $\therefore -(p \& q)$

6. $-(p \lor q)$
   $\therefore -p \& -q$

7. $p \veebar q$
   $\therefore p \veebar (p \& q)$

8. $p \lor q$
   $\therefore p \lor (p \& q)$

9. $p \lor q$
   p
   $\therefore -q$

10. $p \veebar q$
    p
    $\therefore -q$

B. Follow the directions for Set A.

1. $p \& (q \lor r)$
   $\therefore (p \& q) \lor (p \& r)$

2. $(p \& q) \lor (p \& r)$
   $\therefore p \& (q \lor r)$

3. $p \lor (q \& r)$
   $\therefore (p \lor q) \& (p \lor r)$

4. $p \lor (q \& r)$
   $\therefore (p \& q) \lor (p \& r)$

5. $-(p \& q) \lor r$
   $\therefore -p \lor (-q \lor r)$

6. $-(p \lor q) \lor s$
   $\therefore -p \lor s$

7. $-p \lor q$
   $-(q \lor r)$
   $\therefore -p$

8. $p \lor q$
   $r \lor -q$
   $-r$
   $\therefore p$

9. $(p \lor q) \& (r \lor s)$
    $p \lor r$
    $\therefore -q \lor -s$

10. $(p \lor q) \& (r \lor s)$
    $p \lor r$
    $\therefore q \lor s$

C. Prove the truth-functional validity or invalidity of the following arguments using the truth table test.

1. $-A$
    $\therefore -A \lor B$

2. $-A$
    $\therefore -(A \lor B)$

3. $-O \lor P$
    $-P \lor -P$
    $\therefore -O$

4. $E \lor (F \& G)$
    $-F$
    $\therefore E$

5. $H \lor (I \& J)$
    $-(I \lor J) \lor K$
    $\therefore H \lor K$

6. $-A \lor (-B \lor C)$
    $-B \lor -C$
    $\therefore -A$

7. $E \lor F$
    $-F \lor G$
    $-E$
    $\therefore F \& (E \lor G)$

8. $-Q \lor R$
    $-Q \lor S$
    $\therefore R \lor S$

9. $-A \lor (-B \lor C)$
    $-B \lor (-C \lor D)$
    $\therefore -A \lor D$

10. $E \lor F$
    $E \lor G$
    $-E \& -H$
    $\therefore F \& G$

D. Prove the truth-functional validity or invalidity of the following arguments using the truth table test.

1. Oslo is not the capital of both Norway and Sweden. Therefore, it is either not the capital of Norway or not the capital of Sweden.

2. Budapest is either not in Slovenia or not in Romania. Therefore it is in neither Slovenia nor Romania.

3. Russia is rich in gold. It is also rich in either chromium or manganese. Therefore, Russia is rich in gold and chromium or gold and manganese.

4. Zimbabwe does not have both a temperate and a subtropical climate. It has a temperate climate. Therefore, Zimbabwe does not have a subtropical climate.

5. It is not the case that the United States will invade either Nicaragua or El Salvador. The United States will not invade Nicaragua. Therefore, the United States will invade El Salvador.

6. Antananarivo is the capital of either Madagascar, Kenya, or Zimbabwe. It is not the capital of Kenya. Therefore, it is the capital or either Madagascar or Zimbabwe.

7. Fort Providence is on Great Slave Lake or Hudson Bay. Fort Providence is on Great Slave Lake or Great Bear Lake. Therefore, Fort Providence is on Great Slave Lake, and on either Great Bear Lake or Hudson Bay.

8. Fort Providence is on Great Bear Lake or Great Slave Lake. It is in Canada or it is not on Great Slave Lake. It is not on Great Bear Lake. So Fort Providence is in Canada.

9. Rangoon is the capital of either Burma or Thailand, but not both. It is the capital of either Malaysia or Laos, but not both. Rangoon is the capital of either Burma or Malaysia. Therefore, it is either not the capital of Thailand or not the capital of Laos.

10. Rangoon is the capital of either Burma or Thailand, or of either Malaysia or Laos. It is the capital of neither Burma nor Malaya. Therefore, Rangoon is the capital of either Thailand or Laos.

7.4 Logical Truth, Falsity, and Contingency

We have used truth tables to do two things: first, to show how the truth value of a truth-functional compound depends on the truth values of its components; and second, to determine whether a truth-functional argument form is valid or invalid. Truth tables have other uses, as we shall now see.

We have distinguished between arguments and argument forms. There is a parallel distinction between *statements* and *statement forms*. The latter distinction was implicit in the former, since statement forms occupy the place of premises and conclusions in argument forms. A statement form represents the logical structure of a class of statements, which are substitution instances of the form. For example, the statement "The sky is blue and grass is green" is a substitution instance of the statement form $p \ \& \ q$. The statement form that represents all the logical structure of a statement is its specific form; all other forms it possesses are generic forms. "The sky either is or isn't blue" has the form $p \lor q$ as well as the form $p \lor -p$, but the latter is its specific truth-functional form. Even its specific truth-functional form is not the statement's specific form, however, since p does not represent the internal structure of the simple statement "The sky is blue."

Every statement form has an infinitely large class of substitution instances. In the typical case, some substitution instances are true while others are false. Some statement forms, however, have only true substitution instances, while others have only false ones. A statement form is said to be ***logically true*** if all its substitution instances are true, ***logically false*** if all its substitution instances are false, and ***logically contingent*** if some of its substitution instances are true and some false. There are numerous synonyms for these terms, such as "analytic" and "tautologous" for "logically true," "synthetic" for "logically contingent," and "self-contradictory" for "logically false."

Truth tables can be used to determine whether truth-functional statement forms are logically true, false, or contingent. Consider the statement form $p \lor -p$. This has many true substitution instances, such as "2 either is or is not prime" and "The president either is or is not a conservative." We cannot hope to examine all the substitution instances of this or any other form. Fortunately, disjunction and negation are truth-functional, so the truth value of any substitution instance of $p \lor -p$ is completely determined by the truth value of the statement substituted for p. Consequently, there are just two cases to consider: in one, p is true; in the other, p is false. In the first case, the left-hand disjunct of $p \lor -p$ is true, while in the second the right-hand disjunct is true. So in both cases, the disjunction $p \lor -p$ is true. This result is summarized by Table 7-12.

p	$p \lor -p$
T	T
F	T

TABLE 7-12.

Since $p \lor -p$ is true in every case, it is logically true. In contrast, $p \,\&\, -p$ is logically false, having substitution instances like "The president both is and isn't a Republican," and "2 is and is not prime." When p is true, its negation is false, so the conjunction $p \,\&\, -p$ is false because of its right-hand conjunct. When p is false, the left-hand conjunct of $p \,\&\, -p$ is false (see Table 7-13).

p	$p \,\&\, -p$
T	F
F	F

TABLE 7-13.

The truth tables for conjunction, disjunction, and negation show that $p \,\&\, q$, $p \lor q$, $p \veebar q$, and $-p$ are logically contingent. The columns under them in the truth tables have some T's and some F's. Whether or not substitution instances of these forms are true or false is contingent on the specific statements substituted for the variables.

It will seldom be obvious whether a complex statement form is logically true, false, or contingent. Consider $-p \lor [(p \,\&\, q) \lor (p \,\&\, -q)]$. If we work out a truth table, we get Table 7-14.

p	q	$-p \lor [(p \,\&\, q) \lor (p \,\&\, -q)]$
T	T	T
T	F	T
F	T	T
F	F	T

TABLE 7-14.

Since the form comes out true in every row, the form is logically true. Table 7-15 is expanded, with columns for the subcomponents of the statement form being evaluated.

p	q	$-p$	$-q$	$p \,\&\, q$	$p \,\&\, -q$	$[(p \,\&\, q) \lor (p \,\&\, -q)]$	$-p \lor [(p \,\&\, q) \lor (-p \,\&\, -q)]$
T	T	F	F	T	F	T	T
T	F	F	T	F	T	T	T
F	T	T	F	F	F	F	T
F	F	T	T	F	F	F	T
1	2	3	4	5	6	7	8

TABLE 7-15.

We get the values in the third column of Table 7-15 by negating the values in the first column. We get the values in the sixth column by conjoining the values in the first and fourth columns. We get the values in the seventh column by disjoining the values in the fifth and sixth. And finally, we get the values in the eighth column, which represents the statement form we are evaluating, by disjoining the values in the third column with those in the seventh.

Suppose we have a pair of statement forms, one the negation of the other. It follows from our definitions that if one of the statement forms is logically true, the other is logically false. But if one is contingent, the other is also contingent. Since $p \lor -p$ is true in every case, its negation $-(p \lor -p)$ is false in every case. Since $p \,\&\, -p$ is false in every case, its negation is true in every case. And since $p \lor q$ is true in some cases, false in others, its negation $-(p \lor q)$ is also true in some cases, false in others.

Statements vs. Statement Forms. So far in this section we have confined our attention to statement *forms*. A *statement* is said to be logically true, false, or contingent provided its specific form is. Now if any generic form of a statement is logically true or false, then the specific form of the statement must be the same. Hence we can classify "The sky either is or is not blue" as logically true, since it has the logically true form $p \lor -p$. *All* substitution instances of $p \lor -p$ are true, including all those with the specific form of the given statement. Similarly, we can classify "The sky both is and is not blue" as logically false, since it has the logically false form $p \,\&\, -p$. *All* substitution instances of $p \,\&\, -p$ are false, including all those with any more specific form. However, one of a statement's generic forms may be contingent even though its specific form is not: the additional structure represented by the specific form may make a difference. For example, "All men are animals and no men are animals" has the specific truth-functional form $p \,\&\, q$. Even though that form is contingent, the given statement is not, for it has significant structure not represented by $p \,\&\, q$. The form $p \,\&\, q$ has some true substitution instances; but the specific form of the given statement has no true substitution instance. Truth tables, therefore, cannot be used to determine whether or not a statement (as opposed to a statement form) is logically contingent. Even the most specific truth-functional form of a statement will not be its specific form.

Let us say that a statement *is **truth-functionally contingent*** if its specific truth-functional form is contingent. Then "All men are animals and no men are animals" is truth-functionally contingent, even though it is not logically contingent. Truth tables do enable us to determine whether or not a statement is truth-functionally contingent.

To summarize, truth tables can be used to determine whether truth-functional statement forms are logically true, logically false, or logically contingent. We construct a truth table and then see whether the statement form is true in all cases, in no cases, or in some but not all cases. Truth tables can also be used to determine whether statements are logically true, logically false, or truth-functionally contingent. We first represent the statement's specific truth-functional form, and then use truth tables to determine whether that form is logically true, false, or contingent.

A Limitation on the Truth Table Test of Validity. We are now ready to discuss another important limitation on the truth table test of validity. We prove validity using truth tables by constructing a table with rows representing all the possible cases, and finding no row in which the premises are all true and the conclusion false. Every such table shows that it is impossible for the premises of the argument to be true and the conclusion false. But as we saw in §2.4, it may be impossible for the premises of an argument to be true and the conclusion false, without the conclusion of the argument *following* from the premises, and consequently without the argument being valid as we have defined the term. To show that the conclusion follows from the premises, a truth table must show in addition that the premises are *relevant* to the conclusion, by showing that the truth value of the conclusion *depends on* the truth value of the premises. Consider the following argument form.

$$p$$
$$\therefore q \lor -q$$

This form is clearly invalid. One substitution instance is "The sky is blue, therefore the moon either is or is not made of green cheese." This substitution instance is invalid; for the conclusion, which is true, does not follow from the premise, which is also true but completely irrelevant. If we construct a truth table for the argument form, however, we get Table 7-16.

p	q	p	∴q ∨ ~q
T	T	T	T
T	F	T	T
F	T	F	T
F	F	F	T

TABLE 7-16.

There is no row of table 7-16 in which the premise is true and the conclusion false. Indeed, there is no row in which the conclusion is false. We cannot conclude, however, that the argument form is valid. For the conclusion is a logical truth, and as such is necessarily true independently of the premise. Consequently the table fails to show that the truth of the premise is relevant to the truth of the conclusion. Similarly, if the conjunction of the premises of an argument is logically false, then there will be no row of the truth table in which all the premises are true and the conclusion false. This will be so no matter what the conclusion is. Such a table does not show that the premises are relevant to the conclusion, because it fails to show that the truth value of the conclusion depends on the truth value of the premises. Hence such a table does not prove validity.

If it is impossible for the premises of an argument to be true and the conclusion false, we may infer that the conclusion of the argument follows with necessity from the premises *except* when the conclusion of the argument is independently necessary or the conjunction of the premises independently impossible. Consequently, *truth tables do not prove validity if the conclusion of the argument is logically true or if the conjunction of the premises is logically false.* This is not to say that no arguments with logically true conclusions or logically false premises are valid. Many are. But other methods must be used to prove their validity. There is no similar restriction on the truth table test of invalidity. If all the premises are true and the conclusion false in any row, or in all rows, then the argument must be invalid. The conclusion and the premises need not be logically contingent.

Glossary

Logically true: A statement form is logically true if all its substitution instances are true; a statement is logically true if its specific form is logically true.

Logically false: A statement form is logically false if all its substitution instances are false; a statement is logically false if its specific form is logically false.

Logically contingent: A statement form is logically contingent if some of its substitution instances are true while others are false; a statement is logically contingent if its specific form is logically contingent.

Truth-functionally contingent: A statement is truth-functionally contingent if its specific truth-functional form is logically contingent.

Exercises

A. For each statement form in Set A, determine which if any of the statements in Set B are its substitution instances.

1. $p \lor q$
2. $p \lor -p$
3. $p \,\&\, q$
4. $p \,\&\, -p$
5. $(p \,\&\, q) \,\&\, r$
6. $(p \,\&\, -p) \lor q$
7. $p \lor -(r \,\&\, s)$
8. $(p \,\&\, q) \lor -(p \,\&\, r)$

B. For each statement in Set B, determine which if any of the forms in Set A it possesses. Classify any forms it has as its specific truth-functional form or one of its generic truth-functional forms.

a. $(A \,\&\, B) \,\&\, (A \,\&\, C)$
b. $(C \,\&\, D) \lor -(C \,\&\, D)$
c. $(H \,\&\, -H) \,\&\, I$
d. $(C \lor D) \,\&\, -(C \lor D)$
e. $A \lor -A$
f. $(C \,\&\, D) \lor -(C \,\&\, E)$
g. $[(J \lor K) \,\&\, L] \lor -[(J \lor K) \,\&\, M]$
h. $-[(E \,\&\, F) \,\&\, -(E \,\&\, F)]$

C. Use truth tables to determine whether the following statement forms are logically true, false, or contingent.

1. $p \lor (-p \lor q)$
2. $p \lor -(p \lor q)$
3. $-(p \,\&\, q) \lor p$
4. $(p \,\&\, q) \lor (p \,\&\, -q)$
5. $(p \lor q) \lor (-p \,\&\, -q)$
6. $(p \lor q) \,\&\, (-p \,\&\, -q)$
7. $(p \,\&\, q) \lor (-p \,\&\, -q)$
8. $(p \,\&\, q) \lor (-p \lor -q)$
9. $-(-p \lor -q) \lor (-p \,\&\, -q)$
10. $[-(p \,\&\, q) \,\&\, p] \,\&\, q$
11. $[-(p \,\&\, q) \,\&\, p] \,\&\, -q$
12. $-[-(p \,\&\, q) \,\&\, p] \lor -q$
13. $-[(p \lor q) \,\&\, -p] \lor q$
14. $-[(p \lor q) \,\&\, p] \lor -q$
15. $[(p \lor -q) \,\&\, -p] \,\&\, q$
16. $[(p \,\&\, q) \lor (p \,\&\, -q)] \lor [(-p \,\&\, q) \lor (-p \,\&\, -q)]$
17. $-[(p \lor q) \,\&\, (r \lor -q)] \lor (p \lor r)$
18. $[(p \,\&\, q) \lor (p \,\&\, r)] \lor -[p \lor (q \,\&\, r)]$
19. $[(p \lor q) \,\&\, (-q \lor r)] \,\&\, (-p \,\&\, -r)$
20. $-\{[(p \lor q) \,\&\, (r \lor s)] \,\&\, (-p \lor -r)\} \lor (q \lor s)$

D. Use truth tables to determine whether the following statements are logically true, logically false, or truth-functionally contingent.

1. Either Zimbabwe and Russia are both rich in chromium or they are not both rich in the metal.

2. Zimbabwe is rich in chromium, but it is rich in neither oil nor chromium.

3. Either Kenya is rich in both copper and nickel, or it is rich in copper but not nickel.

4. Either no Pakistanis are Hindu, or some Pakistanis are Hindu.

5. Either Paul Martin does not speak French, or he either speaks both French and English or French but not English.

6. Edmonton is not in Alberta, but it is either in both Saskatchewan and Alberta or Alberta but not Saskatchewan.

7. Either Kennedy won the 1960 presidential election, or the following is not the case: either Kennedy or Nixon won the election, but Nixon did not.

8. Either cotton and soybeans are both grown in Alabama, or cotton but not soybeans are grown there, or neither cotton nor soybeans are grown in Alabama.

9. Either Flagstaff is in Arizona, or it is in Arkansas; and it is in the United States or it is not in Arkansas; but Flagstaff is neither in Arizona nor in the United States.

10. Little Rock is in the United States and either in Arkansas or Arizona, but Little Rock is not in both the United States and Arizona.

E. Construct a truth table for the following argument forms, and determine whether the form is valid, invalid, or undetermined.

1. $p \lor q$
   $-p \ \& \ -q$
   $\therefore (-p \lor q) \ \& \ (-q \lor p)$

2. $p \ \& \ (-p \lor -p)$
   $\therefore q \lor (-q \ \& \ -q)$

3. $p \lor (q \lor -p)$
   $\therefore p \ \& \ (q \ \& \ -p)$

4. $p \lor q$
   $-q \ \& \ r$
   $-r \lor -p$
   $\therefore p \ \& \ -q$

5. $-p \lor q$
   $-r \lor q$
   $\therefore -(p \ \& \ r) \lor q$

6. $p \lor r$
   $\therefore q \lor (r \lor -q)$

7.5 Logical Implication, Equivalence, and Incompatibility

Logical Implication and Equivalence. Let F and G be any two statement forms. We shall say that F *logically implies* G, provided the argument form $F \therefore G$ is valid, which means that G follows from F in all instances. It should be evident, for example, that $p \ \& \ q$ logically implies p, which is known as the *simplification* rule. In contrast, p does not logically imply $p \ \& \ q$. Similarly, p logically implies $p \lor q$, which is known as the *addition* rule. But $p \lor q$ does not logically imply p. We can establish that F logically implies G by using truth tables to show that the argument form $F \therefore G$ is valid. This requires showing that there is no case in which F is true while G is false.

We shall say further that F and G are *logically equivalent*, provided that F logically implies G and G logically implies F, which means that the argument forms $F \therefore G$ and $G \therefore F$ are both valid. Logical equivalence, in other words, is *mutual* logical implication. It should be evident that $--p$ is logically equivalent to p, which is the *double negation* rule. Using the equals sign to express logical equivalence, we can write $--p = p$. Other elementary equivalences are the *commutation* and *association* rules. The commutation rules imply that the order of conjunctions and disjunctions is irrelevant: $(p \ \& \ q) = (q \ \& \ p)$ and $(p \lor q) = (q \lor p)$. The association rules imply that the placement of parentheses among more than two disjuncts or more than two conjuncts is also immaterial: $[p \ \& \ (q \ \& \ r)] = [(p \ \& \ q) \ \& \ r]$, and $[p \lor (q \lor r)] = [(p \lor q) \lor r]$. Commutation and association should be familiar from algebra, where we know, for example, that $(x + y) = (y + x)$ and that $[x + (y + z)] = [(x + y) + z]$. Since logical equivalence is mutual logical implication, $p \ \& \ q$ is not logically equivalent to p even though $p \ \& \ q$ logically implies p; for p

does not logically imply p & q. Similarly, p is not logically equivalent to $p \lor q$ even though p logically implies $p \lor q$: for $p \lor q$ does not logically imply p.

We can use truth tables to prove the logical equivalence of F and G, by showing that the argument forms $F \therefore G$ and $G \therefore F$ are both valid. This requires showing that there is no case in which F is true while G is false, and no case in which G is true while F is false, which means that F and G must have the same truth value in all cases. Even though we need to validate two argument forms, only one table is necessary. For example, in §7.1 we observed that there were two equivalent ways to symbolize "Neither p nor q": as either $(p \lor q)$ or $-p$ & $-q$. We can prove that these two statement forms are indeed equivalent by constructing Table 7-17.

p	q	$-p$	$-q$	$p \lor q$	$-(p \lor q)$	$-p$ & $-q$
T	T	F	F	T	F	F
T	F	F	T	T	F	F
F	T	T	F	T	F	F
F	F	T	T	F	T	T

TABLE 7-17.

There are four possible cases: $-(p \lor q)$ and $-p$ & $-q$ are both false in the first three, and both true in the fourth. So $-(p \lor q) = -p$ & $-q$. In a similar way, we can prove that $-(p$ & $q) = -p \lor -q$. These two equivalences are known as the ***De Morgan*** rules, after the nineteenth-century logician and mathematician mentioned in Chapter 6. De Morgan's rules tell us how to distribute negation into conjunctions and disjunctions.

The basic definitions of inclusive and exclusive disjunction are provided by the ***disjunction*** rules. We said that "$p \lor q$" was to mean "p or q or both," so we have: $[p \lor q] = [(p \lor (p$ & $q)]$. Similarly, "$p \veebar q$" was to mean "p or q but not both," which implies: $[p \veebar q] = [(p \lor q)$ & $-(p$ & $q)]$. Table 7-18 verifies the second equivalence.

p	q	$p \veebar q$	$(p \lor q)$ & $-(p$ & $q)$
T	T	F	F
T	F	T	T
F	T	T	T
F	F	F	F

TABLE 7-18.

The ***distribution*** rules tell us how to distribute conjunction into disjunctions and disjunction into conjunctions: $[p$ & $(q \lor r)] = [(p$ & $q) \lor (p$ & $r)]$; and $[p \lor (q$ & $r)] = [(p \lor q)$ & $(p \lor r)]$. Table 7-19 verifies the first equivalence:

p	q	r	p & q	q & r	p v r	p & (q v r)	(p & q) v (p & r)
T	T	T	T	T	T	T	T
T	T	F	T	T	T	T	T
T	F	T	T	T	T	T	T
T	F	F	T	F	T	F	F
F	T	T	T	T	T	F	F
F	T	F	T	T	F	F	F
F	F	T	F	T	T	F	F
F	F	F	F	F	F	F	F

TABLE 7-19.

The distribution rules also have an analogue in algebra, where $a \times (b + c) = (a \times b) + (a \times c)$, which allows us to "factor" in or out a common factor. In algebra, however, the parallel rule that distributes addition into multiplication is invalid: $a + (b \times c) \neq (a + b) \times (a + c)$.

For the sake of contrast, let us look at two statement forms that are not equivalent—namely, $-(p \& q)$ and $-p \& -q$ (see Table 7-20).

p	q	-p	-q	p & q	-(p & q)	-p & -q
T	T	F	F	T	F	F
T	F	F	T	F	T	F
F	T	T	F	F	T	F
F	F	T	T	F	T	T

TABLE 7-20.

The forms $-(p \& q)$ and $-p \& -q$ have different truth values in the second and third case, so they are not equivalent: $-(p \& q) \neq (-p \& -q)$. Now if you examine the last two columns of the table, you will notice that there is no case in which $-p \& q$ is true while $(-p \& q)$ is false. Therefore $-p \& -q$ logically implies $-(p \& q)$. The same table also has two rows in which $-(p \& q)$ is true while $-p \& -q$ *is* false (the second and third), so $-(p \& q)$ does not logically imply $-p \& -q$.

Logical Compatibility and Incompatibility. Two statement forms are *logically incompatible* if the truth of either one logically implies the falsity of the other. Whereas equivalence is mutual implication, incompatibility is mutual exclusion. Every case in which a statement form is true will be a case in which a logically incompatible statement form is false, which means that in no case will incompatible statement forms both be true. There may be cases, though, in which incompatible statement forms are both false. It is obvious from the truth table for negation that a statement form and its negation are logically incompatible. Any case in which p is true is a case in which $-p$ is false; any case in which $-p$ is true is a case in which p is false. It is almost as easy to see that $p \vee q$ and $-p \& -q$ are logically incompatible. For $p \vee q$ is true when p or q or both are true, whereas $-p \& -q$ is true only when both p and q are false. It may not be at all apparent that $(-p \vee q) \& (-q \vee p)$ and $p \& -q$ are logically incompatible, but this can be shown by constructing a truth table and evaluating the two forms in every possible case (see Table 7-21).

p	q	$(-p \lor q) \& (-q \lor p)$	$p \& -q$
T	T	T	F
T	F	F	T
F	T	F	F
F	F	T	F

TABLE 7-21

The statement form $(-p \lor q) \& (-q \lor p)$ is true in the first and the fourth case; $p \& -q$ is false in both those cases. The form $p \& -q$ is true only in the second case; $(-p \lor q) \& (-q \lor p)$ is false in that case. So these two statement forms are logically incompatible. Note that both forms are false in the third case.

Two statement forms are *logically compatible* if they are not logically incompatible. If there is even one case in which two statement forms are both true, then they are logically compatible. Thus $p \lor q$ and $p \& q$ are compatible: they are both true when p and q are both true. The forms $p \lor q$ and $-p \lor -q$ are also compatible: both are true when p is true and q false, or when q is true and p false. In general, two statement forms can be shown to be logically compatible by constructing a truth table, and finding one or more cases in which both statements are true. Any truth table which shows that two statement forms are equivalent, or that one implies the other, will therefore also show that they are compatible. Thus Table 7-19, which proved one of the distribution rules, also showed that $p \& (q \lor r)$ and $(p \& q) \lor (p \& r)$ are compatible: both are true in the first three cases. Table 7-20, which shows that $-p \& -q$ logically implies $-(p \& q)$, but not conversely, also shows that they are compatible: both are true in the fourth case. Two statement forms may be compatible, though, even though neither implies the other. Thus $p \lor q$ and $p \lor r$ are compatible (both are true when p is true, for example) but $p \lor q$ does not imply $p \lor r$ (let q be true and p and r be false), and $p \lor r$ does not imply $p \lor q$ (let r be true and p and q be false).

Statements vs. Statement Forms. Again, we have been focusing on statement *forms*. Two *statements* are logically equivalent if their specific forms are logically equivalent. Thus "I will have steak and either asparagus or broccoli for dinner" is logically equivalent to "I will have either steak and asparagus or steak and broccoli for dinner." For the specific truth-functional forms of the two statements are $p \& (q \lor r)$ and $(p \& q) \lor (p \& r)$, respectively, and these were proven logically equivalent by Table 7-19, Similarly, two statements are logically incompatible if their specific forms are logically incompatible. Thus "It is hot and humid" and "It is hot but not humid" are logically incompatible, because $p \& q$ and $p \& -q$ cannot both be true in the same case. Logical implication and compatibility can be similarly defined for statements in terms of their specific forms.

Two complications must be mentioned, however: First, there are many different ways to represent the form of a statement. For example, the specific truth-functional form of "I will have steak and either asparagus or broccoli for dinner" can be represented by $p \& (q \lor r)$, $q \& (r \lor s)$, $r \& (s \lor t)$, and so on. The statement can be obtained from any of these forms by substituting simple statements for statement variables. Similarly, the truth-functional form of "I will have either steak and asparagus or steak and broccoli for dinner" can be represented by either $(p \& q) \lor (p \& r)$, $(q \& r) \lor (q \& s)$, or $(r \& s) \lor (r \& t)$. However, if we compare $p \& (q \lor r)$ with $(q \& r) \lor (q \& s)$, we find them not logically equivalent. To determine whether two statements are logically equivalent, or stand in other logical relationships, we have to look at *cospecific forms.* The specific forms of two statements are cospecific provided *both* statements can be obtained from the forms by one *consistent* or *uniform* substitution, so that if a simple statement is substituted for a variable in one place, it is substituted for that variable in all places *in both forms.* Thus $p \& (q \lor r)$ and $(p \& q) \lor (p \& r)$ are cospecific forms of my two statements about dinner, for both statements can be obtained by substituting "I will have steak" for every occurrence of *p* in both forms, and by substituting "I will have asparagus" and "I will have broccoli" for every occurrence of *q* and *r*, respectively, in both forms. The forms $q \& (r \vee s)$ and $(q \& r) \vee (q \& s)$ are also cospecific, as are $r \& (s \vee t)$ and $(r \& s) \vee (r \& t)$. But $p \& (q \vee r)$ and $(q \& r) \vee (q \& s)$ are not cospecific forms of the statements about dinner. The requirement that we consider cospecific forms when determining equivalence or other logical relationships among two statements can be easily met in practice by using the same simple statement constants to symbolize both statements, and then using the resulting compound statement constants to represent their cospecific forms. Thus if we use *S* for "I will have steak," *A* for "I will have asparagus," and *B* for "I will have broccoli," we end up with $S \& (A \vee B)$ and $(S \& A) \vee (S \& B)$, which adequately represent the cospecific truth-functional forms of the statements, and can readily be tested for logical equivalence using truth tables.

The second complication is that the specific truth-functional form of a statement is not its specific form. Simple statements always have some structure that is not represented by truth-functional forms. Consequently, while truth tables can prove that statement *forms* are logically inequivalent, they cannot show that *statements* are logically inequivalent. All truth tables can show is that two statements are ***truth-functionally inequivalent***. For example, "No men are reptiles" and "All men are nonreptiles" are logically equivalent, since they are obverses; but they are truth-functionally inequivalent, since their cospecific truth-functional forms are just *p* and *q*. Truth tables can show, however, that two statements are logically equivalent. If the statements' specific truth-functional forms have the same truth values in all cases, then any more specific forms must have the same truth values in all cases. For similar reasons (which you should think through for yourself), truth tables can show that statements are logically incompatible, and truth-functionally compatible, but cannot show that statements are logically compatible.

Glossary

Logically implies: One statement form logically implies another if the argument from the first to the second is valid; one statement logically implies another if its cospecific form logically implies that of the other.

Logically equivalent: Two statement forms are logically equivalent if they logically imply each other; two statements are logically equivalent if their cospecific forms are logically equivalent.

Logically incompatible: Two statement forms are logically incompatible if the truth of one logically implies the falsity of the other; two statements are logically incompatible if their cospecific forms are.

Logically compatible: not logically incompatible.

Cospecific forms: The specific forms of two statements are cospecific provided both statements can be obtained from the forms by one uniform substitution, so that if a simple statement is substituted for a variable in one place, it is substituted for that variable in all places in both forms.

Truth-functionally equivalent: Two statements are truth-functionally equivalent if their cospecific truth-functional forms are logically equivalent.

Simplification: the rule that $p \& q$ logically implies *p*.

Addition: the rule that *p* logically implies $p \vee q$.

Double negation: the rule that $- -p$ is logically equivalent to *p*.

Commutation: the rule that $p \& q$ is logically equivalent to $q \& p$, and that $p \vee q$ is logically equivalent to $q \vee p$.

Association: the rule that $p \& (q \& r)$ is logically equivalent to $(p \& q) \& r$, and that $p \vee (q \vee r)$ is logically equivalent to $(p \vee q) \vee r$.

De Morgan: the rule that $-(p \& q)$ is logically equivalent to $-p \vee -q$, and that $-(p \vee q)$ is logically equivalent to $-p \& -q$.

Disjunction: the rule that $p \vee q$ is logically equivalent to $(p \vee q) \vee (p \& q)$, and that $p \vee q$ is logically equivalent to $(p \vee q) \& -(p \& q)$.

Distribution: the rule that $p \& (q \vee r)$ is logically equivalent to $(p \& q) \vee (p \& r)$, and that $p \vee (q \& r)$ is logically equivalent to $(p \vee q) \& (p \vee r)$.

Exercises

A. For each pair of statement forms below, use truth tables to answer the following questions. Are (a) and (b) logically compatible, or incompatible? Are they equivalent, or inequivalent? Does (a) logically imply (b)? Does (b) logically imply (a)?

1. (a) $-(p \& q)$
    (b) $-p \vee q$

2. (a) $-(p \vee q)$
    (b) $-p \vee -q$

3. (a) $-(p \& q)$
    (b) $-p \& q$

4. (a) $p \vee q$
    (b) $(p \vee q) \vee (p \& q)$

5. (a) $p \vee q$
    (b) $(p \vee q) \vee (p \& q)$

6. (a) $p \vee q$
    (b) $(p \vee q) \& -(p \& q)$

7. (a) p
    (b) $-(p \& q) \vee (p \& -q)$

8. (a) $-(-p \vee q)$
    (b) $-(p \vee -q)$

9. (a) p
    (b) $q \& (-q \vee -p)$

10. (a) $p \vee q$
    (b) $p \vee (p \& q)$

11. (a) p
    (b) $p \vee (q \& -q)$

12. (a) p
    (b) $p \& (q \vee -q)$

13. (a) $(-p \vee q) \& (-q \vee p)$
    (b) $(p \& q) \vee (-p \& -q)$

14. (a) $(p \& -q)$
    (b) $(q \& p) \vee (q \& -p)$

15. (a) $p \vee (q \& r)$
    (b) $(p \vee q) \& (p \vee r)$

13. (a) $p \vee (q \& r)$
    (b) $(p \& q) \vee (p \& r)$

17. (a) $-(p \& q) \vee r$
    (b) $-[-p \vee (-q \vee r)]$

18. (a) $(p \vee q) \& (r \vee -q)$
    (b) $p \vee r$

19. (a) $p \vee (q \& r)$
    (b) $p \vee q$

20. (a) $p \& (q \vee r)$
    (b) $p \& q$

B. Use truth tables to determine whether the following pairs of statements are compatible (truth-functionally) or incompatible (logically), and whether they are equivalent (logically) or inequivalent (truth-functionally).

1. (a) It is not the case that Jameson is from Zimbabwe but not from Africa. (b) Either Jameson is not from Zimbabwe or he is from Africa.

2. (a) Salzburg is in Austria or Germany, but not both. (b) Salzburg is in Austria but not Germany, or in Germany but not Austria.

3. (a) Either Estonia and Latvia both border on the Baltic Sea, or neither does. (b) Either Estonia but not Latvia borders on the Baltic Sea, or Latvia but not Estonia does.

4. (a) Kennedy was elected president in 1960. (b) Either Nixon or Kennedy was elected president in 1960, but it wasn't Nixon.

5. (a) Adlai Stevenson was not elected president in 1956. (b) Eisenhower was elected in 1956, and either Eisenhower or Stevenson was elected in 1956 but not both.

6. (a) Spain does not border on the Atlantic. (b) Spain does border on the Mediterranean, and it borders on either the Atlantic or the Mediterranean.

7. (a) Hungary is west of Romania but not Austria, but it is not west of both Austria and Russia. (b) Either Hungary is west of Romania but not Austria, or it is west of Romania but not Russia.

8. (a) Lake Erie is larger than Lake Ontario, but it is larger than neither Lake Michigan nor Lake Superior. (b) Either Lake Erie is larger than Lake Ontario but not Lake Michigan, or Lake Erie is larger than Lake Ontario but not Lake Superior.

9. (a) Mongolia is part of either Russia or China, but not of India. (b) Either Mongolia is part of India, or it is part of neither Russia nor China.

10. (a) The president visited either Detroit and Chicago or New York and Boston. (b) The president visited Detroit or New York, Detroit or Boston, Chicago or New York, and Chicago or Boston.

7.6 Refutation By Countercase

One row of a truth table suffices to prove invalidity. With complex arguments, however, we may have to work through dozens of rows before such a row is found. A less wasteful method of finding one would be desirable. Each row of a truth table represents an assignment of truth values to all the statement variables in the argument form. To prove invalidity we need an assignment that makes all the premises true and the conclusion false. As it turns out, it is often remarkably easy to simply "figure out" what such an assignment must be. Consider:

$$p \lor r$$
$$q \lor r$$
$$-(r \ \& \ s)$$
$$\therefore p \lor q$$

The full truth table for this would have 16 rows. But all we need is one in which the three premises are true and the conclusion is false. If the conclusion is to be false, then both p and q will have to be false. If p and q are false, then r will have to be true for the first two premises to be true. The third premise will be true only if $r \ \& \ s$ is false. Since we already have r true, s must be false. Here, then, is the one row of the truth table that proves invalidity (see Table 7-22).

p	q	r	s	p v r	q v r	–(r & s)	∴ p v q
F	F	T	F	T	T	T	F

TABLE 7-22

We shall call this procedure ***refutation by countercase.*** A counteracse is an assignment of truth values that makes the premises true and the conclusion false, and thereby shows that an argument form is invalid. Refutation by countercase is essentially the same as refutation by counterinstance, where to show that an argument form is invalid, we find an argument possessing that form with true premises and a false conclusion. We could convert a refutation by countercase into a refutation by counterinstance simply by thinking of appropriate statements to substitute for the statement variables. In our example, we would need three false statements for p, q, and s, and one true statement for r. That is easy:

> Paris is in Germany or France.
> Paris is in Italy or France.
> Paris is not in both France and Spain.
> ∴ Paris is in Germany or Italy.

The premises here are true, and the conclusion is false, so the form of this argument must be invalid. With truth-functional argument forms, it is not necessary to produce a specific instance of the form, since the truth values of the premises and conclusion are completely determined by the truth values of the components. Since it is easier to assign truth values than to think of substitution instances, we shall use refutation by countercase wherever we can.

The example above was particularly easy because only one assignment of truth values made the conclusion false and all the premises true. Trial and error was unnecessary. But consider:

> (p v s) & (–r v q)
> (s & –p) v –q
> q v –p
> ∴ p & q

In this case three different assignments of truth values to p and q will make the conclusion false. So we must try one and see how it works out. Suppose we let p be true and q false. This will make the conclusion false as desired, but will also make the third premise false. So we must try again. Let p and q both be false. Then the third premise comes out true as desired, because –p is true. The second premise also comes out true because –q is true. For the first premise to be true, both p v s and –r v q will have to be true. Since p is false, s will have to be true. And since q is false, –r will have to be true, which means that r will have to be false. So Table 7-23 presents an assignment of truth values that refutes the above argument form.

p	q	r	s	(p v s) & (–r v q)	(s & –p) v –q	q v –p	∴ p & q
F	F	T	T	T	T	T	F

TABLE 7-23

Since there was trial and error, this refutation took more time. But still, it would have taken considerably more time to construct a sixteen-row truth table! Furthermore, the work involved was not as tedious or dull. Incidentally, there are two other countercases besides the one given above: those in which p is false, q true, and s true. Only one countercase is necessary, though.

It is sometimes possible to work out a refutation in your head. But it will generally be necessary to use pencil and paper. An efficient procedure is to write the truth values you assign under the statement variables and logical constants in the argument form you are trying to invalidate. In the preceding example, we started with the conclusion and, after some trial and error, made both p and q false. So write these values under the appropriate variables:

$$(p \vee s) \, \& \, (-r \vee q)$$
$$(s \, \& \, -p) \vee -q$$
$$q \vee -p$$
$$\therefore p \, \& \, q$$
$$\textbf{F F}$$

Then write these values under all other occurrences of *p* and *q*.

$$(p \vee s) \, \& \, (-r \vee q)$$
$$\textbf{F} \qquad\qquad\quad \textbf{F}$$
$$(s \, \& \, -p) \vee -q$$
$$\qquad\quad \textbf{F} \qquad \textbf{F}$$
$$q \vee -p$$
$$\textbf{F} \quad \textbf{F}$$
$$\therefore p \, \& \, q$$
$$\text{F F F}$$

Next observe that without further assignments, the second and third premises are true:

$$(p \vee s) \, \& \, (-r \vee q)$$
$$\text{F} \qquad\qquad\qquad \text{F}$$
$$(s \, \& \, -p) \vee -q$$
$$\qquad \textbf{T} \quad \text{F}\textbf{T}\textbf{T}\text{F}$$
$$q \vee -p$$
$$\text{FT}\;\textbf{T}\text{F}$$
$$\therefore p \, \& \, q$$
$$\text{F F F}$$

Last, observe that to make the first premise true, we have to assign T to *s* and F to *r*.

$$(p \vee s) \, \& \, (-r \vee q)$$
$$\text{F}\,\textbf{T}\,\textbf{T}\,\textbf{T} \quad \textbf{T}\text{F}\textbf{T}\text{F}$$
$$(s \, \& \, -p) \vee -q$$
$$\textbf{T}\,\text{T}\,\text{TF} \; \text{T}\,\text{TF}$$
$$q \vee -p$$
$$\text{F}\;\text{TTF}$$
$$\therefore p \, \& \, q$$
$$\text{F F F}$$

When employing this technique, your assignment of values to variables mast be *consistent*. You cannot have a variable true in one place and false in another in the same argument form, since one statement cannot be both true and false. So make sure that when you write a truth value under one occurrence of a variable, you go through the argument form and write the same value under all occurrences of the same variable. Also, it is advisable to save all *free choices* either until they become forced choices or until the end. Thus, at one point the second premise was true before we assigned a value to *s*. So we had a free choice, which we left free until we got to the first premise; there we saw that *s* had to be true. If you make free choices prematurely, you may have to change them later.

Glossary
Countercase: a consistent assignment of truth values to statement variables in an argument form that makes all the premises true and the conclusion false.
Refutation by countercase: proving that an argument form is invalid by finding a countercase.

Exercises

A. Refute the following argument forms by finding countercases.

1. $p \lor q$
   $q \lor r$
   $\therefore p \lor r$

2. $p \lor q$
   $-p \lor r$
   $\therefore -p \,\&\, (q \lor r)$

3. $p \lor q$
   $p \lor r$
   $-p \lor -s$
   $\therefore q \lor r$

4. $(p \lor q) \,\&\, (r \lor s)$
   $p \lor r$
   $\therefore q \lor s$

5. $-p \lor q$
   $-r \lor s$
   $p \lor s$
   $\therefore q \lor r$

6. $-(p \lor q)$
   $(-p \,\&\, -q) \lor (r \,\&\, s)$
   $-s \lor r$
   $\therefore r$

7. $(p \,\&\, q) \lor r$
   $\therefore p \,\&\, (q \lor r)$

8. $-[p \,\&\, (q \,\&\, r)]$
   $\therefore -p \,\&\, (-q \,\&\, -r)$

9. $-(p \,\&\, q) \lor r$
   $\therefore -p \,\&\, (q \lor r)$

10. $-p \lor (-q \lor r)$
    $-q \lor (-r \lor s)$
    $\therefore -p \lor s$

11. $-(p \,\&\, q) \lor (r \,\&\, s)$
    p
    $\therefore r \,\&\, s$

12. $(p \lor q) \,\&\, (r \lor s)$
    $-p \lor -r$
    $\therefore -q \,\&\, -s$

13. $p \lor -q$
    $-(-r \,\&\, s)$
    $-(-p \,\&\, -s)$
    $\therefore q \lor r$

14. $-(p \,\&\, q) \lor r$
    $-s \lor t$
    $-q \lor s$
    $-(q \,\&\, t)$
    $\therefore (p \,\&\, r) \lor (-p \,\&\, -r)$

15. $[p \& (q \vee r)] \vee [-p \& -(q \vee r)]$
    $[q \& (r \vee p)] \vee [-q \& -(r \vee p)]$
    $[r \& (p \vee q)] \vee [-r \& -(p \vee q)]$
    $-p$
    $\therefore q \vee r$

16. $-p \vee (q \vee r)$
    $-s \vee (t \vee x)$
    $-q \vee (x \vee y)$
    $(-x \vee s) \& (t \vee -s)$
    $-y$
    $\therefore -p \vee (s \vee x)$

17. $-p \vee (q \vee r)$
    $-q \vee (s \vee t)$
    $-t \vee q$
    $-(q \vee s)$
    $\therefore -p$

18. $-p \& (q \& r)$
    $(-q \vee s) \vee -p$
    $-r \vee (-t \vee -s)$
    $(-t \vee x) \& -x$
    $(y \vee -t) \vee -r$
    $\therefore p \vee y$

19. $p \& (q \vee r)$
    $(p \& q) \vee (-p \& -q)$
    $[(r \& s) \vee t] \& [-(r \& s) \vee -t]$
    $(-t \vee u) \& -(x \vee y)$
    $(z \& x) \vee (-z \& -x)$
    $(x \& p) \& (-y \vee r)$
    $\therefore t \vee u$

20. $[-p \vee (-q \& -r)] \& s$
    $[(-q \& s) \vee r] \& (-r \vee t)$
    $-(t \& r) \vee (x \& y)$
    $(x \& p) \vee (p \& -x)$
    $\{[(-p \& -q) \& -r] \& -s\} \vee z$
    $-(z \& -y) \vee (t \& r)$
    $\therefore (p \& t) \vee (-p \& -t)$

B. Refute argument forms 1-10 in Set A by finding counterinstances.

7.7 Conditionals

We now turn to more complex compound statements called **conditionals** (or *hypothetical statements*), which are expressed using the grammatical conjunction *if*. A conditional has two components: one called the **antecedent**, the other called the **consequent**. In the form "If *p, q*" or the equivalent form "*q* if *p*," *p* stands for the antecedent, *q* for the consequent. Thus in "If today is Wednesday, yesterday was Tuesday," or in "Yesterday was Tuesday if today is Wednesday," "Today is Wednesday" is the antecedent, and "Yesterday was Tuesday" is the consequent. We shall use an arrow to symbolize conditionals, pointing from the antecedent to the consequent.

Indicative and Subjunctive Conditionals. Unlike conjunctions, disjunctions and negations, conditionals appear in different *moods,* and the difference can have a significant effect on their truth conditions. Compare "If Oswald did not kill Kennedy, then someone else did" with "If Oswald had not killed Kennedy, then someone else would have." The first conditional is said to be *indicative* because its antecedent and consequent are expressed in the indicative mood. The second is said to be *subjunctive* because its components are in the subjunctive mood. The most obvious logical difference, perhaps, is that the subjunctive conditional presupposes or implies that Oswald did in fact kill Kennedy, whereas the indicative conditional makes no such suggestion. A conditional that implied the falsity of its antecedent is described as a *counterfactual* conditional. Subjunctive conditionals containing "had" or "were" in their antecedents are generally counterfactual. In contrast, those containing "should" in their antecedents are *open*. Whereas, "If I *were* to have a beer, my typing would suffer" implies that I will not have a beer, "If I *should* have a beer, my typing would suffer" leaves it open whether I will or not.

The indicative and subjunctive conditionals about Oswald differ in a deeper respect. For while the indicative conditional is true, the subjunctive conditional is in all probability false. If "someone" is replaced by "no one," then the truth values reverse. So the difference in mood between indicative and subjunctive conditionals can make a difference in truth value. Indicative and subjunctive conditionals nevertheless have nearly the same logical properties. To avoid duplication, and a level of complexity inappropriate in an introductory text, we will restrict our attention to indicative conditionals.

Partial Truth-Functionality. Conditionals differ in one very important way from conjunctions, disjunctions, and negations: *conditionals are only partially truth-functional.* There is at least one case in which the truth value of "If p, q" is uniquely determined by the truth values of p and q, and that is the case in which p is true and q is false. In that case, "If p, q" is false. A statement like "If Bush is a Republican, then Clinton is a Republican" is obviously false, since in fact Bush is a Republican but Clinton is not. "If $2 > 1$ then $2 > 3$" is false for the same reason. Now consider the case in which both p and q are false. We find that "If p, q" could be either true or false, depending on the specific statements substituted for p and q and depending also on the truth of other statements besides p and q. Consider "If Mexicali is in California, then it is in the United States" and "If Mexicali is in California, then it is in Mongolia." These conditionals are alike in that their antecedents and consequents are both false (Mexicali is in Mexico). Nevertheless, the first conditional is true, while the second is false. The first is true because California is part of the United States. The second is false because California is not part of Mongolia. The same lack of truth-functionality exists when the antecedent alone is false. In both "Lemurs are animals if they are insects" and "Lemurs are mammals if they are insects," the antecedent is false and the consequent true; but the first conditional is true while the second is false. Similarly, "If all men are geniuses then some men are" is logically true, while "If no men are geniuses then some men are" is logically false; but in both, the antecedent is false and the consequent true.

Weak and Strong Conditionals. What happens to the truth value of a conditional when its components are both true? We cannot give a simple answer to this question. For there are both *weak* and *strong conditionals*. The word "if" therefore resembles "or." On the strong interpretations, "If p, q" means the same as "If p, *then* q" which says that p implies q or equivalently that q *follows from* p. (Recall that when unaccompanied by "if," "then" is a conclusion leader.) On the weak interpretation, "If p, q" does not express implication and so does not mean the same as "If p, then q." Compare "If you open the refrigerator, it won't explode" with "If you open the refrigerator, then it won't explode." The former statement would most naturally be interpreted in a weaker way than the latter. The latter asserts that your opening the refrigerator would *imply* its not exploding, and is therefore false, at least for normal refrigerators. The conditional would be true, though, for a refrigerator containing a time bomb whose circuit would be broken by opening the door. The former conditional would not ordinarily be interpreted as asserting an implication, and would accordingly be true for normal refrigerators as well as rigged ones. It should be noted, however, that "then" is often deleted purely for stylistic reasons. Thus "If you open the refrigerator, it won't explode" *could* be interpreted as a strong conditional, with "then" understood. *Provided* is a common synonym of "if," but only when the latter expresses a strong conditional. "Provided you open it, the refrigerator will not explode" cannot be interpreted weakly. We shall use the single arrow $\rightarrow$ to symbolize weak conditionals and the double arrow $\Rightarrow$ to symbolize strong conditionals. It is convenient to read $\Rightarrow$ as "implies." If a similar verb is desired for $\rightarrow$, use "weakly implies."

A weak conditional is true when its antecedent and consequent are both true. Given that you will open the refrigerator door and also that it will not explode, it follows that the refrigerator will not explode if you open it. Similarly, suppose you predict and even bet that the Redskins will win if it rains;

your prediction will be proven correct, and you will have won your bet, if it rains and the Redskins win. There need be no connection between the rain and the victory. Your prediction is borne out, and your bet won, whether the Redskins win because of the rain, or in spite of it. Strong conditionals, on the other hand, may be either true or false when their components are both true, depending on whether the antecedent implies the consequent. Thus "If cats are mammals, then they are animals" is true, while "If cats are mammals, then 35 + 27 = 62" is false. Being a mammal implies being an animal, but biological facts imply nothing about arithmetic. Interpreted as a strong conditional, "The Redskins will win if it rains" is true only if rain implies a Redskin victory.

It is commonly assumed that conditionals express *causation*, but not even strong conditionals do. There are many cases, of course, in which a conditional is true because the truth of the antecedent would cause the truth of the consequent. This is the case, for example, with "If you decapitate me, then I will die": decapitation would cause my death. But there are equally many cases in which the consequent would cause the antecedent, as with "If the light came on, then someone flipped the switch": flipping the switch would cause the light to go on. The light's going on would imply, but not cause, the switch's having been flipped. Moreover, conditionals may be true when there is no causal connection whatsoever between antecedent and consequent, as with "If Rich is taller than David, then David is shorter than Rich." Note also that not even the strong conditional expresses *logical* implication. Let C be "Mexicali is in California" and let U be "Mexicali is in the United States." Then $C \Rightarrow U$ is true because C implies U; but C does not logically imply U. Being in California implies being in the United States because California is in fact part of the United States. But Mexicali *could* be in California without being in the United States, and would be if California were still part of Mexico. So being in California does not logically imply being in the United States.

While conditional are not completely truth-functional, they are partially so. The truth value of a conditional is completely determine by the truth values of its components in come, but not all, cases. We can summarize these cases with a partial truth table (see Table 7-24).

p	q	Strong $p \Rightarrow q$	Weak $p \to q$
T	T		T
T	F	F	F
F	T		
F	F		

TABLE 7-24. THE PARTIAL TRUTH TABLE FOR CONDITIONALS

The blank spaces in Table 7-24 indicate cases in which the conditional could be either true or false. We shall say that the conditionals are *undetermined* in these cases.[2]

Since we have two symbols for conditionals, the problem again arises as to which to use in any given case. Sentences of the form "If p then q," with "then" explicit, are seldom if ever given the weak interpretation, and so should uniformly be symbolized as $p \Rightarrow q$. However, sentences of the form "If p, q" or equivalently "q if p," without an explicit "then," can be interpreted either weakly or strongly. And the context will frequently leave it unclear which interpretation is intended. To make our work more manageable, and to avoid duplication, we shall concentrate on the strong conditional. Assume

---

[2] Many logicians—perhaps the majority—do not believe that there are both weak and strong conditionals in English or other natural languages. Among these logicians, however, there is an active controversy over whether conditionals in English are true or undetermined when their components are both true. So some think that all conditionals in English are weak, while the others think all are strong.

that *all* conditionals in the exercises are *strong* conditionals. While we will explicitly discuss only the strong conditional, the logical properties we will study are those shared with the weak conditional. So unless otherwise indicated, what is said henceforth will hold equally well when strong conditionals are replaced by weak ones.

Basic Logical Properties. While conditionals are only partially truth-functional, enough of a truth table exists to validate some of their most important logical properties. First, the table show that $p \Rightarrow q$ is true only if it is *not* the case that p is true and q is false. So the following argument forms are valid, revealing the truth-functional content of conditionals:

The Truth-Functional Content of Conditionals	
$p \Rightarrow q$ $\therefore -(p \ \& \ -q)$	$p \Rightarrow q$ $\therefore -p \lor q$

The conclusions are equivalent by De Morgan's rules and double negation. From the fact that if you play tennis you will exercise, it follows that it is not the case that you will play tennis without exercising, which means that either you won't play tennis or you will exercise. These arguments cannot be reversed. From $-(p \ \& \ -q)$ or $-p \lor q$, it does not follow that $p \Rightarrow q$. is true. For example "Either Hitler was not the thirtieth U.S. president or he was a carrot" is true because its left-hand disjunct is true; but "If Hitler was the thirtieth U.S. president, then he was a carrot" is quite false.

Before going on, we need to complete the truth table for the strong conditional. Let us being with the partial truth table given above, and work our way across rows from left to right. Each case in which $p \Rightarrow q$ is undetermined can be subdivided into two cases: one in which $p \Rightarrow q$ is true, and one in which it is false. The result of this process is a seven-row truth table that summarizes all the possible assignments of truth values to a strong conditional and its components (see Table 7-25).

p	q	$p \Rightarrow q$
T	T	T
T	T	F
T	F	F
F	T	T
F	T	F
F	F	T
F	F	F

TABLE 7-25. THE COMPLETE TRUTH TABLE FOR STRONG CONDITIONALS

Table 7-25 can be generated in another way. If p, q, and $p \Rightarrow q$ were completely independent, there would be a total of eight possible cases, just as if we three statement variables. But these propositions are not totally independent. One assignment of truth values is impossible, the one in which p is true and q false while $p \Rightarrow q$ is true. (The complete truth table for the weak conditional would have only six rows, since $p \Rightarrow q$ must be true when p and q are true.)

As we saw in Chapter 5, the converse of a categorical proposition is obtained by interchanging its subject and predicate. A conditional can be similarly transformed, by interchanging its antecedent and consequent. Thus $q \Rightarrow p$ is the **converse** of $p \Rightarrow q$. The argument form called conversion is:

Conversion (Invalid)
$p \Rightarrow q$
$\therefore q \Rightarrow p$

To see that this is invalid, let $A \Rightarrow C$ be any conditional represented by the fourth row of the complete table, where A is false and C is true. The converse of this conditional is $C \Rightarrow A$; it has a true antecedent and a false consequent, and is therefore false, as represented by the third row of the complete table. Conversion is also easy to refute by the method of counterinstance. "If the president is a pianist, then he is a musician" is true, while its converse "If the president is a musician, then he is a pianist" is false. The invalidity of conversion mean that the *order* of the components in a conditional has an important effect on its truth conditions. This is another respect in which conditionals differ markedly from conjunctions and disjunctions, in which the order of components is logically immaterial.

Let us next examine the valid argument forms known as *modus ponens* and *modus tollens*.[3]

Modus Ponens	Modus Tollens
$p \Rightarrow q$	$p \Rightarrow q$
p	$-q$
$\therefore q$	$\therefore -p$

Suppose you know that if you get an A on the final, then you will get an A in the course. You subsequently learn that you got an A on the final. You could then validly infer that you will get an A in the course. On the other hand, if you learned that you would not get an A in the course, you could validly infer that you did not get an A on the final. The argument "If I got an A on the final, then I will get an A in the course; I got an A on the final; therefore, I will get an A in the course" is a substitution instance of modus ponens. The argument "If I got an A on the final, then I will get an A in the course: I will not get an A in the course; therefore, I did not get an A on the final" is an instance of modus tollens. The validity of modus tollens underlies a common figure of speech. Suppose, while discussing who did or did not get into medical school, Mark says something like "If Andy got in, I'll be a monkey's uncle!" In saying this, Mark is trying to be funny. He is not seriously asserting the obvious falsehood that Andy's getting into medical school implies his becoming a monkey's uncle. Rather, Mark is denying in an oblique and humorous fashion that Andy was admitted. He is relying on it being obvious to all that he will not be a monkey's uncle.

Since $p \Rightarrow q$ means that *if p* is true *then q* is true, it should be evident on reflection that modus ponens and modus tollens are valid. But we can also prove their validity using the complete truth table for conditionals. Take modus ponens. We need to verify that there is no case in which $p \Rightarrow q$ and p are true while q is false. Looking back at the table, we see that there is only one case in which $p \Rightarrow q$ and p are both true: the first. And in that case, q is true too. So modus ponens is valid. Similarly, there is only one case in which $p \Rightarrow q$ and $-q$ are both true: the sixth. And in that case, $-p$ is true. So modus tollens is valid as well.

Modus ponens is sometimes called *affirming the antecedent*, since one premise affirms the antecedent of the other. Modus tollens is similarly known as *denying the consequent*. When, in contrast, the consequent is affirmed, or the antecedent denied, the results are fallacious.

---

[3] Roughly translated from the Latin, these phrases mean "affirming mode" and "denying mode," respectively.

Affirming the Consequent (Invalid)	Denying the Antecedent (Invalid)
$p \Rightarrow q$	$p \Rightarrow q$
q	$-p$
$\therefore p$	$\therefore -q$

Affirming the consequent and denying the antecedent are easily refuted by finding counterinstances, such as:

If whales are fish, then they are aquatic.
Whales are aquatic.
∴ Whales are fish.

If whales are fish, then they are aquatic.
Whales are not fish.
∴ Whales are not aquatic.

Affirming the consequent and denying the antecedent are fallacious because a conditional asserts that the truth of it's antecedent is *sufficient* for the truth of its consequent, but that does not assert that the truth of its antecedent is *necessary*. From the fact that q is true *if p* is true, it does not follow that q is true *only if p* is true. We can also use the complete truth table to show that affirming the consequent and denying the antecedent are invalid. There are two cases in which both $p \Rightarrow q$ and q are true: the first and the fourth. In the latter, p is false. Similarly, there are two cases in which $p \Rightarrow q$ and $-p$ are both true: the fourth and the sixth. In the fourth, $-q$ is false.

The Dilemmas. Disjunctive version of modus ponens and modus tollens are known respectively as the *constructive* and *destructive dilemmas*.

Constructive Dilemma	Destructive Dilemma
$p \Rightarrow q$	$p \Rightarrow q$
$r \Rightarrow s$	$r \Rightarrow s$
$p \lor r$	$-q \lor -s$
$\therefore q \lor s$	$\therefore -p \lor -r$

In a constructive dilemma, we are given that two conditionals are true, and that at least one of their antecedents is true; we can conclude by an extension of modus ponens that at least one of their components is true. Here is an instance:

> If interest rates fall, inflation will increase.
> If interest rates don't fall, unemployment will remain high.
> Interest rates either will or won't fall.
> ∴ Inflation will increase or unemployment will remain high.

Dilemmas are customarily described in metaphorical terms. The two conditionals present the "horns" of the dilemma, and in this case the Federal Reserve Board, the government agency that controls interest rates, would be described as being "impaled on the horns of a dilemma." Dilemmas are valid arguments, so the only way to refute a dilemma is to rebut its premises. If you rebut the disjunctive premise, you are said to escape the dilemma by "going between the horns." In this case, since the disjunctive premise is logically true, going between the horns is out of the question. If you dispute one or both of the conditionals, you are said to be "taking the dilemma by the horns." In this instance, the chairman of the Federal Reserve might take the dilemma by the horns and reject the first premise, that inflation will increase if interest rates fall. He might note that whether inflation rises depends o how fast interest rates fall and on how much demand exists for loans.

Another procedure for refuting a dilemma is called *rebuttal by means of a counterdilemma*, in which another dilemma with a contrary conclusion is presented, such as the following:

> If interest rates fall, unemployment will drop.
> In interest rates don't fall, inflation won't increase.
> Interest rates either will or won't fall.
> ∴ Unemployment will drop or inflation won't increase.

Both arguments are valid, by their form. Since their conclusions are incompatible, their premises cannot all be true. If the premises of the second dilemma are no less plausible then those of the first, the premises and therefore the soundness of the first dilemma have been called into question. Of course, the first dilemma also constitutes a counterdilemma to the second, so the soundness of the second dilemma is no less questionable. What rebuttal by counterdilemma shows is that further evidence and argument is needed on both sides. The presentation of dilemmas and their rebuttal are common rhetorical devices, and standard debating weapons. Note, incidentally, that dilemmas do not necessarily present unpleasant alternatives, as the second dilemma illustrates.

Constructive dilemma can be proven valid by the method of truth tables. The entire table, however, would be excessively large. There must be at least sixteen rows just to represent all the possible assignments to the four variables; and many more rows would be necessary since the truth values of the two conditionals are uniquely determined by only a few of those assignments. However, we can make the table manageable by examining only the rows in which the conclusion $q \vee s$ is false. Only four assignments make $q \vee s$ false (See Table 7-26)

p	q	r	s	$p \Rightarrow q$	$r \Rightarrow s$	$p \vee r$	$\therefore q \vee s$
T	F	T	F	F	F	T	F
T	F	F	F	F		T	F
F	F	T	F		F	T	F
F	F	F	F			F	F

TABLE 7-26

None of the rows in which the conclusion is false is a row in which all the premises are true. So the argument form is valid. It does not matter that $r \Rightarrow s$ is undetermined in the second row (which means that the second row really represents two cases) since the other conditional, $p \Rightarrow q$, is determinately false in that row.

The destructive dilemma is not as common, but here is an example:

> If Bob goes to the party, then Mary will have fun.
> If Tom goes to the party, then Jane will have fun.
> Either Mary or Jane won't have fun.
> ∴ Either Bob or Tom won't go.

The destructive dilemma can also be proven valid using a partial truth table. Again, there are only four cases in which the conclusion $-p \vee -r$ is false: those in which p and r are both true (see Table 7-27).

p	q	r	s	$p \Rightarrow q$	$r \Rightarrow s$	$-q \vee -s$	$\therefore -p \vee -r$
T	T	T	T			F	F
T	T	T	F		F	T	F
T	F	T	T	F		T	F
T	F	F	F	F	F	F	F

TABLE 7-27

In every case with the conclusion false, at least one of the premises is false; so the argument form is valid.

The constructive and destructive dilemmas have invalid counterparts, which are disjunctive versions of affirming the consequent and denying the antecedent. See exercises 9 and 10 in Set F below.

Contraposition and Hypothetical Syllogism. Another extremely common pattern of inference involving conditionals is *hypothetical syllogism*. An instance would be:

> If Alan is in Boston, then he is in Massachusetts.
> If Alan is in Massachusetts, then he is in the United States.
> ∴ If Alan is in Boston, then he is in the United States.

This argument is sound and valid. Its form is simple.

Hypothetical Syllogism
$p \Rightarrow q$
$q \Rightarrow r$
$\therefore p \Rightarrow r$
CONDITION OF VALIDITY: p is compatible with $q \Rightarrow r$.

Like the categorical syllogism rules discussed in Chapter 5, hypothetical syllogism infers a connection between two "terms" p and r by connecting them in the premises to a "middle term" q.

For centuries it was taken for granted that hypothetical syllogism is an *unconditionally* valid argument form. Recent work in logic, however, has shown this assumption to be mistaken. First note that hypothetical syllogism cannot be proven valid by means of a truth table. The premises and conclusion are undetermined in too many cases. The form cannot be classified as a fallacy, however. For its substitution instances are generally valid, like the one about Alan above. Nevertheless, there is a limited subclass of invalid instances. Consequently, it is possible to find counterinstances, such as the following.

> If I play Federer and win, then I will play Federer.
> If I play Federer, then I will lose.
> ∴ If I play Federer and win, then I will lose.

I cannot play world-class tennis, so the second premise is true. The first premise is logically true. The conclusion, however, is logically false. This is admittedly a tricky case. Fortunately, we can explain how it differs from all the valid substitution instances of hypothetical syllogism. The unusual feature of this instance is that the antecedent of the conclusion is incompatible with one of the premises, specifically the second. If the conjunction "I will play Federer and win" is true, then the conditional "If I play Federer, I will lose" must be false. So hypothetical syllogism has a condition of validity (CV): *p must be compatible with q ⇒ r.* Intuitively, the restriction is this: We cannot validly draw a conclusion about what will happen *if* certain conditions obtain from premises that would not be true under those same conditions.

Whereas $q ⇒ p$ is the *converse* of $p ⇒ q$, $-q ⇒ -p$ is its **contrapositive**. The contrapositive of a conditional is obtained by replacing its antecedent with the denial of its consequent, and its consequent with the denial of its antecedent. The argument form called *contraposition* (or *transposition*) is:

Contraposition
$p ⇒ q$
$∴ -q ⇒ -p$
CONDITION OF VALIDITY: $-q$ is compatible with $p ⇒ q$.

Unlike conversion, contraposition has plenty of valid substitution instances, such as:

> If Alan is in Boston, then he is in the United States.
> ∴ If Alan is not in the United States, then he is not In Boston.

Contraposition cannot be invalidated using truth tables, like conversion was, for the premise and conclusion are undetermined in crucial cases. We can find counterinstances, though, in any of the unusual cases in which both p and $-p$ imply q. Imagine the following situation: Geno works for a mob leader named Tony, but has been captured by a rival organization headed by Franco. Franco has threatened to kill Geno unless he reveals certain information. Tony had previously threatened to kill Geno unless he keeps the information secret. Both Tony and Franco are ready, willing, and able to carry out their threats. Now then, consider the following instance of contraposition:

> If Geno does or doesn't talk, then he will die.
> ∴ If Geno doesn't die, then he neither will nor won't talk.

The premise is true because, due to the threats of Tony and Franco, Geno's death is implied by his talking as well as by his not talking. The conclusion, however, is false. Note that the antecedent of the conclusion is once again incompatible with the premise. If "Geno will not die" should be true, then the consequent of the premise would be false while the antecedent would remain logically true. The truth of "Geno will not die" would imply that either Franco's threat or Tony's threat was idle. The condition of validity for contraposition, therefore, is essentially the same as that for hypothetical syllogism: $-q$ *must be compatible with* $p ⇒ q$. We cannot infer a conditional from premises that are incompatible with its antecedent. Since invalid instances of contraposition[4] and hypothetical syllogism are rare in practice, and since it is hard to think up counterinstances even when trying to, you will seldom have to worry about the restrictions on these rules.

Related Constructions. "If" signals the antecedent of the conditional, whether the conditional is expressed by "If *p*, *q*" or "*p* if *q*." Thus "If *p*, *q*" should be symbolized $p ⇒ q$, while "*p* if *q*" should be symbolized $q ⇒ p$ (assuming in either case that a strong conditional is intended). When "if" is preceded by "only," however, things are more complicated. There is a large difference in meaning between "*p*

---

[4] Failures of contraposition are rare with strong conditionals, but are quite common with weak conditionals. There are many cases in which $p → q$ and $-p → q$ are both true: these are cases in which q is true whether or not p is. For example, my television is in good working order and is not affected by the weather. So my television will work whether or not it is humid. It is true, then, that if it is humid, my television will work. But we cannot infer that if my television does not work, it is not humid. For the truth of "My television will not work" would make it false that if it is humid, my television will work.

if *q*" and "*p* only if *q*." The sentence form "*p* if *q*" asserts that the truth of *q* is a *sufficient* condition of the truth of *p*, whereas "*p* only if *q*" asserts that the truth of *q* is a *necessary* condition of the truth of *p*. Accordingly, while you will become president of the United States *only if* you are a U.S. citizen, it does not follow that you will become president of the United States *if* you are a U.S. citizen. Being a citizen is necessary but not sufficient for becoming president. On the other hand, while you will get some exercise *if* you play tennis, it does not follow that you will get some exercise *only if* you play tennis. Playing tennis is sufficient but not necessary for getting exercise.

A necessary condition is a "without-which-not" condition. That is, to say (truly) that you will become president only if you are a citizen is to say that you will *not* become president if you are *not* a citizen. And to say (falsely) that you will get some exercise only if you play tennis is to say that you will *not* get some exercise if you do *not* play tennis. Thus we should symbolize "*p* only if *q*" as $-q \Rightarrow -p$ rather than as $q \Rightarrow p$. As usual, "if" signals the antecedent of the conditional; but the preceding "only" introduces negation into the antecedent and the consequent. To further complicate matters, "if" may precede "only," as in "You will pass *if only* you study." The sentence form "*p* if only *q*" asserts that *q* is a sufficient condition of *p*, and so should be symbolized $q \Rightarrow p$. Whereas "only if" means *not if not*, "if only" means just *if*. So we have:

---

p if $q = q \Rightarrow p$

p if only $q = q \Rightarrow p$

p only if $q = -q \Rightarrow -p$

As discussed earlier, $-q \Rightarrow -p$ is equivalent to its contrapositive $p \Rightarrow q$, except in the unusual case mentioned above. So it will generally make little difference whether "*p* only if *q*" is symbolized $-q \Rightarrow -p$ or $p \Rightarrow q$. However, the fact that exceptions to contraposition do exist makes $-q \Rightarrow -p$ the preferable rendering. Thus "You will become president only if you are a citizen" is equivalent to "If you become president, then you are a citizen"; but "Geno either will or will not talk only if he dies" (which is false) is not equivalent to "If Geno either does or does not talk, he will die" (which is true). Refer back to §5.3, where it was pointed out that "Only *S* are *P*" is equivalent to "All non-*S* are non-*P*" or "All *P* are *S*" rather than to "All *S* are *P*."

"If" also shows up in sentences of the form "*p* if and only if *q*," such as "I will go to the picnic if, and only if, my wife wants to go." The **biconditional**, as this form is called, is simply an abbreviation for the conjunction "*p* if *q*, and *p* only if *q*." The biconditional asserts that the truth of *q* is both sufficient and necessary for the truth of *p*, and should therefore be symbolized $(q \Rightarrow p) \& (-q \Rightarrow -p)$.

---

p if and only if $q = (q \Rightarrow p) \& (-q \Rightarrow -p)$

Assuming that the conditions for contraposition are satisfied, "*p* if and only if *q*" is equivalent to $(q \Rightarrow p) \& (p \Rightarrow q)$, and is therefore said to express equivalence or mutual implication.

"If" is not the only word used to express conditionals in English. We noted above, for example, that *provided* means *if*. *Unless*, on the other hand, means *if not*. Both express strong conditionals. Thus "The picnic will be fun provided it is sunny" means "If it is sunny, then the picnic will be fun," whereas "The picnic will be fun unless it is sunny" means "If it is not sunny, then the picnic will be fun."

---

p provided $q = q \Rightarrow p$

p unless $q = -q \Rightarrow p$

It might be thought that "*p* unless q" also entails "*q* ⇒ –*p*." But the speaker who asserted "The picnic will be fun unless it is sunny" could consistently go on to say "If it is sunny, it might be too hot, in which case all bets are off." The speaker did not commit himself to what will happen if it is sunny, only to what will happen if it is not.

As we have seen several times before, English is full of quirks that make life difficult for the student of logic. One of these is the fact that "if," along with its synonym "provided" is sometimes used as an abbreviation for the cumbersome "if and only if." "Unless" may similarly be short for "if and only if not." For example, in §5.2, the following was offered as a definition of "contradictory": "Two propositions are contradictory if one affirms precisely what the other denies." The context—particularly the fact that a definition was called for—made it clear that "and only if" was intended but left implicit. Or consider an argument run by Gilbert Harman, a noted philosopher at Princeton University, in a book entitled *The Nature of Morality* (Oxford University Press, 1977, p. 77):

> Total pacifism might be a good principle if everyone were to follow it. But not everyone does, so it isn't.

The "if" here could be interpreted as expressing a straightforward conditional. But then the argument would be a blatant instance of the fallacy of denying the antecedent, so that interpretation would be most uncharitable, Harman undoubtedly meant that total pacifism might be a good principle if *and only if* everyone were to follow it. If so, his argument is perfectly valid. In the exercises below, we shall assume that the author's meaning is explicit, and that "if" is not being used as an abbreviation for "if and only if." The same goes for "provided" and "unless."

Glossary

Conditional: a compound statement of the form $p \Rightarrow q$ or $p \rightarrow q$, asserting that q is true *if* p is.

Strong conditional: a conditional of the form $p \Rightarrow q$, which asserts that p implies q, and so is not necessarily true when both p and q are true.

Weak conditional: a conditional of the form $p \rightarrow q$, which is true whenever both p and q are, and so does not assert that p implies q.

Antecedent: the component of a conditional represented by p in $p \Rightarrow q$, $p \rightarrow q$, or q if p.

Consequent: the component of a conditional represented by q in $p \Rightarrow q$, $p \rightarrow q$, or q if p.

Completely truth-functional compound: a compound whose truth value is determined by the truth values of its components in every possible case.

Partially truth-functional compound: a compound whose truth value is determined by the truth values of its components in at least one possible case.

Modus ponens: the valid argument form "$p \Rightarrow q$, p, ∴q", also called "affirming the antecedent."

Modus tollens: the valid argument form "$p \Rightarrow q$, $-q$, ∴ $-p$"; also called "denying the consequent."

Affirming the consequent: the invalid argument form "$p \Rightarrow q$, q, ∴ p."

Denying the antecedent: the invalid argument form "$p \Rightarrow q$, $-p$, ∴ $-q$."

Constructive dilemma: the valid argument form "$p \Rightarrow q$, $r \Rightarrow s$, $p \vee r$, ∴ $q \vee s$."

Destructive dilemma: the valid argument form "$p \Rightarrow q$, $r \Rightarrow s$, $-q \vee -s$, ∴ $-p \vee -r$."

Hypothetical syllogism: the argument form "$p \Rightarrow q, q \Rightarrow r, \therefore p \Rightarrow r$," which is valid on the condition that p is compatible with $q \Rightarrow r$.

Converse: The converse of a conditional is obtained by interchanging its antecedent and consequent; $q \Rightarrow p$ is the converse of $p \Rightarrow q$.

Contrapositive: The contrapositive of a conditional is obtained by interchanging and denying its antecedent and consequent: $-q \Rightarrow -p$ is the contrapositive of $p \Rightarrow q$.

Conversion: the invalid argument form "$p \Rightarrow q, \therefore q \Rightarrow p$."

Contraposition: the argument form "$p \Rightarrow q, \therefore -q \Rightarrow -p$," which is valid on the condition that $-q$ is compatible with $p \Rightarrow q$.

Biconditional: a compound statement of the form "p if and only if q," symbolized $(q \Rightarrow p) \& (-q \Rightarrow -p)$

Exercises

A. Symbolize the following statements. Assume that all conditionals are strong.

1. If the president visits Brazil, he will fly in Air Force One.

2. The president will visit Chile if he visits Brazil.

3. If the president visits Brazil and Chile but not Argentina, the Argentines will be insulted.

4. It is not the case that if the Argentines are insulted, then the U.S. banks will agree to restructure the payment schedule for Argentina's loans.

5. If the U.S. banks do not restructure Argentina's payment schedule, then Argentina will either default and plunge the world into a debt crisis, or find new sources of credit.

6. If Argentina defaults, then Poland and Brazil will default, and if Poland, Argentina, and Brazil default, several major U.S. banks may go under.

7. If the president runs for reelection, then he will have to dump his vice-president if he wishes to be reelected.

8. Unemployment but not inflation will drop if the Federal Reserve Board allows the money supply to increase, whereas inflation but not unemployment will drop if the Federal Reserve Board does not allow the money supply to increase.

9. If unemployment or inflation increases, the president will not be reelected, the Republicans will lose control of the Senate, and the Democrats will not lose any seats in the House.

10. If the president isn't reelected, and the Republicans lose control in the Senate, while the Democrats do not lose any seats in the House, then there will be no chance for any further tax cuts, and neither the attempt to allow prayer in school nor the attempt to prohibit abortion will succeed.

B. Follow the directions for Set A.

1. The world price of oil will rise if Saudi Arabia reduces its level of production.

2. The world price of oil will rise only if Saudi Arabia reduces its level of production.

3. The world price of oil will rise if only Saudi Arabia reduces its level of production.

4. The world price of oil will rise if and only if Saudi Arabia reduces its level of production.

5. The world price of oil will rise if Saudi Arabia reduces its level of production, unless other countries increase their production.

6. There will be no oil crisis in the near future provided the war in the Middle East does not expand.

7. The war in the Middle East will expand if and only if Iran builds nuclear weapons.

8. Only if Iran can purchase enriched uranium or build a nuclear reactor will Iran build nuclear weapons

9. Iran will build nuclear weapons if it can purchase enriched uranium or build a nuclear reactor.

10. Russia will host the Winter Olympics provided the Canadian government withdraws its application, and if Russia hosts the Winter Olympics, Jamaica will not take the gold in bobsledding unless the Swiss team does not compete.

C.   Follow the directions for Set A.

1. You can take exemptions for your spouse if you file a joint return.

2. If you file a separate return, you can take your spouse's exemptions only if your spouse is not filing a return, had no income, and was not the dependent of someone else.

3. You may take one exemption for your spouse if your spouse was neither blind nor 65 or over.

4. You may take two exemptions for your spouse if your spouse was blind or 65 or over.

5. You may take three exemptions for your spouse if your spouse was blind and 65 or over.

6. If at the end of 2005 you were divorced or legally separated, you cannot take an exemption for your former spouse.

7. If your spouse died during 2005 and you did not remarry before the end of 2005, you may take exemptions for your spouse.

8. If you do not file a joint return, you may claim your spouse's exemptions only if your spouse had no income and is not the dependent of another taxpayer.

9. You can file a separate return if both you and your spouse had income, or if either of you did not have income.

10. If you file a separate return and your spouse itemizes deductions, you must also itemize.

D.   Symbolize the following arguments, assuming that all conditionals are strong. Then identify it as having one of the forms named and discussed in this chapter, and determine whether the argument is valid or invalid.

1. If Sirius is brighter than Rigel, then it is brighter than Betelgeuse. Sirius is not brighter than Betelgeuse. So Sirius is not brighter than Rigel.

2. Rigel is brighter than Betelgeuse. And if Rigel is brighter than Betelgeuse, then it is brighter than Sirius. Hence Rigel is brighter than Sirius.

3. If Rigel is brighter than Betelgeuse, then it is brighter than Sirius. If Rigel is brighter than Sirius, it is brighter than Alpha Centauri. Therefore, Rigel is brighter than Alpha Centauri if it is brighter than Betelgeuse.

4. If the atmospheric temperature of Rigel is over 55,000°F, then Rigel is a blue-white star. Rigel is a blue-white star. So the temperature of Rigel is over 55,000°F.

5. The sun is either an orange star or a yellow star. It is not an orange star. Therefore the sun is a yellow star.

6. If the sun is a yellow star, then its atmospheric temperature is about 11,000°F. So if the atmospheric temperature of the sun is not about 11,000°F, then it is not a yellow star.

7. If the sun is an orange star, then metals are present. The sun is not an orange star. So metals are not present.

8. If the sun is an orange star, then metals are present. Therefore, the sun is an orange star if metals are present.

9. If Cepheids are variable stars, then their brightness varies in a periodic fashion. Cepheids are variable stars. So Cepheids vary in brightness in a periodic fashion.

10. If the object we are observing is not revolving around the sun, then it is not Venus. If the object we are observing is Venus and Venus has broken out of the solar system, then the object we are observing is not revolving around the sun. Therefore, if the object we are observing is Venus and Venus has broken out of the solar system, then the object we are observing is not Venus.

11. If Capella is a yellow star, then metals predominate. If it is a white star, then hydrogen predominates. Capella is either a yellow or a white star. So either metals or hydrogen predominates on Capella.

12. If Capella is either a yellow or a white star, then either metals or hydrogen predominates. Capella is either a yellow or a white star. So either metals or hydrogen predominates.

13. If Capella is either a yellow or a white star, then either metals or hydrogen predominates. Hence if neither metals nor hydrogen predominates on Capella, then it is neither a yellow nor a white star.

14. Either hydrogen or metals predominate on Capella. Hydrogen does not predominate. So metals predominate on Capella.

15. Provided metals predominate on Capella, it is a yellow star. It is a white star provided hydrogen predominates, Capella is not a yellow star or it is not a white star. Therefore, either metals or hydrogen do not predominate on Capella.

16. John will either watch television or go to the movies. Either he won't go to the movies or he will spend money. Therefore, John will either watch television or spend money.

17. John will go to the movies only if he spends money. Therefore, he will spend money only if he goes to the movies.

18. If Cepheids are variable stars, then their brightness varies in a periodic fashion. Cepheids do vary in brightness in a periodic fashion. Therefore Cepheids are variable stars.

E. Refute the following argument forms by finding a countercase.

1. $p \lor q$
    $q \lor r$
    $\therefore p \Rightarrow r$

2. $p \lor q$
    $-q \lor r$
    $\therefore r \Rightarrow p$

3. $-(p \mathbin{\&} q)$
    $\therefore p \Rightarrow q$

4. $-(p \Rightarrow q)$
    $\therefore p \mathbin{\&} q$

5. $-[(p \Rightarrow q) \lor (p \Rightarrow r)]$
    $-[q \lor (p \Rightarrow s)]$
    $\therefore r \lor s$

6. $p \lor -q$
    $-(-r \mathbin{\&} s) \mathbin{\&} -(-p \mathbin{\&} -s)$
    $\therefore -q \Rightarrow r$

7. $-p \lor q$
    $-r \lor s$
    $p \lor s$
    $\therefore -p \Rightarrow r$

8. $-p \lor (-q \lor r)$
    $-s \mathbin{\&} -t$
    $-q \lor (s \mathbin{\&} t)$
    $-(q \lor u)$
    $\therefore (p \Rightarrow r) \lor (p \Rightarrow s)$

9. $-p \lor (-q \lor r)$
    $-s \lor (-t \lor u)$
    $-q \lor (s \mathbin{\&} t)$
    $-(q \mathbin{\&} u)$
    $\therefore r \Rightarrow p$

10. $-p \lor (q \lor r)$
    $-s \lor (t \lor u)$
    $-q \lor u$
    $(-u \lor s) \mathbin{\&} (-t \lor -s)$
    $\therefore p \Rightarrow (s \lor u)$

F. Refute the following argument forms by finding a counterinstance. Why can't a countercase be found?

1. $p \Rightarrow q$
    $\therefore p$

2. $p \Rightarrow q$
    $\therefore -p$

3. $-p$
    $\therefore p \Rightarrow q$

4. q
    $\therefore p \Rightarrow q$

5. $p \Rightarrow q$
    $\therefore q$

6. $p \Rightarrow q$
    $\therefore -p \Rightarrow -q$

7. $(p \mathbin{\&} q) \Rightarrow r$
    p
    $\therefore r$

8. $(p \mathbin{\&} q) \Rightarrow r$
    $\therefore p \Rightarrow r$

9. $(p \Rightarrow q) \mathbin{\&} (r \Rightarrow s)$
    $-p \lor -r$
    $\therefore -q \lor -s$

10. $(p \Rightarrow q) \mathbin{\&} (r \Rightarrow s)$
    $q \lor s$
    $\therefore p \lor r$

11. $p \Rightarrow q$
    $q \Rightarrow r$
    $\therefore r$

12. $p \Rightarrow q$
    $q \Rightarrow r$
    r
    $\therefore p$

7.8 Material Implication and Equivalence

Material Conditionals. In §7.7 we discussed two types of conditional that are not completely truth-functional. We focused on the strong conditional, symbolized $p \Rightarrow q$, which expresses implication. Such conditionals are not customarily treated in contemporary logic texts, however. Instead, it is standard to introduce a conditional that is fully truth-functional, called the ***material conditional***, which is symbolized $p \supset q$. The idea of the material conditional can be grasped by focusing on the one case in which the truth value of any conditional is completely determined by the truth values of its components, the case in which the antecedent is true and the consequent false. Since a conditional is false in that case, part of what any conditional asserts is that it is *not* the case that its antecedent is true and its consequent false. In saying "I will go to the picnic if my wife goes," one possibility I have excluded is that my wife will go to the picnic without me. Now this *part* of what any conditional asserts is *all* that a material conditional asserts. That is, $p \supset q$ is defined to be true if, and only if, it is not the case that p is true and q false. By definition, therefore, $p \supset q$ is equivalent to $-(p \& -q)$ which in turn is equivalent to $-p \vee q$ by De Morgan's rule.

$$p \supset q = -(p \& -q) = -p \vee q$$

Given this definition, it is easy to calculate a truth table for the material conditional (see Table 7-28).

p	q	$p \supset q$
T	T	T
T	F	F
F	T	T
F	F	T

TABLE 7-28. **THE TRUTH TABLE FOR THE MATERIAL CONDITIONAL**

The horseshoe symbol $\supset$ may be read *materially implies*. The antecedent of $p \supset q$ is p, and q is the consequent. Note that the material conditional is *completely* truth-functional: its truth value is uniquely determined by its components' truth values in every case. Note also that a material conditional is true in every case *except* that in which its antecedent is true and its consequent false.

Since material conditionals are completely truth-functional, the truth value of any compound containing them is as easy to calculate as a compound containing conjunctions, disjunctions, and negations. Let A and B be true, for example, and let X and Y be false. Then $-\{[(A \& X) \supset -B] \& [(X \vee Y) \supset A]\}$ is false. Since $A \& X$ and $-B$ are both false, $(A \& X) \supset -B$ is true (fourth row). Since $X \vee Y$ is false and A is true, $(X \vee Y) \supset A$ is true (third row). Hence the conjunction in the braces is true, and its negation is false. Two useful shortcuts in such calculations are: *Any material conditional with a false antecedent is true;* and: *Any material conditional with a true consequent is true.* These rules can be verified by examining the truth table.

The logical properties of the material conditional are quite similar to those of the strong (and weak) conditional. Modus ponens, modus tollens, and the dilemmas are valid for material conditionals, for example, while affirming the consequent and denying the antecedent are invalid. That is, the following argument forms are valid:

$$p \supset q$$
$$p$$
$$\therefore q$$

$$p \supset q$$
$$-q$$
$$\therefore -p$$

$$p \supset q$$
$$r \supset s$$
$$p \lor r$$
$$\therefore q \lor s$$

$$p \supset q$$
$$r \supset s$$
$$-q \lor -s$$
$$\therefore -p \lor -r$$

While these are invalid:

$$p \supset q$$
$$q$$
$$\therefore p$$

$$p \supset q$$
$$-p$$
$$\therefore -q$$

The validity or invalidity of each can be proven using truth tables.

The Paradoxes. Because of this match between the logical properties of the material conditional and those of conditionals in English and other natural languages, and because the material conditional is completely truth-functional and therefore logically elementary, the practice has developed in logic of using the horseshoe to symbolize all conditionals. Some logicians treat this practice as a convenient and not too inaccurate idealization. But many—perhaps even the majority—believe that natural language conditionals actually *are* material conditionals, that statements of the form "If p then q" are true if and only if it is not the case that p is true and q false. This practice is recognized by all to be problematic, however. For while many of the material conditional's logical properties are shared by natural language conditionals, there also seem to be many that are not. For example, any material conditional with a false antecedent is true *no matter what the consequent is*. Similarly, any material conditional with a true consequent is true no matter what the antecedent is. In other words, the following argument forms are valid:

The Paradoxes of the Material Conditional	
$-p$	q
$\therefore p \supset q$	$\therefore p \supset q$

These argument forms are called "paradoxes" *not* because there is any doubt about their validity; that is established by truth tables. Rather, their validity presents a paradox if, as is widely believed, $p \supset q$ is equivalent to "If p then q." For the argument forms "$-p$ $\therefore$ if p then q" and "q $\therefore$ if p then q" seem invalid. Suppose someone is pointing at an object in the night sky that happens to be Mars. From the true premise that the object he is pointing at is not a star, it hardly seems to follow that *if* the object *is* a star, then it is an asteroid. And given that the object is a planet, it does not seem to follow that *if* the object is *not* a planet, then it is a planet. Yet these inferences would have to be valid if conditionals in English were material conditionals. It is largely to avoid such problems that this text departs from the usual practice of symbolizing conditionals as material conditionals.

There are other paradoxes. For example, hypothetical syllogism and contraposition are *unconditionally* valid for material conditionals. Yet as argued in §7.7, these argument forms are only conditionally valid for natural language conditionals. The counterinstances to hypothetical syllogism and contraposition have surfaced only in the last several decades, however. The logic of conditionals is one area of logic that is unsettled, and is still the subject of considerable foundational research.

Material Equivalence. Equivalence is mutual implication. If p materially implies q and q also materially implies p then p and q are said to be ***materially equivalent***, a relationship expressed by $p \equiv q$.

$$p \equiv q = (p \supset q) \mathbin{\&} (q \supset p)$$

This definition generates a truth table for material equivalence. When p is true and q false, $p \supset q$ is false. When p is false and q true, $q \supset p$ is false. So $p \supset q$ is true if, and only if p and q have *the same truth value,* either both true or both false.

p	q	$p \equiv q$
T	T	T
T	F	F
F	T	F
F	F	T

TABLE 7-29. THE TRUTH TABLE FOR MATERIAL EQUIVALENCE

Like material implication, material equivalence is completely truth-functional. The expression p ≡ q is customarily used to symbolize English biconditionals, statements of the form "p if and only if q." While this procedure nicely captures many properties of natural language biconditionals, it also presents paradoxes. For any two true statements are materially equivalent, and any two false statements are materially equivalent. But when two arbitrary truths (or falsehoods) are connected by "if and only if," the result often seems absurd, like "Aristotle was a logician if and only if jello is wiggly."

Be careful not to confuse the symbol ≡ for material equivalence with the symbol = for logical equivalence. Two statements are materially equivalent if they have the same truth value in the actual case, but are logically equivalent only if they have the same truth value in all possible cases. To prove that $(p \mathbin{\&} q) \vee (\neg p \mathbin{\&} \neg q) = (p \equiv q)$ for example, you need to construct a four-row truth table, evaluate both $(p \mathbin{\&} q) \vee (\neg p \mathbin{\&} \neg q)$ and $(p \equiv q)$ in all four rows, and then see whether the two forms have the same truth value in all rows.

Glossary

Material conditional: the statement $p \supset q$ which asserts that it is not the case that p is true and q false; "$\supset$" is read "materially implies."

Material equivalence: p and q are materially equivalent provided they materially imply each other, which means that they have the same truth value; symbolized $p \equiv q$.

The paradoxes of the material conditional: the valid argument forms "$\neg p, \therefore p \supset q$" and "$q, \therefore p \supset q$," or equivalently, the fact that a material conditional is true whenever its antecedent is false or its consequent true.

> **The paradoxes of material equivalence:** the fact that any two truths (or any two falsehoods) are materially equivalent.

Exercises

A. Determine whether the following statements are true or false.

1. Paris is in France ⊃ Paris is in Asia.

2. Paris is in Asia ⊃ Paris is in France.

3. $(2+2 = 5) \supset (2 + 2 = 4)$.

4. $(2 + 2 = 4) \supset$ copper conducts electricity.

5. $(3 \times 17 = 51) \supset 51$ is not a prime number.

6. Grass is green ≡ snow is white.

7. Berlin is in France ≡ Paris is in Germany.

8. Triangles have three sides ≡ squares have five sides.

9. Squares have five sides ≡ triangles have three sides.

10. Squares have five sides ⊃ triangles have three sides.

B.   Assume that *A, B,* and *C* are true statements, and that *X, Y,* and *Z* are false. Then determine whether the following compound statements are true or false.

1. $(A \& B) \supset (A \& Z)$
2. $-(Z \supset A)$
3. $(A \& Z) \supset -(A \& Y)$
4. $-(A \& B) \equiv (B \lor C)$
5. $-[(A \& B) \equiv (B \lor C)]$
6. $(A \supset B) \equiv (B \supset A)$
7. $(A \supset Z) \equiv (Z \supset A)$
8. $(X \equiv Y) \supset (X \equiv Z)$
9. $A \supset [Z \supset (B \supset Y)]$
10. $(A \& B) \equiv [(Z \& A) \equiv (A \equiv X)]$

C. Prove the validity or invalidity of the following argument forms. The common name for the form is given if there is one.

1. Modus Ponens

   $p \supset q$
   p
   $\therefore q$

2. Modus Tollens

   $p \supset q$
   $-q$
   $\therefore -p$

3. Affirming the Consequent

   $p \supset q$
   q
   $\therefore p$

4. Denying the Antecedent

   $p \supset q$
   $-p$
   $\therefore -q$

5. Conversion
   $p \supset q$
   $\therefore q \supset p$

6. Constructive Dilemma
   $p \supset q$
   $r \supset s$
   $p \vee r$
   $\therefore q \vee s$

7. Contraposition
   $p \supset q$
   $\therefore -q \supset -p$

8. $p \supset q$
   $\therefore -p \supset -q$

9. Hypothetical Syllogism
   $p \supset q$
   $q \supset r$
   $\therefore p \supset r$

10. Absorption
    $p \supset q$
    $\therefore p \supset (p \& q)$

11. Exportation
    $(p \& q) \supset r$
    $\therefore p \supset (q \supset r)$

12. Exportation
    $p \supset (q \supset r)$
    $\therefore (p \& q) \supset r$

13. Conditional Noncontradiction
    $p \supset -q$
    $\therefore -(p \supset q)$

14. Conditional Excluded Middle
    $-(p \supset q)$
    $\therefore p \supset -q$

15. $p \equiv q$
    $\therefore -p \vee q$

16. $p \equiv q$
    $\therefore (p \& q) \vee (-p \& -q)$

17. $p \& q$
    $\therefore p \equiv q$

18. $p \equiv q$
    $\therefore p \& q$

19. $p \vee q$
    $\therefore p \equiv -q$

20. $p \equiv q$
    $\therefore p \vee q$

21. $(p \vee q) \supset r$
    $\therefore p \supset r$

22. $p \supset (q \& r)$
    $\therefore p \supset q$

23. $p \supset r$
    $\therefore (p \vee q) \supset r$

24. $p \supset q$
    $\therefore (p \& r) \supset q$

D. Determine whether the following statement forms are logically true, false, or contingent.

1. $p \supset p$
2. $(p \supset q) \vee (p \supset -q)$
3. $-[(p \supset q) \& (p \supset -q)]$
4. $[(p \supset q) \& (q \supset r)] \supset (p \supset r)$
5. $p \equiv --p$
6. $p \equiv -p$
7. $(p \supset q) \equiv (-q \supset -p)$
8. $(p \supset q) \equiv (q \supset p)$
9. $(p \supset q) \equiv (-q \vee p)$
10. $-(p \equiv q) \equiv (p \equiv -q)$
11. $-(p \supset q) \equiv (p \supset -q)$
12. $(p \vee -p) \supset (q \& -q)$
13. $(q \& -q) \equiv (p \vee -p)$
14. $(p \& q) \supset (p \equiv q)$

15. $(p \equiv q) \supset (p \& q)$ 16. $(p \supset q) \& (-p \supset q)$
17. $q \supset (p \supset q)$ 18. $-[-p \supset (p \supset q)]$

E. Determine whether the following pairs of statements are logically equivalent or inequivalent.

1. (a) $p \supset q$ 2. (a) $p \supset q$
    (b) $q \supset p$ (b) $-q \supset -p$
3. (a) $p \supset q$ 4. (a) $p \supset q$
    (b) $-p \supset -q$ (b) $-p \supset q$
5. (a) $p \equiv q$ 6. (a) $p \equiv q$
    (b) $q \equiv p$ (b) $-p \equiv -q$
7. (a) $-p \equiv q$ 8. (a) $p \supset -q$
    (b) $-(p \equiv q)$ (b) $-(p \supset q)$
9. (a) $p \equiv q$ 10. (a) $p \equiv q$
    (b) $(p \& q) \vee (-p \& -q)$ (b) $(p \vee q) \& (-p \vee -q)$

LSAT Prep Questions

1. If you have no keyboarding skills at all, you will not be able to use a computer. And if you are not able to use a computer, you will not be able to write your essays using a word processing program.

    If the statements above are true, which one of the following must be true?

    (a) If you have some keyboarding skills, you will be able to write your essays using a word processing program.

    (b) If you are not able to write your essays using a word processing program, you have no keyboarding skills.

    (c) If you are able to write your essays using a word processing program, you have at least some keyboarding skills.

    (d) If you are able to use a computer, you will probably be able to write your essays using a word processing program.

    (e) If you are not able to write your essays using a word processing program, you are not able to use a computer.

    Preptest 32, Section 1, Question 7

2. Only if the electorate is moral and intelligent will a democracy function well.

    Which one of the following can be logically inferred from the claim above?

    (a) If the electorate is moral and intelligent, then a democracy will function well.

    (b) Either a democracy does not function well or else the electorate is not moral or not intelligent.

    (c) If the electorate is not moral or not intelligent, then a democracy will not function well.

    (d) If a democracy does not function well, then the electorate is not moral or not intelligent.

(e) It cannot, at the same time, be true that the electorate is moral and intelligent and that a democracy will not function well.

Preptest 9, Section 4, Question 4

3. Joan got A's on all her homework assignments, so if she had gotten an A on her term paper, she could pass the course even without doing the class presentation. Unfortunately, she did not get an A on her term paper, so it is obvious that she will have to do the class presentation to pass the course.

The argument's reasoning is questionable because the argument:

(a) ignores the possibility that Joan must either have an A on her term paper or do the class presentation to pass the course,

(b) presupposes without justification that Joan's not getting an A on her term paper prevents her from passing the course without doing the class presentation,

(c) overlooks the importance of class participation in a student's overall grade,

(d) ignores the possibility that if Joan has to do the class participation to pass the course, then she did not get an A on her term paper,

(e) fails to take into account the possibility that some students get A's on their term papers but do not pass the course.

Preptest 37, Section 2, Question 3

4. Some people have questioned why the Homeowners Association is supporting Cooper's candidacy for mayor. But if the association wants a major who will attract more business to the town, Cooper is the only candidate it could support. So, since the Association is supporting Cooper, it must have a goal of attracting more business to the town.

The reasoning in this argument is in error because:

(a) the reasons the Homeowners Association should want to attract more business to the town are not given,

(b) the Homeowners Association could be supporting Cooper's candidacy for reasons unrelated to attracting businesses to the town,

(c) other groups besides the Homeowners Association could be supporting Cooper's candidacy,

(d) the Homeowners Association might discover that attracting more businesses to the town would not be in the best interests of its members,

(e) Cooper might not have all of the skills that are needed by a mayor who wants to attract businesses to a town.

Preptest 10, Section 1, Question 5

5. Vague laws set vague limits on people's freedom, which makes it impossible for them to know for certain whether their actions are legal. Thus, under vague laws, people cannot feel secure.

The conclusion follows logically if which of the following is assumed?

(a) People can feel secure only if they know for certain whether their actions are legal.

(b) If people do not know for certain whether their actions are legal, they might not feel secure.

(c) If people know for certain whether their actions are legal, they can feel secure.

(d) People can feel secure if they are governed by laws that are not vague.

(e) Only people who feel secure can know for certain whether their actions are legal.

Preptest 36, Section 3, Question 12.

6. Unless negotiations begin soon, the cease–fire will be violated by one of the two sides to the dispute. Negotiations will be held only if other countries have pressured the two sides to negotiate; an agreement will emerge only if other countries continue such pressure throughout the negotiations. But no negotiations will be held until international troops enforcing the cease–fire have demonstrated their ability to counter any aggression from either side, thus suppressing a major incentive for the two sides to resume fighting.

If the statements above are true, and if negotiations between the two sides do begin soon, at the time those negotiations begin each of the following must be true EXCEPT:

(a) The cease–fire has not been violated by either of the two sides.

(b) International troops enforcing the cease–fire have demonstrated that they can counter aggression from either of the two sides.

(c) A major incentive for the two sides to resume hostilities has been suppressed.

(d) Other countries have exerted pressure on the two sides to the dispute.

(e) The negotiations' reaching an agreement depends in part on the actions of other countries.

Preptest 13, Section 4, Question 14

CHAPTER EIGHT

Propositional Logic: Deduction

8.1 The One-Way Rules of Inference

The truth table test of validity has several virtues. First, the test is capable of proving both validity and invalidity. Second, when applied to truth–functional argument forms, the test is guaranteed (if executed properly) to yield the correct result in a finite time. Third, the test is essentially "mechanical" and does not require insight, creativity, genius, or even trial and error. Unfortunately, the truth table test also has severe drawbacks. First, the time required to complete the test, while always finite, may be exceedingly long. An argument form with as few as 8 variables would require at least 256 rows and 10 columns, for 2,560 entries. Second, while the test does not require genius, it does require careful, concentrated, and accurate work. With thousands of entries, mistakes are practically inevitable. Third, the truth table test is dull and tedious precisely because it is so mechanical. In Chapter 7, we developed a swift way of proving invalidity, the method of refutation by countercase, which requires a limited amount of insight and trial and error. In this chapter we will develop a more efficient and engaging way of proving validity, the method of deduction. Deduction was introduced in §5.6 for proving the validity of categorical syllogisms and other arguments containing categorical propositions. The method will now be applied to arguments containing compound propositions,

The Rules. In a *deduction*, an argument is proven valid by deriving the conclusion from the premises using other argument forms known to be valid. The argument forms used in the derivation are called *rules of inference*, and a specific set of rules defines a *system of deduction*. The basic rules of inference in our system will be the following:

Rules of Inference

Conjunction (Conj): From any two statements, infer their conjunction.

$$p$$

$$q$$

$$\therefore p \;\&\; q$$

Addition (Add): From any statement, infer any (inclusive) disjunction of which it is a disjunct.

$$p$$

$$\therefore p \vee q$$

Simplification (Simp): From a conjunction, infer either conjunct

$$p \;\&\; q$$

$$\therefore p$$

Disjunctive Syllogism (DS): From a disjunction and the denial of one disjunct, infer the other disjunct.

$$p \vee q$$

$$-p$$

$$\therefore q$$

Disjunctive Transitivity (DT): From a pair of disjunctions in which a disjunct of one is the denial of a disjunct of the other, infer the disjunction of the other disjuncts.

$$p \vee q$$

$$-q \vee r$$

$$\therefore p \vee r$$

Modus Ponens (MP): From a conditional and its antecedent, infer its consequent.

$$p \Rightarrow q$$

$$p$$

$$\therefore q$$

Modus Tollens (MT): From a conditional and the denial of its consequent, infer the denial of its antecedent.

$$p \Rightarrow q$$

$$-q$$

$$\therefore -p$$

These rules can all be proven valid by truth tables. Indeed, we validated four in the previous chapter: disjunctive syllogism, disjunctive transitivity, modus ponens and modus tollens. The validity of the other three rules should be self-evident. Simplification says that given a conjunction we can infer its conjuncts; this holds because if a conjunction is true then both of its conjuncts are true. Conjunction says that given two statements we can infer their conjunction; this holds because if both conjuncts are true then the conjunction is true. Finally, addition says that from a statement we can infer any inclusive disjunction of which it is a disjunct; this holds because an inclusive disjunction is true as long as at least one of its disjuncts is true. Note that addition does not hold for exclusive disjunction; for if q is true as well as p, then p ⱽ q is false. Disjunctive syllogism and disjunctive transitivity, in contrast, hold for exclusive as well as inclusive disjunction, but we will understand the rules to apply to inclusive disjunctions only. Similarly, modus ponens and modus tollens hold for all types of conditionals, but we will apply them only to strong indicative conditionals. Addition and conjunction tell us one way to derive disjunctions or conjunctions; disjunctive transitivity describes a more complicated way to derive a disjunction. Disjunctive syllogism and simplification tell us how to derive one of the components of a disjunction or a conjunction. Modus ponens and modus tollens show us how to get unconditional information out of conditionals. Note that disjunctive transitivity is in many ways like a categorical syllogism. Indeed, it is useful to think of q as the "middle term." We infer a link between p and r from premises that link p to q and q to r.

Let us work through an example, proving the validity of the following argument:

> Roberts will run for reelection this year. If Roberts runs, he will defeat Martin. If Roberts runs this year and defeats Martin, Kent will run in the next election. If Kent runs next time, he will win. So Kent will win the next election.

The deduction will be greatly facilitated if we symbolize the argument. Let R be "Roberts will run for reelection this year," let M be "Roberts will defeat Martin," let K be "Kent will run in the next election," and let W be "Kent will win the next election." Then the argument looks like this:

$$1. R$$
$$2. R \Rightarrow M$$
$$3. (R \,\&\, M) \Rightarrow K$$
$$4. K \Rightarrow W \qquad /\therefore W$$

From $R \Rightarrow M$ and R we can derive M by modus pollens. From B and M we can derive $R \,\&\, M$ by conjunction. From $R \,\&\, M$ and $(R \,\&\, M) \Rightarrow K$ we can derive K by modus ponens. From K and $K \Rightarrow W$ we can derive W by modus ponens again. Since W is the conclusion, the proof is complete. We write out our deductions as numbered and annotated sequences of steps:

$$1. R$$
$$2. R \Rightarrow M$$
$$3. (R \,\&\, M) \Rightarrow K$$
$$4. K \Rightarrow W \qquad /\therefore W$$
$$5. M \qquad \text{2,1 MP}$$
$$6. R \,\&\, M \qquad \text{1,5 Conj}$$
$$7. K \qquad \text{6,3 MP}$$
$$8. W \qquad \text{7,4 } MP$$

We can use the rules of inference to validate argument forms as well as arguments. The following deduction, for example, proves the validity of "$(p \lor q) \Rightarrow (r \,\&\, s), p, \therefore r$":

$$1. (p \lor q) \Rightarrow (r \,\&\, s)$$
$$2. p \qquad /\therefore r$$
$$3. p \lor q \qquad \text{2 Add}$$
$$4. r \,\&\, s \qquad \text{1,3 MP}$$
$$5. r \qquad \text{4 Simp}$$

When proving the validity of argument forms, we simply treat the variables in the forms as if they were constants. This procedure can be confusing. In the above deduction, for example, we had to think of $p \lor q$ as an instance of p in order to derive line 4. This is legitimate, because in the argument form we are trying to prove valid, $p \lor q$ stands for any disjunction, while in the rules of inference p stands for any statement, including disjunctions.

Variants of the Rules. Each of the inference rules was presented with a single argument form illustrating the rule. It is very important to remember that the variables in these forms stand for *any* statement, no matter how complex. Since the eight forms are valid, *all* their substitution instances are valid. Thus all of the following and more are justified by modus ponens:

$$R \Rightarrow M \qquad\qquad (R \,\&\, M) \Rightarrow K \qquad [K \,\&\, (L \lor M)] \Rightarrow -\{(-W \,\&\, -V) \lor [J \lor (N \,\&\, O)]\}$$
$$R \qquad\qquad\qquad R \,\&\, M \qquad\qquad K \,\&\, (L \lor M)$$
$$\therefore M \qquad\qquad \therefore K \qquad\qquad \therefore -\{(-W \,\&\, -V) \lor [J \lor (N \,\&\, O)]\}$$

Moreover, all of the forms illustrating the rules have **variants**—equivalent but different argument forms representing essentially the same pattern of inference. Each rule of inference, in other words, is a class of equivalent argument forms, only one of which was presented with the list of rules. First, the order in which the premises are stated is logically irrelevant. So the following forms of inference are both sanctioned by disjunctive syllogism:

$$p \lor q \qquad\qquad\qquad\qquad\qquad -p$$
$$-p \qquad\qquad\qquad\qquad\qquad p \lor q$$
$$\therefore q \qquad\qquad\qquad\qquad\qquad \therefore q$$

When justifying a line, the lines from which it was inferred need not be cited in any particular order. Thus the justification for line 5 in the election example could have been "1,2 MP" as well as "2,1 MP."

Most of the rules have additional variants besides those due to the ordering of the premises. For example, there are two equivalent forms of simplification:

$$p \,\&\, q \qquad\qquad\qquad\qquad\qquad p \,\&\, q$$
$$\therefore p \qquad\qquad\qquad\qquad\qquad \therefore q$$

Both are valid because a conjunction is true only if both conjuncts are true. In both, we are inferring a conjunct from a conjunction. While only one form was presented with the list of rules, the choice was arbitrary. It is to be understood that the form selected represents the variant form as well. Thus we may use simplification to derive q as well as p from $p \,\&\, q$. The form representing addition also has a variant:

$$p \qquad\qquad\qquad\qquad\qquad\qquad p$$
$$\therefore p \lor q \qquad\qquad\qquad\qquad\qquad \therefore q \lor p$$

Both argument forms are valid because a disjunction is true as long as either one of its disjuncts is true.

The form representing disjunctive syllogism has three variants in addition to those already discussed:

$$p \lor q \qquad\quad p \lor q \qquad\quad -p \lor q \qquad\quad p \lor -q$$
$$-p \qquad\qquad -q \qquad\qquad p \qquad\qquad q$$
$$\therefore q \qquad\qquad \therefore p \qquad\qquad \therefore q \qquad\qquad \therefore p$$

All are valid because if a disjunction is true and one of its disjuncts is false, then the other disjunct must be true. Let us say that a statement and its negation are **denials** of each other, so that $-p$ is the denial of

p—and p the denial of $-p$. Then disjunctive syllogism in general is the rule that from a disjunction and the denial of one disjunct you can infer the other disjunct. The form representing modus tollens also has three variants:

$$p \Rightarrow q \qquad\qquad p \Rightarrow -q \qquad\qquad -p \Rightarrow q \qquad\qquad -p \Rightarrow -q$$
$$-q \qquad\qquad\qquad q \qquad\qquad\qquad -q \qquad\qquad\qquad q$$
$$\therefore -p \qquad\qquad \therefore -p \qquad\qquad \therefore p \qquad\qquad \therefore p$$

Each of these forms, furthermore, has a variant with the order of the premises reversed. In general, modus tollens is the rule that from a conditional and the denial of its consequent, you can infer the denial of its antecedent. The form representing disjunctive transitivity has three variants:

$$p \lor q \qquad\qquad p \lor q \qquad\qquad q \lor p \qquad\qquad q \lor p$$
$$-q \lor r \qquad\qquad r \lor -q \qquad\qquad -q \lor r \qquad\qquad r \lor -q$$
$$\therefore p \lor r \qquad\qquad \therefore p \lor r \qquad\qquad \therefore p \lor r \qquad\qquad \therefore p \lor r$$

Each in turn has a variant in which p is disjoined with $-q$ while r is disjoined with q and another in which the order of the premises is reversed. These argument forms all represent inferences *from* a pair of disjunctions in which a disjunct of one is the denial of a disjunct of the other, *to* a disjunction formed from the other disjuncts.

As we shall see in the next section, the variants of each rule (other than those due to premise order) are equivalent to the representative form by the rules of commutation or double negation. Once these are included in our system of deduction, it will not be necessary to use variant forms of the inference rules. But doing so will save trivial steps.

Practical Guides. Proving arguments valid by the method of deduction is a *skill*. In many respects, it resembles playing chess or checkers. The first step in learning the "game" of deduction is to learn the rules—in this case, the rules of inference. The rules must be *memorized*. Just as you cannot play good chess if you have to keep looking up how a knight or a bishop moves, so you will fail to construct any but the simplest deductions if you must look back at the rules. You should memorize the general statements of the rules, and the representative form presented with them. Do not try to memorize the variants of the rules: there are too many of them. As your skill improves, you will automatically begin to recognize and use the variants to save yourself trivial steps. After memorizing the rules, the next step in mastering the method of deduction is to develop your ability to recognize complex instances of the rules. The requisite skill here is essentially pattern recognition. You have to practice this step until the rules are so ingrained that you can "see" what follows from a given set of premises and see what premises would be needed to derive a given conclusion, Similarly, in chess you have to know what moves are possible at any given position on the board, and what moves would put you in a better position. The final step in mastering the method of deduction is to construct your own deductions. Practice is essential, As with any skill, "distributed" practice is more effective than "massed" practice. That is, it is better to practice an hour a day five days a week than to practice for five hours one day a week. As your skill develops, you will be able to do progressively more difficult proofs, and do easy proofs more quickly. No matter how good you get, however, some proofs will still stump you (if not in this text, then in more advanced ones). Unlike the truth table test, the method of deduction can be very frustrating. On the other hand, the "Aha!" experience that results when you finally see how to do a proof after a long struggle can be very rewarding.

Glossary

Deduction: deriving a sequence of statements from given statements using argument forms known to be valid.

Rule of inference: a valid argument form (or set of related forms) selected for use in the process of deduction.

System of deduction: the entire set of inference rules used in the process of deduction.

Conjunction: the rule that from any two statements you can infer their conjunction.

Addition: the rule that from a statement you can infer any disjunction of which it is a disjunct.

Simplification: the rule that from a conjunction, you can infer either conjunct.

Disjunctive syllogism: the rule that from a disjunction and the denial of one disjunct, you can infer the other disjunct.

Disjunctive transitivity: the rule that from a pair of disjunctions in which a disjunct of one is the denial of a disjunct of the other, you can infer the disjunction of the other disjuncts.

Modus ponens: the rule that from a conditional and its antecedent, you can infer its consequent.

Modus tollens: the rule that from a conditional and the denial of its consequent, you can infer the denial of its antecedent.

Variants: equivalent but different argument forms sanctioned by the same rule of inference.

Denial: a statement and its negation are denials of each other, so that $-p$ is the denial of p, and p the denial of $-p$.

Exercises

A. For each of the following arguments, state the rule of inference by which the conclusion follows from the premise or premises, if there is one.

1. $(A \& B) \& (C \& D)$
   $\therefore (A \& B)$

2. $(E \vee F)$
   $\therefore (E \vee F) \vee (A \& B)$

3. $(E \vee F) \Rightarrow [F \& (G \& H)]$
   $E \vee F$
   $\therefore F \& (G \& H)$

4. $J \vee (K \Rightarrow I)$
   $-J$
   $\therefore K \Rightarrow I$

5. $A \Rightarrow B$
   $B \Rightarrow C$
   $\therefore (A \Rightarrow B) \& (B \Rightarrow C)$

6. $A \vee (B \& D)$
   $-(B \& D) \vee (D \& E)$
   $\therefore A \vee (D \& E)$

7. $(L \& M) \Rightarrow N$
    $\therefore [(L \& M) \Rightarrow N] \vee [(L \& M) \Rightarrow -N]$

8. $(H \& I) \Rightarrow (J \vee K)$
    $-(J \vee K)$
    $\therefore -(H \& I)$

9. $[(L \& M) \vee -O)] \Rightarrow (R \vee S)$
    $R \vee S$
    $\therefore (L \& M) \vee -O$

10. $(A \Rightarrow B) \vee (C \Rightarrow D)$
    $-(A \Rightarrow B)$
    $\therefore (C \Rightarrow D)$

11. $[(Y \& Z) \Rightarrow A] \vee (B \& C)$
    $-(B \& C) \vee [A \Rightarrow (Y \& Z)]$
    $\therefore [(Y \& Z) \Rightarrow A] \vee [A \Rightarrow (Y \& Z)]$

12. $(F \& G) \vee [H \& (J \& K)]$
    $\therefore F \vee [H \& (J \& K)]$

13. $-(Q \vee R) \Rightarrow -(-S \& -T)$
    $--(-S \& -T)$
    $\therefore - -(Q \vee R)$

14. $-(Q \vee R) \Rightarrow -(-S \& -T)$
    $-(Q \vee R)$
    $\therefore -(-S \& -T)$

15. $[H \vee (J \& K)] \& -(L \vee M)$
    $-J \vee M$
    $\therefore \{[H \vee (J \& K)] \& -(L \vee M)\} \& (-J \vee M)$

16. $[L \Rightarrow (M \& N)] \& [(X \& Y) \Rightarrow Z]$
    $\therefore L \Rightarrow (M \& N)$

17. $(A \& B) \vee (C \Rightarrow D)$
    $(C \Rightarrow D) \vee F$
    $\therefore (A \& B) \vee F$

18. $(A \& P) \Rightarrow (C \& S)$
    $-(A \& P)$
    $\therefore -(C \& S)$

B. Follow the directions for Set A

1. $A \& (B \vee C)$
    $[A \& (B \vee C)] \Rightarrow D$
    $\therefore D$

2. $(F \vee G) \Rightarrow -(A \& B)$
    $A \& B$
    $\therefore -(F \vee G)$

3. $G \Rightarrow A$
    $\therefore (H \vee F) \vee (G \Rightarrow A)$

4. $(A \& B) \vee X$
    $-(A \& B) \vee Y$
    $\therefore X \vee Y$

5. $-(A \vee D)$
    $B \& -C$
    $\therefore (B \& -C) \& -(A \vee D)$

6. $S \& T$
    $-(Q \& R) \vee -(S \& T)$
    $\therefore -(Q \& R)$

7. $-(C \& D)$
    $-(A \vee B) \Rightarrow (C \& D)$
    $\therefore A \vee B$

8. $(A \& B) \vee (C \& -B)$
    $(-A \& B) \vee -(C \& -B)$
    $\therefore (A \& B) \vee (-A \& B)$

9. $[H \lor (J \,\&\, K)] \,\&\, -(L \lor M)$
   $\therefore -(L \lor M)$

10. $(F \Rightarrow G) \lor (M \,\&\, N)$
    $L \lor -(M \,\&\, N)$
    $\therefore L \lor (F \Rightarrow G)$

11. $-A$
    $-A \Rightarrow -(B \lor Q)$
    $\therefore -(B \lor C)$

12. $-A \Rightarrow -(B \lor C)$
    $B \lor C$
    $\therefore A$

13. $F \lor (H \Rightarrow J)$
    $-F \lor (G \Rightarrow H)$
    $\therefore (G \Rightarrow H) \lor (H \Rightarrow J)$

14. $-\{A \lor -[B \Rightarrow (C \Rightarrow D)]\}$
    $\therefore -\{A \lor -[B \Rightarrow (C \Rightarrow D)]\} \lor$
    $\quad -[B \Rightarrow (C \Rightarrow D)]\}$

C. In the following deductions, justify each line that is not a premise.

1. 1. $E \lor F$
    2. $E \lor G$
    3. $-E \,\&\, -H$ $/\therefore F \,\&\, G$
    4. $-E$
    5. F
    6. G
    7. $F \,\&\, G$

2. 1. $E \lor F$
    2. $F \lor G$
    3. $-E$ $/\therefore F \,\&\, (E \lor G)$
    4. F
    5. G
    6. $E \lor G$
    7. $F \,\&\, (E \lor G)$

3. 1. $A \lor B$
    2. $-B \lor C$
    3. $-C \lor D$
    4. $-(A \lor D) \lor E$ $/\therefore E$
    5. $A \lor C$
    6. $A \lor D$
    7. E

4. 1. $(A \lor B) \Rightarrow (C \,\&\, D)$
    2. $E \Rightarrow -(C \lor D)$
    3. A $/\therefore -E$
    4. $A \lor B$
    5. $C \,\&\, D$
    6. C
    7. $C \lor D$
    8. $-E$

5. 1. $L \lor (M \lor N)$
    2. $-N \lor (O \lor R)$
    3. $Q \Rightarrow S$
    4. $[M \lor (O \lor R)] \Rightarrow -S$
    5. $-L$ $/\therefore -S \,\&\, -Q$
    6. $M \lor N$
    7. $M \lor (O \lor R)$
    8. $-S$
    9. $-Q$
    10. $-S \,\&\, -Q$

6. 1. $(A \,\&\, B) \Rightarrow -C$
    2. $(D \Rightarrow E) \Rightarrow C$
    3. $A \Rightarrow (B \,\&\, E)$
    4. $A \,\&\, E$ $/\therefore -(D \Rightarrow E)$
    5. A
    6. $B \,\&\, E$
    7. B
    8. $A \,\&\, B$
    9. $-C$
    10. $-(D \Rightarrow E)$

7. 1. $X \vee Y$
    2. $-X \vee A$
    3. $-Y \vee B$
    4. $(Y \vee A) \Rightarrow (F \& H)$
    5. $(X \vee B) \Rightarrow G$ $/\therefore F \& G$
    6. $X \vee B$
    7. G
    8. $Y \vee A$
    9. $F \& H$
    10. F
    11. $F \& G$

8. 1. $M \Rightarrow O$
    2. $(K \Rightarrow L) \& (L \Rightarrow M)$
    3. $-O \& [-K \Rightarrow (P \vee O)]$ $/\therefore P \vee R$
    4. $-O$
    5. $-M$
    6. $L \Rightarrow M$
    7. $-L$
    8. $K \Rightarrow L$
    9. $-K$
    10. $-K \Rightarrow (P \vee O)$
    11. $P \vee O$
    12. P
    13. $P \vee R$

9. 1. $p \Rightarrow q$
    2. $(p \& q) \Rightarrow (r \vee s)$
    3. $p \& -s$
    4. $(r \& p) \Rightarrow (t \vee -q)$ $/\therefore t$
    5. p
    6. q
    7. $p \& q$
    8. $r \vee s$
    9. $-s$
    10. r
    11. $r \& p$
    12. $t \vee -q$
    13. t

10. 1. $p \Rightarrow q$
    2. $q \rightarrow r$
    3. $s \& -r$
    4. $(t \Rightarrow u) \& (s \Rightarrow -u)$
    5. $-p \Rightarrow (t \vee x)$ $/\therefore x$
    6. s
    7. $-r$
    8. $-q$
    9. $-p$
    10. $t \vee x$
    11. $s \Rightarrow u$
    12. $-u$
    13. $t \Rightarrow u$
    14. $-t$
    15. x

D. Prove the validity of the following arguments and argument forms by the method of deduction.

1. $(A \vee B) \Rightarrow C$
    A
    $\therefore C$

2. $-C \& -D$
    $A \Rightarrow D$
    $\therefore -A$

3. $J \Rightarrow K$
    J
    $\therefore K \vee L$

4. $-O \Rightarrow -(M \& N)$
    $P \& -O$
    $\therefore -(M \& N)$

5. $A \Rightarrow B$
   $-A \Rightarrow C$
   $-B$
   $\therefore C$

6. $A \vee B$
   $-B \& -C$
   $\therefore A$

7. $(p \Rightarrow q) \& (r \Rightarrow s)$
   p
   $\therefore q$

8. $p \Rightarrow q$
   $q \Rightarrow r$
   p
   $\therefore r$

9. p
   $p \Rightarrow q$
   $\therefore p \& q$

10. $p \vee (q \& r)$
    $-p$
    $\therefore r$

11. $K \vee (-K \Rightarrow L)$
    $-K$
    $\therefore L$

12. $(A \vee B) \Rightarrow (A \& B)$
    $A \vee B$
    $\therefore A$

13. $A \vee B$
    $-B \vee -D$
    $D \vee E$
    $\therefore A \vee E$

14. $(-M \vee N) \& (-M \vee O)$
    $-N \vee O$
    $\therefore -M \vee O$

15. $A \& (B \vee C)$
    $F \vee (G \& H)$
    $\{[A \& (B \vee C)] \& [F \vee (G \& H)]\} \Rightarrow [X \vee (Y \vee Z)]$
    $\therefore X \vee (Y \vee Z)$

16. $(F \vee F) \Rightarrow G$
    F
    $\therefore G$

E. Follow the directions for Set D.

1. $A \vee (B \Rightarrow C)$
   $-C \vee A$
   $-A$
   $\therefore -B$

2. $(N \vee O) \Rightarrow P$
   $Q \vee N$
   $-Q$
   $\therefore P$

3. $L \Rightarrow (M \vee N)$
   $L \Rightarrow -N$
   L
   $\therefore M$

4. $(F \Rightarrow G) \& (H \Rightarrow I)$
   $J \vee H$
   $-J$
   $\therefore I$

5. $p \Rightarrow -(q \lor r)$
    $p \lor r$
    q
    $\therefore r$

6. $-p \Rightarrow q$
    $r \Rightarrow p$
    $-p$
    $\therefore q \,\&\, -r$

7. $F \Rightarrow G$
    $(-F \lor -H) \Rightarrow I$
    $-G$
    $\therefore I$

8. $(A \lor B) \Rightarrow (C \,\&\, D)$
    A
    $\therefore D$

9. X
    $-(X \lor Y) \lor (X \Rightarrow Z)$
    $\therefore Z$

10. $F \lor (G \Rightarrow F)$
    $-F \,\&\, -H$
    $\therefore -G$

11. $(F \lor G) \Rightarrow [(F \lor G) \,\&\, -(F \,\&\, G)]$
    $H \Rightarrow (F \lor G)$
    H
    $\therefore -(F \,\&\, G)$

12. $A \Rightarrow B$
    A
    $(B \lor D) \Rightarrow E$
    $\therefore E$

13. $(A \Rightarrow B) \,\&\, (A \Rightarrow C)$
    A
    $\therefore C \lor D$

14. $R \,\&\, (R \Rightarrow T)$
    $(T \Rightarrow S) \,\&\, (S \Rightarrow T)$
    $\therefore T$

15. A
    $A \Rightarrow B$
    $(A \,\&\, B) \Rightarrow C$
    $\therefore C$

16. $-(L \,\&\, M)$
    $(L \,\&\, M) \lor (L \,\&\, N)$
    $N \Rightarrow (O \lor P)$
    $\therefore O \lor P$

17. $L \lor (-M \lor N)$
    $L \lor (-N \lor O)$
    $-L$
    $\therefore -M \lor O$

18. $(H \lor I) \,\&\, (H \lor J)$
    $J \lor K$
    $-I \lor -J$
    $\therefore H \lor K$

F.   Follow the directions for Set D.

1. $[A \lor (B \lor C)] \,\&\, [-B \lor (C \lor D)]$
    $B \,\&\, (-A \,\&\, E)$
    $\therefore (B \lor C) \lor (C \lor D)$

2. $(-T \Rightarrow U) \,\&\, [(U \,\&\, V) \Rightarrow W]$
    $(-S \Rightarrow V) \,\&\, (-T \,\&\, -S)$
    $\therefore W$

3. $A \Rightarrow (B \& C)$
    $C \Rightarrow (D \& E)$
    $E \Rightarrow [F \& (G \lor H)]$
    $A \& -G$
    $\therefore H$

4. $(A \lor D) \Rightarrow (C \& D)$
    $(C \Rightarrow E) \& (D \Rightarrow F)$
    A
    $\therefore E \& F$

5. $p \Rightarrow q$
    $r \Rightarrow s$
    $-q \& -s$
    $\therefore -p \& -r$

6. $(p \lor q) \Rightarrow (r \lor s)$
    $(r \lor t) \Rightarrow (t \lor u)$
    $p \& -s$
    $\therefore t \lor u$

7. $(-F \lor G) \& (-H \lor I)$
    $-J \lor K$
    $(F \lor J) \& (H \lor L)$
    $\therefore G \lor K$

8. $L \Rightarrow M$
    $-M \lor N$
    $-N \& -O$
    $\therefore -L \& -O$

9. $A \Rightarrow (B \& C)$
    $(B \& C) \lor D$
    $-(B \& C) \Rightarrow (-B \lor -C)$
    $(D \& -A) \Rightarrow [-E \& (-C \Rightarrow E)]$
    $-(B \& C)$
    $\therefore -B$

10. $C \lor -A$
    $-D \lor B$
    $(A \lor D) \& -(B \& E)$
    $(C \lor B) \Rightarrow (F \& G)$
    $F \Rightarrow [(H \lor I) \Rightarrow (B \& E)]$
    $\therefore -(H \lor I)$

G. Prove the validity of the following arguments by the method of deduction.

1. Mary won the lottery. If she won the lottery, then she won a million dollars. If she won a million dollars, then she will quit her job. Therefore, Mary will quit her job.

2. If Clay is happy, then he won a tennis match. Clay played tennis, but did not win. Therefore, Clay is not happy.

3. If Alan is a lawyer, then he works long hours and makes a lot of money. Alan is a lawyer. So he works long hours.

4. Jack will travel to either France or Germany this summer. He will tour the vineyards in Bordeaux or he will not go to France. He will tour the vineyards in the Rhine Valley or he will not go to Germany. If Jack tours the vineyards in either Bordeaux or the Rhine Valley, then he will taste a lot of dry red wines or a lot of sweet white wines. Therefore, Jack will taste a lot of dry red wines or a lot of sweet white wines.

5. Kathy will fly to either Copenhagen or Berlin. She will fly Lufthansa or she will not fly to Berlin. She will pay the maximum fare or she will not fly Lufthansa. Kathy will not pay the maximum fare. So she will fly to Copenhagen.

6. If Alan went to the law school of his choice, then he went to Harvard. If Alan went to either Harvard or Yale, then he got a job at a prestigious law firm. Alan did go to the law school of his choice. So he got a job at a prestigious law firm.

7. Either Mary is in Detroit, or she is in Hanover or Boston. She is not in Detroit, and not in Boston. So Mary is in Hanover.

8. If Mary traveled to Detroit or Boston, then she went by either car or plane. Mary went to Detroit, but not by car. Therefore, she went by plane.

9. If Alan visits, then we will drink a lot of Irish whiskey. If Jack visits, then we will drink a lot of Scotch. If we drink a lot of either Irish whiskey or Scotch, then we will have a good time but will be hung over. Alan and Ouida will visit. Therefore, we will be hung over.

10. Jameson likes football and basketball. If he likes football, then he watched the Superbowl. If he likes basketball, then he watched the NCAA finals. Therefore Jameson watched both the Superbowl and the NCAA finals.

11. You can file a separate return if both you and your spouse had income, or if either of you did not have income. You had income, but not your spouse. Therefore you can file a separate return.

12. Russia will host the Winter Olympics provided the Canadian government withdraws its application. If Russia hosts the Winter Olympics, Jamaica will not take the gold in bobsledding unless the Swiss team does not compete. The Canadian government will withdraw its application but the Swiss team will compete. Hence Russia will host the Winter Olympics and Jamaica will not take the gold in bobsledding.

8.2 The Rules of Replacement

The system of deduction introduced in the last section is *incomplete*. Many valid arguments cannot be proven valid using just those seven rules. For example, none of the rules allows the trivial inference from A to $--A$. To make the system more complete, we will add further rules of inference, such as double negation. It would be very inefficient, however, to formulate double negation as the rule that from a statement its double negation may be inferred. While this would allow us to infer $--A$ from A, it would not allow us to infer A from $--A$. More significantly, the rule would not enable us to infer $--A$ & B from A & B or A & B from $--A$ & B nor $C \lor (--A$ & $B)$ from $C \lor (A$ & $B)$ or $C \lor (A$ & $B)$ from $C \lor (--A$ & $B)$. Yet all of these inferences are valid for the same reason: the equivalence of $--A$ and A. Let X be any compound statement containing p, and let Y be the result of replacing p in X with $--p$, leaving everything else in X unchanged. Then we want to be able to infer X from Y and Y from X. We will therefore define double negation as a ***rule of replacement***, stating that p and $--p$ may replace each other *wherever* they occur. A rule of replacement is simply an economical way of describing an infinitely large set of related rules of inference. We shall now add to our system of deduction double negation and a few other rules of replacement (see the box below). We met the commutation, association, distribution, and De Morgan rules in §7.5. The double disjunction and double conjunction rules are new, but need no explanation.

The Rules Of Replacement

Any two statements equivalent by one of the following rules (or variants thereof) may replace each other wherever they occur.

Double Negation (DN): $--p = p$

Double Disjunction (DD): $p \lor p = p$

Double Conjunction (DC): $p \& p = p$

> **Commutation (Com):** p & q = q & p
>
> p ∨ q = q ∨ p
>
> **Association (Assn):** p ∨ (q ∨ r) = (p ∨ q) ∨ r
>
> p & (q & r) = (p & q) & r
>
> **Distribution (Dist):** p & (q ∨ r) = (p & q) ∨ (p & r)
>
> p ∨ (q & r) = (p ∨ q) & (p ∨ r)
>
> **De Morgan (DM):** –(p & q) = –p ∨ –q
>
> –(p ∨ q) = –p & –q

Keep in mind the important operational difference between the rules (if replacement and the other rules of inference, which we shall henceforth call **one-way rules**. First of all, one-way rules enable us to move in one direction only. For example, while we can infer $p \vee q$ from p by addition, we cannot infer p from $p \vee q$. Second, one-way rules can be applied to *whole lines* only, whereas rules of replacement can be applied to *parts* of lines as well. For example, the commutation rule enables us to infer $(B \& A) \Rightarrow C$ from $(A \& B) \Rightarrow C$ as well as $(B \Rightarrow C) \& A$ from $A \& (B \Rightarrow C)$. The simplification rule, in contrast, allows us to infer A or $B \Rightarrow C$ from $A \& (B \Rightarrow C)$ but not from $(A \& B) \Rightarrow C$, which is good, because the later inference would be invalid. Commutation can be applied to conjunctions wherever they occur. Simplification can be applied only when a whole line is a conjunction.

Let us work through a proof to illustrate how the rules of replacement operate. We shall validate the following argument:

$$A \Rightarrow [(B \& D) \vee (D \& C)]$$
$$–(–A \vee E)$$
$$\therefore D$$

We can apply De Morgans rule to the second premise, giving us $– –A \& –E$. Applying double negation to $– –A \& –E$ yields $A \& –E$. We can simplify $A \& –E$ to give us A. A together with $A \Rightarrow [(B \& D) \vee (D \& C)$ yields $(B \& D) \vee (D \& C)$ by modus ponens. Given $(B \& D) \vee (D \& C)$, we can commute $B \& D$ to get $(D \& B) \vee (D \& C)$. We can apply distribution to $(D \& B) \vee (D \& C)$ to get $D \& (B \vee C)$. Now we simplify to get D. We –write out the proof as follows:

1.	$A \Rightarrow [(B \& D) \vee (D \& C)]$	
2.	$–(–A \vee E)$	$/\therefore D$
3.	$– –A \& –E$	2 DM
4.	$A \& –E$	3 DN
5.	A	4 Simp
6.	$(B \& D) \vee (D \& C)$	1,5 MP
7.	$(D \& B) \vee (D \& C)$	6 Com
8.	$D \& (B \vee C)$	7 Dist
9.	D	8 Simp

Even with the seven rules of replacement, our system of deduction is incomplete. None of the rules, for example, applies to *exclusive* disjunctions. We could easily remedy this particular lack, beginning with the addition of the disjunction rule: $p \vee q = (p \vee q) \& –(p \& q)$. However, since this is an introductory text, we will keep the system simple. Our goal is to understand the method of deduction. This requires learning how to use rules of replacement, but does not require mastering a complete system of deduction.

Variants of the Rules. It was said in §8.1 that since variants of the rules are equivalent to the representative forms by commutation and double negation, we never have to use any of the variants. Let us now examine this point. Take disjunctive syllogism, for example. The representative form is:

$$p \vee q$$
$$-p$$
$$\therefore q$$

We can use this form to validate an instance of one of its variants as follows:

1.	$A \vee -B$	
2.	B	$\therefore A$
3.	$-B \vee A$	1 Com
4.	$--B$	2 DN
5.	A	3,4 DS

In the selected form of disjunctive syllogism, the second premise is the negation of the left-hand disjunct of the first premise, which is why commutation and double negation are necessary here. You can save two trivial steps, however, if you can recognize variants of the rule. Thus the following is perfectly acceptable, since B is the denial of $-B$, and since disjunctive syllogism is the rule that from a disjunction and the denial of one disjunct, you can infer the other disjunct:

1.	$A \vee -B$	
2.	B	$/\therefore A$
3.	A	1,2 DS

When uncertain whether you have a genuine variant of one of the one–way rules of inference, don't guess; just use the representative forms and the rules of replacement. Better a few extra steps than an invalid proof.

Distribution and De Morgan also have a number of variants. The variants of distribution are generated by applying commutation one or more times:

$$p \,\&\, (q \vee r) = (p \,\&\, q) \vee (p \,\&\, r) \qquad\qquad p \vee (q \,\&\, r) = (p \vee q) \,\&\, (p \vee r)$$
$$p \,\&\, (q \vee r) = (q \,\&\, p) \vee (r \,\&\, p) \qquad\qquad p \vee (q \,\&\, r) = (q \vee p) \,\&\, (r \vee p)$$
$$(q \vee r) \,\&\, p = (q \,\&\, p) \vee (r \,\&\, p) \qquad\qquad (q \,\&\, r) \vee p = (q \vee p) \,\&\, (r \vee p)$$
$$(q \vee r) \,\&\, p = (p \,\&\, q) \vee (p \,\&\, r) \qquad\qquad (q \,\&\, r) \vee p = (p \vee q) \,\&\, (p \vee r)$$

In general, distribution is the rule that *a conjunction composed of p and the disjunction of q and r is equivalent to a disjunction composed of the conjunction of p and q and the conjunction of p and r;* and: *a disjunction composed of p and the conjunction of q and r is equivalent to a conjunction composed of the disjunction of p and q and the disjunction of p and r.* The variants of De Morgan are produced by applying double negation one or more times:

$$-(p \,\&\, q) = -p \vee -q \qquad\qquad -(p \vee q) = -p \,\&\, -q$$
$$-(-p \,\&\, q) = p \vee -q \qquad\qquad -(-p \vee q) = p \,\&\, -q$$
$$-(p \,\&\, -q) = -p \vee q \qquad\qquad -(p \vee -q) = -p \,\&\, q$$
$$-(-p \,\&\, -q) = p \vee q \qquad\qquad -(-p \vee -q) = p \,\&\, q$$

The general rule is: *the denial of a conjunction is equivalent to a disjunction composed of the denials of the original conjuncts, and the denial of a disjunction is equivalent to a conjunction composed of the denials of the original disjuncts.* Again, do not try to memorize the variants, and do not use a variant when you have any doubt about it. The variants represent shortcuts to be used when, and only when, your deductive skills progress to the point that you feel burdened by trivial commutations and double negations.

There is one more shortcut we shall allow. Any one rule of replacement may be applied to several different parts of a line in any one step. For example, from $(A \,\&\, B) \vee (C \,\&\, D)$ we can derive $(B \,\&\, A) \vee$

(*D* & *C*) by commutation in one step instead of first deriving (*B* & *A*) ∨ (*C* & *D*) and from that deriving (*B* & *A*) ∨ (*D* & *C*). However, the same rule may not be applied twice to the same part of a line in one step. For example, do not go straight from –[(*A* & *B*) ∨ *C*] to (–*A* ∨ –*B*) & –*C* by De Morgan: first deduce –(*A* & *B*) & –*C* by De Morgan, and then deduce (–*A* ∨ –*B*) & –*C*, again by De Morgan. When the same rule is applied more than once to the same part of a line, it is too easy to make mistakes and too difficult to check proofs.

Practical Guides. A key feature of the truth table test is its completely mechanical nature. The method of deduction is markedly different. While the *checking* of proofs is essentially mechanical, their *construction* is not. Checking a proof requires only the ability to recognize substitution instances of the inference rules, which is basically a matter of pattern recognition. Given the formal character of the rules, you do not need to recognize "intuitively" even the most elementary valid argument, and you do not even need to know what the symbols & or ∨ mean. To check a proof, it is not necessary to memorize the rules of inference: you could do an exhaustive search of the rules for each line of the proof. There are no mechanical rules, though, for the construction of proofs. You have to understand the conclusion and the premises of the argument you are trying to validate, and the rules must be firmly enough ingrained so that you can "figure out" how to derive the conclusion from the premises. This often requires considerable insight, and patient trial and error. Your level of skill will depend on how many steps you can "see" in advance. It is not theoretically necessary to memorize the rules of inference. But as a practical matter, you simply cannot progress very far unless you do. Despite the lack of a mechanical procedure for constructing proofs, the method of deduction is generally faster and easier than the method of truth tables, which might require hundreds or even thousands of rows.

While no rules tell us how to construct proofs, several rules of thumb or vague strategies may provide some guidance.

1. *Work forward blindly from the premises.* If you have no idea how to get from the premises to the conclusion, start deriving whatever you can from the premises. One of the new lines you derive may provide the key to deriving the conclusion.

2. *Work backward from the conclusion.* Examine the conclusion, and see what you would need to derive it. Then see what you would need to derive that, and so on. Keep this up until you see something you can derive from the premises. Then retrace your steps to the conclusion. You might even make a "shopping list" as you do this, reminding yourself to "get this" or "get that." In working backward, it is often helpful to see if the conclusion appears in one of the premises; then figure out what you need to get that component out of the premise. For example, if the conclusion to be derived is *C*, and one of the premises is *A* ⇒ *C*, you know that if you could somehow get *A*, you could derive *C* by modus ponens. You might then observe that you can get *A* out of another premise, say *A* & *B*' by simplification.

3. *Eliminate unwanted statements.* The premises will generally have components that do not appear in the conclusion. Try getting rid of them. For example, if your conclusion is *C* and you have *C* ∨ (*A* & *B*) in the premises, you can get rid of the unwanted *B* by distribution and simplification, which will give you *C* ∨ *A*. Then maybe you will notice –*A* elsewhere in the premises, enabling you to get *C* by disjunctive syllogism. Similarly, disjunctive transitivity enables you to eliminate the common "middle term" of two disjunctions, as when going from *A* ∨ *B* and –*B* ∨ *C* to *A* ∨ *C*.

4. *Introduce desired statements by addition.* If your conclusion is *C*, and *C* does not appear in the premises, try adding *C* onto something.

5. As a variation on the previous rule, *if the conclusion is a disjunction, try deriving just one of the disjuncts, and then add on the other.* Thus if your conclusion is *B* v *C*, you might be able to see how to derive *B*: given *B*, addition will give you *B* v *C*.

6. Similarly, *if the conclusion is a conjunction, derive each conjunct separately, then conjoin.* Thus if the conclusion *A* & *B* does not occur in the premises, you might try deducing *A*, and then *B*; given both, conjunction will give you *A* & *B*.

7. *Always do something.* Never just stare at the premises and conclusion waiting for the whole proof to arrive in a flash of inspiration. In difficult proofs, it generally won't. At best you will get tired and frustrated; at worst, you will develop a mental block against the problem. There are other useful rules of thumb besides these. Perhaps you will be able to devise your own.

Glossary

Rule of replacement: a rule of inference that allows you to infer the result of replacing a statement, wherever it occurs, with a logically equivalent statement.

One-way rule: a rule of inference other than a rule of replacement.

Double negation: the rule that you can replace $--p$ with p (and vice versa).

Double disjunction: the rule that you can replace p v p with p (and vice versa).

Double conjunction: the rule that you can replace p & p with p (and vice versa).

Commutation: the rule that you can replace p & q with q & p and p v q with q v p (and vice versa).

Association: the rule that you can replace p v (q v r) with (p v q) v r, and p & (q & r) with (p & q) & r (and vice versa).

Distribution: the rule that you can replace a conjunction composed of p and the disjunction of q and r with a disjunction composed of the conjunction of p and q and the conjunction of p and r, and replace a disjunction composed of p and the conjunction of q and r with a conjunction composed of the disjunction of p and q and the disjunction of p and r (and vice versa).

De Morgan: the rule that you can replace the denial of a conjunction with a disjunction composed of the denials of the original conjuncts, and replace the denial of a disjunction with a conjunction composed of the denials of the original disjuncts (and vice versa).

Exercises

A. For each of the following arguments, identify the rule of inference by which the conclusion follows from the premise, if there is one.

1. (*A* & *B*) v –(*C* & *D*)
    ∴(*A* & *B*) v (–*C* v –*D*)

2. *E* & [(*F* & *G*) & (*H* ⇒ *I*)]
    ∴[*E* & (*F* & *G*)]& (*H* ⇒ *I*)

3. [(*H* & *I*) & *K*] ⇒(*J* & –*L*)
    ∴[(*I* & *H*) & *K*] ⇒ (*J* & –*L*)

4. (*A* & *B*) v (*F* & *G*)
    ∴ [(*A* & *B*) v *F*] & [(*A* & *B*) v *G*]

5. –(*M* & *N*) v – –*L*
    ∴–[(*M* & *N*) & –*L*]

6. *Q* & (*P* v *R*)
    ∴(*Q* & *P*) v *R*

7. $[(F \Rightarrow G) \& (F \Rightarrow H)] \lor [(F \Rightarrow G) \& (F \Rightarrow I)]$
    $\therefore (F \Rightarrow G) \& [(F \Rightarrow H) \lor (F \Rightarrow I)]$

8. $(A \& B) \lor (C \Rightarrow D)$
    $\therefore [(A \& B) \lor (C \Rightarrow D)] \& [(A \& B) \lor (C \Rightarrow D)]$

9. $-[E \Rightarrow (F \lor G)] \& -[E \Rightarrow (H \lor I)]$
    $\therefore -\{[E \Rightarrow (F \lor G)] \lor [E \Rightarrow (H \lor I)]\}$

10. $(A \& B) \lor [(A \& -B) \lor (-A \& B)]$
    $\therefore [(A \& B) \lor (A \& -B)] \lor (-A \& B)$

11. $[F \Rightarrow (G \& H)] \& (F \& I)$
    $\therefore F \Rightarrow [(G \& H) \& I]$

12. $(A \Rightarrow B) \lor (A \Rightarrow B)$
    $\therefore A \Rightarrow B$

13. $[L \Rightarrow -(M \& N)] \& [L \Rightarrow (J \& K)]$
    $\therefore [L \Rightarrow (-M \lor -N)] \& [L \Rightarrow (J \& K)]$

14. $[L \Rightarrow (-M \lor -N)] \& [L \Rightarrow (J \& K)]$
    $\therefore [L \Rightarrow (-N \lor -M)] \& [L \Rightarrow (J \& K)]$

15. $-(A \& B) \& (C \& D)$
    $\therefore -(A \& B) \& --(C \& D)$

16. $[H \& (I \lor J)] \lor [H \& (K \Rightarrow -L)]$
    $\therefore H \& [(I \lor J) \lor (K \Rightarrow -L)]$

17. $(F \Rightarrow G) \& [(F \Rightarrow H) \lor (F \Rightarrow I)]$
    $\therefore [(F \Rightarrow H) \lor (F \Rightarrow I)] \& (F \Rightarrow G)$

18. $-[(R \& S) \& -(U \lor V)]$
    $\therefore -(R \& S) \lor --(U \lor V)]$

19. $-[-(F \lor G) \& -(H \lor I)]$
    $\therefore (F \lor G) \lor (H \lor I)$

20. $(-F \lor G) \& (-H \lor G)$
    $\therefore (-F \& -H) \lor G$

21. $--(F \lor G) \& --(H \lor I)$
    $\therefore (F \lor G) \& (H \lor I)$

22. $-(L \& M) \Rightarrow -(N \& O)$
    $\therefore (-L \lor -M) \Rightarrow (-N \lor -O)$

23. $(C \& D) \Rightarrow [E \lor (F \& G)]$
    $\therefore [E \lor (F \& G)] \Rightarrow (C \& D)$

24. $(C \& D) \Rightarrow [E \lor (F \& G)]$
    $\therefore (D \& C) \Rightarrow [E \lor (G \& F)]$

25. $-\{[X \Rightarrow (Y \& Z)] \& [(Y \& Z) \Rightarrow X]\}$
    $\therefore -[X \Rightarrow (Y \& Z)] \& -[(Y \& Z) \Rightarrow X]$

26. $(A \Rightarrow B) \& [(C \Rightarrow D) \lor (E \Rightarrow F)]$
    $\therefore [(A \Rightarrow B) \lor (C \Rightarrow D)] \& [(A \Rightarrow B) \lor (E \Rightarrow F)]$

B. In the following deductions, justify each line that is not a premise.

1. 1 $(A \& B) \Rightarrow C$
    2. $(-C \& B) \lor (-C \& D)$ $/ \therefore -A \lor -B$
    3. $-C \& (B \lor D)$
    4. $-C$
    5. $-(A \& B)$
    6. $-A \lor -B$

2. 1. $E \Rightarrow -(F \& G)$
    2. $(H \lor F) \& (H \lor G)$
    3. $(E \& H) \lor (E \& -H)$ $/ \therefore H$
    4. $E \& (H \lor -H)$
    5. E
    6. $-(F \& G)$
    7. $H \lor (F \& G)$
    8. H

3. 1. $(H \lor -I) \lor J$
    2. $(I \& -H) \lor -H$ $/ \therefore -I \lor J$
    3. $(-H \lor I) \& (-H \lor -H)$

4. 1. $(A \lor B) \Rightarrow (O \& P)$
    2. $-O$ $/ \therefore -A$
    3. $-O \lor -P$

4. $-H$ v $-H$

5. $-H$

6. H v $(-I$ v $J)$

7. $-I$ v J

4. $-(O \& P)$

5. $-(A$ v $B)$

6. $-A \& -B$

7. $-A$

5. 1. $-[A \& (B$ v $C)]$
    2. $(-A$ v $-C) \Rightarrow [D \& (E \& F)]$ $/ \therefore D \& E$
    3. $-[(A. \& B)$ v $(A \& C)]$
    4. $-(A \& B) \& -(A \& C)$
    5. $-(A \& C)$
    6. $-A$ v $-C$
    7. $D \& (E \& F)$
    8. $(D \& E) \& F$
    9. $D \& E$

6. 1. $-(M \& N)$
    2. $(-N$ v $-M) \Rightarrow (-O$ v $-P)$
    3. $-R \Rightarrow (P \& O)$ $/ \therefore R$
    4. $-M$ v $-N$
    5. $-N$ v $-M$
    6. $-O$ v $-P$
    7. $-(O \& P)$
    8. $-(P \& O)$
    9. $--R$
    10. R

7. 1. $-[(X \Rightarrow Y)$ v $(Y \Rightarrow X)]$
    2. U v $[V$ v $(Y \Rightarrow X)]$
    3. $-Z \Rightarrow -(V$ v $U)$ $/ \therefore Z$
    4. $-(X \Rightarrow Y) \& -(Y \Rightarrow X)$
    5. $-(Y \Rightarrow X)$
    6. $(U$ v $V)$ v $(Y \Rightarrow X)$
    7. U v V
    8. V v U
    9. $--(V$ v $U)$
    10. $--Z$
    11. Z

8. 1. $A \Rightarrow -(B$ v $C)$
    2. $-B \Rightarrow [D$ v $(F \& G)]$
    3. $A \& -F$ $/ \therefore D$
    4. A
    5. $-(B$ v $C)$
    6. $-B \& -C$
    7. $-B$
    8. D v $(F \& G)$
    9. $(D$ v $F) \& (D$ v $G)$
    10. D v F
    11. $-F$
    12. D

9. 1. $(Q$ v $R) \Rightarrow S$
    2. $-S$ v $(-S \& T)$
    3. $-Q \Rightarrow [-R \Rightarrow (U \& V)]$ $/ \therefore V \& U$
    4. $(-S$ v $-S) \& (-S$ v $T)$
    5. $-S$ v $-S$
    6. $-S$
    7. $-(Q$ v $R)$
    8. $-Q \& -R$
    9. $-Q$
    10. $-R \Rightarrow (U \& V)$

10. 1. $(F \& G)$ v $(H \& I)$
    2. $[H$ v $(F \& G)] \Rightarrow -(J$ v $-K)$
    3. $K \Rightarrow [L$ v $(J$ v $M)]$ $/ \therefore L$ v M
    4. $[(F \& G)$ v $H] \& [(F \& G)$ v $I]$
    5. $(F \& G)$ v H
    6. H v $(F \& G)$
    7. $-(J$ v $-K)$
    8. $-J \& --K$
    9. $-J \& K$
    10. $K \& -J$

11. –R
12. U & V
13. V & U

11. K
12. L v (J v M)
13. (L v J) v M
14. (J v L) v M
15. J v (L v M)
16. –J
17. L v M

C. Prove the validity of the following arguments and argument forms by the method of deduction.

1. A & – –B
    –(A & B) v C
    ∴ C

2. X v Y
    ∴ X v (Y v Z)

3. –[(A & B) & C]
    ∴ (–A v –B) v –C

4. (X & Y) ⇒ Z
    Y & X
    ∴ Z

5. –(F & G) v H
    ∴ –F v (–G v H)

6. –O v P
    –P v –P
    ∴ –O

7. –(p v q)
    ∴ –p

8. –p
    ∴ –(p & q)

9. p v q
    p v r
    ∴ p v (q & r)

10. p
    ∴ (p v q) & (p v –q)

11. p v (q & r)
    ∴ p v q

12. [M & (N & O)] ⇒ (P & Q)
    (M & N) & O
    ∴ P & Q

13. (A & B) v (C & D)
    –(C & D) v (A & B)
    ∴ A & B

14. A v B
    C v D
    ∴ [(A v B) & C] v [(A v B) & D]

15. (A & B) v [(C & D) v (E & F)]
    –(C & D) & –(E & F)
    ∴ (A & B)

16. [X ⇒ (Y & Z)] v –(Y & Z)
    –[X ⇒ (Y & Z)]
    ∴ –Y v –Z

D. Follow the directions for Set C.

1. $-A \lor (-B \lor C)$
    $-C$
    $\therefore -(A \,\&\, B)$

2. $F \lor (G \lor H)$
    $\therefore H \lor (G \lor F)$

3. $-T \lor U$
    $-(U \lor V)$
    $\therefore -T$

4. $-W \lor X$
    $-Y \lor X$
    $\therefore -(W \lor Y) \lor X$

5. $(p \lor q) \Rightarrow r$
    $-r$
    $\therefore -p$

6. $-p \lor q$
    $-(q \,\&\, s)$
    $\therefore -(p \,\&\, s)$

7. $-(p \lor q)$
    $\therefore -p \lor -q$

8. $p \lor -(q \lor r)$
    $\therefore p \lor -q$

9. $[(A \,\&\, B) \,\&\, C] \,\&\, D$
    $\therefore (D \,\&\, A) \,\&\, (B \,\&\, C)$

10. $-(-A \lor -B) \lor C$
    $-(A \,\&\, B)$
    $\therefore C \lor -B$

11. $-(A \Rightarrow B) \lor (A \Rightarrow C)$
    $-[(A \Rightarrow C) \lor (A \Rightarrow D)]$
    $\therefore -(A \Rightarrow B)$

12. $(I \,\&\, J) \lor I$
    $\therefore I$

E. Follow the directions for Set C.

1. $-(A \lor B)$
    $\therefore -(A \,\&\, B)$

2. $(F \lor G) \Rightarrow (H \,\&\, I)$
    $G \lor (E \,\&\, F)$
    $\therefore H$

3. $E \lor F$
    $E \lor G$
    $-(E \lor H)$
    $\therefore F \,\&\, G$

4. $(-F \lor G) \,\&\, (H \lor -I)$
    $-G \lor I$
    $(F \,\&\, -H) \lor G$
    $\therefore G$

5. $-A \lor (B \,\&\, -C)$
    $(-D \lor A) \,\&\, (-D \lor G)$
    $\therefore -D$

6. $F \Rightarrow -(G \,\&\, H)$
    $(-H \lor -G) \Rightarrow I$
    $(F \,\&\, I) \lor (F \,\&\, -I)$
    $\therefore I$

7. $H \Rightarrow I$
    $J \Rightarrow K$
    $-(I \lor K)$
    $\therefore -(H \lor J)$

8. $-A \lor B$
    $\therefore -(A \,\&\, C) \lor B$

9. $(B \lor T) \lor (M \lor L)$
    $-(B \lor M)$
    $\therefore T \lor L$

10. $(A \lor B) \Rightarrow (C \& D)$
    $-(C \lor D)$
    $\therefore -A$

11. $-[(E \& -F) \& -G]$
    $-(F \lor G)$
    $\therefore -E$

12. $-[(F \& G) \lor (F \& -G)] \lor (-F \& -G)$
    $\therefore -F \lor G$

F. Follow the directions for Set C.

1. The president will not visit both France and Germany on his next European trip. He will visit France. So he will not visit Germany.

2. The president will visit Europe or he will not visit France. He will visit Europe or he will not visit Germany. The president will visit either France or Germany. So he will visit Europe.

3. The president will cut taxes or he won't carry out all his campaign promises. The president will balance the budget or he won't carry out all his campaign promises. The president will not both cut taxes and balance the budget. So he will not carry out all of his campaign promises.

4. If Kathy goes to McDonald's and has a Big Mac, she will get indigestion. If she goes to McDonald's and has a large fries, she will get fat. Kathy will go to McDonald's, and she will have a Big Mac and a large fries. So she will get indigestion and get fat.

5. If either Jackson or Smith do not play, then the basketball team will not win. The team will win. So Jackson will play.

6. Either Bill will start studying, or he will fail both biology and chemistry. He will not fail biology. So he will start studying.

7. Skip will fly to Colorado or he will not ski on his vacation. He will fly to Florida or he will not play tennis. Skip is either going to ski or he is going to play tennis and lie on the beach. So Skip will fly to Colorado or Florida.

8. If Skip goes to Florida and lies on the beach for the entire vacation, he will get a marvelous suntan. Skip will go to Florida, but he will not get a marvelous suntan. Therefore he will not lie on the beach for the entire vacation.

9. Bill will either work over vacation, or go skiing in Colorado or Vermont. He is not going to go skiing in Colorado. So he will either work or go skiing in Vermont.

10. Mary is going to stay home for vacation, and she is going to either work or study. She is not going to study. So she is going co stay home and work but not stay home and study.

11. You are married and are filing a separate return. Your spouse had no income but is the dependent of someone else. If you file a separate return, you can take your spouse's exemptions only if your spouse had no income and was not the dependent of someone else. So you cannot take your spouse's exemptions.

12. If unemployment or inflation worsens, the president will not be reelected, and the Republicans will lose control of the Senate while the Democrats will not lose any seats in the House. The Republicans will

lose control of the Senate and the Democrats will not lose any seats in the House, but the president will be reelected. Consequently, unemployment will not worsen.

8.3 Proving Logical Truth and Falsity

Axioms and Theorems. We have been using the method of deduction exclusively to prove the validity of arguments. The method can be put to other uses, however, such as proving that statements are logically true or false. Using the truth table test, a statement is shown to be logically true if it comes out true in every row of the table. Using the method of deduction, we can prove a statement to be logically true by deducing it from other statements already known to be logically true. Those logical truths that are used to prove other logical truths, but are not themselves proven by the method of deduction are called *axioms*. Statements deducible from the axioms are called *theorems*. A body of statements consisting of axioms and theorems is called a *deductive system*. Euclidean geometry and Newtonian mechanics are famous examples of deductive systems. The set of logical truths can also be organized as a deductive system. We shall illustrate the process by selecting as axioms three very simple logical truths that have played a prominent role in the history of logic (see the box below). According to the law of identity, if Rover is a dog then he is a dog. According to the law of excluded middle, Rover either is or is not a dog. According to the law of noncontradiction, Rover is not both a dog and not a dog. Note that the laws of excluded middle and noncontradiction are equivalent by De Morgans rules. Both laws can be proven logically true by means of truth tables. We cannot use truth tables to prove that $p \Rightarrow p$ is logically true, but it is no less evident that $p \Rightarrow p$ is true in every possible case.

The Axioms

All substitution instances of the following logical truths are axioms, and may be introduced as separate lines at any point in a proof of logical truth.

The Law of Identity (ID): $p \Rightarrow p$

The Law of Excluded Middle (EM): $p \lor -p$

The Law of Noncontradiction (NC): $-(p \,\&\, -p)$

The Laws of Thought. The laws of identity, excluded middle, and noncontradiction are generally referred to collectively as the *laws of thought.* This is somewhat inaccurate, since they are not psychological laws and make no reference to thought. The name is not completely inappropriate, however, for anyone who denies the laws, in speech or in thought, immediately lapses into incoherence. It used to be claimed that the laws of thought provide the foundation for all of logic and mathematics. But advances in logic over the last century or so have shown this view to be mistaken. Our goal here, however, is simply to learn how axioms can be used to prove logical truths, so we do not need a complete systematization.

While the laws of thought should be self-evident, they are often misunderstood. The law of identity has been rejected by some (e.g., Heraclitus) on the grounds that things change. But the law does not deny the existence of change. A politician can certainly change from being a liberal to being a conservative. All the law says is that *if* the politician is a liberal then he is a liberal, and furthermore *if* he is a conservative then he is a conservative. A liberal *is* a liberal, although he may *become* a conservative. The law of excluded middle is sometimes rejected on the grounds that some things are not "black or white." A given politician may be neither a conservative nor a liberal, to continue our example, But we need to recall the distinction drawn in Chapter 5 between contradictories and contraries. "Conservative" and 'liberal" are contrary but not contradictory classifications, which is why some politicians cannot be classified as either. "Liberal" and "not liberal," in contrast, are contradictory. All the law of excluded middle asserts is that, either a politician is liberal or he is not liberal, Finally, the law of noncontradiction has been rejected (e.g., by Hegelians) on the grounds that conflicting forces operate in nature and society. But again, the law of noncontradiction does not deny such an obvious fact. Liberalism and conservatism are certainly conflicting forces at work in American political life. The law of noncontradiction only asserts that a politician is not both liberal and not liberal, nor both conservative and not conservative. The law of noncontradiction is also sometimes denied on the grounds that an object may have a given property in one respect, or in one sense, but not in another. For example, President Kennedy's policies were liberal in some respects, but not in others. And Huey Long (governor of Louisiana 1928–1932, US Senator 1932–1935) is a liberal in the current sense, but not in the nineteenth–century sense. But the law denies none of this. It says merely that nothing both does and does not have a given property at the same time, in the same respect, and in the same sense. Such misunderstandings can be avoided by remembering that in any substitution instance of the above statement forms, the same statement must be substituted for both occurrences of p.

Proving Logical Truth. Now, how do we go about using our axioms to prove logical truth? Suppose, for example, we wish to prove the following to be logically true.

$$/ \therefore [(A \ \& \ B) \lor (-A \ \& \ B)] \lor [(A \ \& \ -B) \lor (-A \ \& \ -B)]$$

We start with one or more axioms, which function as premises; then we deduce the proposition we wish to prove logically true, which functions as our conclusion. Since the proposition we want to prove involves A, $-A$, B, and $-B$, let us start with $A \lor -A$ and $B \lor -B$, two instances of the law of excluded middle.

1.	$A \lor -A$	EM
2.	$B \lor -B$	EM
3.	$(A \lor -A) \ \& \ (B \lor -B)$	1,2 Conj
4.	$[(A \lor -A) \ \& \ B] \lor [(A \lor -A) \ \& \ -B]$	3 Dist
5.	$[(A \ \& \ B) \lor (-A \ \& \ B)] \lor [(A \ \& \ -B) \lor (-A \ \& \ -B)]$	4 Dist

Since line 5 follows validly from statements that are logically true, line 5 must also be logically true. In proving a logical truth, we have to start our deduction with an axiom. Axioms are the only statements we can "justify" without referring to earlier lines of the proof. But there is no need to introduce all the axioms we are going to use at the beginning of the proof. We can introduce axioms at any point, as needed.

In constructing a deduction, it is always important to have a clear picture of what you want to deduce. Unless you know exactly where you want to go, it will be hard to figure out how to get there. So write the statement you wish to derive above your deduction, or off to the side of the first step. Prefix the statement with $/ \therefore$, which in this context can be read to prove. The major difficulty is to figure out where to begin the deduction. One helpful technique is to work backward from the "conclusion." That is, use the rules of replacement on the logical truth to be proven, until an equivalent is found that either has the form of one of the axioms, or can be easily derived from one or more of the axioms. Thus, given the task of proving [(A & B) ∨ (–A & B)] ∨ [(A & –B) ∨ (–A & –B)], we might have noted that it is equivalent by distribution to [(A ∨ –A) & B] ∨ [(A ∨ –A) & –B],which in turn is equivalent by distribution to (A ∨ –A) & (B ∨ –B), which can easily be derived from the law of excluded middle. Having done this preliminary "scratch work," we then start at the beginning and work the deduction out in proper sequence.

Proving Logical Falsity. A statement is logically false if its denial is logically true. So we can prove that a statement is logically false by the method of deduction by deriving its denial from the axioms. Suppose, for example, we wish to prove that $[(A \& B) \& C] \& -(B \vee C)$.is logically false. We can do so by proving that its denial is logically true.

$$/\therefore -\{[(A \& B) \& C] \& -(B \vee C)\}$$

This is equivalent to $-[(A \& B) \& C] \vee (B \vee C)$, by De Morgan, and is equivalent by two more applications of the same rule to $[-(A \& B) \vee -C] \vee (B \vee C)$ and $[(-A \vee -B) \vee -C] \vee (B \vee C)$, which can easily be derived from $-C \vee C$ (or from $-B \vee B$) by addition, association, and commutation. The deduction then goes as follows:

1.	$-C \vee C$	EM
2.	$(-C \vee C) \vee (-A \vee -B)$	1 Add
3.	$(-A \vee -B) \vee (-C \vee C)$	2 Com
4.	$\{(-A \vee -B) \vee (-C \vee C)\} \vee B$	3 Add
5.	$\{[(-A \vee -B) \vee -C] \vee C\} \vee B$	4 Assn
6.	$[(-A \vee -B) \vee -C] \vee (C \vee B)$	5 Assn
7.	$[-(A \& B) -C] \vee (C \vee B)$	6 DM
8.	$-[(A \& B) \& C] \vee (C \vee B)$	7 DM
9.	$-\{[(A \& B) \& C] \& -(C \vee B)\}$	8 DM
10.	$-\{[(A \& B) \& C] \& -(B \vee C)\}$	9 Com

Remember: to prove that a statement is logically true, derive it from the axioms. But to prove that a statement is logically false, derive its denial from the axioms.

Proving Logical Contingency. We cannot use the method of deduction to prove that a statement form is logically contingent. Mere failure to prove a statement logically true or false does not prove it contingent. Truth tables may be used for truth–functional forms, of course. And fortunately, it is not necessary to work out an entire truth table. All we need is one assignment of truth values to the variables that makes the statement form true, and another assignment that makes it false. The general method employed in §7.6 can be used efficiently here. For example, suppose we wish to show that $[p \& (q \& r)]$ $\vee [-p \& (-q \& -r)]$ is logically contingent. This form comes out true if p, q, and r are all true; it comes out false if p is true while q and r are false. So the form is contingent. In other words, to prove that a truth–functional form is contingent, find one positive case and one countercase.

Glossary

Axiom: statements not proven by the method of deduction that are used to deduce other statements.

Theorem: a statement deduced from the axioms.

Deductive system: a system of statements some of which are selected as axioms from which the other statements are deduced as theorems.

Law of identity: the principle that all substitution instances of $p \Rightarrow p$ are true.

Law of excluded middle: the principle that all substitution instances of $p \vee -p$ are true.

Law of noncontradiction: the principle that all substitution instances of $-(p \& -p)$ are true.

The laws of thought: the laws of identity, excluded middle, and noncontradiction.

Exercises

A. Prove that the following statements are logically true, using the method of deduction.

1. $(C \& D) \lor (-C \lor -D)$
2. $[(L \& M) \lor (L \& N) \lor -[L \& (M \lor N)]$
3. $--A \Rightarrow A$
4. $[(A \& B) \lor (A \& -B)] \Rightarrow [A \& (B \lor -B)]$
5. $A \lor (-A \lor B)$
6. $(P \& -Q) \lor (Q \lor -P)$
7. $[F \& -(G \& H)] \Rightarrow [(F \& -G) \lor (F \& -H)]$
8. $-[(A \& B) \lor C] \Rightarrow [(-A \& -C) \lor (-B \& -C)]$
9. $-A \lor [(A \lor B) \& (A \lor C)]$
10. $[Q \lor (-Q \lor R)] \& [(S \& T) \lor (-S \lor -T)]$
11. $[A \& (B \& -C)] \Rightarrow -[C \lor -(B \& A)]$
12. $-[-(F \lor G) \& F]$

B. Prove that the following statements are logically false, using the method of deduction.

1. $(X \& Y) \& (-X \lor -Y)$

2. $-(A \Rightarrow --A)$

3. $-\{[(M \& N) \Rightarrow (N \& M)] \& [(N \& M) \Rightarrow (M \& N)]\}$

4. $-\{-[H \& I) \& (J \& K) \Rightarrow [(-H \lor -I) \lor (-J \lor -K)]\}$

5. $-[-(-P \lor Q) \lor (Q \lor -P)]$

6. $[(F \& -F) \& G] \lor [F \& (G \& -G)]$

7. $-[-(A \& B) \lor A]$

8. $-\{[(X \& Y) \lor (-X \& -Y)] \lor [(X \& -Y) \lor (-X \& Y)]\}$

9. $-\{-(-P \lor Q) \lor [-(Q \& -R) \lor -(R \& P)]\}$

10. $-\{[(-A \& B) \lor (A \lor -B)] \& [(C \& -D) \lor (-C \lor D)]\}$

11. $-(A \lor -B) \& -B$

12. $-\{[A \lor (B \lor C) \Rightarrow [C \lor (B \lor A)]\}$

C. Prove that each of the following statement forms is logically contingent by finding one case in which it is true and one in which it is false.

1. $-[(p \lor q) \& p] \lor -q$
2. $[(p \& q) \lor -(r \lor s)] \& (t \& -q)$
3. $[(p \lor q) \& (-q \lor r)] \& (p \& -r)$
4. $-[-(p \& q) \& p] \lor q$
5. $[(p \lor q) \& r] \lor -[(p \lor q) \& s]$
6. $[(p \& q) \lor (r \& p)] \& -(r \& s)$
7. $[-(p \lor q) \lor s] \& (-p \lor s)$
8. $-[p \lor (q \& r)] \lor [(p \& q) \lor (p \& r)]$
9. $-(p \lor q) \lor [p \lor (q \& r)]$
10. $-\{[(p \lor q) \& (r \lor s)] \& (-p \lor -r)\} \lor (-q \& -s)$

8.4 Conditional Proof

The axioms selected in the previous section provide very limited means for proving the logical truth of conditionals. The only conditionals that can be deduced from the axioms are those whose antecedents and consequents are logically equivalent. The selected axioms provide no way to prove even a simple logical truth like $(A \,\&\, B) \Rightarrow A$. One way to remedy this lack, of course, is to expand the list of axioms. There is another way of proving conditionals logically true, however, called **conditional proof.** In a conditional proof, the logical truth of a conditional is proven by deducing the consequent from the antecedent. That is, $p \Rightarrow q$ is proven logically true by using the method of deduction to prove that the argument "$p \therefore q$" is valid, which means that p logically implies q. If q can be deduced from p using our rules of inference, then q follows with necessity from p, and so p implies q in all possible cases. For example, A follows from $A \,\&\, B$ by the rule of simplification; so $(A \,\&\, B) \Rightarrow A$ is logically true. The following two–step proof shows that $[(A \,\&\, B) \vee (A \,\&\, -B)] \Rightarrow A$ is logically true.

1.	$(A \,\&\, B) \vee (A \,\&\, -B)$	$/ \therefore A$
2.	$A \,\&\, (B \vee -B)$	1 Dist
3.	A	2 Simp

Any time we prove an argument valid by the method of deduction, we have also proven that a conditional is logically true—namely, the conditional whose antecedent is the premise of the argument (or the conjunction of the premises if the argument has more than one premise) and whose consequent is the conclusion.

Proving Logical Equivalence. We can prove in a similar fashion that two statements are logically equivalent by deducing one from the other. That is, to prove that $X = Y$ it suffices to prove the validity of the two arguments "$X \therefore Y$" and "$Y \therefore X$." The validity of "$X \therefore Y$" means that X logically implies Y, and the validity of "$Y \therefore X$" means that Y logically implies X. Thus to prove that $A = A \,\&\, (A \vee B)$ two simple proofs suffice:

1. A		$/ \therefore A \,\&\, (A \vee B)$	1. $A \,\&\, (A \vee B)$		$/ \therefore A$
2. $A \vee B$		1 Add	2. A		1 Simp
3. $A \,\&\, (A \vee B)$		1,2 Conj			

The deduction on the left shows that A logically implies $A \,\&\, (A \vee B)$. The deduction on the right shows that $A \,\&\, (A \vee B)$ logically implies A. Since the two statements logically imply each other, they are logically equivalent.

Proving Logical Compatibility and Incompatibility. If one statement logically implies another, the two must be compatible. So either of the above deductions shows that A and $A \,\&\, (A \vee B)$ are compatible. Whereas two deductions are necessary to prove equivalence, one suffices to prove compatibility. When proving the compatibility of any two statements p and q– first try deducing q from p. If that fails, try deducing p from q. The method of conditional proof provides only limited means to establish compatibility, however. For as we saw in Chapter 7, two statements may be compatible even though neither implies the other. In that event, their compatibility cannot be established by a conditional proof.

Two statements are logically incompatible provided the truth of one logically implies the falsity of the other. So the method of conditional proof can be used to establish their incompatibility by picking *either* statement and deducing the *denial* of the other. Thus we can prove the incompatibility of $(R \vee C) \,\&\, -I$ and $I \vee (-R \,\&\, -C)$ by deducing $-[I \vee (-R \,\&\, -C)]$ from $(R \vee C) \,\&\, -I$ as below, or by deducing $-[(R \vee C) \,\&\, -I]$ from $I \vee (-R \,\&\, -C)$.

1.	$(R \vee C) \,\&\, -I$	$/ \therefore -[I \vee (-R \,\&\, -C)]$
2.	$-I \,\&\, (R \vee C)$	1 Com
3.	$-I \,\&\, --(R \vee C)$	2 DN
4.	$-I \,\&\, -(-R \,\&\, -C)$	3 DM
5.	$-[I \vee (-R \,\&\, -C)]$	4 Dist

Only one deduction is necessary to prove that two statements are incompatible. So we have a choice of strategies to pursue. Bear in mind that failure to prove incompatibility does not establish compatibility, and that failure to prove compatibility does not establish incompatibility,

---

Glossary

> **Conditional proof:** proving a conditional logically true by deducing its consequent from its antecedent.

Exercises

A. Prove the logical truth of the following conditional statement forms, using the method of deduction.

1. $p \Rightarrow (p \lor q)$
3. $(p \& q) \Rightarrow (p \lor q)$
5. $-p \Rightarrow -(p \& -q)$
7. $[p \lor (q \& r)] \Rightarrow (p \lor (q \lor r)]$
9. $\{[(p \lor q) \Rightarrow (r \& s)] \& -r\} -p$
11. $[(-p \lor q) \& (-p \lor r)] \Rightarrow [-(p \& r) \lor q]$

2. $[p \& (p \Rightarrow q)] \Rightarrow q$
4. $-(p \lor q) \Rightarrow -p$
6. $[p \& -(p \& q)] \Rightarrow -q$
8. $\{[(-p \Rightarrow q) \& (-r \Rightarrow s)] \& -(p \lor r)\} \Rightarrow (q \& s)$
10. $[(p \lor q) \& (p \lor -q)] \Rightarrow p$
12. $\{[(p \lor q) \& (r \lor s)] \& -(q \& s)\} \Rightarrow \{[(p \lor q) \& r] \lor [p \& (s \lor t)]\}$

B. Prove the following logical equivalences using the method of deduction.

1. $p \& (-p \lor q) = (p \& q)$
3. $-(p \& q) \lor r = -p \lor (-q \lor r)$
5. $-[p \& -(-p \lor r)] = -p \lor r$
7. $p \& [(p \Rightarrow q) \& (q \Rightarrow p)] = q \& [(p \Rightarrow q) \& (q \Rightarrow p)]$

2. $-[(p \& q) \& (r \& s)] = (-p \lor -q) \lor (-r \lor -s)$
4. $-[(p \& q) \lor r] = (-p \& -r) \lor (-q \& -r)$
6. $-[(p \lor q) \& r] \lor -s = [-p \lor -(r \& s)] \& [-q \lor -(r \& s)]$
8. $[(p \& q) \& -(p \& q)] = [(p \& -p) \& q] \lor [p \& (q \& -q)]$

C. Prove the compatibility or incompatibility of the following pairs of statement forms using the method of deduction.

1. (a) $-(p \lor q)$
   (b) $-p \lor -q$
3. (a) p
   (b) $(p \& q) \lor (p \& -q)$
5. (a) p
   (b) $q \& (-q \lor -p)$
7. (a) $-[(p \lor q) \& (-p \lor -q)]$
   (b) $-[(p \& q) \lor (-p \& -q)]$

2. (a) $-(p \lor q)$
   (b) $(p \lor q) \lor (p \& q)$
4. (a) $-(-p \lor q)$
   (b) $-(p \lor -q)$
6. (a) $p \lor (q \& r)$
   (b) $(p \& q) \lor (p \& r)$
8. (a) $p \& -(-q \lor r)$
   (b) $-(p \& q) \lor r$

8.5 Indirect Proof

Proving Validity. We have been studying one method of deduction known as **direct proof.** In a direct proof, an argument is shown to be valid by deriving the conclusion from the premises, using other arguments already known to be valid. A direct proof of validity consists of a sequence of lines, each of which is either a premise or a line that follows from preceding lines by the rules of inference and whose last line is the conclusion. There is another method of deduction, however, known as **indirect proof**– or proof by *reductio ad absurdum.* In an indirect proof an argument is shown to be valid by deriving a contradiction from the premises together with the denial of the conclusion. Any statements that jointly lead to a contradiction cannot all be true. If the premises and the conclusion's denial cannot all be true, then it is impossible for the premises to be true and the conclusion false. So in an indirect proof, you prove an argument to be valid by reducing to absurdity the proposition that the conclusion might be false even if the premises are true.

Theoretically, an indirect proof could terminate in any logical falsehood. It is customary, however, to require that an indirect proof terminate in a self–contradiction, a logical falsehood of the form p & $-p$. Essentially, then, we shall prove an argument "$P \therefore C$" to be valid indirectly by proving another argument of the form "$P, -C, \therefore p$ & $-p$" to be valid directly. An indirect proof will therefore differ from a direct proof in only two ways: One line of an indirect proof will be the denial of the conclusion, which generally will neither be a premise nor follow validly from the premises. And the last line of an indirect proof will be a contradiction rather than the conclusion. The first step in an indirect proof is to write out and number the premises, putting the conclusion after the last premise as usual. The second step is to introduce the denial of the conclusion as one of the lines of the proof. We will mark this line "IP" to indicate that we are constructing an indirect proof, and that the line is not supposed to follow from preceding lines. The denial of the conclusion may be introduced immediately after the premises (if you know in advance that you are going to try an indirect proof), or later (if you try a direct proof first, and then realize that an indirect proof would be better). The final step—the hard one—is to derive a line of the form p & $-p$. Each line after the one marked IP must be justified in the usual manner, by citing the previous lines it follows from and the rule it follows by.

Let us work through the following example again:

> Roberts will run for reelection this year. If Roberts runs, he will defeat Martin. If Roberts runs this year and defeats Martin, Kent will run in the next election. If Kent runs next time, he will win. So Kent will win the next election.

At the beginning of this chapter we symbolized this argument and proved its validity by the method of direct proof, as follows:

1.	R	
2.	$R \Rightarrow M$	
3.	$(R \& M) \Rightarrow K$	
4.	$K \Rightarrow W$	$/ \therefore W$
5.	M	2,1 MP
6.	$R \& M$	1,5 Conj
7.	K	6,3 MP
8.	W	7,4 MP

This argument can also be proven valid by the method of indirect proof. We write in the premises and the conclusion as usual; so steps 1-4 stay the same. But line 5—the next line after the premises—will be the denial of the conclusion in an indirect proof. Then from the premises, together with the denial of the conclusion, we seek to derive a contradiction.

1.	R	
2.	$R \Rightarrow M$	
3.	$(R \& M) \Rightarrow K$	
4.	$K \Rightarrow W$	$/\therefore W$
5.	$-W$	IP
6.	$-K$	4,5 MT
7.	M	1–2 MP
8.	$R \& M$	1,7 Conj
9.	K	3,8 MP
10.	$K \& -K$	6,9 Conj

In this case, the indirect proof was longer, so we would naturally prefer the direct proof. But both methods are equally legitimate, and in other cases the direct proof may be longer or even impossible. In this particular indirect proof, the last line is the conjunction of a simple statement and its negation; this is not essential. The last line of an indirect proof may be *any* substitution instance of $p \& -p$. The following is just as good an indirect proof.

1.	R	
2.	$R \Rightarrow M$	
3.	$(R \& M) \Rightarrow K$	
4.	$K \Rightarrow W$	$/\therefore W$
5.	$-W$	IP
6.	$-K$	4,5 MT
7.	$-(R \& M)$	3,6 MT
8.	M	1,2 MP
9.	$R \& M$	1,8 Conj
10.	$(R \& M) \& -(R \& M)$	7,9 Conj

The method of indirect proof greatly extends the power of our system of deduction. For many arguments that cannot be proven valid directly using our rules of inference can be proven valid indirectly. Consider constructive dilemma, for example, whose validity we established by truth tables in Chapter 7.

1.	$p \Rightarrow q$	
2.	$r \Rightarrow s$	
3.	$p \vee r$	$/\therefore q \vee s$

It seems as if we should be able to prove this valid directly by modus ponens, but we cannot. The other rules are no more helpful. An indirect proof, however, is quite easy:

4.	$-(q \vee s)$	IP
5.	$-q \& -s$	4 DM
6.	$-q$	5 Simp
7.	$-p$	1,6 MT
8.	r	3,7 DS
9.	s	2,8 MP
10.	$-s$	5 Simp
11.	$s \& -s$	9,10 Conj

Destructive dilemma can be proven valid indirectly in a similar fashion.

Indirect proof can be used to derive some of our rules from the others. For example, modus tollens can be derived from modus ponens, as follows:

1.	$p \Rightarrow q$	
2.	$-q$	$/\therefore -p$
3.	p	IP

4.	q	1,3
5.	$q \& -q$	2,4 Conj

And disjunctive transitivity can be proven valid indirectly using disjunctive syllogism.

1.	$p \vee q$	
2.	$-q \vee r$	$/ \therefore p \vee r$
3.	$-(p \vee r)$	IP
4.	$-p \& -r$	3 DM
5.	$-p$	4 Simp
6.	q	1,5 DS
7.	r	2,6 DS
8.	$-r$	4 Simp
9.	$r \& -r$	7,8 Conj

The redundancy in our system of deduction is inelegant theoretically. But it is advantageous from a practical standpoint, because it makes the construction of proofs easier. Each use of disjunctive transitivity, for example, represents a savings of at least eight steps.

Proving Logical Truth. The method of indirect proof can also be used to prove logical truth. In a direct proof, a statement is proven logically true by deriving it from the axioms. In an indirect proof, a statement is proven logically true by deriving a contradiction from its denial. If denying a statement would lead to a contradiction, the statement must be logically true. Suppose, for example, we wish to prove that $A \vee -(A \& B)$ is logically true. In a direct proof, we might try to derive this from $A \vee -A$, an instance of the law of excluded middle. In an indirect proof, we would try to derive a contradiction from $-[A \vee -(A \& B)]$.

1.	$-[A \vee -(A \& B)]$	IP
2.	$-A \& (A \& B)$	1 DM
3.	$(-A \& A) \& B$	2 Assn
4.	$-A \& A$	3 Simp

In this example, we did not introduce any axioms. But we may do so in any proof of logical truth, whether direct or indirect. Consider an indirect proof of $[(A \& B) \vee (-A \& B)] \vee [(A \& -B) \vee (-A \& -B)]$, which was proven directly in §8.3.

1. $-\{[(A \& B) \vee (-A \& B)] \vee [(A \& -B) \vee (-A \& -B)]\}$ I		P
2. $-[(A \& B) \vee (-A \& B)] \& -[(A \& -B) \vee (-A \& -B)]$		1 DM
3. $-[(A \& B) \vee (-A \& B)]$		2 Simp
4. $-(A \& B) \& -(-A \& B)$		3 DM
5. $(-A \vee -B) \& (A \vee -B)$		4 DM
6. $-[(A \& -B) \vee (-A \& -B)]$		2 Simp
7. $-(A \& -B) \& -(-A \& -B)$		6 DM
8. $(-A \vee B) \& (A \vee B)$		7 DM
9. $-A \vee B$		8 Simp
10. $-A \vee -B$		5 Simp
11. $(-A \vee B) \& (-A \vee -B)$		9,10 Conj
12. $-A \vee (B \& -B)$		11 Dist
13. $-(B \& -B)$		NC
14. $-A$		12,13 DS
15. $A \vee B$		8 Simp
16. $A \vee -B$		5 Simp
17. B		14,15 DS
18. $-B$		14,16 DS
19. $B \& -B$		17,18 Conj

An instance of the law of noncontradiction was introduced as line 13. In this case the indirect proof was longer, but in other cases, a direct proof will be longer or even impossible.

Proving Logical Falsity. In a direct proof of logical falsehood, we derive denial of a statement from the axioms. In an indirect proof– we derive a contradiction from the statement itself. Any statement that logically implies a contradiction must be logically false. Thus we can prove that $[(A \& B) \& C] \& -(B \lor C)$ is logically false by reducing it to absurdity.

1.	$[(A \& B) \& C] \& -(B \lor C)$	IP
2.	$-(B \lor C)$	1 Simp
3.	$-B \& -C$	2 DM
4.	$(A \& B) \& C$	1 Simp
5.	C	4 Simp
6.	$-C$	3 Simp
7.	$C \& -C$	5,6 Conj

In this case, the indirect proof was one step shorter than the direct proof given in §8.3. But more importantly, the indirect proof was much easier, because we knew exactly where to begin.

A statement is logically true if, and only if, its denial is logically false. Thus any proof that a statement is logically true is a proof that its denial is logically false, and any proof that a statement is logically false is a proof that its denial is logically true. Thus the first deduction in the previous subsection also shows that $-[A \lor -(A \& B)]$ is logically false, and the deduction just constructed shows that $-\{[(A \& B) \& C] \& -(B \lor C)\}$ is logically true. To keep straight what to reduce to absurdity when proving what, the following rule should be memorized: *To show that a statement is logically true, derive a contradiction from its denial. To show that a statement is logically false, derive a contradiction from the statement itself.*

A Limitation on Indirect Proofs of Validity. We are now in a position to discuss an important limitation on indirect proofs of validity, where we prove an argument valid by deducing a contradiction from the premises, together with the conclusion's denial. Such a proof always shows that it is impossible for the premises to be true and the conclusion false. But if the conclusion is logically true, or if the conjunction of the premises is logically false, an indirect proof may not show that the argument is valid. It may only show that the conclusion is logically true, or that the conjunction of the premises is logically false. Consider once again the invalid argument form "$p \therefore q \lor -q$" and the following indirect "proof" of its validity:

1.	p	$/ \therefore q \lor -q$
2.	$-(q \lor -q)$	IP (WRONG)
3.	$-q \& q$	2 DM

The premise played absolutely no role in this deduction. The contradiction was deduced solely from the denial of the conclusion. Hence the deduction only shows that the conclusion is logically true. Consider next the argument form "$p \Rightarrow q, -q \& p, \therefore r$" and an apparent indirect proof.

1.	$p \Rightarrow q$	$/\therefore r$
2.	$-q \& p$	
3.	$-r$	IP (WRONG)
4.	$-q$	2 Simp
5.	$-p$	1,4 MT
6.	p	2 Simp
7.	$p \& -p$	5,6 Conj

Note that the conclusion's denial (step 3) was not used at all. The contradiction was deduced entirely from the premises. So all the deduction shows is that the conjunction of the premises is logically false.

Whereas the method of indirect proof can always he used to prove logical truth or falsehood, it can be used to establish validity only under certain conditions. These conditions can be met by adhering to the following rule: *Use IP to establish validity only when the conclusion and the conjunction of the premises are logically contingent.* The IP steps in the above deductions violate this condition and are therefore incorrect. In practice, you will often be unable to ascertain the satisfaction of this condition in advance. You will have to review your deduction after constructing it to see if it proves that the conclusion is logically true or the conjunction of the premises logically false.

Glossary

Direct proof: proving an argument valid by deducing the conclusion from the premises, or proving a statement logically true (or logically false) by deducing it (or its denial) from the axioms.

Indirect proof: proving an argument valid by deducing a contradiction from the premises and the denial of the conclusion, or proving a statement logically true (or logically false) by deducing a contradiction from its denial (or from it).

Exercises

A. Prove the validity of the following arguments and argument forms by the method of indirect proof.

1. $(A \lor B) \,\&\, (C \lor D)$
   $-A \lor -C$
   $\therefore B \lor D$

2. $-E \lor -F$
   $-(G \,\&\, -E)$
   $\therefore -G \lor -F$

3. $(A \lor B) \Rightarrow (O \,\&\, P)$
   $-O$
   $\therefore -A$

4. $-A \lor B$
   $\therefore -(A \,\&\, C) \lor B$

5. $p \Rightarrow (q \,\&\, -q)$
   $\therefore -p$

6. $(p \lor -p) \Rightarrow q$
   $\therefore q$

7. $p \lor q$
   $p \lor -q$
   $\therefore p$

8. $p \lor q$
   $r \lor s$
   $-p \lor -r$
   $\therefore q \lor s$

9. $-p \lor q$
   $\therefore -p \lor (p \,\&\, q)$

10. $p \Rightarrow q$
    $\therefore -p \lor q$

11. $H \lor (I \,\&\, J)$
    $-(I \lor J) \lor K$
    $\therefore H \lor K$

12. $(B \lor T) \,\&\, -(B \,\&\, T)$
    $(M \lor L) \,\&\, -(M \,\&\, L)$
    $B \lor M$
    $\therefore -T \lor -L$

13. $-(Q \,\&\, R) \lor (S \Rightarrow T)$
    $-(S \Rightarrow T) \lor -T$
    $\therefore -(Q \,\&\, R) \lor -T$

14. $-(M \,\&\, -N)$
    $-[M \,\&\, (N \,\&\, -O)]$
    $\therefore -(M \,\&\, -O)$

15. $[(A \& B) \Rightarrow C] \& [(A \& -B) \Rightarrow D]$
    A
    $\therefore C \lor D$

16. $(F \lor G) \Rightarrow (H \& I)$
    $G \lor (E \& F)$
    $\therefore H$

17. $-(M \& N)$
    $(-N \lor -M) \Rightarrow (-O \lor -P)$
    $-R \Rightarrow (P \& O)$
    $\therefore R$

18. $E \Rightarrow -(F \& G)$
    $(H \lor F) \& (H \lor G)$
    $(E \& H) \lor (E \& -H)$
    $\therefore H$

19. $-[(X \Rightarrow Y) \lor (Y \Rightarrow X)]$
    $-Z \Rightarrow -(V \lor U)$
    $U \lor [V \lor (Y \Rightarrow X)]$
    $\therefore Z$

20. $A \Rightarrow -(B \lor C)$
    $A \& -F$
    $-B \Rightarrow [D \lor (F \& G)]$
    $\therefore D$

21. $A \Rightarrow B$
    $B \Rightarrow C$
    $A \lor B$
    $\therefore C \lor E$

22. $(A \lor B) \Rightarrow (C \& D)$
    $-(C \lor D)$
    $\therefore -A$

23. $-[(E \& -F) \& -G]$
    $-(F \lor G)$
    $\therefore -E$

24. $T \& (U \lor V)$
    $T \Rightarrow [U \Rightarrow (W \& X)]$
    $(T \& V) \Rightarrow -(W \lor X)$
    $\therefore (W \& X) \lor (-W \& -X)$

B. Prove the logical truth of the following statements by the method of indirect proof

1. $-[(X \& Y) \& (-X \lor -Y)]$
2. $-(A \& B) \lor B$
3. $-(A \& B) \Rightarrow (-A \lor -B)$
4. $-\{[(H \lor -I) \& -H] \& I\}$
5. $[F \& -(G \& H) \Rightarrow [(F \& -G] \lor (F \& -H)]$
6. $-\{[(P \lor Q) \& (-Q \lor R)] \& (-P \& -R)\}$
7. $-\{[-F \lor G) \lor -[-F \lor (G \& F)]\}$
8. $-[(P \lor Q) \& (R \lor -Q)] \lor (P \lor R)$
9. $-\{[E \lor (F \& G)] \& -F\} \lor E$
10. $-\{[(A \lor B) \& (C \lor -A) \& -(C \lor B)\}$
11. $-(-P \lor Q) \lor [(Q \& R) \lor -(R \& P)]$
12. $-(-A \lor B) \lor [-(-B \lor C) \lor (-A \lor C)]$

C. Prove the logical falsehood of the following statements by the method of indirect proof.

1. $-[(C \& D) \lor (-C \lor -D)]$
2. $-[A \lor (-A \lor B)]$
3. $-[(P \& -Q) \lor (Q \lor -P)]$
4. $(F \lor G) \& (-F \& -G)$
5. $-\{-A \lor [(A \lor B) \& (A \lor C)]\}$
6. $-\{-[-P \lor (-Q \lor R)] \lor [-(-P \lor Q) \lor (-P \lor R)]\}$
7. $-\{-[-(-A \lor B) \lor B] \lor (A \lor B)\}$
8. $-\{-A \lor [A \& (A \lor B)]\}$
9. $-\{-[A \& (A \lor B)] \lor A\}$
10. $-(A \& -B) \& [A \& -(A \& B)]$

D. If possible, use the method of indirect proof to establish the validity of the following arguments. If IP cannot be used, explain why not.

1. $p \lor (q \lor -p)$

    $\therefore p \ \& \ (q \ \& \ -p)$

2. $p \lor r$

    $\therefore q \lor (r \lor -q)$

3. $p \lor q$

    $-p \ \& \ -q$

    $\therefore (-p \lor q) \ \& \ (-q \lor p)$

4. $-p \lor q$

    $-r \lor q$

    $\therefore -(p \ \& \ r) \lor q$

5. p

    $-p \lor -p$

    $\therefore q \lor (-q \ \& \ -q)$

6 $p \lor q$

    $-q \ \& \ r$

    $-r \lor -q$

    $\therefore p \ \& \ -q$

LSAT Prep Questions

Bird-watchers explore a forest to see which of the following kinds of birds—grosbeak, harrier, jay, martin, shrike, wren—it contains. The findings are consistent with the following conditions:
If harriers are in the forest, grosbeaks are not.
If jays, martins, or both are in the forest, then so are harriers.
If wrens are in the forest, then so are grosbeaks.
If jays are not in the forest, then shrikes are.

1. Which one of the following could be a complete and accurate list of the birds NOT in the forest?

    (a) jays, shrikes

    (b) harriers, grosbeaks

    (c) grosbeaks, jays, martins

    (d) grosbeaks, martins, shrikes, wrens

    (e) martins, shrikes

2. If both martins and harriers are in the forest, then which of the following must be true?

    (a) Shrikes are the only other birds in the forest.

    (b) Jays are the only other birds in the forest.

    (c) The forest contains neither jays nor shrikes.

    (d) There are at least two other kinds of birds in the forest.

    (e) There are at most two other kinds of birds in the forest.

3. If jays are not in the forest, then which of the following must be false?

    (a) Martins are not in the forest.

    (b) Harriers are in the forest.

    (c) Neither martins nor harriers are in the forest.

    (d) Neither martins nor shrikes are in the forest.

    (e) Harriers and shrikes are the only birds in the forest.

4. Which one of the following pairs of birds CANNOT be among those birds contained in the forest?

    (a) jays, wrens

    (b) jays, shrikes

    (c) shrikes, wrens

    (d) jays, martins

    (e) shrikes, martins

5. If grosbeaks are in the forest, then which one of the following must be true?

    (a) Shrikes are in the forest.

    (b) Wrens are in the forest.

    (c) The forest contains both wrens and shrikes.

    (d) At most two kinds of birds are in the forest.

    (e) At least three kinds of birds are in the forest.

6. Suppose the condition is added that if shrikes are in the forest, then harriers are not. If all other conditions remain in effect, then which of the following could be true?

    (a) The forest contains both jays and shrikes.

    (b) The forest contains both wrens and shrikes.

    (c) The forest contains both martins and shrikes.

    (d) Jays are not in the forest, whereas martins are.

    (e) Only two of the six kinds of birds are not in the forest.

Preptest 33, Section 4, Questions 6–8, 10–12

CHAPTER NINE

Quantification Theory

9.1 Singular Statements

Quantification Theory. In Chapters 7 and 8 we studied the logic of compound statements. We analyzed them into conjunctions, disjunctions, negations, and conditionals formed from simple statements. In Chapters 5 and 6 we studied the logic of simple statements, analyzing them into subjects, predicates, quantifiers, and copulas. We developed separate systems of deduction for syllogistic logic and propositional logic. Neither system, obviously, is complete. We could simply put the two systems together in order to prove the validity of arguments like the following:

> John is in New York. If John is in New York, then no one from the company is in Philadelphia. Bill is in the company. Therefore, Bill is not in Philadelphia.

As in chapter 5, we would first symbolize "John is in New York" as "j is an N" and "Bill is from the company" as "b is a C," and so on.

j is an N.	
(j is an N) $\Rightarrow$ (No C is a P).	
b is a C.	/∴ b is not a P.
No C is a P.	1, 2 MP
Every C is a non-P.	4 Obv
b is a non-P.	5, 3 SCS
b is not a P.	6 Obv

While we could integrate propositional and syllogistic logic in this way, a much more efficient and powerful system has been developed known as ***quantification theory.*** Gottlob Frege (1848–1925) and Bertrand Russell (1872–1970) were two prominent figures in its development. Basically, we keep the system of deduction for propositional logic intact, and add five more rules dealing with quantifiers.

Before we can formulate these new rules, however, we need to develop a more economical and more general method of symbolizing categorical propositions.

Symbolizing Singular Statements. We begin with those statements that have the simplest logical structure—namely, affirmative singular statements like:

> Giuliani is a conservative.

U statements, as we called them, have general terms as their predicates and singular terms as their subjects; there is no quantifier, and no "not" in the copula. We previously abbreviated such statements by using lower-case letters for subject terms, and capital letters for predicate terms. Using g for "Giuliani," and C for "conservative," we get:

> g is a C.

We will continue to use lower-case letters to abbreviate singular subject terms, but we will now use capital letters to abbreviate *the entire predicate* rather than just the *predicate term*. Thus, we shall let C stand for the whole phrase "is a conservative." You might expect us to write gC, but it is customary in quantification theory, by analogy with function notation in mathematics, to reverse the order and write the predicate constant before the subject constant:

> Cg

Some authors increase the analogy even further by writing $C(g)$. The parentheses here carry no information, however, so we forego them to minimize parentheses.

Next, consider a negative singular statement, a **Y** statement:

> Giuliani is not a conservative.

We would previously have used the same constants, giving us:

> g is not a C.

Since "Giuliani is not a conservative" is obviously the negation of "Giuliani is a conservative," we shall now simply use the negation sign to represent the "not" in the copula. This gives us:

> $-Cg$

In general, we abbreviate "s is P" still further to "Ps," and we reduce "s is not P" to "$-Ps$."

U	s is $P = Ps$
Y	s is not $P = -Ps$

The extreme brevity of our new symbolism will be quite helpful in seeing how to prove the validity of complex arguments. But such brevity has an obvious drawback. We have departed so far from English that it is hard to attach any meaning to an expression like Cg. It should help to continue reading this as "g is C."

Compactness is not the only virtue of our new method of representation. We noted in §5.1 that the forms we were using to represent categorical propositions had some accidental features. For not all predicates explicitly contain general terms, and not all are in the present tense. While it was easy to ignore as irrelevant the difference between nominative, adjectival, and verbal predicates, we could not similarly ignore differences in tense. We had to be content with the fact that what we said about present-tense categorical propositions would hold for all other categorical propositions. Since we are now abbreviating the entire predicate, these differences will no longer bother us. Thus consider:

> John loves coffee.

We do not now have to think of this us meaning "John is a coffee lover." We can simply let L mean "loves coffee," and represent the statement as

> *Lj*

We can also view *Lj* as representing "John is a coffee lover," of course, since "is a coffee lover" and "love coffee" do not differ in meaning. When we do have predicates that differ in meaning, we use different constants to represent them. Thus consider:

> Bob is a prisoner.
> Bob was a prisoner.

Since these statements are not equivalent, we cannot symbolize them in the same way. But all we have to do is pick different letters, say I and W, to represent "is a prisoner" and "was a prisoner" respectively.

> *Ib*
> *Wb*

In general, be guided by the following rule: *Sentences should be symbolized in the same way if, and only if, they have the same reference and meaning.* Ignore grammatical distinctions except insofar as they make for semantic distinctions.

Compound predicates. In Chapter 5, we represented the forms of the following two statements differently:

> Giuliani is not a liberal.
> Giuliani is a nonliberal.

We focused on the difference in the copulas, and classified the first statement as negative, the second as affirmative. However, we noted that since the affirmative statement had a negative predicate, the two statements were equivalent by obversion. To avoid a special symbol for the complement of a predicate, we shall simply treat both of the above as saying that it is not the case that Giuliani is a liberal, which is symbolized by:

> *–Lg*

In general, both "*s* is not *P*" and "*s* is non-*P*" become *–Ps*.

$$\boxed{s \text{ is non-}P = -Ps}$$

Given an affirmative singular statement, we can form its negation in English by putting either a "not" in the copula or a "non" in the predicate.

In the forms discussed in Chapters 5 and 6, the predicate term could have any degree of complexity. Thus, as instances of "*s* is *P*" we could have:

> John is a wise man.
> John is a bourbon or Scotch drinker.

By using single letters to represent complex predicates, however, we failed to represent some important logical structure. As a result, we were unable to prove the validity of many valid arguments. For example, there is no way using the methods of Chapters 5 or 6 to validate the following disjunctive syllogism: "John is a bourbon or Scotch drinker; he is not a bourbon drinker; therefore, John is a Scotch drinker." We shall now analyze predicates as much as we can. Since "John is a bourbon or Scotch drinker" means that either John is a bourbon drinker or John is a Scotch drinker, we symbolize the statement as a disjunction:

Bj ∨ *Sj*

Similarly, since "John is a wise man" means that John is both wise and a man, we symbolize it as a conjunction:

Wj & *Mj*

As usual, care must be taken to understand the statement before symbolizing it. "Derek Jeter is a baseball player" does not mean that he is both a baseball and a player; hence we should not analyze it as a conjunction. So we abbreviate it simply as Bd, where B means "is a baseball player." Even with our new symbolism, we will not be able to represent all the structure in relational predicates until §9.9. Thus, we will for now abbreviate a sentence like "Jack loves Mary" as Lj (L for "loves Mary"), and a sentence like "Bill gave the flower to Jane" as Gb (G for "gave the flower to Jane").

Predicate and Individual Constants. Symbols used to abbreviate particular predicates are called ***predicate constants***. In Chapters 7 and 8, we used capital letters as simple statement constants. Henceforth we shall use them as simple predicate constants. The context will always make clear which interpretation is intended, for predicate and individual symbols always occur together in statements or statement forms. Furthermore, once we begin representing statements using predicate and individual constants, there is no reason to continue using statement constants. Symbols used to abbreviate particular singular terms are called ***individual constants***. We shall use lower-case letters (other than *x*) as individual constants. Note that we are using the term "individual" in a very broad sense: individual constants may represent the names of places and things as well as people. Since Chapter 7, we have been confining our attention to propositions that are either true or false, which we have called statements. In Chapter 6, however, we observed that singular propositions whose subject terms refer to nonexistent things, such as "Your dodo is big," are neither true nor false. We shall continue to restrict out attention to statements, so we stipulate that individual constants are to represent singular terms referring to *existing* things.

In the rules of propositional logic, the letters *p*, *q*, *r*, and *s* are statement variables. Since these variables stand for any statement or statement constant, they stand for *Ca, Fb, –Fb, Ca & Cb, Cb & (Fb ∨ Vb)*, and so on. Consequently, you must learn to recognize "*Ca, Ca ⇒ Ma, ∴ Ma*" as an instance of modus ponens, "*Fa ∨ Va, –Va, ∴Fa*" as an instance of disjunctive syllogism, "*Fa, ∴Fa ∨ Va*" as an instance of addition, and so on. Simply treat the combination of a predicate constant followed by an individual constant as a unit representing a statement.

Glossary

Quantification theory: a system of deduction that combines the rules of propositional logic with the quantification rules and the rules of quantifier negation, from which the rules of syllogistic logic can be derived.

Predicate constants: symbols like *A*, *B*, and *C* that are used to abbreviate particular simple predicates when combined with individual constants.

Individual constants: symbols like *a*, *b*, and *c* that are used to abbreviate particular singular terms when combined with predicate constants.

Exercises

A. Symbolize the following statements, using individual and predicate constants.

1. Ted Kennedy is a Democrat.

2. The prime minister of England is not a man.

3. John Kerry is either a liberal or a conservative.

4. Either Kerry or Dean will win.

5. Trudeau speaks French and English, but not German.

6. Neither England nor Italy is landlocked.

7. If Smith is in London, then he is in England.

8. The sun is a yellow star, not an orange star.

9. Capella either is or isn't a variable star.

10. Rostropovich was a cellist and a conductor; he was also a pianist.

11. The price of oil will increase if Saudi Arabia reduces its level of production.

12. The price of oil will increase only if Saudi Arabia reduces its level of production.

13. Monaco is on the Mediterranean, but Greece and Italy are not both on the Mediterranean.

14. Monaco is on the Mediterranean, but Greece and Italy are both not on the Mediterranean.

15. It is not the case that neither Greece nor Italy is on the Mediterranean.

16. If Argentina defaults, then Poland and Brazil will default, and if Poland, Argentina, and Brazil default, Citicorp may go bankrupt.

17. If the president visits Brazil and Chile but not Argentina, then he will insult a friendly nation.

18. Moscow will try to host the Winter Olympics if Toronto doesn't build a new stadium or can't renovate their old stadium.

19. If the sun is a yellow star, then it has an atmospheric temperature of about 11,000 degrees but if it is an orange star, then it has an atmospheric temperature of about 7,500 degrees.

20. If Capella is a white or a blue-white star, then hydrogen or helium predominates.

B. Identify the rule of inference (if there is one) by which the conclusion follows from the premises in the following arguments.

1. $Ba \ \& \ Ca$
    $\therefore Ca$

2. Aa
    $\therefore Aa \lor Ba$

3. $Fa \Rightarrow Ga$
    Fa
    $\therefore Ga$

4. $Ha \Rightarrow Ib$
    $-Ib$
    $\therefore -Ha$

5. *(Ba & Ca) & Db*
    ∴*(Ca & Ba) & Db*

6. *(Ba & Ca) & Db*
    ∴ *Ba & (Ca & Db)*

7. *–(Fc & Gd)*
    ∴ *–Fc* ∨ *–Gd*

8. *Je & (Ke* ∨ *Le)*
    ∴ *(Je & Ke)* ∨ *(Je & Le)*

9. *Fa & Ga*
    Fb & Gc
    ∴ *(Fa & Ga) & (Fb & Gc)*

10. *(Fa & Ga)* ∨ *Hb*
    –(Fa & Ga)
    ∴ *Hb*

11. *(Ma* ∨ *Na)* ⇒ *–Kb*
    Ma ∨ *Na*
    ∴ *–Kb*

12. *Ab* ∨ *Bd*
    –Bd ∨ *Ce*
    ∴ *Ab* ∨ *Ce*

13. *Ba*
    ∴ *Ba* ∨ *c*

14. *Ba*
    ∴ *B*

15. *–(Fj* ∨ *Gk)*
    ∴ *–Fj & –Gk*

16. *–Fj* ∨ *– –Gk*
    ∴ *–Fj* ∨ *Gk*

17. *Fa*
    ∴ *Fa* ∨ *Fa*

18. *Fa*
    ∴ *Fa* ∨ *Fb*

19. *Fa*
    ∴ *Fa & Fa*

20. *Fa*
    ∴ *Fa & Fb*

C. Prove the validity of the following arguments, using the rules of propositional logic.

1. *Ba & Ca*
    –(Ba & Ca) ∨ *(Bb & Cb)*
    ∴ *Bb*

2. *–Aa*
    ∴ *–(Aa & Ba)*

3. *Fc*
    ∴ *(Fc* ∨ *Gc) & (Fc* ∨ *–Gc)*

4. *Ma* ∨ *Mb*
    Ma ∨ *Mc*
    ∴ *Ma* ∨ *(Mb & Mc)*

5. *(Ka* ∨ *Lb)* ⇒*Mc*
    Ka & La
    ∴*Mc*

6. *– (Cj* ∨ *Ck)*
    ∴ *–Cj*

7. *–Ab* ∨ *(–Bb* ∨ *Cb)*
    –Cb
    ∴*–(Ab & Bb)*

8. *(Ea* ∨ *Fa)* ⇒ *Eb*
    –Eb
    ∴ *–Fa*

9. *–Tm* ∨ *Vm*
    –(Um ∨ *Vm)*
    ∴ *–Tm*

10. *Xa* ∨ *(Ya* ∨ *Aa)*
    –Xa & (Za ∨ *–Aa)*
    ∴ *Ya* ∨ *Za*

11. –(*Fb* ∨ *Fc*)
    ∴ –(*Fc* & *Fb*)

12. (*Fa* ∨ *Ga*) ⇒ (*Hb* & *Hc*)
    Ga ∨ (*Ea* & *Fa*)
    ∴*Hb*

13. *Ma* ∨ *Mb*
    –(*Mb* & *Nb*)
    Nb ∨ *Na*
    ∴ *Ma* ∨ *Na*

14. (*Ab* ∨ *Ba*) ⇒ (*Cc* & *Dc*)
    –(*Cc* ∨ *Db*)
    ∴ –*Ab*

9.2 General Statements

Statement Functions. We have analyzed singular statements and devised an efficient method of symbolizing them. We turn next to general statements. But first we have to introduce some new concepts. The same predicate can appear in a singular statement with any singular term as subject. Consider for example:

> *Cb:* Bach was a composer.
> *Cc:* Chopin was a composer
> *Cd:* Debussy was a composer.

In order to represent the common structure of these statements, we use the letter *x*, which will function as an ***individual variable***, holding a place for any individual constant.

> *Cx: x* was a composer.

In Chapter 5, we used *s* as an individual variable, to emphasize that it stood for the subject of a categorical proposition. In quantification theory, however, it is customary to use *x*, by analogy with algebra. We will *never* use *x* as an individual constant. In §9.9, when relational statements like "John loves Mary" are analyzed in greater depth, it will be necessary to introduce other individual variables. But until then, *x* will be our only individual variable.

It would be natural at this point to introduce the notion of a predicate variable. But we can achieve greater precision and generality by using a more complex type of variable. It will be evident that *Cx* is a statement *form,* three of whose substitution instances are above. Such a statement form, from which statements result when individual constants are substituted for variables, is called a ***statement function***. Statement functions contain predicate constants and individual variables. Some statement functions are simple, like *Cx*. But others are compound, being composed of other statement functions, like *Cx* ∨ –*Cx*, *Bx* & *Cx*, *Ax* ⇒ *Cx*, and –[(*Ax* & *Bx*) ⇒ *Cx*]. *Cx* ∨ –*Cx* is a statement function because statements result when constants replace the individual variable *x*. Thus when *a* is substituted for *x* the result is *Ca* ∨ –*Ca*: when *b* is substituted for *x*, the result is *Cb* ∨ –*Cb*; and so on. *Cx* ∨ –*Cx* is a compound statement function because it is composed of the statement functions *Cx* and –*Cx*. A formula like *Cx* ∨ *Ca* also counts as a compound statement function. For when constants are substituted for the individual variable *x*, statements like *Ca* ∨ *Ca*, *Cb* ∨ *Ca,* and *Cc* ∨ *Ca* result. *Cx* ∨ *Ca* is compound, because one of its components is the statement function *Cx*. We shall use *Px* (and occasionally *Mx* and *Sx*) as a ***statement function variable***, which stands for *any* statement function in which *x* is the only variable. Thus *Px* stands for *Ax*, *Bx*, *Cx*, *Cx* ∨ –*Cx*, *Bx* & *Cx*, *Ax* ⇒ *Cx*, –[(*Ax* & *Bx*) ⇒ *Cx*], *Cx* ∨ *Ca*, and so on.

The Universal and Existential Quantifiers. Let us examine a simple type of general statement, consisting of "everything" followed by a simple predicate, such as:

Everything is blue.

You might expect us to symbolize this by symbolizing the predicate and the quantifier, and putting the quantifier symbol next to the predicate constant where an individual constant would normally go. Unfortunately, this natural procedure cannot be generalized to more complex general statements, as we will see later. Instead, we symbolize "Everything is blue" by symbolizing the following:

Everything is such that it is blue.

Clearly, this is just a long–winded way of saying that everything is blue. We abbreviate "Everything is such that" by using the symbol ∀, called the ***universal quantifier***. We represent the pronoun "it," when it refers back to a quantifier, with the symbol x. This gives us:

∀Bx

The expression ∀Bx should be read "Everything is such that it is B," or more simply "Everything is B." "All things are B" is another possible reading. We shall refer to x as *the universal quantification of the statement function Bx*. A statement function is a statement form whose substitution instances are obtained by substituting individual constants for variables. The universal quantification of any statement function asserts that *every* substitution instance of the statement function is true. Thus ∀Bx asserts that Ba is true *and* Bb is true and Bc is true and so on for all individuals. Hence ∀Bx is often read "For all (or every) x, Bx" or "Given any x, Bx." The universal quantifier ∀ is an upside-down "A" for "All." We put the letter in an unusual orientation so that it will not be confused with a predicate constant.

Consider next:

Something is blue.

Again, we symbolize this indirectly, by symbolizing:

Something is such that it is blue.

We will abbreviate "Something is such that" with the symbol ∃ (for "Exists"), called the ***existential quantifier***. Symbolizing "it is blue" as Bx gives us:

∃Bx

This may be read "Something is such that it is B," or more simply "Something is B." "There exists something such that it is B" or "There exists a B" are alternative readings. ∃Bx is *the existential quantification of the statement function Bx*. The existential quantification of any statement function asserts that *some* substitution instance of the statement function is true, which means that there exists at least one true substitution instance. Thus ∃Bx asserts that Ba is true *or* Bb is true or Bc is true, and so on for all individuals. Hence ∃Bx is often read "For some x, Bx"" or "There exists an x such that Ba."

We have often noted that statements like "Everything is not blue" are ambiguous, meaning either "Everything is nonblue," or more commonly "Not everything is blue." Both meanings can be expressed unambiguously in our new notation. The statement function "x is nonblue" would be abbreviated –Bx. So "Everything is nonblue" would be symbolized ∀–Bx, which says that everything is such that it is not B, or in other words, that –Bx is true for every individual. "Not everything is blue," on the other hand, is simply the negation of "Everything is blue," and so would be symbolized –∀Bx.

In Chapters 5 and 6 we had a third quantifier, as in the following negative universal statement:

Nothing is blue.

Rather than introduce a special symbol meaning "Nothing is such that," it is customary in quantification theory to view this statement as equivalent to its obverse:

> Everything is nonblue.

As discussed in the previous paragraph, this would be symbolized:

$$\forall -Bx$$

You may, if you like, treat $\forall-$ as a unit, reading it "Nothing is such that" or simply "Nothing." Finally, the particular negative statement "Something is not blue," or equivalently its obverse "Something is nonblue," should be symbolized $\exists -Bx$.

Statements of the form "Everything is P," "Nothing is P," "Something is P," and "Something is not P" can be viewed as special Aristotelian categoricals whose subject term is "thing," that most general of all terms applying to absolutely everything in existence. We never have to worry about the presuppositions of such statements: as long as we are around contemplating propositions, there are some things. We symbolize both universal propositions with the universal quantifier, both particular propositions with the existential quantifier. We symbolize negative propositions by applying the quantifier to a negation. All the relationships of the Aristotelian square of opposition hold (see Figure 9-1).

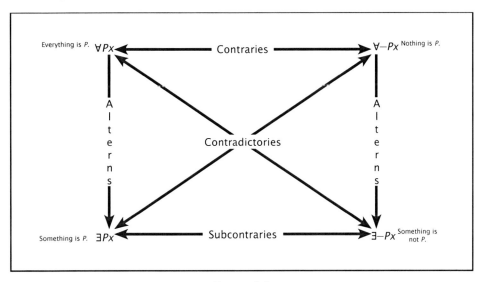

FIGURE 9-1

$\forall Px$ and $\forall-Px$ are contraries. Consequently, at most one is true. $\exists Px$ and $\exists-Px$, on the other hand, are subcontraries, so at least one is true. $\forall Px$ and $\exists Px$ are alterns, so if $\forall Px$ is true then $\exists Px$ must be true too. Similarly $\forall-Px$ and $\exists-Px$, are alterns: if $\forall-Px$ is true, then $\exists-Px$ is true.

$\forall Px$ and $\exists-Px$ are contradictories, so one must be true, the other false. Since two statements are contradictory if one denies what the other affirms, the following equivalences can be read off the square of opposition:

$$\forall Px = -\exists -Px$$
$$\exists -Px = -\forall Px$$

The first equivalence tells us that "Everything is blue" is equivalent to "It is not the case that something is not blue." The second says that "Something is not blue" is equivalent to "Not everything is blue." $\forall-Px$ and $\exists Px$ are also contradictory, so the following equivalences hold as well:

$$\forall -Px = -\exists Px$$
$$\exists Px = -\forall -Px$$

"Nothing is blue" (or "Everything is nonblue") is equivalent to "It is not the case that something is blue." And "Something is blue" is equivalent to "It is not the case that nothing is blue" (or "Not everything is nonblue"). These four equivalences are referred to collectively as the rules of ***quantifier negation***, since they tell us how to exchange quantifiers and make compensating changes with negations. The rules also show that we could theoretically get by with just one quantifier. If we chose the universal quantifier, we could symbolize "Something" as $-\forall-$. If we chose the existential quantifier, we could symbolize "Everything" as $-\exists-$.

We have been illustrating the use of quantifiers in connection with simple statement functions and their negations. But quantifiers can be used with statement functions of any complexity. Thus "Everything either is or is not blue" would be symbolized $\forall (Bx \lor -Bx)$. "Something is both a watch and a calculator" would be $\exists(Wx \ \& \ Cx)$. "Nothing is indestructible if it is either living or man–made" would be $\forall-[(Lx \lor Mx) \Rightarrow -Dx]$. The rules of quantifier negation hold, no matter how complex Px is.

In English, quantifiers behave in many respects like singular terms. There are crucial differences, however. For example, "The car either is or is not blue" is equivalent to "Either the car is blue or the car is not blue." Hence both can be symbolized $Bc \lor -Bc$. However, "Everything either is or is not blue," which is logically true, is not equivalent to "Either everything is blue or everything is not–blue," which is false. We symbolize the former $\forall(Bx \lor -Bx)$, which says that everything is such that it is either B or $-B$. We symbolize the latter $\forall Bx \lor \forall-Bx$, which says that either everything is such that it is B or everything is such that it is $-B$. We say that the quantifier *has within its scope* the entire disjunction $Bx \lor -Bx$ in $\forall(Bx \lor -Bx)$, whereas the first quantifier in $\forall Bx \lor \forall-Bx$ has within its scope only Bx. To be more explicit, $\forall Bx \lor \forall-Bx$ might be written out $\forall(Bx) \lor \forall(-Bx)$. But as with the negation sign, we economize on parentheses by stipulating that a quantifier applies to the smallest possible unit to its right.

In a quantified statement like $\forall(Bx \lor -Bx)$. we say that the two occurrences of the variable x are ***bound*** by the quantifier. In $\forall Bx \lor \forall-Bx$, on the other hand, the first occurrence of the bound variable x is bound by the first quantifier, while the second occurrence is bound by the second quantifier. When variables are not bound by quantifiers, they are said to be ***free***. In the statement form $Bx \lor -Bx$, both occurrences of x are free. A free variable is functioning as a genuine variable. It is being used to represent a form, and substitution instances of the form can be obtained by replacing the variable with any individual constant. Thus, $Bx \lor -Bx$ has substitution instances like $Ba \lor -Ba$, $Bb \lor -Bb$, and $Bc \lor -Bc$. Bound variables are not functioning as variables. $\forall(Bx \lor -Bx)$ is a *statement*, not a statement *form*. $\forall(Bx \lor -Bx)$ does not have any substitution instances at all. In particular, $\forall(Ba \lor -Ba)$, $\forall(Bb \lor -Bb)$, and $\forall(Bc \lor -Bc)$ cannot be obtained by substitution from $\forall(Bx \lor -Bx)$ and do not even make much sense. Whereas free variables are functioning as *blanks* that may be filled by individual constants, bound variables are functioning as *pronouns* that refer back to the quantifiers that bind them. The two bound variables in $\forall(Bx \lor -Bx)$ can be regarded as referring back to the quantifier in the same way the two "it's" in "Everything is such that it is blue or it is not blue" refer back to "Everything."

Venn Categoricals. The Venn categoricals we discussed in Chapter 6 are quantified statements with conjunctive predicates. Thus "Nothing is a man and a reptile" would be symbolized $\forall -(Mx \ \& \ Rx)$, while "Nothing is a man and not an animal" would be symbolized $\forall -(Mx \ \& \ -Ax)$. Similarly, "Something is a man and a genius" would be symbolized $\exists(Mx \ \& \ Gx)$, while "Something is a man and not a genius" would be $\exists(Mx \ \& \ -Gx)$. In general, we have the following:

A*	Nothing is *S* and not *P*	= ∀–(*Sx* & –*Px*)
E*	Nothing is *S* and *P*	= ∀–(*Sx* & *Px*)
I*	Something is *S* and *P*	= ∃(*Sx* & *Px*)
O*	Something is *S* and not *P*	= ∃(*Sx* & –*Px*)

When the rules of replacement are considered, it will be evident that conversion is valid for **E*** and **I*** but not for **A*** and **O*** propositions. For example, ∀–(*Px* & *Sx*) is the converse of ∀ –(*Sx* & *Px*); these are equivalent by commutation. In contrast, ∀–(*Sx* & –*Px*) is not equivalent to its converse ∀–(*Px* & –*Sx*) by any rule. Similarly, contraposition is valid for **A*** and **O*** but not for **E*** and **I*** propositions. Thus ∀– (*Sx* & –*Px*) is equivalent to its contrapositive ∀–(–*Px* & – –*Sx*) by commutation and double negation. The validity of obversion is reflected in our practice of symbolizing both "not" and "non" by the negative sign –. Thus both "Nothing is an *S* and not a *P*" and its obverse "Nothing is an *S* and a non–*P*" would be symbolized ∀–(*Sx* & –*Px*).

It will also be evident that the Venn square of opposition is weaker than the Aristotelian square because the predicates are not the same in all four *Venn* categoricals (see Figure 9–2).

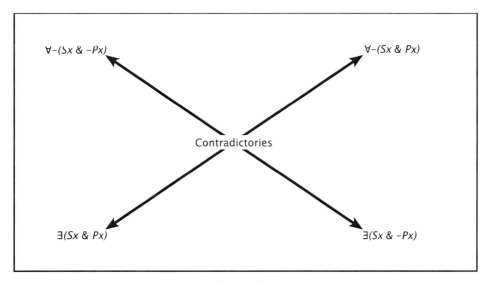

FIGURE 9-2

Opposing **A*** and **I*** propositions are not alterns. For while ∀ (*Sx* & –*Px*) is equivalent to ∀ (–*Sx* ∨ *Px*) by De Morgan's rules, and ∀ (–*Sx* ∨ *Px*) does entail ∃(–*Sx* ∨ *Px*) by subalternation, it is evident that ∃(–*Sx* ∨ *Px*) does not imply ∃(*Sx* & *Px*). Similar reasoning shows that opposing **E*** and **O*** propositions are not alterns either. Opposing **A*** and **E*** propositions are not contrary, because both will be true when ∀–*Sx* ("Nothing is an *S*") is true. Opposing **I*** and **O*** propositions are not subcontrary, because both will be false when ∀–*Sx* is true. Opposing **A*** and **O*** propositions are contradictory, however, as are opposing **E*** and **I*** propositions. These contradictions follow from the rules of quantifier negation, as can be seen by viewing the formulas in parentheses after the quantifiers as units—that is, as conjunctive statement functions. The **A*** and the **O*** propositions involve the same conjunction (*Sx* & –*Px*), while the **E*** and the **I*** propositions share a different conjunction (*Sx* & *Px*).

Compounds of General Statements. General statements as well as singular statements may be components of compound statements. We have already looked at some negations of general statements—namely: $-\forall Bx$ ("Not everything is blue"), and $-\exists(Mx \& Rx)$ ("It is not the case that something is both a man and a reptile"). We have also looked at a disjunction of general statements: $\forall Bx \lor \forall -Bx$ ("Either everything is blue or everything is not blue"). There are conjunctions of general statements: $\exists Cx \& \exists Dx$ ("Something is a cat and something is a dog") and conditionals involving them: $\forall Bx \Rightarrow \exists Dx$ ("If everything is blue, then something is blue"). And there are mixed compounds involving both general and singular statements, such as: $\forall Bx \Rightarrow Bc$ ("If everything is blue, then my car is blue") and $Bc \Rightarrow \exists Bx$ ("If my car is blue, then something is blue").

Glossary

Individual variable: a symbol like x, which stands for any individual constant in a statement form.

Statement functions: statement forms like Cx, $-Bx$, and $Cx \& -Bx$, from which statements result when individual constants are substituted for individual variables.

Statement function variables: compound symbols like Px, which stand for any statement function in which x is the only free variable.

Universal quantifier: a symbol like $\forall$, abbreviating "Everything is such that," which combines with a statement function to form a statement saying that every substitution instance of the statement function is true.

Existential quantifier: a symbol like $\exists$, abbreviating "Something is such that," which combines with a statement function to form a statement saying that some substitution instance of the statement function is true.

Bound variable: a variable within the scope of a quantifier, which functions as a pronoun referring back to that quantifier.

Free variable: a variable that is not within the scope of a quantifier, and which functions as a genuine variable holding a place where any individual constant may go.

Quantifier negation: a rule of replacement based on the following equivalences: $\forall Px = -\exists -Px$, $-\forall Px = \exists -Px$, $\forall -Px = -\exists Px$, and $-\forall -Px = \exists Px$.

Exercises

Symbolize the following statements, using quantifiers and statement functions.

1. Everything is a material object.
2. Nothing is a nonmaterial object.
3. There is an honest politician.
4. Not everything is important.
5. Something is an aggressive, bloodthirsty predator.
6. Nothing is a skunk and not a mammal.
7. Everything is either a rodent or a nonmouse.

8. Something is a mouse and a rodent.

9. Something is an even–toed hoofed mammal and a hippopotamus.

10. Not everything is a plant or an animal.

11. It is not the case that something is wrong.

12. Either everything is material, or something is immaterial.

13. Everything is either material or immaterial.

14. If anything is a rodent, then it is a mammal.

15. If everything is alive, then the moon is alive.

16. If the moon is not alive, then something is not alive.

17. If anything is wrong, then John will help.

18. If something is wrong, then John will help.

19. If something is evil, then not everything is good.

20. If anything is an apple or an orange, then it is delicious and nutritious.

21. Either the president's policies will work, or nothing will work.

22. Everything was tried, but nothing worked.

23. The house was unlocked, but nothing was taken.

24. An object is a hexagon if, and only if, it is a six-sided polygon.

25. Something is a square if and only if it is a four-sided equilateral polygon.

9.3 Quantifier Negation

Now that we have an economical and general method of symbolizing categorical propositions, we can extend the system of deduction developed for propositional logic to cover syllogistic logic. Quantification theory consists of the rules of propositional logic together with five more rules dealing with the logical properties of quantifiers. Our first additional rule will be quantifier negation, which formulates the fact that propositions at opposite corners of the square of opposition are contradictory. Quantifier negation is a rule of replacement, since it allows us to interchange four pairs of logically equivalent expressions wherever they occur.

Quantifier Negation (QN)
Any two statements equivalent by one of the following rules may replace each other wherever they occur.

$$\forall Px = {-}\exists{-}Px$$
$$-\forall Px = \exists{-}Px$$
$$\forall{-}Px = {-}\exists Px$$
$$-\forall{-}Px = \exists Px$$

Bear in mind that Px stands for any statement function here, no matter how complex. To illustrate how quantifier negation operates, consider the following argument:

> If John is the mechanic, then everything will work properly. Something will not work properly. Therefore John is not the mechanic.

We can symbolize the argument and prove it valid as follows:

$$
\begin{array}{lll}
1. & Mj \Rightarrow \forall Wx & \\
2. & \exists -Wx /\therefore\ -Mj & \\
3. & -\forall Wx & \text{2 QN} \\
4. & -Mj & \text{1,3 MT}
\end{array}
$$

Note that step 3 is essential. Modus tollens does not apply directly to lines 1 and 2.

The rules of replacement apply anywhere, to parts of lines as well as whole lines. This means that the original rules of replacement (double negation, commutation, and so on) apply even within the scope of a quantifier. Thus $\exists(Cx\ \&\ Ax)$ can be inferred from $\exists(Ax\ \&\ Cx)$ by commutation. And $\forall(-Mx \lor Ax)$ can be inferred from $\forall -(Mx\ \&\ -Ax)$ by De Morgan's rules. In contrast, the one–way rules of inference (modus ponens, addition, and so on) apply only to whole lines, and so cannot be applied within the scope of a quantifier. Consequently, we cannot infer $\exists Bx$ from $\exists(Ax \lor Bx)$ and $\exists -Ax$ by disjunctive syllogism, for example. This is good, for the argument "Something is in box A or box B; something is not in box A; hence something is in box B" is invalid. Suppose that box A contains a hat, and that box B is empty. The first premise is then true; a hat is in box A, and therefore in box A or B. The second premise is also true, because lots of things other than the hat, such as a cat, are not in box A. Nevertheless, the conclusion is false: box B is empty.

It is not theoretically necessary to include all four QN rules in any system of deduction. Any one of the equivalences suffices, along with double negation. Suppose we are given the first QN equivalence: $\forall Px = -\exists -Px$. And suppose $-\forall Px$ appears in a proof. We could replace $-\forall Px$ with $\exists -Px$ in two steps. For $-\forall Px$ is equivalent to $--\exists -Px$ by the given QN rule. And $--\exists -Px$ is equivalent to $\exists -Px$ by double negation. But as usual, we shall tolerate redundancy in order to save steps in our deductions.

Exercises

A. Identify the rule of inference (if there is one) by which the conclusions of the following arguments follow from the premises.

1. $\exists Fx \lor \exists -Fx$
    $\therefore\ \exists Fx \lor -\forall Fx$

2. $-(\exists Fx\ \&\ \exists -Fx)$
    $\therefore\ -\exists Fx \lor -\exists -Fx$

3. $-\exists Fx \lor -\exists -Fx$
    $\therefore\ -\exists Fx \lor \forall Fx$

4. $-\exists Fx \lor \forall Fx$
    $-\forall Fx$
    $\therefore\ -\exists Fx$

5. $\forall Fx \Rightarrow \exists Fx$
    $\forall Fx$
    $\therefore \exists Fx$

6. $\forall(Fx \Rightarrow Gx)$
    $\forall Fx$
    $\therefore\ \forall Gx$

7. $\exists Fx\ \&\ \exists Gx$
    $\therefore \exists Fx$

8. $\exists(Fx\ \&\ Gx)$
    $\therefore\ \exists Fx$

9. $\forall Fx$
    $\therefore \forall Fx \lor Ga$

10. $\forall Fx$
    $\therefore \forall (Fx \lor Ga)$

11. $\forall -(Fx \& Gx)$
    $\therefore \forall (-Fx \lor -Gx)$

12. $\forall -(Fx \& Gx)$
    $\therefore --\forall -(Fx \& Gx)$

13. $\forall Fx \& (\forall Gx \lor \forall Hx)$
    $\therefore (\forall Fx \& \forall Gx) \lor (\forall Fx \& \forall Hx)$

14. $\forall [Fx \& (Gx \lor Hx)]$
    $\therefore \forall [(Fx \& Gx) \lor (Fx \& Hx)]$

15. $\forall Fx$
    $\forall Gx$
    $\therefore \forall Fx \& \forall Gx$

16. $\forall Fx$
    $\forall Gx$
    $\therefore \forall (Fx \& Gx)$

17. $-(\exists Fx \Rightarrow -\forall Gx)$
    $\therefore -(\exists Fx \Rightarrow \exists -Gx)$

18. $-(\exists Fx \Rightarrow -\forall Gx)$
    $\therefore \forall -Fx \Rightarrow -\forall Gx$

19. $-\forall -Fx$
    $\therefore \forall Fx$

20. $-\forall Gx$
    $\therefore -\exists Gx$

21. $\forall Fx \lor \exists Gx$
    $-\exists Gx \lor \forall -Gx$
    $\therefore \forall Fx \lor \forall -Gx$

22. $\forall (Mx \lor Nx)$
    $\forall (-Nx \lor Ox)$
    $\therefore \forall (Mx \lor Ox)$

B. Prove the validity of the following arguments by the method of deduction.

1. $-\forall (-Ax \lor Bx)$
    $\therefore \exists (Ax \& -Bx)$

2. $-\exists (Mx \lor Nx)$
    $\therefore \forall (-Mx \& -Nx)$

3. $-(\forall Mx \lor \forall -Mx)$
    $\therefore \exists -Mx \& \exists Mx$

4. $-\forall Fx$
    $\therefore -(\forall Fx \& \forall Gx)$

5. $\exists (Ix \& -Jx)$
    $\therefore -\forall (-Ix \lor Jx)$

6. $-\forall -(-Ux \& -Vx)$
    $\therefore \exists -(Vx \lor Ux)$

7. $-\exists [Fx \& (Gx \lor Hx)]$
    $\therefore \forall [(-Fx \lor -Gx) \& (-Fx \lor -Hx)]$

8. $Aa \& Ba$
    $Aa \Rightarrow (\exists Ax \& \exists Cx)$
    $\therefore \exists Cx$

9. $\forall [-Ax \lor (-Bx \& -Cx)]$
    $\therefore -\exists [(Ax \& Bx) \lor (Ax \& Cx)]$

10. $\exists Ax \lor \exists Bx$
    $\exists -Cx \lor \exists Dx$
    $-\exists Bx \lor -\exists Dx$
    $\therefore \exists Ax \lor -\forall Cx$

11. Aa
    $(Aa \lor Ab) \Rightarrow \exists Ax$
    $\therefore -\forall -Ax$

12. $(Aa \lor Ab) \Rightarrow \exists Cx$
    $Ab \Rightarrow -Ca$
    $-Aa \& Ab$
    $\therefore \exists Cx \& -Ca$

13. $-\exists(Gx \mathbin{\&} -Hx)$
     $\forall(-Gx \lor Hx) \Rightarrow \exists (Sx \mathbin{\&} -Tx)$
     $\therefore -\forall(-Sx \lor Tx)$

14. $-(\exists Fx \mathbin{\&} \exists Gx)$
     $-(\forall Fx \lor \forall -Fx)$
     $\therefore \forall -Gx$

15. $-\forall Ex \lor \forall Fx$
     $-\forall Ex \lor \forall Gx$
     $-(\exists -Ex \lor \exists -Hx)$
     $\therefore \forall Gx \mathbin{\&} \forall Fx$

16. $(\forall Gx \lor \forall Fx) \Rightarrow -\exists -(Gx \lor Fx)$
     $\forall(Gx \lor Fx) \Rightarrow (Ge \mathbin{\&} Fe)$
     $-Ge$
     $\therefore -\forall Gx$

17. $\exists Cx \Rightarrow Ca$
     $\exists Dx \Rightarrow Da$
     $-(Ca \lor Da)$
     $\therefore \forall -Cx \mathbin{\&} \forall -Dx$

18. $\forall Cx \Rightarrow Ca$
     $\forall Dx \Rightarrow Da$
     $-(Ca \lor Da)$
     $\therefore -(\forall Cx \lor \forall Dx)$

C. Symbolize the following arguments, and then prove their validity using the method of deduction.

1. It is not the case that something is both a plant and an animal. Therefore, everything is either not a plant or not an animal.

2. It is not the case that either something is in box A or something is in box B. Therefore, nothing is in box A.

3. It is not the case that either everything is good or everything is evil. Therefore, either something is not good, or something is not evil.

4. Either the sky is blue or not everything is blue. Either grass is blue or not everything is blue. The sky and the grass are not both blue. Therefore, not everything is blue.

5. If everything is a unicorn, then something is as unicorn. Everything is a nonunicorn. Therefore, not everything is a unicorn.

6. Either nothing has a soul, or everything does. If it is not the case that something has a soul, then I do not have a soul. I do have a soul. So everything has a soul.

7. If either Mars or Venus has a circular orbit, then something has a circular orbit. Nothing has a circular orbit. So Mars does not have a circular orbit.

8. It is not the case that either everything is black or nothing is black. It is not the case that either everything is white or nothing is white. Therefore, something is white and something is not black.

9. If there is a god, then there is a perfect being. If there is a perfect being, then there is no evil. Something is evil. Therefore nothing is a god.

10. If there is an omnipotent being, then something is able to make a round square. If something is able to make a round square, then something can be contradictory. Nothing can be contradictory. Therefore, nothing is an omnipotent being.

9.4 Quantification Rules: UI and EG

Universal Instantiation and Existential Generalization. Suppose we wish to prove the validity of the argument: "If anything is human, then it is mortal. Alan is human. Therefore Alan is mortal."

$$1. \; \forall(Hx \Rightarrow Mx)$$
$$2. \; Ha \qquad\qquad /\therefore Ma$$

This argument seems to involve an application of modus ponens. But that rule applies only to whole lines, and so does not apply to the conditional embedded in premise 1. However, we can infer from premise 1 that if Alan is human, then he is mortal. Given that $Hx \Rightarrow Mx$ is true no matter what constant replaces x—which is what premise 1 says—we can infer $Ha \Rightarrow Ma$. Now from $Ha \Rightarrow Ma$ and Ha we can infer Ma by modus ponens

$$3. \; Ha \Rightarrow Ma \qquad\qquad 1. \; \text{UI}$$
$$4. \; Ma \qquad\qquad\qquad 2, 3 \; \text{MP}$$

In general, $\forall Px$ means that every substitution instance of Px is true. Consequently, given a statement of the form $\forall Px$, we can infer $Pa, Pb, Pc,$ and so on. This rule is known as ***universal instantiation,*** since it says that we can infer any instance of a universal generalization.

Consider now a **UUΛ*3** syllogism: "Mercury is a metal. Mercury is a liquid. Therefore something is both a metal and a liquid."

$$1. \; Mm$$
$$2. \; Lm \qquad\qquad /\therefore \exists(Mx \,\&\, Lx)$$

The two premises entail $Mm \,\&\, Lm$ by conjunction. But none of our previous rules enables us to get from $Mm \,\&\, Lm$ to $\exists(Mx \,\&\, Lx)$. This inference is clearly valid, however. $\exists(Mx \,\&\, Lx)$ is true as long as at least one substitution instance of $Mx \,\&\, Lx$ is true. And we have just such a substitution instance in $Mm \,\&\, Lm$.

$$3. \; Mm \,\&\, Lm \qquad\qquad 1,2 \; \text{Conj}$$
$$4. \; \exists(Mx \,\&\, Lx) \qquad\qquad 3 \; \text{EG}$$

In general, we can infer $\exists Px$ from any substitution instance of Px. This rule is known as ***existential generalization.*** Statements of the form "Something is P" are not commonly called "generalizations," so the name is somewhat misleading. But since the rule enables us to infer one sort of general statement from a singular statement, its name is not totally inappropriate.

Universal instantiation and existential generalization are two of four rules of inference known as ***quantification rules,*** since they formulate inferences that are possible between quantifications of statement functions and their substitution instances. Universal instantiation allows us to infer any substitution instance of Px from the universal quantification of Px. Existential generalization allows us to infer the existential quantification of Px from any substitution instance of Px.

Quantification Rules Ui And Eg

Universal Instantiation (UI): From ∀*Px*, infer any substitution instance of *Px* in which *x* is replaced by any constant *s*.

$$∀Px$$

$$∴ Ps$$

Existential Generalization (EG): From any substitution instance of *Px* in which *x* replaced by any constant *s*, infer ∃*Px*.

$$Ps$$

$$∴∃Px$$

In the argument forms accompanying UI and EG, *Ps* stands for the result of replacing *x* with *s* in the statement function quantified in a line of the form ∀*Px* or ∃*Px*; *s* may be *any* constant, and *Px* may be *any* statement function. Thus from ∀(*Fx* ∨ −*Gx*), we can infer *Fa* ∨ −*Ga*, *Fb* ∨ −*Gb*, and *Fc* ∨ −*Gc* by UI. From *Fa* ∨ −*Ga*, *Fb* ∨ −*Gb*, or *Fc* ∨ −*Gc*, we can infer ∃(*Fx* ∨ −*Gx*) by EG.

While the rules of quantifier negation are rules of replacement, which apply to parts of lines as well as whole lines, the quantification rules are one–way rules, and so apply to whole lines only. For example, we cannot use UI to go from ∀*Mx* ⇒ ∀*Ax* ("If everything is a man, then everything is an animal") to *Mp* ⇒ ∀*Ax* ("If the president is a man, then everything is an animal"). Since the first quantifier in ∀*Mx* ⇒ ∀*Ax* applies only to *Mx*, ∀*Mx* ⇒ ∀*Ax* does not have the form ∀*Px*, and so UI does not apply. We could, in contrast, use UI to go from ∀(*Mx* ⇒ ∀*Ax*) ("If anything is a man, then everything is an animal") to *Mp* ⇒ ∀*Ax*. For ∀(*Mx* ⇒ ∀*Ax*) does have the form ∀*Px*: *Px* in this case is the statement function *Mx* ⇒ ∀*Ax*, whose substitution instances include *Ma* ⇒ ∀*Ax* and *Mb* ⇒ ∀*Ax* as well as *Mp* ⇒ ∀*Ax*. Note especially that universal instantiation cannot be applied to negations of quantified statements. For example, from −∀*Mx* ("Not everything is a man"), we cannot infer −*Mp* ("The president is not a man") by universal instantiation.

The Square of Opposition. Using both universal instantiation and existential generalization, we can prove the validity of subalternation for quantified statements:

1. ∀*Px*	/∴∃*Px*
2. *Pa*	1 UI
3. ∃*Px*	2 EG

Indeed, it is useful to think of ∀*Px*, *Ps*, and ∃*Px* as differing only in quantity (universal, singular, and particular, respectively), and to insert *Ps* between the alterns in the square of opposition (see Figure 9–3).

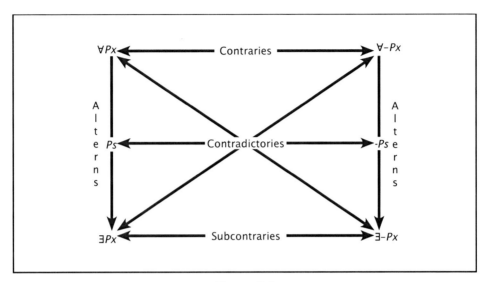

FIGURE 9-3

Using all three of our new rules, we can show that $\exists Px$ and $\exists -Px$ are subcontraries. To show that one of these must be true, it suffices to show that the truth of one follows from the falsity of the other. We can show that if $\exists Px$ is not true, then $\exists -Px$ must be true as follows:

1. $-\exists Px$	$/\therefore \exists -Px$
2. $\forall -Px$	1 QN
3. $-Pa$	2 UI
4. $\exists -Px$	3 EG

As an exercise, try deriving $\exists Px$ from $-\exists -Px$ in a similar fashion. We can also show that $\forall Px$ and $\forall -Px$ are contraries, by deducing $-\forall -Px$ from $\forall Px$:

1. $\forall Px$	$/\therefore -\forall -Px$
2. Pa	1 UI
3. $\exists Px$	2 EG
4. $-\forall -Px$	3 QN

$-\forall Px$ can be derived from $\forall -Px$ just as easily, as you should verify for yourself.

Singular Categorical Syllogism. The rule called singular categorical syllogism in Chapter 5 contained two syllogisms involving singular propositions, **AUU1** and **UUI3**. Universal instantiation is essentially the special case of the **AUU1** syllogism in which the middle term is "thing." Existential generalization similarly represents the **UUI3** syllogism in which the minor term is "thing." To see this, think of "s is a thing" as an obvious suppressed premise. Then UI and EG become:

Everything is P.	s is P.
(s is a thing.)	(s is a thing.)
$\therefore$ s is P.	$\therefore$ Something is P.

Given UI and EG, however, we can prove the validity of *all* **AUU1** and **UUI3** syllogisms and their Venn transforms. We proved above the validity of the **UUI*3** syllogism "Mercury is a metal, mercury is a liquid, therefore something is both a metal and a liquid." Consider now an **A*UU1** syllogism: "Nothing is a man and not an animal. The president is a man. Therefore, the president is an animal." We can symbolize the argument and prove its validity as follows:

    1. ∀ –(Mx & –Ax)
    2. Mp   /∴ Ap
    3. –(Mp & –Ap)   1 UI
    4. –Mp ∨ Ap   3 DM
    5. Ap   2,4 DS

We will consider arguments involving Aristotelian categoricals in a later section.

Glossary

Quantification rules: the rules known as universal instantiation, existential generalization, existential instantiation, and universal generalization, which specify the inferences possible between quantifications of a statement function and substitution instances of that function.

Universal instantiation (UI): the rule that from a statement of the form ∀Px, you can infer any substitution instance of Px in which x is replaced by any constant s.

Existential generalization (EG): the rule that from any substitution instance of a statement function Px in which x is replaced by any constant s, you can infer ∃Px.

Exercises

A. Identify the rule of inference (if there is one) by which the conclusions of the arguments below follow from the premises.

1. ∀(–Fx ∨ Gx)   2. –Fa ∨ Ga
    ∴ –Fa ∨ Ga   ∴ ∃(–Fx ∨ Gx)

3. ∀(–Kx & Jx)   4. ∀ –Kx & ∀Jx
    ∴ –Kb & Jb   ∴ –Kb & Jb

5. –Kb & Jb   6. –Kb & Jb
    ∴ ∃(–Kx & Jx)   ∴ ∃ –Kx & ∃Jx

7. ∀(Cx ∨ Dx)   8. Ci ⇒ ∃Cx
    –Ci   Ci
    ∴ Di   ∴ ∃Cx

9. ∀[Lx ∨ (Mx & Nx)]   10. La ∨ (Ma & Na)
    ∴ La ∨ (Mb & Nb)   ∴ ∃[Lx ∨ (Ma & Na)]

11. –∀(Qx ⇒ Rx)   12. –∀(Qx ⇒ Rx)
    ∴ –(Qa ⇒ Ra)   ∴ ∃ –(Qx ⇒ Rx)

13. ∀(Cx ∨ Dx)   14. Ca ∨ Da
    ∴ ∀(Ca ∨ Da)   ∴ ∃ (Ca ∨ Da)

15. ∀ –{–[(Ax & Bx) ⇒ Cx] ∨ [Cx ⇒ (Ax ∨ Bx)]} 16. ∀[Mx ∨ (Qx & Rx)] ⇒ [Ma ∨ (Qa & Ra)]
    ∴ –{–[(Aj & Bj) ⇒ Cj] ∨ [Cj ⇒ (Aj & Bj)]}   ∴[Ma ∨ (Qa & Ra)] ⇒ ∃[Mx ∨ (Qx & Rx)]

B. Prove the validity of the following arguments.

1. $\forall(Fx \vee Gx)$
    $-Fa$
    $\therefore Ga$

2. Rd
    $\therefore \exists(Qx \vee Rx)$

3. $Fa \Rightarrow Ga$
    $\forall Fx$
    $\therefore \exists Gx$

4. $\forall[Fx \& (Gx \vee Hx)]$
    $\therefore \exists[(Fx \& Gx) \vee (Fx \& Hx)]$

5. $\forall(Mx \vee Nx)$
    $\therefore -\forall-(Mx \vee Nx)$

6. $\forall(Ax \Rightarrow Bx)$
    $\forall Ax$
    $\therefore Bk$

7. $\exists Gx \Rightarrow \exists(Hx \& Ix)$
    $\forall(Gx \& Jx)$
    $\therefore \exists(Hx \& Ix)$

8. $\forall(Rx \vee -Cx)$
    Fa
    $\therefore \exists[(Fx \& Rx) \vee (Fx \& -Cx)]$

9. $-\exists(Mx \& -Nx)$
    Ma
    $\therefore Na$

10. $\forall(Bx \vee Cx)$
    $\forall -Cx$
    $\therefore \exists Bx$

C. Symbolize the following arguments, and then prove their validity.

1. If anything is a terrier, then it is a dog. Morris is not a dog. Therefore, Morris is not a terrier.

2. If anything is a Buick, then it was made by General Motors. If anything is a Skylark, then it is a Buick. John's car is a Skylark. Therefore, John's car was made by General Motors.

3. Nothing is gold and not soluble in aqua regia. This ring is not soluble in aqua regia. Therefore, it is not gold.

4. If anything is a chimpanzee, then it is a primate. Both Washoe and Gua are chimps. Therefore, Washoe and Gua are primates.

5. Nothing is both liquid and solid. This material is liquid or it is not mercury. It is solid or it is not aluminum. Therefore, something is not both mercury and aluminum.

6. If something is in box A, and something is in box B, then not everything is in box C. The marble is in box A, and the shell is in box B. Therefore, not everything is in box C.

7. If everything is a material object, then everything has a gravitational field. Everything is a material object. Therefore, the sun and the moon have a gravitational field.

8. Everything has the body of a horse or it is not a centaur. Everything has the head and torso of a man or it is not a centaur. Nothing has both the body of a horse and the head and torso of man. Therefore, not everything is a centaur.

9. If one files a separate return and has an itemizing spouse, then one must also itemize. One files a separate return unless one files a joint return. John is not filing a joint return. He does have an itemizing spouse, so John must itemize.

10. If there is a god, then there is a perfect being. If there is a perfect being, then nothing is evil. God is a god. Therefore, the Holocaust was not evil.

D. Prove the validity of the following arguments.

1. $\forall(Ax \Rightarrow Bx)$
   $\forall Cx \; \& \; \forall Ax$
   $\therefore Bn$

2. $\forall Fx \Rightarrow \exists Gx$
   $\exists Gx \Rightarrow \forall Hx$
   $- Ha$
   $\therefore -\forall Fx$

3. $\exists Fx \Rightarrow \exists Rx$
   $\exists Rx \Rightarrow \exists Gx$
   $\forall Fx$
   $\therefore \exists Gx$

4. $\forall(-Mx \lor -Rx)$
   $Rc \lor Vc$
   $\forall Mx$
   $\therefore \exists Vx$

5. $\forall(Ax \; \& \; Bx) \Rightarrow \exists Cx$
   $(Ka \lor Kb) \Rightarrow -\exists Cx$
   $Kb \; \& \; Kc$
   $\therefore \exists -(Ax \; \& \; Bx)$

6. $\forall Fx \; \& \; Ga$
   $\exists Fx \Rightarrow \exists Hx$
   $\therefore \exists Gx \; \& \; \exists Hx$

7. $\exists(Hx \lor Ix) \Rightarrow \forall[Jx \; \& \; (Kx \; \& \; Lx)]$
   Ia
   $\therefore \exists(Jx \; \& \; Kx)$

8. $\exists Fx \Rightarrow \forall(Gx \lor -Fx)$
   $Fa \; \& \; -Gb$
   $\therefore \exists Gx \; \& \; \exists -Fx$

9. $\forall -(Mx \; \& \; -Px)$
   $\forall -(Sx \; \& \; -Mx)$
   $\therefore \exists(-Sx \lor Px)$

10. $\exists Mx \Rightarrow \forall(Bx \lor Cx)$
    $\forall(Dx \lor -Cx)$
    $\forall Mx$
    $\therefore \exists(Bx \lor Dx)$

9.5 Quantification Rules: EI and UG

The quantification rules introduced so far formulate basic facts about the logic of categorical propositions that should be familiar from Chapters 5 and 6. If the rules seem very different, that is undoubtedly because of the new and compact symbolism. The new rules' main advantage lies in the way they can be used with the rules of propositional logic. The extra power is tremendous.

Existential Instantiation. The next two rules are genuinely new. Let us examine the following argument: "If anything is a koala bear, then it is a marsupial. Something is a koala bear. Therefore something is a marsupial."

$$1. \; \forall(Kx \Rightarrow Mx)$$
$$2. \; \exists Kx \quad /\therefore \exists Mx$$

Again, the argument seems valid by modus ponens. But that rule does not apply within the scope of quantifiers. We can prove the validity of the argument by focusing on the second premise, which says that there is at least one koala bear. Let the constant i designate one of the koala bears in virtue of which the second premise is true. What do we know about i? We have stipulated that Ki is true. And from the first premise we can infer by UI that $Ki \Rightarrow Mi$ is also true. Finally, $Ki \Rightarrow Mi$ together with Ki entails Mi by modus ponens. But if Mi is true, then $\exists Mx$ is true by EG. Here, then, is our proof.

3. Ki 2 EI
4. $Ki \Rightarrow Mi$ 1 UI
5. Mi 3,4 MP
6. $\exists Mx$ 5 EG

What is the justification for step 3? From the fact that *something* is K, we cannot infer that any particular individual is K. However, we can infer that at least one substitution instance of Kx is true. We are then *stipulating* that Ki is to be one of the true substitution instances of Kx. We can do this as long as the constant i has not previously been given a meaning. If we had been using i to abbreviate "Italy," say, we could hardly stipulate that i is a koala bear. But as long as i is an unused constant, we can give it any meaning we like. Looked at another way, since the constant i was arbitrarily selected, by deriving the conclusion from Ki, we have shown that the conclusion can be derived from any of the substitution instances of Kx. Since the truth of $\exists Kx$ requires the truth of at least one of those substitution instances, we have established the conclusion.

The rule used to get step 3 is known as ***existential instantiation***. The rule says that given a line of the form $\exists Px$, we can infer a substitution instance of Px under certain conditions. Like universal instantiation, existential instantiation allows us to take off a quantifier and replace a variable with a constant. Unlike universal instantiation, there are restrictions on the constant we can choose. Intuitively, the restriction is that the constant be *previously unused*. The constant must not have been used in symbolizing the argument to be proven, and must not have been used in any line of the proof prior to its introduction by existential instantiation. If it has been used in either way, we are not free to stipulate that the constant designates one of the individuals making the existential statement true. If either restriction is violated, we are liable to "prove" invalid arguments valid. Consider the invalid argument: "Something is a carrot. If anything is a carrot, it is a vegetable. Therefore Baltimore is a vegetable." Let us use b to abbreviate "Baltimore." Then we can symbolize the conclusion as Vb. Consider now the following "proof":

1. $\exists Cx$
2. $\forall(Cx \Rightarrow Vx)$ $/\therefore Vb$
3. Cb 1 EI (WRONG)
4. $Cb \Rightarrow Vb$ 2 UI
5. Vb 3,4 MP

The only illegitimate step is line 3. Since we used the constant b to abbreviate "Baltimore" in symbolizing the conclusion, we cannot assume that b is an object making $\exists Cx$ true. Existential instantiation can be applied to premise 1, but we have to use a constant other than b. If we do, we cannot derive Vb.

Existential instantiation may be used several times in one proof, but each time a different constant must be used. Consider the invalid argument: "Something is a cat. Something is a dog. Therefore, something is both a cat and a dog." If the restriction on EI is violated, we could prove this argument to be valid.

1. $\exists Cx$
2. $\exists Dx$ $/\therefore \exists(Cx \& Dx)$
3. Ch 1 EI
4. Dh 2 EI (WRONG)
5. $Ch \& Dh$ 3,4 Conj
6. $\exists(Cx \& Dx)$ 5 EG

Step 3 is fine. Since premise 1 says that something is a C, we can legitimately let h designate one of the Cs. Premise 2 says similarly that something is a D. But we cannot assume that h is a D, because we have already stipulated that h is a C. EI can be applied to line 2 only if we use a constant other than h. If we do, we will not be able to derive $\exists(Cx \& Dx)$.

In the koala bear argument, we had both a universal and an existential premise. We instantiated both with respect to the same constant i, applying EI before UI. If we had applied UI before EI, we would have violated the restriction on EI, for *i* would have appeared in line 3 before EI was used to introduce *Ki* in line 4. In this context, no harm would have been done by violating the restriction on EI, which means that we could theoretically weaken the restriction somewhat. However, the rule would become overly cumbersome if we sought to make the restriction as weak as possible. It is better to keep the rule uncomplicated, and simply apply EI before UI when instantiating both an existential and a universal statement with respect to the same constant.

Universal Generalization. To introduce the final quantification rule, let us try to prove the validity of: "If anything is a material object, then it is not conscious. Everything is a material object. Therefore, nothing is conscious."

$$1. \; \forall(Mx \Rightarrow -Cx)$$
$$2. \; \forall Mx \qquad\qquad\qquad /\!\therefore \forall -Cx$$

Once again, modus ponens does not apply because of the quantifiers. We can, however, universally instantiate both premises. Indeed, let *a* be any individual. By UI we can infer *Ma* and *Ma* $\Rightarrow$ *-Ca*. By modus ponens, we can infer *-Ca*. Now nothing was special about our choice of *a* here. The same sequence of steps would lead to the same result for any other individual. That is, two applications of UI and an application of modus ponens would lead to *-Cb*, to *-Cc*, to *-Cd*, and so on. We have therefore shown that *-Cx* is true for every individual, which establishes the conclusion we set out to prove. In general, if we can prove that *Px* is true for an *arbitrarily selected* individual, then we can infer $\forall Px$. We complete our proof as follows:

$$3. \; Ma \Rightarrow -Ca \qquad\qquad 1 \; UI$$
$$4. \; Ma \qquad\qquad\qquad\quad\; 2 \; UI$$
$$5. \; -Ca \qquad\qquad\qquad\quad 3,4 \; MP$$
$$6. \; \forall -Cx \qquad\qquad\qquad 5 \; UG$$

UG stands for ***universal generalization***, the rule that we can infer $\forall Px$ from a substitution instance of *Px* in which *x* is replaced by an arbitrarily selected constant *s*. The name derives from the fact that the rule allows us to move from a singular statement to a universally general statement. Like existential generalization, universal generalization involves putting on a quantifier. Unlike existential generalization, there is a restriction on the singular statements we can universally generalize. Intuitively, the restriction is that the constant *s*, which replaces *x* in *Px*, must be "arbitrarily selected." What does this mean? The legitimacy of universal generalization requires that the sequence of steps used to derive *Ps* be repeatable for any other individual. This requires that no *special* information about s be used in the derivation. We can ensure that no information about *s* is used other than the fact that *s* is an individual, by requiring that *s* not be used in the premises or in any line introduced by existential instantiation. By requiring that the constant selected not be used in the premises, we block "proofs" like the following:

$$1. \; Vh \qquad /\!\therefore \forall Vx \qquad\qquad 1. \; \forall(Vx \Rightarrow Mx)$$
$$2. \; \forall Vx \qquad 1 \; UG \; (WRONG) \qquad 2. \; Vh \qquad\qquad\qquad /\!\therefore \forall Mx$$
$$\qquad\qquad\qquad\qquad\qquad\qquad\qquad 3. \; Vh \Rightarrow Mh \qquad 1 \; UI$$
$$\qquad\qquad\qquad\qquad\qquad\qquad\qquad 4. \; Mh \qquad\qquad\quad 2,3 \; MP$$
$$\qquad\qquad\qquad\qquad\qquad\qquad\qquad 5. \; \forall Mx \qquad\qquad 4 \; UG \; (WRONG)$$

To see that the arguments are invalid, let *h* be "Heifetz," v be "violinist," and *M* be "musician." From the fact that Heifetz is a violinist, we cannot infer that everything is. And given that if anything is a violinist then it is a musician, and that Heifetz is a violinist, we cannot infer that everything is a musician, By requiring that the constant selected not appear in any line introduced by existential instantiation, we block "proofs" like this one:

1. $\exists Vx$ /∴$\forall Vx$
2. Va 1 EI
3. $\forall Vx$ 2 UG (WRONG)

From the fact that something is a violinist, we cannot infer that everything is.

We now complete the quantification rules with the following formulations of existential instantiation and universal generalization.

Quantification Rules EI and UG

Existential Instantiation (EI): From $\exists Px$, infer any substitution instance of Px in which x is replaced by a constant s that is not used in the conclusion or in any previous line.

$$\exists Px$$
$$\therefore Ps$$

Universal Generalization (UG): From any substitution instance of Px in which x is replaced by a constant s that is not used in the premises or in any line introduced by EI, infer $\forall Px$.

$$Ps$$
$$\therefore \forall Px$$

Bear in mind that unlike UI and EG, EI and UG are permitted only under certain conditions. While the argument forms presented with UI and EG are unconditionally valid, those with EI and UG are only conditionally valid. Whereas in UI and EG there are no restrictions on the constant s selected, there are stringent restrictions on s in EI and UG. EI and UG are like UI and EG, however, in applying only to whole lines. Thus we cannot directly instantiate the negation of an existential statement. For example, we cannot go from $-\exists Ux$ ("It is not the case that something is a unicorn") to $-Um$ ("Morris is not a unicorn") by EI. We must first apply quantifier negation, to get $\forall -Ux$, then apply UI to get $-Um$. And from $-\forall Mx$ ("Not everything is a man") we cannot infer $-Mp$ ("The president is not a man"). We must first apply QN to get $\exists -Mx$. We can then apply EI, but not to get $-Mp$, if p designates the president, for p will violate the restrictions on EI.

General Categorical Syllogism. With the addition of universal generalization and existential instantiation, we can validate Venn transforms of the two argument forms comprising Chapter 5's general categorical syllogism rule. Consider the **A*I*I*1** syllogism: "Nothing is a man and not an animal. Something is a violinist and a man. Therefore, something is a violinist and an animal." We can symbolize the argument and prove its validity as follows.

1. $\forall -(Mx \, \& \, -Ax)$
2. $\exists(Vx \, \& \, Mx)$ /∴$\exists(Vx \, \& \, Ax)$
3. $Vi \, \& \, Mi$ 2 EI
4. $-(Mi \, \& \, -Ai)$ 1 UI
5. $-Mi \lor Ai$ 4 Dm
6. Mi 3 Simp
7. Ai 5,6 DS
8. Vi 3 Simp
9. $Vi \, \& \, Ai$ 7,8 Conj
10. $\exists(Vx \, \& \, Ax)$ 9 EG

Whereas disjunctive syllogism is used to prove **A*I*I*1** syllogisms, disjunctive transitivity is used to prove **A*A*A*1** syllogisms. Consider: "Nothing is a cat and not a mammal. Nothing is a mammal and not an animal. Therefore, nothing is a cat and not an animal."

1. ∀–(Cx & –Mx)
2. ∀–(Mx & –Ax)   /∴ ∀–(Cx & –Ax)
3. –(Ca & –Ma)   1 UI
4. –(Ma & –Aa)   2 UI
5. –Ca ∨ Ma   3 DM
6. –Ma ∨ Aa   4 DM
7. –Ca ∨ Aa   5,6 DT
8. –(Ca & –Aa)   7 DM
9. ∀–(Cx & –Ax)   8 UG

Indirect Proofs. The quantification rules can be used in indirect as well as direct proofs (see §8.5). The first step of an indirect proof after the premises is to assume the denial of the conclusion; then the quantification rules are used as usual to derive a contradiction. An indirect proof of the **A*A*A*I** syllogism just proven directly would go as follows:

1. ∀(Cx & –Mx)
2. ∀–(Mx & –Ax)   /∴ ∀–(Cx & –Ax)
3. –∀–(Cx & –Ax)   IP
4. ∃(Cx & –Ax)   3 QN
5. Ca & –Aa   4 EI
6. –(Ca & –Ma)   1 UI
7. –(Ma & –Aa)   2 UI
8. –Ca ∨ Ma   6 DM
9. –Ma ∨ Aa   7 DM
10. Ca   5 Simp
11. Ma   8,10 DS
12. Aa   9,11 DS
13. –Aa   5 Simp
14. Aa & –Aa   12,13 Conj

The indirect proof was longer, but no less legitimate. The exercise problems are designed to be solved by direct proof, unless otherwise indicated. But you may use an indirect proof whenever you please.

Glossary

Existential instantiation (EI): the rule that from a statement of the form ∃Px, you can infer any substitution instance of Px in which x is replaced by a constant s that is not used in the conclusion of the argument being proven valid or in any previous line of the proof.

Universal generalization (UG): the rule that from any substitution instance of a statement function Px in which x is replaced by a constant s that is not used in the premises of the argument being proven valid or in any line of the proof introduced by EI, you can infer ∀Px.

Exercises

A. Identify the errors in the following deductions, if there are any.

1. 1. ∀(Ax ⇒ Px)
    2. ∀Ax   /∴ ∀Px
    3. Aa   2 UI
    4. Aa ⇒ Pa   1 UI
    5. Pa   3,4 MP

2. 1. ∃Ax
    2. ∃Bx   /∴ ∀(Ax & Bx)
    3. Ad   1 EI
    4. Bd   2 EI
    5. Ad & Bd   3,4 Conj

	6. $\forall Px$	5 UG	

3.	1. $\forall(Kx \Rightarrow Mx)$	
	2. Kj	$/\therefore \forall Mx$
	3. $Kj \Rightarrow Mj$	UI
	4. Mj	2,3 MP
	5. $\forall Mx$	4 UG

5.	1. $-\forall(Cx \& Dx)$	
	2. $\exists Cx$	$/\therefore \exists -Dx$
	3. $-(Ca \& Da)$	1 UI
	4. $-Ca \vee -Da$	3 DM
	5. Ca	2 EI
	6. $-Da$	4,5 DS
	7. $\exists -Dx$	6 EG

7.	1. $\exists(Qx \vee Rx)$	
	2. $-Qa$	$/\therefore Ra$
	3. $Qa \vee Ra$	1 EI
	4. Ra	2,3 DS

9.	1. $\forall Bx \Rightarrow \forall Kx$	
	2. $\forall(Bx \& Cx)$	$/\therefore Kj$
	3. $Bj \& Cj$	2 UI
	4. Bj	3 Simp
	5. $\forall Bx$	4 UG
	6. $\forall Kx$	5,1 MP
	7. Kj	6 UI

4.	1. $\exists Ax$	
	2. $\forall(Ax \Rightarrow Cx)$	$/\therefore Am \& Cm$
	3. Am	1 EI
	4. $Am \Rightarrow Cm$	2 UI
	5. Cm	3,4 MP
	6. $Am \& Cm$	3,5 Conj

6.	1. $\exists(Mx \& -Px)$	
	2. $\exists(Sx \& -Mx)$	$/\therefore \exists(Sx \& -Px)$
	3. $Ma \& -Pa$	1 EI
	4. $Sa \& -Ma$	2 EI
	5. Sa	4 Simp
	6. $-Pa$	3 Simp
	7. $Sa \& -Pa$	5,6 Conj
	8. $\exists(Sx \& -Px)$	7 EG

8.	1. $\forall(Qx \vee Rx)$	
	2. $\exists -Qx$	$/\therefore \forall Rx$
	3. $-Qa$	2 EI
	4. $Qa \vee Ra$	1 UI
	5. Ra	3,4 DS
	6. $\forall Rx$	5 UG

10.	1. $\exists -Sx$	
	2. $\forall (Tx \Rightarrow Sx)$	$/\therefore -\exists Tx$
	3. $Ta \Rightarrow Sa$	2 UI
	4. $-Sa$	1 EI
	5. $-Ta$	3,4 MT
	6. $-\exists Tx$	5 EG

B. Prove the validity of the following arguments.

1. $\forall Fx$
   $\therefore \forall(Fx \vee Gx)$

2. $\exists(Fx \& Gx)$
   $\therefore \exists Fx$

3. $\forall(Qx \vee Rx)$
   $\forall -Qx$
   $\therefore \forall Rx$

4. $\forall Fx$
   $\forall Gx$
   $\therefore \forall(Fx \& Gx)$

5. $\forall(Bx \Rightarrow Cx)$
   $\exists Bx$
   $\therefore \exists Cx$

6. $\forall(Sx \vee Mx)$
   $\forall(-Mx \vee Px)$
   $\therefore \forall(Sx \vee Px)$

7. $\exists(Mx \Rightarrow Nx)$

8. $\forall(Bx \Rightarrow Cx)$

∀–Nx   ∀Bx & ∀Dx
∴ –∀Mx   ∴ ∀Cx

9. ∀[(Jx ∨ Kx) ⇒ –Lx]   10. ∀(Mx ⇒ –Rx)
    ∃Lx   ∃(Rx ∨ Vx)
    ∴ ∃ –Jx   ∀Mx
                                                 ∴ ∃Vx

11. ∀Ax   12. ∀(Fx ⇒ Gx)
     ∃Ax ⇒ –∃Bx   ∀(Fx & Hx)
     ∀Cx ⇒ Bd   ∴∀(Gx & Hx)
     ∴ –∀Cx

13. ∀(Hx ∨ Ix) ⇒ ∃[Jx & (Kx &Lx)]   14. ∀[(Mx ∨ Nx) ⇒ (Ox & Px)]
     ∀Hx   –∀Ox
     ∴∃(Jx & Kx)   ∴∃ –Mx

15. ∀(Bx ⇒ Tx)   16. ∃(Nx & Sx)
     ∃ (Gx & Ix)   ∀(Vx ⇒ Tx)
     ∀ –(Ix & Tx)   ∀(Sx ⇒ Vx)
     ∴ ∃(Gx & –Bx)   ∴ ∃(Nx & Tx)

17. ∀Gx ⇒ ∃(Hx & Jx)   18. ∃Hx
     ∀(Gx & Jx)   ∀(Tx ⇒ Wx)
     ∴ ∃(Hx & Gx)   ∀(Hx ⇒ –Rx)
                                                 ∀(–Rx ⇒ –Wx)
                                                 ∴ ∃(Hx & –Tx)

19. ∃(Nx & Sx)   20. ∀–(Tx & –Wx)
     ∀(–Vx ∨ Tx)   ∀–(Hx & Rx)
     ∀ –(Sx & –Vx)   ∀(–Wx ∨ Rx)
     ∴∃(Nx & Tx)   ∴ ∀–(Hx & Tx)

C. Prove the validity of the following syllogistic forms using quantification theory.

1. **A*YY2**   2. **E*I*O*1**
3. **E*A*E*1**   4. **E*UY2**
5. **I*A*I*4**   6. **A*E*E*4**

D. Prove the validity of arguments 1-8 in Set B above, using the method of indirect proof.

9.6 Aristotelian Categoricals

We cannot directly symbolize Aristotelian categoricals using the notation of quantification theory. We can, however, symbolize both their Venn transforms and their presuppositions. Consider "All men are animals." Its Venn transform ("Nothing is both a man and not an animal") can be symbolized $\forall{-}(Mx$ $\&\ {-}Ax)$. Its presupposition ("Something is a man") can be symbolized $\exists Mx$. Similarly, "Some men are geniuses" has $\exists(Mx\ \&\ Gx)$ as its Venn transform, and $\exists Mx$ as its presupposition. In general:

Aristotelian Categorical	Venn Transform	Presupposition
A All S are P	$\forall{-}(Sx\ \&\ {-}Px)$	$\exists Sx$
E No S are P	$\forall{-}(Sx\ \&\ Px)$	$\exists Sx$
I Some S are P	$\exists(Sx\ \&\ Px)$	$\exists Sx$
O Some S are not P	$\exists(Sx\ \&\ {-}Px)$	$\exists Sx$

We observed in §6.4 that if its presupposition is true, an Aristotelian categorical is equivalent to its Venn transform, and that if its presupposition is false, an Aristotelian categorical is neither true nor false. To prove the validity of an argument, we need to show that if the premises are all true, then the conclusion must be true. For an argument containing Aristotelian categoricals, this can be done by deducing the Venn transform and presupposition of the conclusion from those of the premises. The Venn transforms of the two particular propositions entail their presuppositions. Hence their presuppositions can be ignored as redundant when proving validity. So we symbolize the conjunction of the Venn transform and presupposition of each **A** or **E** proposition, and the Venn transform of each **I** or **O** proposition, and then prove the validity of the resulting argument.

Let us validate the **AII1** syllogism, one of the argument forms used as a rule of inference in Chapter 5.

> All *M* are P.
> Some *S* are *M*.
> ∴ Some *S* are P.

We symbolize and conjoin the Venn transform and presupposition of the universal premise, and we symbolize the Venn transform of the particular premise and of the conclusion. The following argument results:

> $\forall(Mx\ \&\ {-}Px)\ \&\ \exists Mx$
> $\exists(Sx\ \&\ Mx)$
> ∴ $\exists(Sx\ \&\ Px)$

These two arguments are not equivalent in all respects. For example, if there is no *S*, then the first argument's conclusion will be neither true nor false, while the second argument's conclusion will be false. However, the two arguments are *equivalent with regard to validity:* one is valid if and only if the other is. Consequently, we can prove the validity of the first argument by proving the validity of the second. This can be done as follows:

> 1. $\forall{-}(Mx\ \&\ {-}Px)\ \&\ \exists Mx$
> 2. $\exists(Sx\ \&\ Mx)$ /∴ $\exists(Sx\ \&\ Px)$
> 3. $\forall{-}(Mx\ \&\ {-}Px)$ 1 Simp
> 4. $Sa\ \&\ Ma$ 2 EI
> 5. ${-}(Ma\ \&\ {-}Pa)$ 3 UI
> 6. ${-}Ma\ \lor\ Pa$ 5 DM
> 7. Ma 4 Simp

$$8.\ Pa \qquad\qquad 6,7 \text{ DS}$$
$$9.\ Sa \qquad\qquad 4 \text{ Simp}$$
$$10.\ Sa \ \& \ Pa \qquad\qquad 8,9 \text{ Conj}$$
$$11.\ \exists(Sx \ \& \ Px) \qquad\qquad 10 \text{ EG}$$

In this case, the presupposition of the universal premise played no role in the deduction. In other cases, the presupposition is essential. Consider the rule of subalternation:

All S are P.
∴ Some S are P.

We symbolize and prove the validity of this argument form as follows:

$$1.\ \forall{-}(Sx \ \& \ {-}Px) \ \& \ \exists Sx$$
$$2.\ \forall{-}(Sx \ \& \ {-}Px) \qquad\qquad /\therefore \ \exists(Sx \ \& \ Px)$$
$$3.\ \exists Sx \qquad\qquad 1 \text{ Simp}$$
$$4.\ Sa \qquad\qquad 3 \text{ EI}$$
$$5.\ {-}(Sa \ \& \ {-}Pa) \qquad\qquad 2 \text{ UI}$$
$$6.\ {-}Sa \lor Pa \qquad\qquad 5 \text{ DM}$$
$$7.\ Pa \qquad\qquad 4,6 \text{ DS}$$
$$8.\ Sa \ \& \ Pa \qquad\qquad 4,7 \text{ Conj}$$
$$9.\ \exists(Sx \ \& \ Px) \qquad\qquad 8 \text{ EG}$$

The proof could not have proceeded without line 3. Consider, finally, the **AAA1** syllogism, another argument form used as a rule of inference in Chapter 5.

All M are P.
All S are M.
∴ All S are P.

We symbolize the argument, and prove its validity, as follows:

$$1.\ \forall(Mx \ \& \ {-}Px) \ \& \ \exists Mx$$
$$2.\ \forall{-}(Sx \ \& \ {-}Mx) \ \& \ \exists Sx \qquad\qquad /\therefore \ \forall{-}(Sx \ \& \ {-}Px) \ \& \ \exists Sx$$
$$3.\ \exists Sx \qquad\qquad 2 \text{ Simp}$$
$$4.\ \forall{-}(Mx \ \& \ {-}Px) \qquad\qquad 1 \text{ Simp}$$
$$5.\ \forall{-}(Sx \ \& \ {-}Mx) \qquad\qquad 2 \text{ Simp}$$
$$6.\ {-}(Ma \ \& \ {-}Pa) \qquad\qquad 4 \text{ UI}$$
$$7.\ {-}(Sa \ \& \ {-}Ma) \qquad\qquad 5 \text{ UI}$$
$$8.\ {-}Ma \lor Pa \qquad\qquad 6 \text{ DM}$$
$$9.\ {-}Sa \lor Ma \qquad\qquad 7 \text{ DM}$$
$$10.\ {-}Sa \lor Pa \qquad\qquad 8,9 \text{ DT}$$
$$11.\ {-}(Sa \ \& \ {-}Pa) \qquad\qquad 10 \text{ DM}$$
$$12.\ \forall{-}(Sx \ \& \ {-}Px) \qquad\qquad 11 \text{ UG}$$
$$13.\ \forall{-}(Sx \ \& \ {-}Px) \ \& \ \exists Sx \qquad\qquad 3,12 \text{ Conj}$$

We have not considered compounds of Aristotelian categoricals. Since this is an introductory text we shall not discuss them in any detail. But here, briefly, is how to proceed: Let the Venn transform of any conjunction, disjunction, or other compound containing Aristotelian categoricals be defined as the conjunction, disjunction, or other compound formed from their Venn transforms. Thus the Venn transform of "All dogs are animals and all cats are animals would be $\forall{-}(Dx \ \& \ {-}Ax) \ \& \ \forall{-}(Cx \ \& \ {-}Ax)$. The presupposition of Aristotelian compounds is generally the conjunction of the components' presuppositions. Thus the presupposition of "All dogs are animals and all cats are animals" would be $\exists Dx \ \& \ \exists Cx$. (There are exceptions to this general rule. For example, "All unicorns, if' there are any, have a horn" does not presuppose that any unicorns exist: the if-clause "cancels" that presupposition.) Then to prove the validity of an argument containing compounds of Aristotelian categoricals, deduce the Venn transform and presupposition of the conclusion from those of the premises.

Exercises

A. Symbolize both the Venn transform and the presupposition of the following Aristotelian categoricals, using quantifiers and statement functions.

1. All skunks are mammals.

2. Some rodents are not mice.

3. Some even-toed hoofed mammals are rhinoceroses.

4. No rhinoceros is a hippopotamus.

5. Every black-footed ferret is a member of the weasel family.

6. Some aggressive, bloodthirsty predators are wolverines.

7. Any violet growing on the moon is blue.

8. No men over 300 years old drink gin.

9. Some foxes are not male vixen.

10. All governments restrain and rule people.

11. Some authors can write only if they are inebriated.

12. An athlete can play well only if he or she is not inebriated.

13. Some students can pass only if they cheat.

14. Some students pass if and only if they study hard.

15. Some students pass but do not study hard.

16. Not all expensive cars are beautiful or long-lasting.

17. Some cars that are expensive are neither beautiful nor long-lasting.

18. Any car that is a Mercedes-Benz is both expensive and long-lasting.

19. A Porsche is an expensive and beautiful high-performance car, but it is not very roomy.

20. Some, but not all, cars are expensive.

21. Vegas and Pintos were inexpensive cars.

22. Porsches or Jaguars are expensive cars.

B. Prove the validity of the following arguments, using the rules of quantification theory.

1. Some fish are not sharks, so some nonsharks are fish.

2. Some saints are martyrs, so some martyrs are not nonsaints.

3. All men are animals, so some animals are men.

4. All socialists are pacifists. There are some nonpacificists. So no nonpacifists are socialists.

5. No scientist is a philosopher, so some nonphilosopher is not a nonscientist.

6. There are some nonmetals. But every steel is a metal. So no nonmetal is a steel.

7. No apple is a vegetable, so some nonvegetable is an apple.

8. There are some poisons. But all chemicals are nonpoisons. So some poisons are not chemicals.

9. Every nonathlete is a bookworm, some bookworm is not an athlete.

10. Every nonathlete is a bookworm. But not everything is a bookworm. So some nonbookworm is an athlete.

C. Follow the directions for Set B.

1. No representative is a senator. Dennis Hastert is a representative. Therefore Dennis Hastert is not a senator.

2. Mick Jagger is a singer. Mick Jagger is not a pianist. Therefore, some singers are not pianists.

3. Hilary Clinton is not a musician. All rock singers are musicians. Therefore Hilary Clinton is not a rock singer.

4. Zinc is a metal. No organic compound is a metal. Therefore zinc is not an organic compound.

5. Every senator is a member of Congress. Ted Kennedy is a senator. Therefore, Ted Kennedy is a member of Congress.

6. Every executive is hard driving. Some woman is an executive. Therefore, some woman is hard driving.

7. Henry Kissinger is a famous American. Every famous American is wealthy. Therefore, Henry Kissinger is wealthy.

8. All flowers are plants. All roses are flowers. Therefore, some roses are plants.

9. Some plants are roses. All roses are flowers. Therefore, some flowers are plants.

10. Every flower is a plant. Some flower is a rose. Therefore, some rose is a plant.

11. Every ape is a primate. Every ape is a mammal. Therefore, some mammal is a primate.

12. No whales are fish. Some mammals are whales. Therefore, some mammals are not fish.

13. Some parents are understanding. No parents are nonadults. Therefore, some adults are understanding.

14. Every television is an electronic instrument. No model F21 is an electronic instrument. Therefore, no model F21 is a television.

D. Follow the directions for Set B.

1. k is not an A.
   All non-A are B.
   ∴ k is a B.

2. c is a J.
   c is a K.
   Every K is an L.
   ∴ Some J is an L.

3. *d* is an *A*.
    No *A* is a *B*.
    d is a *C*.
    ∴ Some *C* is a non-*B*.

5. *c* is not an *H*.
    Every non-*G* is an *H*.
    ∴ *c* is a *G*.

7. Some *N* is an *S*.
    Every *v* is a *T*.
    No *S* is a non-*V*.
    ∴ Some *N* is a *T*.

9. All *T* are *W*.
    No *H* are *R*.
    All *W* are *R*.
    ∴ No *H* are *T*.

11. No *T* is a *W*.
    No non-*W* is a *C*.
    Each *K* is a *T*.
    ∴ No *K* is a *C*.

4. *f* is an *X*.
    Every *Y* is a non-*X*.
    ∴ *f* is not a *Y*.

6. All *C* are *D*.
    i is not a non-*G*.
    No *G* are non-*C*.
    ∴ *i* is a *D*.

    Every *Q* is an *N*.
    Each *D* is a *Q*.
    No *N* is a *W*.
    ∴ No *D* is a *W*.

10. No *B* is a non-*T*.
    Some *G* is an *I*.
    No *I* is a *T*.
    ∴ Some *G* is a non-*B*.

12. All *C* are *T*.
    No *L* are non-*O*.
    No *O* are non-*C*.
    ∴ All *L* are *T*.

E. It is customary in modern logic to symbolize universal Aristotelian categoricals using the material conditional, which was introduced in §7.8. By definition, the material conditional $p \supset q$ is equivalent to $-(p \& -q)$. The Venn transform of "All *S* are *P*" is $\forall -(Sx \& -Px)$; using the material conditional, this can be expressed as $\forall (Sx \supset Px)$. The Venn transform of "No *S* are *P*" is $\forall -(Sx \& Px)$; this is equivalent by double negation to $\forall -(Sx \& --Px)$, which in turn can be expressed as $\forall (Sx \supset -Px)$. Symbolize the Venn transforms of the universal propositions in Set A, using material conditionals.

9.7 Proving Logical Truth

The rules of quantification theory can be used along with the laws of thought (or other axioms) to prove that statements are logically true or logically false, according to the procedure explained in §8.3–5. The laws of thought were formulated as rules for introducing compound propositions of certain forms, such as p ∨ –p, which is the law of excluded middle. This allows us to introduce statements like "Alan either is or is not bald," "Bob either is or is not bald," and even "k either is or is not bald," where k is an arbitrarily selected constant. We can then use UG to infer "Everything either is or is not bald." Indeed, using EM with an arbitrary constant and then UG, we can prove any substitution instance of $\forall (Px \lor -Px)$, which is another common way of formulating the law of excluded middle.

/∴ $\forall (Px \lor -Px)$
1. $Pk \lor -Pk$ EM
2. $\forall (Px \lor -Px)$ 1 UG

The other laws have similar corollaries. The law of identity entails $\forall (Px \Rightarrow Px)$ ("If anything is *P*, then it is *P*"), and the law of noncontradiction entails $\forall -(Px \& -Px)$ ("Nothing both is and is not *P*"). Conditionals formulating basic implications summarized in the square of opposition can be proven just as directly. For example, we can introduce $\forall Px \Rightarrow \forall Px$ by the law of identity. Then we can deduce $\forall Px \Rightarrow -\exists -Px$ by quantifier negation.

$$/\therefore \; \forall Px \Rightarrow -\exists \, -Px$$
1. $\forall Px \Rightarrow \forall Px$ ID
2. $\forall Px \Rightarrow -\exists \, -Px$ 1 QN

Other implications require a conditional proof. For example, to prove $\forall Px \Rightarrow \exists Px$, we deduce $\exists Px$ from $\forall Px$, using UI and then EG.

1. $\forall Px$ $/\therefore \; \exists Px$
2. Pa 1 UG
3. $\exists Px$ 2 EG

Finally, the method of indirect proof can be used to prove that a quantified statement is logically true by deducing a contradiction from its denial. For example, to prove that $-\exists (Px \;\&\; -Px)$ is logically true, it suffices to deduce a contradiction from $\exists (Px \;\&\; -Px)$.

$$/\therefore \; -\exists (Px \;\&\; -Px)$$
1. $\exists (Px \;\&\; -Px)$ IP
2. $Pa \;\&\; -Pa$ 1 EI

In short, we prove quantified statements to be logically true (or false) in exactly the same ways we prove unquantified statements to be logically true (or false). Of course, not all proofs will be as simple as the examples given above. For instance, to show that $(-\exists Fx \lor Ga) \Rightarrow \forall (-Fx \lor Ga)$ is logically true, a ten-step indirect conditional proof is necessary:

1. $-\exists Fx \lor Ga$ $/\therefore \; \forall (-Fx \lor Ga)$
2. $-\forall (-Fx \lor Ga)$ IP
3. $\exists -(-Fx \lor Ga)$ 2 QN
4. $-(-Fb \lor Ga)$ 3 EI
5. $Fb \;\&\; -Ga$ 4 DM
6. Fb 5 Simp
7. $\exists Fx$ 6 EG
8. Ga 1,7 DS
9. $-Ga$ 5 Simp
10. $Ga \;\&\; -Ga$ 8,9 Conj

Exercises

Prove that the following statements are logically true.

1. $\forall Fx \lor \exists \, -Fx$ 2. $\exists Fx \lor \forall -Fx$

3. $-\forall (Fx \;\&\; Gx) \Rightarrow \exists (-Fx \lor -Gx)$ 4. $\forall [(Fx \lor Gx) \lor -Gx]$

5. $\forall (Fx \lor -Fx) \;\&\; -\exists (Gx \;\&\; -Gx)$ 6. $(\forall Fx \;\&\; -\forall Gx) \lor (\exists Gx \lor \exists -Fx)$

7. $\forall Fx \lor -\forall (Fx \;\&\; Gx)$ 8. $\forall (Fx \lor Gx) \lor \exists (-Fx \lor -Gx)$

9. $\exists (Fx \;\&\; Gx) \Rightarrow (\exists Fx \;\&\; \exists Gx)$ 10. $\forall (Fx \;\&\; Ga) \Rightarrow (\forall Fx \;\&\; Ga)$

11. $(\forall Fx \;\&\; \forall Gx) \Rightarrow \forall (Fx \;\&\; Gx)$ 12. $(\forall Fx \lor \forall Gx) \Rightarrow \forall (Fx \lor Gx)$

13. $\forall (-Ga \lor Fx) \Rightarrow (-Ga \lor \forall Fx)$ 14. $\forall (-Fx \lor Ga) \Rightarrow (-\exists Fx \lor Ga)$

9.8 Refutation By Countercase

The rules of quantification theory can be used to prove validity, but not invalidity. How can we invalidate an argument form like **A*A*A*2**?

$$\forall{-}(Px \ \& -Mx)$$
$$\forall \ {-}(Sx \ \& -Mx)$$
$$\therefore \ \forall \ {-}(Sx \ \& -Px)$$

One method is refutation by counterinstance. For example, let Px be "x is a panther," let Sx be "x is a squirrel," and let Mx be "x is a mammal." Then we have a substitution instance with true premises and a false conclusion, which shows that the argument form is invalid. While refutation by counterinstance can often be used swiftly and effectively, a more formal method of proving invalidity would be desirable.

Singular Statements. The method of countercase was developed in §7.6 for argument forms consisting entirely of statement variables and truth-functional connectives. A countercase is defined as a consistent assignment of truth values to the statement variables that makes the premises true and the conclusion false. In an argument like the **A*A*A*2** syllogism, however, we have statement function variables rather than statement variables, and we have quantifiers in addition to truth-functional connectives. So the definition of a countercase does not apply. However, the definition does apply to argument forms consisting entirely of *singular* statement variables and truth-functional connectives, such as the following.

$$-(Pa \ \& -Ma)$$
$$-(Sa \ \& -Ma)$$
$$\therefore -(Sa \ \& -Pa)$$

We have been using Px, and occasionally Mx and Sx, as statement function variables. We have also been using Pa to stand for the result of replacing the variable x with the constant a in Px. Pa, then, is a **singular statement variable**, since it represents all statements that can be made about a. Since $Pa, Ma,$ and Sa are statement variables, the definition of a countercase applies without modification: a countercase is a consistent assignment of truth values to the statement variables that makes the premises true and the conclusion false. There is only one countercase in this example: the one in which Sa and Ma are true, and Pa false.

Singular Equivalents of Universal Statements. We can apply the method of countercase to argument forms involving general statements by first finding a **singular equivalent** of the argument form. A quantified statement of the form $\forall Px$ is true if and only if *all* substitution instances of the statement function Px are true, which means that *Pa and Pb and Pc,* and so on for all individuals, are true. Now consider the possible case in which a is the only individual. Then $\forall Px$ is true if and only if Pa is true. If only two individuals exist, a and b, then $\forall Px$ is true if and only if $Pa \ \& \ Pb$ is true. With three individuals $a, b,$ and c, $\forall Px$ is true if and only if $Pa \ \& \ Pb \ \& \ Pc$ is true. In general, if there are n individuals (where n is any finite integer greater than 1), $\forall Px$ is equivalent to a conjunction of singular statements containing n conjuncts. We shall say that Pa is the singular equivalent of $\forall Px$ for the case in which a is the only individual; $Pa \ \& \ Pb$ is the singular equivalent of $\forall Px$ for the case in which a and b are the only individuals; $Pa \ \& \ Pb \ \& \ Pc$ is the singular equivalent of $\forall Px$ for the case in which $a, b,$ and c are the only individuals; and so on.

To produce the singular equivalent of an *argument* form containing quantified statement forms, for a given set of individuals, we replace every quantified statement form with its singular equivalent for that set of individuals. Thus, the singular equivalent for one individual *a* of the **A*A*A*2** syllogism is the singular argument examined above:

$$-(Pa\ \&\ -Ma)$$
$$-(Sa\ \&\ -Ma)$$
$$\therefore\ -(Sa\ \&\ -Pa)$$

The singular equivalent of the same general argument for two individuals *a* and *b* is:

$$-(Pa\ \&\ -Ma)\ \&\ -(Pb\ \&\ -Mb)$$
$$-(Sa\ \&\ -Ma)\ \&\ -(Sb\ \&\ -Mb)$$
$$\therefore\ -(Sa\ \&\ -Pa)\ \&\ -(Sb\ \&\ -Pb)$$

And its singular equivalent for three individuals *a, b,* and *c* is:

$$-(Pa\ \&\ -Ma)\ \&\ -(Pb\ \&\ -Mb)\ \&\ -(Pc\ \&\ -Mc)$$
$$-(Sa\ \&\ -Ma)\ \&\ -(Sb\ \&\ Mb)\ \&\ -(Sc\ \&\ -Mc)$$
$$\therefore -(Sa\ \&\ -Pa)\ \&\ -(Sb\ \&\ -Pb)\ \&\ -(Sc\ \&\ -Pc)$$

Now to prove that an rgument is invalid, we need to show that there is a possible case in which the premises of the argument are all true and the conclusion false. Hence, we can prove that an argument form containing quantified statement forms is invalid by using the method of countercase to show that one of the singular equivalents of the argument form is invalid. Thus, in refuting the singular equivalent of the **A*A*A*2** syllogism for one individual, we have refuted the argument. For we have described a possible case (one individual *a, Sa* and *Ma* true, and *Pa* false) in which the premises of the argument are true and the conclusion false.

Singular Equivalents of Existential Statements. We still must define the notion of a singular equivalent for existentially quantified statements. ∃*Px* is true if and only if *at least one* substitution instance of the statement function *Px* is true, which means that *Pa or Pb or Pc,* and so on for all individuals, is true. If there is only one individual *a,* ∃*Px* is equivalent to *Pa; Pa,* then, is the singular equivalent of ∃*Px* for the case in which *a* is the only individual. If there are two individuals *a* and *b,* ∃*Px* is equivalent to *Pa* v *Pb; Pa* v *Pb* is the singular equivalent of ∃*Px* for the case in which *a* and *b* are the only individuals. If there are three individuals a, *b,* and c, then ∃*Px* is equivalent to *Pa* v *Pb* v *Pc,* which is the singular equivalent of ∃*Px* for the case in which *a, b,* and *c* are the only individuals. In general, the singular equivalent of ∃*Px* for *n* individuals is a disjunction with *n* disjuncts. Note that the singular equivalent of a *universal* statement is a *conjunction,* while the singular equivalent of an *existential* statement is a *disjunction.* To produce the singular equivalent (for a given set of individuals) of an argument form containing existential statements, we replace every existential statement with its singular equivalent (for that same set of individuals). Consider now the **I*I*I*1** syllogism:

$$\exists(Mx\ \&\ Px)$$
$$\exists(Sx\ \&\ Mx)$$
$$\therefore\ \exists(Sx\ \&\ Px)$$

Its singular equivalent for one individual *a* is:

$$Ma\ \&\ Pa$$
$$Sa\ \&\ Ma$$
$$\therefore\ Sa\ \&\ Pa$$

Its singular equivalent for two individuals *a* and *b* is:

$$(Ma\ \&\ Pa)\ \text{v}\ (Mb\ \&\ Pb)$$
$$(Sa\ \&\ Ma)\ \text{v}\ (Sb\ \&\ Mb)$$
$$\therefore\ (Sa\ \&\ Pa)\ \text{v}\ (Sb\ \&\ Pb\ )$$

Its singular equivalent for three individuals *a, b,* and *c* is:

$$(Ma \,\&\, Pa) \lor (Mb \,\&\, Pb) \lor (Mc \,\&\, Pc)$$
$$(Sa \,\&\, Ma) \lor (Sb \,\&\, Mb) \lor (Sc \,\&\, Mc)$$
$$\therefore (Sa \,\&\, Pa) \lor (Sb \,\&\, Pb) \lor (Sc \,\&\, Pc)$$

To refute the **I*I*I*1** syllogism by the method of countercase, we refute any one of its singular equivalents. Consider the singular equivalent for one individual *a.* To make the conclusion false, we have to let either *Sa* or *Pa* be false. But then one of the premises will also be false. So we cannot refute the singular equivalent for one individual. We must move on, therefore, to the singular equivalent for two individuals. This can be refuted as follows:

$$(Ma \,\&\, Pa) \lor (Mb \,\&\, Pb)$$
$$\text{T} \quad \text{T} \quad \text{T} \quad \text{T} \quad \text{F} \quad \text{F} \quad \text{F}$$
$$(Sa \,\&\, Ma) \lor (Sb \,\&\, Mb)$$
$$\text{F} \quad \text{F} \quad \text{T} \quad \text{T} \quad \text{T} \quad \text{T}$$
$$\therefore (Sa \,\&\, Pa) \lor (Sb \,\&\, Pb)$$
$$\text{F} \quad \text{F} \quad \text{T} \quad \text{F} \quad \text{T} \quad \text{F} \quad \text{F}$$

For invalid argument forms consisting exclusively of quantifiers, truth-functional connectives, and a finite number *n* of statement functions, it is theoretically sufficient to consider the singular equivalent for any 2^n individuals. So if such an argument form contains three statement functions, its singular equivalent for any eight individuals can always be refuted by the method of countercase. (The proof of this fact is something that would be taken up in advanced logic courses.) Fortunately, it is seldom necessary in practice to consider such a large singular equivalent. In general, when trying to refute an argument containing general statements by the method of countercase, it is most efficient to consider the singular equivalent for one individual first, then if necessary the singular equivalent for two individuals, then the singular equivalent for three individuals, and so on. It does not matter which individual constants are used, as long as the same constants are used to produce the singular equivalents of all the general statements in the argument. Thus you can use *c, d,* and *e* instead of *a, b,* and *c* if you like, as long as you are consistent.

Mixtures and Compounds. We have applied the method of countercase to argument forms consisting exclusively of singular statement variables, exclusive of universally quantified statements, or exclusively of existentially quantified statements. But the method can also be applied to argument forms containing a mixture of these three types of statements. To produce the singular equivalent of any argument form for a given set of individuals, simply replace all quantified statements with their singular equivalents for that set of individuals. Consider the **I*A*A*2** syllogism:

$$\exists (Px \,\&\, Mx)$$
$$\forall{-}(Sx \,\&\, {-}Mx)$$
$$\therefore \forall{-}(Sx \,\&\, {-}Px)$$

Its singular equivalent for one individual *a* is:

$$Pa \,\&\, Ma$$
$${-}(Sa \,\&\, {-}Ma)$$
$$\therefore {-}(Sa \,\&\, {-}Pa)$$

This cannot be refuted, so we must go on to two individuals:

$$(Pa \,\&\, Ma) \lor (Pb \,\&\, Mb)$$
$${-}(Sa \,\&\, {-}Ma) \,\&\, {-}(Sb \,\&\, {-}Mb)$$
$$\therefore {-}(Sa \,\&\, {-}Pa) \,\&\, {-}(Sb \,\&\, {-}Pb)$$

This can be refuted by letting *Sa, Sb, Ma, Mb,* and *Pb* be true, while letting *Pa* be false. When producing the singular equivalent of a mixed argument, you must remember to replace universal statements with conjunctions, and existential statements with disjunctions.

The method of countercase can also be applied to argument forms containing truth-functional compounds of quantified statements. We simply replace each quantified statement *wherever it occurs* with its appropriate singular equivalent. Consider:

$$\exists Px \lor \forall Px$$
$$\exists Px$$
$$\therefore \forall Px$$

Its singular equivalent for one individual *a* is:

$$Pa \lor Pa$$
$$Pa$$
$$\therefore Pa$$

This cannot be refuted, so we must move on to the singular equivalent for two individuals *a* and *b,* which is:

$$(Pa \lor Pb) \lor (Pa \,\&\, Pb)$$
$$Pa \lor Pb$$
$$\therefore Pa \,\&\, Pb$$

This can be refuted by letting *Pa* be false and *Pb* true. Note that the singular equivalent for two individuals *a* and *b* of $\forall\!-\!Px$ is $-Pa \,\&\, -Pb$, while the singular equivalent for the same two individuals of $-\forall Px$ is $-(Pa \,\&\, Pb)$.

The method of countercase can be applied to arguments containing singular statement variables as well as general statement forms by using the individual constants that appear in the singular statement variables to produce the singular equivalents of the general statements appearing in the argument. Any singular statement variables appearing in the original argument form must appear *as is* in every singular equivalent of the argument form. (Singular statement variables are their own singular equivalents, as it were.) Thus consider the following argument form:

$$\forall\!-\!(Px \,\&\, -Mx)$$
$$Mc \,\&\, Md$$
$$\therefore Pc \,\&\, Pd$$

Since two individuals *c* and *d* are mentioned, the first case we consider is that in which *c* and *d* are the only two individuals. The singular equivalent for this case is:

$$-(Pc \,\&\, -Mc) \,\&\, -(Pd \,\&\, -Md)$$
$$Mc \,\&\, Md$$
$$\therefore Pc \,\&\, Pd$$

The singular equivalent for the case of three individuals *c, d,* and *e* is:

$$-(Pc \,\&\, -Mc) \,\&\, -(Pd \,\&\, -Md) \,\&\, -(Pe \,\&\, -Me)$$
$$Mc \,\&\, Md$$
$$\therefore Pc \,\&\, Pd$$

To refute the argument form, it suffices to consider the case in which *c* and *d* are the only individuals. Let *Pc* and *Pd* be false, and let *Mc* and *Md* be true.

Aristotelian Categoricals. Finally, to apply the method of countercase to arguments containing Aristotelian categoricals, symbolize the conjunction of the Venn transform and presupposition of each **A**

and **E** proposition, and symbolize the Venn transform of each **I** and **O** proposition; then use the method of countercase to prove the invalidity of the resulting argument. Thus consider the **AII2** syllogism:

All *P* are *M*.
Some *S* are *M*.
∴ Some *S* are *P*.

This argument form is invalid if and only if the following argument form is invalid:

∀–(*Px* & –*Mx*) & ∃*Px*
∃(*Sx* & *Mx*)
∴ ∃(*Sx* & *Px*)

This quantified argument form can be refuted by considering the singular equivalent for two individuals *a* and *b*:

[–(*Pa* & –*Ma*) & –(*Pb* & –*Mb*)] & [*Pa* ∨ *Pb*]
(*Sa* & *Ma*) ∨ (*Sb* & *Mb*)
∴ (*Sa* & *Pa*) ∨ (*Sb* & *Pb*)

Let *Sa, Ma, Mb,* and *Pb* be true, and let *Sb* and *Pa* be false.

Glossary

Singular statement variable: a symbol like *Pa* that represents all statements about a given individual.

Singular equivalent: a singular statement that is equivalent to a quantified statement under the assumption that only certain individuals exist. The singular equivalent of a universally quantified statement is a conjunction with one conjunct for each individual, and the singular equivalent of an existentially quantified statement is a disjunction with one disjunct for each individual.

Refutation by countercase: proving that an argument form containing quantified statements is invalid by finding a consistent assignment of truth values to each singular statement variable in any one of the singular equivalents of the argument form that makes the premises true and the conclusion false.

Exercises

A. Prove that the following argument forms are invalid using the method of countercase.

1. ∀–(*Sx* & –*Px*)
    ∴ ∀–(*Px* & –*Sx*)

2. ∃(*Sx* & *Px*)
    ∴ ∀ –(*Sx* & –*Px*)

3. –∃(*Sx* & –*Px*)
    ∴ ∃(*Sx* & *Px*)

4. ∃(*Sx* & *Px*)
    ∴ ∃(*Sx* & –*Px*)

5. ∃(*Sx* & *Px*)
    ∴ ∀(*Sx* & Px)

6. ∀ –(*Sx* & *Px*)
    ∴ ∀–(–*Px* & *Sx*)

7. ∀–(*Sx* & –*Px*)
    Pa
    ∴ *Sa*

8. ∃(*Sx* & *Px*)
    Sa
    ∴ *Pa*

9. $Pa \& Pb$
    $\therefore \forall Px$

10. $-\forall(Sx \lor Px)$
    Sc
    $\therefore -Pc$

11. $\forall-(Mx \& -Px) \& \forall-(Sx \& Mx)$
    $\therefore \forall-(Sx \& Px)$

12. $\forall(-Sx \lor -Mx)$
    $\exists(Px \& -Mx)$
    $\therefore \forall(-Sx \lor Px)$

13. $\forall-(Mx \& Px)$
    $\exists(Mx \& Sx)$
    $\therefore \exists(Sx \& Px)$

14. $\exists(Mx \& Px)$
    $\exists(Mx \& Sx)$
    $\therefore \forall-(Sx \& -Px)$

15. $\forall-(Px \& -Mx)$
    $\forall-(Mx \& -Nx)$
    $\forall-(Nx \& -Sx)$
    $\therefore \forall-(Sx \& -Px)$

16. $\exists(Sx \& Mx)$
    $\exists(Mx \& Nx)$
    $\exists(Nx \& Px)$
    $\therefore \exists(Sx \& Px)$

17. $-\forall(Sx \lor Mx)$
    $\forall Px \lor \exists Mx$
    $\therefore \forall-Sx$

18. $\exists Kx \& \exists Lx$
    $\exists(-Kx \& -Lx)$
    $\therefore \exists(Lx \& -Kx)$

B. Prove the validity or invalidity of the following syllogistic forms, using the methods of quantification theory.

1. **AAA3**
3. **AAI1**
5. **IAI4**
7. **EAE3**
9. **IAI3**
11 **OOO1**

2. **EAE1**
4. **AAI2**
6. **AAI3**
8. **EIO1**
10. **OAO3**
12. **AOO2**

9.9 Relational Statements

Quantification theory provides the tools for analyzing the structure of simple subject-predicate statements, and for proving the validity and invalidity of arguments involving them. The more complete our ability to analyze logical structure, the more complete our ability to prove validity and invalidity. We have not yet provided for a complete analysis of logical structure, however. We have developed no way, for example, of analyzing the predicates in relational statements like the following:

Jack loves Mary.

The best we can do so far with this sentence is to symbolize it Mj, where j abbreviates "Jack" and M abbreviates "loves Mary." This representation is adequate for many purposes, as we have seen. For instance, it enables us to use UI to infer:

Something loves Mary.

Given the suppressed premise that Jack is a person, we can also infer "Someone loves Mary." However, using Mj to represent "Jack loves Mary" does not enable us to infer:

Jack loves something.

To draw this conclusion using the tools so far available, we would have to represent "Jack loves Mary" as Jm, where m abbreviates "Mary," and J abbreviates "Jack loves," or equivalently, "is loved by Jack." Neither way of symbolizing "Jack loves Mary," however, enables us to infer:

Something loves something.

Clearly, in order to represent fully the logical structure of "Jack loves Mary," we need *two* constants, one representing Jack and one representing Mary. We also need a *relational* predicate, say *L*, abbreviating "loves." This gives us: *Ljm*. The symbol *M* in *Mj* is called a *monadic* predicate constant since it abbreviates a predicate that combines with a single individual constant to form a singular proposition. The symbol *L* in *Ljm*, on the other hand, is a *dyadic* predicate constant, since it combines with two individual constants to form a singular statement. If *Gbfj* symbolizes "Bill gave the flower to Jane," then *G* is a *triadic* predicate constant. There can be *n*-adic predicate constants for any integer *n*. In general, when symbolizing relational statements, every singular term can be symbolized by an individual constant; the rest of the sentence can be represented by a relational predicate constant.

Once relational predicate constants are introduced, it is necessary to use more than one individual variable to represent form. For *Ljm* is not a substitution instance of *Lxx*. We cannot substitute different constants for the same variable when obtaining substitution instances. *Lxx* has only substitution instances like *Ljj* ("Jack loves himself") and *Lmm* ("Mary loves herself"). To represent the form of *Ljm*, we must therefore use *Lxy*, where *y* is a variable as well as *x*. *Lxy* is called a *dyadic statement function,* since it contains two different free variables and becomes a statement when all occurrences of both variables are replaced by constants. We also have to expand our stock of quantifiers. "Something loves something" cannot be symbolized ∃*Lxx*, for ∃*Lxx* means "Something is such that it loves itself." or "Something loves itself." ∃*Lxx* is not a statement that follows validly from "Jack loves Mary." To symbolize "Something loves something," we need *two* existential quantifiers, one for each variable in the dyadic statement function *Lxy*. The customary way of generating different quantifiers is to combine the symbols ∃ and ∀ with the different variables used, which gives us ∃*x*, ∃*y*, ∀*x*, ∀*y*, and so on as quantifiers. Then "Something loves something would be symbolized ∃*x*∃*yLxy*, and would be read "Something *x* is such that something *y* is such that *x* loves *y*." or "For some *x* and for some *y*, *x* loves *y*." The variables in dyadic statement functions that are bound by quantifiers continue to function as pronouns. The variables that are part of the quantifiers (which are also called bound variables) tell you which quantifier is the antecedent of which pronoun. The cross-referencing function of the variables that are part of the quantifiers is especially crucial when both existential and universal quantifiers are applied to the same polyadic statement function. For example, ∀*x*∃*yLxy* ("Everything loves something") has a very different meaning from ∃*x*∀*yLxy* ("Something loves everything").

Relational statements can be universally and existentially generalized, and multiply general statements, with two or more quantifiers, can be universally and existentially instantiated. However, the rules governing these operations are considerably more complicated than the rules developed in §9.4-5. The four quantification rules developed above apply only when *Px* is a statement function in which *x* is the only variable. Those rules are invalid if *Px* contains other variables besides *x*. All four rules must be restricted by additional conditions before they can be validly used with any statement function. That part of quantification theory which deals exclusively with statement functions containing only one variable is known as *monadic quantification theory*. Complete and rigorous treatments of general quantification theory can be found in more advanced logic texts.

CHAPTER TEN

The Outskirts of Logic

10.1 Modal Logic

Modal logic is the study of necessity, possibility, actuality, and related concepts. The basic laws of modal logic were worked out by Aristotle, but major advances have been made in this century, notably by C. I. Lewis (1883-1964) and Saul Kripke (1940-).

Modal Operators. Necessity is typically expressed by prefixing a sentence with "It is necessary that" or by modifying its main verb with the adverb "necessarily," as in "It is necessary that my brother is male," "Necessarily, my brother is male," or "My brother is necessarily male," The symbol $\Box$ is used to abbreviate "It is necessary that" or "necessarily," and is prefixed to a statement constant or variable. Thus if Mb symbolizes "My brother is male," $\Box Mb$ symbolizes "Necessarily, my brother is male." Possibility is similarly expressed by "It is possible that" and "possibly," which are abbreviated $\Diamond$. The symbols $\Box$ and $\Diamond$ are called ***modal operators***, and function syntactically like the symbol – for negation. $\Box p$ and $\Diamond p$ are compound propositions formed from a single proposition p. Actuality can be expressed in English by the prefix "It is actually the case that" or by the adverb "actually." But "The sky is *actually* blue" is equivalent to "The sky *is* blue": "actual" only serves to emphasize a contrast with "necessary" or "possible." So no special symbol is used in modal logic for actuality. "Actually p" is just symbolized "p."

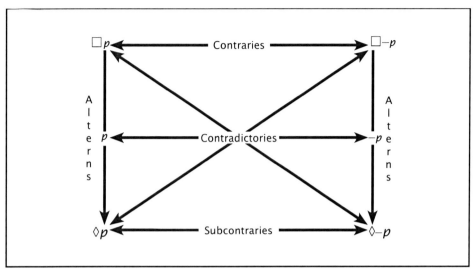

FIGURE 10-1. THE SQUARE OF MODAL OPPOSITION

Necessity is also expressed by the auxiliary verbs "must," "have to," and "need to," and possibility by "can," "could," and "might." "Impossible" and "unnecessary" combine modality and negation. "It is impossible that p" is equivalent to "It is not possible that p," and so can be symbolized $-\diamond p$. "It is unnecessary that p" is similarly equivalent to "It is not necessary that p," which would be symbolized $-\square p$. "Cannot" and "might not" also combine possibility and negation, but in different ways. "Might not" means "possibly not," as you would expect from the order of the words. "Cannot," however, means "not possibly." Thus "John might not have won" would be symbolized $\diamond-Wj$, whereas "John cannot have won" would be $-\diamond Wj$. "Must not" is predictable, meaning "necessarily not," while "need not" means "not necessarily." So "John must not have won" would be symbolized $\square-Wj$, whereas "John need not have won" would be $-\square Wj$.

Modal Opposition. Propositions differing only in modality or quality are **_opposed._** Opposing modal propositions stand in the same relationships as opposing categorical propositions (see Figure 10-1). $\square p$ and $\diamond-p$ are contradictory, so one must be true, the other false. This means that $\square p$ and $-\diamond-p$ are equivalent. The necessary is what cannot possibly be otherwise. To say that the light bulb must be burned out is to say that it is not possible that it is not burned out. $\diamond p$ and $\square-p$ are also contradictory, so that $\diamond p$ and $-\square-p$ are equivalent. The possible is what is not necessarily otherwise. Bill may live another year if and only if he will not necessarily not live another year. $\square p$ and $\square-p$ are contrary: they cannot both be true, although they might both be false. If "The coin necessarily will fall heads" is true, then "It necessarily won't fall heads" must be false. However, both statements may be false as they will be if the coin is normal. $\diamond p$ and $\diamond-p$, on the other hand, are sub-contrary: they cannot both be false, although they might both be true. The coin necessarily either may or may not fall heads. Falling heads and not falling heads cannot both be impossible, no matter what the coin is like: but if it is normal, both alternatives are possible.

Propositions that differ in modality alone are alterns. $\square p$ logically implies p, which in turn implies $\diamond p$. What is necessary is actual, and what is actual is possible. If the light bulb must be burned out, then it follows that it is burned out, and follows further that it might be burned out. The converse implications do not hold: what is possible may or may not be actual, and what is actual may or may not be necessary. The coin I just flipped could have come up heads, but it actually came up tails. These relationships are summarized in Table 10-1. $\diamond p$ is true in every case in which p is true, but $\square\, p$ is false in every case in which p is false, but $\diamond p$ is true in some, false in others. $\diamond p$ is true in every case in which $\square p$ is true, but $\square p$ is not true in every case in which $\diamond p$ is true. As Table 10-1 shows, *the modal operators are partially but not completely truth-functional.* The truth value of a modal statement is completely determined by the truth value of its component in some cases, but not in all.

As the square of modal opposition suggests, $\square p$ resembles an **A** proposition, $\square{-}p$ resembles an **E**, $\diamond p$ an **I**, $\diamond{-}p$ an **O**, p a **U**, and $-p$ a **Y**. These resemblances are more than skin deep, for each modal proposition is equivalent to a categorical statement about *possible cases* (or "possible worlds"). For example, the statement that it necessarily either will or will not rain is equivalent to the statement that it either will or will not rain in *every* possible case, which is in an **A** proposition. The statement that it may rain is equivalent to the **I** proposition that it will rain in *some* possible case. The statement that it will rain, finally, is equivalent to the **U** statement that it will rain in the *actual* case, which of course is a possible case. The complete set of equivalences follows:

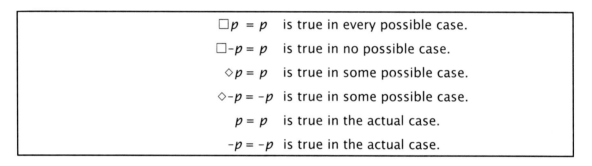

$$\square p = p \quad \text{is true in every possible case.}$$
$$\square{-}p = p \quad \text{is true in no possible case.}$$
$$\diamond p = p \quad \text{is true in some possible case.}$$
$$\diamond{-}p = -p \quad \text{is true in some possible case.}$$
$$p = p \quad \text{is true in the actual case.}$$
$$-p = -p \quad \text{is true in the actual case.}$$

These equivalences are associated with Gottfried Leibniz (1646-1716), the philosopher and mathematician famous for having said that God created this world because it is "the best of all possible worlds." The Leibnizian equivalences have made it possible to reduce modal logic to quantification theory. The principle that p follows from $\square p$ has its basis in UI, for example, and the principle that $\square p$ is equivalent to $-\diamond{-}p$ has its basis in the analogous rule of quantifier negation. We cannot pursue this development further in an introductory text, however.

Logical, Empirical, and Epistemic Necessity. There are many different types of necessity and possibility. A statement is said to be ***logically necessary*** if it is logically true, and ***logically possible*** if it is either logically true or logically contingent. A statement is logically true, recall, if all substitution instances of its specific form are true, and logically contingent if some, but not all, substitution instances of its specific form are true. A logically possible case, then, is one in which all logical truths are true. Thus it is logically possible that lead bars float, and logically necessary that lead bars either do or do not float. A statement is said to be ***empirically necessary*** (or "naturally necessary") if it is either a logical truth or a law of nature. An empirically possible case is one in which all the laws of nature and all the logical truths hold, and a statement is empirically possible if it is true in some empirically possible case. Thus, it is empirically as well as logically necessary that lead bars either do or do not float, since this is a logical truth. But while it is empirically necessary that lead bars sink, since this is a law of nature, it is not logically necessary, since it is not a logical truth. We must turn to science, of course, to determine exactly what the laws of nature are. The laws of modal logic, such as those represented by the square of modal opposition, hold whether $\square$ and $\diamond$ are interpreted as expressing the logical or empirical modalities.

Logical and empirical necessity and possibility are *absolute* modalities: a proposition that has such a modality at one time has it at all times. There are also *relative* necessities and possibilities. A statement is **epistemically (or deductively) necessary** if it is logically implied by the data, and possible if its negation is not logically implied by the data. An epistemically possible case is one in which all the data obtains. Epistemic necessities are things that can be validly deduced from the data. The *data* consists of all the *given* facts, propositions that are *known* to be true and are not in question ('Epistemic' derives from the Greek term for knowledge). The given facts will typically include, but not be limited to, some logical truths and laws of nature. Thus suppose it is given that all balls in an urn are red, and that a ball will be drawn. Then it is epistemically necessary that the ball will be red, and possible but not necessary that it will be plastic. It is neither logically nor empirically necessary, however, that the ball is red. For "The ball is red" is neither a logical truth nor a law of nature. This statement is epistemically necessary, though, because it is logically implied by the given fact that the ball will be drawn from an urn containing only red balls.

The given facts relative to which statements are assessed as epistemically necessary or possible may change from occasion to occasion. Suppose it is learned that the ball will be drawn from an urn containing only plastic balls, and forgotten that all balls in the urn are red. Then it is epistemically necessary that the ball will be plastic, and possible but not necessary that the ball will be red. Despite the importance of knowing precisely what the given facts are, they are seldom completely and explicitly specified when statements about relative necessity and possibility are made. When they are specified, it is usually by giving them as premises from which modal conclusions are drawn. The premises of such arguments must be understood as elliptical, with "It is given that...." understood. One might argue, for example, that the drawn ball must be red since all balls in the urn are red. But the conclusion that it is epistemically necessary for the drawn ball to be red does not follow simply from the fact that all balls in the urn are red, but from its being part of the data that all are red. The laws of modal logic also hold when $\Box$ and $\Diamond$ are interpreted as expressing relative necessity, but only so long as the same factual basis is assumed for all modal statements.

Logical, empirical, and epistemic necessity and possibility may be described as *descriptive or factual* modalities. There are, in addition, various *prescriptive* or *normative* modalities, such as moral and legal necessity. People may legally drive 50 mph on interstate highways, and they must legally have a driver's license. All the relationships represented in the square of opposition hold for prescriptive modalities *except* subalternation. Given that some people do drive 80 mph on interstate highways, it does not follow that they legally may. And the fact that every driver legally must have a license does not imply that every driver does. The logical properties of the prescriptive modalities are studied in a branch of modal logic known as *deontic logic*. We will concentrate on descriptive modality.

Compound Modal Statements. Great care must be taken when symbolizing statements in which modal operators and other logical connectives are mixed. We have already observed, for example, that "John may not win" is not equivalent to "John cannot win." The former would be symbolized $\Diamond -Wj$, while the latter would be $-\Diamond Wj$. There is a difference, in other words, between the possibility of a negation and the negation of a possibility. A similar distinction exists between the necessity of a disjunction and a disjunction of necessities. lit is logically necessary that the coin either will or will not fall heads: $\Box(Hc \lor -Hc)$ is true; but it is neither logically necessary that the coin will fall heads nor logically necessary that it won't: $\Box Hc \lor \Box -Hc$ is false. As with the negation sign, it is understood that a modal operator applies to the smallest possible unit to its right. Thus $\Box Rb \& Pb$ means $(\Box Rb) \& Pb$ rather than $\Box(Rb \& Pb)$.

The order of quantifiers and modal operators is also crucial. Suppose God is going to pick one but only one object random and destroy it. Then $\forall \Diamond Dx$ is true: no matter what object you pick, it may be destroyed by God. $\Diamond \forall Dx$, in contrast, is false: it is not possible that every object in existence will be destroyed by God, since it is given that just one is to be destroyed. ∀◇x expresses the universality of a possibility, while ◇∀Dx expresses the possibility of a universality. Unfortunately, an English sentence like "Every object may be destroyed by God" is ambiguous, and could mean either ∀◇Dx or ◇∀Dx. "Each object may be destroyed" and "Any object may be destroyed" are unequivocal, meaning only ∀◇Dx. And "Each and every object may be destroyed" means the conjunction ∀◇Dx & ◇∀Dx.

English conditionals with modal operators can be ambiguous too. Consider "If it rains, then it necessarily will rain." As normally interpreted, this is true. The sentence could mean either $R \Rightarrow \Box R$ or $\Box(R \Rightarrow R)$. However, $R \Rightarrow \Box R$ is false: actuality does not imply necessity. $\Box(R \Rightarrow R)$, on the other hand, is true: every statement necessarily implies itself. The latter interpretation is normally the one intended, therefore, even though the former is most straightforward. As a general rule, sentences of the form "If p then necessarily q" should be symbolized $\Box(p \Rightarrow q)$ rather than $p \Rightarrow \Box q$. Exceptions to the rule occur when the antecedents as well as the consequents of conditionals are modalized. For example, "If the ball is necessarily both red and plastic, then it is necessarily red" should be symbolized straightforwardly as $\Box(Rb \& Pb) \Rightarrow \Box Rb$. Conditionals with the possibility operator do not present the same problem. "If p then possibly q" should generally be symbolized $p \Rightarrow \Diamond q$, although occasionally $\Diamond(p \Rightarrow q)$ is appropriate.

Rules of Inference. The method of deduction can be used to prove the validity of arguments involving modal statements by selecting some valid modal argument forms to serve as rules of inference, and using them together with the rules of propositional logic and quantification theory. The first argument forms we shall select are based on the fact that $\Box p$, p, and $\Diamond p$ are alterns.

Modal Subalternation (MS)
From $\Box p$ infer p, from p infer $\Diamond p$, and from $\Box p$ infer $\Diamond p$.

$\Box p$　　　　p　　　　$\Box p$
$\therefore p$　　　$\therefore \Diamond p$　　$\therefore \Diamond p$

Modal subalternation is a one-way rule, and functions just like simplification or addition. The first form listed is analogous to UI, since it involves taking off the necessity operator; the second is analogous to EG, since it involves putting on the possibility operator. The third form is superfluous given the other two, but its use will save trivial steps.

We shall add a rule of replacement based on the fact that $\Box p$ and $\Diamond -p$ are contradictory, as are $\Box -p$ and $\Diamond p$. Since $\Box p$ and $-\Diamond -p$ are logically equivalent, they may replace each other wherever they occur. A similar rule holds for each of the equivalences that can be read off the square of modal opposition.

Modality Negation (MN)
Any two statements equivalent by one of the following rules may replace each other wherever they occur.

$$\Box p = -\Diamond -p$$
$$-\Box p = \Diamond -p$$
$$\Box -p = -\Diamond p$$
$$-\Box -p = \Diamond p$$

Modality negation operates just like quantifier negation.

The final rules we shall select are grounded on the unconditional validity of the one-way rules of propositional logic. Consider modus ponens, for example, which enables us to infer B from $A \Rightarrow B$ and A. Since modus ponens is unconditionally valid, B must be true in every possible case in which $A \Rightarrow B$ and A are true. If $A \Rightarrow B$ and A are themselves true in every possible case, then B must also be true in every possible case. So we can also infer $\Box B$ from $\Box(A \Rightarrow B)$ and $\Box A$. This latter inference is an instance not of modus ponens itself, but of what we will call the *modal extension* of modus ponens. We will call the rule *modal modus ponens* (MMP). Note that $\Box B$ follows from A and $A \Rightarrow \Box B$ by modus ponens, not by its extension. Every other one-way rule of propositional logic (and indeed every other unconditionally valid rule) also has a modal extension.

The Modal Extension Rules

If a statement can be inferred from other statements by any of the one-way rules of propositional logic, then the necessity of the statement can be inferred from the necessity of the other statements.

MConj	MAdd	MSimp	MDS
$\Box p$	$\Box p$	$\Box(p \mathbin{\&} q)$	$\Box(p \lor q)$
$\Box q$	$\therefore \Box(p \lor q)$	$\therefore \Box p$	$\Box -p$
$\therefore \Box(p \mathbin{\&} q)$			$\therefore \Box q$

MDT	MMP	MMT
$\Box(p \lor q)$	$\Box(p \Rightarrow q)$	$\Box(p \Rightarrow q)$
$\Box(-q \lor r)$	$\Box p$	$\Box -q$
$\therefore \Box(p \lor r)$	$\therefore \Box q$	$\therefore \Box -p$

We do not need modal extensions of the replacement rules in propositional logic or quantification theory. For they already tell us that specified statements may replace each other *wherever they occur*. So $\Box(A \mathbin{\&} B)$ can be inferred from $\Box(B \mathbin{\&} A)$ by commutation. And $\Diamond \forall -Px$ can be inferred from $\Diamond -\exists Px$ by quantifier negation.

Our modal extension rules all involve necessity. There are similar but slightly different rules involving possibility: if a statement follows from other statements by any rule of propositional logic, then the possibility of the statement follows from the *joint* possibility of the other statements. For example, while $\Diamond(p \lor r)$ follows from $p \lor q$ and $-q \lor r$ disjunctive transitivity, $\Diamond(p \lor r)$ does not follow from $\Diamond(p \lor q)$ and $\Diamond(-q \lor r)$. To see this, let p be "Bachelors are married", q be "It will rain'" and r be "Vixen are male." While there is a possible case in which "Bachelors are married or it will rain," is true (any case in which it rains), and another in which "It will not rain or vixen are male" is true (any case in which it does not rain), there is no case in which "Bachelors are married or vixen are male" is true. The problem is that "Bachelors are married or it will rain" and "It will not rain or vixen are male" are true only in *different* possible cases. To infer $\Diamond(p \lor r)$ by an extension of DT we must be given $\Diamond[(p \lor q) \mathbin{\&} (-q \lor r)]$ which requires that $p \lor q$ and $-q \lor r$ *both* be true in the *same* possible case. Many of the extension rules involving possibility can be derived using the extension rules involving necessity together with the other rules of our system; this will be done in the exercises. The system is not complete, but we shall not complicate it further.

The modal extensions of three of the four quantification rules are not unconditionally valid. Consider UI, which allows us to infer Ps from $\forall Px$, where s is any constant. The modal extension of UI would allow us to infer $\Box Ps$ from $\Box \forall Px$. $\Box \forall Px$ says that everything in every possible case is P. $\Box Ps$ says that s is P in every possible case. Now s is P in every possible case only if s *exists* in every possible case. But the existence of s in a given case is not guaranteed by the fact that everything is P in that case.

The convention governing the use of constants in quantification theory requires that constants designate objects existing in the actual case; but there is no requirement that constants designate objects existing in every possible case. Modal UI is valid, in other words, only under the special condition that any individual existing in the actual case exists in all possible cases, which would mean that any individual that does exist must exist. Modal UG, which would allow us to infer $\square \forall Px$ from $\square Ps$, where s is an arbitrarily selected constant, is valid only under the converse condition that any individual existing in any possible case exists in the actual case, which would mean that any individual that could exist does exist. Both rules are valid under the condition that the same objects exist in all possible cases.

Modal EI, which would allow us to infer $\square Ps$ from $\square \exists Px$, where s is a new constant, is not valid under any useful conditions. For while $\square \exists Px$ says that something is P in every possible case, it does not require that the same thing is P in every possible case. But $\square Ps$ requires that s is P in every possible case. Consider a game in which it is necessary that someone will win; it need not be a game in which any particular person will necessarily win. The only quantification rule whose modal extension is unconditionally valid is EG: $\square Ps$ logically implies $\square \exists Px$. If s is P in every possible case, then something is P in every possible case. $\diamond Ps$ similarly implies $\diamond \exists Px$. We shall not use modal EG as a rule of inference.

Glossary

Modal operators: the symbols $\square$ and $\diamond$, which abbreviate "necessarily" and "possibly."

Opposing modal propositions: those differing only in modality or quality.

Logical necessity: A statement is logically necessary if it is a logical truth.

Empirical necessity: A statement is empirically necessary if it is either a logical truth or a law of nature.

Epistemic (or Deductive) necessity: A statement is epistemically (or deductively) necessary if it is logically implied by the data.

Modal subalternation (MS): the rule that p and $\diamond p$ may be inferred from $\square p$, and that $\diamond p$ may be inferred from p.

Modality negation (MN): the rule that any two statements equivalent by one of the following rules may replace each other wherever they occur: $\square p = -\diamond -p$, $-\square p = \diamond -p$, $\square -p = -\diamond p$, $-\square -p = \diamond p$.

Modal extension rules: a set of rules specifying that if a statement can be inferred from other statements by any of the one-way rules of propositional logic, then the necessity of the statement can be inferred from the necessity of the other statements.

Exercises

A. Symbolize the following modal statements using the symbols of quantification theory and modal logic.

1. The next president may be a woman.

2. The current president is actually a man.

3. The president is necessarily either a man or a woman.

4. The president cannot be a foreigner.

5.   The next president need not be a Republican.

6.   The quarterback must either run or pass.

7.   Either the quarterback must run or he must pass.

8.   The quarterback must run if he does not pass.

9.   The quarterback cannot both run and pass.

10. If the quarterback can pass then he will pass.

11. Necessarily everything either is or is not red.

12. Everything necessarily either is or is not red.

13. It is impossible for something to be both red and nonred.

14. George might win if he runs.

15. Anything might go wrong.

16. Everything might go wrong.

17. Something might go wrong.

18. Something might not go wrong.

19. Nothing can go wrong.

20. Nothing can't go wrong.

B.   Assuming that the numbered statements below are true, determine whether the lettered statements are true, false, or undetermined, and explain why in terms of the square of modal opposition.

1.   The next president might be a woman.

   (a) The next president might not be a woman.

   (b) The next president must be a woman.

   (c) The next president necessarily won't be a woman.

2.   The Yankees have to have won.

   (a) The Yankees might not have won.

   (b) The Yankees might have won.

   (c) The Yankees must have not won.

3.   It is possible that God exists.

   (a) It is necessary that God exists.

   (b) It is possible that God does not exist.

   (c) It is necessary that God does not exist.

4. Something possibly won't go wrong.

    (a) Something possibly will go wrong.

    (b) Something necessarily will go wrong.

    (c) Something necessarily won't go wrong.

C. Assuming that the numbered statements in Set B are false, determine whether the lettered statements are true, false, or undetermined.

D. Determine which of the following pairs of statements are equivalent or inequivalent, compatible or incompatible.

1. (a) The next president might be a woman.
    (b) The next president might not be a woman.
2. (a) The Yankees must have won.
    (b) The Yankees could not have won.
3. a) The Tigers could not have won.
    (h) The Tigers must not have won.
4. (a) It is not impossible to succeed.
    (b) It is possible to succeed.
5. (a) John will not necessarily succeed.
    (b) John cannot possibly succeed.
6. (a) Bill will necessarily not succeed.
    (b) It is not possible for Bill to succeed.
7. (a) Your car may not rust.
    (b) Your car cannot rust.
8. (a) I will not necessarily not come.
    (b) I may possibly come.
9. (a) A student cannot possibly not study.
    (b) A student can study.
10. (a) The quarterback does not have to be tall.
    (b) The quarterback is tall.

E. Identify the rule of inference (if there is one) by which the conclusions of the following arguments follow from the premises.

1. $\Box(Ra \,\&\, Rb)$
    $\therefore Ra \,\&\, Rb$

2. $\Box(Ra \,\&\, Rb)$
    $\therefore \Box Ra$

3. $\Diamond Fi \lor \Diamond -Fi$
    $\therefore \Diamond Fi \lor -\Box Fi$

4. $\Diamond Ga$
    $\therefore Ga$

5. Ga
    $\therefore \Diamond Ga$

6. $\Diamond(Fa \Rightarrow Ga)$
    Fa
    $\therefore \Diamond Ga$

7. $Fa \Rightarrow \Diamond Ga$
    Fa
    $\therefore \Diamond Ga$

8. $\Box(Fa \Rightarrow Ga)$
    $\Box{-}Ga$
    $\therefore \Box{-}Fa$

9. $\Box Fa$
    $\Box Ga$
    $\therefore \Box(Fa \& Ga)$

10. $\Box Fa$
    $\Box Ga$
    $\therefore \Box Fa \& \Box Ga$

11. $\Box Am$
    $\therefore \Box(Am \vee An)$

12. $\Box Am$
    $\therefore \Box Am \vee An$

13. $-\Box{-}(Bk \vee Ck)$
    $\therefore \Diamond(Bk \vee Ck)$

14. $-\Box({-}Bk \vee Ck)$
    $\therefore \Diamond(Bk \vee Ck)$

15. $-\Box(Ra \& Rb)$
    $\therefore -(Ra \& Rb)$

16. $\Box{-}(Ra \& Rb)$
    $\therefore -(Ra \& Rb)$

17. $\Box(At \vee Bt)$
    $\Box({-}Bt \vee Ct)$
    $\therefore \Box(At \vee Ct)$

18. $\Diamond(At \Rightarrow Bt)$
    $\Diamond At$
    $\therefore \Diamond Bt$

19. $\Box\forall{-}(Fx \vee Gx)$
    $\therefore \Box\forall({-}Fx \& {-}Gx)$

20. $\Box(At \Rightarrow Bt)$
    $\therefore \Diamond(At \Rightarrow Bt)$

F. Prove: the validity of the following arguments using the method of deduction.

1. $-\Diamond Fa$
    $\therefore -Fa$

2. $-Fa$
    $\therefore -\Box Fa$

3. $\Box({-}Ra \& {-}Sa)$
    $\therefore -\Diamond(Ra \vee Sa)$

4. $\Box\forall Fx$
    $\therefore -\Diamond\exists{-}Fx$

5. $Ra \vee Sa$
    $\Box{-}Sa$
    $\therefore \Diamond Ra$

6. $\Box{-}Me$
    $-\Diamond Ne$
    $\therefore \Diamond{-}(Me \vee Ne)$

7. $\Box(Pa \& Qa)$
    $\therefore \Box Pa \& \Box Qa$

8. $\Box(Fa \vee Ga)$
    $-\Diamond Fa$
    $\therefore \Diamond Ga$

9. $\Box Fa$
    $\therefore \Diamond\exists Fx$

10. $\Box\forall Fx$
    $\therefore \Diamond Fa$

11. $-\Diamond\exists Fx$
    $\therefore -Fa$

12. $\Box(As \vee Bs)$
    $\Box({-}Bs \vee {-}Cs)$
    $-\Diamond{-}Cs$
    $\therefore \Box As$

13. $\Box(Fa \& Ga)$
    $-\Diamond(Fb \vee Gb)$
    $\therefore \Box(Fa \& {-}Fb)$

14. $-\Diamond(Bc \& Bd)$
    $\Box(Ac \& Bc)$
    $\therefore -\Diamond Bd$

15. $\square(\forall Rx \lor \exists Bx)$
    $-\lozenge\forall Rx$
    $\therefore \lozenge\exists Bx$

16. $\square Sj \lor \square Tj$
    $\lozenge -Tj$
    $\therefore \square(Sj \lor Tj) \, \& \, \square(Sj \lor -Tj)$

17. $\square\forall(Fx \Rightarrow Gx)$
    $\square Fa$
    $\therefore \lozenge Ga$

18. $\forall\square(Cx \lor Dx)$
    $-\lozenge\exists Cx$
    $\therefore \lozenge\exists Dx$

G. Symbolize the following arguments, then prove their validity using the method of deduction.

1. It is not possible for something to be both red and green all over. Therefore, it is not the case that something is red and green all over.

2. Not everything is good. Therefore, it is not necessary for everything to be good.

3. Necessarily, nothing is both a plant and an animal. Therefore, the slime mold is not both a plant and an animal.

4. Nothing can be both a wave and a particle. Therefore, light is either not a wave or not a particle.

5. Necessarily both Alan and Bob failed. Therefore, necessarily either Alan or Bob failed.

6. Necessarily everything is in space. Therefore, it is possible that something is in space.

7. If John crosses the river, then he will have to swim. He can't swim. So he won't cross the river.

8. If anything can go wrong, it will go wrong. The computer circuitry in new cars can go wrong, so it will.

9. If it is possible for Kerry to be nominated, then it is possible for McCain to be. Kerry will in fact be nominated. Therefore it is not impossible for McCain to be nominated.

10. If something is the will of God, then it must be good. The Holocaust was evil. If anything is evil, then it necessarily isn't good. Therefore the Holocaust was not the will of God.

H. Prove the validity of the following modal extension rules, using the method of indirect proof.

1. $\lozenge(p \, \& \, q)$
   $\therefore \lozenge p$

2. $\lozenge p$
   $\therefore \lozenge(p \lor q)$

3. $\lozenge[(p \lor q) \, \& \, (-q \lor r)]$
   $\therefore \lozenge(p \lor r)$

4. $\square(p \lor q)$
   $\lozenge(-q \lor r)$
   $\therefore \lozenge(p \lor r)$

5. $\square(p \Rightarrow q)$
   $\lozenge p$
   $\therefore \lozenge q$

6. $\square(p \Rightarrow q)$
   $\lozenge -q$
   $\therefore \lozenge -p$

7. $\square(p \lor q)$
   $\lozenge -p$
   $\therefore \lozenge q$

8. $\lozenge(p \lor q)$
   $\square -p$
   $\therefore \lozenge q$

10.2 Probability

The study of probability is on the borderline between logic and mathematics, having close links with both disciplines. Rigorous courses in probability theory are customarily taught by mathematicians, who seek to prove new theorems and develop new applications. Logicians are especially interested in the connections between probability theory and inductive logic, and in the logical foundations of probability theory. Probability theory was developed by numerous mathematicians, including Blaise Pascal (1623-1662), Jakob Bernoulli (1654-1705), Laplace (1749-1827), and A. N. Kolmogorov (1903-1987). The laws of probability were discovered by studying games of chance, but their applicability is universal.

There are two kinds of probability statement. *Qualitative* probability statements, like "It is probable that it will rain," state that something is probable or improbable, without specifying a degree of probability. *Quantitative* probability statements, like "The probability that it will rain is .9," specify how probable something is. Qualitative probability statements could be represented by probability operators analogous to the modal operators. We will focus on quantitative probability statements, however, which are symbolized using the functional notation of mathematics. We shall use "$P(p)$" to represent the probability of any given statement p. If R is the statement that it will rain, "$P(R) = .9$" is the statement that the probability of rain is .9. "Probability," of course, has the synonyms "chance" and "likelihood."

The Probability Calculus. The basic laws of probability form an interrelated system called the *probability calculus*, since it enables us to calculate unknown probabilities on the basis of known probabilities. The probability calculus can be presented as a *deductive system*, in which certain laws are selected as *axioms* from which the remaining laws can be deduced as *theorems*. Many different choices of axioms are possible. We shall select a set that emphasizes the links between probability theory and logic. The first axiom is that the probability of any statement is a number between 0 and 1.

Axiom 1: $0 \leq P(p) \leq 1$.

Probabilities, in other words, are nonnegative quantities with a maximum value, which is conventionally selected as the unit. Probabilities can be expressed equivalently as percentages, fractions, or decimals. Thus we may say indifferently that the probability of rain is 90 percent, or 9/10, or .9, for 90 percent $= 90/100 = 9/10 = .9$. The second axiom says that the highest degree of probability is possessed by necessary truths.

Axiom 2: $P(p) = 1$ if p is necessary.

Thus the probability is 1 that it either will or will not rain, and that tomorrow is not both Saturday and Sunday. The necessity referred to in axiom 2 may be of any sort (logical, empirical, or deductive), But when we derive theorems using axiom 2, p will be a logical necessity, since we can prove that something is logically necessary by purely logical techniques. Note that axiom 2 is not intended as a biconditional: it does not say that p has probability 1 *only if p* is necessary. Axiom 3 states that equivalent propositions have the same probability.

Axiom 3: $P(p) = P(q)$ if p and q are equivalent

The probability that it will be hot and humid is the same as the probability that it will be humid and hot (commutative rule): the probability that it will not be both hot and humid is the same as the probability that it will either not be hot or not be humid (De Morgan's rule); and so on. Axiom 3 functions like a rule of replacement. It holds, however, whether p and q are logically equivalent, or only equivalent relative to the evidence.

Probabilities may change over time. The principles of the probability calculus hold only when all probabilities are referred to the same time. Clearly, the probability in 1979 that John and Bill will live another thirty years need not equal the probability in 1999 that Bill and John will live another thirty years.

Axiom 4 relates disjunction to addition, and is called the *addition rule*.

The Addition Rule
Axiom 4: $P(p \lor q) = P(p) + P(q)$ if p and q are incompatible.

Getting a one on a single roll of a fair die is incompatible with getting a two. Since the probability of a one is 1/6, and the probability of a two is also 1/6, the probability of a one or a two is 2/6. Getting an ace of spades when drawing a single card from a standard deck is incompatible with getting a diamond. Since the probability of an ace of spades is 1/52 and the probability of a diamond is 13/52, the probability of an ace of spades or a diamond is 14/52. Axiom 4 is stated for disjunctions containing only two disjuncts. Three or more propositions are incompatible if each one is incompatible with each of the others. Any disjunction formed from such propositions will be incompatible with any other disjunction formed from them. By repeatedly applying axiom 4, it can be seen that the addition rule holds for disjunctions of any length. Thus let A, B, C, and D be incompatible. Then $A \lor B$ and $C \lor B$ are also incompatible. Hence $P[(A \lor B) \lor (C \lor D)] = P(A) + P(B) + P(C) + P(D)$. So an immediate corollary of axiom 4 *is* that *the probability of a disjunction of incompatible propositions is the sum of the probabilities of the disjuncts.* In the course of our logical investigations, we have proven that many statement forms are logically necessary, equivalent, and incompatible. Axioms 2, 3, and 4 enable us to use these results to prove theorems in the probability calculus.

Our fifth and final axiom relates conjunction to multiplication, and is called the *multiplication rule*.

The Multiplication Rule
Axiom 5: $P(p \;\&\; q) = P(p) \times P(q/p)$

$P(q/p)$ is the probability of q if (or *given*) p, and is called a *conditional probability*. (It is customary in probability theory to use a slash or a comma for conditional probability rather than an arrow.) By the commutative rule, $P(q \;\&\; p) = P(p \;\&\; q)$ so it is a corollary of axiom 5 that $P(p \;\&\; q)$ is also equal to $P(q) \times P(p/q)$. Hence the multiplication rule says that the probability of a conjunction is equal to the probability that one of its conjuncts is true multiplied by the probability that the other conjunct is true if the first is. Suppose that two cards will be drawn from a full deck. The probability that the first will be an ace is 4/52. The probability that the second will be an ace, given that the first is an ace, is 3/51. So by axiom 5, the probability that both the first and the second cards will be aces is $(4/52) \times (3/51) = 12/2652$.

Axiom 5 can be solved for $P(q/p)$ by dividing both sides by $P(p)$. This yields $P(q/p) = P(p \;\&\; q)/P(p)$, which relates conditional probability to division. Since this formula enables us to calculate conditional probabilities given certain unconditional probabilities, it is often called the ***reduction rule***. Suppose a pair of dice is rolled. The probability that both the first and the second die will come up six is 1/36; the probability that the first die will come up six is 1/6; so the probability that the second die will come up six if the first one does is $(1/36)/(1/6) = 1/6$. Since it is impossible to divide by zero, the reduction rule cannot be used when $P(p) = 0$.

Axiom 4 says that the probability of a disjunction of mutually exclusive alternatives is the sum of the probabilities of its disjuncts. If a set of alternatives is jointly exhaustive, their disjunction is necessarily true, and so by axiom 2 the probability of their disjunction is 1. It follows that if a set of alternatives is both mutually exclusive and jointly exhaustive, then their probabilities sum to 1.

> **Theorem 1:** $P(p) + P(q) + \ldots + P(z) = 1$ if $p, q, \ldots, z$ are mutually exclusive and jointly exhaustive.

The alternatives of getting a one on the roll of a die (O) getting a six (S), and getting neither a one nor a six are mutually exclusive and jointly exhaustive. So $P(O) + P(S) + P(-O \& -S) = 1$. Now any proposition and its negation are mutually exclusive and jointly exhaustive, so as a special case of theorem 1 we have $P(p) + P(-p) = 1$. When this is solved for $P(-p)$, we obtain a formula that relates negation to subtraction.

> **Theorem 2:** $P(-p) = 1 - P(p)$.

Since the probability of getting a one on the roll of a die is $1/6$, the probability of not getting a one is $5/6$. If the probability of rain is 75 percent, the probability of no rain is 25 percent. According to axiom 2, the probability of any necessity is 1. Now if a proposition is necessary, then its negation is impossible. So it follows from theorem 2 that the probability of any impossibility is 0.

> **Theorem 3:** $P(p) = 0$ if p is impossible.

Since it is impossible to both win and not win a game, the probability of both winning and not winning is zero. Since it is impossible to get both heads and tails on a single coin toss, the probability of getting both is 0.

Odds. Probabilities are often expressed in terms of ratios called **odds**. The *odds of an event occurring* are said to be $a{:}b$ (read "*a* to *b*") when *a* divided by *b* is equal to the probability of the event occurring divided by the probability of it not occurring: $a/b = P(E)/P(-E)$. Theorem 2 entails that the odds of an event occurring are $a{:}b$ when the probability of the event occurring is $a/(a + b)$, which means that the probability of the event not occurring is $b/(a + b)$.

> The odds of E occurring are $a{:}b$ when $P(E) = a/(a + b)$ and $P(-E) = b/(a + b)$.

Thus to say that the odds of getting an A are 3:5 is to say that the probability of an A is 3/8, which means that the probability of not getting an A is 5/8. The odds *against* an event occurring are the odds of its not occurring. So if the odds in favor of getting an A are 3:5, then the odds against getting an A are 5:3. The odds against an event are always the reciprocal of the odds in favor of the event. Now when b is many times greater than a, $a + b$ will be approximately equal to b, and hence a/b will be approximately equal to $a/(a + b)$. In most lotteries and commercial contests, for example, the odds of winning are on the order of 1:1,000,000 or even 1:10,000,000. The probability of winning in such cases can be given with sufficient accuracy as 1/1,000,000 or 1/10,000,000. The stated odds in lotteries and the like are usually estimates anyway.

If you bet on an event occurring, then the odds of it occurring equal the ratio of the probability of your winning to the probability of your losing. Unfortunately, this whole terminology of odds can be very confusing. For when someone announces "the odds" for an event, you may not know whether he is giving the odds of the event occurring or *the odds for betting on the event,* which equal the ratio of what you will win if the event occurs to what you will lose if it does not Suppose you will receive $3 if you win and pay $1 if you lose; then the betting odds are 3:1. Now betting odds on an event are considered *fair* if they are the odds *against* your winning, which are the odds of your losing. So betting odds of 3:1 are fair if the odds of losing are 3:1. Since you are 3 times more likely to lose than to win, it is considered fair if you stand to win three times what you might lose. Betting odds are *favorable* when greater than fair odds, *unfavorable* when less. If the odds of winning are 1:3, then betting odds of 4:1 are favorable, while betting odds of 2:1 are unfavorable. The probability calculus was discovered in large part because of the efforts of Pascal and others to determine fair betting odds for various games of chance.

Qualitative Probability Statements. We are now in a position to define the qualitative probability operators in terms of quantitative probabilities. *Certainty* is the highest possible degree of probability. So a statement is certain provided its probability is 1. Certainty in this sense is *complete,* or *absolute,* certainty. "Certainty" is also commonly used in a weaker sense, however, to denote a degree of probability *near* 1. Thus it is certain in the weak sense that a normal coin will come up heads at least once in 1,000 tosses, even though it is not completely certain that it will. A statement is *probable,* or *likely,* if it is more likely than not to be true. If $P(p) > P(-p)$ then it follows from theorem 2 that $P(p) > 1/2$. So a statement is probable provided there is better than a "50-50 chance," or "even odds," that it is true. A statement is *improbable,* or *unlikely,* if its negation is probable, which means that its probability is less than ½. Thus it is improbable that a die will come up six, and probable though not certain that it will not come up six. It is neither probable nor improbable that a fair coin will come up heads. There is *a chance* that a statement is true, finally, as long as its probability is greater than zero. Thus there is a chance that a normal coin will come up heads 100 times in a row, but no chance that it will come up both heads and tails.

It is certain that p:	$P(p) = 1$.
It is probable that p:	$P(p) > 1/2$.
It is improbable that p:	$P(p) < 1/2$.
There is a chance that p:	$P(p) > 0$.

These equivalences, together with axiom 2 and theorem 3, give us the modal ordering presented in §2.2: necessity implies certainty, certainty implies probability, and probability implies possibility. Similarly, impossibility implies improbability, lack of certainty, and lack of necessity.

The Probability Calculus (Continued). Let us return to axiom 4, relating disjunction to addition, Axiom 4 applies only when the disjuncts are incompatible or mutually exclusive. The addition rule can be generalized however, to cover all disjunctions.

Theorem 4: $P(p \lor q) = P(p) + P(q) - P(p \& q)$.

Intuitively, P(*p*) already reflects the probability that *p* is true with *q,* but P(*q*) also reflects the probability that *q* is true with *p.* To avoid double-counting the probability that both *p* and *q* are true, P(*p* & *q*) must be subtracted from P(*p*) + P(*q*). When *p* and q are incompatible, P(*p* & *q*) = 0, so this adjustment is unnecessary. More rigorously, theorem 4 is based on two equivalences that can be proven by truth tables: *p* v *q* = (*p* & –*q*) v *q*, and *p* = (*p* & *q*) v (*p* & –*q*). Applying axiom 3, we get the following two equations:

$$P(p \vee q) = P[(p \& {-q}) \vee q]$$

$$P(p) = P[(p \& q) + P(p \& {-q})]$$

Now *q* is incompatible with *p* & –*q*, and *p* & *q* is incompatible with *p* & –*q*. So axiom 4 can be applied to the right side of both equations, yielding:

$$P(p \vee q) = P(p \& {-q}) + P(q)$$

$$P(p) \quad = P(p \& q) + P(p \& {-q})$$

The second equation here can be solved for P(*p* & –*q*), giving us P(*p* & –*q*) = P(*p*) – P(*p* & *q*). P(*p*) – P(*p* & *q*) can therefore be substituted for P(*p* & –*q*) in the first equation, giving us P(*p* v *q*) = P(*p*) – P(*p* & *q*) + P(*q*), which is equivalent to theorem 4. To illustrate the application of theorem 4, suppose that two regular dice are tossed, and that we wish to calculate the probability of getting a one on the first die *or* on the second. Getting a one on the first die is compatible with getting a one on the second. So theorem 4 must be applied instead of axiom 4. The probability of a one on the first die is 1/6; the probability of a one on the second die is also 1/6. The probability of a one on both dice is 1/36. So the probability of getting a one on the first die or the second is 1/6 + 1/6 – 1/36 = 11/36, which is slightly less than 1/3.

We saw above that P(*p*) = P(*p* & *q*) + P(*p* & –*q*). This can be solved for P(*p* & *q*), giving us P(*p* & *q*) = P(*p*) – P(*p* & –*q*). Now, by axiom 1, P(*p* & *q*) is nonnegative. It follows, then, that P(*p* & *q*) ≤ P(*p*). It can similarly be shown that P(*p* & *q*) ≤ P(*q*). *The probability* of *a conjunction is always less than or equal to the probability* of *either conjunct.* Hence the probability of a conjunction is less than or equal to the probability of the *least* likely conjunct. It follows that if a conjunction is certain, then each conjunct is certain, and that if a conjunction is probable, then each conjunct is probable, which are probabilistic versions of the simplification rule. Look now at theorem 4. Since P(*q*) ≥ P(*p* & *q*) by the above rule, P(*q*) – P(*p* & *q*) ≥ 0. Consequently, *the probability of a disjunction is always greater than or equal to the probability of either disjunct.* The probability of a disjunction is greater than or equal to that of the *most* likely disjunct. It follows that if any disjunct is certain (or probable), then the whole disjunction is certain or probable), which is analogous to the addition rule of propositional logic. Indeed, a probabilistic analogue of the truth tables for the logical connectives can be calculated, with probabilities one and zero in place of truth and falsity (see Table 10-2).

P(*p*)	P(*q*)	P(-*p*)	P(*p* & *q*)	P(*p* v *q*)	P(*q* / *p*)
1	1	0	1	1	1
1	0	0	0	1	0
0	1	1	0	1	
0	0	1	0	0	

TABLE 10-2

The third column of Table 10-2 can be derived from the first by theorem 2. The entries in the first three rows of the fifth column can be derived from those in the first two columns by the rule that the probability of a disjunction is greater than or equal to that of the most probable disjunct. The last entry in column 5 (and 4) can be determined using theorem 4: when $P(p)$ and $P(q)$ are 0, $P(p \lor q) = -P(p \& q)$; but this can hold only if both $P(p \lor q)$ and $P(p \& q)$ are 0, since probabilities are nonnegative numbers by axiom 1. The fourth column can be calculated from the first, second, and fifth by solving theorem 4 for $P(p \& q)$, which gives: $P(p \& q) = P(p) + P(q) - P(p \lor q)$. The last column can be calculated from the first and fourth by solving axiom 5 for $P(q/p)$, which gives: $P(p/q) = P(p \& q)/P(p)$. It is impossible to divide by zero, so $P(q/p)$ is undetermined when $P(p) = 0$. The last column indicates that conditional probability corresponds to the weak conditional, not the strong conditional (or the material conditional).

Two events are said to be ***independent*** if the occurrence or nonoccurrence of one is uncorrelated with the occurrence or nonoccurrence of the other. Thus the possible outcomes of successive coin tosses are independent, while the possible outcomes of one coin toss are not. If two events are independent, then the unconditional probability that one will occur is equal to the conditional probability that it will occur if the other occurs: $P(p) = P(p/q)$. Thus the probability of heads on the second toss of a coin is the same as the probability of heads on the second toss given tails on the first toss. But whereas the probability of heads on the second toss is 1/2, the probability of heads given tails on the same toss is 0. It follows from the definition that if p and q are independent, then $-p$ and $-q$ are also. Since getting heads on one toss is independent of getting heads on another toss, not getting heads on the one toss is independent of not getting heads on the other. A simple version of the multiplication role (axiom 5) holds for independent propositions:

Theorem 5: $P(p \& q) = P(p) \times P(q)$ if p and q are independent.

Since the outcomes of two successive coin tosses are independent, the probability of getting heads on both tosses is $1/2 \times 1/2 = 1/4$. The outcome of rolling one die is independent of the outcome of rolling another. So the probability of a pair of sixes is $1/6 \times 1/6 = 1/36$. The definition of independence, and theorem 5, can be extended to any number of propositions. Three or more events are independent if each one is uncorrelated with any combination of the others. And in general, the probability of a conjunction of independent propositions is the product of the probabilities of its conjuncts.

The principles discussed so far enable us to calculate probabilities when other probabilities are already given. Only axiom 2 and theorem 3 give us any initial probabilities. The probability calculus would have little utility, however, if there were no other way to arrive at initial probabilities. In many of the calculations above, it was assumed that the probability of getting a six on a roll of a die is 1/6. How was this determined? There are six possible outcomes if a die is rolled: one could come up, two could come up and so on. These outcomes are mutually exclusive and jointly exhaustive, so by theorem 1 the sum of their probabilities is 1. These alternatives, furthermore, are *equally probable*. Since there are six equal probabilities whose sum is 1, each probability must be 1/6. What is the probability of a three or better? There are four ways of getting a three or better: by getting a three, a four, a five, or a six. Since these ways are incompatible, the probability of getting a three, a four, a five, or a six is $1/6 + 1/6 + 1/6 + 1/6$, or 4/6. The probability, of getting a three or better is therefore 4/6. The general procedure is summarized by theorem 6, which we shall call the *ratio rule*.

The Ratio Rule

Theorem 6: $P(p) = s/n$ where n is the total number of mutually exclusive, jointly exhaustive, and equally probable cases, and s is the number of cases in which p is true.

It is common to think of *s* here as the number of "successes," since if you bet on *p* you will win in every case in which *p* is true. The practical utility of the ratio rule is limited by our ability to identify equally probable cases. Judgments of equiprobability are commonly based on observed *symmetries,* as with coins and dice, on various procedures like shuffling and mixing designed to insure *random selection,* and on the observation of *equal frequencies* of occurrence. Warning: we can seldom if ever he sure that two outcomes are *exactly* equiprobable. A coin's symmetry, for example, is hardly perfect. As a result, the precision of most probability estimates, including those we have been using for illustrative purposes, should be taken with a grain of salt. While the ratio rule is simple in concept, its application is often difficult because it requires the mathematics of combinations and permutations. To calculate the probability of drawing a full house from a full deck of cards, for example we need to know how many different combinations of 5 cards can be drawn from 52 cards, and how many different permutations or orders each can be arranged in.

The Statistical Syllogism. Another common method for arriving at initial probabilities does not seem to involve the ratio rule. Let us return to John, a 25-year-old American male applying for life insurance. Since 86 percent of all 25-year-old American men live to be 50, the insurance company might infer that John will probably live to be 50. This pattern of inference, discussed in §3.3, is called the statistical syllogism. But the insurance company might also infer, from the same data, that the probability of John living to be 50 is 86 percent. In general, from the premise that percentage *r* of population *P* has attribute *A*, we may under certain conditions infer not only the qualitative conclusion that a particular member of that population probably does (or does not) have *A*, but also the quantitative conclusion that the probability of the member having *A* is *r* percent, We may accordingly distinguish between the *qualitative* and *quantitative forms* of the statistical syllogism.

The Statistical Syllogism: Quantitative Form
r% of all *P* have *A*.
i is *P*.
∴ P(*i* has *A*) = *r*%.
CV: *i* is a single object randomly selected from the population of *P*s.

This argument form is especially useful in practice because the percentage of the population having *A* can either be observed directly, or can be inferred from the percentage observed in a limited sample using enumerative induction. The statistical syllogism can also be used to estimate probabilities in connection with coin tosses and the like. Suppose we toss a coin 100 times and observe that heads came up 51 percent of the time. We can consider our 100 coin tosses to be a sample drawn from the population of all tosses of that coin. Then using enumerative induction, we can infer that 51 percent of all tosses of that coin will come up heads. And using the quantitative form of the statistical syllogism, we can infer that the probability of heads in the next toss is 51 percent.

Appearances to the contrary, the quantitative form of the statistical syllogism is based on the ratio rule. For a condition of validity on the statistical syllogism is that the inference object be *randomly selected* from the population. If the insurance company suspects that the processes that bring applicants to its doors are not random—if, say, the company attracts mainly men with serious illnesses—then it cannot infer the probability of John living to be 50 from the percentage of the population at large living to be that age. If the selection is random, however, then every member of the population has an equal chance of being the inference object. Let there be *n* members of the population. Then *i* could be the first member of the population, the second member, ..., or the *n*th member: these are the *n* mutually exclusive, jointly exhaustive, and equally probable cases required for application of the ratio rule. If *s* is the number of members having attribute *A*, then the ratio *s/n* equals *r* percent, the percentage of the population having *A*. Let *p* be the proposition that *i* has *A*, and the conclusion can be drawn by the ratio rule that $P(i$ has $A) = r\%$. The condition that *i* be randomly selected requires that *i* not be known to belong to any particular subgroup of the population, for every member of the population must have an equal chance to be *r*. If a 25-year-old man is known to have a serious illness, for example, we cannot infer the probability that he will live to be 50 from the percentage of all 25-year-old men that do. Actually, this condition can be relaxed somewhat. It will not matter if *i* is known to belong to an *irrelevant* subgroup, one in which the same percentage *r* possesses *A*. For in that case, the premise of the argument could simply be restated. It is all right if John is known to have blond hair, for example, as long as 86 percent of all 25-year-old American males with blond hair live to be 50.

The conditions of validity on the qualitative and quantitative forms of the statistical syllogism differ. First, in order to infer by the qualitative form that *i* probably has *A*, the percentage of the population having *A* must be over 50 percent. But with the quantitative form, there is no restriction on the percentage. Since 19 percent of all 25-year-old American males live to be 80, we can infer that there is a 19 percent chance that John will, even though we cannot infer that he probably will reach 80. Second, the inference group in a qualitative statistical syllogism may consist of more than one object, although with larger inference groups the conclusion is less probable. We may infer that both John and George will live to be 50, for example, if both are 25-year-olds. But the quantitative form can only be used directly with one inference object. We may infer that there is an 86 percent chance that John will live to be 50, and an 86 percent chance that George will, but not that there is an 86 percent chance that both will live to be 50. We can, however, *calculate* the probability that both will live to be 50 by using the multiplication rule. Assuming independence, the probability that both will reach 50 is .86 x .86 = .74. The probability that John and George as well as Tom and Dick will all reach 50 would be 55 percent (.55 = .86 x .86 x .86 x .86). The probability of any five 25-year-old American men living to be 50 would be .47, so an inference group of four is the maximum for a qualitative statistical syllogism in this case.

Inductive and Empirical Probability. There are two different types of probability, both governed by the probability calculus. The type directly relevant to logic is called ***inductive probability*** (or *logical probability*), and is analogous to epistemic (or deductive) necessity. The inductive probability of a proposition is determined by the degree to which it is supported by the data. A proposition that follows from the data by a deductively valid argument (and is therefore deductively necessary) has a probability of 1. A proposition that follows from the data by an inductively valid argument has a probability greater than 1/2 but less than 1. A proposition that is supported by the data, but whose negation is supported equally well, has a probability of 1/2. A proposition whose negation follows from the data by either a deductively or an inductively valid argument has a probability less than 1/2. If everything were *known*, then the probability of every proposition would be either 1 or 0. Fractional inductive probabilities exist, therefore, only because our knowledge is incomplete. *Inductive probability is a measure of rational belief*. It is not rational to believe a proposition unless it is probable on the evidence, or to withhold belief from a proposition that is probable on the evidence. The greater the probability of a proposition, the more certain we may and should be that it is true.

The inductive probability of a proposition is determined by *all* the available evidence, not just part of it. This is called the ***principle of total evidence***. We observed in §3.4 that while an argument is invalid if it excludes any undermining evidence, an inductively valid argument need not include all the evidence in its premises. While the omission of some evidence may make the conclusion seem more or less probable than it really is, the validity of an argument requires only that the conclusion is *at least probable* if the premises are true. But when the exact degree of probability is at issue, all the evidence must be considered. The principle of total evidence therefore applies to quantitative assessments of inductive probability and not to qualitative assessments of inductive validity. The principle also applies to deductive necessity. A proposition that is not logically implied by selected parts of the data is still deductively necessary as long as it is implied by all of it.

In addition to inductive probability, there is ***empirical probability*** (or *statistical probability*). The empirical probability of an event is determined by how frequently it tends to occur in a given situation. *Empirical probability is a measure of long-run relative frequency.* To say that the empirical probability of a coin falling heads is 1/2 is to say that the coin has a tendency to fall heads half the times it is tossed. If the coin is tossed just a few times, it may fall heads much more or less than 50 percent of the time. But if it were tossed again and again hundreds and thousands of times (with no wear-and-tear), the relative frequency of heads (the number of heads divided by the number of tosses) would tend to come closer and closer to 1/2. If a coin tends to fall heads 60 percent of the time, then the probability of heads is .6 rather than .5, and the coin is said to be biased.

The inductive probability of an event will typically be equal to the empirical probability, especially since the observed frequency of an event in the past is important evidence as to whether it will occur again in the future. But inductive and empirical probabilities are often different. Suppose we are presented with a coin that *appears* to be normal, but *unbeknownst to us* is actually weighted so that it is biased towards heads. Then the inductive probability of heads is 1/2, since the coin looks symmetrical and looks just like a million other coins that have been observed to fall heads as often as tails. But since the coin is actually biased toward heads, the empirical probability of heads is greater than 1/2. Suppose now that the coin is tossed and that the percentage of heads is observed to gradually approach 60 percent. The inductive probability of heads will increase from 50 percent to 60 percent as the data comes in. But the empirical probability of heads will not change appreciably from toss to toss.

As these examples illustrate, the inductive probability of heads depends on the available *evidence* about the coin, whereas the empirical probability of heads depends on the *properties of* the coin. Thus the empirical probability depends on whether the coin is symmetrical, while the inductive probability depends on whether it is *known* to be symmetrical. And the empirical probability depends on how the coin is *disposed* to fall in the future, while the inductive probability depends on how it has been *observed* to fall in the past. The empirical probability does not change significantly from toss to toss, because the coin suffers little wear-and-tear. But the inductive probability may change from toss to toss because each successive toss constitutes new evidence about future tosses.

Empirical probability statements have been playing an increasingly important role in scientific theories since the end of the nineteenth century, as in genetics, statistical mechanics, and quantum theory. To take a simple example, the *half-life* of a radioactive element is based on the empirical probability of radioactive decay. A half-life of 3 minutes, for instance, means that the empirical probability is 1/2 that any given atom will decay within 3 minutes. Inductive probability statements, in contrast, appear not *within* scientific theories, but in their *evaluation*. The claim that the theory of evolution is more probable than the theory of special creation is an inductive probability statement. The notion of empirical probability is not even applicable to a proposition like the theory of evolution since it does not describe a *repeatable* event. It simply makes no sense to say that the theory of evolution has a tendency to occur, or even to be true, a certain proportion of the time. Propositions that do not describe repeatable events have no empirical probability at all (not even the probability of zero). The empirical probability function is said to be *undefined* for them.

Insufficient Reason vs. Equal Evidence. Laplace is justly esteemed for his many valuable contributions to the mathematical theory of probability and its applications. But he is also infamous for having laid down what he called the ***principle of insufficient reason***, according to which *any set of mutually exclusive and jointly exhaustive alternatives are equally likely if the available evidence does* *not support one more than any other.* This principle seems very plausible, and has been used by many able thinkers to justify application of the ratio rule. Suppose an urn is known to contain only red and white balls. And suppose that 100 balls are drawn, 50 of which are red. What is the probability that the next ball will be red? The available evidence does not support the proposition that the ball will be red any more than the proposition that it be white. So the principle of insufficient reason rules that they are equally likely, which means that the probability of another red ball is 1/2. While the principle seems to give the correct results in this case, it yields contradictory results in other cases. Suppose we are told that the ratio of men to women at a school is somewhere between .5 and 1 (i.e., somewhere between one man for every two women and one man for every woman). Then the following two propositions are mutually exclusive and jointly exhaustive on the evidence: the ratio of men to women is between .5 and .75; and the ratio of men to women is between .75 and 1. The available evidence does not support one of these propositions more than the other, since .75 is halfway between .5 and 1. So by the principle of insufficient reason, they are equally probable; hence both have probability 1/2. Again, this seems plausible. But now consider that if the ratio of men to women is between .5 and 1, then the ratio of women to men is between 2 and 1 (if there is one man for every two women, then there are two women for every man). So on the same evidence, two other propositions are also mutually exclusive and jointly exhaustive: the ratio of women to men is between 2 and 1.5; and the ratio of women to men is between 1.5 and 1. Neither of these two propositions is supported by the evidence more than the other, since 1.5 is halfway between 2 and 1. So they are equally likely by the principle of insufficient reason, which implies that both have probability 1/2. But now observe that if the ratio of men to women is .75, then the ratio of women to men must be 1.3, the reciprocal of .75. So the principle of insufficient reason has led us to the absurd result that it is equally likely that the ratio of women to men is between 1.3 and 1 as it is that the ratio is between 1.5 and 1. This could be only if the probability were zero that the ratio is between 1.3 and 1.5. But another application of the principle rules that the probability of the ratio being in that interval is 1/5 (divide the interval between 1 and 2 into 5 equal subintervals of length .2). Since a contradiction has been derived from the principle of insufficient reason, it has been proven false by the method of *reductio ad absurdum.*

The principle of insufficient reason is fallacious for much the same reason that arguments from ignorance are fallacious. Just as we cannot infer that a proposition is true from the fact that there is no evidence that it is false, so we cannot infer that a proposition has any particular probability from the fact that contrary propositions are not supported the evidence. It is instructive in this regard to compare closely the two cases presented in the previous paragraph. In the urn example, there was plenty of evidence that the next ball would be red, since 50 previous balls were red. There was, however, an equal amount of evidence that the next ball would be white, since 50 previous balls were white. But in the school example, there was no evidence at all that the ratio of women to men was between 1 and 1.5, and there was no evidence that it was not between 1 and 1.5. The principle of insufficient reason is false, therefore, because it applies when there is no evidence at all supporting any of the possible alternatives as well as when the alternatives are all supported by the evidence to an equal extent. "Insufficient reason," in other words, includes "no reason" as well as "equally good reason." When the principle is properly restricted, it becomes what we shall call the ***principle of equal evidence:*** *Any set of mutually exclusive and jointly exhaustive alternatives are equally likely if they are supported by the evidence and supported equally.* This principle holds only for inductive probability. It does not apply to empirical probability, because that depends on the actual properties of things and not on our evidence about them. When there is no evidence supporting a proposition, it has no inductive probability. The inductive probability function is undefined, therefore, for the proposition that the ratio of women to men is between 1 and 1.5 as well as for the proposition that it is between 1 and 1.3.

Subjective Probability. Both inductive and empirical probability are *objective* in the sense that the probability that an event will occur is independent of whether or not any particular person believes that it will. Inductive probabilities depend on the logical relations between a proposition and the available data, while empirical probabilities generally depend on the physical properties of things. It was said above that certainty is the highest degree of probability. But the term "certainty" has a subjective as well as an objective sense. Compare the following two statements:

> It is certain that the coin will fall heads.
> I am certain that the coin will fall heads.

The first statement may be true even though the second is false (I may not realize that the coin is two-headed), and the second may be true even though the first is false (I may mistakenly think the coin is two-headed). "Certainty" has its objective sense in the first statement, its subjective sense in the second. Objective certainty is the highest degree of objective probability. Subjective certainty, on the other hand, is the highest degree of *belief*; so it is natural and increasingly common to refer to belief as *subjective probability*. The calculus of probability holds for both types of objective probability, but not for subjective probability. While many principles of the probability calculus are plausible for subjective probability (such as the theorem that a disjunction is no less certain than either disjunct), others are implausible (such as the axiom that all necessary truths are certain—no one knows all the necessary truths). It can be said, however, that the beliefs of a perfectly rational person *would* conform to the probability calculus. For inductive probability is a measure of *rational* belief.

Glossary

Probability calculus: the basic laws of probability, which form a deductive system, and enable the calculation of unknown probabilities given known probabilities.

Odds: The odds of an event occurring are the ratio of the probability of the event occurring to the probability of its not occurring; the betting odds for an event are the ratio of what the bettor will win if the event occurs to what he will lose if it does not. Betting odds of $a:b$ for an event are fair if the odds of the event occurring are $b:a$.

Addition rule: the principle that the probability of a disjunction of incompatible propositions is the sum of their probabilities, and that in general $P(p \lor q) = P(p) + P(q) - P(p \& q)$.

Multiplication rule: the principle that the probability of a conjunction of independent events is the product of their probabilities, and that in general $P(p \& q) = P(p) \times P(q/p)$.

Reduction rule: the principle reducing conditional probabilities to unconditional, according to which $P(p/q) = P(p \& q)/P(q)$.

Independence: Two events are independent if the occurrence or nonoccurrence of one is uncorrelated with the occurrence or nonoccurrence of the other, so that $P(p) = P(p/q)$ and $P(p \& q) = P(p) \times P(q)$.

Ratio rule: $P(p) = s/n$, where n is the total number of mutually exclusive, jointly exhaustive, and equally probable cases, and s is the number of cases in which p is true.

Statistical syllogism, quantitative form: the argument in which the conclusion that $P(i \text{ has } A) = r\%$ is drawn from the premises that i is P and that $r\%$ of all P have A; to be valid, i must be a single object randomly selected from the population of Ps.

Inductive probability: the type of probability that is determined by the degree to which a proposition is supported by the data, and is therefore a measure of rational belief.

> **Empirical probability:** the type of probability that is determined by how frequently an event tends to occur in a given situation, and that is therefore a measure of long-run relative frequency.
>
> **Subjective probability:** degree of belief.
>
> **Principle of total evidence:** the principle that the inductive probability (and deductive necessity) of a proposition is determined by all available data.
>
> **Principle of insufficient reason:** the fallacious principle that any set of mutually exclusive and jointly exhaustive alternatives are equally likely if the available evidence does not support one more than any other.
>
> **Principle of equal evidence:** the principle that any set of mutually exclusive and jointly exhaustive alternatives are equally likely (inductively) if they are supported by the evidence and supported equally.

Exercises

A. Determine whether the following statements are compatible or incompatible, and if compatible whether one implies the other.

1. (a) Bill is certain to win.
   (b) Bill is likely to win.
2. (a) Rain is improbable.
   (b) There is a chance of rain.
3. (a) Rain is likely.
   (b) Rain is not unlikely.
4. (a) It is probable that the hurricane will not strike land.
   (b) It is improbable that the hurricane will strike land.
5. (a) It is probable that the hurricane will strike land.
   (b) It is probable that the hurricane will not strike land.
6. (a) There is a chance that Bill will win.
   (b) It is not certain that Bill won't win.
7. (a) Bill is likely to win.
   (b) It is probable that either Bill or John will win.
8. (a) It will probably be hot, and it will probably be humid.
   (b) It is probably going to be both hot and humid.
9. (a) It is probable that it will be hot and humid.
   (b) It is probable that it will be hot if it is humid.
10. (a) It will probably be hot and humid.
    (b) It will probably be hot or humid.
11. (a) It is probable that either Mary or Jane will succeed.
    (b) It is probable that Mary and Jane will not both fail.
12. (a) I am likely to have fish and either peas or spinach.
    (b) I am likely to have either fish and peas or fish and spinach.

B. Use the probability calculus to find the unknown probabilities below on the basis of the given information.

1. GIVEN: the probability of rain (R) is 3/4, the probability of hail (H) is 1/8, and rain and hail are independent. Find:

(a) P(–H).
(b) P(–R).
(c) P(R & H).
(d) P(R & –H).
(e) P(H & –R).
(f) P(–H & –R).
(g) P(R ∨ H).
(h) P(R ∨ –H).
(i) P(–R ∨ H).
(j) P(–R ∨ –H).

(k) P(H/R).
(1) P(R/H).
(m) P(–R/H).
(n) P(H/–R).
(o) P[(R & –H) ∨ (R & H)].
(p) P[R & (–H ∨ H)].
(q) P[R/(H ∨ –H)]
(r) P[(R & –H) ∨ (–R & –H)].
(s) P[R & (H & –R)].
(t) P[(R & –H) ∨ (–R & H) ∨ (–R & –H)].

2. GIVEN: the probability of rain (R) is 1/2, the probability of lightning (L) is 1/2, and the probability of lightning given rain is 3/4. Find:

(a) P(–L).
(b) P(R & L).
(c) P(R ∨ L).
(d) P[–(R ∨ L)].
(e) P(–R & –L).
(f) P(–R/–L).
(g) P[(R & L) ∨ (-R & -L)].

(h) P[(R & L) ∨ (R & –L)].
(i) P(R & –L).
(j) P(R/ –L).
(k) P(–L/R).
(1) P[L/(R & –L)].
(m) P[R/(R & L)].

3. GIVEN: a normal coin tossed several times. Find the probability of the following outcomes:
(a) Heads on the first three tosses.
(b) Heads on the first toss, and tails on the second and third.
(c) Heads on either the first or the second toss.
(d) Heads on the first but not the second toss.
(e) Heads on the first toss and on either the second or third.
(f) Heads on neither the first nor the second toss.

4. GIVEN: a normal pair of dice tossed once. Find the probability of the following outcomes:
(a) A five on both dice.
(b) A five on at least one die.
(c) A five on exactly one die.
(d) A five on at most one die.
(e) A five or a six on the first die.
(g) A five on the first die or a six on the second.

5. GIVEN: a normal deck of cards from which a single card is drawn. Find the probability of getting the following:
(a) A king.
(b) Anything but a queen.
(c) A king or a nonqueen.

(d) A black queen or a red king.

(e) A spade and a diamond.

(f) A king and a spade.

(g) A king or a spade.

(h) An even numbered card.

(i) A face card.

(j) A face card or an even numbered card.

(k) A face card but not an even numbered card.

6.   GIVEN: a normal deck of cards from which three cards are drawn in succession and then discarded. Find the probability of getting the following:

(a) Three aces.

(b) An ace and then two kings.

(c) Two kings and then an ace.

(d) An ace, followed by a king and then a queen.

(e) A three, followed by a seven and then an eight.

C. Convert probabilities to odds and odds to probabilities. (Convert to odds of occurrence rather than betting odds.)

1.   The probability of heads is 1/2.

2.   The probability of not getting a six is 5/6.

3.   The probability of drawing an ace is 4/52.

4.   The probability of drawing three aces in a row is 24/132,600.

5.   The odds of getting a five on both dice are 1:35.

6.   The odds of Blue Sky winning are 6:1.

7.   The odds of Midnight Magic winning are 1:100.

8.   The odds against rain are 4:3.

9.   The fair odds for betting on the Tigers are 2:3.

10. The fair odds for betting on the Cubs are 3:2.

D. Prove the following theorems.

Theorem 7: $P(p) = P(p \& q) + P(p \& -q)$.

Theorem 8: $P(p) = [P(p/q) \times P(q)] + [P(p/-q) \times P(-q)]$.

Theorem 9: $P(-q/p) = 1 - P(q/p)$, provided $P(p) > 0$.

Theorem 10: ("Bayes's Theorem"): $P(q/p) = P(p/q) \times [P(q)/P(p)]$, provided $P(p) > 0$. (Hint: $P(q \& p) = P(p \& q)$.)

Theorem 11: $P(p \& q) = P(q)$ if p is necessary.

Theorem 12: $P(p/q) = 1$ if p is necessary and $P(q) > 0$. (Hint: use axiom 4.)

Theorem 13: $P(p/q) = P(p)$ if q is necessary. (Hint: use theorems 10 and 12.)

Theorem 14: $P(p) \leq P(q)$ if p logically implies q.

Theorem 15: $P(q/p) = 1$ if p logically implies q (when $P(q) > 0$).

Theorem 16: $P(p/q) = s_{p\&q}/s_q$ where $s_{p\&q}$ is the number of equally likely, jointly exhaustive, and mutually exclusive cases in which $p \& q$ is true, and s_q is the number of those in which q is true, provided $P(q) > 0$.

Theorem 17: If $P(p) = P(p/q)$, then $P(q) = P(q/p)$, provided $P(p) > 0$.

Theorem 18: If $P(p) = P(p/q)$, then $P(-p) = P(-p/-q)$, provided $P(-q) > 0$.

Theorem 19: $P(p \vee q \vee r) = P(p) + P(q) + P(r) - P(p \& q) - P(p \& r) - P(q \& r) + P(p \& q \& r)$. (Hint: apply axiom 4, letting q be $q \vee r$.)

Theorem 20: $P(p \& q \& r) = P(p) \times P(q/p) \times P(r/p \& q)$.

10.3 Binary Logic Circuits

The design of digital computers is a branch of computer engineering. The basic circuits of a digital computer, however, perform operations that represent the truth-functional connectives of propositional logic, and are therefore called *logic circuits*. Logic circuits have provided the "brain power" since the first digital computers were developed in the 1940s by Howard Aiken and IBM, by J. Presper Eckert and John W. Mauchly, and by John von Neumann.

The word *digital* means that all information is represented by *discrete* variables, whose values can therefore be represented by digits. Digital systems are opposed to *analog* systems, in which information is represented by *continuous* variables. Everyone should be familiar by now with the two different kinds of clock. Digital clocks represent the time by a sequence of four digits, two representing the hour and two the minute. Analog clocks represent the time by the position of two hands as they rotate around in a circle. While analog computers are possible, digital computers have been more successful in practice because of the physical restrictions of the hardwire components and also because of the logical propensities of computer designers. Modern computers are electronic, representing all information by electrical signals. They are furthermore *binary,* meaning that only two different signals are used, such as high and low voltage (or equivalently, current). High voltage (or "on") is represented by 1, and low voltage (or "off") by 0. All information is represented by a sequence of 1's and 0's, which are called *binary digits,* or for short, *bits*.

Gates. The basic processing in a modern digital computer is done by logic circuits called *gates*. Gates are silicon chips or other electronic components that take one or more signals as inputs and produce a single signal as output. Different gates have different input-output functions. One gate with two inputs, for example produces a high voltage output only when *both* inputs are high-voltage signals. Since the input-output function of this gate is analogous to the truth function of conjunction (which produces a true "output" only when both "inputs" are true), it is called an *AND-gate.* We shall represent the inputs by the variables x and y, and the output by the compound $x \& y$, which we shall call a *logic formula.* The input-output function of an AND-gate can be summarized by a *logic table* that is analogous to the truth table for conjunction (see Table 10-3).

x	y	x & y
1	1	1
1	0	0
0	1	0
0	0	0

TABLE 10-3. AND-GATE

Two other gates are called **OR-gates** and **inverters**. OR-gates also have two inputs but produce a high-voltage output as long as *either* input is high, and therefore represent inclusive disjunction; we will symbolize the output by the logic formula $x \vee y$. Inverters have a single input and produce a high-voltage output only when the input is low, and so could be called NOT-gates; we will represent the output by $-x$ (see Table l0-4). There are AND-gates and OR-gates with more than two inputs, but we will concentrate on the simplest case.

x	y	x ∨ y
1	1	1
1	0	1
0	1	1
0	0	0

x	−x
1	0
0	1

TABLE 10-4. OR-GATE AND INVERTER

Compound Logic Circuits. AND-gates, OR-gates, and inverters suffice to perform all the computations of a computer. More complex logic circuits can be constructed by *combining* these three gates. To illustrate this process, let us use the symbols in Figures 10-2, 10-3, and 10-4 for our basic logic circuits.

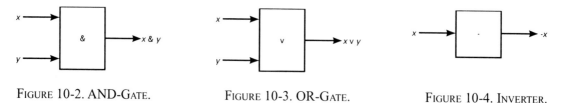

FIGURE 10-2. AND-GATE.   FIGURE 10-3. OR-GATE.   FIGURE 10-4. INVERTER.

Suppose we want to construct a logic circuit that takes x and y as input and produces $-(x \, \& \, y)$ as output, and which would therefore have the input-output function in Table 10-5:

x	y	-(x & y)
1	1	0
1	0	1
0	1	1
0	0	1

TABLE 10-5. NAND-GATE

We could construct such a circuit by combining an AND-gate with an inverter in such a way that the output of the AND-gate becomes the input of the inverter. This circuit, called a NAND-gate, is represented by the *logic diagram* in Figure 10-5.

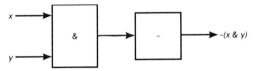

FIGURE 10-5. NAND-GATE.

Suppose two high-voltage inputs are fed into the NAND-gate. The AND-gate will produce a high-voltage output, which will then be fed into the inverter. The inverter will convert the high-voltage input into a low-voltage output. So the NAND-gate satisfies the first row of the logic table. Verify for yourself that it also satisfies the remaining rows.

   Any binary input-output function can he realized by a combination of AND-gates, OR-*gates, and inverters.* If the input-output function is specified by a logic formula like $-(x \& y)$, $-(x \lor y)$, or $x \lor (-x \& -y)$, then it should be easy, given your study of propositional logic, to diagram a logic circuit with that input-output function by combining AND-gates, OR-gates, and inverters just as they are combined in the logic formula. If the input-output function is given by a logic table, we can proceed as follows: First find a logic formula which would have that logic table. Then diagram the circuit by combining the basic gates as they are combined in the formula. Suppose we want to diagram a circuit with the input-output function represented in Table 10-6.

x	y	?
1	1	0
1	0	1
0	1	1
0	0	0

TABLE 10-6

The desired circuit must have high output when either x or y but not both have high output. So one logic formula with this logic table is the exclusive disjunction $x \lor y$, which is equivalent to $(x \lor y) \& -(x \& y)$. Now, given the formula $(x \lor y) \& -(x \& y)$, we can diagram the appropriate logic circuit (see Figure 16-6).

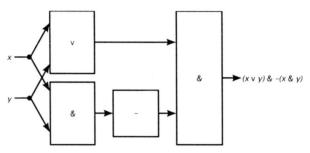

FIGURE 10-6. XOR-GATE.

We shall call this the XOR-gate. Note a new element in this diagram: the inputs branch off and enter two different gates. A dot indicates a connection point where one signal passes to two or more wires. Lines that cross without a dot are unconnected. (The size of a gate box has no significance.)

There are two systematic procedures for producing a logic formula for any given logic table without trial and error. The first is to form a *disjunction of conjunctions,* with one conjunction for every row in which the output is 1. This method yields $(x \& -y) \vee (-x \& y)$ for Table 10-6, since the desired circuit has high output when $x \& -y$ has high output (second row) or when $-x \& y$ has high output (third row). The other method for inducing logic formulas from logic tables is to form a *conjunction of negations,* with one negation for every row in which the output is 0. This method yields $-(x \& y) \& -(-x \& -y)$ for Table 10-6, since the desired circuit has 0 output when either $x \& y$ (first row) or $-x \& y$ (fourth row) has high output. The different circuits represented by the three formulas $(x \vee y) \& -(x \& y)$, $(x \& -y) \& (-x \& y)$ and $-(x \& y) \& -(-x \& -y)$ are said to be ***equivalent,*** since they all have the same logic table. Even though the two methods produce equivalent results, the disjunctive method is easier when there are more high outputs then low; the conjunctive method is easier when there are more low outputs.

In pure logic, costs are irrelevant. In engineering, however, they are a major factor influencing design. If two different circuits can do the same job, the less expensive is preferable. Logic circuits "do the same job" if they have the same input-output function. For every logic circuit, there is an infinite number of equivalent circuits. Let us assume that our basic AND-, OR-, and NOT-gates are the only circuit elements with significant costs, and that they are equally costly (these may not be realistic assumptions). Then, given any logic circuit, an engineer will try to find an equivalent circuit with fewer gates. We can use the basic equivalences and techniques of propositional logic to find equivalent circuits. Thus $-x \& -y$ is equivalent to $-(x \vee y)$ by De Morgan's rule, and $x \& (y \vee z)$ is equivalent to $(x \& y) \vee (x \& z)$ by distribution. Furthermore, we can measure the cost of a circuit by counting the number of logical connectives—that is, the number of &'s, ∨'s, and –'s, Thus $(x \vee y) \& -(x \& y)$ has a cost factor of 4, $(x \& -y) \vee (-x \& y)$ has a cost factor of 5, and $-(x \& y) \& -(-x \& -y)$ has a cost factor of 6; so $(x \vee y) \& -(x \& y)$ is the least costly of these equivalent circuits. There are automatic routines that will yield the simplest equivalent of any formula without trial and error, but we shall not pursue the matter further.

The Binary Number System. We have seen how digital computers process electronic signals. This processing is completely meaningless, however, unless a ***binary code*** has been set up specifying what a given sequence of 1's and 0's represents. Computers are best known for their ability to do millions, billions, and even trillions of arithmetic computations in seconds. One binary code used for arithmetic is the *binary,* or *base 2, number system.* The number system in everyday use is the decimal, or base 10, system: all numbers are represented by strings of ten digits 0, 1 , 2, 3, … , 9. Counting from the right: The first digit specifies the number of ones ($1 = 10^0$); the second digit specifies the number of tens ($10 = 10^1$); the third digit specifies the number of hundreds ($100 = 10^2$); the fourth digit specifies the number of thousands ($1,000 = 10^3$); and so on (the nth digit specifies the number of 10^{n-1}s). Thus 1011 in the decimal system represents 1 one plus 1 ten plus 0 hundreds plus 1 thousand, or $(1 \times 1) + (1 \times 10) + (0 \times 100) + (1 \times 1000)$. The string 435 in the decimal system represents $(5 \times 1) + (3 \times 10) + (4 \times 100)$. In the binary number system, all numbers are represented by strings of the two digits 0 and 1. Again counting from the right: The first digit specifies the number of ones ($1 = 2^0$); the second represents the number of twos ($2 = 2^1$); the third represents the number of fours ($4 = 2^2$); the fourth represents the number of eights ($8 = 2^3$) and so on (the nth digit represents the number of 2^{n-1}s). Thus 1011 in the binary system represents 1 one plus 1 two plus 0 fours plus 1 eight, or $(1 \times 1) + (1 \times 2) + (0 \times 4) + (1 \times 8)$, which is 11 in the decimal system. For practice, verify in this way that each binary string in Table 10-7 represents the same number as the decimal string to its right.

Binary	Decimal
111	7
101	5
110	6
1110	14
1010	10
1101	13
11111	31

TABLE 10-7

The binary system is less economical for humans because too many digits are required to represent even small numbers. But computers operate better with just two digits—that is, two signals.

Other binary codes for decimal numbers are possible. One system in common use, for example, represents 31 by the string 0011 0001, which is formed from the binary numbers for 3 and 1. Furthermore, a binary code is possible for any set of elements: letters of the alphabet, musical notes, chess pieces and positions, members of Congress, whatever. We shall focus on the binary number system to see how computers use logic circuits to do arithmetic.

The Half-Adder. The simplest arithmetic operation is the addition of two numbers. In early grade school, we memorize the sums of any two (decimal) digits: 1 plus 1 is 2, 1 plus 2 is 3, and so on for the rest of the "addition table." We then learn a systematic procedure, or *algorithm,* for adding two numbers of any length: add the ones digits, then the tens digits, and so on. Thus when we add 437 and 561, we say to ourselves "7 and 1 is 8, 3 and 6 is 9, and 4 and 5 is 9, so the sum is 998":

$$\begin{array}{r} 437 \\ +561 \\ \hline 998 \end{array}$$

Addition is complicated by the occasional need to "carry" digits from one column to the next. If we add 7 and 6 we *enter* 3 in the ones column and *carry* 1 to the tens column, to get 13 as the result. If we add 57 and 56, we first add 7 and 6, entering 3 in the ones column and carrying 1 to the tens column; we then add 1 5, and 5, entering 1 in the tens column and carrying 1 to the hundreds column; the result is 113.

$$\begin{array}{r} 7 \\ +6 \\ \hline 13 \end{array} \qquad \begin{array}{r} {}^{1}57 \\ +56 \\ \hline 113 \end{array}$$

To add three or more numbers, we usually add two numbers at a time, adding the next number to the sum of all previous numbers. Thus we can add 1, 5, and 5 by first adding 1 and 5 to get 6, and then adding 6 and 5 to get 11.

If we were learning to add in the binary number system, we would first have to memorize the binary addition table, which gives the sum of each of the two binary digits (see Table 10-8).

0	1	0	1
+0	+0	+1	+1
00	01	01	10

TABLE 10-8. BINARY ADDITION

We are not interested in doing binary addition ourselves, however. Rather, we seek to design a computer that will do it for us. For practical purposes, a 0 in the twos column is superfluous and can be deleted. But for our purposes it will be essential to treat the sum of any two digits x and y as a two-digit number composed of a carry digit c and an entry digit e.[1] Thus, when we add 1 and 1, we enter 0 and carry 1. When we add 1 and 0 (in either order), we enter 1 and carry 0. When we add 0 and 0, we enter 0 and carry 0. A logic circuit that will add binary digits, called a *half-adder*, must therefore have the logic table presented in Table 10-9.

x	y	ce
1	1	10
1	0	01
0	1	01
0	0	00

TABLE 10-9. HALF-ADDER

The output of our basic logic circuits, the AND-, OR-, and NOT-gates, is only a single digit. A half-adder, therefore, will have to combine two simpler circuits, one giving the carry digit c as output, the other producing the entry digit e. Table 10-9 should therefore be thought of as combining two separate logic tables, one giving c as a function of x and y; the other giving e as a function of x and y. Note that $c = (x \mathbin{\&} y)$, which is simply the AND-gate, while $e = [(x \mathbin{\&} -y) \lor (-x \mathbin{\&} y)] = (x \lor y)$, which is the XOR-gate diagramed in Figure 10-6. So to add binary digits x and y, we feed them into both an AND-gate and an XOR-gate. We shall represent the XOR-gate by putting ∨ in a box, abbreviating the logic diagram in Figure 10-6.

---

[1] The entry digit is usually called the "sum" digit, a misleading term since it does not represent the total sum of the numbers being added.

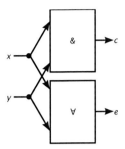

FIGURE 10-7. LOGIC DIAGRAM FOR THE HALF-ADDER

The Full-Adder. A half-adder does only one of the two basic operations involved in adding two binary numbers of any length. We also must be able to add two digits *plus a carry digit.* When we add 11 and 11, we first add 1 and 1, entering 0 and carrying 1; then we must add 1 and 1 and 1, entering 1 and carrying 1; the result is 110.

$$
\begin{array}{r}
11 \\
+11 \\
\hline
110
\end{array}
$$

A circuit capable of adding three binary digits is called a *full-adder.* Table 10-10 is its logic table.

x	y	z	CE
1	1	1	11
1	1	0	10
1	0	1	10
1	0	0	01
0	1	1	10
0	1	0	01
0	0	1	01
0	0	0	00

TABLE 10-10. FULL-ADDER

We can use the half-adder to add x and y. The result will be a two-digit number $c'e'$. Next we add $c'e'$ to z, which can be done by using the half-adder to add e and z; the result will be a two-digit number $c''e''$. e'' is the number we enter in the E column. We carry 1 to the C column if either c' or c'' is 1 (they will not both be 1.) Thus suppose we wish to add 1, 0, and 1 as in the third row. We first add 1 and 0: we enter 1 and carry 0 to get 01. Then we add 01 and 1 to get 10. Next, suppose we wish to add 1, 1, and 1. First we add 1 and 1, entering 0 and carrying 1 to get 10. Then we add 10 and 1 to get 11. The full-adder is diagrammed to Figure 10-8. The blocks labeled HA are half-adders.

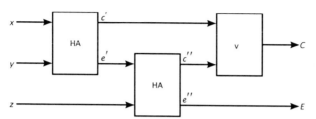

FIGURE 10-8. LOGIC DIAGRAM FOR THE FULL-ADDER.

The Four-Bit Parallel Adder. Our final task is to design a circuit that will add two binary numbers of any length. Let us focus on four-digit binary numbers. Suppose we are to add 1101 and 1001. We first add the digits in the first column (from the right), entering 0 and carrying 1 to the second column. We then add the second column, entering 1 and carrying 0. Then we add the third column, entering 1 and carrying 0. Finally, we add the fourth column, entering 0 and carrying 1. The result is 10110.

$$\begin{array}{r} 1101 \\ +1001 \\ \hline 10110 \end{array}$$

In general, we wish to add any two four-digit binary numbers $A_4A_3A_2A_1$ and $B_4B_3B_2B_1$. This can be done with four full-adders, one for each column, connected so that the carry digit output from one full-adder becomes an input for the next full-adder. The result is called a *four-bit parallel adder* (see Figure 10-9).

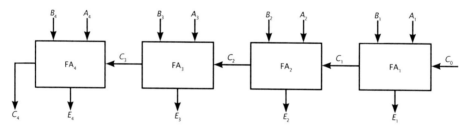

FIGURE 10-9. THE FOUR-BIT PARALLEL ADDER.

C_0, the third input to the full-adder for the first column, is 0 (there is never anything to carry into the ones column from previous columns).

To add n-digit numbers for any length n, we can simply connect together n full-adders. In practice, four-bit parallel adders are mass produced as *integrated circuits,* single silicon chips with a total of fourteen terminals or leads: four terminals for the As, four for the Bs, four for the Es, and one each for C_0 and C_4. Two four-bit adders are combined to add up to eight digits, and three are combined to add up to twelve digits. C_4 from the first four-bit adder becomes C_0 of the second, C_4 of the second becomes C_0 of the third, and so on.

General Procedure. We have examined how circuits are designed to do a simple operation—namely, addition. The same general approach leads to the design of circuits for other operations. The first step is to devise a binary code for the material. The second is to break the operation into a sequence of basic operations, and to find the logic table for each of the basic operations. The basic logic circuits are then constructed from AND-gates, OR-gates, and inverters. Finally, the basic logic circuits are combined into a circuit for the whole operation.

Glossary

Logic circuits: the basic circuits of a digital computer, which perform operations representing the truth-functional connectives of propositional logic.

Digital: a system in which all information is represented by discrete (as opposed to continuous) variables.

Binary: a digital system whose information-carrying variables have only two discrete values.

Binary digits: 1 and 0, represented in a computer by high voltage ("on") and low ("off"); called "bits."

Gate: a logic circuit that takes one or more signals as input and produces a single signal as output.

AND-gate: a gate whose output is 1, provided both (or all) inputs are 1.

OR-gate: a gate whose output is 1, provided either (or any) input is 1.

Inverter: a gate whose output is 1 (or 0), provided the input is 0 (or 1).

Logic formula: an algebraic equation expressing an input-output function.

Logic table: a table representing an input-output function.

Logic diagram: a diagram representing how a complex logic circuit is formed from simpler logic circuits.

Equivalent circuits: those whose input-output functions are the same.

Binary code: a code specifying what numbers, letters, or other items a sequence of binary digits represents.

Exercises

A. Construct the logic tables and logic diagrams for each of the following logic formulas.

1. $-x \vee -y$
2. $-(x \vee y)$
3. $x \mathbin{\&} (-x \vee y)$
4. $(x \mathbin{\&} y) \vee (-x \mathbin{\&} -y)$
5. $x \mathbin{\&} (y \vee z)$
6. $(x \mathbin{\&} y) \vee z$

B. Find a logic formula for the following logic tables.

1.

x	y	?
1	1	0
1	0	0
0	1	1
0	0	0

2.

x	y	?
1	1	1
1	0	0
0	1	1
0	0	1

3.

x	y	?
1	1	1
1	0	0
0	1	1
0	0	0

4.

x	y	?
1	1	1
1	0	1
0	1	0
0	0	0

5.

x	y	z	?
1	1	1	0
1	1	0	0
1	0	1	1
1	0	0	0
0	1	1	0
0	1	0	1
0	0	1	0
0	0	0	0

6.

x	y	z	?
1	1	1	1
1	1	0	1
1	0	1	1
1	0	0	0
0	1	1	0
0	1	0	1
0	0	1	1
0	0	0	1

C. For each of the following numbered logic formulas, determine which of the lettered formulas represents the least costly but equivalent circuit.

1. $-(x \mathbin{\&} -y)$
    (a) $-(-y \mathbin{\&} x)$
    (b) $y \mathbin{\&} x$
    (c) $-x \lor - -y$
    (d) $-x \lor y$

2. $(x \mathbin{\&} y) \lor (-x \mathbin{\&} y)$
    (a) $y \lor (x \mathbin{\&} -x)$
    (b) y
    (c) $y \mathbin{\&} (x \lor -x)$
    (d) x

3. $-[-x \lor (-y \lor -x)]$
    (a) $x \mathbin{\&} -(-y \lor -x)$
    (b) $x \mathbin{\&} (y \mathbin{\&} x)$
    (c) $x \mathbin{\&} y$
    (d) x

4. $-\{-x \mathbin{\&} [(-y \lor -z) \mathbin{\&} (-x \lor -z)]\}$
    (a) $x \lor -[(-y \lor -z) \mathbin{\&} (-x \lor -z)]$
    (b) $x \lor [-(-y \lor -z) \lor -(-x \lor -z)]$
    (c) $x \lor [(y \mathbin{\&} x) \lor (x \mathbin{\&} z)]$
    (d) $x \lor [(y \mathbin{\&} x) \lor z]$

D. Design a "one-bit multiplier," a logic circuit that will multiply any two binary digits.

E. Design a "two-bit multiplier," a logic circuit that will multiply any two two-digit binary numbers. (Hint: recall how you would ordinarily multiply two two-digit binary numbers; then use a combination of one-bit multipliers and half-adders to design the circuit.)

10.4 Definition

As our study of formal logic has shown, we can often determine that an argument is valid, and sometimes even sound, without understanding any of the terms used besides logical constants like "and," "or," "all," and "some." Identifying the form may be all that is necessary to evaluate an argument. But we have also seen that validity frequently depends, and soundness nearly always depends, on the specific nonlogical terms in the premises and conclusions. We can evaluate such arguments only to the extent that we *understand* the premises and conclusions. An essential aspect of critical thinking, therefore, is the striving for conceptual clarity.

Descriptive Categorical Definitions. One way to increase our understanding of a term is to have it *defined*. There are many different ways to define a term, as we shall see. Our study will begin with one of the most common and useful ways, which we shall call a ***descriptive categorical definition.*** A descriptive categorical definition is *a statement asserting that the application of one general or singular term (in a given sense) is necessary and sufficient for the application of another.* A definition is said to be *descriptive* if it *states*—rather than *stipulates*—the conditions for the use of a term. Stipulative definitions will be discussed later. Until then, we will drop the adjective "descriptive." The application of *P* is said to be *necessary* for the application of *S* when *S* applies *only if P* does. Finally, to say that a term "*T*" *applies* to an object is to say that the object *is T*. To illustrate, "A vixen is a female fox" is a definition of the most common sense of the general term "vixen." That is, it asserts that an object is a vixen if and only if it is a female fox. Now the term "vixen" is ambiguous. In one of its other senses, "vixen" means "shrewish woman" rather than "female fox." A definition always defines just one sense of a term. Separate definitions must be given, therefore, for each meaning of an ambiguous term. Categorical definitions can be used for singular terms as well as general terms. "The president is the chief executive of the U.S. government" is a categorical definition of a singular term, for it asserts that "the president" applies to a person if and only if "the chief executive of the U.S. government" applies.

Every categorical definition is about two terms. The term being defined is called the ***definiendum*** (plural: "definienda"). The defining term is called the ***definiens*** (plural: "definientia"). In "A vixen is a female fox," "vixen" is the definiendum, "female fox" the definiens. In "The president is the chief executive of the U.S. government," "the president" is the definiendum, and "the chief executive of the U.S. government" is the definiens. The definiens and definiendum may have any degree of logical complexity. Thus an isosceles right triangle may be defined as a three-sided polygon with two equal sides and a right angle. And an independent congressman may be defined as a male member of either the House of Representatives or the Senate who is not a member of any political party.

As the above examples illustrate, a categorical definition can appear in several different but equivalent forms. We shall say that "A vixen is a female fox" is in *categorical form*, since it has the form of a categorical (or subject-predicate) statement. "An object is a vixen if and only if it is a female fox" is in *conditional form*, since it is a conjunction of conditionals.

Descriptive Categorical Definitions
Conditional Form: An object is *S* if and only if it is *P*.
Categorical Form: S is *P*.

In the vixen example, *S* is "vixen" while *P* is "female fox." In the president example, *S* is "the president" while *P* is "the chief executive of the U.S. government." Thus *S* stands for the definiendum, *P* for the definiens. Definitions of functions and other singular terms in mathematics and science are commonly expressed using the equals sign. Thus the square of a number might be defined as $n^2 = n \times n$. This can be expressed verbally in a categorical form ("The square of a number is that number multiplied by itself") or in conditional form ("Something is the square of a number if and only if it is that number multiplied by itself").

The categorical form is more common than the conditional, and is certainly more compact. Unfortunately, a sentence with the form "*S* is *P*" is ambiguous when *S* is a general term. It can be interpreted either as a categorical definition, or as an Aristotelian categorical. For example, "A square is a four-sided polygon" can be interpreted either as a false definition (not all four-sided polygons are squares) or as a true **A** proposition (all squares are four-sided polygons). When "*S* is *P*" expresses an *A* proposition, it means simply "*All S are P.*" When "*S* is *P*" is used to define a general term, it implies "All *and only S* are *P*" (if there are any *S*). Another difference between a categorical definition and an Aristotelian categorical is that *definitions do not presuppose existence.* A griffin may be defined as a beast with the head and wings of an eagle and the body of a lion without implying in any way that griffins exist. Similarly, defining the president as the chief executive of the U.S. government does not presuppose that there is currently a president. The categorical form of a definition should always be understood as an abbreviation for the conditional form. The conditional form is also commonly shortened by deleting the "only if." Thus one might define "vixen" by saying "An object is a vixen if it is a female fox." The "only if" must be understood, however. A categorical definition, we might say, is a biconditional statement that can be abbreviated as a categorical statement. Finally, the term "object" in the conditional form is often replaced by a more specific term implied by *P*, as in "A person is the president if and only if he or she is the chief executive of the U.S. government."

A categorical definition is defined as a statement *about terms.* Consequently, definitions with different definienda or definientia are different definitions *even if the terms are synonymous.* Thus "A positive integer is a whole number greater than 0" and "A positive whole number is an integer greater than 0" are different definitions, even though "integer" and "whole number" have the same meaning. That definitions are about words is not explicit in either of the commonly used forms given above. The most explicit formulation of a categorical definition would therefore go as follows: *"S" applies to an object if and only if "P" does.* The conditional and categorical forms should both be regarded as abbreviations of this. The fact that definitions are about words does not imply, however, that they are not also about things. Since definitions tell us *when words apply to things,* they are about words *and* things. The sentence "Triangles are three-sided polygons" makes a statement not only about the word "triangles" but also about the things to which it applies.

Breadth and Narrowness. A categorical definition is a statement and, like any other statement, can be either true or false. Since a categorical definition states that the application of the definiens is both necessary and sufficient for the application of the definiendum, there are two ways a categorical definition can be incorrect. If the application of the definiens is *not sufficient* for the application of the definiendum, the definition is said to be ***too broad*** (or *too weak).* Thus "A square is a four-sided polygon" is too broad. Being a polygon with four sides is necessary but not sufficient for being a square, since a square must also have equal sides. If the application of the definiens is *not necessary* for the application of the definiendum, the definition is said to be ***too narrow*** (or *too strong).* Thus "A rectangle is a polygon with four equal sides" is too narrow. Being a polygon with four equal sides is sufficient but not necessary for being a rectangle, since a rectangle does not have to have equal sides. In a correct definition, the definiens and definiendum must apply to the same class of objects. If the definiens applies to more things than the definiendum does, as in Figure 10-10, the definition is too broad. If the definiens applies to fewer things than the definiendum does, as in Figure 10-11, the definition is too narrow.

A definition may be *both* too broad and too narrow, as depicted in Figure 10-12. An example would be "*A* vixen is a young fox." Being a young fox is neither necessary nor sufficient for being a vixen.

Consequently, some young foxes are not vixens (the male ones), and some vixens are not young foxes (the old ones).

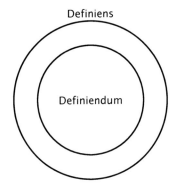

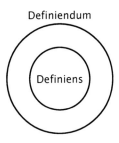

FIGURE 10-10. TOO BROAD, BUT NOT TOO NARROW.   FIGURE 10-11. TOO NARROW, BUT NOT TOO BROAD.

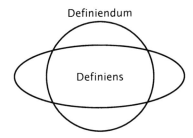

FIGURE 10-12. TOO BROAD AND TOO NARROW.

Ambiguity and Vagueness. Like any other term, the definiens may be *ambiguous* or *vague*. These attributes tend to defeat the purpose of a definition, which is to clarify the defiendum. A term is **ambiguous** if it has more than one meaning. If we misinterpret an ambiguous definition, it will not increase our understanding of the definiendum. Suppose a candidate is defined as a man running for office. This definition is ambiguous, since the term "man" can mean either "person" or "male person." On the gender-neutral interpretation, the definition is correct. On the gender-specific interpretation, it is too narrow. It would be better, therefore, to define a candidate as a *person* running for office. Some ambiguities cause no trouble, however. The term "running" is also ambiguous, for instance, but one of its senses is so unlikely in the context of "for office" that the chances of misunderstanding the definition are negligible.

A term is **vague** if it is impossible to determine whether it applies in some cases, no matter how much information we have. The term "middle-age" is vague, for example, since there is no precise age at which middle-age ends and old-age begins. Does middle-age end at 60 or 65? How about 59 years 300 days and 56 minutes? There is no way to tell. Our uncertainty about whether a 65-year-old man is middle-aged is not due to lack of information about the man. In contrast, we are uncertain whether there is extraterrestrial life mainly because we do not have enough information about other planets and solar systems, not because the term "life" is vague (although it is). It is easy to describe evidence that would conclusively prove the existence of extraterrestrial life (such as telescopic observation of herds of elephants on Mars). Note that vagueness is different from ambiguity. The term "animal" is vague because of organisms like the slime mold, which are on the borderline between the plant and animal kingdoms. "Animal" is ambiguous because it can mean "brutish person" as well as "member of the animal kingdom."

Since a definition is supposed to tell us the conditions under which the defiendum applies, a vague definiens is unsatisfying. Suppose love is defined as the ultimate mystical union of two spirits. This does little to increase our understanding of love. For the definiens is so vague it is hard to say whether it ever applies. Pick any two people at random. How would you begin to determine whether they are united by the ultimate mystical union? The definiens here needs definition more than the definiendum. *Metaphors* and other figures of speech are common sources of serious vagueness. C. S. Pierce once defined belief as "the demi-cadence which closes a musical phrase in the symphony of our intellectual life."[2] This is a wonderful metaphor. But since it is hard to determine exactly what Pierce had in mind, the definition does little to clarify the meaning of "belief." A vague definiens must be used, however, when the definiendum itself is vague. Thus "A middle-aged person is one who is *roughly* between 40 and 60 years of age" cannot be criticized On the grounds that the definiens is too vague, since it is no vaguer than the definiendum.

Circularity. Any statement can suffer from falsity, ambiguity, and vagueness. A defect peculiar to definitions is **circularity**. A definition is circular if the definiendum appears in the definiens. Thus *"An explanation is a statement that provides an explanation of something"* is circular. This definition is perfectly *true*. Indeed, it is tautological. But since the term "explanation" appears in the definiens, the definition cannot increase our understanding of "explanation."

A sequence of definitions forms a *chain* if all or part of the definiens of the first is the definiendum of a second, all or part of the definiens of the second is the definiendum of the third, and so on. Newtonian physics contains a well-known chain of definitions: Acceleration is defined as change of velocity; velocity is defined as rate of motion in a given direction; and motion is defined as change of place. A chain of definitions is circular if the definiendum of the first definition is in the definiens of the last. Thus if psychology is defined as what psychologists study (a common definition), and psychologists are defined as professionals in the field of psychology, we are running in a definitional circle. Note that this chain is circular even though neither link of the chain is circular. Dictionaries abound in such circles. A circular chain may be perfectly true, but since the initial definiendum is ultimately defined in terms of itself, the chain cannot increase our understanding of that term.

Circularity in a definition is not always a defect. It is when the definition cannot be understood without a previous understanding of the definiendum; the circularity is then said to be **vicious**. One sort of nonviciously circular definition is called a *recursive* definition. Suppose we wished to define "descendent." A descendent is an offspring, an offspring of an offspring, an offspring of an offspring of an offspring, *and so on*. A descendent may therefore be defined as either (1) an offspring or (2) an offspring of a descendent. Clause (1) specifies an initial class of descendents; it is the *initiating clause*. Clause (2) when applied to any class of descendents specifies a larger class of descendents. It is called a *recursion clause* since it can be applied over and over again to yield larger and larger classes of objects denoted by the definiendum. A recursive definition in general is one containing an initiating clause and one or more recursion clauses. Such a definition is circular, since the definiendum appears in the definiens. But the circularity is not vicious. For the initiating clause enables us to find some objects denoted by the definiendum *without any previous understanding of the definiendum*. And the recursion clause enables us to find all the other objects denoted by the definiendum, given only that initial class. A recursion clause, in other words, is simply a compact and precise way of formulating *and so on*.

[2] This example comes from I. M. Copi, *Introduction to Logic*, 6th ed. (Macmillan, 1982), p. 172.

Recursive definitions resemble a deductive proof procedure known as *mathematical induction.* Using mathematical induction, we can prove that *all* positive integers have a certain property by proving first that 1 has it, and second that if any integer i has it, then $i + 1$ has it. This procedure essentially employs a recursive definition of a positive integer as either 1 (the initiating clause) or any positive integer plus 1 (the recursion clause).

Definition by Genus and Differentia. When a quadrilateral is defined as a four-sided polygon, it is said to be defined *by genus and differentia.* Polygons comprise a *genus* of which quadrilaterals are a *species.* Being four-sided is the *differentia,* the property that differentiates the species of quadrilaterals from all other species in the genus of polygons. "A square is a quadrilateral with equal sides" is another definition by genus and differentia, except this time quadrilaterals comprise the genus, squares the species, and equal-sidedness the differentia. In biology, the terms "genus" and "species" refer to fixed ranks in a taxonomic classification. A species is a group of animals capable of interbreeding; a genus is a group of species; a family is group of genera; and so on for orders, classes, phyla, and kingdoms. Humans fall in the species *Homo sapiens,* the genus *Homo*, the order of primates, the class of mammals, and the kingdom of animals. In logic, however, "genus" and "species" are relative terms like "premise" and "conclusion." The **species** is the set of objects denoted by the definiendum; the **genus** (plural "genera") is the set of objects mentioned in the definiens of which the species is assorted to be a subset; and the **differentia** (plural: "differentiae") is the property used to differentiate members of the species from other members of the genus. One and the same set may be the species in one definition and the genus another, as we saw above with the set of quadrilaterals. When a species is defined by genus and differentia, and the genus is in turn defined by genus and differentia, and so on, the result is a hierarchy of concepts constituting a systematic classification.

A definition by genus and differentia is a categorical definition in which the definiens P denotes the objects in genus G that have the differentia D.

Definition by Genus and Differentia
Categorical Form: S is G & D.
Conditional Form: An object is S if and only if it is G & D.

Such a definition identifies the set $\{S\}$ of all objects to which the definiendum applies as the intersection of sets $\{G\}$ and $\{D\}$, as shown in the Venn diagram of Figure 10-13.

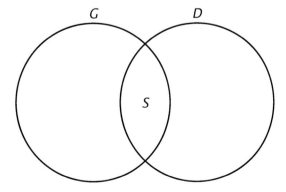

FIGURE 10-13. S IS G & D.

As the symmetry of Figure 10-13 indicates, for every definition in genus and differentia form, there is an equivalent definition in which the roles of genus and differentia are switched. Thus instead of defining a vixen as a fox that is female (genus: foxes; differentia: being female), we could equally well define a vixen as a female that is a fox (genus: females; differentia: being a fox).

While we have focused on definitions of general terms, definitions of singular terms can also be given in genus and differentia form. The winner of a baseball game can be defined as the team that has the most runs after nine or more complete innings. Then the genus is *team,* the differentia is *having the most runs after nine or more complete innings,* and the species is *winner of the baseball game.* The only difference here is the presupposition that the species has only a single member.

Categorical definitions need not be in genus and differentia form. "A descendent is either an offspring or a descendent of an offspring" is not, for example, nor is "A whole number is an integer." But any categorical definition can be put in genus and differentia form by using as genus the class of all *objects,* or some other more specific but suitably general class. Thus an offspring may be defined equivalently as an object (or more specifically a living being) that is either an offspring or a descendent of an offspring. Then *object* (or *living being*) is the genus, and *being either an offspring or a descendent of an offspring* is the differentia.

Definition by Example. The genus and differentia form is especially useful as a guide for the *construction* of definitions. It tells us that as the first step in defining a term, we may select any more general term. The second step is to find a property that differentiates the objects denoted by the definiendum from all other objects denoted by the more general term selected. The first step is easy. The second step may be exceedingly difficult, however, and for this reason most terms in common use are hard to define precisely by genus and differentia. Consider the term "dog." *Mammal* would be a suitable genus, as would *animal* or *living being.* But the precise properties differentiating dogs from all other mammals are hard to specify, especially for the layman. Dogs are carnivores with four legs and a tail, of course, but so are cats and wolves. One way to get around this problem is to find a dog, point to it, and say "A dog is a mammal *like this"* (or something to that effect). Then the differentia is *being like this.* The dog referred to is serving as an *example* of the species. Instead of an actual dog, we could just as well use a picture of a dog. In place of the demonstrative pronoun, a proper name or definite description could be used. We might define a dog as *an animal like Lassie.* Kinds of examples may be mentioned instead of particular examples, as in "A dog is an animal like a collie." A definition whose definiens refers to one or more examples of the species being defined, is called a definition *by example.* When the examples are indicated by a gesture like pointing, such a definition is called an *ostensive* definition.[3]

In practice, definitions by example can be very effective. Their utility is severely limited by their *vagueness,* however. For the "like this" in a definition by example does not simply mean "like this in *some* respect." Rather, it means "like this in *certain* respects." Because those respects have not been specified, the definitions are vague. Consider, "A dog is an animal like Lassie." Lassie has hair. Does any animal with hair count as an animal like Lassie? If so, then the definition is too broad. Lassie is a collie. Does any dog other than a collie count as an animal like Lassie? If not, then the definition is too narrow. The vagueness of a definition by example can be reduced by increasing the number of examples. Thus a better definition of "dog" can be constructed by gathering together dogs of all breeds, and saying "Dogs are animals like these." Some vagueness will remain, however, unless *all possible* examples are enumerated, which is usually impossible. Ostensive definitions, furthermore, are highly *ambiguous* unless the sort of object being pointed at is specified. Thus "A dog is an *object* like this" is ambiguous, a speaker whose finger is aimed at Lassie may be pointing at Lassie, at Lassie's head, at Lassie's left ear,

---

[3] The root of "ostensive" is a Latin word meaning "to show."

at the fly on Lassie's left ear, or even at Lassie's dog house. This ambiguity can be eliminated easily, by saying that a dog is a *mammal* like this.

Semantic vs. Nonsemantic Definitions. All definitions are designed to *clarify* the meaning of the definiendum. Not all definitions, however, *state* the meaning of the definiendum. This point requires some explanation. Let us say that two terms are ***equivalent*** if the application of one is necessary and sufficient for the application of the other. Then a correct categorical definition clarifies the meaning of the definiendum by specifying another equivalent term. Two terms may be equivalent, however, even though they do not have the same meaning. Terms with the same meaning are ***synonymous***. *Synonymous terms must be equivalent, but equivalent terms need not be synonymous.* "Vixen" and "female fox" are synonymous, for example, and consequently are equivalent. But consider "three-sided polygon," "three-angled polygon," and "polygon whose angles add up to 180°." These terms are not synonymous, since the first specifies a number of sides, the second a number of angles, and the third the sum of the angles. Nevertheless, the terms are equivalent, for a polygon has three sides if and only if it has three angles, and has three angles if and only if its angles add up to 180°. Consequently, triangles can be defined correctly as three-sided polygons, as three-angled polygons, or as polygons whose angles add up to 180°. Definitions in which the definiens and definiendum are not synonymous are very common in science. A chemist may define gold, for example, as the element whose atomic number is 79. This definition is correct even though "gold" and "the element whose atomic number is 79" are not synonymous. That they are not synonymous is shown by the fact that most people who know what "gold" is do not know that it denotes an element whose atomic number is 79. Many do not even have the concept of an atomic number. The fact that gold is the element whose atomic number is 79 was an important scientific discovery. The realization that vixens are female foxes, in contrast, does not constitute much of a discovery and is certainly not a scientific one. Even dictionary entries are frequently not synonymous with the terms they are used to define.

Some definitions, however, do state that the definiens and definiendum have the same meaning. We shall call them ***semantic definitions***.[4] *"Vixen* means *female fox"* is a semantic definition. It is a categorical definition, since it asserts by implication that the application of "female fox" is necessary and sufficient for the application of "vixen." But it is also a semantic definition, since it asserts in addition that "vixen" and "female fox" have the same meaning. We shall say that *"Vixen* means *female fox"* is a categorical definition in *semantic form*.

Semantic Definitions
Semantic Form: S means *P* (in *L*).

A variant on the semantic form is *P is called S*. Thus "vixen" may be defined by saying "A female fox is called a vixen." While all semantic definitions can be put in semantic form, they do not always appear in it. The conditional and categorical forms are also used to give semantic definitions. Sometimes the intention to offer a semantic definition is indicated explicitly by inserting *by definition* into the categorical or conditional forms. But sometimes no explicit indication is given, and we must infer from the context whether or not a semantic definition is intended. We noted above that when the conditional or categorical forms are used to give definitions, it is implicit that a statement is being made about words. When the semantic form is used, this fact is explicit.

Semantic definitions are false if they are either too broad or too narrow. Thus *"Vixen* means *fox,"* *"Vixen* means *young female fox,"* and *"Vixen* means *young fox"* are all incorrect definitions. The first

---

[4] Nonsemantic definitions are often called "real" definitions.

is too broad, the second too narrow, and the third both. Terms that are not equivalent cannot have the same meaning. A semantic definition may also be false, however, even if it is neither too broad nor too narrow. For terms may be equivalent without having the same meaning. Thus *"Triangle means polygon whose angles add up to 180°"* is false even though it is neither too broad nor too narrow. For the definiens and definiendum are not synonymous. Their lack of synonymy is shown by the fact that many who know what the term "triangle" means, who talk intelligently about triangles and understand talk about them, do not have the slightest idea what the angles of a triangle add up to. Children generally learn what triangles are before entering grade school. They learn that a triangle's angles add up to 180° in high school.

Synonymous terms must be equivalent, although equivalent terms need not be synonymous. It follows that if *"S means P"* is true, then *"S is P"* and *"An object is S if and only if it is P"* must also be true (although the converse does not hold). Moreover, if *"S means P"* is true, then *"S is P"* and *"An object is S if and only if it is P"* are *logically true.* Since "vixen" means "female fox," for example. "A vixen is a female fox" is true in all possible cases, for it states simply that a female fox is a female fox. "An object is a vixen if and only if it is a female fox" is similarly a logical truth. The truth of the semantic form, that is, implies the logical truth of the conditional and categorical forms. This is so even though no substitution instance of the semantic form itself is logically true. A word could always have meant something other than what it does mean. In English as it is actually spoken, "vixen" means "female fox." But there is a logically possible case in which "vixen" means "young cow." In that case, the sentence "A vixen is a female fox" would express the false statement that a young cow is a female fox. As used in modern English, however, the sentence "A vixen is a female fox" expresses a logical truth. For there is no possible case in which a female fox is anything but a female fox. When the semantic form is false, the conditional and categorical forms need not be logically true. It is true but not logically true, for example, that gold is the element whose atomic number is 79. Semantic definitions, therefore, serve the additional purpose of helping us to identify which sentences express logical truths.

Conventional vs. Speaker's Meaning. To say that "vixen" means "female fox," without qualification, is to say that "vixen" means "female fox" *in English.* To say that "cheval" means "horse" is to say that "cheval" means "horse" *in French.* In general, *"S means P"* (without qualification) says that *S means P in the language S belongs to.* Now what words mean in a given language is determined by *conventional usage.* "Vixen" means "female fox" in English be-cause speakers of English commonly use the word "vixen" to mean "female fox." "Cheval" means "horse" in French because speakers of French customarily use "cheval" to express the idea of a horse. If everyone speaking English began using the word "vixen" to mean "horse," that is what "vixen" would mean: English would change. Not all usage is conventional, however. People speak in code, make up nonce words, and create their own terminology. Even though "vixen" means "female fox" in conventional English usage, John may use "vixen" to mean "female tennis player." Mary may use it to mean "a Colt 45 revolver." The terms *word meaning* and *speaker's meaning* are often used to mark the distinction we are noting. The *word* "vixen" means "female fox," for example, while the *speaker* John means "female tennis player" by "vixen." Word meaning is also called *conventional meaning,* since it is determined by conventional speaker's meaning. Between the extremes of private codes and common usage there is technical usage and slang. For example, "pencil" means "a one-parameter family of two- or three-dimensional figures" *in mathematics,* even though "pencil" has a very different meaning in common usage. While it is conventional among English-speaking mathematicians to use "pencil" in that sense, it is not common among English-speaking people at large. And "vixen" means "sexy lady" in slang English but not in standard English.

The parenthetical "in L" after the semantic form stands for prepositional phrases like "in John's usage," "in Mary's code," "in slang usage," and "in mathematics," as well as "in English" or "in French."

A semantic definition may assert that the definiens and definiendum are synonymous *in any established usage*. In order to evaluate a semantic definition, we need to know which usage is being defined. If a particular speaker's usage is being defined, we have to look at how he or she uses the definiendum. If standard English usage is being defined, we have to look at how speakers of English commonly use the term.

Noncategorical Definitions. We have focused on *categorical* definitions, which state that the application of the definiens is necessary and sufficient for the application of the definiendum. The definiens and definiendum in a categorical definition are either general or singular terms. Other sorts of terms exist, however, such as logical connectives and quantifiers. Since logical terms cannot appear as predicates in categorical propositions, they cannot be said to *apply* to objects. A general term like "horse" is said to apply to Secretariat, because Secretariat is a horse. Similarly, "the president elected in 1980" applies to Ronald Reagan, because he *was* the president elected in 1980. But it makes no sense to say that something is an and or an all, so the quantifier "all" and the connective "and" cannot be said to apply to objects. We cannot therefore define a logical term by stating necessary and sufficient conditions for its *application*. We can, nevertheless, define such a term by stating necessary and sufficient conditions for its *correct use*. Thus "unless" may be defined as follows:

"*p* unless *q*" is true if and only if "*p* if not-*q*" is true.

This defines "unless" *in context*. For it says that any substitution instance of the form "*p* unless *q*" is true provided the corresponding substitution instance of "*p* if not-*q*" is true. This definition enables us to determine whether any statement of the form "*p* unless *q*" is true on the basis of our understanding of the corresponding statement "*p* if not-*q*." Thus if we know that Mary will go to the picnic if it does not rain, then we can say correctly that Mary will go to the picnic unless it rains. Such a definition cannot be expressed in categorical form: nothing can be put for *S* and *P* in "*S* is *P*." It can however be expressed in semantic form. For we can say that "unless" means "if not," or more explicitly, "if it is not the case that." Note that categorical definitions also state conditions for the correct use of terms. For the conditional form is equivalent to: "*x is S*" *is true if and only if* "*x is P*" *is true*, where *x* stands for any individual. So the term "definition" denotes *any statement of truth conditions*, any statement, that is, which asserts necessary and sufficient conditions for the correct use of an expression.

Stipulative Definitions. Not all definitions, however, are *statements*. Many are *stipulations*, commands of a certain sort. Thus when setting up her code, Mary may say: *Let* "vixen" mean "Colt 45 revolver," *let* "stag" mean "M-16 rifle," and *let* " "the zoo keeper" mean "the man suspected of illegal gunrunning." She might later say, in code, "Murphy bought three vixens and two stags from the zoo keeper." Definitions that state the meaning of a term or the conditions of its use are **descriptive** (they are also called *reportive* or *lexical*). Definitions that stipulate the meaning or use of a term are **stipulative**. Stipulative definitions may be either categorical or noncategorical, and stipulative categorical definitions may occur in categorical or conditional form in addition to the semantic form illustrated in the example of Mary.

Stipulative Categorical Definitions	
Semantic Form:	Let *S* mean *P*.
Categorical Form.:	Let *S* be *P*.
Conditional Form:	Let an object be *S* if and only if it is *P*.

As in the descriptive forms, *S* stands for the definiendum, *P* for the definiens. Stipulative definitions can also be given by prefixing *I stipulate that* to any form used to give descriptive definitions. Mary could have set up her code by saying "I stipulate that a vixen is a Colt 45 revolver, a stag is an M-16 rifle, and the zoo keeper is the man suspected of illegal gunrunning." The fact that a definition is stipulative may also be *understood*. Mary might simply have said "A vixen is a Colt 45 revolver…," leaving us to infer from the context that she is stipulating.

Descriptive definitions are statements about an established use of a term, and therefore can be evaluated as correct or incorrect in relation to that usage. Stipulative definitions, in contrast, are not concerned with existing usage, and do not make any sort of statement at all. Consequently, *stipulative definitions cannot be evaluated as true or false, correct or incorrect, too broad or too narrow.* A stipulatively defined term applies to just those things it is stipulated to apply to. One cannot criticize Mary on the grounds that a revolver is not a vixen, for example, since she is not claiming that Colt 45's are vixens in the common sense of the term. Stipulative definitions can be circular, but that is not a defect since they are not intended to increase our understanding of an established sense of a term. Thus Mary cannot be faulted if she expands her code by saying "Let 'truck' mean 'truck.'" She is free to stipulate that in her code certain terms are to have their usual senses. This immunity to criticism is a *special* feature of stipulative definitions. Unfortunately, a widespread and pernicious misconception about definitions is that they *all* share this feature. Stipulative definitions are immune to criticism only because they are not concerned with existing usage. As a result, they cannot increase our understanding of any established sense of the definiendum. If we want to know when human life begins, for instance, in the conventional English sense of "human life," a stipulative definition will not help. A second insidious misconception about definitions is that *all* can increase our understanding of established senses of terms. That is a special feature of descriptive definitions. Personal semantic definitions are often confused with stipulative definitions. Indeed, a person who says "By *apple* I mean *red fruit*" might be stipulating, and if so cannot be criticized. But such a person might also be describing his or her own usage (already established), and may or may not have done so correctly.

While stipulative definitions cannot increase our understanding of existing usage, they can do many useful things. For example, they can:

1. *Set up secret codes.* This may seem like a frivolous pursuit, but it is vital in war and business, where secrets need to be kept.

2. *Introduce technical terms.* The scientist often has to name something for which no common name is suitable. Back in the seventeenth century, for example, physicists needed a term for the product of the force applied to an object times the distance through which it is applied. The ordinary English term "work" had roughly, but not exactly, the right meaning. We do more work, for example, if we push a car up a hill than if we roll a ball up the hill; but thinking is often hard work in the ordinary sense, even though no forces are applied through distances. Rather than introduce a totally unfamiliar term for force times distance, physicists simply stipulated that it be called "work." This sense has subsequently become standard in physics. Sometimes a term more general than any existing term is needed. In American law, for instance, no term denoted all loan agreements in which property was given as security or collateral. Instead, there was an array of terms like "chattel mortgage," "conditional sale," and "trust receipt" whose application depended on the type of property put up and other particulars. If the wrong term was used, the loan agreement was invalid; lenders stood to lose their money and debtors their property. So the Uniform Commercial Code introduced the term "security agreement," which was defined to cover all loan agreements involving collateral.

3. *Name new objects.* Babies have to be named, as do inventions and discoveries. An old term may be given a new sense (as when yet another baby is named "John Smith"), or a new term introduced (like

"television"). The term introduced may be totally new, as when the mathematician Edward Kasner named 10^{100} "googol" at the suggestion of his grandson.

4. *Abbreviate complex terms.* Whenever a lengthy expression must be used repeatedly, time and space can be saved by abbreviating. Mathematicians, for example, often have to express the product of all positive integers up to, and including, some integer n. The expression $n!$ (read "n factorial") abbreviates that product. 12! can be used in place of:

$$1 \times 2 \times 3 \times 4 \times 5 \times 6 \times 7 \times 8 \times 9 \times 10 \times 11 \times 12$$

At first, abbreviations reduce comprehension. But once they become familiar, comprehension is improved. Anyone familiar with factorial notation will know at a glance what 12! means, but will have to check each digit in the long product above, And finally, because abbreviations save time and space, they save money in business. The cost of a telegram or a book is determined by the number of symbols used, not their content.

5. *Avoid unwanted associations.* As a result of centuries of oppression in America, the term "Negro" became almost as offensive to Americans of African descent as the emotive term "nigger." So the term "black" was introduced to replace it. Similarly, women averse to being categorized on the basis of their relationship to men introduced the title "Ms." as a replacement for "Miss or Mrs."

6. *Fix an unambiguous meaning.* Ambiguous terms are liable to be misinterpreted. To avoid this, an author can stipulate that a term be given one of its established senses. This is common in legal documents, where misinterpretation can be costly. In connection with loans, for example, "pledge" has two applicable senses. It could mean merely a formal promise to pay back, or the actual delivery of goods as collateral. A loan agreement might stipulate that "pledge" have the second meaning. The fixing of unambiguous meanings is also common in logic and mathematics texts. It is often stipulated, for instance, that "or" is to mean inclusive disjunction.

7. *Fix a precise meaning.* Nearly all common words are vague in one respect or another. Consider the term "adult." It is clear that a 30-year-old person is an adult, and that a 10-year-old is not. But in its standard English sense, it is not possible to determine the precise age at which a person becomes an adult. Since the laws governing adults and minors differ, this situation is legally intolerable. Consequently the law stipulates that an adult is a person who has reached a certain age, usually 18. This stipulation does not alter the common English sense of "adult," or increase our understanding thereof, but it does create a precise legal sense of the term. Taxonomists confronting organisms on the borderline between the plant and animal kingdoms may stipulate more precise senses for "plant" and "animal" so that the organisms can be classified.

8. *Lay down rules, standards, or criteria.* Suppose you intend to hold a beer-drinking contest, and offer a prize to the winner. Before the contest, you must stipulate what is to count as winning. Drinking a specified amount the fastest? Drinking the most in a specified amount of time? Before government meat inspectors can do their job, the criteria for determining what is Prime, Choice, or Good need to be specified. These criteria may need to be revised periodically if the general quality of meat improves, or if the methods of testing become more sophisticated.

Definitions in General. We have now discussed and defined many different types of definition. In general, a ***definition*** *either states or stipulates a necessary and sufficient condition for the correct use of a term in a given sense.* The tree in Figure 10-14 represents the major classifications discussed. The omitted classifications, such as ostensive, recursive, and genus and differentia would require many further branches at the end of most of the current branches. One feature of this tree requires some comment—namely, the nonsemantic branches on the stipulative limb. Most stipulative definitions are semantic: they specify meanings for terms. But when stipulative definitions are used to lay down rules, standards, or criteria, they are nonsemantic. When you set up a beer-drinking contest, you do not stipulate what "winning" means, you only stipulate what counts as winning. Similarly, a change in the meat inspectors' code may change the degree of leanness necessary for meat to qualify as Prime, but it will not change the meaning of "Prime," which is simply "the highest U.S. government grade of meat."

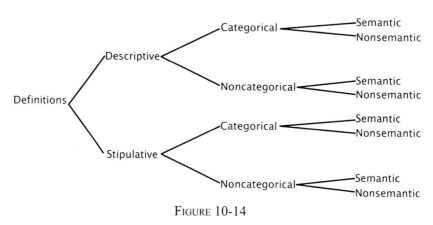

FIGURE 10-14

Undefined Terms. Once the virtues of "defining your terms" are grasped, it is natural to propose as an ideal that *all* terms be defined. This is impossible. To define one term, as we have seen, another term must be used. To define that term, another must be used. And so on. The attempt to define all terms would therefore result in either an infinite series or a circle of definitions. An infinite series is impossible since our lives are limited, and since languages contain only a finite number of noncompound words. And a circle of definitions cannot increase our understanding. So the fact must be faced: *some terms must always remain undefined.* They are said to be *primitive.* We talked about *deductive systems* in earlier chapters. Deductive systems are set up by selecting some unproven statements as axioms, and then using them to derive theorems. Definitions are also common components of deductive systems. They function as axioms: they are unproven in the system and are used as initial premises in proofs of theorems. Just as any deductive system must contain some unproven principles, so it must contain some primitive, or undefined terms. The process of definition, therefore, can never increase our understanding above the level to which our primitive terms are understood,

Glossary

Definition: a statement or stipulation of a necessary and sufficient condition for the correct use of a term in a given sense.

Definiendum: the term being defined.

Definiens: the defining term.

Descriptive definition: one that states conditions for the use of a term in an established sense.

Stipulative definition: one that stipulates conditions for the use of a term.

Categorical definition: a definition that states or stipulates that the application of one general or singular term is necessary and sufficient for the application of another.

Semantic definition: a definition that states or stipulates the meaning of a term.

Too broad: a definition is too broad if the application (or correct use) of the definiens is not sufficient for the application of the definiendum.

Too narrow: a definition is too narrow if the application (or correct use) of the definiens is not necessary for the application of the definiendum.

Circular: A definition is circular if the definiendum appears in the definiens. A chain of definitions is circular if the definiendum of the first definition appears in the definiens of the last.

Viciously circular: A circular definition (or chain of definitions) is viciously circular if the definition cannot be used without a previous understanding of the definiendum.

Ambiguous: A term is ambiguous if it has more than one meaning.

Vague: A term is vague if there are some cases in which it is impossible to determine whether it applies, no matter how much information we have.

Definition by genus and differentia: a categorical definition in which the definiens P denotes the objects in a given class G that have property D.

Species: in a definition by genus and differentia, the set of objects denoted by the definiendum.

Genus: in a definition by genus and differentia, the set of objects mentioned in the definiens of which the species is said to be a subset.

Differentia: in a definition by genus and differentia, the property mentioned in the definiens that is used to differentiate members of the species from other members of the genus.

Equivalent terms: Terms are equivalent if the application (or correct use) of one is necessary and sufficient for the application of the other.

Synonymous terms: Terms are synonymous if they have the same meaning.

Exercises

A. The following definitions are in one of three forms: conditional, categorical, or semantic. Reexpress each in the other two forms.

1. A drake is a male duck.

2. "Duckling" means "young duck."

3. A cow is a female bovine animal.

4. An animal is a tomcat if and only if it is a male cat.

5. A square is a four-sided equilateral polygon.

6. "Rectangle" means "polygon with four right angles."

7. A logical truth is a statement that is true in all possible cases.

8. Two statements are contrary provided they are incompatible statements about the same subject.

B. Define each of the species listed below in terms of one of the genera listed and an appropriate differentia. Check your definition against a dictionary.

Genera: person, horse, deer, chicken, sheep, number, polygon.

Species: man, woman, boy, girl, baby, child, teen-ager, adult, bachelor, husband, wife, mother, father, employer, employee, widow, widower, stallion, mare, colt, foal, doe, buck, fawn, ewe, ram, lamb, rooster, hen, chick, odd number, even number, prime number, composite number, rational number. irrational number, pentagon, hexagon, regular polygon, parallelogram, trapezoid.

C. Determine whether the following definitions are defective because they are too broad, too narrow, or circular, and whether any form circular chains.

1. A spinster is an unmarried woman.

2. Relatives are people with a common ancestor.

3. Let "relatives" mean "people with a common ancestor."

4. A kitten is a young male cat.

5. A cat is an offspring of a cat.

6. A cause is an event that has an effect.

7. An effect is an event that has a cause.

8. "p and q" is true if and only if both p and q are true.

9. A conjunction is true if and only if all conjuncts are true.

10. A disjunction is true if and only if all disjuncts are true.

11. To hope for something is to want it to occur.

12. To decide to do something is to do it.

13. To desire to do something is to have a tendency to do it.

14. Let "desire to do something" mean "tendency to do it."

15. To punish a person is to do something to him that he does not like.

16. To love a person is to enjoy being with him or her.

17. Murder is the killing of one person by another.

18. Homicide is the killing of one person by another.

19. A table is a man-made object consisting of a flat, level surface and supports, intended to support smaller objects.

20. A table is a piece of furniture used as a table,

21. "Furniture" means "moveable man-made objects intended to be used in a human habitation, which can support the weight of the human body, or support or store other, smaller objects."

22. A man is a rational animal (one with the ability to reason).

23. A man is a featherless biped.

24. A man is a primate with an opposing thumb.

25. A man is an animal capable of using language.

26. An animal is a conscious living being capable of locomotion.

27. Let "animal" mean "member of the animal kingdom."

28. An object is red if and only if it looks red.

29. Orange is the color between red and yellow the spectrum.

30. Yellow is the color between orange and green in the spectrum.

31. Something is necessary if and only if its negation is impossible.

32. Something is impossible if and only if its negation is necessary.

D. The following definitions are philosophically controversial. Try to determine whether they are too broad or too narrow.

1. Knowledge is true belief.

2. Knowledge is justified belief.

3. Knowledge is true justified belief.

4. Knowledge is true belief based on sense-perception or on a chain of reasoning based ultimately on sense-perception.

5. Truth is correspondence to reality.

6. Truth is coherence with one's beliefs.

7. To be is to be perceived.

8. To be is to be capable of being perceived.

9. A law of nature is a true universal statement.

10. A law of nature is a true universal statement that is both necessary and a posteriori.

11. C caused E if and only if C preceded E, and whenever an event like C occurs, an event like E occurs.

12. C caused E if and only if C preceded E, and if C had not occurred, E would not have occurred.

13. The meaning of a term is the object or set of objects it applies to.

14. The meaning of a term is the idea it is used to express.

15. To be happy is to have whatever one wants.

16. To be happy is to lead a good life.

17. An action is morally right provided it will lead to the greatest happiness for all people.

18. An action is morally right provided it is commanded by God.

19. Justice is when everyone gets the same as everyone else.

20. Justice is when everyone gets what one deserves.

SOLUTIONS

1.1, Set A

1. PREMISE: Mental life is bound up with brain structure and organized bodily energy. CONCLUSION: Mental life ceases when bodily life ceases. CONCLUSION LEADER: Therefore.

3. PREMISE: We perceive space as three-dimensional, and to three-dimensional space we can conceive no boundaries. CONCLUSION: By the very forms of our perceptions, we must feel as if we lived somewhere in infinite space. CONCLUSION LEADER: Therefore.

5. PREMISE: The circumpolar stars have a circular motion. PREMISE: Other stars always rise and set at the same points of the horizon. CONCLUSION: The heavens is a sphere, turning round a fixed axis. PREMISE LEADER: As may be proved by and by. ARGUER: Ptolemy.

7. PREMISE: The administration's referee proposal will deal not only with registrations, but also with voting itself. PREMISE: It does no good to be able to register if you cannot vote. CONCLUSION: The administration's referee proposal is far superior to the well-intentioned, but less effective recommendation of the Civil Rights Commission. PREMISE LEADER: Because.

9. PREMISE: All governments restrain and rule people. PREMISE: Totalitarianism refers to a centralized form of government in which those in control grant neither recognition nor tolerance to parties differing in opinion. PREMISE: Authoritarianism is a system of governing that calls for unquestioning submission to authority submission to authority. CONCLUSION: All governments are totalitarian and authoritarian to one extent or another. CONCLUSION LEADER: Therefore.

11. PREMISE: Prosperity in the modern sense is attainable only by cultivating such drives of human nature as greed and envy, which destroy intelligence, happiness, serenity, and thereby the peacefulness of man. CONCLUSION: The foundations of peace cannot be laid by universal prosperity in the modern sense. PREMISE LEADER: Because.

13. PREMISE: The criteria conventionally used for measuring aggregate economic damage do not account for either the indirect or the long-term consequences of widespread destruction for both the society and the economy. CONCLUSION: The criteria significantly understate the destructiveness of nuclear attacks. PREMISE LEADER: Since. ARGUER: The authors of the cited report, with Zuckerman agreeing.

15. PREMISE: To be effective, deterrence must be credible. PREMISE: To be credible, a deterrent posture must convince potential enemies beyond any reasonable potential doubt that aggression would bring them no gains proportionate to the damage that they would suffer. PREMISE: Deterrence requires the willingness to follow through on your threats if you are subjected to nuclear aggression. CONCLUSION: In a free society political leaders entrusted with responsibility to maintain a credible deterrent and to carry out war-fighting strategies need public support. CONCLUSION LEADER: This means that.

17. PREMISE: All behavior springs from desire. CONCLUSION: It is clear that ethical notions can have no importance except as they influence desire. PREMISE LEADER: Since.

19. PREMISE: Stock and bond prices are set in the open market—and the market rewards risk. CONCLUSION: Over the long run, stocks should outperform bonds. PREMISE LEADER: The reason is that.

1.1, Set B

1. PREMISE: To live a good life in the fullest sense a man must have a good education, etc. PREMISE: All these things, in varying degrees depend upon the community and are helped or hindered by political events. CONCLUSION: The good life must be lived in a good society and is not fully possible otherwise.

3. PREMISE: Without soil, land plants as we know them could not grow, and without plants no animals could survive. CONCLUSION: The soil controls our own existence and that of every other animal of the land.

5. PREMISE: Even the most necessary laws are considered by some to be a challenge and an intrusion. PREMISE: Legislation in this area tends to provoke the extremists on both sides. PREMISE: It can have the effect of silencing moderate and constructive elements that have been trying for years—by education and persuasion and the force of example—to bring justice and harmony into our racial picture. CONCLUSION: There are drawbacks to efforts to achieve racial progress by way of law.

7. PREMISE: We could create any number of jobs (such as digging and refilling holes), but many of them would be useless and unrewarding. PREMISE: Our real objective is not just jobs but productive jobs—jobs that will mean more goods and services to consume. CONCLUSION: The

creation of jobs is not desirable in and of itself, regardless of what the persons employed do. [Note: There are other legitimate ways to divide up the premises of this argument.]

9. PREMISE: There are people who have died needlessly as a result of reading persuasive books recommending dangerous diets and fake medical cures. PREMISE: The idiocies of Hitler were strengthened in the minds of the German people by crackpot theories of anthropology. PREMISE: In recent years many children have become seriously disturbed by reading books and seeing movies about haunted houses and demon possession. PREMISE: Psychotic mothers have killed their children in attempts to exorcise devils. CONCLUSION: Books on worthless science, promoted into best-sellers by cynical publishers, do considerable damage in areas like medicine, health, and anthropology.

11. PREMISE: Those who hold and those who are without property have ever formed distinct interests in society. PREMISE: Those who are creditors, and those who are debtors, fall under a like discrimination. PREMISE: A landed interest, a manufacturing interest, a mercantile interest, a moneyed interest, with many lesser interests, grow up of necessity in civilized nations, and divide them into different classes, actuated by different sentiments and views. CONCLUSION: The most common and durable source of factions has been the various and unequal distribution of property.

13. PREMISE: Teams of trained and well-paid workers, moving from dwelling to dwelling, engineering technologically advanced cleaning machinery, could swiftly and efficiently accomplish what the present-day house wife does so arduously and primitively. CONCLUSION: The nature of house work could be radically transformed.

15. PREMISE: The very able mayors of San Francisco and Houston, who happen to be women, won reelection with whopping margins. PREMISE: Incumbent black mayors kept their jobs by comfortable margins, and several promising new figures from Philadelphia and Charlotte, NC joined their ranks. PREMISE: Hispanic big-city mayors are fewer in number, but carry weight by their evident quality. CONCLUSION: The record of black, Hispanic, and female candidates this year has indeed been impressive.

17. PREMISE: The President will have only the occasional command of such part of the militia of the nation as by legislative provision may be called into the actual service of the Union. PREMISE: The king of Great Britain and the governor of New York have at all times the entire command of all the militia within their several jurisdictions. CONCLUSION: In this article, … the power of the President would be inferior to that of … the monarch.

19. PREMISE: The Executive not only dispenses the honors, but holds the sword of the community. PREMISE: The legislature not only commands the purse, but prescribes the rules by which the duties and rights of every citizen are to be regulated. PREMISE: The judiciary, on the contrary, has no influence over either the sword or the purse; no direction either of the strength or of the wealth of the society; and can take no active resolution whatever. CONCLUSION: It may truly be said to have neither FORCE nor WILL, but merely judgment; and must ultimately depend upon the aid of the executive arm even for the efficacy of its judgments.

Solutions to LSAT Prep Questions

1. (d). "Ambiguity requires interpretation" is the conclusion of the argument.

1.2

1. Historical narrative.

3. Explanation.

5. Series of unsupported assertions.

7. PREMISE: These small amounts of pesticides are cumulatively stored and only slowly excreted. CONCLUSION: The threat of chronic poisoning and degenerative changes of the liver and other organs is very real. [This might be interpreted as an explanation.]

9. Explanation.

11. Conditional.

13. General statement plus example.

15. Comparison.

17. PREMISE: Both affirmation and denial of God are possible. CONCLUSION: We are faced with stalemate, indecision.

19. CONCLUSION: American foreign policy must be defensible in moral terms, as well as in expediential ones. PREMISE: Our nation is founded on moral propositions regarding the "rights of man," not simply the rights of Americans.

1.3, Set A

1. [1] Over the long run—and it may be very long—stocks should outperform bonds. *The reason is that* [2] stock and bond prices are set in the open market—and the market, over the long run, rewards risk. [3] From 1926 to 1975, the total compounded annual rate of return you would have had from buying risk-free United States Treasury bills was 2.3 percent; the return from slightly riskier corporate bonds would have been 3.89 percent, and the return from stocks would have been 9 percent.

$$[3] \longrightarrow [2] \longrightarrow [1]$$

3. [1] If someone says that there is no God, this cannot be positively refuted….*For* [2] this negative statement rests in the last resort on a decision, a decision that is connected with the fundamental decision for reality as a whole….And [3] if someone says that there is a God, this, too, cannot be positively refuted….[4] The affirmation of God also rests, in the last resort, on a decision, which, again, is connected with the fundamental decision for reality as a whole

$$[2] \longrightarrow [1]$$
$$[4] \longrightarrow [3]$$

5. [1] Tolstoy condemned all war; others have held the life of a soldier doing battle for the right to be very noble. [2] Here there was probably involved a real difference as to ends. [3] Those who praised the soldier usually consider the punishment of sinners a good thing in itself; Tolstoy did not think so. [4] On such a matter no argument is possible; [5] I can only state my view and hope that as many as possible will agree.

$$[3] \longrightarrow [2]$$
$$[4] \longrightarrow [5]$$

7. [1] Every increase of courage in the ruling caste was used to increase the burdens on the oppressed, and *therefore* [2] to increase the grounds for fear in the oppressors, and *therefore* [3] to leave the causes of cruelty undiminished.

$$[1] \longrightarrow [2] \longrightarrow [3]$$

9. [1] Differences in the mass of the rock on the sea floor result in variations in gravity; seamounts have a high gravity field and trenches have a low field. *Hence* [2] water tends to "pile up" over seamounts and do the opposite over trenches. *Therefore* [3] the ocean bottom can be inferred from the height of the sea trenches.

$$[1] \longrightarrow [2] \longrightarrow [3]$$

11. [1] Government actions affect your daily life beginning with the moment you wake up in the morning. [2] The clock radio that awakens you is subject to many manufacturing and sales regulations. [3] The music set off by the alarm mechanism comes from a station that is able to broadcast only because it has been granted a special government license; it must comply with the government's idea of "good programming" or run the risk of having its license revoked.

$$\{[2][3]\} \longrightarrow [1]$$

13. [1] In 1960, 37 percent of the voting age population did not vote. [2] In the 1976 presidential election, the figure had grown to 45 percent. *That means that* [3] almost 70 million eligible voters did not participate in the last presidential election. *It also means that* [4] Jimmy Carter was, at best, the choice of about one-fourth of the eligible voters (a little more than half of the 54 percent who voted).

15. [1] Nothing, or anyhow not much, lasts forever. But [2] what is well established is likely to last for a time. *So* [3] the forces that have shaped past policy (or which past policy has resisted), if they have been correctly identified in this history, will, one may assume, continue to operate for at least a while in the future. [41 They are, in the fullest sense, historical imperatives. *This means that [5]* they are not matters for ideological preference as commonly imagined.

$$[2] \longrightarrow [3] \longrightarrow [4] \longrightarrow [5]$$

17. [1] I cannot sit idly by in Atlanta and not be concerned about what happens in Birmingham. [2] Injustice anywhere is a threat to justice everywhere. [3] We are caught in an inescapable network of mutuality, tied in a single garment of destiny. [4] Whatever affects one directly, affects all indirectly. [5] Never again can we afford to live with the narrow, provincial "outside agitator" idea. [6] Anyone who lives inside the United States can never be considered an outsider anywhere within its bounds.

$$\{[4]\ [3]\} \longrightarrow [2] \longrightarrow [1]$$
$$[6] \longrightarrow [5]$$

19. [1]If and when a historian sets the record straight on the experiences of enslaved black women, she (or he) will have performed an inestimable service. [2] It is not for the sake of historical accuracy alone that such a study should be conducted, *for* [3] lessons can be gleaned from the slave era that will shed light upon black women's and all women's current battle for emancipation.

1.3, Set B

1. [1] What we call our "thoughts" seem to depend upon the organization of tracks in the brain in the same sort of way in which journeys depend upon roads and railways. [2] The energy used in thinking seems to have a chemical origin; for instance, a deficiency of iodine will turn a clever man into an idiot. [3] Mental phenomena seem to be bound up with material structure. If this be so, [4] we cannot suppose that a solitary electron or proton can "think";

we might as well expect a solitary individual to play a football match. [5] We also cannot suppose that an individual's thinking survives bodily death, *since* [6] that destroys the organization of the brain and dissipates the energy that utilized the brain tracks.

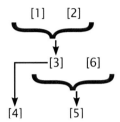

3. [1] The belief in such a supernatural reality itself can neither be proved nor disproved by experience. [2] The arguments or its existence are metaphysical, and to me conclusive. They turn on the fact that even to think and act in the natural world we have to assume something beyond it and even assume that we partly belong to that something. [4] In order to think we must claim for our own reasoning a validity which is not credible if our own thought is merely a function of our brain, and our brains a byproduct of irrational physical processes. [5] In order to act, above the level of mere impulse, we must claim a similar validity for our judgments of good and evil.

$$\{[4][5]\} \longrightarrow [3] \longrightarrow [2]$$

5. But [1] that command method can be the exclusive or even principal method of organization only in a very small group. [2] Not even the most autocratic head of a family can control every act of other family members entirely by order. [3] No sizable army can really be run entirely by command. [4] The general cannot conceivably have the information necessary to direct every moment of the lowliest private. [5] At every step in the chain of command, the soldier, whether officer or private, must have discretion to take into account information about specific circumstances that his commanding officer could not have.

$$[4] \longrightarrow [5] \longrightarrow [3] \atop [2] \Big\} \longrightarrow [1]$$

7. [1] While the materialist is mainly interested in goods, the Buddhist is mainly interested in liberation. But [2] Buddhism is "The Middle Way" and therefore [3] in no way antagonistic to physical well-being. [4] It is not wealth that stands in the way of liberation but the attachment to wealth; not the enjoyment of pleasurable things, but the craving for them. [5] The keynote of Buddhist economics, therefore, is simplicity and nonviolence.

$$\{[1][4]\} \longrightarrow [5]$$
$$[2] \longrightarrow [3]$$

9. [1] There are again two methods of removing the causes of faction: the one, by destroying the liberty which is essential to its existence; the other, by giving to every citizen the same opinions, the same passions, and the same interests. [2] It could never be more truly said than of the first remedy, that it was worse than the disease. [3] Liberty is to faction what air is to fire, an ailment without which it instantly expires. [4] But it could not be less folly to abolish liberty, which is essential to political life, because it nourishes faction, than it would be to wish the annihilation of air, which is essential to animal life, because it imparts to fire its destructive agency.

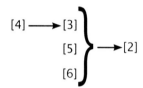

Solutions to LSAT Prep Questions

1. (e). A new section in the rattle is formed when the rattlesnake molts. To tell the age of a rattlesnake by the number of sections in its rattle, it would have to molt in regular time intervals.

2. (e). If they learned crucial details from a third source, then they would not have <u>independently</u> discovered calculus.

3. (b). PREMISE: no one has been able to prove it. PREMISE INDICATOR: since. INTERMEDIATE CONCLUSION: this alleged theorem simply cannot be proved.

    MAIN CONCLUSION: it is likely that Fermat was either lying or else mistake when he made his claim. Conclusion indicator: therefore.

4. (c). BACKGROUND INFORMATION: Antarctica has generally been thought to have been covered by ice for at least the past 14 million years.

    PREMISE: Three-million-year-old fossils of a kind previously found only in ocean-floor sediments were discovered under the ice sheet covering central Antarctica.

    CONCLUSION: About three million years ago the Antarctic ice sheet must temporarily have melted. CONCLUSION INDICATOR: therefore.

5. (a). CONCLUSION: Almost anyone can be an expert.

    EXPLICIT PREMISE: there are no official guidelines determining what an expert must know.

EXPLICIT PREMISE: Anybody who manages to convince some people of his or her qualifications in an area—whatever those may be—is an expert

SUPPRESSED PREMISE: Almost anyone can convince some people of his or her qualifications in some area.

6. (b). CONCLUSION: Marian Anderson, the famous contralto, did not take success for granted.

EXPLICIT PREMISE: Anderson had to struggle early in life.

EXPLICIT PREMISE: Anyone who has to struggle early in life is able to keep a good perspective on the world.

SUPPRESSED PREMISE: Anyone who is able to keep a good perspective on the world does not take success for granted.

2.1

1. Sound.

3. Sound.

5. Nonstarter.

7. Non sequitur.

9. Question-begger.

11. Non sequitur.

13. Non sequitur.

15. Sound.

17. Non sequitur.

19. Non sequitur.

21. Non sequitur.

23. Sound.

25. Nonstarter.

27. Nonstarter.

29. Sound.

31. Nonstarter.

Solutions to LSAT Prep Questions

1. (b). This assumption negates a third possibility. Without negating this third possibility, the conclusion—a two-part disjunction—would not follow.

2.2 Set A

1. (a) Stronger.
   (b) Weaker.
   (c) Undetermined.
   (d) Weaker.
   (e) Stronger.
   (f) Undetermined.
   (g) Weaker.

2.2 Set B

1. Necessity; "can(not)."

3. Necessity; "cannot."

5. Probability; "rational to suppose."

7. Possibility; "could."

9. Certainty; "surely." [The "should" expresses a normative modality.]

11. Actuality.

13. Probability; "should."

15. Necessity; "can(not)."

17. Normative modality; "should."

19. Certainty; "bound to."

21. Probability; "certainly doubtful."

23. Possibility; "may be."

Solutions to LSAT Prep Questions

1. (d). "…words also <u>have the power</u> to change the way we see and the way we act." MODALITY: possibility

    The answer (d) ("may help") reflects the modality of possibility.

2.3

1. Deductively sound.

3. Inductively sound.

5. Inductively sound.

7. Deductively sound.

9. Deductively sound.

11. Inductively sound.

13. Inductively sound.

15. Inductively sound.

17. Inductively sound.

19. Deductively sound.

2.4

1. Deductively valid; sound.

3. Invalid; fallacious.

5. Invalid; fallacious.

7. Deductively valid; fallacious.

9. Deductively valid; fallacious.

11. Inductively valid; fallacious.

13. Inductively valid; sound.

15. Deductively valid; fallacious.

17. Deductively valid; fallacious.

19. Invalid; fallacious.

21. Invalid; fallacious.

23. Deductively valid; fallacious.

25. Deductively valid; sound.

27. Invalid; fallacious.

29. Inductively valid; fallacious.

2.5

1. True.

3. False.

5. False.

7. True.

9. False.

11. True.

13. False.

15. True.

17. False.

19. False.

21. False.

23. True.

25. True.

27. False.

29. True.

31. True.

33. True.

35. False.

37. False.

39. False.

41. True.

43. True.

45. True.

47. False.

49. True.

51. True.

53. False.

55. False.

2.6

1. Begging the question.

3. Fallacy of equivocation.

5. *Ad hominem* argument.

7. Begging the question.

9. Poisoning the well.

11. None.

13. Popular appeals ("loyal American Democrats," "able loyal Democrats").

15. *Ad hominem* argument.

17. None (legitimate conclusion drawn from lack of information).

19. None: the ad contains many clever ambiguities, but no fallacy of equivocation.

21. Poisoning the well ("Any morally minded citizen").

23. None: this may be a non sequitur, but it is not one of the fallacies discussed in §2.6.

25. Fallacy of equivocation.

Solutions to LSAT Prep Questions

1. (b). Ad hominem: the city council member argues against the Mayor's position on real estate development fees by highlighting the Mayor's potential conflict of interest rather than evaluating the merits of the Mayor's position on the issue.

2. (c). Attorney's argument commits the fallacy of argument from ignorance.

3. (c). CONCLUSION: Cotrell is, at best, able to write magazine articles of average quality.

   PREMISE: "...since [premise indicator] Cotrell...is incapable of writing an article that is better than average."

   FALLACY: begging the question.

3.1

1. SOURCE: Annual Reports. INFO: Information regarding the numbers and assets of oil companies in 1921.

3. Mere report of opinion.

5. SOURCE: Grant Hague, M.D. Info: There are two million people in New York with some gonorrhea and syphilis. Such venereal diseases are responsible for congenital birth defects. Women do not appreciate the significance of the problem. Critique: Grant Hague is not an epidemiologist. He does not cite a relevant authority in the field. His conclusion that the relevant venereal diseases are responsible for congenital birth defects is not the consensus view. Nor does he cite any further evidence to establish this connection. He provides no specific sources to back up the claim that women do not appreciate the significance of the spread of venereal disease. He claims that no one but a physician can appreciate the consequences of these infections while at the same time accusing young women and mothers (who presumably are not physicians) of not appreciating these consequences.

7. Mere report of opinion.

9. SOURCE: 1998 memo from ExxonMobil. INFO: There are two significant conclusions: (1) It is unknown whether global climate change is occurring, and (2) it is unknown whether or not humans have any impact on the climate at all (not just climate change). CRITIQUE: First, neither conclusion is the consensus of the scientific community. Second, ExxonMobil is not a relevant authority on weather or climate change. Third, ExxonMobil is in the petroleum industry. The use of petroleum products, specifically their extraction and burning, is considered a chief cause of global warming. ExxonMobil has strong economic interests in avoiding the charge that its products contribute to global warming. This is evidence that the memo may be biased. This violates a condition of validity for arguments from authority.

11. Report of statement plus criticism.

13. Mere report of opinion.

15. SOURCE: Charles Ball. INFO: One young woman carried her infant in a knapsack all day while working, etc.

17. SOURCE: The primary source is Keith F. Pinsoneault, and the secondary source is *The Wall Street Journal*. INFO: Technical factors will move the market higher in January. CRITIQUE: Pinsoneauit's credentials seem good, but there is seldom if ever a consensus on stock market predictions.

19. SOURCE: Lawrence Garfinkel. INFO: Passive smoking had very little if any effect on lung cancer rates among non-smokers. CRITIQUE: This argument cannot be criticized on the grounds that R. J. Reynolds Tobacco Co. is biased, for it is not the source.

21. SOURCE: Astronomers Liverrier and Newcomb. INFO: Newton's theory of motion does not predict the observed perihelial motion of Mercury.

23. SOURCE: Dr. Galton. INFO: When parents who are taller than average reproduce, the difference in height between their children and the average child is less than the difference in height between the parents and the average person. Furthermore, the cause of this regression can be attributed to hereditary drag. CRITIQUE: First, the claim that hereditary drag is the cause of this regression is not the consensus view among scientists. Second, while the genes of the parents affect the height of the offspring, more recent confounding evidence suggests environmental factors, including nutrition, play a large role. Third, it is well known that 'regression to the mean' occurs in any purely random process.

25. SOURCE: Timothy P. King. INFO: "Rich Scotch" is better. CRITIQUE: King is not a relevant authority, and was presumably paid for his testimonial.

27. SOURCE: The unnamed author of the manuscript. INFO: A large round silver thing like a disk flew slowly over the people of Byland Abbey. CRITIQUE: We know nothing of the author of the manuscript, and cannot even rule out the possibility that he was stone drunk during the great portent. Incidentally, it is a long leap from a "large round silver thing like a disc" to a "flying saucer."

Solutions to LSAT Prep Questions

1. (d). The survey asks consumers, who are not knowledgeable sources on how much market-share a product has. Thus, we are not justified in believing what they affirm.

2. (e). The allegation in the advertisement is that other assessors are biased. Answer (e) remedies this potential bias.

3. (c). To undermine an argument from authority, an authority denying what another authority affirms must be equally reliable.

3.2, Set A

1. DATA GROUP: Hitler and Stalin. INFERENCE GROUP: Willie. PROJECTED ATTRIBUTE: Being evil (committing atrocities). SIMILARITIES: Having a moustache. DETAILS: Straight and pure. CRITIQUE: The only noted similarity between Hitler, Stalin, and Willie is that each has a moustache. The projected attribute is being evil. It is unlikely that having a moustache makes someone evil (given all the non-evil, mustachioed people in the world). This violates the condition of validity that requires the DATA GROUP and the inference object to be similar in the relevant respects.

3. DATA GROUP: The various animal and plant species mentioned. INFERENCE GROUP: The animals and plants humans choose to selectively breed. SIMILARITIES: Being part of nature, and similarly subject to the 'mysterious laws of correlation'. PROJECTED ATTRIBUTE: Unpredictable or mysterious changes in physiological structures which result from continued selection for 'peculiarities'. DETAILS: Straight and Pure (perhaps Cautious).

5. DATA GROUP: Me. INFERENCE GROUP: Other human beings. SIMILARITIES: Having similar bodies and exhibiting similar acts and other outward signs. PROJECTED ATTRIBUTE: Having feelings.

DETAILS: Straight, *pure.* CRITIQUE: The DATA GROUP is small, but the similarities are highly relevant. [This argument is one of the major solutions proposed for the philosophical "Problem of Other Minds"; its evaluation is controversial.]

7. DATA GROUP: Modern man. INFERENCE GROUP: *Homo erectus.* PROJECTED ATTRIBUTE: Being an excellent walker. SIMILARITIES: Having fundamentally similar skeletons, and scarcely distinguishable leg bones. DETAILS: Straight, pure.

9. Not an argument from analogy.

11. DATA GROUP: Mars. INFERENCE GROUP: The other planets. PROJECTED ATTRIBUTE: Being correctly described by Kepler's laws. DETAILS: Straight, pure. CRITIQUE: Small data group.

13. DATA GROUP: The two vaccinated dogs. INFERENCE GROUP: All people. PROJECTED ATTRIBUTE: Being immune to rabies. DETAILS: Straight, pure.

15. Not an argument from analogy.

17. Not an argument from analogy, but rather an argument attempting to establish an analogy.

19. DATA GROUP: The last 365 billion days. INFERENCE GROUP: Tomorrow. PROJECTED ATTRIBUTE: Rising. DETAILS: Straight and pure.

21. DATA GROUP: Chablis. INFERENCE GROUP: Soave. PROJECTED ATTRIBUTE: Being loved by you. DETAILS: Rash and pure. CRITIQUE: Fallacious because rash.

23. Not an argument from analogy, but rather an argument trying to establish an analogy.

25. Mere simile.

27. Mere statement of similarity.

29. DATA GROUP: Lines. INFERENCE GROUP: Time. PROJECTED ATTRIBUTE: One dimensionality. SIMILARITIES: The relations between points in time are similar to the relations between points on a line. We can talk about time the way we talk about lines: points, long and short segments, beginnings, ends, portions, etc.

31. Not an argument from analogy.

3.2, Set B

1. (a) Weakens, by decreasing the size of the data group. (b) Strengthens, by increasing the size of the data group. (c) Weakens, by reducing the proportion of the data group that has the projected attribute. (d) Weakens, by reducing the similarity between the data group and the inference group. (e) Strengthens, by increasing the similarity between the data group and the inference group. (f) Weakens, by reducing the similarity between the data group and the inference group. (g) Strengthens, by increasing the variety in the data group. (h) Weakens, by reducing *the* variety in the data group. (i) Strengthens, by increasing the similarity between the data group and the inference group. (j) Strengthens, by increasing the similarity between the data group and the inference group. (k) No effect: irrelevant difference. (l) No effect: irrelevant similarity. (m) Weakens, by strengthening the conclusion. (n) Strengthens,

by weakening the conclusion. (o) Strengthens, by strengthening the attribution premise. (p) Weakens, by strengthening the conclusion. (q) Weakens, by increasing the size of the inference group, and thereby strengthening the conclusion. (r) No effect: irrelevant similarity. (s) No effect: irrelevant difference.

Solutions to LSAT Prep Questions

1. (a). Analogizes coloring films to basing a movie on a novel.

2. (b). Draws a conclusion about other planetary systems based on our planetary system without justifying that these systems possess relevant similarities.

3. (d). The proponent of off-shore drilling analogizes the opponent's argument to an argument maintaining that new farms should be prohibited.

4. (a). This weakens the analogy by demonstrating that the two cases—drilling new wells and building new farms—are not similar in relevant respects.

5. (a). Both arguments assert that, because the original painting/speech contained mistakes, accurate reproductions of the mistaken originals are not possible.

6. (a). This is an example of indirect reasoning: Sedley assumes Beckstein's reasoning to be valid and then shows the unfavorable consequences of that assumption.

3.3, Set A

1. Vaguely statistical argument from analogy.

3. Pure argument from analogy.

5. Pure argument from analogy.

7. Pure enumerative induction.

9. Pure argument from analogy.

11. Pure argument from analogy.

13. Statistical enumerative induction.

15. Statistical argument from analogy.

17. Pure syllogism.

3.3, Set B

(a) Strengthens, by increasing the size of the data group. (b) Weakens, by reducing the size of the data group. (c) Weakens, by reducing the variety in the data group. (d) Strengthens, by increasing the variety in the data group. (e) Strengthens, by increasing the variety in the data group. (f) Weakens, by reducing the variety in the data group. (g) Weakens, by reducing the variety in the data group. (h) Strengthens, by increasing the variety in the data group. (i) No effect: irrelevant characteristic. (j) Weakens, by reducing the variety in the data group. (k) Strengthens (slightly), by increasing the variety in the data group. (l) Strengthens, by weakening the conclusion. (m) Strengthens, by weakening the conclusion. (n) Weakens, by strengthening the conclusion. (o) Weakens, by strengthening the conclusion.

Solutions to LSAT Prep Questions

1. (e). Hasty generalization.

2. (d). Sixty-nine percent (38% for some media + 31% for all advertising) of those surveyed favored some sort of ban on cigarette advertising. Because the sample is representative of the general population, we can infer that a similar percentage holds true for the population as a whole.

3. (c). The background of some researchers has no bearing on the results of the study.

4. (b). Although <u>1984</u> was second, in a <u>relative</u> ordering, the conclusion makes a claim about the absolute number (the book "has exercised much influence on a great number of this newspaper's readers"). Whether this is true depends on how many readers chose other books, including the Bible.

3.4

1. Analogy; exclusion: the president has appointment powers through the Constitution of the United States which other persons (citizens or not) do not possess.

3. Authority; exclusion: billions of mothers have been nonvirgins, there have been no proven cases of virgin mothers, and elementary facts of biology prove that it is impossible for virgins to have babies.

5. Authority; exclusion: anthropologists, paleontologists, and geologists overwhelmingly support evolution, and their assent is based on evidence that is too voluminous to cite here.

7. Authority; no exclusion.

9. Analogy; no exclusion.

11. Analogy; exclusion: pennies are symmetrical, and so are just as likely to come up tails as heads on any toss.

13. Analogy; exclusion: every deck of cards contains one ace of spades.

15. Enumerative induction; exclusion: the damaging effects in question are cumulative and take many years to show up.

17. Analogy; exclusion: all humans before now have died eventually, even those who have lived over 10,000 days.

19. Analogy; no exclusion.

21. Enumerative induction and authority; exclusion: there is no causal connection between the chance mechanisms that resulted in your being born on a certain date, and the chance mechanisms that produce winners in lotteries and the like.

23. Probably analogy (with moving fast on the surface of the earth); exclusion: all things held on earth by gravity, like us and the air, are traveling at the same speed the earth is.

25. Analogy (and hypothetical induction—see §4.2); exclusion: first, there are no proven cases to date of an intelligent being capable of creating an eye; second, all the data supporting the theory of evolution undermines the conclusion of this argument.

27. Authority; exclusion: the consensus of scientists, based on vast evidence, supports global warming.

Solutions to LSAT Prep Questions

1. (e). The different uses for pyramids in each civilization are not the only possible link between civilizations.

2. (e). The argument contends that the use of nonaddictive drugs by athletes should be allowed, but the use of addictive drugs should be banned since they are physically harmful. If taking massive doses of nonaddictive drugs (such as aspirin or vitamins) is harmful, then this undermines the conclusion by making the nonaddictive drugs more like addictive drugs.

3. (d). The question is asked from the environmentalist's perspective and requires justifying why methanol should replace gasoline if both cause cancer.

4.1

1. SUSPECTED CAUSE: Mother flies. EFFECT: Maggots and new flies. FORM: Causal induction. METHOD: Difference. STUDY: Experimental. TEST GROUP: The open jar. CONTROL GROUP: The covered jar.

3. There are two arguments here: (I) SUSPECTED CAUSE: Preexisting little animals. EFFECT: New little animals. FORM: Causal induction. METHOD: Difference. STUDY: Experimental. TEST GROUP: The corked flasks. CONTROL GROUP: The sealed and boiled flasks. (ii) SUSPECTED CAUSE: Boiling for an hour. EFFECT: All little animals dead. FORM: Difference and concomitant variation. STUDY: Experimental. TEST GROUP: The flasks boiled for an hour. CONTROL GROUP: The flasks boiled less than an hour and the unboiled flasks.

5. SUSPECTED CAUSE: The drive of fear. EFFECT: Stopping vocal behavior. FORM: Causal induction. METHOD: Agreement. STUDY: Correlational.

7. SUSPECTED CAUSE: Gravitational potential. EFFECT: Spectral lines shifted toward the red end of the spectrum. FORM: Other.

9. SUSPECTED CAUSE: The moral decadence of a civilization. EFFECT: The decline and extinction of that civilization. FORM: *Post hoc* reasoning.

11. SUSPECTED CAUSES: The dozen or twenty different mosquitoes. EFFECT: Malaria. FORM: Causal elimination.

13. SUSPECTED CAUSE: The multipage insert in *Life*. EFFECT: Three years later there was no longer any doubt about the size of the company and its resources. FORM: *Post hoc* reasoning.

15. SUSPECTED CAUSE: Receiving the fourth reinforcement. EFFECT: The swift acceleration to the maximum rate of bar pressing. FORM: Hard to classify. It appears to be a *post hoc* argument. But the rate of response accelerated to the maximum when and only when the fourth response was received, so a correlation was established; and the "Skinner Box" is a carefully controlled environment, so there are no obvious confounding variables. Hence, this is best classified as a causal induction employing the method of difference. STUDY: Also hard to classify. The Skinner Box is a carefully controlled environment, and Skinner determined whether a response would be reinforced. Nevertheless, Skinner had no control over when any response would occur, and the fourth reinforcement was selected as the suspected cause only because it was correlated with the effect. So this should be classified as a correlational study. However, the rat whose behavior is being analyzed is part of the test group of a larger experimental study (see exercise 16) employing causal induction and the method of difference which showed that reinforcing every response (the suspected cause) produces a high and constant rate of response after a few reinforcements (the effect). The control group in this study consisted of rats who were never reinforced, or who were reinforced on a different schedule.

17. SUSPECTED CAUSE: The new bacillus. EFFECT: Diphtheria. FORM: Causal elimination.

19. SUSPECTED CAUSE: Passive/secondhand smoke. EFFECT: Development of lymphoma, risk of lymphoma in cats. FORM: Causal induction. METHOD: Concomitant variation. STUDY:

Correlational. TEST GROUP: Cats exposed to passive smoke. CONTROL GROUP: Cats which were not exposed.

21. SUSPECTED CAUSE: Exposure to radiation from the atomic bombs. EFFECT: Increased incidence of leukemia. FORM: Causal induction. METHOD: Concomitant variation. STUDY: Correlational.

23. SUSPECTED CAUSE: The pronounced economic and industrial surge in the sixteenth and seventeenth centuries. EFFECT: The rise of modern science in the sixteenth and seventeenth centuries. FORM: *Post hoc* reasoning. This could also be classified as a causal induction, since the rise of modern science occurred when and only when the economic surge occurred. But even if it is, the argument still commits the fallacy of *post hoc reasoning*, since two of the conditions of validity on causal induction are violated: the rise of modern science is a possible cause of the economic surge, and there are countless confounding variables.

25. FORM: Other. A causal conclusion could be drawn here in accordance with the method of concomitant variation; but Newton drew a noncausal conclusion.

27. SUSPECTED CAUSE: Heating wine to 55°C, thereby killing the microorganisms responsible for diseases. EFFECT: Excellent flavor after ten months. FORM: Causal induction. METHOD: Difference. STUDY: Experimental. TEST GROUP: The heated wine. CONTROL GROUP: The unheated wine.

Solutions to LSAT Prep Questions

1. (d). A mere correlation between two events, without more, does not establish causation. See requirements for causal induction.

2. (a). By arguing that removing the regulations will cause the banks to loan more money, the argument assumes that there is no alternative cause (such as less available money to loan) that is sufficient to produce the effect (banks loaning less money).

3. (b). Confounds sufficiency and necessity. That a particular cost-cutting plan is <u>sufficient</u> to decrease expenditures by a required amount does not mean that it is the only way to reduce expenditures by that amount.

4. (d). Causal elimination. Potential cause: Number of calories one consumes. Effect: Body fat gain.

5. (a). Causal elimination: e occurred without c (<u>in b</u>). Since the skeptic controlled for only one possible cause in each of the three different experiments, the skeptic would be justified in concluding only that the cause tested for in that experiment was not the cause <u>in that particular experiment</u> (that is, in circumstances b).

6. (e). Causal induction: Mill's Method of Difference. Cause: Presence of Apo-A-IV-2 gene. Effect: Inhibiting elevation of blood cholesterol.

7. (e). Smoking, drinking, and exercise are factors influenced by lifestyle. The premises indicate that these factors influence the level of cholesterol in the blood, and the level of cholesterol in the blood, in turn, affects the risk of having a fatal heart attack.

8. (d). Insulin is linked to the production of body fat, and the study indicates that a high intake of carbohydrates causes the body to overproduce insulin.

4.2

1. DATA: The extreme amount of diversity and variation observed in plants and animals. HYPOTHESIS: There are no limitations on the extent to which a species can vary. COMPETING HYPOTHESIS: There are limitations on the extent to which a species can vary.

3. DATA: The curious slow turning of the elliptical path traced by Mercury in its plane (the perihelion of Mercury). HYPOTHESIS: Einstein's formulas of general relativity. COMPETING HYPOTHESIS: Presumably the standard Newtonian astronomical theories of the day.

5. DATA: The similarity of embryological development throughout the animal kingdom. HYPOTHESIS: Heritable and successive slight variations.

7. DATA: From post-hypnotic suggestion, dreams, and slips. HYPOTHESIS: There are unconscious mental processes. COMPETING HYPOTHESIS: All mental processes are conscious.

9. DATA: Polarization. HYPOTHESIS: Light consists of corpuscles with different properties in two perpendicular directions. COMPETING HYPOTHESIS: Light consists of waves.

11. DATA: Two or more substances with quite different chemical properties can be composed of the same numbers of the same atoms. HYPOTHESIS: The atoms are arranged differently in the different isomers.

13. DATA: The diphtheria soup killed rabbits even though no bacillus could be found in the rabbits. HYPOTHESIS: The bacillus produces a toxin that causes diphtheria. COMPETING HYPOTHESIS: The bacillus itself causes diphtheria. TEST: Inject filtered diphtheria soup into rabbits. NEW DATA: The filtered soup also caused diphtheria.

15. DATA: Large deflection of cathode rays in a magnetic field; sharp outlines of their beam; their ability to penetrate gold leaf; the magnetic deflection's independence of the nature of the gas in the discharge tube; the results of the thermopile experiment showing high velocity and charge to mass ratio of 10^7. HYPOTHESIS: Cathode rays consist of particles 1,000 times smaller than hydrogen atoms and traveling at great velocities. COMPETING HYPOTHESIS: Cathode rays consist of charged atoms of the gas in the discharge tube traveling at low velocities. TEST: The thermopile experiment.

17. DATA: The majority of the alpha particles were scattered through only a few degrees, but a small proportion actually bounced back. HYPOTHESIS: The atom consists of a tiny, massive, positively charged nucleus, around which the electrons revolve. COMPETING HYPOTHESIS: The atom consists of a diffuse sphere of positive charge in which the electrons are embedded. TEST: The twelve months of experiments by Geiger and Marsden. NEW DATA: About eight times as many particles were scattered between 60° and 120° as between 120° and 180°.

19. DATA: Differences in the position, manner of operation, and other details of the orifices of certain air-breathing species (of crustaceans). HYPOTHESIS: Species belonging to distinct

families living in different conditions slowly adapted (via natural selection) to live more and more out of water and breathe air.

Solutions to LSAT Prep Questions

1. (e). The explanation must resolve why something that apparently limits a disease's symptoms and duration without producing side effects is nevertheless dangerous for widespread use.

2. (b). The explanation must resolve why trees living in an area with better nutrients and more moisture are younger than those in a more hostile environment. No other answer choice is even relevant to this conflict.

3. (a). For a hypothetical induction to be valid, no competing hypothesis can explain the data as well as the proffered hypothesis. This argument attacks the original claim by offering a competing hypothesis that fully explains the data.

4.4

1. Explanatory power.

3. Explanatory power.

5. No comparison.

7. Explanatory power.

9. Explanatory power.

13. Explanatory power.

15. Explanatory power and consistency.

17. Explanatory power.

Solutions to LSAT Prep Questions

1. (e). (e) explains why people in North America several thousand years ago would continue producing a crop that was not, by itself, sufficient to maintain their heath. (b), (c), and (d) are irrelevant to complete the explanation. (a) does not resolve the continued reliance on that variety of corn despite the health problems caused when consuming only that food.

2. (c). First becoming depressed in middle age (which, as phrased in this argument, implies continued depression as one gets older) does not explain why those who are younger and depressed have more fear of dying than those who are older and depressed.

3. (c). The phenomenon being explained is why, other things being equal, a running track with a hard surface produces a greater speed under dry conditions than a soft one. (c) gives further reasons why this is the case. (a), (b), and (d) are irrelevant to analyzing this phenomenon. (e) is also irrelevant since the type of maintenance procedure required to

keep the track in good condition has no bearing on whether that track produces a faster speed than a type of track with a different maintenance procedure.

5.1, Set A

1. FORM: **A**; QUANTITY: universal; QUALITY: affirmative; SUBJECT: mammal; PREDICATE: vertebrate.

3. **E**, universal negative, *S*: businessman, *P*: politician.

5. **O**, particular negative, *S*: Republicans *P*: liberals.

7. **A**, universal affirmative, *S*: senator, *P*: congressman.

9. **A**, universal affirmative, *S*: woman, *P*: female.

5.1, Set B

1. **A**, universal affirmative, *S*: behavior, *P*: (thing which) springs from desire.

3. **I**, particular affirmative, *S*: politicians, *P*: very fine people.

5. **E**, universal negative, *S*: society, *P*: (thing which) operates entirely on the command principle.

7. **I**, particular affirmative, *S*: animals, *P*: (things) we find and kill.

9. **I**, particular affirmative, *S*: elements, *P*: solids at room temperature.

11. **A**, universal affirmative, *S*: variety of wine, *P*: (thing which) has its own peculiar maladies.

13. **A**, universal affirmative, *S*: governments. *P*: (things which are) totalitarian and authoritarian to one extent or another.

15. **A**, universal affirmative, *S*: technological developments, *P*: (things which) derive from common basic scientific knowledge.

17. **A**, universal affirmative, *S*: social phenomenon, *P*: fluid product of human history.

19. **A**, universal affirmative, *S*: bodies in motion, *P*: (things which) continue to move in a straight line…force.

21. **A**, universal affirmative, *S*: man's beneficent ideals, *P*: rationalizations of…nature.

23. **O**, particular negative, *S*: students, *P*: (people) able to get through school without…grief.

5.1, Set C

1. **A**, *S*: atheists, *P*: hedonists.

3. **E**, *S*: atheists, *P*: hedonists.

5. **A**, *S*: unborn babies, *P*: (beings which) have the right to life.

7. **A**, *S*: expectant mothers, *P*: (people who) have the right to choose an abortion.

9. **A**, *S*: comet, *P*: (thing) made mostly of ice.

11. **I**, *S*: insecticides, *P*: (things which) remain in the soil for years. (The quantity could be universal, or something weaker, like "commonly.")

13. **I**, *S*: the most necessary laws, *P*: (things) considered a challenge and an intrusion.

15. **O**, *S*: payroll-savings plans, *P*: (things) to be sniffed at.

17. **E**, *S*: individual in prison, *P*: (person who) loses the right to have rights.

19. **A**, *S*: transactions in a free-trade world, *P*: (things which) take place among private entities.

21. **A**, *S*: politician's decisions and actions, *P*: (things which) flow naturally from his mental convictions.

23. **E**, *S*: my dogs, *P*: (thing) dead as a result of the vaccine.

25. **A**, *S*: (place) where the zanzarone mosquito buzzes, *P*: (place) where there is malaria.

27. **I**, *S*: tests conducted by Pasteur, *P*: (things which) show that the rabies vaccine is effective.

29. **A**, *S*: the craters on the moon, *P*: depressions rather than mounds.

31. **I**, *S*: giant fireball, *P*: (thing) moving rapidly across the sky.

33. **A**, *S*: feelings, *P*: (things) created by what you put into your own mind.

35. **A**, *S*: those other worlds in space, *P*: (worlds in which) there are events in progress that will determine their futures.

37. **A**, *S*: earthquake, *P*: (thing) followed by aftershocks.

39. **A**, *S*: (one who) lives by the sword, *P*: (one who) dies by the sword.

41. **A**, *S*: these things—a good education, friends, love,...and work, *P*: (things which) depend upon the community and are helped or hindered by political events.

5.2, Set A

1. (a) is false: it is the contrary of (1) and contraries cannot both be true; (b) is true: it is the subaltern of (1) and the subaltern must be true if the superaltern is; (c) is false: it is the contradictory of (1) and contradictories cannot both be true.

3. (a) is undetermined: it is the subcontrary of (3) and subcontraries may but need not both be true; (b) is undetermined: it is the superaltern of (3) and the superaltern may but need not be true if the subaltern is; (c) is false: it contradicts (3) and contradictories cannot both be true.

5.2, Set B

1. (a) is undetermined because it is the contrary of (1) and contraries may but need not both be false; (b) is undetermined because it is the subaltern of (1) and the subaltern may, but need not, be false if the superaltern is; (c) is true because it contradicts (1), and contradictories, cannot both be false.

3. (a) is true because it is the subcontrary of (3) and subcontraries cannot both be false; (b) is false because it is the superaltern of (3) and the superaltern must be false if the subaltern is; (c) is true because it contradicts (3) and contradictories cannot both be false.

5.2, Set C

1. Valid: The subaltern must be true if the superaltern is.

3. Invalid: Subcontraries may but need not both be true.

5. Invalid: The superaltern need not be true if the subaltern is.

7. Valid: "Some ducks are widgeons" and "No ducks are widgeons" are contradictory, and so cannot both be true.

9. Valid: "All widgeons are ducks" and "No widgeons are ducks" are contrary, and so cannot both be true.

5.2, Set D

1. Contraries.

3. Alterns.

5. Subcontraries.

7. Contraries.

9. Contradictories.

11. Subcontraries.

13. Contraries.

5.3, Set A

1. CONV: Every vertebrate is a mammal. OBV: No mammal is a nonvertebrate. CONTR: Every nonvertebrate is a nonmammal.

3. CONV: Some liberals are Republicans. OBV: Some Republicans are not nonliberals. CONTR: Some nonliberals are non-Republicans.

5.3, Set B

1. CONV: Everyone who is corrupt is a politician. OBV: No politician is noncorrupt. CONTR: Everyone who is not corrupt is a nonpolitician.

3. CONV: Some beautiful individuals are women. OBV: Some women are not non-beautiful. CONTR: Some nonbeautiful individuals are nonwomen.

5.3, Set C

1. CONV: Every singer is a soprano. OBV: No soprano is a nonsinger. CONTR: Every nonsinger is a nonsoprano.

3. CONV: Some liars are people. OBV: Some people are not nonliars. CONTR: Some nonliars are nonpeople.

5.3, Set D

1. CONV: Every individual who votes Republican is a true patriot. OBV: No true patriot is an individual who does not vote Republican. CONTR: Every individual who does not vote Republican is other than a true patriot.

3. CONV: Some solids are elements at room temperature. OBV: Some elements at room temperature are not nonsolids. CONTR: Some nonsolids are things other than elements at room temperature.

5.3, Set E

1. CONV: All things springing from desire are behavior. OBV: No behavior is a thing not springing from desire. CONTR: Everything not springing from desire is nonbehavior.

3. CONV: Everything having its own peculiar maladies is a variety of wine. OBV: No variety of wine is lacking its own peculiar maladies. CONTR: Everything lacking its own peculiar maladies is something other than a variety of wine.

5. CONV: No things that continue moving indefinitely are terrestrial objects. OBV: All terrestrial objects are objects that do not continue to move indefinitely. CONTR: No objects that do not continue to move indefinitely are nonterrestrial objects.

7. CONV: Some beings still oppressed by the idea…are humans. OBV: Some humans are not beings not still oppressed by the idea… CONTR: Some beings not still oppressed by the idea…are nonhumans.

9. CONV: Some individuals able to get through school without cheating and plagiarizing are not students. OBV: Some students are unable to get through school without cheating and

plagiarizing. CONTR: Some individuals unable to get through school without cheating and plagiarizing are not nonstudents.

11. CONV: Everywhere there are mosquitoes, there is malaria. OBV: Nowhere there is malaria are there no mosquitoes. CONTR: Everywhere there are no mosquitoes, there is no malaria.

5.3, Set F

1. (a) is undetermined: an **A** is not convertible; (b) is true: all propositions are obvertible; (c) is true: an **A** is contraposable; (d) is false: contraries cannot both be true; (e) is true: the subaltern is true if the superaltern is.

3. (a) is undetermined: the superaltern may but need not be true if the subaltern is; (b) is true: an **I** is convertible; (c) is true: all propositions are obvertible; (d) is undetermined: subcontraries may but need not both be true; (e) is undetermined: an **I** is not contraposable.

5. (a) is true: an **E** is convertible; (b) is true: all propositions are obvertible; (c) is undetermined: an **E** is not contraposable; (d) is false: contradictories cannot both be true; (e) is true: the subaltern is true if the superaltern is.

5.3, Set G

1. (a) is undetermined: an **A** is not convertible; (b) is false: all propositions are obvertible; (c) is false: an **A** is contraposable; (d) is undetermined: contraries may but need not both be false; (e) is undetermined: the subaltern may but need not be false if the superaltern is.

3. (a) is false: the superaltern must be false if the subaltern is; (b) is false: an **I** is convertible; (c) is false: all propositions are obvertible; (d) is true: subcontraries cannot both be false; (e) is undetermined: an **I** is not contraposable.

5. (a) is false: an **E** is convertible; (b) is false: all propositions are obvertible: (c) is undetermined: an **E** is not contraposable; (d) is true: contradictories cannot both be false; (e) is undetermined: the subaltern may but need not be false if the superaltern is.

5.3, Set H

1. Invalid: an **A** is not convertible.

3. Valid: an **A** is contraposable.

5. Valid: an **I** is convertible.

7. Invalid: subcontraries may but need not both be true.

9. Valid: an **O** is contraposable.

11. Valid: all propositions are obvertible.

13. Invalid: an **E** is not contraposable.

15. Invalid: the converse of a true **A** may but need not be false.

5.3, Set I

1. All students who pass are those who study.

3. Some, but not all, students who pass study—i.e., some students who pass study but some students who pass do not study.

5. All those who pass are students who study.

7. Some, but not all, amateurs are eligible for the Olympics—i.e., some amateurs are eligible for the Olympics but some amateurs are not eligible for the Olympics.

9. All triangles are three-sided figures and all three-sided figures are triangles.

11. All three-sided figures are triangles.

5.4

1. **AIO1**

3. **IAI1**

5. **AII2**

7. **EEE3**

9. **AEO1**

5.5, Set A

1. All mammals are animals and some cats are mammals, so some cats are not animals.

3. Some cats are dogs, for some animals are dogs and all cats are animals.

5. Some cats are animals. All dogs are animals. Therefore, some cats are dogs.

7. No dogs are mammals, for no snakes are mammals and no snakes are dogs.

9. Every cat is an animal. No dog is a cat, so some dog is not an animal.

5.5, Set B

1. All dogs are animals and all mammals are animals, so all mammals are dogs.

3. No mammals are reptiles and some mammals are cats, so some cats are reptiles.

5. All cats are mammals and all cats are animals, so all animals are mammals.

7. All cats are animals and all cats are mammals, so no mammals are animals.

9. No cats are birds and some animals are cats, so all animals are birds.

11. No cats are men and some cats are mammals, so all mammals are men.

13. Some mammals are dogs and some mammals are cats, so all cats are dogs.

15. Some birds are animals and no cats are birds, so no cats are animals.

17. All mammals are animals and some cats are mammals, so some cats are not animals.

19. Some plants are not animals and all cats are animals, so all cats are plants.

5.5, Set C

1. Some animals are cats, therefore all animals are cats.

3. Some animals are not cats, therefore no animals are cats.

5. All cats are animals, therefore no cats are animals.

7. No cat is a dog, therefore no nondog is a noncat.

9. Some animals are not cats, therefore some cats are not animals.

11. Some cats are mammals, therefore only some cats are mammals.

13. All cats are animals, therefore all noncats are nonanimals.

15. Some cats are mammals, some mammals are animals, some animals are dogs, therefore some cats are dogs.

17. Some animals are rats, no cats are nonanimals, therefore some cats are rats.

5.6, Set A

1. Subalternation

2. Conversion

3. General categorical syllogism

7. General categorical syllogism

9. Double negation

11. General categorical syllogism

5.6, Set B

1. Contr

2. GCS

3. Obv

7. Sub

9. Obv

11. GCS

5.6, Set C

1. 2. 1 Obv

    3. 2 Contr

    4. 3 Sub

3. 2. 1 Sub

    3. 2 Obv

    4. 3 Conv

5. 3. 1 Obv

    4. 2,3 GCS

    5. 4 Obv

7. 3. 2 Conv

    4. 3 Obv

    5. 1,4 GCS

    6. 5 Contr

5.6, Set D

1. 3. 1,2 GCS

    4. 3 Conv

3. 3. 2 Contr

    4. 1,3 GCS

    5. 4 Obv

    6. 5 Conv

5. 3. 1 Obv

    4. 3 Conv

    5. 2,4 GCS

    6. 5 Conv

    7. 6 Obv

    8. 7 DN

7.   5. 1,4 GCS

    6. 5 Contr

    7. 2,6 GCS

    8. 3,7 GCS

5.6, Set E

1.   1. All men are animals.   /∴ Some animals are men.

    2. Some men are animals.   1 Sub

    3. Some animals are men.   2 Conv

3.   1. No scientist is a philosopher.   /∴ Some nonphilosopher is not a nonscientist.

    2. Some scientist is not a philosopher.   1 Sub

    3. Some nonphilosopher is not a nonscientist.   2 Contr

5.   1. Some fish are not sharks.   /∴ Some nonsharks are fish.

    2. Some fish are nonsharks.   1 Obv

    3. Some nonsharks are fish.   2 Conv

7.   1. No apple is a vegetable.   /∴ Some nonvegetable is an apple.

    2. Every apple is a nonvegetable.   1 Obv

    3. Some apple is a nonvegetable.   2 Sub

    4. Some nonvegetable is an apple.   3 Conv

9.   1. Every nonathlete is a bookworm.   /∴ Some nonbookworm is not a nonathlete.

    2. Every nonbookworm is an athlete.   1 Contr

    3. Some nonbookworm is an athlete.   2 Sub

    4. Some nonbookworm is not a nonathlete.   3 Obv

5.6, Set F

1.
  1. All flowers are plants.
  2. All roses are flowers.   /∴ Some roses are plants.
  3. All roses are plants.   1,2 GCS
  4. Some roses are plants.   3 Sub

3.
  1. Every flower is a plant.
  2. Some flower is a rose.   /∴ Some rose is a plant.
  3. Some rose is a flower.   2 Conv
  4. Some rose is a plant.   1,3 GCS

5.
  1. Every ape is a primate.
  2. Every ape is a mammal.   /∴ Some mammal is a primate.
  3. Some ape is a mammal.   2 Sub
  4. Some mammal is an ape.   3 Conv
  5. Some mammal is a primate.   4,1 GCS

7.
  1. Some parents are understanding people.
  2. No parents are nonadults.   /∴ Some adults are understanding people.
  3. Some understanding people are parents. 1 Conv
  4. All parents are adults.   2 Obv
  5. Some understanding people are adults. 3,4 GCS
  6. Some adults are understanding people. 5 Conv

9.
  1. No nonbirds are ducks.
  2. All nonducks are nonmallards.   /∴ All mallards are birds.
  3. All mallards are ducks.   2 Contr
  4. No ducks are nonbirds.   1 Conv
  5. All ducks are birds.   4 Obv
  6. All mallards are birds.   3,5 GCS

5.6, Set G

1. 1. Some A is a B.

    2. Every A is a C.   / ∴ Some C is a B.

    3. Some B is an A.   1 Conv

    4. Some B is a C.   3,2 GCS

    5. Some C is a B.   4 Conv

    [A stands for "member of the House of Representatives who has served on the armed forces subcommittee for many years"; B for "Republican from the Finger Lakes region of upstate New York"; C for "congressman with enormous political clout in matters concerning military procurement."]

3. 1. Every A is a B.

    2. No B is a C.   / ∴ No C is an A.

    3. Every B is a non-C.   2 Obv

    4. Every A is a non-C.   3,1 GCS

    5. No A is a C.   4 Obv

    6. No C is an A.   5 Conv

    [A stands for "left-handed tennis player who has ever won at Wimbledon"; B stands for "individual who has a good chance of making it into the tennis Hall of Fame"; C for "football player, hockey player, or professor."]

5. 1. No A is a B.

    2. Every C is a B.   / ∴ No C is an A.

    3. Every non-B is a non-C.   2 Contr

    4. Every A is a non-B.   1 Obv

    5. Every A is a non-C.   4,3 GCS

    6. No A is a C.   5 Obv

    7. No C Is an A.   6 Conv

    [A stands for "one who has carefully studied the problem of hunger in the United States"; B for "(one who) holds that the problem is negligible" C for "member of the committee appointed by President Reagan to study hunger in America"]

7. 1. Every S is an L.

    2. Every F is an S.

3. No *Y* is an *L*.	/∴No *Y* is an *F*.
4. Every *F* is an *L*.	1,2 GCS
5. No *L* is a *Y*.	3 Conv
6. Every *L* is a non-*Y*.	5 Obv
7. Every *F* is a non-*Y*.	4,6 GCS
8. Every *Y* is a non-*F*.	7 Contr
9. No *Y* is an *F*.	8 Obv

[*S* for "one who is sane"; *L* for "(person) able to do logic"; *F* for "(person) fit to serve on a jury"; *Y* for "your sons."]

5.6, Set H

1.
1. Some *N* is an *S*.	
2. Every *V* is a *T*.	
3. No *S* is a non-*V*.	/∴Some *N* is a *T*.
4. Every *S* is a *V*.	3 Obv
5. Some *N* is a *V*.	1,4 GCS
6. Some *N* is a *T*.	5,2 GCS

3.
1. All *T* are *W*.	
2. No *H* are *R*.	
3. All *W* are *R*.	/∴No *H* are *T*.
4. No *R* are *H*.	2 Conv
5. All *R* are non-*H*.	4 Obv
6. All *W* are non-*H*.	3,5 GCS
7. All *T* are non-*H*.	1,6 GCS
8. No *T* are *H*.	7 Obv
9. No *H* are *T*.	8 Conv

5.
1. No *T* is a *W*.	
2. No non-*W* is a *C*.	
3. Each *K* is a *T*.	/∴No *K* is a *C*.
4. Every *T* is a non-*W*.	1 Obv

5. Every K is a non-W.	3,4 GCS
6. Every non-W is a non-C.	2 Obv
7. Every K is a non-C.	5,6 GCS
8. No K is a C.	7 Obv

7.   1. No T is a non-W.

2. No H is an R.

3. Every non-R is a non-W.	$/ \therefore$ Some H is not a T.
4. Every H is a non-R.	2 Obv
5. Every H is a non-W.	4,3 GCS
6. No non-W is a T.	1 Conv
7. Every non-W is a non-T.	6 Obv
8. Every H is a non-T.	5,7 GCS
9. Some H is a non-T.	8 Sub
10. Some H is not a T.	9 Obv

9.   1. All F are non-R.

2. No A are non-T.

3. All W are R.

4. All T are F.	$/ \therefore$ No W are A.
5. All T are non-R.	4,1 GCS
6. All non-R are non-W.	3 Contr
7. All T are non-W.	5,6 GCS
8. All A are T.	2 Obv
9. All A are non-W.	8,7 GCS
10. No A are W.	9 Obv
11. No W are A.	10 Conv

5.7, Set A

1.   **U**, singular affirmative, s: Ted Kennedy P: Democrat.

3.   **A**, universal affirmative, s: taxpayers, P: (people who are) advised to read the IRS manual carefully.

5. **Y**, singular negative, *s*: Steffi Graf, *P*: left-handed.

7. **U**, singular affirmative, *s*: Arabic, *P*: (language) spoken in Syria.

9. **U**, singular affirmative, *s*: the Nile, *P*: (thing) longer than any other river.

5.7, Set B

1. Ted Kennedy is not a non-Democrat.

3. No taxpayers are unadvised to read the IRS manual carefully.

5. Steffi Graf is non-left–handed.

7. Arabic is not unspoken in Syria.

9. The Nile is not a thing that is not longer than any other river.

5.7, Set C

1. **AYY1**

3. **EUU1**

5. **YUO3**

7. **IUU1**

9. **EUY2**

5.7, Set D

1. SCS

3. Obv

5. SCS

7. SCS

9. SCS

5.7, Set E

1. Invalid: Every woman is a human being. George Bush is not a woman. Therefore, George Bush is not a human being.

3. Invalid: The Nile is a river. No river is a lake. Therefore, the Nile is a lake.

5. Valid:

    1. Mick Jagger is a singer.

    2. Mick Jagger is not a pianist.   /∴ Some singers are not pianists.

    3. Mick Jagger is a nonpianist.   2, Obv

    4. Some singers are nonpianists.   1,3 SCS

    5. Some singers are not pianists.   4 Obv

7.   Invalid: The earth is a planet. Some planets are moonless. Therefore the earth is moonless.

9.   Valid:

    1. Zinc is a metal.

    2. No organic compound is a metal.   /∴ Zinc is not an organic compound.

    3. No metal is an organic compound.   2 Conv

    4. Every metal is a non(organic compound).   3 Obv

    5. Zinc is a non(organic compound).   1,4 SCS

    6. Zinc is not an organic compound.   5 Obv

5.7, Set F

1.   1. k is not an A.

    2. All non-A are B.   /∴ k is a B.

    3. k is a non-A.   1 Obv

    4. k is a B.   3,2 SCS

3.   1. d is an A.

    2. No A is a B.

    3. d is a C.   /∴ Some C is a non-B.

    4. Every A is a non-B.   2 Obv

    5. Some C is an A.   3,1 SCS

    6. Some C is a non-B.   5,4 GCS

5.   1. c is not an H.

    2. Every non-G is an H.   /∴ c is a G.

    3. c is a non-H.   1 Obv

    4. Every non-H is a G.   2 Contr

5. *c* is a *G*.   3,4 SCS

7. 1. *b* is an *F*.

2. Every *F* is a *G*.

3. No *G* is an *H*.   / ∴ *b* is not an *H*.

4. *b* is a *G*.   1,2 SCS

5. Every *G* is a non-*H*.   3 Obv

6. *b* is a non-*H*.   4,5 SCS

7. *b* is not an *H*.   6 Obv

9. 1. No T is a *W*.

2. No non-*W* is a *C*.

3. Every *K* is a *T*.

4. *b* is a *K*.   / ∴ *b* is not a *C*.

5. *b* is a *T*.   4,3 SCS

6. Every *T* is a non-*W*.   1 Obv

7. *b* is a non-*W*.   5,6 SCS

8. Every non-*W* is a non-*C*.   2 Obv

9. *b* is a non-*C*.   7,8 SCS

10. *b* is not a *C*.   9 Obv

5.7, Set G

1. 1. *l* is *C*.

2. No *C* is a non-*A*.   / ∴ *l* is an *A*.

3. Every *C* is an *A*.   2 Obv

4. *l* is an *A*.   1,3 SCS

[*l* stands for "Liechtenstein"; *C* for "country in which taxes are low"; and *A* for "(thing that) attracts the headquarters of many international corporations."]

3. 1. *v* is an *A*.

2. Any *A* is a *B*.

3. Any *B* is a *C*.

4. Any *C* is a *D*.   / ∴ *v* is a *D*.

5. *v* is a *B*.   1,2 SCS

6. *v* is a *C*.   3,5 SCS

7. *v* is a *D*.   4,6 SCS

[*v* stands for "the Sacramento-San Joaquin Valley system"; *A* for "(thing) located in central California"; *B* for "(thing) located in California"; *C* for "(thing) located in the United States"; and *D* for "(thing) safe from foreign invasion."]

5. 1. *g* is a *W*.

2. No non-*O* is an *A*.

3. No non-*A* is a *W*.   /∴ *g* is an *O*.

4. Every non-*O* is a non-*A*.   2 Obv

5. Every non-*A* is a non-*W*.   3 Obv

6. Every *W* is an *A*.   5 Contr

7. *g* is an *A*.   1,6 SCS

8. Every *A* is an *O*.   4 Contr

9. *g* is an *O*.   7,8 SCS

[g stands for "my gardener"; W for "(one) well worth listening to on military subjects"; O for "very old (person)"; A for "(one) able to remember the battle of Waterloo."]

Solutions to LSAT Prep Questions

1. (b). Modality of conclusion: probability ("unlikely"). Only answers (b) and (d) have a modality of probability. The form of the original argument is "A, except B in circumstances C" and "Circumstances C do not apply"; therefore, A. Answer (b) has this form.

5.8

1. Suppressed premise: All whales are mammals.

1. All *W* are *M*.

2. All *W* are *A*.   /∴ Some *M* are *A*.

3. Some *W* are *A*.   2 Sub

4. Some *A* are *W*.   3 Conv

5. Some *A* are *M*.   1,4 GCS

6. Some *M* are *A*.   5 Conv

3. Suppressed premise: No four-cylinder cars are six-cylinder cars.

    1. No *F* are *S*.

    2. All *A* are *F*.

    3. All *M* are *S*.   / ∴ All *M* are non-*A*.

    4. No *S* are *F*.   1 Conv

    5. All *S* are non-*F*.   4 Obv

    6. All non-*F* are non-*A*.   2 Contr

    7. All *S* are non-*A*.   6,5 GCS

    8. All *M* are non-*A*.   3,7 GCS

5. Suppressed premise: No one who should avoid alcohol should drink martinis.

    1. No *A* are *M*.

    2. All *P* are *A*   / ∴ No *P* are *M*.

    3. All *A* are non-*M*.   1 Obv

    4. All *P* are non-*M*.   2,3 GCS

    5. No *P* are *M* .   4 Obv

7.   Suppressed premises: Everything 115 feet long is over 100 feet long; all blue whales are whales.

    1. Every *F* is an *O*.

    2. All *B* are *W*.

    3. Some *B* are *F*.   / ∴ Some *W* are *O*.

    4. Some *B* are *O*.   1,3 GCS

    5. Some *O* are *B*.   4 Conv

    6. Some *O* are *W*.   2,5 GCS

    7. Some *W* are *O*.   6 Conv

9. Suppressed premises: The tail of Halley's Comet is a comet's tail; nothing that streams away from the sun streams toward it.

    1. *t* is a *C*.

    2. No *A* is a *T*.

    3. Every *C* is an *A*.   / ∴ *t* is not a *T*.

    4. *t* is an *A*.   1,3 SCS

5. Every *A* is a non-*T*.	2 Obv
6. *t* is a non-*T*.	4,5 SCS
7. *t* is not a *T*.	6 Obv

Solutions to LSAT Prep Questions

1. (a). These people believe that the following proposition is false:

    Some legally permissible actions are not moral.

    This is an **O** proposition, so if it is false, the opposed **A** proposition must be true:

    All legally permissible actions are moral.

    If this proposition is true, then its contrapositive must be true as well.

    All immoral actions are legally impermissible.

    Which is just what (a) denies.

2. (b). Let *C* be "chordate"; *T* be "tracheophyte"; *P* be "member of Pteropsida"; and *H* be "member of Hominidae." We then have:

    1. No *C* is a *T*.

    2. Every *P* is a *T*.

    3. ?   /∴ No *P* is an *H*.

    The conclusion is equivalent (by obversion) to:

    Every *P* is a non-*H*.

4.	No *T* is a *C*.	1 Conv
5.	Every *T* is a non-*C*.	4 Obv
6.	Every *P* is a non-*C*.	2,5 GCS

    We can apply GCS to 6. to get "every *P* is a non-*H*" if we introduce:

    3. Every non-*C* is a non-*H*.

    Which is the contrapositive of (b) and so logically equivalent to it.

3. (c). Let *F* be "contemporary poet whose poetry is formal"; *P* be "politically progressive"; and *C* be "person who is performing a politically conservative act." The premise of the argument is:

P   Some *F* is a *P*.

The intended conclusion is:

C   It is false that every *F* is a *C*.

Which is equivalent to saying that its contradictory is true, or:

C   Some *F* is not a *C*.

For C to follow from P, it must be the case that:

P*   No *P* is a *C*.

1. Some *F* is a *P*.

2. No *P* is a *C*.   /∴ Some *F* is not a *C*.

3. Every *P* is a non-*C*.   P* Obv

4. Some *F* is a non-*C*.   1,3 GCS

5. Some *F* is not a *C*.   4 Obv

Which is what (c) asserts.

4. (c). Let *D* be "person who does not believe that others distrust them"; *A* be "person who is confident in his own abilities"; *T* be "person who tends to trust others"; and *C* be "person who thinks of a difficult task as a challenge rather than a threat."

The argument, then, is:

1. Every *D* is an *A*.

2. Every *A* is a *C*.

3. ?   /∴ Every *T* is a *C*.

1. and 2. allow us to derive:

4. Every *D* is a *C*.   1,2 GCS

So, in order to derive the conclusion, we need.

3. Every *T* is a *D*.

Which gives us:

5. Every *T* is a *C*.   3,4 GCS

And (c) is equivalent to 3.

5. (e). Let *M* be "most beautiful cat"; *P* be "Persian cat"; *R* be "pompous cat"; and *I* be "irritating cat." We are told:

    1. Some *M* is a *P*.

    2. Every *P* is an *R*.

    3. Every *R* is an *I*.

    From which we can derive:

4. Some *M* is an *R*.	1,2 GCS
(a) Some *M* is an *I*.	3,4 GCS
(b) Some *I* is an *M*.	(a) Conv
5. Every *P* is an *I*.	2,3 GCS
(c) Every non-*I* is a non-*P*.	5 Contr
(d) Some *R* is an *M*.	4 Conv

    This gives us (e) by process of elimination.

6. (e). From the premise "Behavior that appears to be altruistic <u>can be understood</u> [to be self-interested]" (modality: possibility), the argument concludes, "There <u>is</u> no genuinely altruistic behavior" (modality: actuality).

6.1, Set A

1. **A***

3. **I***

5. **I***

7. **E***

9. **I***

6.1, Set B

1. Nothing is a mammal and not a vertebrate.

3. Nothing is a businessman and a politician.

5. Something is a Republican and not a liberal.

7. Nothing is a senator and not a Congressman.

9. Nothing is a woman and not a female.

6.1, Set C

1. Something is a politician and a downright evil being.

3. Nothing is a society and an entity that operates entirely on the command principle.

5. Something is an element at room temperature and a solid.

7. Something is a moon and a thing so close that its planet covers half the sky.

9. Nothing is a free transaction and not a thing that takes place among private entities.

6.1, Set D

1. Obverses; equivalent.

3. Obverses; equivalent.

5. Converses; equivalent.

7. Contrapositives; inequivalent.

9. Converses; inequivalent.

6.1, Set E

1. **A*I*O*1**.

3. **I*A*I*1**.

5. **E*E*E*3**.

7. **I*E*O*4**.

9. **A*I*I*1**.

6.2, Set A

1. {Twenty-toed mammals} = Ø.

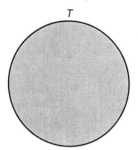

3. {Nonmaterial objects} = Ø.

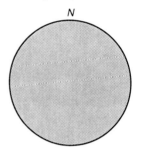

5. {Free lunches} = Ø.

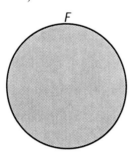

7. {Skunks} ∩ {Mammals}′ = Ø; **A***.

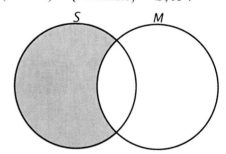

9. {Mice} ∩ {Rodents} ≠ Ø; **I***.

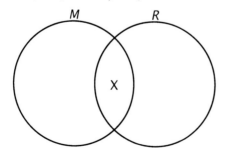

11. {Rhinos} ∩ {Hippos}′ = Ø; **A***.

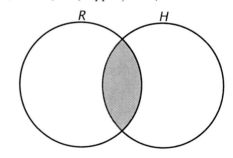

13. {Members of the weasel family} ∩
{Aggressive, bloodthirsty predators}' =
Ø; **A***.

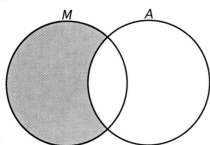

15. {Eagles} ∩ {Hawks}' = Ø; **A***.

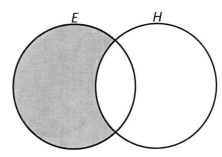

17. {Nonhawks} ∩ {Noneagles}' = Ø; **A***.

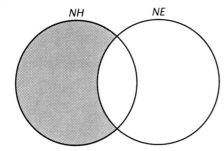

19. {Hawks} ∩ {Non-osprey}' ≠ Ø; **O***.

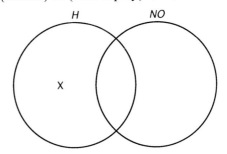

21. {Hard-rock groups} ∩ {Musical groups}
= Ø; **E***.

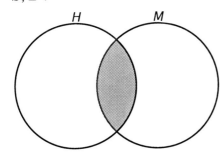

23. {Rock groups} ∩ {Country music groups}
≠ Ø; **I***.

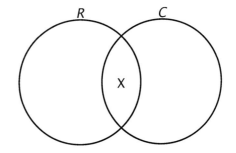

25. {Violations of property rights} ∩
{Violations of human rights}' = Ø; **A***.

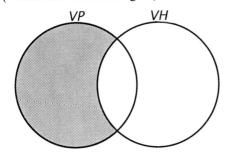

27. {Violations of human rights} ∩
{Violations of property rights}' ≠ Ø; **O***.

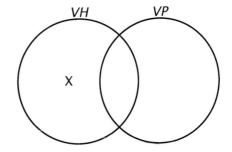

29. {Governments} ∩ {Things that rule and constrain people}′ = Ø; **A***.

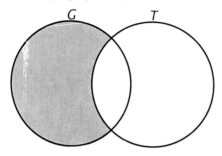

6.2, Set B

1. (a)

3. (a)

5. (a)

7. (a)

9. (a)

11. (c)

13. (c)

15. (a)

17. (b)

19. (d)

6.3, Set A

1   (a) Yes (it is diagrammed); (b) No (it is not diagrammed); (c) No; (d) No; (e) Yes; (f) Yes

3.   (a) Yes; (b) Yes; (c) No; (d) Yes; (e) No; (f) Yes

6.3, Set B

1. Valid.

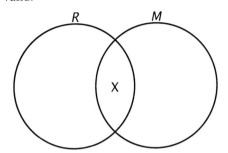

3. Valid.

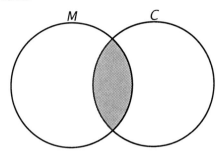

5. Invalid.

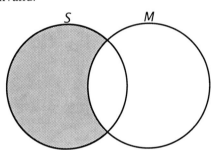

7. Invalid.

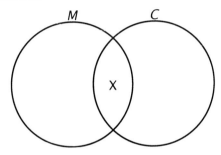

9. Invalid.

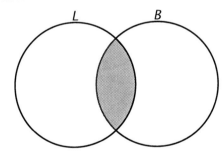

11. Valid.

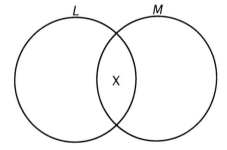

13. Invalid.

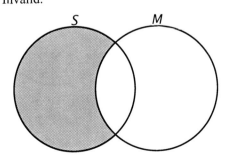

15. Valid.

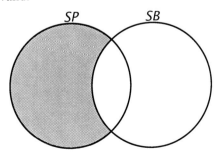

17. Invalid.

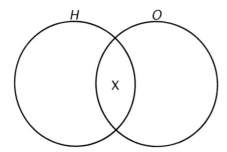

6.3, Set C

1. Invalid.

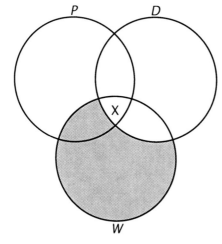

3. Invalid.

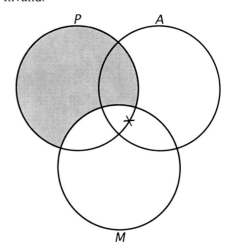

5. Invalid.

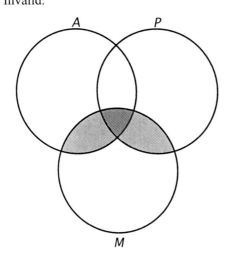

7. Valid.

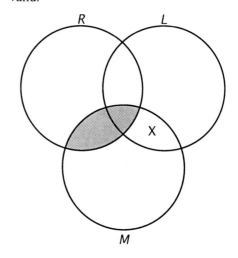

9. Valid.

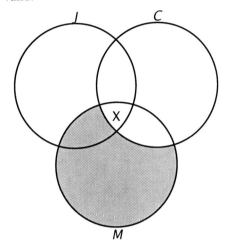

6.3, Set D

1. Invalid.   3. Invalid.

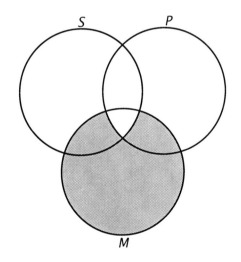   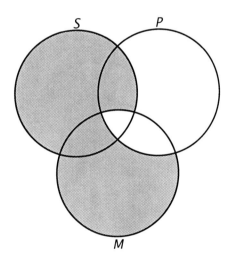

5. Valid.

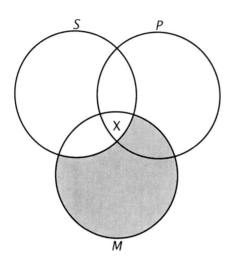

7. Invalid.

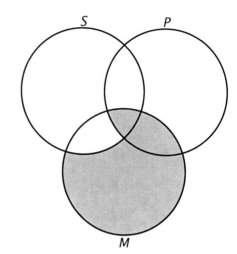

9. Valid.

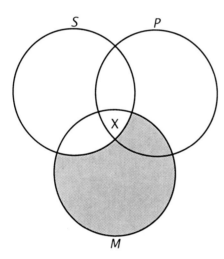

11. Invalid.

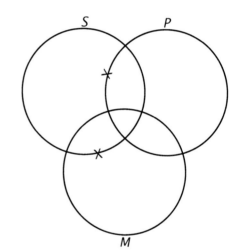

13. Valid.

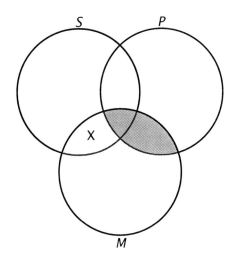

15. Invalid.

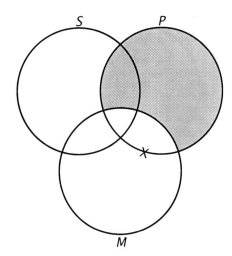

17. Valid.

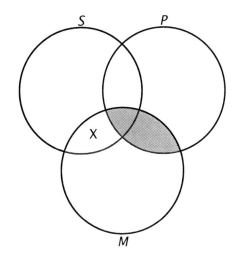

19. Invalid.

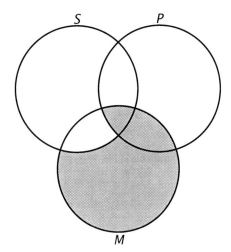

21. Invalid.

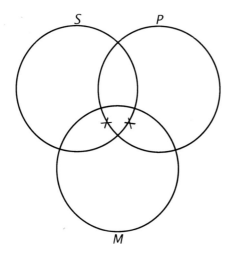

6.4, Set A

1. Something is a mammal.

3. There are Republicans.

5. No presupposition (other than that there is a thing).

7. The United States exists.

9. Something is a male vixen.

6.4, Set B

1. Neither.

3. True.

5. Neither.

7. False.

9. Neither.

6.4, Set C

1. Line 2.

3. Lines 3 and 4.

5. None.

6.5, Set A

1.

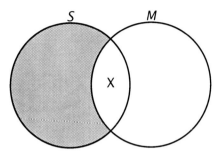

3.

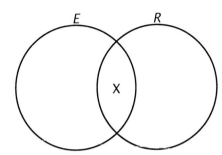

5.

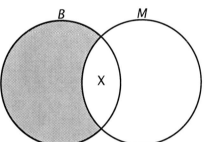

7.

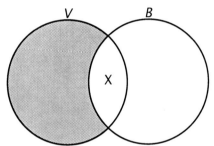

9.

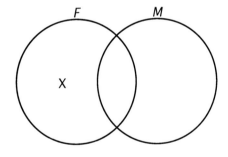

6.5, Set B

1. Valid.

3. Invalid.

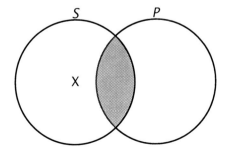

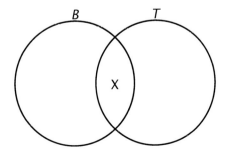

5. Invalid.

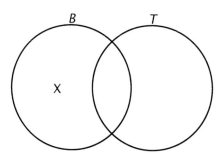

7. Invalid.

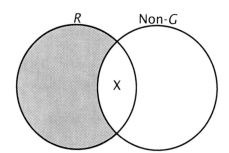

9. Invalid.

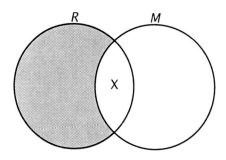

6.5, Set C

1. Invalid.

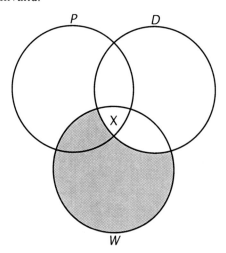

3. Valid.

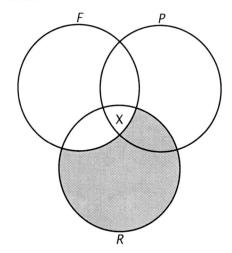

5. Invalid.

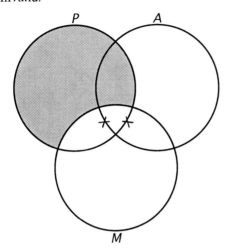

7. Valid.

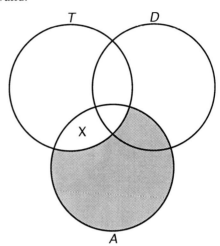

9. Valid.

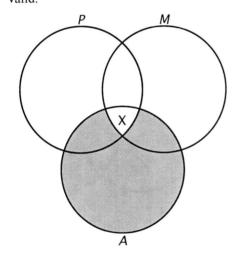

6.5, Set D

1. Valid.

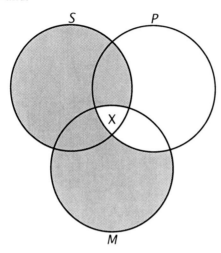

3. Invalid.

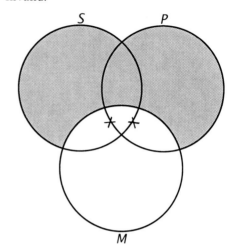

5. Valid.

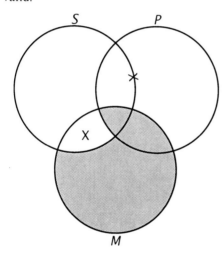

7. Invalid.

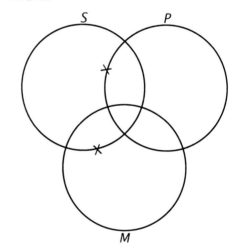

9. Valid.

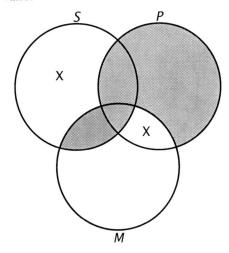

1. Valid.   3. Valid.

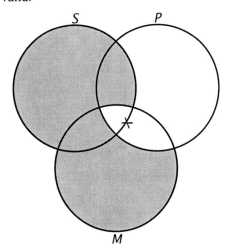   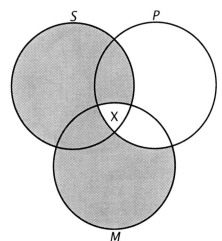

5. Valid.

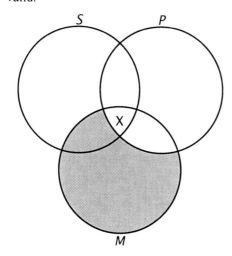

7. Valid.

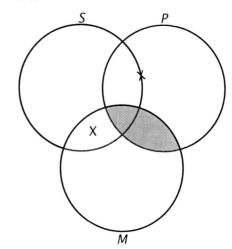

6.6, Set A

1. $k \in$ {Democrats}.

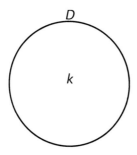

3. {Slime molds} $\neq \emptyset$.

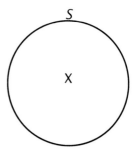

5. $m \notin$ {Right-handers}.

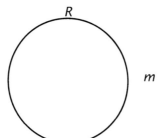

7. $e \notin$ {Beautiful languages}.

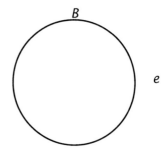

9. $c \in$ {Major religions in Italy}.

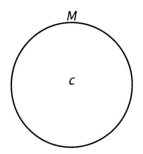

6.6, Set B

1. Invalid.

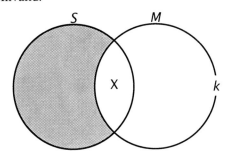

3. Invalid.

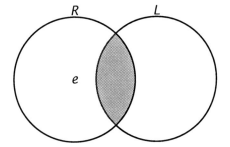

5. Valid.

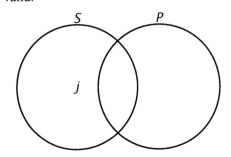

7. Invalid.

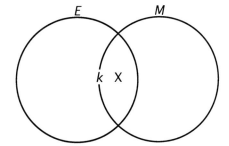

9. Valid.

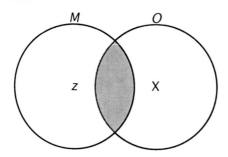

6.6, Set C

AUU2: Invalid.   **UUA3:** Invalid.

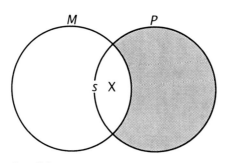

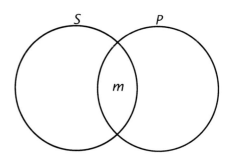

IUU1: Invalid.   **IUU2:** Invalid.

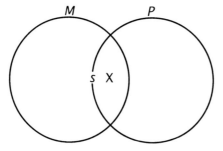

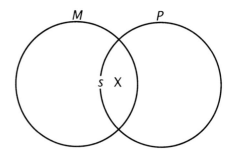

OUU1: Invalid.   **OUU2:** Invalid.

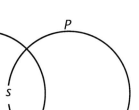 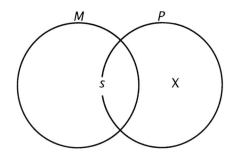

UUO3: Invalid.

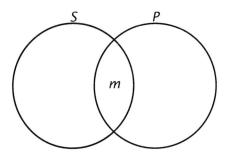

Solutions to LSAT Prep Questions

1. (e). Let "P" = "planning committee member," "F" = "person having significant financial interests in the committee's decisions," and "L" = "person who lives in the suburbs."

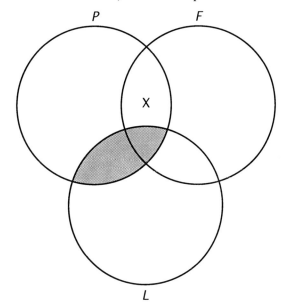

The diagram shows that some F is not an L, which is just what (e) asserts.

2. (d). Let "S" be "person who supports the tax plan," "E' be "person who has a chance of being elected," and "U" be "person who truly understand economics."

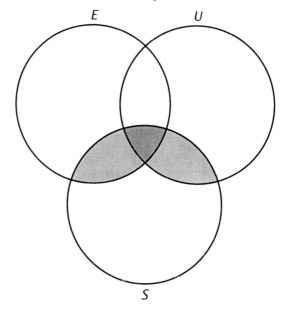

The conclusion states that:

Only U are E.

Which is equivalent to saying that:

Every E is a U.

But this is not diagrammed. According to our diagram, there might be an E that is not U, or someone who does not support the tax plan and does not truly understand economics, which is what (D) asserts.

3. (e). Let "E" be "expert in some branch of psychology," let "U" be "someone who could understand why Patrick is behaving irrationally," let "C" be "someone who is certain of being able to solve someone else's problems," and let "c" be Charles.

Recall that:

Only Es are Us = Every U is an E

So for premises we have:

Every U is an E.
No E is a C.

(e) asks us to suppose that c is a C.

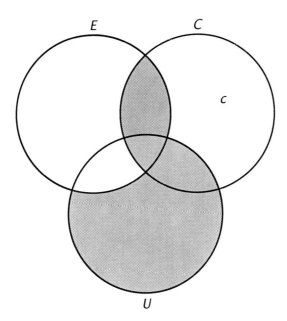

Clearly, if c is a C, c is not a U, which is what (E) asserts.

4. (b). Since we have four terms, we need a four-term diagram. Let "A" be "actor," "E" be "exuberant person," "X" be "extrovert," and "S" be "shy person."

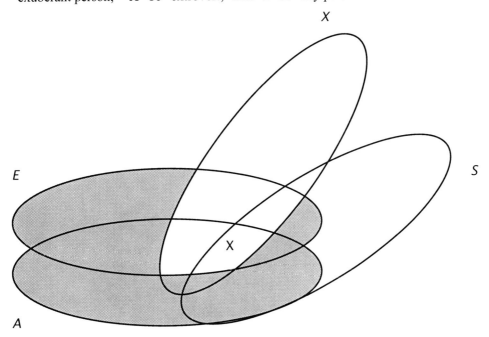

Notice that the diagram is not composed of circles and that every possible subset is represented.

(c) need not be true–there are no x's outside the S ellipse.

7.1, Set A

1. *I* & *G*; true.
    T T T

3. −*E*; true.
    T F

5. *I* & −*G*; false.
    T F FT

7. *E* & (*G* ∨ *I*); false.
    F F T T T

9. −(*G* & *E*); true.
    T T F F

11. −(*G* ∨ *E*) or −*G* & −*E*; false.
    F T T F   FT F TF

13. (*G* ∨ *E*) ∨ (*G* & *E*) or (*G* ∨ *E*); true.
    T T F T T F F   T T F

15. −*M* & −*E*; false.
    FT F TF

17. *M* & −(*G* & *I*); false.
    T F FT T T

19. *M* & −(*G* ∨ *I*) or *M* & (−*G* & −*I*); false.
    T F FT T T   T F FT F FT

21. (*B* & *E*) & (−*G* & −*I*); false.
    F F F F   FT F FT

23. (*E* ∨ *B*) ∨ (*E* ∨ *G*); true.
    F F F T F T T

25. −[(*E* & *F*) ∨ (*B* & *G*)]; true.
    T F FT F F F T

27. [(*E* & *G*) ∨ (*E* & −*G*)] & [(*B* & *F*) ∨ (*F* & −*B*)]; false.
    F F T F FFFT   F   FFT T T TTF

7.1, Set B

1. Ford or General Motors raised prices.

3. Ford but not General Motors raised prices.

5. Ford and General Motors did not both raise prices.

7. Ford or GM raised prices, but not both.

9. Either Ford and GM both raised prices, or both did not.

11. Either Ford and GM both raised prices, or Ford did but GM didn't.

7.1, Set C

1. $-A \lor B$; true.
   FT T T

3. $-Y \lor Z$; true.
   TF T F

5. $-(Y \& Z)$; true.
   T F F F

7. $-Y \lor -Z$; true.
   TF T TF

9. $A \lor Z$; true.
   T T F

11. $A \lor B$; true.
    T T T

13. $-(A \lor C)$; true.
    T T F T

15. $(A \lor B) \& -(A \& B)$; false.
    T T T F F T T T

17. $(A \lor B) \lor (A \lor B)$; true.
    T T T T T F T

19. $-[(A \lor B) \& (A \lor C)]$; false.
    F T T T T T T T

21. $-[-(A \lor B) \& -(X \lor Y)]$; true.
    TFTT T F T FFF

23. $(-\{[(A \lor C) \lor X] \lor Y\} \& C) \& A$; false.
    F T T T T F TF F T F T

25. $-\{-[(B \& -C) \lor (Y \& -C)] \& [(-B \lor X) \lor (B \lor -Y)]\}$; false.
    F T T F FT F FF FT T FTFF TT T TF

7.1, Set D

1. $A \vee P$; true.
    T T

3. $X \vee P$; undet.
    F

5. $-(A \vee Q)$; false.
    F T T

7. $-A \& P$; false.
    F T F

9. $(X \& P) \vee (X \& Q)$; false.
    F F   F F F

11. $(A \vee P) \vee (A \& P)$; true.
    T T   T T

13. $P \vee -P$; true.
    T T F T or
    F T T F

15. $(P \& Q) \vee -(P \& Q)$; true.
    T   T F   T or
    F   T T   F

7.2, Set A

1. b, g.

3. a, j.

5. None.

7. a, b, g, j.

9. g.

7.2, Set B

a. Generic: 7; specific: 3.

c. Generic: 8; specific: 4.

e. Generic: none; specific: none.

g. Generic: 1,7; specific: 9.

i. Generic: 8; specific: 6.

k. Generic: 6, 8; specific: none.

7.3, Set A

1. Valid.

p	*q*	*p*	∴*p* ∨ *q*
T	T	T	T
T	F	T	T
F	T	F	T
F	F	F	F

3. Valid.

p	*q*	*p* & *q*	∴*p*
T	T	T	T
T	F	F	T
F	T	F	F
F	F	F	F

5. Valid.

p	*q*	−*p* & −*q*	∴−(*p* & *q*)
T	T	F	F
T	F	F	T
F	T	F	T
F	F	T	T

7. Invalid.

p	*q*	*p* ∀ *q*	∴*p* ∀ (*p* & *q*)
T	T	F	F
T	F	T	T
F	T	T	F
F	F	F	F

9. Invalid.

p	*q*	*p* ∨ *q*	*p*	∴−*q*
T	T	T	T	F
T	F	T	T	T
F	T	T	F	F
F	F	F	F	T

7.3, Set B

1. Valid.

p	q	r	p & (q ∨ r)	∴(p & q) ∨ (p & r)
T	T	T	T	T
T	T	F	T	T
T	F	T	T	T
T	F	F	F	F
F	T	T	F	F
F	T	F	F	F
F	F	T	F	F
F	F	F	F	F

3. Valid.

p	q	r	p ∨ (q & r)	∴(p ∨ q) & (p ∨ r)
T	T	T	T	T
T	T	F	T	T
T	F	T	T	T
T	F	F	T	T
F	T	T	T	T
F	T	F	F	F
F	F	T	F	F
F	F	F	F	F

5. Valid.

p	q	r	-(p & q) ∨ r	∴-p ∨ (-q ∨ r)
T	T	T	T	T
T	T	F	F	F
T	F	T	T	T
T	F	F	T	T
F	T	T	T	T
F	T	F	T	T
F	F	T	T	T
F	F	F	T	T

7. Valid.

p	q	r	-p ∨ q	-(q ∨ r)	∴-p
T	T	T	T	F	F
T	T	F	T	F	F
T	F	T	F	F	F
T	F	F	F	T	F
F	T	T	T	F	T
F	T	F	T	F	T
F	F	T	T	F	T
F	F	F	T	T	T

9. Valid.

p	q	r	s	(p ∨ q) & r ∨ s	p ∨ r	∴ −q ∨ −s
T	T	T	T	F	F	F
T	T	T	F	F	F	T
T	T	F	T	F	T	F
T	T	F	F	F	T	T
T	F	T	T	F	F	T
T	F	T	F	T	F	F
T	F	F	T	T	T	T
T	F	F	F	F	T	F
F	T	T	T	F	T	F
F	T	T	F	T	T	T
F	T	F	T	T	F	F
F	T	F	F	F	F	T
F	F	T	T	F	T	T
F	F	T	F	F	T	F
F	F	F	T	F	F	T
F	F	F	F	F	F	F

7.3, Set C

1. Valid.

A	B	−A	∴ −A ∨ B
T	T	F	T
T	F	F	F
F	T	T	T
F	F	T	T

3. Valid.

O	P	−O ∨ P	−P ∨ −P	∴ −O
T	T	T	F	F
T	F	F	T	F
F	T	T	F	T
F	F	T	T	T

5. Valid.

H	I	J	K	H v (I & J)	~(I v J) v K	∴ H v K
T	T	T	T	T	T	T
T	T	T	F	T	F	T
T	T	F	T	T	T	T
T	T	F	F	T	F	T
T	F	T	T	T	T	T
T	F	T	F	T	F	T
T	F	F	T	T	T	T
T	F	F	F	T	T	T
F	T	T	T	T	T	T
F	T	T	F	T	F	F
F	T	F	T	F	T	T
F	T	F	F	F	F	F
F	F	T	T	F	T	T
F	F	T	F	F	F	F
F	F	F	T	F	T	T
F	F	F	F	F	T	F

7. Valid.

E	F	G	E v F	~F v G	~E	∴ ~F & (E v G)
T	T	T	T	T	F	T
T	T	F	T	F	F	T
T	F	T	T	T	F	F
T	F	F	T	T	F	F
F	T	T	T	T	T	T
F	T	F	T	F	T	F
F	F	T	F	T	T	F
F	F	F	F	T	T	F

9. Invalid.

A	B	C	D	–A v (–B v C)	–B v (–C v D)	∴–A v D
T	T	T	T	T	T	T
T	T	T	F	T	F	F
T	T	F	T	F	T	T
T	T	F	F	F	T	F
T	F	T	T	T	T	T
T	F	T	F	T	T	F

7.3, Set D

1. Valid.

N	S	–(N & S)	∴–N v –S
T	T	F	F
T	F	T	T
F	T	T	T
F	F	T	T

3. Valid.

G	C	M	G	C v M	∴(G & C) v (G & M)
T	T	T	T	T	T
T	T	F	T	T	T
T	F	T	T	T	T
T	F	F	T	F	F
F	T	T	F	T	F
F	T	F	F	T	F
F	F	T	F	T	F
F	F	F	F	F	F

5. Invalid.

N	E	–(N v E)	–N	∴E
T	T	F	F	T
T	F	F	F	F
F	T	F	T	T
F	F	T	T	F

7. Invalid (the rest is unnecessary).

S	H	M	S v H	S v B	∴ S & (B v H)
T	T	T	T	T	T
T	T	F	T	T	T
T	F	T	T	T	T
T	F	F	T	T	F

9. Valid.

B	T	M	L	(B v T) & -(B & T)	(M v L) & -(M & L)	B v M	∴-T v -L
T	T	T	T	F	F	T	F
T	T	T	F	F	T	T	T
T	T	F	T	F	T	T	F
T	T	F	F	F	F	T	T
T	F	T	T	T	F	T	T
T	F	T	F	T	T	T	T
T	F	F	T	T	T	T	T
T	F	F	F	T	F	T	T
F	T	T	T	T	F	T	F
F	T	T	F	T	T	T	T
F	T	F	T	T	T	F	F
F	T	F	F	T	F	F	T
F	F	T	T	F	F	T	T
F	F	T	F	F	T	T	T
F	F	F	T	F	T	F	T
F	F	F	F	F	F	F	T

7.4, Set A

1. b, e, f, g.

3. a, c, d.

5. a, c.

7. b, f, g.

7.4, Set B

a. Generic: 3, 5; specific: none.

c. Generic: 3, 5; specific: none.

e. Generic: 1; specific: 2.

g. Generic: 1, 7, 8; specific: none.

7.4, Set C

1. True.

3. True.

5. True.

7. Contingent.

9. Contingent.

11. Contingent.

13. True.

15. False.

17. True.

19. False.

7.4, Set D

1. True.

3. Contingent.

5. True.

7. True.

9. False.

7.4, Set E

1. Undetermined.

p	q	$p \lor q$	$-p \& -q$	$\therefore (-p \lor q)$ & $(-q \lor p)$
T	T	T	F	T
T	F	T	F	F
F	T	T	F	F
F	F	F	T	T

3. Invalid.

p	q	$p \lor (q \lor -p)$	$\therefore p \& (q \& -p)$
T	T	T	F
T	F	T	F
F	T	T	F
F	F	T	F

5. Valid.

p	q	r	−p ∨ q	−r ∨ q	∴ −(p & r) ∨ q
T	T	T	T	T	T
T	T	F	T	T	T
T	F	T	F	F	F
T	F	F	F	T	T
F	T	T	T	T	T
F	T	F	T	T	T
F	F	T	T	F	T
F	F	F	T	T	T

7.5, Set A

1. Compat, Equiv, Yes, Yes.

p	q	−(p & q)	−p ∨ −q
T	T	F	F
T	F	T	T
F	T	T	T
F	F	T	T

3. Compat, Inequiv, No, Yes.

p	q	−(p & q)	−p & q
T	T	F	F
T	F	T	F
F	T	T	T
F	F	T	F

5. Compat, Equiv, Yes, Yes.

p	q	p ∨ q	(p ∨ q) ∨ (p & q)
T	T	T	T
T	F	T	T
F	T	T	T
F	F	F	F

7. Compat, Equiv, Yes, Yes.

p	q	p	(p & q) ∨ (p & −q)
T	T	T	T
T	F	T	T
F	T	F	F
F	F	F	F

9. Incompat, Inequiv, No, No.

p	q	p	q & (−q ∨ −p)
T	T	T	F
T	F	T	F
F	T	F	T
F	F	F	F

11. Compat, Equiv, Yes, Yes.

p	q	p	p ∨ (q & −q)
T	T	T	T
T	F	T	T
F	T	F	F
F	F	F	F

13. Compat, Equiv, Yes, Yes.

p	q	(-p ∨ q) & (-q ∨ p)	(p & q) ∨ (-p & -q)
T	T	T	T
T	F	F	F
F	T	F	F
F	F	T	T

15. Compat, Equiv, Yes, Yes.

p	q	r	(p ∨ q) & r	(p ∨ q) & (p ∨ r)
T	T	T	T	T
T	T	F	T	T
T	F	T	T	T
T	F	F	T	T
F	T	T	T	T
F	T	F	F	F
F	F	T	F	F
F	F	F	F	F

17. Incompat, Inequiv, No, No.

p	q	r	-(p & q) ∨ r	-[-p ∨ (-q ∨ r)]
T	T	T	T	F
T	T	F	F	T
T	F	T	T	F
T	F	F	T	F
F	T	T	T	F
F	T	F	T	F
F	F	T	T	F
F	F	F	T	F

19. Compat, Inequiv, Yes, No.

p	q	r	p ∨ (q & r)	p ∨ q
T	T	T	T	T
T	T	F	T	T
T	F	T	T	T
T	F	F	T	T
F	T	T	T	T
F	T	F	F	T
F	F	T	F	F
F	F	F	F	F

7.5, Set B

1. Compat and Equiv.

Z	A	-(Z & -A)	-Z ∨ A
T	T	T	T
T	F	F	F
F	T	T	T
F	F	T	T

2. Incompat and Inequiv.

E	L	(E & L) ∨ (-E & -L)	(E & -L) ∨ (L & -E)
T	T	T	F
T	F	F	T
F	T	F	T
F	F	T	F

5. Compat and Inequiv.

E	S	-S	E & [(E v S) & -(E & S)]
T	T	F	F
T	F	T	T
F	T	F	F
F	F	T	F

7. Compat and Equiv.

R	A	U	R & -(A & U)	(R & -A) v (R & -U)
T	T	T	F	F
T	T	F	T	T
T	F	T	T	T
T	F	F	T	T
F	T	T	F	F
F	T	F	F	F
F	F	T	F	F
F	F	F	F	F

9. Incompat and Inequiv.

R	C	I	(R v C) & -I	I v (-R & -C)
T	T	T	F	T
T	T	F	T	F
T	F	T	F	T
T	F	F	T	F
F	T	T	F	T
F	T	F	T	F
F	F	T	F	T
F	F	F	F	T

7.6, Set A

1.

p	q	r
F	T	F

3.

p	q	r	s
T	F	F	F

5.

p	q	r	s
F	F	F	T

7.

p	q	r	
F	T	T	or
F	F	T	

9.

p	q	r	
T	F	T	or
T	F	F	or
T	T	T	or
F	F	F	

11.

p	q	r	s	
T	F	F	T	or
T	F	F	F	or
T	F	T	F	

13.

p	q	r	s
T	F	F	F

15.

p	q	r
F	F	F

17.

p	q	r	s	t
T	F	T	F	F

19.

p	q	r	s	t	u	x	y	z	
T	T	T	T	F	F	T	T	T	or
T	T	T	T	F	F	T	F	T	

7.6, Set B

1. Paris is in Germany or France. Paris is in France or England.

   ∴ Paris is in Germany or England.

3. Paris is in France or Germany. Paris is in France or England.

   Paris is cither not in France or not in Italy.

   ∴ Paris is in Germany or England.

5. Paris is not in Italy or it is in Germany. Paris is not in England or it is in France. Paris is in Italy or France.

∴ Paris is in Germany or England.

7. Paris is either in Germany and Italy or in France.

∴ Paris is in Germany and in either Italy or France.

9. Paris is either not in both France and Germany, or it is in England.

∴ Paris is not in France, but it is in either Germany or England.

7.7, Set A

1. $B \Rightarrow F$

3. $[(B \& C) \& -A] \Rightarrow I$

5. $-R \Rightarrow [(D \& P) \vee F]$

7. $R \Rightarrow (W \Rightarrow D)$

9. $(U \vee I) \Rightarrow [-P \& R \& -D]$

7.7, Set B

1. $S \Rightarrow W$

3. $S \Rightarrow W$

5. $-O \Rightarrow (S \Rightarrow W)$

7. $(N \Rightarrow E) \& (-N \Rightarrow -E)$

9. $(U \vee R) \Rightarrow N$

7.7, Set C

1. $J \Rightarrow E$

3. $-[B \vee (S \vee O)] \Rightarrow F$

5. $[B \& (S \vee O)] \Rightarrow B$

7. $(D \& -M) \Rightarrow E$

9. $[(Y \& Z) \vee (-Y \vee Z) \Rightarrow K$

(E: "exemptions for spouse"; F: "one exemption for spouse"; G: "two exemptions"; H: "three exemptions"; J: "file jointly"; K: "file separately"; Y: "you had income"; Z: "your spouse had income.")

7.7, Set D

1. $R \Rightarrow B$

    $-B$

    $\therefore -R$

    Modus tollens, valid.

3. $B \Rightarrow S$

    $S \Rightarrow A$

    $\therefore B \Rightarrow A$

    Hypothetical syllogism, valid.

5. $O \vee Y$

    $-O$

    $\therefore Y$

    Disjunctive syllogism, valid.

7. $O \Rightarrow M$

    $-O$

    $\therefore -M$

    Denying the antecedent, invalid.

9. $V \Rightarrow B$

    V

    $\therefore B$

    Modus ponens, valid.

11. $Y \Rightarrow M$

    $W \Rightarrow H$

    $Y \vee W$

    $\therefore M \vee H$

    Constructive dilemma, valid.

13. $(Y \vee W) \Rightarrow (M \vee H)$

    $\therefore -(M \vee H) \Rightarrow -(Y \vee W)$

    Contraposition, valid.

15. $M \Rightarrow Y$

   $H \Rightarrow W$

   $-Y \lor -W$

   $\therefore -M \lor -H$

   Destructive dilemma, valid.

17. $-S \Rightarrow -M$

   $\therefore -M \Rightarrow -S$

   Conversion, invalid.

7.7 Set E

1.

p	q	r
T	T	F

3.

p	q
T	F

5.

p	q	r	s
T	F	F	F

7.

p	q	r	s	
F	T	F	T	or
F	F	F	T	

9.

p	q	r	s	t	u	
F	F	T	F	F	F	or many others

7.7 Set F

1. If Paris is in China, then it is in Asia.

   $\therefore$ Paris is in Asia.

3. Paris is not in Germany.

   $\therefore$ If Paris is in Germany, then it is in Asia.

5. If Paris is in Scotland, then it is in Great Britian.

   $\therefore$ Paris is in Great Britain.

7. If Paris is in Europe and Scotland, then it is in Great Britain.

Paris is in Europe.

∴ Paris is in Great Britain.

9. If Paris is in Germany, then it is in Europe, and if Paris is in Italy, then it is in the Eastern Hemisphere.

Either Paris is not in Germany or it is not in Italy.

∴ Either Paris is not in Europe or it is not in the Eastern Hemisphere.

11. If Paris is near Edinburgh, then it is in Scotland.

If Paris is in Scotland, then it is in Great Britain.

∴ Paris is in Great Britain.

The two reasons why countercases cannot be found for these forms are illustrated by (1) and (3). With regard to (1), no assignment of truth values will make the premise $p \Rightarrow q$ definitely true. As for (3), one assignment of truth values will make the conclusion $p \Rightarrow q$ definitely false, but that assignment makes the premise $-p$ false too.

7.8, Set A

1. False.

3. True.

5. True.

7. True.

9. False.

7.8, Set B

1. False.

3. True.

5. False.

7. False.

9. True.

7.8, Set C

1. Valid.

3. Invalid.

5. Invalid.

7. Valid.

9. Valid.

11. Valid.

13. Invalid.

15. Valid.

17. Valid.

19. Valid.

21. Valid.

23. Invalid.

7.8, Set D

1. True.

3. Contingent.

5. True.

7. True.

9. Contingent.

11. Contingent.

13. True.

15. Contingent.

17. True.

7.8, Set E

1. Inequiv.

3. Inequiv.

5. Equiv.

7. Equiv.

9. Equiv.

Solutions to LSAT Prep Questions

1. (c). The two sentences in the exercise form the premises of a hypothetical syllogism, allowing us to conclude:

    > If you have no keyboarding skills at all, you will not be able to write your essays using a word processing program.

    The contrapositive of this is:

    > If you are able to write your essays using a word processing program, then it is not the case that you have no keyboarding skills at all.

    Which is just what (c) asserts.

2. (c). *p* only if *q* = $-q \Rightarrow -p$. Thus, the original claim is equivalent to:

    > If the electorate is not (moral and intelligent), then a democracy will not function well.

    De Morgan's rules tell us that $-(p \ \& \ q) = -p \lor -q$. Thus, this claim is equivalent to:

    > If the electorate is (not moral or not intelligent), then a democracy will not function well.

    Which is (c).

3. (b). This is an example of the fallacy of denying the antecedent. The claim is that if Joan gets an A, she does not have to do the presentation. It is then inferred that she has to do the presentation because she did not get an A.

    $$p \Rightarrow q$$
    $$-p$$
    $$\therefore -q$$

    This is an invalid inference, so the argument must presuppose: $-p \Rightarrow -q$, which is just what (b) asserts.

4. (b). This is an example of the fallacy of affirming the consequent. The claim is that if the homeowners want to attract business, they will support Cooper. It is then inferred that since the homeowners are supporting Cooper, they must want to attract business.

    $$p \Rightarrow q$$
    $$q$$
    $$\therefore p$$

    It may be that the homeowners know that if they want to reduce crime, they should support Cooper ($r \Rightarrow q$) and that they support him because they want to reduce crime. $p \Rightarrow q$ does not rule out $r \Rightarrow q$. Thus (b) is the right answer.

5. (a). Let "*L*" be "laws are vague," let "*P*" be "people feel secure," let "*K*" be "people know for certain whether their actions are legal."

    The argument is:

    $$L \Rightarrow -K$$
    $$\therefore L \Rightarrow -P$$

Thus, for this argument to be valid, we need $-K \Rightarrow -P$. (a) tells us that P only if K and we know that:

P only if $K = -K \Rightarrow -P$

So (a) makes the argument valid.

6. (a). Let "N" be "negotiations begin soon," "V" be "the cease-fire will be violated by one of the two sides to the dispute," "P" be "other countries have pressured the two sides to negotiate," "A" be "an agreement will emerge," "C" be "other countries continue pressure throughout the negotiations," "I" be "international troops enforcing the cease-fire have demonstrated their ability to counter aggression from either side," and "S" be "a major incentive for the two sides to resume hostilities has been suppressed."

Thus, we have:

$(1) -N \Rightarrow V$
$(2) -P \Rightarrow -N$
$(3) -C \Rightarrow -A$
$(4) -I \Rightarrow -N$
$(5) I \Rightarrow S$
$(6) N$

(b) says that I is true, which follows from (6) and (4) by modus tollens.

(c) says that S is true, which follows from (b) and (5) by modus ponens.

(d) says that P is true, which follows from (6) and (2) by modus tollens.

(e) says that the actions of other countries are a necessary condition for an agreement to be reached. But p is a necessary condition of q if $-p$ implies $-q$. So (2) implies (e).

Moreover, (a) says that $-V$ is true, and to infer this from N and $-N \Rightarrow V$ would be the fallacy of denying the antecedent.

8.1, Set A

1. Simp
5. Conj
9. None.
13. MT
17. None.

3. MP
7. Add
11. DT
15. Conj

8.1, Set B

1. MP
5. Conj
9. Simp
13. DT

3. Add
7. MT
11. MP

8.1, Set C

1. 4. 4,3 Simp
    5. 1,4 DS
    6. 2,4 DS
    7. 5,6 Conj

5. 6. 5,1 DS
    7. 2,6 DT
    8. 4,7 MP
    9. 3,8 MT
    10. 8,9 Conj

9. 5. 3 Simp
    6. 1,5 MP
    7. 5,6 Conj
    8. 2,7 MP
    9. 3 Simp
    10. 8,9 DS
    11. 5,10 Conj
    12. 4,11 MP
    13. 6,12 DS

3. 5. 1,2 DT
    6. 3,5 DT
    7. 4,6 DS

7. 6. 1,3 DT
    7. 5,6 MP
    8. 1,2 DT
    9. 4,8 MP
    10. 9 Simp
    11. 7,10 Conj

8.1, Set D

1. 1. $(A \lor B) \Rightarrow C$
   2. A $/\therefore C$
   3. $A \lor B$ 2 Add
   4. C 1,3 MP

5. 1. $A \Rightarrow B$
   2. $-A \Rightarrow C$
   3. $-B$ $/\therefore C$
   4. $-A$ 1,3 MT
   5. C 4,2 MP

9. 1. p
   2. $p \Rightarrow q$ $/\therefore p \& q$
   3. q 1,2 MP
   4. $p \& q$ 1,3 Conj

13. 1. $A \lor B$
    2. $-B \lor -D$
    3. $D \lor E$ $/\therefore A \lor E$
    4. $A \lor -D$ 1,2 DT
    5. $A \lor E$ 3,4 DT

15. 1. $A \& (B \lor C)$
    2. $F \lor (G \& H)$
    3. $\{[A \& (B \lor C)] \& [F \lor (G \& H)]\} \Rightarrow [X \lor (Y \lor Z)]$ $/\therefore X \lor (Y \lor Z)$
    4. $[A \& (B \lor C)] \& [F \lor (G \& H)]$ 1,2 Conj
    5. $X \lor (Y \lor Z)$ 3,4 MP

3. 1. $J \Rightarrow K$
   2. J $/\therefore K \lor L$
   3. K 1,2 MP
   4. $K \lor L$ 3 Add

7. 1. $(p \Rightarrow q) \& (r \Rightarrow s)$
   2. $p / \therefore q$
   3. $p \Rightarrow q$ 1 Simp
   4. q 2,3 MP

11. 1. $K \lor (-K \Rightarrow L)$
    2. $-K$ $/\therefore L$
    3. $-K \Rightarrow L$ 1,2 DS
    4. L 2,3 MP

8.1, Set E

1. 1. $A \lor (B \Rightarrow C)$
   2. $-C \lor A$
   3. $-A$ $/\therefore -B$
   4. $-C$ 2,3 DS
   5. $B \Rightarrow C$ 1,3 DS
   6. $-B$ 4,5 MT

5. 1. $p \Rightarrow -(q \lor r)$
   2. $p \lor r$
   3. q $/\therefore r$
   4. $q \lor r$ 3 Add
   5. $-p$ 1,4 MT
   6. r 2,5 DS

3. 1. $L \Rightarrow (M \lor N)$
   2. $L \Rightarrow -N$
   3. L $/\therefore M$
   4. $-N$ 2,3 MP
   5. $M \lor N$ 1,3 MP
   6. M 4,5 DS

7. 1. $F \Rightarrow G$
   2. $(-F \lor -H) \Rightarrow I$
   3. $-G$ $/\therefore I$
   4. $-F$ 1,3 MT
   5. $-F \lor -H$ 4 Add
   6. I 5,2 MP

9. 1. X
    2. $-(X \lor Y) \lor (X \Rightarrow Z)$ / ∴ Z
    3. $X \lor Y$ 1 Add
    4. $X \Rightarrow Z$ 2,3 DS
    5. Z 1,4 MP

11. 1. $(F \veebar G) \Rightarrow [(F \lor G) \& -(F \& G)]$
    2. $H \Rightarrow (F \veebar G)$
    3. H / ∴ $-(F \& G)$
    4. $F \veebar G$ 2,3 MP
    5. $(F \lor G) \& -(F \& G)$ 1,4 MP
    6. $-(F \& G)$ 5 Simp

13. 1. $(A \Rightarrow B) \& (A \Rightarrow C)$
    2. A / ∴ $C \lor D$
    3. $A \Rightarrow C$ 1 Simp
    4. C 2,3 MP
    5. $C \lor D$ 4 Add

15. 1. A
    2. $A \Rightarrow B$
    3. $(A \& B) \Rightarrow C$ / ∴ C
    4. B 1,2 MP
    5. $A \& B$ 1,4 Conj
    6. C 3,5 MP

17. 1. $L \lor (-M \lor N)$
    2. $L \lor (-N \lor O)$
    3. $-L$ / ∴ $-M \lor O$
    4. $-M \lor N$ 1,3 DS
    5. $-N \lor O$ 2,3 DS
    6. $-M \lor O$ 4,5 DT

8.1 Set F

1. 1. $[A \lor (B \lor C)] \& [-B \lor (C \lor D)]$
    2. $B \& (-A \& E)$ / ∴ $(B \lor C) \lor (C \lor D)$
    3. B 2 Simp
    4. $-B \lor (C \lor D)$ 1 Simp
    5. $C \lor D$ 3,4 DS
    6. $(B \lor C) \lor (C \lor D)$ 5 Add

3. 1. $A \Rightarrow (B \& C)$
    2. $C \Rightarrow (D \& E)$
    3. $E \Rightarrow [F \& (G \lor H)]$
    4. $A \& -G$ / ∴ H
    5. A 4 Simp
    6. $B \& C$ 1,5 MP
    7. C 6 Simp
    8. $D \& E$ 2,7 MP
    9. E 8 Simp
    10. $F \& (G \lor H)$ 3,9 MP
    11. $G \lor H$ 10 Simp
    12. $-G$ 4 Simp
    13. H 11,12 DS

5. 1. $p \Rightarrow q$
    2. $r \Rightarrow s$
    3. $-q \& -s$ / ∴ $-p \& -r$
    4. $-q$ 3 Simp
    5. $-p$ 1,4 MT
    6. $-s$ 3 Simp
    7. $-r$ 2,6 MT
    8. $-p \& -r$ 5,7 Conj

7. 1. $(-F \lor G) \& (-H \lor I)$
    2. $-J \lor K$
    3. $(F \lor J) \& (H \lor L)$ / ∴ $G \lor K$
    4. $F \lor J$ 3 Simp
    5. $F \lor K$ 2,4 DT
    6. $-F \lor G$ 1 Simp
    7. $G \lor K$ 5,6 DT

9. 1. $A \Rightarrow (B \& C)$
    2. $(B \& C) \lor D$
    3. $-(B \& C) \Rightarrow (-B \lor -C)$
    4. $(D \& -A) \Rightarrow [-E \& (-C \Rightarrow E)]$
    5. $-(B \& C)$ $/\therefore -B$
    6. D 2,5 DS
    7. $-A$ 5,1 MT
    8. $D \& -A$ 6,7 Conj
    9. $-E \& (-C \Rightarrow E)$ 4,8 MP
    10. $-E$ 9 Simp
    11. $-C \Rightarrow E$ 9 Simp
    12. C 10,11 MT
    13. $-B \lor -C$ 3,5 MP
    14. $-B$ 12,13 DS

8.1, Set G

1. 1. L
    2. $L \Rightarrow M$
    3. $M \Rightarrow Q$ $/\therefore Q$
    4. M 1,2 MP
    5. Q 4,3 MP

3. 1. $L \Rightarrow (W \& M)$
    2. L $/\therefore W$
    3. $W \& M$ 1,2 MP
    4. W 3 Simp

5. 1. $C \lor B$
    2. $L \lor -B$
    3. $M \lor -L$
    4. $-M$ $/\therefore C$
    5. $-L$ 3,4 DS
    6. $-B$ 2,5 DS
    7. C 1,6 DS

7. 1. $D \lor (H \lor B)$
    2. $-D \& -B$ $/\therefore H$
    3. $-D$ 2 Simp
    4. $H \lor B$ 1,3 DS
    5. $-B$ 2 Simp
    6. H 4,5 DS

9. 1. $A \Rightarrow I$
    2. $J \Rightarrow S$
    3. $(I \lor S) \Rightarrow (G \& H)$
    4. $A \& O$ $/\therefore H$
    5. A 5 Simp
    6. I 1,5 MP
    7. $I \lor S$ 6 Add
    8. $G \& H$ 3,7 MP
    9. H 8 Simp

11. 1. $[(I \& J) \lor (-I \lor -J)] \Rightarrow S$
    2. $I \& -J$ $/\therefore S$
    3. $-J$ 2 Simp
    4. $-I \lor -J$ 3 Add
    5. $(I \& J) \lor (-I \lor -J)$ 4 Add
    6. S 1,5 MP

8.2 Set A

1. DM
5. DM
9. DM

3. Com
7. Dist
11. None.

13. DM
17. Com
21. DN
25. None.

15. DN
19. DM
23. None.

8.2 Set B

1. 3. 2 Dist
    4. 3 Simp
    5. 1,4 MT
    6. 5 DM

5. 3. 1 Dist
    4. 3 DM
    5. 4 Simp
    6. 5 DM
    7. 2,6 MP
    8. 7 Assn
    9. 8 Simp

9. 4. 2 Dist
    5. 4 Simp
    6. 5 DD
    7. 1,6 MT
    8. 7 DM
    9. 8 Simp
    10. 3,9 MP
    11. 8 Simp
    12. 10,11 MP
    13. 12 Com

3. 3. 2 Dist
    4. 3 Simp
    5. 4 DD
    6. 1 Assn
    7. 5,6 DS

7. 4. 1 DM
    5. 4 Simp
    6. 2 Assn
    7. 5,6 DS
    8. 7 Com
    9. 8 DN
    10. 3,9 MT
    11. 10 DN

8.2, Set C

1. 1. $A \,\&\, --B$
    2. $-(A \,\&\, B) \lor C$ $/\therefore C$
    3. $A \,\&\, B$ 1 DN
    4. C 2,3 DS

5. 1. $-(F \,\&\, G) \lor H$ $/\therefore -F \lor (-G \lor H)$
    2. $(-F \lor -G) \lor H$ 1 DM
    3. $-F \lor (-G \lor H)$ 2 Assn

3. 1. $-[(A \,\&\, B) \,\&\, C)]$ $/\therefore (-A \lor -B) \lor -C$
    2. $-(A \,\&\, B) \lor -C$ 1 DM
    3. $(-A \lor -B) \lor -C$ 2 DM

7. 1. $-(p \lor q)$ $/\therefore -p$
    2. $-p \,\&\, -q$ 1 DM
    3. $-p$ 2 Simp

9. 1. $p \lor q$
    2. $p \lor r$ /∴ $p \lor (q \& r)$
    3. $(p \lor q) \& (p \lor r)$ 1,2 Conj
    4. $p \lor (q \& r)$ 3 Dist

11. 1. $p \lor (q \& r)$ /∴ $p \lor q$
    2. $(p \lor q) \& (p \lor r)$ 1 Dist
    3. $p \lor q$ 2 Simp

13. 1. $(A \& B) \lor (C \& D)$
    2. $-(C \& D) \lor (A \& B)$ /∴ $A \& B$
    3. $(A \& B) \lor (A \& B)$ 1,2 DT
    4. $A \& B$ 3 DD

15. 1. $(A \& B) \lor [(C \& D) \lor (E \& F)]$
    2. $-(C \& D) \& -(E \& F)$ /∴ $A \& B$
    3. $-[(C \& D) \lor (E \& F)]$ 2 DM
    4. $A \& B$ 1,3 DS

8.2, Set D

1. 1. $A \lor -(B \lor C)$
    2. $-C$ /∴ $-(A \& B)$
    3. $(-A \lor -B) \lor C$ 1 Assn
    4. $-A \lor -B$ 2,3 DS
    5. $-(A \& B)$ 4 DM

3. 1. $-T \lor U$
    2. $-(U \lor V)$ /∴ $-T$
    3. $-U \& -V$ 2 DM
    4. $-U$ 3 Simp
    5. $-T$ 1,3 DS

5. 1. $(p \lor q) \Rightarrow r$
    2. $-r$ /∴ $-p$
    3. $-(p \lor q)$ 1,2 MT
    4. $-p \& -q$ 3 DM
    5. $-p$ 4 Simp

7. 1. $-(p \lor q)$ /∴ $-p$
    2. $-p \& -q$ 1 DM
    3. $-p$ 2 Simp
    4. $-p \lor -q$ 3 Add

9. 1. $[(A \& B) \& C] \& D$ /∴ $(D \& A) \& (B \& C)$
    2. $D \& [(A \& B) \& C]$ 1 Com
    3. $D \& [A \& (B \& C)]$ 2 Assn
    4. $(D \& A) \& (B \& C)$ 3 Assn

11. 1. $-(A \Rightarrow B) \lor (A \Rightarrow C)$
    2. $-[(A \Rightarrow C) \lor (A \Rightarrow D)]$ /∴ $-(A \Rightarrow B)$
    3. $-(A \Rightarrow C) \& -(A \Rightarrow D)$ 2 DM
    4. $-(A \Rightarrow C)$ 3 Simp
    5. $-(A \Rightarrow B)$ 1,4 DS

8.2, Set E

1. 1. –(A ∨ B)   /∴ –(A & B)
    2. –A & –B   1 DM
    3. –A   2 Simp
    4. –A ∨ –B   3 Add
    5. –(A & B)   4 DM

3. 1. E ∨ F
    2. E ∨ G
    3. –(E ∨ H)   /∴ F & G
    4. –E & –H   3 DM
    5. –E   4 Simp
    6. F   1,5 DS
    7. G   2,5 DS
    8. F & G   6,7 Conj

5. 1. –A ∨ (B & –C)
    2. (–D ∨ A) & (–D ∨ C)   /∴ –D
    3. (–A ∨ B) & (–A ∨ –C)   1 Dist
    4. –A ∨ –C   3 Simp
    5. –(A & C)   4 DM
    6. –D ∨ (A & C)   3 Dist
    7. –D   5,6 DS

7. 1. H ⇒ I
    2. J ⇒ K
    3. –(I ∨ K)   /∴ –(H ∨ J)
    4. –I & –K   3 DM
    5. –I   4 Simp
    6. –H   1,5 MT
    7. –K   4 Simp
    8. –J   2,7 MT
    9. –H & –J   6,8 Conj
    10. –(H ∨ J)   9 DM

9. 1. (B ∨ T) ∨ (M ∨ L)
    2. –(B ∨ M)   /∴ T ∨ L
    3. –B & –M   2 DM
    4. –B   3 Simp
    5. B ∨ [T ∨ (M ∨ L)]   1 Assn
    6. T ∨ (M ∨ L)   5,4 DS
    7. T ∨ (L ∨ M)   6 Com
    8. (T ∨ L) ∨ M   7 Assn
    9. –M   3 Simp
    10. T ∨ L   8,9 DS

11. 1. –[(E & –F) & –G]
    2. –(F ∨ G)   /∴ –E
    3. –(E & –F) ∨ G   1 DM
    4. (–E ∨ F) ∨ G   3 DM
    5. –F & –G   2 DM
    6. –G   5 Simp
    7. –E ∨ F   4,6 DS
    8. –F   5 Simp
    9. –E   7,8 DS

8.2, Set F

1. 1. –(F & G)
    2. F   /∴ –G
    3. –F ∨ –G   1 DM
    4. –G   2,3 DS

3. 1. T ∨ –P
    2. B ∨ –P
    3. –(T & B)   /∴ –P
    4. (T ∨ –P) & (B ∨ –P)   1,2 Conj
    5. (T & B) ∨ –P   4 Dist
    6. –P   3,5 DS

5. 1. $(-J \vee -S) \Rightarrow -W$
    2. W $/\therefore J$
    3. $-(-J \vee -S)$ 1,2 MT
    4. $J \& S$ 3 DM
    5. J 4 Simp

9. 1. $W \vee (C \vee V)$
    2. $-C$ $/\therefore W \vee V$
    3. $W \vee (V \vee C)$ 1 Com
    4. $(W \vee V) \vee C$ 3 Assn
    5. $W \vee V$ 2,4 DS

7. 1. $C \vee -S$
    2. $F \vee -T$
    3. $S \vee (T \& L)$ $/\therefore C \vee F$
    4. $(S \vee T) \& (S \vee L)$ 3 Dist
    5. $S \vee T$ 4 Simp
    6. $C \vee T$ 1,5 DT
    7. $C \vee F$ 2,6 DT

11. 1. $M \& S$
    2. $-I \& D$
    3. $S \Rightarrow [-(-I \& -D) \Rightarrow -E]$ $/\therefore -E$
    4. S 1 Simp
    5. $-(-I \& -D) \Rightarrow -E$ 3,4 MP
    6. $(I \vee D) \Rightarrow -E$ 5 DM
    7. D 2 Simp
    8. $I \vee D$ 7 Add
    9. $-E$ 6,8 MP

8.3, Set A

1. 1. $(C \& D) \vee -(C \& D)$ EM
    2. $(C \& D) \vee (-C \vee -D)$ 1 DM

3. 1. $A \Rightarrow A$ ID
    2. $--A \Rightarrow A$ 1 DN

5. 1. $A \vee -A$ EM
    2. $(A \vee -A) \vee B$ 1 Add
    3. $A \vee (-A \vee B)$ 2 Assn

7. 1. $[F \& -(G \& H)] \Rightarrow [F \& -(G \& H)]$ ID
    2. $[F \& -(G \& H)] \Rightarrow [F \& (-G \vee -H)]$ 1 DM
    3. $[F \& -(G \& H)] \Rightarrow [(F \& -G) \vee (F \& -H)]$ 2 Dist

9. 1. $A \vee -A$ EM
    2. $(A \vee -A) \vee (B \& C)$ 1 Add
    3. $(-A \vee A) \vee (B \& C)$ 2 Com
    4. $-A \vee [A \vee (B \& C)]$ 3 Assn
    5. $-A \vee [(A \vee B) \& (A \vee C)]$ 4 Dist

11. 1. $[A \& (B \& -C)] \Rightarrow [A \& (B \& -C)]$ ID
    2. $[A \& (B \& -C)] \Rightarrow [(A \& B) \& -C]$ 1 Assn
    3. $[A \& (B \& -C)] \Rightarrow [-C \& (A \& B)]$ 2 Com
    4. $[A \& (B \& -C)] \Rightarrow [-C \& (B \& A)]$ 3 Com
    5. $[A \& (B \& -C)] \Rightarrow -[C \vee -(B \vee A)]$ 4 DM

8.3, Set B

1. 1. $-[(X \& Y) \& -(X \& Y)]$ NC
    2. $-[(X \& Y) \& (-X \lor -Y)]$ 1 DM

3. 1. $(M \& N) \Rightarrow (M \& N)$ ID
    2. $(M \& N) \Rightarrow (N \& M)$ 1 Com
    3. $(N \& M) \Rightarrow (M \& N)$ 1 Com
    4. $[2] \& [3]$ 2,3 Conj

5. 1. $-(-P \lor Q) \lor (-P \lor Q)$ EM
    2. $-(-P \lor Q) \lor (Q \lor -P)$ 1 Com

7. 1. $-A \lor A$ EM
    2. $-B \lor (-A \lor A)$ 1 Add
    3. $(-B \lor -A) \lor A$ 2 Assn
    4. $-(B \& A) \lor A$ 3 DM
    5. $-(A \& B) \lor A$ 4 Com

9. 1. $R \lor -R$ EM
    2. $(R \lor -R) \lor -P$ 1 Add
    3. $R \lor (-R \lor -P)$ 2 Assn
    4. $-Q \lor [R \lor (-R \lor -P)]$ 3 Add
    5. $(-Q \lor R) \lor (-R \lor -P)$ 4 Assn
    6. $-(-P \lor Q) \lor [(-Q \lor R) \lor (-R \lor -P)]$ 5 Add
    7. $-(-P \lor Q) \lor [-(Q \& -R) \lor -(R \& P)]$ 6 DM

11. 1. $B \lor -B$ EM
    2. $A \lor (B \lor -B)$ 1 Add
    3. $A \lor (-B \lor B)$ 2 Com
    4. $(A \lor -B) \lor B$ 3 Assn
    5. $--[(A \lor -B) \lor B]$ 4 DN
    6. $-[-(A \lor -B) \& -B]$ 5 DM

8.3, Set C

1.

p	q	
T	F	True
T	T	False

3.

p	q	r	
T	F	F	True
F	T	T	False

5.

p	q	r	s	
T	T	T	T	True
T	T	F	T	False

7.

p	q	s	
T	T	T	True
T	T	F	False

9.

p	*q*	*r*	
T	T	T	True
F	T	F	False

Many other pairs of assignments are possible.

8.4, Set A

1. 1. *p*   /∴ *p* ∨ *q*   3. 1. *p* & *q*   /∴ *p* ∨ *q*
    2. *p* ∨ *q*   1 Add   2. *p*   1 Simp
                                                            3. *p* ∨ *q*   2 Add

5. 1. −*p*   /∴ −(*p* & −*q*)   7. 1. *p* ∨ (*q* & *r*)   /∴ *p* ∨ (*q* ∨ *r*)
    2. −*p* ∨ *q*   1 Add   2. (*p* ∨ *q*) & (*p* ∨ *r*) 1 Dist
    3. −(*p* & −*q*)   2 DM   3. *p* ∨ *q*   2 Simp
                                                            4. (*p* ∨ *q*) ∨ *r*   3 Add
                                                            5. *p* ∨ (*q* ∨ *r*)   4 Assn

9. 1. [(*p* ∨ *q*) ⇒ (*r* & *s*)] & − *r*   /∴ −*p*   11. 1. (−*p* ∨ *q*) & (−*p* ∨ *r*) /∴ −(*p* & *r*) ∨ *q*
    2. (*p* ∨ *q*) ⇒ (*r* & *s*)   1 Simp   2. −*p* ∨ *q*   1 Simp
    3. −*r*   1 Simp   3. −*r* ∨ (−*p* ∨ *q*)   2 Add
    4. −*r* ∨ −*s*   3 Add   4. (−*r* ∨ −*p*) ∨ *q*   3 Assn
    5. −(*r* & *s*)   4 DM   5. −(*r* & *p*) ∨ *q*   4 DM
    6. −(*p* ∨ *q*)   2,5 MT   6. −(*p* & *r*) ∨ *q*   5 Com
    7. −*p* & −*q*   6 DM
    8. −*p*   7 Simp

8.4, Set B

1. 1. *p* & (−*p* ∨ *q*)   /∴ *p* & *q*   1. *p* & *q*   /∴ *p* & (−*p* ∨ *q*)
    2. *p*   1 Simp   2. *p*   1 Simp
    3. −*p* ∨ *q*   1 Simp   3. *q*   1 Simp
    4. *q*   2,3 DS   4. −*p* ∨ *q*   3 Add
    5. *p* & *q*   2,4 Conj   5. *p* & (−*p* ∨ *q*)   2,4 Conj

3. 1. −(*p* & *q*) ∨ *r*   /∴ −*p* ∨ (−*q* ∨ *r*) 1. −*p* ∨ (−*q* ∨ *r*)   /∴ −(*p* & *q*) ∨ *r*
    2. (−*p* ∨ −*q*) ∨ *r*   1 DM   2. (−*p* ∨ −*q*) ∨ *r*   1 Assn
    3. −*p* ∨ (−*q* ∨ *r*)   2 Assn   3. −(*p* & *q*) ∨ *r*   2 DM

5. 1. −[*p* & −(−*p* ∨ *r*)]   /∴ −*p* ∨ *r*   1. −*p* ∨ *r*   /∴ −[*p* & −(−*p* ∨ *r*)]
    2. −*p* ∨ (−*p* ∨ *r*)   1 DM   2. (−*p* ∨ −*p*) ∨ *r*   1 DD
    3. (−*p* ∨ −*p*) ∨ *r*   2 Assn   3. −*p* ∨ (−*p* ∨ *r*)   2 Assn
    4. −*p* ∨ *r*   3 DD   4. −[*p* & −(−*p* ∨ *r*)]   3 DM

7. 1. p & $[(p \Rightarrow q)$ & $(q \Rightarrow p)]$ /∴ q & $[(p \Rightarrow q)$ & $(q \Rightarrow p)]$
    2. p 1 Simp
    3. $(p \Rightarrow q)$ & $(q \Rightarrow p)$ 1 Simp
    4. $p \Rightarrow q$ 3 Simp
    5. q 2,4 MP
    6. q & $[(p \Rightarrow q)$ & $(q \Rightarrow p)]$ 5,3 Conj

    1. q & $[(p \Rightarrow q)$ & $(q \Rightarrow p)]$ /∴ p & $[(p \Rightarrow q)$ & $q \Rightarrow p)]$
    2. q 1 Simp
    3. $(p \Rightarrow q)$ & $(q \Rightarrow p)$ 1 Simp
    4. $q \Rightarrow p$ 3 Simp
    5. p 2,4 MP
    6. p & $[(p \Rightarrow q)$ & $(q \Rightarrow p)]$ 5,3 Conj

8.4, Set C

1. Compatible.
    1. $-(p \vee q)$ /∴ $-p \vee -q$
    2. $-p$ & $-q$ 1 DM
    3. $-p$ 2 Simp
    4. $-p \vee -q$ 3 Add

3. Compatible.
    1. $(p$ & $q) \vee (p$ & $-q)$ /∴ p
    2. p & $(q \vee -q)$ 1 Dist
    3. p 2 Simp

5. Incompatible.
    1. q & $(-q \vee -p)$ /∴ p
    2. q 1 Simp
    3. $-q \vee -p$ 1 Simp
    4. $-p$ 2,3 DS

7. Incompatible.
    1. $-[(p$ & $q) \vee (-p$ & $-q)]$ /∴ $(p \vee q)$ & $(-p \vee -q)$
    2. $-(p$ & $q)$ & $-(-p$ & $-q)$ 1 DM
    3. $-(p$ & $q)$ 2 Simp
    4. $-p \vee -q$ 3 DM
    5. $-(-p$ & $-q)$ 2 Simp
    6. $p \vee q$ 5 DM
    7. $(p \vee q)$ & $(-p \vee -q)$ 4,6 Conj

8.5, Set A

1.
1. $(A \lor B) \& (C \lor D)$
2. $-A \lor -C$ $/\therefore B \lor D$
3. $-(B \lor D)$ IP
4. $-B \& -D$ 3 DM
5. $-B$ 4 Simp
6. $A \lor B$ 1 Simp
7. A 5,6 DS
8. $-C$ 2,7 DS
9. $C \lor D$ 1 Simp
10. D 8,9 DS
11. $B \lor D$ 10 Add
12. $(B \lor D) \& -(B \lor D)$ 3,11 Conj

3.
1. $(A \lor B) \Rightarrow (O \& P)$
2. $-O$ $/\therefore -A$
3. A IP
4. $A \lor B$ 3 Add
5. $O \& P$ 1,4 MP
6. O 5 Simp
7. $O \& -O$ 6,2 Conj

5.
1. $p \Rightarrow (q \& -q)$ $/\therefore -p$
2. p IP
3. $q \& -q$ 1,2 MP

7.
1. $p \lor q$
2. $p \lor -q$ $/\therefore p$
3. $-p$ IP
4. q 1,3 DS
5. q 2,3 DS
6. $q \& -q$ 4,5 Conj

9.
1. $-p \lor q$ $/\therefore -p \lor (p \& q)$
2. $-[-p \lor (p \& q)]$ IP
3. $p \& -(p \& q)$ 2 DM
4. $-(p \& q)$ 3 Simp
5. $-p \lor -q$ 4 DM
6. p 3 Simp
7. $-q$ 5,6 DS
8. q 1,6 DS
9. $q \& -q$ 7,8 Conj

11.
1. $H \lor (I \& J)$
2. $-(I \lor J) \lor K$ $/\therefore H \lor K$
3. $-(H \lor K)$ IP
4. $-H \& -K$ 3 DM
5. $-H$ 4 Simp
6. $I \& J$ 1,5 DS
7. I 6 Simp
8. $I \lor J$ 7 Add
9. K 2,8 DS
10. $-K$ 4 Simp
11. $K \& -K$ 9,10 Conj

13.
1. $-(Q \& R) \vee (S \Rightarrow T)$
2. $-(S \Rightarrow -T) \vee -T$ $/\therefore -(Q \& R) \vee -T$
3. $-[-(Q \& R) \vee -T]$ IP
4. $(Q \& R) \& T$ 3 DM
5. T 4 Simp
6. $-(S \Rightarrow T)$ 2,5 DS
7. $-(Q \& R)$ 1,6 DS
8. $Q \& R$ 4 Simp
9. $(Q \& R) \& -(Q \& R)$ 8,7 Conj

15.
1. $[(A \& B) \Rightarrow C] \& [(A \& -B) \Rightarrow D]$
2. A $/\therefore C \vee D$
3. $-(C \vee D)$ IP
4. $-C \& -D$ 3 DM
5. $(A \& B) \Rightarrow C$ 1 Simp
6. $-C$ 4 Simp
7. $-(A \& B)$ 5,6 MT
8. $(A \& -B) \Rightarrow D$ 1 Simp
9. $-D$ 4 Simp
10. $-(A \& -B)$ 8,9 MT
11. $-A \vee B$ 10 DM
12. B 11,2 DS
13. $-A \vee -B$ 7 DM
14. $-B$ 2,13 DS
15. $B \& -B$ 13,14 Conj

17.
1. $-(M \& N)$
2. $(-N \vee M) \Rightarrow (-O \vee -P)$
3. $-R \Rightarrow (P \& O)$ $/\therefore R$
4. $-R$ IP
5. $P \& O$ 3,4 MP
6. $(-N \vee -M) \Rightarrow -(O \& P)$ 2 DM
7. $O \& P$ 5 Com
8. $-(-N \vee -M)$ 6,7 MT
9. $N \& M$ 8 DM
10. $M \& N$ 9 Com
11. $(M \& N) \& -(M \& N)$ 1,10 Conj

19.
1. $-[(X \Rightarrow Y) \vee (Y \Rightarrow X)]$
2. $U \vee [V \vee (Y \Rightarrow X)]$
3. $-Z \Rightarrow -(V \vee U)$ $/\therefore Z$
4. $-Z$ IP
5. $-(V \vee U)$ 3,4 MP
6. $(U \vee V) \vee (Y \Rightarrow X)$ 2 Assn
7. $-(U \vee V)$ 5 Com
8. $Y \Rightarrow X$ 6,7 DS
9. $-(X \Rightarrow Y) \& -(Y \Rightarrow X)$ 1 DM
10. $-(Y \Rightarrow X)$ 9 Simp
11. $(Y \Rightarrow X) \& -(Y \Rightarrow X)$ 8,10 Conj

21.
1. $A \Rightarrow B$
2. $B \Rightarrow C$
3. $A \vee B$ $/\therefore C \vee E$
4. $-(C \vee E)$ IP
5. $-C \& -E$ 4 DM
6. $-C$ 5 Simp
7. $-B$ 2,6 MT
8. $-A$ 1,7 MT
9. B 3,8 DS
10. $B \& -B$ 7,9 Conj

22.
1. $-[(E \& -F) \& -G]$
2. $-(F \vee G)$ $/\therefore -E$
3. E IP
4. $-[E \& (-F \& -G)]$ 1 Assn
5. $-[E \& -(F \vee G)]$ 4 DM
6. $-E \vee (F \vee G)$ 5 DM
7. $F \vee G$ 3,6 DS
8. $(F \vee G) \& -(F \vee G)$ 2,7 Conj

8.5, Set B

1. 1. $(X \& Y) \& (-X \lor -Y)$ IP
    2. $(X \& Y) \& -(X \& Y)$ 1 DM

3. 1. $-[-(A \& B) \Rightarrow (-A \lor -B)]$ IP
    2. $-[-(A \& B) \Rightarrow -(A \& B)]$ 1 DM
    3. $-(A \& B) \Rightarrow -(A \& B)$ ID
    4. [2] & [3]   2,3 Conj

5. 1. $-\{[F \& -(G \& H)] \Rightarrow [(F \& -G) \lor (F \& -H)]\}$ IP
    2. $-\{[F \& -(G \& H)] \Rightarrow [(F \& (-G \lor -H)]\}$ 1 Dist
    3. $-\{[F \& -(G \& H)] \Rightarrow [(F \& -(G \& H)]\}$ 2 DM
    4. $[(F \& -(G \& H)] \Rightarrow [(F \& -(G \& H)]$ ID
    5. [4] & [3]   4,3 Conj

7. 1. $(-F \lor G) \& -[-F \lor (G \& F)]$ IP
    2. $-F \lor G$ 1 Simp
    3. $-[-F \lor (G \& F)]$ 1 Simp
    4. $F \& -(G \& F)$ 3 DM
    5. $F \& (-G \lor -F)$ 4 DM
    6. F 5 Simp
    7. $-G \lor -F$ 5 Simp
    8. $-G$ 6,7 DS
    9. $-F$ 2,8 DS
    10. $F \& -F$ 6,9 Conj

9. 1. $-[-\{[E \lor (F \& G)] \& -F\} \lor E]$ IP
    2. $\{[E \lor (F \& G)] \& -F\} \& -E$ 1 DM
    3. $-E$ 2 Simp
    4. $[E \lor (F \& G)] \& -F$ 2 Simp
    5. $E \lor (F \& G)$ 4 Simp
    6. $F \& G$ 3,5 DS
    7. F 6 Simp
    8. $-F$ 4 Simp
    9. $F \& -F$ 7,8 Conj

11. 1. $-\{-(-P \lor Q) \lor [(Q \& R) \lor -(R \& F)]\}$ IP
    2. $(-P \lor Q) \& -[(Q \& R) \lor -(R \& P)]$ 1 DM
    3. $-P \lor Q$ 2 Simp
    4. $-[(Q \& R) \lor -(R \& P)]$ 2 Simp
    5. $-(Q \& R) \& (R \& P)$ 4 DM
    6. $-(Q \& R)$ 5 Simp
    7. $-Q \lor -R$ 6 DM
    8. $-R \lor -P$ 3,7 DT
    9. $R \& P$ 5 Simp
    10. $-(R \& P)$ 8 DM
    11. $(R \& P) \& -(R \& P)$ 9,10 Conj

8.5, Set C

1.　1. $-[(C \,\&\, D) \vee (-C \vee -D)]$　　IP
　　2. $-(C \,\&\, D) \,\&\, -(-C \vee -D)$　　1 DM
　　3. $(-C \vee -D) \,\&\, -(-C \vee -D)$　　2 DM

3.　1. $-[(P \,\&\, -Q) \vee (Q \vee -P)]$　　IP
　　2. $-(P \,\&\, -Q) \,\&\, -(Q \vee -P)$　　1 DM
　　3. $(-P \vee Q) \,\&\, -(Q \vee -P)$　　2 DM
　　4. $(Q \vee -P) \,\&\, -(Q \vee -P)$　　3 Com

5.　1. $-\{-A \vee [(A \vee B) \,\&\, (A \vee C)]\}$　　IP
　　2. $A \,\&\, -[(A \vee B) \,\&\, (A \vee C)]$　　1 DM
　　3. $-[(A \vee B) \,\&\, (A \vee C)]$　　2 Simp
　　4. $-(A \vee B) \vee -(A \vee C)$　　3 DM
　　5. $(-A \,\&\, -B) \vee (-A \,\&\, -C)$　　4 DM
　　6. $-A \,\&\, (-B \vee C)$　　5 Dist
　　7. $-A$　　6 Simp
　　8. A　　2 Simp
　　9. $A \,\&\, -A$　　7,8 Conj

7.　1. $-\{-[-(-A \vee B) \vee B] \vee (A \vee B)\}$　　IP
　　2. $[-(-A \vee B) \vee B] \,\&\, -(A \vee B)$　　1 DM
　　3. $-(A \vee B)$　　2 Simp
　　4. $-A \,\&\, -B$　　3 DM
　　5. $-A$　　4 Simp
　　6. $-B$　　4 Simp
　　7. $-(-A \vee B) \vee B$　　2 Simp
　　8. $-(-A \vee B)$　　7,6 DS
　　9. $A \,\&\, -B$　　8 DM
　　10. A　　9 Simp
　　11. $A \,\&\, -A$　　5,10 Conj

9.　1. $-\{-[A \,\&\, (A \vee B)] \vee A\}$　　IP
　　2. $[A \,\&\, (A \vee B)] \,\&\, -A$　　1 DM
　　3. $-A$　　2 Simp
　　4. $A \,\&\, (A \vee B)$　　2 Simp
　　5. A　　4 Simp
　　6. $A \,\&\, -A$　　3,5 Conj

8.5, Set D

1. The conclusion is logically false and the premise is logically true (hence the argument is invalid).

3. The conjunction of the premises is logically false.

5. The conclusion is logically true and the conjunction of the premises is logically false.

Solutions to LSAT Prep Questions

1. (d). The rules tell us:

$$1. H \Rightarrow -G$$
$$2. (J \vee M) \Rightarrow H$$
$$3. W \Rightarrow G$$
$$4. -J \Rightarrow S$$

(a) tells us:

$$5. (-J \& -S)$$

which allows us to derive:

6. $-J$	5 Simp
7. $-S$	5 Simp
8. S	4,6 MP

A contradiction, so (a) is eliminated.

(b) tells us:

$$5. (-H \& -G)$$

which allows us to derive:

6. $-H$	5 Simp
7. $-G$	5 Simp
8. $-W$	3,7 MT

So the (b) list cannot be complete and (b) is eliminated.

(c) tells us:

$$5. [-G \& (-J \& -M)]$$

which allows us to derive:

6. $-G$	5 Simp
7. $-W$	4,6 MT

So the (c) list is not complete and (c) is eliminated.

(e) tells us:

$$5. (-M \& -S)$$

which allows us to derive:

6. $-S$	5 Simp
7. J	4,6 MT
8. $(J \lor M)$	7 Add
9. H	2,8 MP
10. $-G$	1,9 MP

So the (e) list is not complete and (e) is eliminated, leaving only (d).

2.   (e). Again, the rules tell us:

$$1. H \Rightarrow -G$$
$$2. (J \lor M) \Rightarrow H$$
$$3. W \Rightarrow G$$
$$4. -J \Rightarrow S$$

The new condition tells us:

$$5. M$$
$$6. H$$

which allows us to derive:

7. $-G$	1,6 MP
8. $-W$	3,7 MT

Since there are only 6 types of birds, this means there are at most two other kinds of birds in the forest.

3. (d). The rules tell us:

$$1. H \Rightarrow -G$$
$$2. (J \lor M) \Rightarrow H$$
$$3. W \Rightarrow G$$
$$4. -J \Rightarrow S$$

The new condition tells us:

$$5. -J$$

which allows us to derive:

6. S	4,5 MP

Which is inconsistent with (d).

4. (a). The rules tell us:

$$1. H \Rightarrow -G$$
$$2. (J \lor M) \Rightarrow H$$
$$3. W \Rightarrow G$$
$$4. -J \Rightarrow S$$

(a) tells us:

$$5. J$$
$$6. W$$

which allows us to derive:

7. $J \lor M$	5 Add
8. H	2,7 MP
9. $-G$	1,8 MP
10. $-W$	3,9 MT

which contradicts (6).

5. (a). The rules tell us:

$$1. H \Rightarrow -G$$
$$2. (J \lor M) \Rightarrow H$$
$$3. W \Rightarrow G$$
$$4. -J \Rightarrow S$$

The new conditions tell us:

$$5. G$$

which allows us to derive:

6. $-H$	1,5 MT
7. $-(J \lor M)$	2,6 MT
8. $-J \& -M$	7 DM
9. $-J$	8 Simp
10. S	4,9 MP

6. (b). The old rules tell us:

$$1. H \Rightarrow -G$$
$$2. (J \lor M) \Rightarrow H$$
$$3. W \Rightarrow G$$
$$4. -J \Rightarrow S$$

The new rule tells us:

$$5. S \Rightarrow -H$$

(a) tells us:

$$6. J$$
$$7. S$$

which allows us to derive:

8. –H	5,7 MP
9. J v M	6 Add
10. H	2,9 MP

So (a) cannot be true.

(c) tells us:

6. M
7. S

which allows us to derive:

8. J v M	6 Add
9. H	2,8 MP
10. –H	5,7 MP

So (c) cannot be true.

(d) tells us:

6. –J
7. M

Which allows us to derive:

8. S	4,6 MP
9. –H	5,8 MP
10. J v M	7 Add
11. H	2,10 MP

So (d) cannot be true.

(e) tells us that four of the six kinds of birds are in the forest. We know that H is either in or not in the forest. If H is in the forest, then:

6. H	
7. –G	1,6 MP
8. –S	5,6 MT
9. –W	3,7 MT

So, if H is in the forest, there are at most three birds in the forest.

If H is not in the forest, then:

6. –H	
7. –(J v M)	2,6 MT
8. –J & –M	7 DM

So if H is not in the forest, there are at most three birds in the forest. Thus, there are at most three birds in the forest, which is inconsistent with (e), leaving only (b).

9.1, Set A

1. *Dk*
3. *Lk* ∨ *Ck*
5. (*Ft* & *Et*) & –*Gt*
7. *Ls* ⇒ *Es*
9. *Vc* ∨ –*Vc*
11. *Rs* ⇒ *Ip*
13. *Mm* & –(*Mg* & *Mi*)
15. –(–*Mg* & –*Mi*)
17. [(*Bp* & *Cp*) & –*Ap*] ⇒ *Ip*
19. (*Ys* ⇒ *Es*) & (*Os* ⇒ *Ss*)

9.1, Set B

1. Simp
3. MP
5. Com
7. DM
9. Conj
11. MP
13. None.
15. DM
17. DD or Add
19. DC

9.1, Set C

1.
   1. *Ba* & *Ca*
   2. –(*Ba* & *Ca*) ∨ (*Bb* & *Cb*)   /∴ *Bb*
   3. *Bb* & *Cb*   1,2 DS
   4. *Bb*   3 Simp

3.
   1. *Fc*   /∴ (*Fc* ∨ *Gc*) & (*Fc* ∨ –*Gc*)
   2. *Fc* ∨ *Gc*   1 Add
   3. *Fc* ∨ –*Gc*   1 Add
   4. (*Fc* ∨ *Gc*) & (*Fc* ∨ –*Gc*)   2,3 Conj

5.
   1. (*Ka* ∨ *Lb*) ⇒ *Mc*
   2. *Ka* & *La*   /∴ *Mc*
   3. *Ka*   2 Simp
   4. *Ka* ∨ *Lb*   3 Add
   5. *Mc*   1,4 MP

7.
   1. –*Ab* ∨ (–*Bb* ∨ *Cb*)
   2. –*Cb*   /∴ –(*Ab* & Bb)
   3. (–*Ab* ∨ –*Bb*) ∨ *Cb*   1 Assn
   3. –*Ab* ∨ –*Bb*   2,3 DS
   4. –(*Ab* & Bb)   4 DM

9.
   1. –*Tm* ∨ *Vm*
   2. –(*Um* ∨ *Vm*)   /∴ –*Tm*
   3. –*Um* & –*Vm*   2 DM
   4. –*Vm*   3 Simp
   5. –*Tm*   1,4 DS

11. 1. –(Fb ∨ Fc)   /∴ –(Fc ∨ & Fb)
     2. –Fb & –Fc   1 DM
     3. –Fb   2 Simp
     4. –Fc ∨ –Fb   3 Add
     5. –(Fc & Fb)   4 DM

13. 1. Ma ∨ Mb
     2. –(Mb & Nb)
     3. Nb ∨ Na   /∴ Ma ∨ Na
     4. –Mb ∨ –Nb   2 DM
     5. Ma ∨ –Nb   1,4 DT
     6. Ma ∨ Na   1,4 DT

9.2

1. ∀Mx   3. ∃(Hx & Px)
5. ∃(Ax & Bx & Px)   7. ∀(Rx ∨ –Mx)
9. ∃[(Ex & Hx & Mx) & Hx]   11. –∃Wx
13. ∀(Mx ∨ –Mx)   15. ∀Ax ⇒ Am
17. ∀(Wx ⇒ Hj), or ∃Wx ⇒ Hj   19. ∃Ex ⇒ –∀Gx
21. Wp ∨ ∀–Wx   23. Uh & ∀–Tx
25. ∀{[(Fx & Ex & Px) ⇒ Sx] & [–(Fx & Ex & Px) ⇒ –Sx]}

9.3, Set A

1. QN   3. QN   5. MP   7. Simp
9. Add   11. DM   13. Dist   15. Conj
17. QN   19. None.   21. DT

9.3, Set B

1. 1. –∀(–Ax ∨ Bx)   /∴ (Ax & –Bx)
    2. ∃–(–Ax ∨ Bx)   1 QN
    3. ∃(Ax & –Bx)   2 DM

3. 1. –(∀Mx ∨ ∀–Mx)   /∴ ∃–Mx & ∃Mx
    2. –∀Mx & –∀–Mx   1 DM
    3. ∃–Mx & ∃Mx   2 QN

5. 1. ∃(Ix & –Jx)   /∴ –∀(–Ix ∨ Jx)
    2. –∀–(Ix & –Jx)   1 QN
    3. –∀(–Ix ∨ Jx)   2 DM

7. 1. $-\exists[Fx \,\&\, (Gx \lor Hx)]$ $/\therefore\ \forall[(-Fx \lor Gx) \,\&\, (-Fx \lor -Hx)]$
    2. $\forall-[Fx \,\&\, (Gx \lor Hx)]$ 1 QN
    3. $\forall[-Fx \lor -(Gx \lor Hx)]$ 2 DM
    4. $\forall[-Fx \lor (-Gx \,\&\, -Hx)]$ 3 DM
    5. $\forall[(-Fx \lor -Gx) \,\&\, (-Fx \lor -Hx)]$ 4 Dist

9. 1. $\forall[-Ax \lor (-Bx \,\&\, -Cx)]$ $/\therefore\ -\exists[(Ax \,\&\, Bx) \lor (Ax \,\&\, Cx)]$
    2. $-\exists-[-Ax \lor (-Bx \,\&\, -Cx)]$ 1 QN
    3. $-\exists[Ax \,\&\, -(-Bx \,\&\, -Cx)]$ 2 DM
    4. $-\exists[Ax \,\&\, (Bx \lor Cx)]$ 3 DM
    5. $-\exists[(Ax \,\&\, Bx) \lor (Ax \,\&\, Cx)]$ 4 Dist

11. 1. Aa
    2. $(Aa \lor Ab) \Rightarrow \exists Ax$ $/\therefore\ -\forall-Ax$
    3. $Aa \lor Ab$ 1 Add
    4. $\exists Ax$ 2,3 MP
    5. $-\forall-Ax$ 4 QN

13. 1. $-\exists(Gx \,\&\, -Hx)$
    2. $\forall(-Gx \lor Hx) \Rightarrow \exists(Sx \,\&\, -Tx)$ $/\therefore\ -\forall(-Sx \lor Tx)$
    3. $\forall-(Gx \,\&\, -Hx)$ 1 QN
    4. $\forall(-Gx \lor Hx)$ 3 DM
    5. $\exists(Sx \,\&\, -Tx)$ 2,4 MP
    6. $-\forall-(Sx \,\&\, -Tx)$ 5 QN
    7. $-\forall(-Sx \lor Tx)$ 6 DM

15. 1. $-\forall Ex \lor \forall Fx$
    2. $-\forall Ex \lor \forall Gx$
    3. $-(\exists-Ex \lor \exists-Hx)$ $/\therefore\ \forall Gx \,\&\, \forall Fx$
    4. $-\exists-Ex \,\&\, -\exists-Hx$ 3 DM
    5. $-\exists-Ex$ 4 Simp
    6. $\forall Ex$ 5 QN
    7. $\forall Fx$ 1,6 DS
    8. $\forall Gx$ 2,6 DS
    9. $\forall Gx \,\&\, \forall Fx$ 7,8 Conj

17. 1. $\exists Cx \Rightarrow Ca$
    2. $\exists Dx \Rightarrow Da$
    3. $-(Ca \lor Da)$ $/\therefore\ \forall-Cx \,\&\, \forall-Dx$
    4. $-Ca \,\&\, -Da$ 3 DM
    5. $-Ca$ 4 Simp
    6. $-\exists Cx$ 1,5 MT
    7. $-Da$ 4 Simp
    8. $-\exists Dx$ 2,7 MT
    9. $-\exists Cx \,\&\, -\exists Dx$ 6,8 Conj
    10. $\forall-Cx \,\&\, \forall-Dx$ 9 QN

9.3, Set C

1. 1. $-\exists(Px\ \&\ Ax)$ $/\therefore\ \forall(-Px\ \lor\ -Ax)$
    2. $\forall-(Px\ \&\ Ax)$ 1 QN
    3. $\forall(-Px\ \lor\ -Ax)$ 2 DM

5. 1. $\forall Ux \Rightarrow \exists Ux$
    2. $\forall-Ux$ $/\therefore\ -\forall Ux$
    3. $-\exists Ux$ 2 QN
    4. $-\forall Ux$ 1,3 MT

9. 1. $\exists Gx \Rightarrow \exists Px$
    2. $\exists Px \Rightarrow -\exists Ex$
    3. $\exists Ex$ $/\therefore\ \forall-Gx$
    4. $-\exists Px$ 2,3 MT
    5. $-\exists Gx$ 1,4 MT
    6. $\forall-Gx$ 5 QN

3. 1. $-(\forall Gx \lor \forall Ex)$ $/\therefore\ \exists-Gx \lor \exists-Ex$
    2. $-\forall Gx\ \&\ -\forall Ex$ 1 DM
    3. $-\forall Gx$ 2 Simp
    4. $\exists-Gx$ 3 QN
    5. $\exists-Gx \lor \exists-Ex$ 4 Add

7. 1. $(Cm \lor Cv) \Rightarrow \exists Cx$
    2. $\forall-Cx$ $/\therefore\ -Cm$
    3. $-\exists Cx$ 2 QN
    4. $-(Cm \lor Cv)$ 1,3 MT
    5. $-Cm\ \&\ -Cv$ 4 DM
    6. $-Cm$ 5 Simp

9.4, Set A

1. UI
3. UI
5. EG
7. None.
9. None.
11. None.
13. None.
15. UI

9.4, Set B

1. 1. $\forall(Fx \lor Gx)$
    2. $-Fa$ $/\therefore\ Ga$
    3. $Fa \lor Ga$ 1 UI
    4. Ga 2,3 DS

5. 1. $\forall(Mx \lor Nx)$ $/\therefore\ -\forall-(Mx \lor Nx)$
    2. $Ma \lor Na$ 1 UI
    3. $\exists(Mx \lor Nx)$ 2 EG
    4. $-\forall-(Mx \lor Nx)$ 3 QN

9. 1. $-\exists(Mx\ \&\ -Nx)$
    2. Ma $/\therefore\ Na$
    3. $\forall-(Mx\ \&\ -Nx)$ 1 QN
    4. $-(Ma\ \&\ -Na)$ 3 UI
    5. $-Ma \lor Na$ 4 DM
    6. Na 2,5 DS

3. 1. $Fa \Rightarrow Ga$
    2. $\forall Fx$ $/\therefore\ \exists Gx$
    3. Fa 2 UI
    4. Ga 1,3 MP
    5. $\exists Gx$ 4 EG

7. 1. $\exists Gx \Rightarrow \exists(Hx\ \&\ Ix)$
    2. $\forall(Gx\ \&\ Jx)$ $/\therefore\ \exists(Hx\ \&\ Ix)$
    3. $Ga\ \&\ Ja$ 2 UI
    4. Ga 3 Simp
    5. $\exists Gx$ 4 EG
    6. $\exists(Hx\ \&\ Ix)$ 1,5 MP

9.4, Set C

1. 1. $\forall(Tx \Rightarrow Dx)$
    2. $-Dm$ $/\therefore -Tm$
    3. $Tm \Rightarrow Dm$ 1 UI
    4. $-Tm$ 2,3 MT

5. 1. $\forall-(Lx \& Sx)$
    2. $Lt \lor -Mt$
    3. $St \lor -At$ $/\therefore \exists-(Mx \& Ax)$
    4. $-(Lt \& St)$ 1 UI
    5. $-Lt \lor -St$ 4 DM
    6. $-Mt \lor St$ 2,5 DT
    7. $-Mt \lor -At$ 3,6 DT
    8. $-(Mt \& At)$ 7 DM
    9. $\exists-(Mx \& Ax)$ 8 EG

9. 1. $\forall[(Sx \& Ix) \Rightarrow Mx]$
    2. $\forall(-Jx \Rightarrow Sx)$
    3. $-Jj$
    4. Ij $/\therefore Mj$
    5. $-Jj \Rightarrow Sj$ 2 UI
    6. Sj 3,5 MP
    7. $Sj \& Ij$ 4,6 Conj
    8. $(Sj \& Ij) \Rightarrow Mj$ 1 UI
    9. Mj 7,8 MP

3. 1. $\forall-(Gx \& -Sx)$
    2. $-Sr$ $/\therefore -Gr$
    3. $-(Gr \& -Sr)$ 1 UI
    4. $-Gr \lor Sr$ 3 DM
    5. $-Gr$ 2,4 DS

7. 1. $\forall Mx \Rightarrow \forall Gx$
    2. $\forall Mx$ $/\therefore Gs \& Gm$
    3. $\forall Gx$ 1,2 MP
    4. Gs 3 UI
    5. Gm 3 UI
    6. $Gs \& Gm$ 4,5 Conj

9.4, Set D

1. 1. $\forall(Ax \Rightarrow Bx)$
    2. $\forall Cx \& \forall Ax$ $/\therefore Bn$
    3. $An \Rightarrow Bn$ 1 UI
    4. $\forall Ax$ 2 Simp
    5. An 4 UI
    6. Bn 3,5 MP

3. 1. $\exists Fx \Rightarrow \exists Rx$
    2. $\exists Rx \Rightarrow \exists Gx$
    3. $\forall Fx$ $/\therefore \exists Gx$
    4. Fa 3 UI
    5. $\exists Fx$ 4 EG
    6. $\exists Rx$ 1,5 MP
    7. $\exists Gx$ 2,6 MP

5. 1. ∀(*Ax* & *Bx*) ⇒ ∃*Cx*
   2. (*Ka* ∨ *Kb*) ⇒ –∃*Cx*
   3. *Kb* & *Kc*   /∴ ∃–(*Ax* & *Bx*)
   4. *Kb*   3 Simp
   5. *Ka* ∨ *Kb*   4 Add
   6. –∃*Cx*   2,5 MP
   7. –∀(*Ax* & *Bx*)   1,6 MT
   8. ∃–(*Ax* & *Bx*)   7 QN

7. 1. ∃(*Hx* ∨ *Ix*) ⇒ ∀[*Jx* & (*Kx* & *Lx*)]
   2. *Ia*   /∴ ∃(*Jx* & *Kx*)
   3. *Ha* ∨ *Ia*   2 Add
   4. ∃(*Hx* ∨ *Ix*)   3 EG
   5. ∀[*Jx* & (*Kx* & *Lx*)]   1,4 MP
   6. *Ja* & (*Ka* & *La*)   5 UI
   7. (*Ja* & *Ka*) & *La*   6 Assn
   8. *Ja* & *Ka*   7 Simp
   9. ∃(*Jx* & *Kx*)   8 EG

9. 1. ∀–(*Mx* & –*Px*)
   2. ∀–(*Sx* & –*Mx*)   /∴ ∃(–*Sx* ∨ Px)
   3. –(*Ma* & –*Pa*)   1 UI
   4. –(*Sa* & – *Ma*)   2 UI
   5. –*Ma* ∨ *Pa*   3 DM
   6. –*Sa* ∨ *Ma*   4 DM
   7. –*Sa* ∨ *Pa*   5,6 DT
   8. ∃(–*Sx* ∨ *Px*)   7 EG

9.5, Set A

1. None.

3. Line 5 (*j* was used in premise 2).

5. Line 3 (you can't UI part of a line); line 5 (*a* was used in lines 3 and 4).

7. Line 3 (*a* was used in line 2).

9. None.

9.5, Set B

1. 1. ∀*Fx*   /∴ ∀(*Fx* ∨ *Gx*)
   2. *Fa*   1 UI
   3. *Fa* ∨ *Ga*   2 Add
   4. ∀(*Fx* ∨ *Gx*)   3 UG

3.   1. $\forall(Qx \lor Rx)$
     2. $\forall{-}Qx$ $/\therefore \forall Rx$
     3. $-Qa$ 2 UI
     4. $Qa \lor Ra$ 1 UI
     5. Ra 3,4 DS
     6. $\forall Rx$ 5 UG

5.   1. $\forall(Bx \Rightarrow Cx)$
     2. $\exists Bx$ $/\therefore \exists Cx$
     3. Ba 2 EI
     4. $Ba \Rightarrow Ca$ 1 UI
     5. Ca 3,4 MP
     6. $\exists Cx$ 5 EG

7.   1. $\exists(Mx \Rightarrow Nx)$
     2. $\forall{-}Nx$ $/\therefore -\forall Mx$
     3. $Ma \Rightarrow Na$ 1 EI
     4. $-Na$ 2 UI
     5. $-Ma$ 3,4 MT
     6. $\exists{-}Ma$ 5 EG
     7. $-\forall Mx$ 6 QN

9.   1. $\forall[(Jx \lor Kx) \Rightarrow -Lx]$
     2. $\exists Lx$ $/\therefore \exists{-}Jx$
     3. La 2 EI
     4. $(Ja \lor Ka) \Rightarrow -La$ 1 UI
     5. $-(Ja \lor Ka)$ 3,4 MT
     6. $-Ja \& -Ka$ 5 DM
     7. $-Ja$ 6 Simp
     8. $\exists{-}Jx$ 7 EG

11. 1. $\forall Ax$
     2. $\exists Ax \Rightarrow -\exists Bx$
     3. $\forall Cx \Rightarrow Bd$ $/\therefore -\forall Cx$
     4. Aa 1 UI
     5. $\exists Ax$ 4 EG
     6. $-\exists Bx$ 2,5 MP
     7. $\forall{-}Bx$ 6 QN
     8. $-Bd$ 7 UI
     9. $-\forall Cx$ 3,8 MT

13. 1. $\forall(Hx \lor Ix) \Rightarrow \exists[Jx \& (Kx \& Lx)]$
    2. $\forall Hx$ $/\therefore \exists(Jx \& Kx)$
    3. Ha 2 UI
    4. $Ha \lor Ia$ 3 Add
    5. $\forall(Hx \lor Ix)$ 4 UG
    6. $\exists[Jx \& (Kx \& Lx)]$ 1,5 MP
    7. $Jb \& (Kb \& Lb)$ 6 EI
    8. $(Jb \& Kb) \& Lb$ 7 Assn
    9. $Jb \& Kb$ 8 Simp
    10. $\exists(Jx \& Kx)$ 9 EG

15. 1. $\forall(Bx \Rightarrow Tx)$
    2. $\exists(Gx \& Ix)$
    3. $\forall-(Ix \& Tx)$ $/\therefore \exists(Gx \& -Bx)$
    4. $Ga \& Ia$ 2 EI
    5. $-(Ia \& Ta)$ 3 UI
    6. $-Ia \lor -Ta$ 5 DM
    7. Ia 4 Simp
    8. $-Ta$ 6,7 DS
    9. $Ba \Rightarrow Ta$ 1 UI
    10. $-Ba$ 8,9 MT
    11. Ga 4 Simp
    12. $Ga \& -Ba$ 10,11 Conj
    13. $\exists(Gx \& -Bx)$ 12 EG

17. 1. $\forall Gx \Rightarrow \exists(Hx \& Jx)$
    2. $\forall(Gx \& Jx)$ $/\therefore \exists(Hx \& Gx)$
    3. $Ga \& Ja$ 2 UI
    4. Ga 3 Simp
    5. $\forall Gx$ 4 UG
    6. $\exists(Hx \& Jx)$ 1,5 MP
    7. $Hb \& Jb$ 6 EI
    8. Hb 7 Simp
    9. $Gb \& Jb$ 2 UI
    10. Gb 9 Simp
    11. $Hb \& Gb$ 8,10 Conj
    12. $\exists(Hx \& Gx)$ 11 EG

19. 1. ∃(*Nx* & *Sx*)
    2. ∀(–*Vx* ∨ *Tx*)
    3. ∀–(*Sx* & –*Vx*)   /∴ ∃(*Nx* & *Tx*)
    4. *Na* & *Sa*   1 EI
    5. –*Va* ∨ *Ta*   2 UI
    6. –(*Sa* & –*Va*)   3 UI
    7. –*Sa* ∨ *Va*   6 DM
    8. –*Sa* ∨ *Ta*   5,7 DT
    9. *Sa*   4 Simp
    10. *Ta*   8,9 DS
    11. *Na*   4 Simp
    12. *Na* & *Ta*   10,11 Conj
    13. ∃(*Nx* & *Tx*)   12 EG

9.5, Set C

1. 1. ∀–(*Px* & –*Mx*)
    2. –*Ms*   /∴ –*Ps*
    3. –(*Ps* & –*Ms*)   1 UI
    4. –*Ps* ∨ *Ms*   3 DM
    5. –*Ps*   2,4 DS

3. 1. ∀–(*Mx* & *Px*)
    2. ∀–(*Sx* & –*Mx*)   /∴ ∀–(*Sx* & *Px*)
    3. –(*Ma* & *Pa*)   1 UI
    4. –(*Sa* & –*Ma*)   2 UI
    5. –*Ma* ∨ –*Pa*   3 DM
    6. –*Sa* ∨ *Ma*   4 DM
    7. –*Sa* ∨ –*Pa*   5,6 DT
    8. –(*Sa* & *Pa*)   7 DM
    9. ∀–(*Sx* & *Px*)   8 UG

5. 1. ∃(*Px* & *Mx*)
    2. ∀–(*Mx* & –*Sx*)   /∴ ∃(*Sx* & *Px*)
    3. *Pa* & *Ma*   1 EI
    4. –(*Ma* & –*Sa*)   2 UI
    5. –*Ma* ∨ *Sa*   4 DM
    6. *Ma*   3 Simp
    7. *Sa*   5,6 DS
    8. *Pa*   3 Simp
    9. *Sa* & *Pa*   7,8 Conj
    10. ∃(*Sx* & *Px*)   9 EG

9.5, Set D

1.
1. ∀Fx	/∴ ∀(Fx v Gx)
2. –∀(Fx v Gx)	IP
3. ∃–(Fx v Gx)	2 QN
4. –(Fa v Ga)	3 EI
5. –Fa & –Ga	4 DM
6. –Fa	5 Simp
7. Fa	1 UI
8. Fa & –Fa	6,7 Conj

3.
1. ∀(Qx v Rx)	
2. ∀–Qx	/∴ ∀Rx
3. –∀Rx	IP
4. ∃–Rx	3 QN
5. –Ra	4 EI
6. Qa v Ra	1 UI
7. Qa	5,6 DS
8. –Qa	2 UI
9. Qa & –Qa	7,8 Conj

5.
1. ∀(Bx ⇒ Cx)	
2. ∃Bx	/∴ ∃Cx
3. –∃Cx	IP
4. ∀–Cx	3 QN
5. Ba	2 EI
6. Ba ⇒ Ca	1 UI
7. Ca	5,6 MP
8. –Ca	4 UI
9. Ca & –Ca	7,8 Conj

7.
1. ∃(Mx ⇒ Nx)	
2. ∀–Nx	/∴ –∀Mx
3. ∀Mx	IP
4. Ma ⇒ Na	1 EI
5. Ma	3 UI
6. Na	4,5 MP
7. –Na	2 UI
8. Na & –Na	6,7 Conj

9.6, Set A

1. ∀–(Sx & –Mx), ∃Sx

3. ∃[(Ex & Hx & Mx) & Rx], ∃(Ex & Hx & Mx)

5. ∀–[(Bx & Fx) & –Wx], ∃(Bx & Fx)

7. ∀–[(Vx & Mx) & –Bx], ∃(Vx & Mx)

9. ∃[Fx & –(Mx & Vx)], ∃Fx

11. ∃[Ax & (–Ix ⇒ –Wx)], ∃Ax

13. ∃[Sx & (–Cx ⇒ –Px)], ∃Sx

15. ∃[Sx & (Px & –Hx)], ∃Sx

17. ∃[(Cx & Ex) & –(Bx v Lx)], ∃(Cx & Ex)

19. ∀–{Px & –[(Ex & Bx & Hx & Cx) & –Rx]}, ∃Px

21. ∀–(Vx & –Ix) & ∀–(Px & –Ix), ∃Vx & ∃Px

9.6, Set B

1.
1. ∃(Fx & –Sx)	/∴ ∃(–Sx & Fx)
2. ∃(–Sx & Fx)	1 Com

3.   1. $\forall -(Mx \,\&\, -Ax) \,\&\, \exists Mx$ /∴ $\exists(Ax \,\&\, Mx)$
     2. $\exists Mx$ 1 Simp
     3. $\forall -(Mx \,\&\, -Ax)$ 1 Simp
     4. Ma 2 EI
     5. $-(Ma \,\&\, -Aa)$ 3 UI
     6. $-Ma \lor Aa$ 5 DM
     7. Aa 4,6 DS
     8. $Aa \,\&\, Ma$ 4,7 Conj
     9. $\exists(Ax \,\&\, Mx)$ 8 EG

5.   1. $\forall -(Sx \,\&\, Px) \,\&\, \exists Sx$ /∴ $\exists(-Px \,\&\, --Sx)$
     2. $\exists Sx$ 1 Simp
     3. Sa 2 EI
     4. $\forall -(Sx \,\&\, Px)$ 1 Simp
     5. $-(Sa \,\&\, Pa)$ 4 UI
     6. $-Sa \lor -Pa$ 5 DM
     7. $-Pa$ 3,6 DS
     8. $-Pa \,\&\, Sa$ 3,7 Conj
     9. $\exists(-Px \,\&\, Sx)$ 8 EG
     10. $\exists(-Px \,\&\, --Sx)$ 9 DN

7.   1. $\forall -(Ax \,\&\, Vx) \,\&\, \exists Ax$ /∴ $\exists(-Vx \,\&\, Ax)$
     2. $\exists Ax$ 1 Simp
     3. Aa 2 EI
     4. $\forall -(Ax \,\&\, Vx)$ 1 Simp
     5. $-(Aa \,\&\, Va)$ 4 UI
     6. $-Aa \lor -Va$ 5 DM
     7. $-Va$ 3,6 DS
     8. $-Va \,\&\, Aa$ 3,7 Conj
     9. $\exists(-Vx \,\&\, Ax)$ 8 EG

9.   1. $\forall -(-Ax \,\&\, -Bx) \,\&\, \exists -Ax$ /∴ $\exists(Bx \,\&\, -Ax)$
     2. $\exists -Ax$ 1 Simp
     3. $-Aa$ 2 EI
     4. $\forall -(-Ax \,\&\, -Bx)$ 1 Simp
     5. $-(-Aa \,\&\, Ba)$ 4 UI
     6. $Aa \lor Ba$ 5 DM
     7. Ba 3,6 DS
     8. $Ba \,\&\, -Aa$ 3,7 Conj
     9. $\exists(Bx \,\&\, -Ax)$ 8 EG

9.6, Set C

1. 1. ∀–(Rx & Sx) & ∃Rx
    2. Rg   /∴ –Sg
    3. ∀–(Rx & Sx)   1 Simp
    4. –(Rg & Sg)   3 UI
    5. –Rg ∨ –Sg   4 DM
    6. –Sg   2,5 DS

3. 1. –Mt
    2. ∀–(Rx & –Mx) & ∃Rx   /∴ –Rt
    3. ∀–(Rx & –Mx)   2 Simp
    4. –(Rt & –Mt)   3 UI
    5. –Rt ∨ Mt   4 DM
    6. –Rt   1,5 DS

5. 1. ∀–(Sx & –Cx) & ∃Sx
    2. Sk   /∴ Ck
    3. ∀–(Sx & –Cx)   1 Simp
    4. –(Sk & –Ck)   3 UI
    5. –Sk ∨ Ck   4 DM
    6. Ck   2,5 DS

7. 1. Fk & Ak
    2. ∀–[(Fx & Ax) & –Wx] & ∃(Fx & Ax)   /∴ Wk
    3. ∀–[(Fx & Ax) & –Wx]   2 Simp
    4. –[(Fk & Ak) & –Wk]   3 UI
    5. –(Fk & Ak) ∨ Wk   4 DM
    6. Wk   1,5 DS

9. 1. ∃(Px & Rx)
    2. ∀–(Rx & –Fx) & ∃Rx   /∴ ∃(Fx & Px)
    3. Pa & Ra   1 EI
    4. ∀–(Rx & –Fx)   2 Simp
    5. –(Ra & –Fa)   4 UI
    6. –Ra ∨ Fa   5 DM
    7. Ra   3 Simp
    8. Fa   6,7 DS
    9. Pa   3 Simp
    10. Fa & Pa   8,9 Conj
    11. ∃(Fx & Px)   10 EG

11. 1. ∀–(Ax & –Px) & ∃Ax
     2. ∀–(Ax & –Mx) & ∃Ax   /∴ ∃(Mx & Px)
     3. ∃Ax   1 Simp
     4. Aa   4 EI
     5. ∀–(Ax & –Px)   1 Simp
     6. ∀–(Ax & –Mx)   2 Simp
     7. –(Aa & –Pa)   5 UI
     8. –(Aa & –Ma)   6 UI
     9. –Aa ∨ Pa   7 DM
     10. –Aa ∨ Ma   8 DM
     11. Pa   4,9 DS
     12. Ma   4,10 DS
     13. Ma & Pa   11,12 Conj
     14. ∃(Mx & Px)   13 EG

13. 1. ∃(Px & Ux)
     2. ∀–(Px & –Ax) & ∃Px   /∴ ∃(Ax & Ux)
     3. Pa & Ua   1 EI
     4. ∀–(Px & –Ax)   2 Simp
     5. –(Pa & –Aa)   4 UI
     6. –Pa ∨ Aa   5 DM
     7. Pa   3 Simp
     8. Aa   6,7 DS
     9. Ua   3 Simp
     10. Aa & Ua   8,9 Conj
     11. ∃(Ax & Ux)   10 EG

9.6, Set D

1.   1. –Ak
     2. ∀–(–Ax & –Bx) & ∃–Ax   /∴ Bk
     3. ∀–(–Ax & –Bx)   2 Simp
     4. –(–Ak & Bk)   3 UI
     5. Ak ∨ Bk   4 DM
     6. Bk   1,5 DS

3.   1. Ad
     2. ∀–(Ax & Bx) & ∃Ax
     3. Cd   /∴ ∃(Cx & –Bx)
     4. ∀–(Ax & Bx)   2 Simp
     5. –(Ad & Bd)   4 UI
     6. –Ad ∨ –Bd   5 DM
     7. –Bd   1,6 DS
     8. Cd & –Bd   3,7 Conj
     9. ∃(Cx & –Bx)   8 EG

5. 1. $-Hc$
    2. $\forall -(-Gx \,\&\, -Hx) \,\&\, \exists -Gx$ $/\therefore\ Gc$
    3. $\forall -(-Gx \,\&\, -Hx)$ 2 Simp
    4. $-(-Gc \,\&\, -Hc)$ 3 UI
    5. $Gc \lor Hc$ 4 DM
    6. Gc 1,5 DS

7. 1. $\exists (Nx \,\&\, Sx)$
    2. $\forall -(Vx \,\&\, -Tx) \,\&\, \exists Vx$
    3. $\forall -(Sx \,\&\, -Vx) \,\&\, \exists Sx$ $/\therefore\ \exists (Nx \,\&\, Tx)$
    4. $Na \,\&\, Sa$ 1 EI
    5. $\forall -(Vx \,\&\, -Tx)$ 2 Simp
    6. $-(Va \,\&\, -Ta)$ 5 UI
    7. $-Va \lor Ta$ 6 DM
    8. $\forall -(Sx \,\&\, -Vx)$ 3 Simp
    9. $-(Sa \,\&\, -Va)$ 8 UI
    10. $-Sa \lor Va$ 9 DM
    11. Sa 4 Simp
    12. Va 10,11 DS
    13. Ta 7,12 DS
    14. Na 4 Simp
    15. $Na \,\&\, Ta$ 13,14 Conj
    16. $\exists (Nx \,\&\, Tx)$ 15 EG

9. 1. $\forall -(Tx \,\&\, -Wx) \,\&\, \exists Tx$
    2. $\forall -(Hx \,\&\, Rx) \,\&\, \exists Hx$
    3. $\forall -(Wx \,\&\, -Rx) \,\&\, \exists Wx$ $/\therefore\ \forall -(Hx \,\&\, Tx) \,\&\, \exists Hx$
    4. $\forall -(Tx \,\&\, -Wx)$ 1 Simp
    5. $\forall -(Hx \,\&\, Rx)$ 2 Simp
    6. $\forall -(Wx \,\&\, -Rx)$ 3 Simp
    7. $-(Ta \,\&\, -\text{Wa})$ 4 UI
    8. $-(Ha \,\&\, Ra)$ 5 UI
    9. $-(Wa \,\&\, -Ra)$ 6 UI
    10. $-Ta \lor Wa$ 7 DM
    11. $-Ha \lor -Ra$ 8 DM
    12. $-Wa \lor Ra$ 9 DM
    13. $-Ha \lor -Wa$ 11,12 DT
    14. $-Ha \lor -Ta$ 10,13 DT
    15. $-(Ha \,\&\, Ta)$ 14 DM
    16. $\forall -(Hx \,\&\, Tx)$ 15 UG
    17. $\exists Hx$ 2 Simp
    18. $\forall -(Hx \,\&\, Tx) \,\&\, \exists Hx$ 16,17 Conj

11. 1. ∀–(*Tx* & *Wx*) & ∃*Tx*
     2. ∀–(–*Wx* & *Cx*) & ∃–*Wx*
     3. ∀–(*Kx* & –*Tx*) & ∃*Kx*   /∴ ∀–(*Kx* & *Cx*) & ∃*Kx*
     4. ∀–(*Tx* & *Wx*)   1 Simp
     5. ∀–(–*Wx* & *Cx*)   2 Simp
     6. ∀–(*Kx* & –*Tx*)   3 Simp
     7. –(*Ta* & *Wa*)   4 UI
     8. –(–*Wa* & *Ca*)   5 UI
     9. –(*Ka* & –*Ta*)   6 UI
     10. –*Ta* ∨ –*Wa*   7 DM
     11. *Wa* ∨ –*Ca*   8 DM
     12. –*Ka* ∨ *Ta*   9 DM
     13. –*Ta* ∨ –*Ca*   10,11 DT
     14. –*Ka* ∨ –*Ca*   12,13 DT
     15. –(*Ka* & *Ca*)   14 DM
     16. ∀–(*Kx* & *Cx*)   15 UG
     17. ∃*Kx*   3 Simp
     18. ∀–(*Kx* & *Cx*) & ∃*Kx*   16,17 Conj

9.6, Set E

1. ∀(*Sx* ⊃ *Mx*)   5.   ∀[(*Bx* & *Fx*) ⊃ *Wx*]   7.   ∀[(*Vx* & *Mx*) ⊃ *Bx*]
19. ∀{*Px* ⊃ [(*Ex* & *Bx* & *Hx* & *Cx*) & –*Rx*]}   21. ∀(*Vx* ⊃ *Ix*) & ∀(*Px* ⊃ *Ix*)

9.7

1. 1. ∀*Fx* ∨ –∀*Fx*   EM
    2. ∀*Fx* ∨ ∃–*Fx*   1 QN

3. 1. –∀(*Fx* & *Gx*) ⇒ –∀(*Fx* & *Gx*)   ID
    2. –∀(*Fx* & *Gx*) ⇒ ∃–(*Fx* & *Gx*)   1 QN
    3. –∀(*Fx* & *Gx*) ⇒ ∃(–*Fx* ∨ –*Gx*)   2 DM

5. 1. *Fa* ∨ –*Fa*   EM
    2. ∀(*Fx* ∨ –*Fx*)   1 UG
    3. –(*Ga* & –*Ga*)   NC
    4. ∀–(*Gx* & –*Gx*)   3 UG
    5. –∃(*Gx* &–*Gx*)   4 QN
    6. ∀(*Fx* ∨ –*Fx*) & –∃(*Gx* & –*Gx*)   2,5 Conj

7. 1. $-[\forall Fx \lor -\forall(Fx \ \& \ Gx)]$ — IP
    2. $-\forall Fx \ \& \ \forall(Fx \ \& \ Gx)$ — 1 DM
    3. $-\forall Fx$ — 2 Simp
    4. $\exists-Fx$ — 3 QN
    5. $-Fa$ — 4 EI
    6. $\forall(Fx \ \& \ Gx)$ — 2 Simp
    7. $Fa \ \& \ Ga$ — 6 UI
    8. Fa — 7 Simp
    9. $Fa \ \& \ -Fa$ — 5,8 Conj

9. 1. $\exists(Fx \ \& \ Gx)$ — $/\therefore \ \exists Fx \ \& \ \exists Gx$
    2. $Fa \ \& \ Ga$ — 1 EI
    3. Fa — 2 Simp
    4. $\exists Fx$ — 3 EG
    5. Ga — 2 Simp
    6. $\exists Gx$ — 5 EG
    7. $\exists Fx \ \& \ \exists Gx$ — 4,6 Conj

11. 1. $\forall Fx \ \& \ \forall Gx$ — $/\therefore \ \forall(Fx \ \& \ Gx)$
    2. $\forall Fx$ — 1 Simp
    3. $\forall Gx$ — 1 Simp
    4. Fa — 2 UI
    5. Ga — 3 UI
    6. $Fa \ \& \ Ga$ — 4,5 Conj
    7. $\forall(Fx \ \& \ Gx)$ — 6 UG

13. 1. $\forall(-Ga \lor Fx)$ — $/\therefore \ -Ga \lor \forall Fx$
    2. $-(-Ga \lor \forall Fx)$ — IP
    3. $Ga \ \& \ -\forall Fx$ — 2 DM
    4. $-\forall Fx$ — 3 Simp
    5. $\exists-Fx$ — 4 QN
    6. $-Fb$ — 5 EI
    7. $-Ga \lor Fb$ — 1 UI
    8. $-Ga$ — 6,7 DS
    9. Ga — 3 Simp
    10. $Ga \ \& \ -Ga$ — 8,9 Conj

9.8, Set A

1. $-(Sa \ \& \ -Pa)$
    $\therefore \ -(Pa \ \& \ -Sa)$

Sa	Pa
F	T

3. $-(Sa \ \& \ -Pa)$
    $\therefore \ (Sa \ \& \ Pa)$

Sa	Pa
F	T

5. $(Sa \ \& \ Pa) \lor (Sb \ \& \ Pb)$
    $\therefore \ (Sa \ \& \ Pa) \lor (Sb \ \& \ Pb)$

Sa	Sb	Pa	Pb
F	T	T	T

7. $-(Sa \& -Pa)$
   Pa
   $\therefore Sa$

Sa	Pa
F	T

9. $Pa \& Pb$
   $\therefore Pa \& Pb \& Pc$

Pa	Pb	Pc
T	T	F

11. $-(Ma \& Pa) \& -(Sa \& Ma)$
    $\therefore -(Sa \& Pa)$

Ma	Pa	Sa
F	T	T

13. $-(Ma \& -Pa)$
    $Ma \& Sa$
    $\therefore Sa \& Pa$

Sa	Ma	Pa
T	T	F

15. $-(Pa \& -Ma)$
    $-(Ma \& -Na)$
    $-(Na \& -Sa)$
    $\therefore -(Sa \& -Pa)$

Sa	Ma	Na	Pa
T	T	T	F

17. $-[(Sa \lor Ma) \& (Sb \lor Mb)]$
    $(Pa \& Pb) \lor (Ma \lor Mb)$
    $\therefore -Sa \& -Sb$

Sa	Sb	Ma	Mb	Pa	Pb
T	F	T	F	T	T

9.8, Set B

1. $[-(Ma \& -Pa) \& -(Mb \& -Pb)] \& (Ma \lor Mb)$
   $[-(Ma \& -Sa) \& -(Mb \& -Sb)] \& (Ma \lor Mb)$
   $\therefore [-(Sa \& -Pa) \& -(Sb \& -Pb)] \& (Sa \lor Sb)$

Sa	Sb	Ma	Mb	Pa	Pb
T	T	F	T	F	T

3.
   1. $\forall -(Mx \& -Px) \& \exists Mx$
   2. $\forall -(Sx \& -Mx) \& \exists Sx$ $/ \therefore \exists (Sx \& Px)$
   3. $\exists Sx$ 2 Simp
   4. Sa 3 EI
   5. $\forall -(Sx \& -Mx)$ 2 Simp
   6. $-(Sa \& -Ma)$ 5 UI
   7. $-Sa \lor Ma$ 6 DM
   8. Ma 4,7 DS
   9. $\forall -(Mx \& -Px)$ 1 Simp
   10. $-(Ma \& -Pa)$ 9 UI
   11. $-Ma \lor Pa$ 10 DM
   12. Pa 8,11 DS
   13. $Sa \& Pa$ 4,12 Conj
   14. $\exists (Sx \& Px)$ 13 EG

5. 1. ∃(Px & Mx)
    2. ∀–(Mx & –Sx) & ∃Mx   / ∴ ∃(Sx & Px)
    3. Pa & Ma   1 EI
    4. ∀–(Mx & –Sx)   2 Simp
    5. –(Ma & –Sa)   4 UI
    6. –Ma ∨ Sa   5 DM
    7. Ma   3 Simp
    8. Sa   6,7 DS
    9. Pa   3 Simp
    10. Sa & Pa   8,9 Conj
    11. ∃(Sx & Px)   10 EG

7. [–(Ma & Pa) & –(Mb & Pb)] & (Ma ∨ Mb)
    [–(Ma & –Sa) & –(Mb & –Sb)] & (Ma ∨ Mb)
    ∴ [–(Sa & Pa) & –(Sb & Pb)] & (Sa ∨ Sb)

Sa	Sb	Ma	Mb	Pa	Pb
T	T	F	T	T	F

9. 1. ∃(Mx & Px)
    2. ∀–(Mx & –Sx) & ∃Mx   / ∴ ∃(Sx & Px)
    3. Ma & Pa   1 EI
    4. ∀–(Mx & –Sx)   2 Simp
    5. –(Ma & –Sa)   4 UI
    6. –Ma ∨ Sa   5 DM
    7. Ma   3 Simp
    8. Sa   6,7 DS
    9. Pa   3 Simp
    10. Sa & Pa   8,9 Conj
    11. ∃(Sx & Px)   10 EG

11. (Ma & –Pa) ∨ (Mb & –Pb)
    (Sa & –Ma) ∨ (Sb & –Mb)
    ∴ (Sa & –Pa) & (Sb & –Pb)

Ma	Mb	Sa	Sb	Pa	Pb
F	T	T	F	T	F

10.1, Set A

1. ◊*Wn*
3. □(*Mp* ∨ *Wp*)
5. −□*Rn*
7. □*Rq* ∨ □*Pq*
9. −◊(*Rq* & *Pq*)
11. □∀(*Rx* ∨ −*Rx*)
13. −◊∃(*Rx* & −*Rx*)
16. ∀◊*Wx*
17. ∃◊*Wx*
19. ∀−◊*Wx*

10.1, Set B

1. (a) Undetermined; subcontrary; (b) undetermined; superaltern; (c) false; contradictory.

3. (a) Undetermined; superaltern; (b) undetermined; subcontrary; (c) false; contradictory.

10.1, Set C

1. (a) True; (b) false; (c) true.
3. (a) False; (b) true; (c) true.

10.1, Set D

1. Compatible but inequivalent.
3. Compatible and equivalent.
5. Compatible but inequivalent.
7. Compatible but inequivalent.
9. Compatible but inequivalent.

10.1, Set E

1. MS
3. MN
5. MS
7. MP
9. MConj
11. MAdd
13. MN
15. None.
17. MDT
19. DM

10.1, Set F

1. 1. −◊*Fa*   /∴ −*Fa*
    2. □−*Fa*   1 MN
    3. −*Fa*   2 MS

3. 1. □(−*Ra* & −*Sa*)   /∴ −◊(*Ra* ∨ *Sa*)
    2. □−(*Ra* ∨ *Sa*)   1 DM
    3. −◊(*Ra* ∨ *Sa*)   2 MN

5. 1. *Ra* ∨ *Sa*
    2. □−*Sa*   /∴ ◊*Ra*
    3. −*Sa*   2 MS
    4. *Ra*   1,3 DS
    5. ◊*Ra*   4 MS

7. 1. □(*Pa* & *Qa*)   /∴ □*Pa* & □*Qa*
    2. □*Pa*   1 MSimp
    3. □*Qa*   1 MSimp
    4. □*Pa* & □*Qa*   2,3 Conj

9. 1. □*Fa*   /∴ ◊∃*Fx*
    2. *Fa*   1 MS
    3. ∃*Fx*   2 EG
    4. ◊∃*Fx*   3 MS

11. 1. −◊∃*Fx*   /∴ −*Fa*
    2. □−∃*Fx*   1 MN
    3. −∃*Fx*   2 MS
    4. ∀−*Fx*   3 QN
    5. −*Fa*   4 UI

13. 1. □(*Fa* & *Ga*)
    2. −◊(*Fb* ∨ *Gb*)   /∴ □(*Fa* & −*Fb*)
    3. □*Fa*   1 MSimp
    4. □−(*Fb* ∨ *Gb*)   2 MN
    5. □(−*Fb* & −*Gb*)   4 DM
    6. □−*Fb*   5 MSimp
    7. □(*Fa* & −*Fb*)   3,6 MConj

15. 1. □(∀*Rx* ∨ ∃*Bx*)
    2. −◊∀*Rx*   /∴ ◊∃*Bx*
    3. □−∀*Rx*   2 MN
    4. −∀*Rx*   3 MS
    5. ∀*Rx* ∨ ∃*Bx*   1 MS
    6. ∃*Bx*   4,5 DS
    7. ◊∃*Bx*   6 MS

17. 1. □∀(*Fx* ⇒ *Gx*)
    2. □*Fa*   /∴ ◊*Ga*
    3. ∀(*Fx* ⇒ *Gx*)   1 MS
    4. *Fa* ⇒ *Ga*   3 UI
    5. *Fa*   2 MS
    6. *Ga*   4,5 MP
    7. ◊*Ga*   6 MS

10.1, Set G

1. 1. −◊(*Rx* & *Gx*)   /∴ −∃(*Rx* & *Gx*)
    2. □−∃(*Rx* & *Gx*)   1 MN
    3. −∃(*Rx* & *Gx*)   2 MS

3. 1. □∀−(*Px* & *Ax*)   /∴ −(*Ps* & *As*)
    2. ∀−(*Px* & *Ax*)   1 MS
    3. −(*Ps* & *As*)   2 UI

5. 1. □(*Fa* & *Fb*)   /∴ □(*Fa* ∨ *Fb*)
    2. □(*Fa*   1 MSimp
    3. □(*Fa* ∨ *Fb*)   2 MAdd

7. 1. □(*Cj* ⇒ *Sj*)
    2. −◊*Sj*   /∴ −*Cj*
    3. □−*Sj*   2 MN
    4. □−*Cj*   1,3 MMT
    5. −*Cj*   4 MS

9. 1. ◊*Nk* ⇒ ◊*Nm*
    2. *Nk*   /∴ − −◊*Nm*
    3. ◊*Nk*   2 MS
    4. ◊*Nm*   1,3 MP
    5. − −◊*Nm*   4 DN

10.1, Set H

1. 1. ◊(p & q)   / ∴ ◊p
    2. −◊p   IP
    3. □−p   2 MN
    4. □(−p ∨ −q)   3 MAdd
    5. □−(p & q)   4 DM
    6. −◊(p & q)   5 MN
    7. ◊(p & q) & −◊(p & q)   1,6 Conj

3. 1. ◊[(p ∨ q) & (−q ∨ r)]   / ∴ ◊(p ∨ r)
    2. −◊(p ∨ r)   IP
    3. □−(p ∨ r)   2 QN
    4. □(−p & −r)   3 DM
    5. □[(−p & −r) ∨ (q & −r)]   4 MAdd
    6. □[−(p ∨ r) ∨ −(−q ∨ r)]   5 DM
    7. □−[(p ∨ q) & (−q ∨ r)]   6 DM
    8. −◊[(p ∨ q) & (−q ∨ r)]   7 MN
    9. {1} & {8}   1,8 Conj

5. 1. □(p ⇒ q)
    2. ◊p   / ∴ ◊q
    3. −◊q   IP
    4. □−q   3 MN
    5. □−p   1,4 MMT
    6. −◊p   5 MN
    7. ◊p & −◊p   2,6 Conj

7. 1. □(p ∨ q)
    2. ◊−p   / ∴ ◊q
    3. −◊q   IP
    4. □−q   3 MN
    5. □p   1,4 MDS
    6. −◊−p   5 MN
    7. ◊−p & −◊−p   2,6 Conj

10.2, Set A

1. (a) implies (b).   3. (a) implies (b).   5. Incompatible.
7. (a) implies (b).   9. (a) implies (b).   11. Equivalent.

10.2, Set B

1. (a) $P(-H) = 1 - P(H) = 1 - \frac{1}{8} = \frac{7}{8}$
   (b) $P(-R) = 1 - P(R) = 1 - \frac{3}{4} = \frac{1}{4}$
   (c) $P(R \,\&\, H) = P(R) \times P(H) = \frac{3}{4} \times \frac{1}{8} = \frac{3}{32}$
   (d) $P(R \,\&\, -H) = P(R) \times P(-H) = \frac{3}{4} \times \frac{7}{8} = \frac{21}{32}$
   (e) $P(H \,\&\, -R) = P(H) \times P(-R) = \frac{1}{8} \times \frac{1}{4} = \frac{1}{32}$
   (f) $P(-H \,\&\, -R) = P(-H) \times P(-R) = \frac{7}{8} \times \frac{1}{4} = \frac{7}{32}$
   (g) $P(R \lor H) = P(R) + P(H) - P(R \,\&\, H) = \frac{3}{4} + \frac{1}{8} - \frac{3}{32} = \frac{25}{32}$
   (h) $P(R \lor -H) = P(R) + P(-H) - P(R \,\&\, -H) = \frac{3}{4} + \frac{7}{8} - \frac{21}{32} = \frac{31}{32}$
   (i) $P(-R \lor H) = P(-R) + P(H) - P(-R \,\&\, H) = \frac{1}{4} + \frac{1}{8} - (\frac{1}{4} \times \frac{1}{8}) = \frac{11}{32}$
   (j) $P(-R \lor -H) = P(-R) + P(-H) - P(-R \,\&\, -H) = \frac{1}{4} + \frac{7}{8} - \frac{7}{32} = \frac{28}{32}$
   (k) $P(H/R) = P(H \,\&\, R)/P(R) = (\frac{3}{32})/(\frac{3}{4}) = \frac{1}{8}$; or, $P(H/R) = P(H) = \frac{1}{8}$, since H and R are independent.
   (l) $P(R/H) = P(R) = \frac{3}{4}$
   (m) $P(-R/H) = P(-R) = \frac{1}{4}$
   (n) $P(H/-R) = P(H)\ \frac{1}{8}$
   (o) $P[(R \,\&\, -H) \lor (R \,\&\, H)] = P(R \,\&\, -H) + P(R \,\&\, H) = \frac{21}{32} + \frac{3}{32} = \frac{24}{32} = \frac{3}{4}$
   (p) $P[R \,\&\, (-H \lor H)] = P[(R \,\&\, -H) \lor (R \,\&\, H)] = \frac{3}{4}$
   (q) $P[R/(H \lor -H)] = P[R \,\&\, (H \lor -H)]/P(H \lor -H) = (\frac{3}{4})/1 = \frac{3}{4}$
   (r) $P[(R \,\&\, -H) \lor (-R \,\&\, -H)] = P(R \,\&\, -H) + P(-R \,\&\, -H) = \frac{21}{32} + \frac{7}{32} = \frac{28}{32} = \frac{7}{8}$
   (s) $P[R \,\&\, (H \,\&\, -H)] = 0$
   (t) $P[(R \,\&\, -H) \lor (-R \,\&\, H) \lor (-R \,\&\, -H)] = P(R \,\&\, -H) + P(-R \,\&\, H) + P(-R \,\&\, -H) = \frac{21}{32} + \frac{1}{32} + \frac{7}{32} = \frac{29}{32}$

3. (a) $P = P(H \text{ on 1st}) \times P(H \text{ on 2nd}) \times P(H \text{ on 3rd}) = \frac{1}{2} \times \frac{1}{2} \times \frac{1}{2} = \frac{1}{8}$
   (b) $P = P(H \text{ on 1st}) \times P(T \text{ on 2nd}) \times P(T \text{ on 3rd}) = \frac{1}{2} \times \frac{1}{2} \times \frac{1}{2} = \frac{1}{8}$
   (c) $P = P(H \text{ on 1st}) + P(H \text{ on 2nd}) - P(H \text{ on 1st and 2nd}) = \frac{1}{2} + \frac{1}{2} - (\frac{1}{2} \times \frac{1}{2}) = \frac{3}{4}$
   (d) $P = P(H \text{ on 1st}) \times P(\text{not } H \text{ on 2nd}) = \frac{1}{2} \times \frac{1}{2} = \frac{1}{4}$
   (e) $P = P(H \text{ on 1st}) \times P(H \text{ on 2nd or 3rd}) = \frac{1}{2} \times [P(H \text{ on 2nd}) + P(H \text{ on 3rd}) - P(H \text{ on 2nd and 3rd})] = \frac{1}{2} \times [\frac{1}{2} + \frac{1}{2} - (\frac{1}{2} \times \frac{1}{2})] = \frac{3}{8}$
   (f) $P = P(\text{not } H \text{ on 1st}) \times P(\text{not } H \text{ on 2nd}) = \frac{1}{2} \times \frac{1}{2} = \frac{1}{4}$

5. (a) $P = \frac{4}{52}$
   (b) $P = 1 - P(Q) = 1 - \frac{4}{52} = \frac{48}{52}$
   (c) $P = P(K) + P(-Q) - P(K \,\&\, -Q) = P(K) + P(-Q) - P(K) = P(-Q) = \frac{48}{52}$
   (d) $P = P(\text{black } Q) + P(\text{red } K) = \frac{2}{52} + \frac{2}{52} = \frac{4}{52}$
   (e) $P = 0$
   (f) $P = P(K) \times P(S) = \frac{4}{52} \times \frac{1}{4} = \frac{1}{52}$
   (g) $P = P(K) + P(S) - P(K \,\&\, S) = \frac{4}{52} + \frac{13}{52} - \frac{1}{52} = \frac{16}{52} = \frac{4}{13}$
   (h) $P = \frac{20}{52}$ (There are five even–numbered cards in each of the four suits.)
   (i) $P = \frac{12}{52}$ (There are three face cards in each suit.)
   (j) $P = \frac{12}{52} + \frac{20}{52} = \frac{32}{52}$

(k) P = P(face card) x P(not even–numbered card/face card) = $^{12}/_{52}$ x 1 = $^{12}/_{52}$

10.2, Set C

1. The odds are 1:1.
3. The odds are 4:48.
5. P = $^1/_{36}$.
7. P = $^1/_{101}$.
9. P(Tigers win) = $^3/_5$.

10.2, Set D

Theorem 7. p = [(p & q) ∨ (p & –q)], so P(p) = P[(p & q) ∨ (p & –q)] by axiom 3. p & q and p & –q are incompatible, so P(p) = P(p & q) + P(p & –q) by axiom 4.

Theorem 9. P(p) = P(p & q) + P(p & –q) by theorem 7. Hence P(p) = [P(p) x P(q/p)] + [P(p) x P(–q/p)] by theorem 5. Dividing by P(p) yields 1 = P(q/p) + P(–q/p). Hence P(–q/p) = 1 – P(q/p). The proviso on theorem 9 is necessary because we cannot divide by 0.

Theorem 11. By axiom 4, P(p ∨ q) = P(p) + P(q) – P(p & q). By axiom 2, if p is necessary, then P(p) = 1. Furthermore, p ∨ q is necessary if p is, so P(p ∨ q) = 1. Plugging these values into theorem 4 yields 1 = 1 + P(q) – P(p &q), from which it follows that P(p & q) = P(q).

Theorem 13. Since q is necessary, P(q) = 1. Then by theorem 10, P(p/q) = [P(p)/P(q)] x P(q/p). Hence P(p/q) = 0 when P(p) = 0. Now assume that P(p) > 0. Then by theorem 12, P(q/p) = 1. So P(p/q) = [P(p)/1] x 1 = P(p).

Theorem 15. If q logically implies p, then q = (p & q). Hence P(q) = P(p & q) by axiom 3. P(p/q) = P(p & q)/P(q) by axiom 5, as long as P(q) > 0. So P(p/q) = 1.

Theorem 17. Assume P(p) = P(p/q). Then P(p & q) = P(p) x P(q) by axiom 5. It follows that P(q) = P(q & p)/P(p) = P(q/p) as long as P(p) > 0.

Theorem 19. By theorem 4, P(p ∨ q ∨ r) = P(p) + P(q ∨ r) – P[p & (q ∨ r)], and P(q ∨ r) = P(q) + P(r) – P(q & r). By axiom 3, P[p & (q ∨ r)] = P[(p & q) ∨ (p & r)], which by theorem 4 equals P(p & q) + P(p & r) – P[(p & q) & (p & r)]. P[(p & q) & (p & r)] = P(p & q & r) by axiom 3. Putting all these results together gives P(p ∨ q ∨ r) = P(p) + [P(q) + P(r) – P(q & r)] – [P(p & q) + P(p & r) – P(p & q & r)] = P(p) + P(q) + P(r) – P(p & q) – P(p & r) – P(q & r) + P(p & q & r).

10.3, Set A

1.

x	y	–x ∨ –y
1	1	0
1	0	1
0	1	1
0	0	1

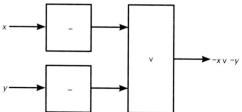

3.

x	y	x & (–x ∨ y)
1	1	1
1	0	0
0	1	0
0	0	0

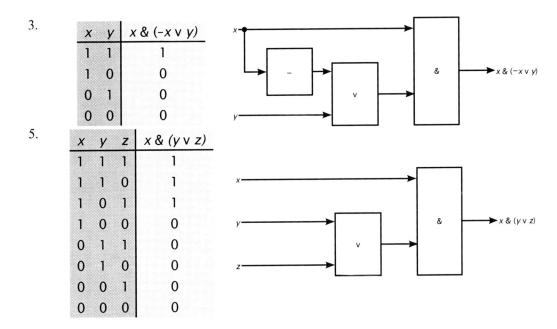

5.

x	y	z	x & (y ∨ z)
1	1	1	1
1	1	0	1
1	0	1	1
1	0	0	0
0	1	1	0
0	1	0	0
0	0	1	0
0	0	0	0

10.3, Set B

1. –x & y

3. (x & y) ∨ (–x & y) or –(x & –y) & –(–x & –y)

5. [(x & z) & –y] ∨ [y & (–x & –z)]

10.3, Set C

1. d   3. c

10.3, Set D

First construct a multiplication table for one-digit binary numbers, then convert it to a logic table. Using $x \cdot y$ to symbolize the product of x and y, the result is:

x	y	x • y
1	1	1
1	0	0
0	1	0
0	0	0

The logic table for multiplication makes it clear that $x \cdot y = x \& y$, so that the AND-gate is a one-bit multiplier.

10.3, Set E

Let *AB* and *YZ* be any two-digit binary numbers. We would multiply them as follows:

$$
\begin{array}{rr}
AB & \text{E.g.} \quad 11 \\
\times\ YZ & \times\ 10 \\
\hline
\end{array}
$$

		A x	*Z*	*B* x *Z*
A x *Y*	*B* x	*Y*		
A x *Y* (*A* x *Z*) + (*B* x *Y*)			*B* x *Z*	

E.g.
```
   11
 x 10
 ----
   00
   11
 ----
  110
```

So a two-bit multiplier can be constructed as follows:

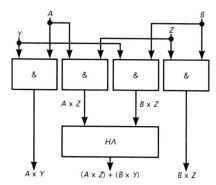

Two-bit multipliers for decimal numbers, or many-bit multipliers for digital numbers, would have to be considerably more complex because of the need to carry digits from one column to another.

10.4, Set A

1. An object is a drake if and only if it is a male duck. "Drake" means "male duck."

3. An object is a cow if and only if it is a female bovine animal. "Cow" means "female bovine animal."

5. An object is a square if and only if it is a four-sided equilateral polygon. "Square" means "four-sided equilateral polygon."

7. An object is a logical truth if and only if it is true in all possible cases. "Logical truth" means "statement that is true in all possible cases."

10.4, Set C

1. Too broad: a spinster must also be beyond the normal age for marriage.

3. Stipulative, so not defective.

5. Circular: and presumably also too narrow, since cats have not existed for all time.

7. Not defective by itself, but forms a circle with 6.

9. Not defective.

11. Too broad: hope also requires uncertainty.

13. Too broad (people have a tendency to make mistakes but do not want to) and too narrow (most people want to live forever but have no tendency to do so).

15. Too broad: punishment requires a certain purpose (accidentally stepping on someone's toe is not punishment).

17. Too broad: murder must also be unlawful.

19. Too broad (desks satisfy the definiens) and too narrow (some tables are intended to support larger objects).

21. Too broad (a refrigerator satisfies the definiens) and too narrow (some furniture is intended to be used outside).

23. This is ambiguous. "Featherless" may mean "genotypically" or "phenotypically" featherless. On the first interpretation, the definition is okay. On the second it is too broad (consider a chicken that has been defeathered).

25. Too narrow (some humans cannot use language because of genetic defects) and too broad (chimpanzees have been taught various sign languages).

27. Stipulative, so not defective.

29. Forms a circle with 30.

31. Forms a circle with 32.

Inductive Logic

Argument from Authority: Simple Form

> a affirmed p.
> $\therefore p$ is true.

CV: a affirmed what he believes, his belief is based on careful observation or sound reasoning, and no equally reliable source denies p.

Argument from Analogy: Simple Form

> d is like i.
> d has A.
> $\therefore i$ has A.

CV: d is sufficiently like i in relevant respects, and is sufficiently large and varied.

Enumerative Induction: Pure Form

> All observed P have A.
> $\therefore$ All P have A.

CV: The group of observed Ps is sufficiently large and varied, and is sufficiently similar to the group of unobserved Ps in relevant respects.

Statistical Syllogism: Qualitative Form

> r% of all P have A.
> i is P.
> $\therefore i$ has A.

CV: r is greater than 50%, and i is a sufficiently small group of objects.

Causal Induction

> c occured when and only when e occured (in b).
> $\therefore c$ caused e (in b).

CV: c is a possible cause of e, e is not a possible cause of c, and there are no confounding factors.

Causal Elimination

> c occured without e, or
> e occured without c (in b).
> $\therefore c$ did not cause e (in b).

Hypothetical Induction

> d is true.
> h would explain d.
> $\therefore h$ is true.

CV: No competing hypothesis explains d as well as h.

General Condition of Validity

There is no undermining counterevidence.

Syllogistic Logic

Subalternation (Sub): From an **A** or an **E** proposition, infer its subaltern.

Every S is a P.
∴ Some S is a P.

No S is a P.
∴ Some S is not a P.

Conversion (Conv): From an **E** or an **I** proposition, infer its converse.

No S is a P.
∴ No P is an S.
CV: There is a P.

Some S is a P.
∴ Some P is not an S.

Contraposition (Contr): From an **A** or an **O** proposition, infer its contrapositive.

Every S is a P.
∴ Every non-P is a non-S.
CV: There is a non-P.

Some S is not a P.
∴ Some non-P is not a non-S.

Obversion (Obv): From any categorical proposition, infer its obverse.

Every S is a P.
∴ No S is a non-P.

No S is a P.
∴ Every S is not a P.

Some S is a P.
∴ Some S is not an non-P.

Some S is not a P.
∴ Some non-S is a non-P.

s is a P.
∴ s is not a non-P.

s is not a P.
∴ s is not a non-P.

General Categorical Syllogism (GCS): Infer any proposition that follows from an **AAA1** or **AII1** syllogism.

Every S is an M.
Every M is a P.
∴ Every S is a P.

Some S is an M.
Every M is a P.
∴ Some S is a P.

Singular Categorical Syllogism (SCS): Infer any proposition that follows from an **AUU1** or **UUI3** syllogism.

s is an M.
Every M is a P.
∴ s is a P.

m is an S.
m is a P.
∴ Some S is a P.

Double Negation (DN): Infer any proposition that results from replacing any general term T with nonnon-T, or nonnon-T with T, wherever it occurs.

$$T = \text{nonnon-}T$$

Propositional Logic

Conjunction (Conj): From any two statements, infer their conjunction.

$$p$$
$$q$$
$$\therefore p \,\&\, q$$

Addition (Add): From any statement, infer any (inclusive) disjunction of which it is a disjunct.

$$p$$
$$\therefore p \lor q$$

Simplification (Simp): From a conjunction, infer either conjunct.

$$p \,\&\, q$$
$$\therefore p$$

Disjunctive Syllogism (DS): From a disjunction and the denial of one disjunct, infer the other disjunct.

$$p \lor q$$
$$-p$$
$$\therefore q$$

Modus Tollens (MT): From a conditional and the denial of its consequent, infer the denial of its antecedent.

$$p \Rightarrow q$$
$$-q$$
$$\therefore -p$$

Modus Ponens (MP): From a conditional and its antecedent, infer the its consequent.

$$p \Rightarrow q$$
$$p$$
$$\therefore q$$

Disjunctive Transitivity (DT): From a pair of disjunctions in which a disjunct of one is the denial of a disjunct in the other, infer the disjunction of the other disjuncts.

$$p \lor q$$
$$-q \lor r$$
$$\therefore p \lor r$$

Axioms: All substitution instances of the following logical truths are axioms, and may be introduced as separate lines at any point in a proof of logical truth.

Law of Identity (ID): $p \Rightarrow p$
Law of Excluded Middle (EM): $p \lor -p$
Law of Noncontradiction (NC): $-(p \,\&\, -p)$

Rules of Replacement: Any two statements equivalent by one of the following rules (or variants thereof) may replace each other wherever they occur.

Double Negation (DN): $--p = p$
Double Disjunction (DD): $p \lor p = p$
Law of Conjunction (DC): $p \,\&\, p = p$
Commutation (Com): $p \,\&\, q = q \,\&\, p$
$ p \lor q = q \lor p$

Association (Assn): $p \lor (q \lor r) = (p \lor q) \lor r$
$ p \,\&\, (q \,\&\, r) = (p \,\&\, q) \,\&\, r$
Distribution (Dist): $p \,\&\, (q \lor r) = (p \,\&\, q) \lor (p \,\&\, r)$
$ p \lor (q \,\&\, r) = (p \lor q) \,\&\, (p \lor r)$
De Morgan (DM): $-(p \,\&\, q) = -p \lor -q$
$ -(p \lor q) = -p \,\&\, -q$

Quantification Theory

Quantifier Negation (QN): Any two statements equivalent by one of the following rules may replace each other wherever they occur.

$$\forall Px = -\exists -Px$$
$$-\forall Px = \exists -Px$$

$$-\forall Px = -\exists Px$$
$$-\forall -Px = \exists Px$$

Universal Instantiation (UI): From $\forall Px$, infer any substitution instance of Px in which x is replaced by any constant s.

$$\forall Px$$
$$\therefore Ps$$

Existential Generalization (EG): From any substitution instance of Px in which x is replaced by any constant s, infer $\exists Px$.

$$Ps$$
$$\therefore \exists Px$$

Existential Instantiation (EI): From $\exists Px$, infer any substitution instance of Px in which x is replaced by any constant s that is not used in the conclusion or in any previous line.

$$\exists Px$$
$$\therefore Ps$$

Universal Generalization (UG): From any substitution instance of Px in which x is replaced by any constant s that is not used in the premises or in any line introduced by EI, infer $\forall Px$.

$$Ps$$
$$\therefore \forall Px$$

Modal Logic

Modal Subalternation (MS): From $\Box p$ infer p, from p infer $\Diamond p$, and from $\Box p$ infer $\Diamond p$.

$$\Box p$$
$$\therefore p$$

$$p$$
$$\therefore \Diamond p$$

$$\Box p$$
$$\therefore \Diamond p$$

Modal Negation (MN): Any two statements equivalent by one of the following rules may replace each other wherever they occur.

$$\Box Px = -\Diamond -Px$$
$$-\Box Px = \Diamond -Px$$

$$-\Box Px = -\Diamond Px$$
$$-\Box -Px = \Diamond Px$$

Modal Extension Rules: If a statement can be inferred from other statements by any of the one-way rules of propositional logic, then the necessity of the statement can be inferred from the necessity of the other statements.

MConj	MAdd	MSimp	MDS	MDT	MMP	MMT
$\Box p$	$\Box p$	$\Box(p \,\&\, q)$	$\Box(p \vee q)$	$\Box(p \vee q)$	$\Box(p \Rightarrow q)$	$\Box(p \Rightarrow q)$
$\Box q$	$\therefore \Box(p \vee q)$	$\therefore \Box p$	$\Box -p$	$\Box(-q \vee r)$	$\Box p$	$\Box -q$
$\therefore \Box(p \,\&\, q)$			$\therefore \Box q$	$\therefore \Box(p \vee r)$	$\therefore \Box q$	$\therefore \Box -p$

Printed in the United States
118400LV00003B/7-34/A